IF FOUND, please notify and arrange return to owner. This written test book is important for the owner's preparation for the Federal Aviation Administration Pilot Knowledge Test for the Private Pilot Certificate. Thank you.

Pilot's Name: _____

Address: _____

_____

City   State   Zip Code

Telephone: (_____) _____

Additional copies of *Private Pilot and Recreational Pilot FAA Written Exam* are available from

Gleim Publications, Inc.
P.O. Box 12848, University Station
Gainesville, Florida 32604
(352) 375-0772 / (800) 87-GLEIM / (800) 874-5346
FAX: (352) 375-6940
Internet: www.gleim.com
E-mail: admin@gleim.com

W9-BON-281

The price is $15.95 (subject to change without notice). Orders must be prepaid. Use the order form on page 326. Shipping and handling charges will be added to telephone orders. Add applicable sales tax to shipments within Florida.

Gleim Publications, Inc. guarantees the immediate refund of all resalable materials returned in 30 days. Shipping and handling charges are nonrefundable.

ALSO AVAILABLE FROM GLEIM PUBLICATIONS, INC.

ORDER FORM ON PAGE 326

Private Pilot Flight Maneuvers and Practical Test Prep
Pilot Handbook
Aviation Weather and Weather Services
FAR/AIM
Private Pilot Syllabus and Logbook
Instrument Pilot Syllabus
Commercial Pilot Syllabus
Flight Computer
Navigational Plotter
Flight Bag

Advanced Pilot Training Books

Instrument Pilot FAA Written Exam
Instrument Pilot Flight Maneuvers and Practical Test Prep

Commercial Pilot FAA Written Exam
Commercial Pilot Flight Maneuvers and Practical Test Prep

Flight/Ground Instructor FAA Written Exam
Fundamentals of Instructing FAA Written Exam
Flight Instructor Flight Maneuvers and Practical Test Prep

Airline Transport Pilot FAA Written Exam

Flight Engineer FAA Written Exam

Gleim's Private Pilot Kit -- see order form on page 326.

REVIEWERS AND CONTRIBUTORS

Karen A. Hom, B.A., University of Florida, is our book production coordinator. Ms. Hom coordinated the production staff and provided production assistance throughout the project.

Barry A. Jones, ATP, CFII, MEI, B.S. in Air Commerce/Flight Technology, Florida Institute of Technology, drafted material in previous editions and for this edition, and provided technical assistance throughout the project.

Joshua B. Moore, CFI, B.A., University of Florida, is our aviation technical research assistant and a flight instructor with Gulf Atlantic Airways in Gainesville, FL. Mr. Moore researched questions, edited answer explanations, and incorporated revisions into the text.

John F. Rebstock, B.S., Fisher School of Accounting, University of Florida, reviewed portions of the edition and composed the page layout.

Jan M. Strickland is our book production assistant. Ms. Strickland reviewed the manuscript and provided assistance throughout the project.

The CFIs who have worked with me throughout the years to develop and improve my pilot training materials.

The many FAA employees who helped, in person or by telephone, primarily in Gainesville, FL; Orlando, FL; Oklahoma City, OK; and Washington, DC.

The many pilots and student pilots who have provided comments and suggestions about *Private Pilot and Recreational Pilot FAA Written Exam*, *Private Pilot Flight Maneuvers and Practical Test Prep* and *Pilot Handbook* during the past 17 years.

A PERSONAL THANKS

This manual would not have been possible without the extraordinary efforts and dedication of Jim Collis and Terry Hall, who typed the entire manuscript and all revisions, as well as prepared the camera-ready pages.

The author also appreciates the proofreading and production assistance of Melissa Gruebel, Kevin Jordan, Jessica Medina, and Shane Rapp.

Finally, I appreciate the encouragement, support, and tolerance of my family throughout this project.

NINTH EDITION
PRIVATE PILOT

AND RECREATIONAL PILOT
FAA WRITTEN EXAM

for the FAA Computer-Based Pilot Knowledge Tests:
Private Pilot - Airplane   Recreational Pilot - Airplane
Private Pilot - Airplane Transition

by Irvin N. Gleim, Ph.D., CFII

ABOUT THE AUTHOR

Irvin N. Gleim earned his private pilot certificate in 1965 from the Institute of Aviation at the University of Illinois, where he subsequently received his Ph.D. He is a commercial pilot and flight instructor (instrument) with multiengine and seaplane ratings, and is a member of the Aircraft Owners and Pilots Association, American Bonanza Society, Civil Air Patrol, Experimental Aircraft Association, and Seaplane Pilots Association. He is also author of flight maneuvers and practical test prep books for the private, instrument, commercial, and flight instructor certificates/ratings, and study guides for the private/recreational, instrument, commercial, flight/ground instructor, fundamentals of instructing, airline transport pilot, and flight engineer FAA knowledge tests. Three additional pilot training books are *Pilot Handbook*, *Aviation Weather and Weather Services*, and *FAR/AIM*.

Dr. Gleim has also written articles for professional accounting and business law journals, and is the author of widely used review manuals for the CIA exam (Certified Internal Auditor), the CMA exam (Certified Management Accountant), the CFM exam (Certified in Financial Management), and the CPA exam (Certified Public Accountant), and the EA exam (IRS Enrolled Agent). He is Professor Emeritus, Fisher School of Accounting, University of Florida, and is a CFM, CIA, CMA, and CPA.

Gleim Publications, Inc.

P.O. Box 12848 • University Station
Gainesville, Florida 32604

(352) 375-0772
(800) 87-GLEIM or (800) 874-5346
FAX: (352) 375-6940

Internet: www.gleim.com
E-mail: admin@gleim.com

ISSN 1080-4900
ISBN 1-58194-128-5
Second Printing: November 2001

This is the second printing of the ninth edition of *Private Pilot and Recreational Pilot FAA Written Exam*. Please e-mail update@gleim.com with PPWE 9-2 in the subject or text. You will receive our current update as a reply.

EXAMPLE:

To: update@gleim.com
From: your e-mail address
Subject: PPWE 9-2

Copyright © 2000-2001 by Gleim Publications, Inc.

ALL RIGHTS RESERVED. No part of this material may be reproduced in any form whatsoever without express written permission from Gleim Publications, Inc.

SOURCES USED IN PRIVATE PILOT AND RECREATIONAL PILOT FAA WRITTEN EXAM

The first lines of the answer explanations contain citations to authoritative sources of the answers. These publications can be obtained from the FAA, the Government Printing Office, and aviation bookstores. These citations are abbreviated as provided below:

AC	Advisory Circular	AWS	Aviation Weather Services
ACL	Aeronautical Chart Legend	FAR	Federal Aviation Regulations
A/FD	Airport/Facility Directory	Fl Comp	Flight Computer
AFH	Airplane Flying Handbook	IFH	Instrument Flying Handbook
AIM	Aeronautical Information Manual	NTSB	National Transportation Safety Board Regulations
AvW	Aviation Weather		
AWBH	Aircraft Weight and Balance Handbook	PHAK	Pilot's Handbook of Aeronautical Knowledge

HELP !!

This is the Ninth Edition designed specifically for potential pilots, student pilots, and private pilots. Please send any corrections and suggestions for subsequent editions to the author, c/o Gleim Publications, Inc. The last page in this book has been reserved for you to make comments and suggestions. It can be torn out and mailed to us.

Two other volumes, *Private Pilot Flight Maneuvers and Practical Test Prep* and *Pilot Handbook*, are also available. *Private Pilot Flight Maneuvers and Practical Test Prep* focuses on your flight training and the FAA practical test, just as this book focuses on the FAA knowledge test. *Pilot Handbook* is a complete private pilot ground school text in outline format with many diagrams for ease in understanding. Save time, money, and frustration -- order these books today! See the order form in the back of this book. Please bring these books to the attention of flight instructors, fixed base operators, and others interested in flying. Wide distribution of these books and increased interest in flying depend on your assistance, good word, etc. Thank you.

NOTE: ANSWER DISCREPANCIES and UPDATES

Our answers have been carefully researched and reviewed. Inevitably, there will be differences with competitors' books and even the FAA. If necessary, we will develop an UPDATE for *Private Pilot and Recreational Pilot FAA Written Exam*. Send e-mail to update@gleim.com as described at the top right of this page, and visit our Internet site for the latest updates and information on all of our products. To continue providing our customers with first-rate service, we request that questions about our books and software be sent to us via mail, e-mail, or fax. The appropriate staff member will give each question thorough consideration and a prompt response. Questions concerning orders, prices, shipments, or payments will be handled via telephone by our competent and courteous customer service staff.

TABLE OF CONTENTS

SECOND PRINTING (11/01) CHANGES
Minor edits have been made throughout the book.

1. Pages 14-18. Updated description of *FAA Test Prep* software.

2. The FAA made revisions to or added the following questions:

   Chapter 8: Q. 39 and Q. 41
   Chapter 9: Q. 7

3. Pages 313-321. Numerous updates to the Subject Matter Knowledge Codes.

To continue providing our customers with first-rate service, we request that questions about our books and software be sent to us via mail, e-mail, or fax. The appropriate staff member will give each question thorough consideration and a prompt response. Questions concerning orders, prices, shipments, or payments will be handled via telephone by our competent and courteous customer service staff.

PREFACE

The primary purpose of this book is to provide you with the easiest, fastest, and least expensive means of passing the private pilot (airplane) knowledge test. We have

1. Reproduced all actual test questions which can possibly appear on your FAA private pilot knowledge test (airplane).

2. Reordered the questions into 109 logical topics.

3. Organized the 109 topics into 11 chapters.

4. Explained the answer immediately to the right of each question.

5. Provided an easy-to-study outline of exactly what you need to know (and no more) at the beginning of each chapter.

Accordingly, you can thoroughly prepare for the FAA pilot knowledge test by

1. Studying the brief outlines at the beginning of each chapter.

2. Answering the question on the left side of each page while covering up the answer explanations on the right side of each page.

3. Reading the answer explanation for each question that you answer incorrectly or have difficulty with.

4. Our *FAA Test Prep* software facilitates this process. See pages 13 through 19.

The secondary purpose of this book is to introduce *Private Pilot Flight Maneuvers and Practical Test Prep* and *Pilot Handbook*.

Private Pilot Flight Maneuvers and Practical Test Prep is designed to help prepare pilots for their flight training and the FAA private pilot practical test. Each task, objective, concept, and requirement is explained, analyzed, illustrated, and interpreted so pilots will be totally conversant with all aspects of the private pilot practical test.

Pilot Handbook is a textbook of aeronautical knowledge presented in easy-to-use outline format. While this book contains only the material needed to pass the FAA pilot knowledge test, *Pilot Handbook* contains the textbook knowledge required to be a safe and proficient pilot.

Most books create additional work for the user. In contrast, my books facilitate your effort. They are easy to use. The outline format, type styles, and spacing are designed to improve readability. Concepts are often presented as phrases rather than as complete sentences.

Read the introductory chapter, The FAA Pilot Knowledge Test, carefully. Also, recognize that this study manual is concerned with **airplane** flight training, not balloon, glider, or helicopter training. I am confident this manual will facilitate speedy completion of your FAA pilot knowledge test. I also wish you the very best as you complete your private pilot certificate, in subsequent flying, and in obtaining additional ratings and certificates.

Enjoy Flying -- Safely!

Irvin N. Gleim

November 2001

INTRODUCTION
THE FAA PILOT KNOWLEDGE TEST

This introduction explains how to obtain a private pilot certificate, and explains the content and procedure of the Federal Aviation Administration (FAA) pilot knowledge test including how to take the test at a computer testing center. The remainder of this Introduction discusses and illustrates the Gleim **FAA Test Prep** software. Achieving a private certificate is fun. Begin today!

Private Pilot and Recreational Pilot FAA Written Exam is one of five books contained in Gleim's Private Pilot Kit. The other four books are

1. *Private Pilot Flight Maneuvers and Practical Test Prep*
2. *Private Pilot Syllabus and Logbook*
3. *Pilot Handbook*
4. *FAR/AIM*

Private Pilot Flight Maneuvers and Practical Test Prep presents each flight maneuver you will perform in outline/illustration format so you will know what to expect and what to do before each flight lesson. This book will thoroughly prepare you to complete your FAA practical (flight) test confidently and successfully.

Private Pilot Syllabus and Logbook is a step-by-step syllabus of ground and flight training lesson plans for your private pilot training. Additionally, to keep everything organized in one place, you may use this book as your logbook.

Pilot Handbook is a complete pilot reference book which combines over 100 FAA books and documents including *AIM*, FARs, ACs and much more. This book more than any other will help make you a better and more proficient pilot.

Gleim's *FAR/AIM* is an easy-to-read reference book containing all of the Federal Aviation Regulations (FARs) applicable to general aviation flying, plus the full text of the FAA's *Aeronautical Information Manual (AIM)*.

If you are planning on purchasing the FAA's books on aviation weather, Gleim's *Aviation Weather and Weather Services* combines all of the information from the FAA's *Aviation Weather* (AC 00-6A), *Aviation Weather Services* (AC 00-45E), and numerous FAA publications into one easy-to-understand book. It will help you study all aspects of aviation weather and provide you with a single weather reference book.

WHAT IS A PRIVATE PILOT CERTIFICATE?

A private pilot certificate is much like a driver's license. A private pilot certificate will allow you to fly an airplane and carry passengers and baggage, although not for compensation or hire. However, operating expenses may be shared with your passengers. The certificate, which is a piece of paper similar to a driver's license, is sent to you by the FAA upon satisfactory completion of your training program, a pilot knowledge test, and a practical test. A sample private pilot certificate is reproduced below. The recreational pilot certificate is the same except it says "recreational."

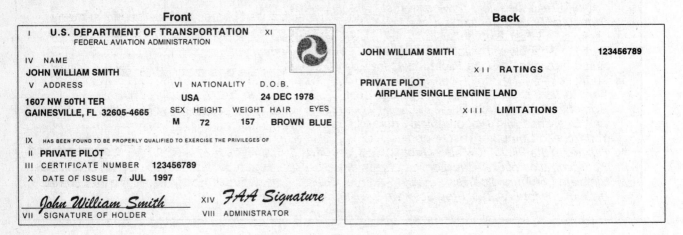

WHAT IS A RECREATIONAL PILOT CERTIFICATE?

The FAA added a recreational pilot certificate in 1989 for those who want to fly locally for fun, i.e., recreation. The objective is to provide only the flight training required for those **NOT** aspiring to fly on trips, at night, with more than one passenger, or to airports with an operating control tower or other airspace requiring air traffic control (ATC) communication. A recreational pilot certificate will take you less time and money to obtain, but your flying privileges will be restricted. The recreational pilot certificate is, however, upgradable to a private pilot certificate.

The recreational pilot knowledge test has 50 questions and includes most of the topics on the private pilot knowledge test. There are 25 questions specific to recreational pilots in Chapter 4, beginning on page 111. For the recreational pilot knowledge test, we suggest you study the entire book except the following:

Module	Module Name
3.2	Beacons and Taxiway Lights
3.6	Collision Avoidance (Qs on night visual scanning)
3.7	ATIS and Ground Control
3.10	Terminal Radar Programs

Module	Module Name
3.13	ATC Traffic Advisories
3.14	ATC Light Signals
Chapter 4 FARs	61.31, 61.113, 91.123, 91.130, 91.131, 91.135, 91.157

REQUIREMENTS TO OBTAIN A PRIVATE PILOT CERTIFICATE

1. Be at least 17 years of age.

2. Be able to read, write, and converse fluently in English (certificates with operating limitations may be available for medically related deficiencies).

3. Obtain at least a third-class FAA medical certificate (see the sample on page 3).

    a. You must undergo a routine medical examination which may be administered only by FAA-designated doctors called aviation medical examiners (AME).

1) For operations requiring a private, recreational, or student pilot certificate, a first-, second-, or third-class medical certificate expires at the end of the last day of the month either

   a) 3 years after the date of examination shown on the certificate, if you have not reached your 40th birthday on or before the date of examination or

   b) 2 years after the date of examination shown on the certificate, if you have reached your 40th birthday on or before the date of examination.

b. Even if you have a physical handicap, medical certificates can be issued in many cases. Operating limitations may be imposed depending upon the nature of the disability.

c. Your certificated flight instructor (CFI) or fixed-base operator (FBO) will be able to recommend an AME.

   1) An FBO is an airport business that gives flight lessons, sells aviation fuel, repairs airplanes, etc.

   2) Also, the FAA publishes a directory that lists all authorized AMEs by name and address. Copies of this directory are kept at most FAA offices, ATC facilities, and Flight Service Stations (FSS). Alternatively, go to the Gleim website at www.gleim.com/Aviation/AMESearch.html.

d. As a student pilot, your medical certificate will also function as your student pilot certificate once it is signed by you and your AME.

   1) Alternatively, a separate student pilot certificate can be obtained from an FAA Flight Standards District Office (FSDO) or any designated pilot examiner.

   a) This would be necessary if your AME issued you a third-class medical certificate instead of a student pilot certificate (you should request a student pilot certificate).

Front   Back

2) The only substantive difference between a regular medical certificate and a medical certificate/student pilot certificate is that the back of the medical certificate/student pilot certificate provides for flight instructor signature.

   a) Also, the combined medical certificate/student pilot certificate is on slightly heavier paper and is yellow instead of white.

3) Note that the back of the student pilot certificate must be signed by your CFI prior to solo flight (flying by yourself).

4) You must be at least 16 years of age to receive a student pilot certificate.

4. Receive and log ground training from an authorized instructor or complete a home-study course (such as studying this book, *Private Pilot Flight Maneuvers and Practical Test Prep*, and *Pilot Handbook*) to learn

   a. Applicable Federal Aviation Regulations ... that relate to private pilot privileges, limitations, and flight operations.

   b. Accident reporting requirements of the National Transportation Safety Board.

   c. Use of the applicable portions of the Aeronautical Information Manual and FAA ACs (advisory circulars).

   d. Use of aeronautical charts for VFR navigation using pilotage, dead reckoning, and navigation systems.

   e. Radio communication procedures.

   f. Recognition of critical weather situations from the ground and in flight, windshear avoidance, and the procurement and use of aeronautical weather reports and forecasts.

   g. Safe and efficient operation of aircraft, including collision avoidance, and recognition and avoidance of wake turbulence.

   h. Effects of density altitude on takeoff and climb performance.

   i. Weight and balance computations.

   j. Principles of aerodynamics, powerplants, and aircraft systems.

   k. Stall awareness, spin entry, spins, and spin recovery techniques for the airplane...category ratings.

   l. Aeronautical decision making and judgment.

   m. Preflight action that includes

      1) How to obtain information on runway lengths at airports of intended use, data on takeoff and landing distances, weather reports and forecasts, and fuel requirements.

      2) How to plan for alternatives if the flight cannot be completed or delays are encountered.

5. Pass a knowledge test with a score of 70% or better. All FAA tests are administered at FAA-designated computer testing centers. The private pilot knowledge test consists of 60 multiple-choice questions selected from all of the airplane-related questions among the questions in the FAA's private pilot knowledge test bank; the remaining questions are for balloons, helicopters, etc. Each of the FAA's airplane questions is reproduced in this book with complete explanations to the right of each question.

6. Accumulate flight experience (FAR 61.109). Receive a total of 40 hr. of flight instruction and solo flight time, including

   a. 20 hr. of flight training from an authorized flight instructor, including at least

      1) 3 hr. of cross-country, i.e., to other airports

       2)   3 hr. at night, including

          a)   One cross-country flight of over 100 NM total distance
          b)   10 takeoffs and 10 landings to a full stop at an airport

       3)   3 hr. of instrument flight training in an airplane

       4)   3 hr. in airplanes in preparation for the private pilot practical test within 60 days prior to that test

NOTE: A maximum of 2.5 hr. of instruction may be accomplished in an FAA-approved flight simulator or flight training device representing an airplane.

   b.   10 hr. of solo flight time in an airplane, including at least

       1)   5 hr. of cross-country flights

       2)   One solo cross-country flight of at least 150 NM total distance, with full-stop landings at a minimum of three points and with one segment of the flight consisting of a straight-line distance of at least 50 NM between the takeoff and landing locations

       3)   Three solo takeoffs and landings to a full stop at an airport with an operating control tower

7.   Receive flight instruction and demonstrate skill (FAR 61.107).

   a.   Obtain a logbook sign-off by your CFI on the following areas of operations:

       1)   *Preflight preparation*
       2)   *Preflight procedures*
       3)   *Airport and seaplane base operations*
       4)   *Takeoffs, landings, and go-arounds*
       5)   *Performance maneuvers*
       6)   *Ground reference maneuvers*
       7)   *Navigation*
       8)   *Slow flight and stalls*
       9)   *Basic instrument maneuvers*
       10) *Emergency operations*
       11) *Night operations*
       12) *Postflight procedures*
       13) *Multiengine operations (for only multiengine airplanes)*

   b.   Alternatively, enroll in an FAA-certificated pilot school that has an approved private pilot certification course (airplane).

       1)   These are known as Part 141 schools or Part 142 training centers because they are authorized by Part 141 or Part 142 of the FARs.

          a)   All other regulations concerning the certification of pilots are found in Part 61 of the FARs.

8.   Successfully complete a practical (flight) test which will be given as a final exam by an FAA inspector or designated pilot examiner. The practical test will be conducted as specified in the FAA's Private Pilot Practical Test Standards (FAA-S-8081-14, dated May 1995, with Change 1, dated April 28, 1997).

   a.   FAA inspectors are FAA employees and do not charge for their services.

   b.   FAA-designated pilot examiners are proficient, experienced flight instructors and pilots who are authorized by the FAA to conduct practical tests. They do charge a fee.

   c.   The FAA's Private Pilot Practical Test Standards are outlined and reprinted in Gleim's *Private Pilot Flight Maneuvers and Practical Test Prep*.

FAA PILOT KNOWLEDGE TEST

1.   This book is designed to help you prepare for the following FAA knowledge tests:

   a.   Private Pilot-Airplane (PAR), which consists of 60 questions and has a time limit of 2 hr. 30 min.

   b.   Recreational Pilot-Airplane (RPA), which consists of 50 questions and has a time limit of 2 hr.

   c.   Private Pilot-Airplane Transition (PAT), which consists of 30 questions and has a time limit of 1 hr. 30 min. (to upgrade from recreational to private)

NON-AIRPLANE TESTS

If you are using this book to study for a non-airplane pilot knowledge test, you should skip all of the obviously airplane-related questions. Then, go to www.gleim.com/Aviation/nonairplane/ for the appropriate non-airplane questions.

---

2.   In an effort to develop better test questions, the **FAA frequently pretests questions** on pilot knowledge tests by adding up to 5 "pretest" questions. Thus, rather than the number of questions listed above, you may be required to answer up to 5 extra pretest questions. The pretest questions will not be graded. You will NOT know which questions are "real" and which are "pretest." Accordingly, you must attempt to answer all questions correctly.

3.   All of the questions in the FAA's private pilot knowledge test bank that are applicable to airplanes have been grouped into the following 11 categories, which are the titles of Chapters 1 through 11:

Chapter 1: Airplanes and Aerodynamics
Chapter 2: Airplane Instruments, Engines, and Systems
Chapter 3: Airports, Air Traffic Control, and Airspace
Chapter 4: Federal Aviation Regulations
Chapter 5: Airplane Performance and Weight and Balance
Chapter 6: Aeromedical Factors

Chapter 7: Aviation Weather
Chapter 8: Aviation Weather Services
Chapter 9: Navigation: Charts, Publications, Flight Computers
Chapter 10: Navigation Systems
Chapter 11: Cross-Country Flight Planning

   Note that the FAA's questions are **not** grouped together by topic. We have unscrambled them for you in this book.

4.   Within each of the chapters listed, questions relating to the same subtopic (e.g., duration of medical certificates, stalls, carburetor heat, etc.) are grouped together to facilitate your study program. Each subtopic is called a module.

5.   To the right of each question are

   a.   The correct answer
   b.   The FAA question number
   c.   A reference for the answer explanation

      1)   See page iv for a listing of abbreviations used for authoritative sources.
      2)   EXAMPLE: *FTH Chap 1* means *Flight Training Handbook*, Chapter 1.

6.   Each chapter begins with an outline of the material tested on the FAA knowledge test. The outlines in this part of the book are very brief and have only one purpose: to help you pass the FAA knowledge test for the private pilot certificate.

   a.   **CAUTION:** The **sole purpose** of this book is to expedite your passing the FAA knowledge test for the private pilot certificate. Accordingly, all extraneous material (i.e., not directly tested on the FAA knowledge test) is omitted even though much more information and knowledge are necessary to fly safely. This additional material is presented in two related books: Gleim's *Private Pilot Flight Maneuvers and Practical Test Prep* and *Pilot Handbook*.

Follow the suggestions given throughout this chapter and you will have no trouble passing the pilot knowledge test the first time you take it.

HOW TO PREPARE FOR THE FAA PILOT KNOWLEDGE TEST

1. Begin by carefully reading the rest of this chapter. You need to have a complete understanding of the examination process prior to beginning to study for it. This knowledge will make your studying more efficient.

2. After you have spent an hour studying this chapter, set up a study schedule, including a target date for taking your knowledge test.

    a. Do not let the study process drag on because it will be discouraging, i.e., the quicker the better.

    b. Consider enrolling in an organized ground school course at your local FBO, community college, etc.

    c. Determine where and when you are going to take your pilot knowledge test.

3. Work through each of Chapters 1 through 11.

    a. Each chapter begins with a list of its module titles. The number in parentheses after each title is the number of FAA questions that cover the information in that module. The two numbers following the parentheses are the page numbers on which the outline and the questions for that particular module begin, respectively.

    b. Begin by studying the outlines slowly and carefully.

    c. Next, answer the multiple-choice questions under exam conditions. Cover the answer explanations on the right side of each page with the Gleim bookmark provided at the back of this book while you answer the multiple-choice questions.

        1) Remember, it is very important to the learning (and understanding) process that you honestly commit yourself to an answer. If you are wrong, your memory will be reinforced by having discovered your error. Therefore, it is crucial to cover up the answer and make an honest attempt to answer the question before reading the answer.

        2) Study the answer explanation for each question that you answer incorrectly, do not understand, or have difficulty with.

        3) Use our *FAA Test Prep* software to assure that you do not refer to answers before committing to an answer AND to simulate actual computer testing center exam conditions.

4. Note that this test book (in contrast to most other question and answer books) contains the FAA questions grouped by topic. Thus, some questions may appear repetitive, while others may be duplicates or near-duplicates. Accordingly, do not work question after question (i.e., waste time and effort) if you are already conversant with a topic and the type of questions asked.

5. As you move from module to module and chapter to chapter, you may need further explanation or clarification of certain topics. You may wish to obtain and use the following Gleim books described on page 1.

    a. *Private Pilot Flight Maneuvers and Practical Test Prep*
    b. *Pilot Handbook*

6. Keep track of your work!!! As you complete a module in Chapters 1 through 11, grade yourself with an A, B, C, or ? (use a ? if you need help on the subject) next to the module title at the front of the respective chapter.

    a. The A, B, C, or ? is your self-evaluation of your comprehension of the material in that module and your ability to answer the questions.

      A   means a good understanding.

      B   means a fair understanding.

      C   means a shaky understanding.

      ?   means to ask your CFI or others about the material and/or questions and read the pertinent sections in *Private Pilot Flight Maneuvers and Practical Test Prep* and/or *Pilot Handbook*.

b.   This procedure will provide you with the ability to quickly see (by looking at the first page of Chapters 1 through 11) how much studying you have done (and how much remains) and how well you have done.

c.   This procedure will also facilitate review. You can spend more time on the modules you had difficulty with.

d.   *FAA Test Prep* software provides you with your historical performance data.

WHEN TO TAKE THE PILOT KNOWLEDGE TEST

1.   You must be at least 15 years of age to take the private pilot knowledge test.

2.   You must prepare for the test by successfully completing a ground instruction course, or you may use this book as your self-developed home study course.

    a.   See "Authorization to Take the Pilot Knowledge Test," on page 9.

3.   Take the pilot knowledge test within the next 30 days.

    a.   Get your pilot knowledge test behind you.

4.   Your practical test must follow within 24 months

    a.   Or you will have to retake your pilot knowledge test.

COMPUTER TESTING CENTERS

The FAA has contracted with several computer testing services to administer FAA pilot knowledge tests. Each of these computer testing services has testing centers throughout the country. You register by calling an 800 number. Call the following testing services for information regarding the location of testing centers most convenient to you and the time allowed and cost to take the private pilot (airplane) knowledge test.

CATS	(800) 947-4228, (650) 259-8559
LaserGrade	(800) 211-2754, (360) 896-9111

Also, about twenty Part 141 schools use the AvTEST computer testing system, which is very similar to the computer testing services described above.

GLEIM'S *FAA TEST PREP* SOFTWARE

Computer testing is consistent with aviation's use of computers (e.g., DUATS, flight simulators, computerized cockpits, etc.). All FAA knowledge tests are administered by computer.

Computer testing is natural after computer study. Computer assisted instruction is a very efficient and effective method of study. Gleim's *FAA Test Prep* software is designed to prepare you for computer testing. *FAA Test Prep* software contains all of the questions in this book, context-sensitive outline material, and on-screen charts and figures. You choose either Study Mode or Test Mode.

In Study Mode, the software provides you with an explanation of each answer you choose (correct or incorrect). You design each study session:

Topic(s) you wish to cover	Questions marked from last session -- test, study, or both
Number of questions	Questions missed from last session -- test, study, or both
Order of questions -- FAA, Gleim, or random	Questions missed from all sessions -- test, study, or both
Order of answers to each question -- FAA or random	Questions never answered correctly

In Test Mode, you decide the format -- CATS, LaserGrade, AvTEST, or Gleim. When you finish your test, you can study the questions missed and access answer explanations. The software emulates the operation of the FAA-approved computer testing companies. Thus, you have a complete understanding of how to take an FAA knowledge test and know exactly what to expect before you go to a computer testing center.

For more information on Gleim's *FAA Test Prep* software, see page 14.

PART 141 SCHOOLS WITH PILOT KNOWLEDGE TEST EXAMINING AUTHORITY

The FAA permits some FAR Part 141 schools to develop, administer, and grade their own pilot knowledge tests as long as they use the FAA pilot knowledge test questions, i.e., the same questions as in this book. The FAA does not provide the correct answers to the Part 141 schools, and the FAA only reviews the Part 141 school test question selection sheets. Thus, some of the answers used by Part 141 test examiners may not agree with the FAA or those in this book. The latter is not a problem but may explain why you may miss a question on a Part 141 knowledge test using an answer presented in this book.

AUTHORIZATION TO TAKE THE PILOT KNOWLEDGE TEST

Before taking the private pilot knowledge test, you must receive an endorsement from an authorized instructor who conducted the ground training or reviewed your home-study in the areas listed in item 4. on page 4, certifying that you are prepared to pass the knowledge test.

Recreational pilots have a similarly worded requirement. For your convenience, a standard authorization form for both the private and recreational pilot knowledge tests are reproduced on page 327, which can be easily completed, signed by a flight or ground instructor, torn out, and taken to the test site.

FORMAT OF THE PILOT KNOWLEDGE TEST

The FAA's private pilot knowledge test for airplanes consists of 60 multiple-choice questions selected from the questions that appear in the next 11 chapters.

Note that the FAA test will be taken from exactly the same questions that are reproduced in this book. If you study the next 11 chapters, including all the questions and answers, **you should be assured of passing your FAA knowledge test.**

Additionally, all of the FAA legends and figures are contained in a book titled *Computer Testing Supplement for Recreational Pilot and Private Pilot*, which you will be given for your use at the time of your test. All of the airplane-related figures and legends are reproduced in this book.

We need your help identifying which questions the FAA is pretesting (but not grading - see page 6). After you take your exam, please e-mail, fax, or mail us a description of these questions so we can anticipate their future use by the FAA.

Additionally, all of the FAA legends and figures are contained in a book titled *Computer Testing Supplement for Recreational Pilot and Private Pilot*, which you will be given for your use at the time of your test. All of the FAA legends and figures that are applicable to airplanes are reproduced in this book.

WHAT TO TAKE TO THE FAA PILOT KNOWLEDGE TEST

1. The same flight computer that you have used to solve the test questions in this book, i.e., one you are familiar with and have used before

2. Navigational plotter

3. A pocket calculator you are familiar with and have used before (no instructional material for the calculator allowed)

4. Authorization to take the knowledge test (see page 327)

5. Picture identification of yourself

NOTE: Paper and pencils are supplied at the examination site.

COMPUTER TESTING PROCEDURES

To register for the pilot knowledge test, you should call one of the computer testing services listed in "Computer Testing Centers," on page 8, or you may call one of their testing centers. These testing centers and telephone numbers are listed in Gleim's *FAA Test Prep* software under Vendors in the main menu. When you register, you will pay the fee with a credit card.

When you arrive at the computer testing center, you will be required to provide positive proof of identification and documentary evidence of your age. The identification presented must include your photograph, signature, and actual residential address, if different from the mailing address. This information may be presented in more than one form of identification. Next, you will sign in on the testing center's daily log. Your signature on the logsheet certifies that, if this is a retest, you meet the applicable requirements (see "Failure on the Pilot Knowledge Test," on page 12) and that you have not passed this test in the past 2 years. Finally, you will present your logbook endorsement or authorization form from your instructor, which authorizes you to take the test. A standard authorization form is provided on page 327 for your use.

Next, you will be taken into the testing room and seated at a computer terminal. A person from the testing center will assist you in logging on the system, and you will be asked to confirm your personal data (e.g., name, Social Security number, etc.). Then you will be prompted and given an online introduction to the computer testing system and you will take a sample test. If you have used our *FAA Test Prep* software, you will be conversant with the computer testing methodology and environment, and you will probably want to skip the sample test and begin the actual test immediately. You will be allowed 2.5 hr. to complete the actual test. This is 2.5 minutes per question. Confirm the time permitted when you call the testing center to register to take the test by computer. When you have completed your test, an Airman Computer Test Report will be printed out, validated (usually with an embossed seal), and given to you by a person from the testing center. Before you leave, you will be required to sign out on the testing center's daily log.

Each computer testing center has certain idiosyncrasies in its paperwork, scheduling, and telephone procedures, as well as in its software. It is for this reason that our *FAA Test Prep* software emulates each of these FAA-approved computer testing companies.

FAA QUESTIONS WITH TYPOGRAPHICAL ERRORS

Occasionally, FAA test questions contain typographical errors such that there is no correct answer. The FAA test development process involves many steps and people, and as you would expect, glitches occur in the system that are beyond the control of any one person. We indicate "best" rather than correct answers for some questions. Use these best answers for the indicated questions.

Note that the FAA corrects (rewrites) defective questions as they are discovered; these changes are explained in our updates -- see page iv. However, problems due to faulty or out-of-date figures printed in FAA Computer Testing Supplements are expensive to correct. Thus, it is important to carefully study questions that are noted to have a best answer in this book. Even though the best answer may not be completely correct, you should select it when taking your test.

YOUR AIRMAN COMPUTER TEST REPORT

1. You will receive your Airman Computer Test Report upon completion of the test. An example computer test report is reproduced below.

    a. Note that you will receive only one grade as illustrated.

    b. The expiration date is the date by which you must take your FAA practical test.

    c. The report lists the FAA subject matter knowledge codes of the questions you missed, so you can review the topics you missed prior to your practical test.

Federal Aviation Administration
Airman Computer Test Report

EXAM TITLE: Private Pilot Airplane

NAME: Jones David John

ID NUMBER: 123456789   TAKE: 1

DATE: 08/14/01   SCORE: 82   GRADE: Pass

Knowledge area codes in which questions were answered incorrectly. See appropriate FAA Study Guide. A code may represent more than one incorrect response.

A23 B07 H04 H66 I41 J03

EXPIRATION DATE: 08/31/03

DO NOT LOSE THIS REPORT

Authorized instructor's statement. (If Applicable)

I have given Mr./Ms. _____ additional instruction in each subject area shown to be deficient and consider the applicant competent to pass the test.

Last _____ Initial _____ Cert. No. _____ Type _____
(Print Clearly)

Signature _____

CTD's Embossed Seal

2. Use the FAA List of Subject Matter Knowledge Codes on pages 309 to 312 to determine which topics you had difficulty with.

    a. Look them over and review them with your CFI so (s)he can certify that (s)he reviewed the deficient areas and found you competent in them when you take your practical test.

3. Keep your Airman Computer Test Report in a safe place, as you must submit it to the FAA examiner when you take your practical test.

FAILURE ON THE PILOT KNOWLEDGE TEST

1. If you fail (less than 70%) the pilot knowledge test (virtually impossible if you follow the above instructions), you may retake it after your instructor endorses the bottom of your Airman Computer Test Report certifying that you have received the necessary ground training to retake the test.

2. Upon your retaking the test, you will find that the procedure is the same except that you must also submit your Airman Computer Test Report indicating the previous failure to the computer testing center.

3. Note that the pass rate on the private pilot knowledge test is about 92%, i.e., less than 1 out of 10 fail the test initially. Reasons for failure include

    a. Failure to study the material tested (contained in the outlines at the beginning of Chapters 1 through 11 of this book);

    b. Failure to practice working the FAA questions under test conditions (all of the FAA questions on airplanes appear in Chapters 1 through 11 of this book); and

    c. Poor examination technique, such as misreading questions and not understanding the requirements.

REORGANIZATION OF FAA QUESTIONS

1. The questions in the FAA's private pilot knowledge test bank are numbered 3001 to 3955. The FAA questions appear to be presented randomly.

    a. We have reorganized and renumbered the FAA questions into chapters and modules.

    b. The FAA question number is presented in the middle of the first line of the explanation of each answer.

2. Pages 313 through 321 contain a list of the FAA questions numbers 3001 to 3955 with cross-references to the FAA's subject matter knowledge codes and the chapters and question numbers in this book.

    a. For example, we have coded question 3001 as A01 and 4-1, which means it is covered under the FAA subject code, "FAR Part 1, General Definitions," and is found in Chapter 4 as question 1 in this book.

    b. Note that, although 3001 to 3955 implies more questions than those in this book, numerous FAA questions have two or more questions using the same question number.

        1) The remaining questions relate to helicopters, gliders, balloons, etc., and have been omitted from this book.

            a) These questions are indicated as NA in the answer column in our cross-reference table beginning on page 313.

    c.   In June 2001, the FAA test bank was released without the familiar four-digit FAA question numbers. We identified all of the new questions and added them to the end of our cross-reference chart using our own question numbering system.

        1)   The first four digits of this code refer to the month and year the question first appeared. The remaining digits identify the question number used in that particular FAA test bank release.

With this overview of exam requirements, you are ready to begin the easy-to-study outlines and rearranged questions with answers to build your knowledge and confidence and PASS THE FAA's PRIVATE PILOT KNOWLEDGE TEST.

The feedback we receive from users indicates that our books and software reduce anxiety, improve FAA test scores, and build knowledge. Studying for each test becomes a useful step toward advanced certificates and ratings.

SIMULATED FAA PRACTICE TEST

Appendix A, Private Pilot Practice Test, beginning on page 301, allows you to practice taking the FAA pilot knowledge test without the answers next to the questions. This test has 60 questions that have been randomly selected from the airplane-related questions in the FAA's private pilot knowledge test bank. Topical coverage in this practice test is similar to that of the FAA private pilot test.

It is very important that you answer all 60 questions at one sitting. You should not consult the answers, especially when being referred to figures (charts, tables, etc.) throughout this book where the questions are answered and explained. Analyze your performance based on the answer key which follows the practice test.

Also rely on Gleim's *FAA Test Prep* software to simulate actual computer testing conditions including the screen layouts, instructions, etc., for CATS, LaserGrade, and AvTEST.

INSTRUCTIONS FOR THE *FAA TEST PREP* SOFTWARE

To install *FAA Test Prep*, put your CD-ROM in your CD-ROM drive. If an autoplay window appears after you insert the CD, follow the Setup wizard. If no screen appears after you have inserted the CD, click on the Windows Start button, and select "Run" from a list of options. Type x:\setup.exe (if x is the drive letter of your CD-ROM), and click "OK." Follow the on-screen instructions to finalize the installation.

Gleim Publications requires all *FAA Test Prep* users to register their software for unlimited use, free updates, and technical support. To register, simply use the Personal Registration Number and Library Passkey(s) that were shipped with your CD-ROM, call (800) 87-GLEIM, or register online at (http://www.gleim.com/license.html).

Once you have installed *FAA Test Prep* onto your system, you can begin studying at any time by clicking on the icon placed on your desktop or the Windows Start Menu. Use the Tutorial in the HELP menu to go step by step through the Test Prep study process, or start studying right away by clicking on Create Session. *FAA Test Prep* allows you to customize your study process using several different options.

Study Session

Study Sessions give you immediate feedback on why your answer selection for a particular FAA question is correct or incorrect and allows you to access the context-sensitive outline material that helps to explain concepts related to the question. Choose from several different question sources: all questions available for that library, questions from a certain topic (chapters and modules from Gleim books), questions that you missed or marked in the last session you created, questions that you have never answered correctly, questions from certain FAA subject codes, etc. You can mix up the questions by selecting to randomize the question and/or answer order so that you do not memorize answer letters.

You may then grade your study sessions and track your study progress using the performance analysis charts and graphs. The Performance Analysis information helps you to focus on areas where you need the most improvement, saving you time in the overall study process. You may then want to go back and study questions that you missed in a previous session, or you may want to create a study session of questions that you marked in the previous session, and all of these options are made easy with *FAA Test Prep*'s Study Sessions.

After studying the outlines and questions in a Study, you can switch to a Test Session. In a Test Session, you will not know which questions you have answered correctly until the session is graded. You can further test your skills with a Standard Test Session, which gives you the option of taking your pilot knowledge test under actual testing conditions using one of the emulations of the major testing centers.

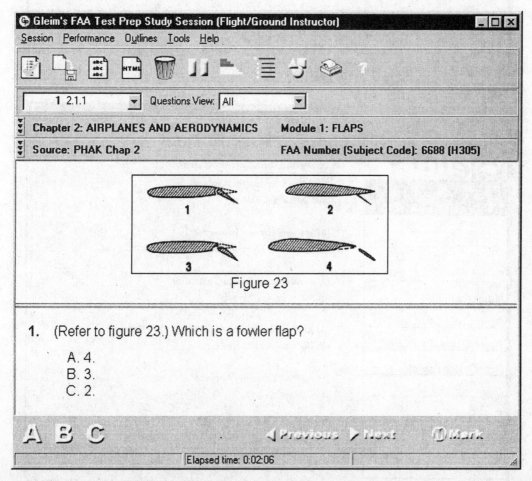

Standard Test Session

Take an exam in the actual testing environment of any of the major testing centers: CATS, AvTest, or Lasergrade. *FAA Test Prep* emulates the testing formats of these testing centers making it easy for you to study FAA questions under actual exam conditions. After studying with *FAA Test Prep*, you will know exactly what to expect when you go in to take your pilot knowledge test.

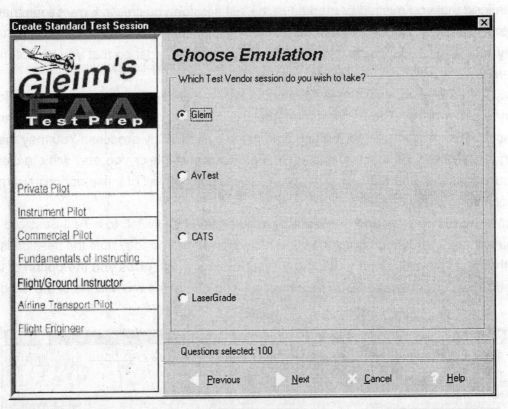

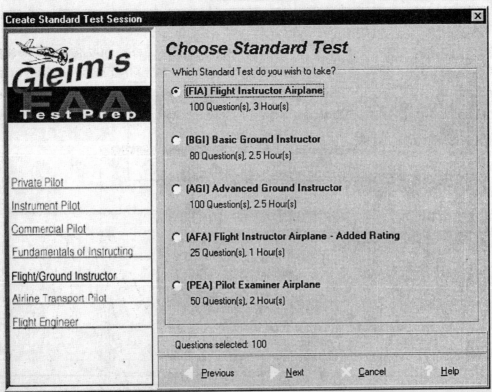

On-Screen Charts and Figures

One of the most convenient features of *FAA Test Prep* is the easily accessible on-screen charts and figures. Several of the FAA questions refer to drawings, maps, charts, and other pictures that provide information to help answer the question. In *FAA Test Prep*, you can pull up any of these figures with the click of a button. You can increase or decrease the size of the images, and you may also use our drawing feature to calculate the true course between two given points (required only on the private pilot knowledge test).

Instructor Print Options

FAA Test Prep is also a useful tool for instructors who want to create quizzes and assignments for their students. An instructor may mark questions in a session and then choose to print marked questions to create a quiz or test. (S)he may select to print an answer sheet, a blank answer sheet, and a renumbered printout of questions marked and any instructions that go along with the quiz or test.

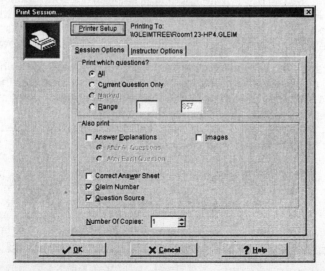

INSTRUCTOR SIGN-OFF SHEETS

FAA Test Prep is capable of generating an instructor sign-off for FAA knowledge tests which require one. This sign-off has been approved by the FAA, and can be presented at the computer testing center as authorization to take your test—you do NOT need an additional endorsement from your instructor.

In order to obtain the instructor sign-off sheet for your test, you must first answer all questions in *FAA Test Prep* correctly. Then, select "Instructor Sign-Off Sheets" under the PERFORMANCE menu and select the appropriate test acronym using the index tabs (test acronyms are explained on page 6). If you have answered all of the required questions, the instructor sign-off sheet will appear for you to print. If you have not yet answered all required questions, a list of the unanswered questions, along with their location, will appear.

FAA Test Prep also contains a listing by state of all major testing center locations for CATS, AvTest, and LaserGrade. Gleim's *FAA Test Prep* is an all-in-one program designed to help anyone with a computer, Internet access, and an interest in flying to pass the pilot knowledge tests.

FREE Updates and Technical Support

Gleim offers FREE technical support to all registered users. Call (800) 87-GLEIM, send e-mail to support@gleim.com, or fill out the technical support request form online (www.gleim.com/techform.html). Gleim's new Online Updates feature makes updating your software and libraries even easier than before. Simply connect to the Internet, start the Gleim software, select Online Updates from the Test Prep Tools screen, and follow the on-screen instructions. Downloadable library updates will also be available online (www.gleim.com/updates.html) free to registered users of our CD-ROM software. For more information on our update service by e-mail, turn to page 367.

Obtain your copy of *FAA Test Prep* today. Order online at http://www.gleim.com/Aviation/IndivOrderForm.html or call 800 87-GLEIM.

If this Gleim test book saves you time and frustration in preparing for the FAA private pilot knowledge test, you should use Gleim's *Private Pilot Flight Maneuvers and Practical Test Prep* to prepare for the FAA practical test. *Private Pilot Flight Maneuvers and Practical Test Prep* will assist you in developing the competence and confidence to pass your FAA practical (flight) test, just as this book organizes and explains the knowledge needed to pass your FAA private pilot knowledge test.

Also, flight maneuvers are quickly perfected when you understand exactly what to expect before you get into an airplane to practice the flight maneuvers. You must be ahead of (not behind) your CFI and your airplane. Gleim's flight maneuvers books explain and illustrate all flight maneuvers so the maneuvers and their execution are intuitively appealing to you.

END OF INTRODUCTION

Gleim Publications, Inc.

(352) 375-0772

(800) 87-GLEIM
FAX # (352) 375-6940
P. O. Box 12848 • University Station
Gainesville, Florida 32604

TO: Users of Our Written Test Books

FROM: Irvin N. Gleim

TOPIC: Our **Flight Maneuvers and Practical Test Prep** Books

Before pilots take their FAA knowledge (written) test, they want to understand the answer to every FAA test question. Our test books and software are widely used because they help pilots learn and understand exactly what they need to know to do well on the FAA knowledge test.

To help you and all other pilots do well on your FAA practical (flight) test(s), we have developed a series of **Flight Maneuvers and Practical Test Prep** books (a book for each certificate and rating). An easy-to-understand, comprehensive explanation of all knowledge and skill required on your instrument pilot practical test is essential to you because

1. We outline and illustrate each flight maneuver you will perform during your flight training. You will know what to expect and what to do before your instructor demonstrates the maneuver. You will learn faster because you understand what to do.

2. We have included discussion of common errors made during each flight maneuver. This will help you learn from others' mistakes.

3. Each FAA practical test task is explained in terms of what your FAA-designated examiner may expect you to interpret or demonstrate. You will be thoroughly prepared to complete your practical test confidently and successfully.

4. Finally, we help you focus on gaining *practical test standard* proficiency as quickly as possible to prep you for your FAA practical (flight) test.

Private Pilot Flight Maneuvers and Practical Test Prep will help you be a better and safer pilot. It is also an excellent reference after you earn your certificate.

If your FBO or aviation bookstore does not have **Private Pilot Flight Maneuvers and Practical Test Prep**, call **(800) 87-GLEIM** to order your copy today.

Thank you for recommending our **FAA Written Exam** books, **FAA Test Prep** software, and **Flight Maneuvers and Practical Test Prep** books to your friends and colleagues.

CHAPTER ONE
AIRPLANES AND AERODYNAMICS

This chapter contains outlines of major concepts tested, all FAA test questions and answers regarding the basics of aerodynamics, and an explanation of each answer. Each module, or subtopic, within this chapter is listed above with the number of questions from the FAA pilot knowledge test pertaining to that particular module. For each module, the first number following the parentheses is the page number on which the outline begins, and the next number is the page number on which the questions begin.

CAUTION: Recall that the **sole purpose** of this book is to expedite your passing the FAA pilot knowledge test for the private pilot certificate. Accordingly, all extraneous material (i.e., topics or regulations not directly tested on the FAA pilot knowledge test) is omitted, even though much more information and knowledge are necessary to fly safely. This additional material is presented in *Pilot Handbook* and *Private Pilot Flight Maneuvers and Practical Test Prep*, available from Gleim Publications, Inc. See the order form on page 326.

1.1 FLAPS AND RUDDER (Questions 1-3)

1. One of the main functions of flaps during the approach and landing is to increase wing lift, which allows an increase in the angle of descent without increasing airspeed.

2. The rudder is used to control the yaw about the airplane's vertical axis.

1.2 AERODYNAMIC FORCES (Questions 4-6)

1. The four aerodynamic forces acting on an airplane during flight are

    a. Lift -- the upward-acting force
    b. Weight -- the downward-acting force
    c. Thrust -- the forward-acting force
    d. Drag -- the rearward-acting force

2. These forces are at equilibrium when the airplane is in unaccelerated flight:

   Lift = Weight
   Thrust = Drag

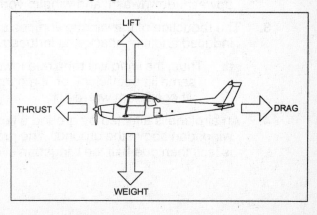

1.3 ANGLE OF ATTACK (Questions 7-10)

1. The angle of attack is the angle between the wing chord line and the direction of the relative wind.

    a. The wing chord line is an imaginary straight line from the leading edge to the trailing edge of the wing.

    b. The relative wind is the direction of airflow relative to the wing when the wing is moving through the air.

2. The angle of attack at which a wing stalls remains constant regardless of weight, airplane loading, etc.

1.4 STALLS AND SPINS (Questions 11-13)

1. An airplane can be stalled at any airspeed in any flight attitude. A stall results whenever the critical angle of attack is exceeded.

2. An airplane in a given configuration will stall at the same indicated airspeed regardless of altitude because the airspeed indicator is directly related to air density.

3. An airplane spins when one wing is less stalled than the other wing.

    a. To enter a spin, an airplane must always be stalled first.

1.5 FROST (Questions 14-16)

1. Frost forms when the temperature of the collecting surface is at or below the dewpoint of the adjacent air, and the dewpoint is below freezing.

    a. The water vapor sublimates directly as ice crystals on the wing surface.

2. Frost on wings disrupts the smooth airflow over the airfoil by causing early airflow separation from the wing. This

    a. Decreases lift, and
    b. Causes friction and increases drag.

3. Frost may make it difficult or impossible for an airplane to take off.

4. Frost should be removed before attempting to take off.

1.6 GROUND EFFECT (Questions 17-20)

1. Ground effect is the result of the interference of the ground (or water) surface with the airflow patterns about an airplane.

2. The vertical component of the airflow around the wing is restricted, which alters the wing's upwash, downwash, and wingtip vortices.

3. The reduction of the wingtip vortices alters the spanwise lift distribution and reduces the induced angle of attack and induced drag.

    a. Thus, the wing will require a lower angle of attack in ground effect to produce the same lift coefficient, or, if a constant angle of attack is maintained, an increase in the lift coefficient will result.

4. An airplane is affected by ground effect when it is within the length of the airplane's wingspan above the ground. The ground effect is most often recognized when the airplane is less than one-half the wingspan's length above the ground.

5. Ground effect may cause an airplane to float on landings or permit it to become airborne with insufficient airspeed to stay in flight above the area of ground effect.

    a. An airplane may settle back to the surface abruptly after flying through the ground effect if the pilot has not attained recommended takeoff airspeed.

1.7 AIRPLANE TURN (Question 21)

1. The horizontal component of lift makes an airplane turn.

    a. To attain this horizontal component of lift, the pilot coordinates rudder, aileron, and elevator.

2. The rudder on an airplane controls the yaw, i.e., rotation about the vertical axis, but does not cause the airplane to turn.

1.8 AIRPLANE STABILITY (Questions 22-26)

1. An inherently stable airplane returns to its original condition (position or attitude) after being disturbed. It requires less effort to control.

2. The location of the center of gravity (CG) with respect to the center of lift determines the longitudinal stability of an airplane.

3. Airplanes (except a T-tail) normally pitch down when power is reduced (and the controls not adjusted) because the downwash on the elevators from the propeller slipstream is reduced and elevator effectiveness is reduced. This allows the nose to drop.

4. When the CG in an airplane is located at, or rear of, the aft CG limit, the airplane

    a. Develops an inability to recover from stall conditions, and
    b. Becomes less stable at all airspeeds.

1.9 TORQUE AND P-FACTOR (Questions 27-29)

1. The torque effect (left-turning tendency) is greatest at low airspeed, high angles of attack, and high power, e.g., on takeoff.

2. P-factor (asymmetric propeller loading) causes the airplane to yaw to the left when at high angles of attack because the descending right side of the propeller (as seen from the rear) has a higher angle of attack (than the upward-moving blade on the left side) and provides more thrust.

1.10 LOAD FACTOR (Questions 30-35)

1. Load factor refers to the additional weight carried by the wings due to the airplane's weight plus the centrifugal force.

    a. The amount of excess load that can be imposed on an airplane's wings varies directly with the airplane's speed and the excess lift available.

        1) At low speeds, very little excess lift is available, so very little excess load can be imposed.

        2) At high speeds, the wings' lifting capacity is so great that the load factor can quickly exceed safety limits.

    b. An increased load factor will result in an airplane stalling at a higher airspeed.

    c. As bank angle increases, the load factor increases. The wings not only have to carry the airplane's weight, but the centrifugal force as well.

2. On the exam, a load factor chart is given with the amount of bank on the horizontal axis (along the bottom of the graph), and the load factor on the vertical axis (up the left side of the graph). Additionally, a table which provides the load factor corresponding to specific bank angles is found on the left side of the chart. Use this table to answer load factor questions.

   a. Compute the load factor by multiplying the airplane's weight by the load factor which corresponds to the given angle of bank. For example, the wings of a 2,000 lb. airplane in a 60° bank must support 4,000 lb. (2,000 x 2.000).

   b. Example load factor chart:

ANGLE OF BANK ϕ	LOAD FACTOR n
0°	1.0
10°	1.015
30°	1.154
45°	1.414
60°	2.000
70°	2.923
80°	5.747
85°	11.473
90°	∞

LOAD FACTOR CHART

3. Load factor (or G units) is a multiple of the regular weight or, alternatively, a multiple of the force of gravity.

   a. Straight-and-level flight has a load factor at 1.0. (Verify on the chart above.)

   b. A 60° level bank has a load factor of 2.0. Due to centrifugal force, the wings must hold up twice the amount of weight.

   c. A 50° level bank has a load factor of about 1.5.

QUESTIONS AND ANSWER EXPLANATIONS

All the FAA questions from the pilot knowledge test for the private pilot certificate relating to the basics of aerodynamics and the material outlined above are reproduced on the following pages in the same modules as the outlines. To the immediate right of each question are the correct answer and answer explanation. You should cover these answers and answer explanations while responding to the questions. Refer to the general discussion in the Introduction on how to take the FAA pilot knowledge test.

Remember that the questions from the FAA pilot knowledge test bank have been reordered by topic, and organized into a meaningful sequence. Accordingly, the first line of the answer explanation gives the FAA question number and the citation of the authoritative source for the answer.

1.1 Flaps and Rudder

1.
3220. What is one purpose of wing flaps?

A—To enable the pilot to make steeper approaches to a landing without increasing the airspeed.
B—To relieve the pilot of maintaining continuous pressure on the controls.
C—To decrease wing area to vary the lift.

Answer (A) is correct (3220). *(PHAK Chap 2)*
Extending the flaps increases the wing camber and the angle of attack of the wing. This increases wing lift and induced drag, which enables the pilot to make steeper approaches to a landing without an increase in airspeed.
Answer (B) is incorrect because trim tabs (not wing flaps) help relieve control pressures. Answer (C) is incorrect because wing area usually remains the same, except for certain specialized flaps which increase (not decrease) the wing area.

2.
3219. One of the main functions of flaps during approach and landing is to

A—decrease the angle of descent without increasing the airspeed.
B—permit a touchdown at a higher indicated airspeed.
C—increase the angle of descent without increasing the airspeed.

Answer (C) is correct (3219). *(PHAK Chap 2)*
Extending the flaps increases the wing camber and the angle of attack of the wing. This increases wing lift and induced drag, which enables the pilot to increase the angle of descent without increasing the airspeed.
Answer (A) is incorrect because extending the flaps increases lift and induced drag, which enables the pilot to increase (not decrease) the angle of descent without increasing the airspeed. Answer (B) is incorrect because flaps increase lift at slow airspeed, which permits touchdown at a lower (not higher) indicated airspeed.

3.
3213. What is the purpose of the rudder on an airplane?

A—To control yaw.
B—To control overbanking tendency.
C—To control roll.

Answer (A) is correct (3213). *(PHAK Chap 1)*
The rudder is used to control yaw, which is rotation about the airplane's vertical axis.
Answer (B) is incorrect because the ailerons (not the rudder) control overbanking. Overbanking tendency refers to the outside wing traveling significantly faster than the inside wing in a steep turn, and generating incremental lift to raise the outside wing higher unless corrected by aileron pressure. Answer (C) is incorrect because roll is movement about the longitudinal axis and is controlled by ailerons.

1.2 Aerodynamic Forces

4.
3201. The four forces acting on an airplane in flight are

A—lift, weight, thrust, and drag.
B—lift, weight, gravity, and thrust.
C—lift, gravity, power, and friction.

Answer (A) is correct (3201). *(PHAK Chap 1)*
Lift is produced by the wings and opposes weight, which is the result of gravity. Thrust is produced by the engine/propeller and opposes drag, which is the resistance of the air as the airplane moves through it.
Answer (B) is incorrect because gravity reacts with the airplane's mass, thus producing weight which opposes lift. Answer (C) is incorrect because gravity results in weight, power produces thrust, and friction is a cause of drag. Power, gravity, velocity, and friction are not aerodynamic forces in themselves.

5.
3202. When are the four forces that act on an airplane in equilibrium?

A—During unaccelerated flight.
B—When the aircraft is accelerating.
C—When the aircraft is at rest on the ground.

Answer (A) is correct (3202). *(PHAK Chap 1)*
The four forces (lift, weight, thrust, and drag) that act on an airplane are in equilibrium during unaccelerated flight.
Answer (B) is incorrect because thrust must exceed drag in order for the airplane to accelerate. Answer (C) is incorrect because, when the airplane is at rest on the ground, there are no aerodynamic forces acting on it other than weight (gravity).

6.
3205. What is the relationship of lift, drag, thrust, and weight when the airplane is in straight-and-level flight?

A—Lift equals weight and thrust equals drag.
B—Lift, drag, and weight equal thrust.
C—Lift and weight equal thrust and drag.

1.3 Angle of Attack

7.
3204. The term "angle of attack" is defined as the angle

A—between the wing chord line and the relative wind.
B—between the airplane's climb angle and the horizon.
C—formed by the longitudinal axis of the airplane and the chord line of the wing.

8.
3317. Angle of attack is defined as the angle between the chord line of an airfoil and the

A—direction of the relative wind.
B—pitch angle of an airfoil.
C—rotor plane of rotation.

9.
3203. (Refer to figure 1 below.) The acute angle A is the angle of

A—incidence.
B—attack.
C—dihedral.

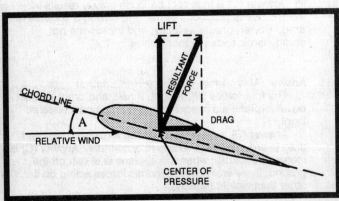

FIGURE 1.—Lift Vector.

Answer (A) is correct (3205). *(PHAK Chap 1)*
When the airplane is in straight-and-level flight (assuming no change of airspeed), it is not accelerating, and therefore lift equals weight and thrust equals drag.
Answer (B) is incorrect because lift equals weight and drag equals thrust. Answer (C) is incorrect because lift and weight are equal and thrust and drag are equal, but the four are not equal to each other.

Answer (A) is correct (3204). *(PHAK Chap 1)*
The angle of attack is the angle between the wing chord line and the direction of the relative wind. The wing chord line is a straight line from the leading edge to the trailing edge of the wing. The relative wind is the direction of airflow relative to the wing when the wing is moving through the air.
Answer (B) is incorrect because the angle between the airplane's climb angle and the horizon does not describe any term. Answer (C) is incorrect because the angle formed by the longitudinal axis of the airplane and the chord line of the wing is the angle of incidence (not attack).

Answer (A) is correct (3317). *(PHAK Chap 1)*
The angle of attack is the angle between the wing chord line and the direction of the relative wind. The wing chord line is a straight line from the leading edge to the trailing edge of the wing. The relative wind is the direction of airflow relative to the wing when the wing is moving through the air.
Answer (B) is incorrect because pitch is used in conjunction with the aircraft or longitudinal axis, not the chord line of the airfoil. Answer (C) is incorrect because rotor plane of rotation deals with helicopters, not fixed-wing aircraft.

Answer (B) is correct (3203). *(PHAK Chap 1)*
The angle between the relative wind and the wing chord line is the angle of attack. The wing chord line is a straight line from the leading edge to the trailing edge of the wing.
Answer (A) is incorrect because the angle of incidence is the acute angle formed by the chord line of the wing and the longitudinal axis of the airplane. Answer (C) is incorrect because the dihedral is the angle at which the wings are slanted upward from the wing root to the wingtip.

10.
3311. The angle of attack at which an airplane wing stalls will

A—increase if the CG is moved forward.
B—change with an increase in gross weight.
C—remain the same regardless of gross weight.

Answer (C) is correct (3311). *(PHAK Chap 1)*
A given airplane wing will always stall at the same angle of attack regardless of airspeed, weight, load factor, or density altitude. Each wing has a particular angle of attack (the critical angle of attack) at which the airflow separates from the upper surface of the wing and the stall occurs.
Answer (A) is incorrect because a change in CG will not change the wing's critical angle of attack. Answer (B) is incorrect because the critical angle of attack does not change when gross weight changes.

1.4 Stalls and Spins

11.
3263. As altitude increases, the indicated airspeed at which a given airplane stalls in a particular configuration will

A—decrease as the true airspeed decreases.
B—decrease as the true airspeed increases.
C—remain the same regardless of altitude.

Answer (C) is correct (3263). *(AC 61-67B)*
All the performance factors of an airplane are dependent upon air density. As air density decreases, the airplane stalls at a higher true airspeed. However, you cannot detect the effect of high density altitude on your airspeed indicator. Accordingly, an airplane will stall in a particular configuration at the same indicated airspeed regardless of altitude.
Answer (A) is incorrect because true airspeed increases, not decreases, with increased altitude, and indicated airspeed at which an airplane stalls remains the same (not decreases). Answer (B) is incorrect because the indicated airspeed of the stall does not change with increased altitude.

12.
3309. In what flight condition must an aircraft be placed in order to spin?

A—Partially stalled with one wing low.
B—In a steep diving spiral.
C—Stalled.

Answer (C) is correct (3309). *(AC 61-67B)*
In order to enter a spin, an airplane must always first be stalled. Thereafter, the spin is caused when one wing becomes less stalled than the other wing.
Answer (A) is incorrect because the aircraft must first be fully stalled. Answer (B) is incorrect because a steep diving spiral has a relatively low angle of attack and thus does not produce a stall.

13.
3310. During a spin to the left, which wing(s) is/are stalled?

A—Both wings are stalled.
B—Neither wing is stalled.
C—Only the left wing is stalled.

Answer (A) is correct (3310). *(AC 61-67B)*
In order to enter a spin, an airplane must always first be stalled. Thereafter, the spin is caused when one wing is less stalled than the other wing. In a spin to the left, the right wing is less stalled than the left wing.
Answer (B) is incorrect because both wings must be at least partially stalled through the spin. Answer (C) is incorrect because both wings are stalled; the right wing is simply less stalled than the left.

1.5 Frost

14.
3206. How will frost on the wings of an airplane affect takeoff performance?

A—Frost will disrupt the smooth flow of air over the wing, adversely affecting its lifting capability.
B—Frost will change the camber of the wing, increasing its lifting capability.
C—Frost will cause the airplane to become airborne with a higher angle of attack, decreasing the stall speed.

Answer (A) is correct (3206). *(PHAK Chap 1)*
Frost does not change the basic aerodynamic shape of the wing, but the roughness of its surface spoils the smooth flow of air, thus causing an increase in drag and an early airflow separation over the wing, resulting in a loss of lift.
Answer (B) is incorrect because frost will decrease (not increase) lift during takeoff and has no effect on the wing camber. Answer (C) is incorrect because a layer of frost on an airplane will increase drag which increases (not decreases) the stall speed.

15.
3431. Why is frost considered hazardous to flight?

A—Frost changes the basic aerodynamic shape of the airfoils, thereby decreasing lift.
B—Frost slows the airflow over the airfoils, thereby increasing control effectiveness.
C—Frost spoils the smooth flow of air over the wings, thereby decreasing lifting capability.

Answer (C) is correct (3431). *(AvW Chap 10)*
Frost does not change the basic aerodynamic shape of the wing, but the roughness of its surface spoils the smooth flow of air, thus causing an increase in drag and an early airflow separation over the wing, resulting in a loss of lift.
Answer (A) is incorrect because frost is thin and does not change the basic aerodynamic shape of the airfoil. Answer (B) is incorrect because the smooth flow of air over the airfoil is affected, not control effectiveness.

16.
3432. How does frost affect the lifting surfaces of an airplane on takeoff?

A—Frost may prevent the airplane from becoming airborne at normal takeoff speed.
B—Frost will change the camber of the wing, increasing lift during takeoff.
C—Frost may cause the airplane to become airborne with a lower angle of attack at a lower indicated airspeed.

Answer (A) is correct (3432). *(AvW Chap 10)*
Frost that is not removed from the surface of an airplane prior to takeoff may make it difficult to get the airplane airborne at normal takeoff speed. The frost disrupts the airflow over the wing, which increases drag.
Answer (B) is incorrect because the smoothness of the wing, not its curvature, is affected and lift is decreased (not increased). Answer (C) is incorrect because ground effect (not frost) may cause an airplane to become airborne with a lower angle of attack at a lower indicated airspeed.

1.6 Ground Effect

17.
3312. What is ground effect?

A—The result of the interference of the surface of the Earth with the airflow patterns about an airplane.
B—The result of an alteration in airflow patterns increasing induced drag about the wings of an airplane.
C—The result of the disruption of the airflow patterns about the wings of an airplane to the point where the wings will no longer support the airplane in flight.

Answer (A) is correct (3312). *(PHAK Chap 4)*
Ground effect is due to the interference of the ground (or water) surface with the airflow patterns about the airplane in flight. As the wing encounters ground effect, there is a reduction in the upwash, downwash, and the wingtip vortices. The result is a reduction in induced drag. Thus, for a given angle of attack, the wing will produce more lift in ground effect than it does out of ground effect.
Answer (B) is incorrect because the result of the alteration in airflow patterns about the wing decreases, not increases, the induced drag. Answer (C) is incorrect because the disruption of the airflow patterns about the wing decreases induced drag, which causes an increase, not decrease, in lift at a given angle of attack.

18.
3313. Floating caused by the phenomenon of ground effect will be most realized during an approach to land when at

A—less than the length of the wingspan above the surface.
B—twice the length of the wingspan above the surface.
C—a higher-than-normal angle of attack.

Answer (A) is correct (3313). *(PHAK Chap 4)*
Ground effect is most usually recognized when the airplane is within one-half of the length of its wingspan above the surface. It may extend as high as a full wingspan length above the surface. Due to an alteration of the airflow about the wings, induced drag decreases, which reduces the thrust required at low airspeeds. Thus, any excess speed during the landing flare may result in considerable floating.
Answer (B) is incorrect because ground effect generally extends up to only one wingspan length, not two. Answer (C) is incorrect because floating will occur with excess airspeed, which results in a lower-than-normal, not higher-than-normal, angle of attack.

19.
3314. What must a pilot be aware of as a result of ground effect?

A—Wingtip vortices increase creating wake turbulence problems for arriving and departing aircraft.
B—Induced drag decreases; therefore, any excess speed at the point of flare may cause considerable floating.
C—A full stall landing will require less up elevator deflection than would a full stall when done free of ground effect.

Answer (B) is correct (3314). *(PHAK Chap 4)*
Ground effect reduces the upwash, downwash, and vortices caused by the wings, resulting in a decrease in induced drag. Thus, thrust required at low airspeeds will be reduced and any excess speed at the point of flare may cause considerable floating.
Answer (A) is incorrect because wingtip vortices are decreased, not increased. Answer (C) is incorrect because a full stall landing will require more, not less, up elevator deflection since the wing will require a lower angle of attack in ground effect to produce the same amount of lift.

20.
3315. Ground effect is most likely to result in which problem?

A—Settling to the surface abruptly during landing.
B—Becoming airborne before reaching recommended takeoff speed.
C—Inability to get airborne even though airspeed is sufficient for normal takeoff needs.

Answer (B) is correct (3315). *(PHAK Chap 4)*
Due to the reduction of induced drag in ground effect, the airplane may seem capable of becoming airborne well below the recommended takeoff speed. However, as the airplane rises out of ground effect (a height greater than the wingspan) with a deficiency of speed, the increase in induced drag may result in very marginal initial climb performance. In extreme cases, the airplane may become airborne initially, with a deficiency of airspeed, only to settle back on the runway when attempting to fly out of the ground effect area.
Answer (A) is incorrect because the airplane will experience a little extra lift on landing due to the reduction in induced drag, causing it to float rather than settle abruptly. Answer (C) is incorrect because ground effect would not hamper the airplane from becoming airborne if the airspeed were sufficient for normal takeoff. Ground effect may allow the airplane to become airborne before reaching the recommended takeoff speed.

1.7 Airplane Turn

21.
3301. What force makes an airplane turn?

A—The horizontal component of lift.
B—The vertical component of lift.
C—Centrifugal force.

Answer (A) is correct (3301). *(AFH Chap 4)*
When the wings of an airplane are not level, the lift is not entirely vertical and tends to pull the airplane toward the direction of the lower wing. An airplane is turned when the pilot coordinates rudder, aileron, and elevator to bank in order to attain a horizontal component of lift.
Answer (B) is incorrect because the vertical component of lift opposes weight and controls vertical, not horizontal, movement. Answer (C) is incorrect because the horizontal component of lift opposes centrifugal force, which acts toward the outside of the turn.

1.8 Airplane Stability

22.
3210. An airplane said to be inherently stable will

A—be difficult to stall.
B—require less effort to control.
C—not spin.

Answer (B) is correct (3210). *(PHAK Chap 1)*
An inherently stable airplane will usually return to the original condition of flight (except when in a bank) if disturbed by a force such as air turbulence. Thus, an inherently stable airplane will require less effort to control than an inherently unstable one.
Answer (A) is incorrect because stability of an airplane has an effect on stall characteristic, not on the difficulty level of entering a stall. Answer (C) is incorrect because an inherently stable aircraft will spin.

23.
3211. What determines the longitudinal stability of an airplane?

A—The location of the CG with respect to the center of lift.
B—The effectiveness of the horizontal stabilizer, rudder, and rudder trim tab.
C—The relationship of thrust and lift to weight and drag.

Answer (A) is correct (3211). *(PHAK Chap 1)*
The location of the center of gravity with respect to the center of lift determines, to a great extent, the longitudinal stability of the airplane. Positive stability is attained by having the center of lift behind the center of gravity. Then the tail provides negative lift, creating a downward tail force, which counteracts the nose's tendency to pitch down.
Answer (B) is incorrect because the rudder and rudder trim tab control the yaw, not the pitch. Answer (C) is incorrect because the relationship of thrust and lift to weight and drag affects speed and altitude, not longitudinal stability.

24.
3287. An airplane has been loaded in such a manner that the CG is located aft of the aft CG limit. One undesirable flight characteristic a pilot might experience with this airplane would be

A—a longer takeoff run.
B—difficulty in recovering from a stalled condition.
C—stalling at higher-than-normal airspeed.

25.
3212. What causes an airplane (except a T-tail) to pitch nosedown when power is reduced and controls are not adjusted?

A—The CG shifts forward when thrust and drag are reduced.
B—The downwash on the elevators from the propeller slipstream is reduced and elevator effectiveness is reduced.
C—When thrust is reduced to less than weight, lift is also reduced and the wings can no longer support the weight.

26.
3288. Loading an airplane to the most aft CG will cause the airplane to be

A—less stable at all speeds.
B—less stable at slow speeds, but more stable at high speeds.
C—less stable at high speeds, but more stable at low speeds.

1.9 Torque and P-Factor

27.
3207. In what flight condition is torque effect the greatest in a single-engine airplane?

A—Low airspeed, high power, high angle of attack.
B—Low airspeed, low power, low angle of attack.
C—High airspeed, high power, high angle of attack.

28.
3208. The left turning tendency of an airplane caused by P-factor is the result of the

A—clockwise rotation of the engine and the propeller turning the airplane counterclockwise.
B—propeller blade descending on the right, producing more thrust than the ascending blade on the left.
C—gyroscopic forces applied to the rotating propeller blades acting 90° in advance of the point the force was applied.

Answer (B) is correct (3287). *(PHAK Chap 4)*
The recovery from a stall in any airplane becomes progressively more difficult as its center of gravity moves backward. Generally, airplanes become less controllable, especially at slow flight speeds, as the center of gravity is moved backward.
Answer (A) is incorrect because an airplane with an aft CG has less drag, resulting in a shorter, not longer, takeoff run. Answer (C) is incorrect because an airplane with an aft CG flies at a lower angle of attack, resulting in a lower, not higher, stall speed.

Answer (B) is correct (3212). *(PHAK Chap 1)*
The relative wind on the tail is the result of the airplane's movement through the air and the propeller slipstream. When that slipstream is reduced, the horizontal stabilizer (except a T-tail) will produce less negative lift and the nose will pitch down.
Answer (A) is incorrect because the CG is not affected by changes in thrust or drag. Answer (C) is incorrect because thrust and weight have no relationship to each other.

Answer (A) is correct (3288). *(PHAK Chap 4)*
Airplanes become less stable at all speeds as the center of gravity is moved backward. The rearward center of gravity limit is determined largely by considerations of stability.
Answer (B) is incorrect because an aft CG will cause the airplane to be less stable at all speeds. Answer (C) is incorrect because an aft CG will cause the airplane to be less stable at all speeds.

Answer (A) is correct (3207). *(PHAK Chap 1)*
The effect of torque increases in direct proportion to engine power and inversely to airspeed. Thus, at low airspeeds, high angles of attack, and high power settings, torque is the greatest.
Answer (B) is incorrect because torque effect is the greatest at high (not low) power settings, and high (not low) angle of attack. Answer (C) is incorrect because torque effect is the greatest at low (not high) airspeeds.

Answer (B) is correct (3208). *(PHAK Chap 1)*
Asymmetric propeller loading (P-factor) occurs when the airplane is flown at a high angle of attack. The downward-moving blade on the right side of the propeller (as seen from the rear) has a higher angle of attack, which creates higher thrust than the upward moving blade on the left. Thus, the airplane yaws around the vertical axis to the left.
Answer (A) is incorrect because torque reaction (not P-factor) is a result of the clockwise rotation of the engine and the propeller turning the airplane counterclockwise. Answer (C) is incorrect because gyroscopic precession (not P-factor) is a result of the gyroscopic forces applied to the rotating propeller blades acting 90° in advance of the point the force was applied.

29.
3209. When does P-factor cause the airplane to yaw to the left?

A—When at low angles of attack.
B—When at high angles of attack.
C—When at high airspeeds.

Answer (B) is correct (3209). *(PHAK Chap 1)*
P-factor or asymmetric propeller loading occurs when an airplane is flown at a high angle of attack because the downward-moving blade on the right side of the propeller (as seen from the rear) has a higher angle of attack, which creates higher thrust than the upward moving blade on the left. Thus, the airplane yaws around the vertical axis to the left.
Answer (A) is incorrect because at low angles of attack, both sides of the propeller have similar angles of attack and "pull" the airplane straight ahead. Answer (C) is incorrect because, at high speeds, an airplane is not at a high angle of attack.

1.10 Load Factor

30.
3217. The amount of excess load that can be imposed on the wing of an airplane depends upon the

A—position of the CG.
B—speed of the airplane.
C—abruptness at which the load is applied.

Answer (B) is correct (3217). *(PHAK Chap 1)*
The amount of excess load that can be imposed on the wing depends upon how fast the airplane is flying. At low speeds, the maximum available lifting force of the wing is only slightly greater than the amount necessary to support the weight of the airplane. Thus, any excess load would simply cause the airplane to stall. At high speeds, the lifting capacity of the wing is so great (as a result of the greater flow of air over the wings) that a sudden movement of the elevator controls (strong gust of wind) may increase the load factor beyond safe limits. This is why maximum speeds are established by airplane manufacturers.
Answer (A) is incorrect because the position of the CG affects the stability of the airplane but not the total load the wings can support. Answer (C) is incorrect because it is the amount of load, not the abruptness of the load, that is limited. However, the abruptness of the maneuver can affect the amount of the load.

31.
3218. Which basic flight maneuver increases the load factor on an airplane as compared to straight-and-level flight?

A—Climbs.
B—Turns.
C—Stalls.

Answer (B) is correct (3218). *(PHAK Chap 1)*
Turns increase the load factor because the lift from the wings is used to pull the airplane around a corner as well as to offset the force of gravity. The wings must carry the airplane's weight plus offset centrifugal force during the turn. For example, a 60° bank results in a load factor of 2; i.e., the wings must support twice the weight they do in level flight.
Answer (A) is incorrect because the wings only have to carry the weight of the airplane once the airplane is established in a climb. Answer (C) is incorrect because, in a stall, the wings are not producing lift.

32.
3316. During an approach to a stall, an increased load factor will cause the airplane to

A—stall at a higher airspeed.
B—have a tendency to spin.
C—be more difficult to control.

Answer (A) is correct (3316). *(PHAK Chap 1)*
The greater the load (whether from gross weight or from centrifugal force), the more lift is required. Therefore, an airplane will stall at higher airspeeds when the load and/or load factor is increased.
Answer (B) is incorrect because an airplane's tendency to spin is not related to an increase in load factors. Answer (C) is incorrect because an airplane's stability (not load factor) determines its controllability.

33.
3214. (Refer to figure 2 below.) If an airplane weighs 2,300 pounds, what approximate weight would the airplane structure be required to support during a 60° banked turn while maintaining altitude?

A—2,300 pounds.
B—3,400 pounds.
C—4,600 pounds.

34.
3215. (Refer to figure 2 below.) If an airplane weighs 3,300 pounds, what approximate weight would the airplane structure be required to support during a 30° banked turn while maintaining altitude?

A—1,200 pounds.
B—3,100 pounds.
C—3,960 pounds.

35.
3216. (Refer to figure 2 below.) If an airplane weighs 4,500 pounds, what approximate weight would the airplane structure be required to support during a 45° banked turn while maintaining altitude?

A—4,500 pounds.
B—6,750 pounds.
C—7,200 pounds.

Answer (C) is correct (3214). *(PHAK Chap 1)*
Note on Fig. 2 that, at a 60° bank angle, the load factor is 2. Thus, a 2,300-lb. airplane in a 60° bank would require its wings to support 4,600 lb. (2,300 x 2).
Answer (A) is incorrect because a 1,150-lb. airplane would be required to support a 2,300-lb. load in a 60° banked turn. Answer (B) is incorrect because a 1,700-lb. airplane would be required to support a 3,400-lb. load in a 60° banked turn.

Answer (C) is correct (3215). *(PHAK Chap 1)*
Look on the left side of the chart in Fig. 2 to see that, at a 30° bank angle, the load factor is 1.154. Thus, a 3,300-lb. airplane in a 30° bank would require its wings to support 3,808.2 lb. (3,300 x 1.154). Answer (C) is closest to this value.
Answer (A) is incorrect because a 1,000-lb. airplane would be required to support a 1,200-lb. load in a 30° banked turn. Answer (B) is incorrect because a 2,583-lb. airplane would be required to support a 3,100-lb. load in a 30° banked turn.

Answer (B) is correct (3216). *(PHAK Chap 1)*
Look on the left side of the chart under 45° and note that the load factor curve is 1.414. Thus, a 4,500-lb. airplane in a 45° bank would require its wings to support 6,363 lb. (4,500 x 1.414). Answer (B) is closest to this value.
Answer (A) is incorrect because a 3,000-lb. airplane would be required to support a 4,500-lb. load in a 45° banked turn. Answer (C) is incorrect because a 4,800-lb. airplane would be required to support a 7,200-lb. load in a 45° banked turn.

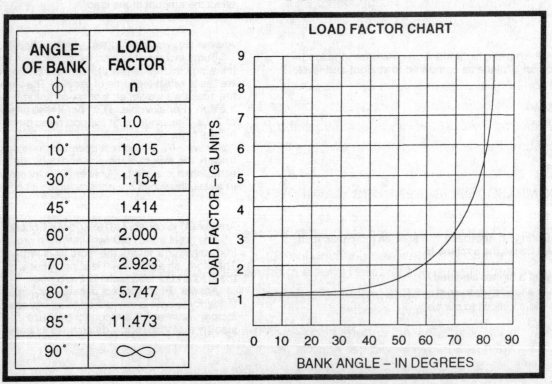

ANGLE OF BANK ϕ	LOAD FACTOR n
0°	1.0
10°	1.015
30°	1.154
45°	1.414
60°	2.000
70°	2.923
80°	5.747
85°	11.473
90°	∞

FIGURE 2.—Load Factor Chart.

END OF CHAPTER

CHAPTER TWO
AIRPLANE INSTRUMENTS, ENGINES, AND SYSTEMS

This chapter contains outlines of major concepts tested, all FAA test questions and answers regarding the major mechanical and instrument systems in an airplane, and an explanation of each answer. Each module, or subtopic, within this chapter is listed above with the number of questions from the FAA pilot knowledge test pertaining to that particular module. For each module, the first number following the parentheses is the page number on which the outline begins, and the next number is the page number on which the questions begin.

CAUTION: Recall that the **sole purpose** of this book is to expedite your passing the FAA pilot knowledge test for the private pilot certificate. Accordingly, all extraneous material (i.e., topics or regulations not directly tested on the FAA pilot knowledge test) is omitted, even though much more information and knowledge are necessary to fly safely. This additional material is presented in *Pilot Handbook* and *Private Pilot Flight Maneuvers and Practical Test Prep*, available from Gleim Publications, Inc. See the order form on page 326.

2.1 COMPASS TURNING ERRORS (Questions 1-7)

1. During flight, magnetic compasses can be considered accurate only during straight-and-level flight at constant airspeed.

2. The difference between direction indicated by a magnetic compass not installed in an airplane and one installed in an airplane is called deviation.

   a. Magnetic fields produced by metals and electrical accessories in an airplane disturb the compass needles.

3. In the Northern Hemisphere, acceleration/deceleration error occurs when on an east or west heading. Remember ANDS: Accelerate North, Decelerate South.

   a. A magnetic compass will indicate a turn toward the north during acceleration when on an east or west heading.

   b. A magnetic compass will indicate a turn toward the south during deceleration when on an east or west heading.

   c. Acceleration/deceleration error does not occur when on a north or south heading.

4. In the Northern Hemisphere, compass turning error occurs when turning from a north or south heading.

    a. A magnetic compass will lag (and at the start of a turn indicate a turn in the opposite direction) when turning from a north heading.

        1) If turning to the east (right), the compass will initially indicate a turn to the west and then lag behind the actual heading until your airplane is headed east (at which point there is no error).

        2) If turning to the west (left), the compass will initially indicate a turn to the east and then lag behind the actual heading until your airplane is headed west (at which point there is no error).

    b. A magnetic compass will lead or precede the turn when turning from a south heading.

    c. Turning errors do not occur when turning from an east or west heading.

5. These errors diminish as the acceleration/deceleration or turns are completed.

2.2 PITOT-STATIC SYSTEM (Questions 8-11)

1. The pitot-static system is a source of pressure for the

    a. Altimeter
    b. Vertical-speed indicator
    c. Airspeed indicator

2. The pitot tube provides impact (or ram) pressure for the airspeed indicator only.

3. When the pitot tube and the outside static vents or just the static vents are clogged, all three instruments mentioned above will provide inaccurate readings.

    a. If only the pitot tube is clogged, only the airspeed indicator will be inoperative.

2.3 AIRSPEED INDICATOR (Questions 12-22)

1. Airspeed indicators have several color-coded markings (Figure 4, page 42).

    a. The white arc is the full flap operating range.

        1) The lower limit is the power-off stalling speed with wing flaps and landing gear in the landing position (V_{S0}).

        2) The upper limit is the maximum full flaps-extended speed (V_{FE}).

    b. The green arc is the normal operating range.

        1) The lower limit is the power-off stalling speed in a specified configuration (V_{S1}). This is normally wing flaps up and landing gear retracted.

        2) The upper limit is the maximum structural cruising speed (V_{NO}) for normal operation.

    c. The yellow arc is airspeed which is safe in smooth air only.

        1) It is known as the caution range.

    d. The red radial line is the speed that should never be exceeded (V_{NE}).

        1) This is the maximum speed at which the airplane may be operated in smooth air (or under any circumstances).

2. The most important airspeed limitation which is **not** color-coded is the maneuvering speed (V_A).

a. The maneuvering speed is the maximum speed at which full deflection of aircraft controls can be made without causing structural damage.

b. It is usually the maximum speed for flight in turbulent air.

2.4 ALTIMETER (Questions 23-26)

1. Altimeters have three hands (e.g., as a clock has the hour, minute, and second hands; Figure 3, page 44).

2. The three hands on the altimeter are the

    a. 10,000-ft. interval (short needle).
    b. 1,000-ft. interval (medium needle).
    c. 100-ft. interval (long needle).

3. Altimeters are numbered 0-9.

4. To read an altimeter,

    a. First, determine whether the short needle points between 0 and 1 (1-10,000), 1-2 (10,000-20,000), or 2-3 (20,000-30,000).

    b. Second, determine whether the medium needle is between 0 and 1 (0-1,000), 1 and 2 (1,000-2,000), etc.

    c. Third, determine at which number the long needle is pointing, e.g., 1 for 100 ft., 2 for 200 ft., etc.

2.5 TYPES OF ALTITUDE (Questions 27-34)

1. Absolute altitude is the altitude above the surface, i.e., AGL.

2. True altitude is the actual distance above mean sea level, i.e., MSL. It is not susceptible to variation with atmospheric conditions.

3. Density altitude is pressure altitude corrected for nonstandard temperatures.

4. Pressure altitude is the height above the standard datum plane of 29.92 in. of mercury. Thus, it is the indicated altitude when the altimeter setting is adjusted to 29.92 in. of mercury (also written 29.92" Hg).

5. Pressure altitude and density altitude are the same at standard temperature.

6. Indicated altitude is the same as true altitude when standard conditions exist and the altimeter is calibrated properly.

7. Pressure altitude and true altitude are the same when standard atmospheric conditions (29.92" Hg and 15°C at sea level) exist.

8. When the altimeter is adjusted on the ground so that indicated altitude equals true altitude at airport elevation, the altimeter setting is that for your location, i.e., approximately the setting you would get from the control tower.

2.6 SETTING THE ALTIMETER (Questions 35-36)

1. The indicated altitude on the altimeter increases when you change the altimeter setting to a higher pressure and decreases when you change the setting to a lower pressure.

    a. This is opposite to the altimeter's reaction due to changes in air pressure.

2. The indicated altitude will change at a rate of approximately 1,000 ft. for 1 in. of pressure change in the altimeter setting.

    a. EXAMPLE: When changing the altimeter setting from 29.15 to 29.85, there is a 0.70 in. change in pressure (29.85 - 29.15). The indicated altitude would increase (due to a higher altimeter setting) by 700 ft. (0.70 x 1,000).

2.7 ALTIMETER ERRORS (Questions 37-41)

1. Since altimeter readings are adjusted for changes in barometric pressure but not for temperature changes, an airplane will be at lower than indicated altitude when flying in colder than standard temperature air when maintaining a constant indicated altitude.

   a. On warm days, the altimeter indicates lower than actual altitude.

2. Likewise, when pressure lowers en route at a constant indicated altitude, your altimeter will indicate higher than actual altitude until you adjust it.

3. Remember, when flying from high to low (temperature or pressure), look out below.

   a. Low to high, clear the sky.

2.8 GYROSCOPIC INSTRUMENTS (Questions 42-45)

1. The attitude indicator, with its miniature aircraft and horizon bar, displays a picture of the attitude of the airplane (Figure 7, page 49).

   a. The relationship of the miniature aircraft to the horizon bar is the same as the relationship of the real aircraft to the actual horizon.

   b. The relationship of the miniature airplane to the horizon bar should be used for an indication of pitch and bank attitude, i.e., nose high, nose low, left bank, right bank.

   c. The gyro in the attitude indicator rotates in a horizontal plane and depends upon rigidity in space for its operation.

   d. An adjustment knob is provided with which the pilot may move the miniature airplane up or down to align the miniature airplane with the horizon bar to suit the pilot's line of vision.

2. The turn coordinator shows the roll and yaw movement of the airplane (Figure 5, page 49).

   a. It displays a miniature airplane which moves proportionally to the roll rate of the airplane. When the bank is held constant, the turn coordinator indicates the rate of turn.

   b. The ball indicates whether the angle of bank is coordinated with the rate of turn.

3. The heading indicator is a gyro instrument which depends on the principle of rigidity in space for its operation (Figure 6, page 49).

   a. Due to gyro precession, it must be periodically realigned with a magnetic compass.

2.9 ENGINE TEMPERATURE (Questions 46-51)

1. Excessively high engine temperature either in the air or on the ground will cause loss of power, excessive oil consumption, and excessive wear on the internal engine.

2. An engine is cooled, in part, by circulating oil through the system to reduce friction and absorb heat from internal engine parts.

3. Engine oil and cylinder head temperatures can exceed their normal operating range because of (among other causes)

   a. Operating with too much power
   b. Climbing too steeply (i.e., at too low an airspeed) in hot weather
   c. Using fuel that has a lower-than-specified octane rating
   d. Operating with too lean a mixture
   e. The oil level being too low

4. Excessively high engine temperatures can be reduced by reversing any of the above situations, i.e., reducing power, climbing less steeply (increasing airspeed), using higher octane fuel, enriching the mixture, etc.

2.10 CONSTANT-SPEED PROPELLER (Questions 52-54)

1. The advantage of a constant-speed propeller (also known as controllable-pitch) is that it permits the pilot to select the blade angle for the most efficient performance.

2. Constant-speed propeller airplanes have both throttle and propeller controls.

    a. The throttle controls power output, which is registered on the manifold pressure gauge.

    b. The propeller control regulates engine revolutions per minute (RPM), which are registered on the tachometer.

3. To avoid overstressing cylinders, excessively high manifold pressure should not be used with low RPM settings.

2.11 ENGINE IGNITION SYSTEMS (Question 55)

1. One purpose of the dual-ignition system is to provide for improved engine performance.

    a. The other is increased safety.

2.12 CARBURETOR ICING (Questions 56-61)

1. Carburetor-equipped engines are more susceptible to icing than fuel-injected engines.

    a. The operating principle of float-type carburetors is the difference in air pressure between the venturi throat and the air inlet.

    b. Fuel-injected engines do not have a carburetor.

2. The first indication of carburetor ice on airplanes with fixed-pitch propellers and float-type carburetors is a loss of RPM.

3. Carburetor ice is likely to form when outside air temperature is between 20°F and 70°F and there is visible moisture or high humidity.

4. When carburetor heat is applied to eliminate carburetor ice in an airplane equipped with a fixed-pitch propeller, there will be a further decrease in RPM (due to the less dense hot air entering the engine) followed by a gradual increase in RPM as the ice melts.

2.13 CARBURETOR HEAT (Questions 62-64)

1. Carburetor heat enriches the fuel/air mixture,

    a. Because warm air is less dense than cold air.

    b. When the air density decreases (because the air is warm), the fuel/air mixture (ratio) becomes richer since there is less air for the same amount of fuel.

2. Applying carburetor heat decreases engine output and increases operating temperature.

2.14 FUEL/AIR MIXTURE (Questions 65-67)

1. At higher altitudes, the fuel/air mixture must be leaned to decrease the fuel flow in order to compensate for the decreased air density, i.e., to keep the fuel/air mixture constant.

    a. If you descend from high altitudes to lower altitudes without enriching the mixture, the mixture will become leaner because the air is denser at lower altitudes.

2. If you are running up your engine at a high-altitude airport, you may eliminate engine roughness by leaning the mixture,

    a. Particularly if the engine runs even worse with carburetor heat, since warm air further enriches the mixture.

2.15 ABNORMAL COMBUSTION (Questions 68-71)

1. Detonation occurs when the fuel/air mixture explodes instead of burning evenly.

2. Detonation is usually caused by using a lower-than-specified grade (octane) of aviation fuel or by excessive engine temperature.

    a. This causes many engine problems including excessive wear and higher than normal operating temperatures.

3. Lower the nose slightly if you suspect that an engine (with a fixed-pitch propeller) is detonating during climbout after takeoff. This will increase cooling and decrease the engine's workload.

4. Pre-ignition is the uncontrolled firing of the fuel/air charge in advance of the normal spark ignition.

2.16 AVIATION FUEL PRACTICES (Questions 72-75)

1. Use of the next-higher-than-specified (octane) grade of fuel is better than using the next-lower-than-specified grade of fuel. This will prevent the possibility of detonation, or running the engine too hot.

2. Filling the fuel tanks at the end of the day prevents moisture condensation by eliminating the airspace in the tanks.

3. In an airplane equipped with fuel pumps, the auxiliary electric fuel pump is used in the event the engine-driven fuel pump fails.

2.17 STARTING THE ENGINE (Questions 76-77)

1. After the engine starts, the throttle should be adjusted for proper RPM and the engine gauges, especially the oil pressure, checked.

2. When starting an airplane engine by hand, it is extremely important that a competent pilot be at the controls in the cockpit.

QUESTIONS AND ANSWER EXPLANATIONS

All the FAA questions from the pilot knowledge test for the private pilot certificate relating to the major mechanical and instrument systems in an airplane and the material outlined previously are reproduced on the following pages in the same modules as the outlines. To the immediate right of each question are the correct answer and answer explanation. You should cover these answers and answer explanations while responding to the questions. Refer to the general discussion in the Introduction on how to take the FAA pilot knowledge test.

Remember that the questions from the FAA pilot knowledge test bank have been reordered by topic, and the topics have been organized into a meaningful sequence. Accordingly, the first line of the answer explanation gives the FAA question number and the citation of the authoritative source for the answer.

2.1 Compass Turning Errors

1.
3282. In the Northern Hemisphere, a magnetic compass will normally indicate a turn toward the north if

A—a right turn is entered from an east heading.
B—a left turn is entered from a west heading.
C—an aircraft is accelerated while on an east or west heading.

Answer (C) is correct (3282). *(PHAK Chap 3)*
In the Northern Hemisphere, a magnetic compass will normally indicate a turn toward the north if an airplane is accelerated while on an east or west heading.
Answer (A) is incorrect because there is no compass turning error on turns from an east heading. Answer (B) is incorrect because there is no compass turning error on turns from a west heading.

2.
3286. During flight, when are the indications of a magnetic compass accurate?

A—Only in straight-and-level unaccelerated flight.
B—As long as the airspeed is constant.
C—During turns if the bank does not exceed 18°.

Answer (A) is correct (3286). *(PHAK Chap 3)*
During flight, the magnetic compass indications can be considered accurate only when in straight-and-level, unaccelerated flight. During acceleration, deceleration, or turns, the compass card will dip and cause false readings.
Answer (B) is incorrect because, even with a constant airspeed, the magnetic compass may not be accurate during a turn. Answer (C) is incorrect because, due to the compass card dip, the compass may not be accurate even during shallow turns.

3.
3279. Deviation in a magnetic compass is caused by the

A—presence of flaws in the permanent magnets of the compass.
B—difference in the location between true north and magnetic north.
C—magnetic fields within the aircraft distorting the lines of magnetic force.

Answer (C) is correct (3279). *(PHAK Chap 3)*
Magnetic fields produced by metals and electrical accessories in the airplane disturb the compass needle and produce errors. These errors are referred to as compass deviation.
Answer (A) is incorrect because a properly functioning magnetic compass is still subject to deviation. Answer (B) is incorrect because the difference in the location between true and magnetic north refers to magnetic variation, not deviation.

4.
3284. In the Northern Hemisphere, if an aircraft is accelerated or decelerated, the magnetic compass will normally indicate

A—a turn momentarily.
B—correctly when on a north or south heading.
C—a turn toward the south.

Answer (B) is correct (3284). *(PHAK Chap 3)*
Acceleration and deceleration errors on magnetic compasses do not occur when on a north or south heading in the Northern Hemisphere. They occur on east and west headings.
Answer (A) is incorrect because acceleration and deceleration errors occur only on easterly and westerly headings. Answer (C) is incorrect because a turn to the north is indicated upon acceleration and a turn to the south is indicated on deceleration when on east or west headings.

5.
3280. In the Northern Hemisphere, a magnetic compass will normally indicate initially a turn toward the west if

A—a left turn is entered from a north heading.
B—a right turn is entered from a north heading.
C—an aircraft is accelerated while on a north heading.

Answer (B) is correct (3280). *(PHAK Chap 3)*
Due to the northerly turn error in the Northern Hemisphere, a magnetic compass will initially indicate a turn toward the west if a right (east) turn is entered from a north heading.
Answer (A) is incorrect because, if a left (west) turn were made from a north heading, the compass would initially indicate a turn toward the east. Answer (C) is incorrect because acceleration/deceleration error does not occur on a north heading.

6.
3283. In the Northern Hemisphere, the magnetic compass will normally indicate a turn toward the south when

A—a left turn is entered from an east heading.
B—a right turn is entered from a west heading.
C—the aircraft is decelerated while on a west heading.

Answer (C) is correct (3283). *(PHAK Chap 3)*
In the Northern Hemisphere, a magnetic compass will normally indicate a turn toward the south if an airplane is decelerated while on an east or west heading.
Answer (A) is incorrect because turning errors do not occur from an east heading. Answer (B) is incorrect because turning errors do not occur from a west heading.

7.
3281. In the Northern Hemisphere, a magnetic compass will normally indicate initially a turn toward the east if

A—an aircraft is decelerated while on a south heading.
B—an aircraft is accelerated while on a north heading.
C—a left turn is entered from a north heading.

Answer (C) is correct (3281). *(PHAK Chap 3)*
In the Northern Hemisphere, a magnetic compass normally initially indicates a turn toward the east if a left (west) turn is entered from a north heading.
Answer (A) is incorrect because acceleration/deceleration errors do not occur while on a south heading, only on an east or west heading. Answer (B) is incorrect because acceleration/deceleration errors do not occur while on a north heading, only on an east or west heading.

2.2 Pitot-Static System

8.
3262. The pitot system provides impact pressure for which instrument?

A—Altimeter.
B—Vertical-speed indicator.
C—Airspeed indicator.

Answer (C) is correct (3262). *(PHAK Chap 3)*
The pitot system provides impact pressure, or ram pressure, for only the airspeed indicator.
Answer (A) is incorrect because the altimeter operates off the static (not pitot) system. Answer (B) is incorrect because the vertical-speed indicator operates off the static (not pitot) system.

9.
3248. Which instrument will become inoperative if the pitot tube becomes clogged?

A—Altimeter.
B—Vertical speed.
C—Airspeed.

Answer (C) is correct (3248). *(PHAK Chap 3)*
The pitot-static system is a source of pressure for the altimeter, vertical-speed indicator, and airspeed indicator. The pitot tube is connected directly to the airspeed indicator and provides impact pressure for it alone. Thus, if the pitot tube becomes clogged, only the airspeed indicator will become inoperative.
Answer (A) is incorrect because the altimeter operates off the static system and is not affected by a clogged pitot tube. Answer (B) is incorrect because the vertical speed indicator operates off the static system and is not affected by a clogged pitot tube.

10.
3247. If the pitot tube and outside static vents become clogged, which instruments would be affected?

A—The altimeter, airspeed indicator, and turn-and-slip indicator.
B—The altimeter, airspeed indicator, and vertical speed indicator.
C—The altimeter, attitude indicator, and turn-and-slip indicator.

Answer (B) is correct (3247). *(PHAK Chap 3)*
The pitot-static system is a source of air pressure for the operation of the altimeter, airspeed indicator, and vertical speed indicator. Thus, if the pitot and outside static vents become clogged, all of these instruments will be affected.
Answer (A) is incorrect because the turn-and-slip indicator is a gyroscopic instrument and does not operate on the pitot-static system. Answer (C) is incorrect because the attitude indicator and turn-and-slip indicator are both gyroscopic instruments and do not operate on the pitot-static system.

11.
3249. Which instrument(s) will become inoperative if the static vents become clogged?

A—Airspeed only.
B—Altimeter only.
C—Airspeed, altimeter, and vertical speed.

Answer (C) is correct (3249). *(PHAK Chap 3)*
The pitot-static system is a source of air pressure for the operation of the airspeed indicator, altimeter, and vertical speed indicator. Thus, if the static vents become clogged, all three instruments will become inoperative.
Answer (A) is incorrect because not only will the airspeed indicator become inoperative, but also the altimeter and vertical speed indicator. Answer (B) is incorrect because not only will the altimeter become inoperative, but also the airspeed and vertical speed indicators.

2.3 Airspeed Indicator

12.
3264. What does the red line on an airspeed indicator represent?

A—Maneuvering speed.
B—Turbulent or rough-air speed.
C—Never-exceed speed.

Answer (C) is correct (3264). *(PHAK Chap 3)*
The red line on an airspeed indicator indicates the maximum speed at which the airplane can be operated in smooth air, which should never be exceeded intentionally. This speed is known as the never-exceed speed.
Answer (A) is incorrect because maneuvering speed is not indicated on the airspeed indicator. Answer (B) is incorrect because turbulent or rough-air speed is not indicated on the airspeed indicator.

13.
3274. What is an important airspeed limitation that is not color coded on airspeed indicators?

A—Never-exceed speed.
B—Maximum structural cruising speed.
C—Maneuvering speed.

Answer (C) is correct (3274). *(PHAK Chap 3)*
The maneuvering speed of an airplane is an important airspeed limitation not color-coded on the airspeed indicator. It is found in the airplane manual (*Pilot's Operating Handbook*) or placarded in the cockpit. Maneuvering speed is the maximum speed at which full deflection of the airplane controls can be made without incurring structural damage. Maneuvering speed or less should be held in turbulent air to prevent structural damage due to excessive loads.
Answer (A) is incorrect because the never-exceed speed is indicated on the airspeed indicator by a red radial line. Answer (B) is incorrect because the maximum structural cruising speed is indicated by the upper limit of the green arc on the airspeed indicator.

14.
3266. (Refer to figure 4 below.) What is the caution range of the airplane?

A—0 to 60 MPH.
B—100 to 165 MPH.
C—165 to 208 MPH.

Answer (C) is correct (3266). *(PHAK Chap 3)*
   The caution range is indicated by the yellow arc on the airspeed indicator. Operation within this range is safe only in smooth air. The airspeed indicator in Fig. 4 indicates the caution range from 165 to 208 MPH.
   Answer (A) is incorrect because 0-60 MPH is less than stall speed. Answer (B) is incorrect because 100-165 MPH is the normal operating airspeed range from maximum flap extension speed to maximum structural cruising speed.

15.
3267. (Refer to figure 4 below.) The maximum speed at which the airplane can be operated in smooth air is

A—100 MPH.
B—165 MPH.
C—208 MPH.

Answer (C) is correct (3267). *(PHAK Chap 3)*
   The maximum speed at which the airplane can be operated in smooth air is indicated by the red radial line. The airspeed indicator in Fig. 4 indicates the red line is at 208 MPH.
   Answer (A) is incorrect because 100 MPH is the maximum flaps-extended speed, the upper limit of the white arc. Answer (B) is incorrect because 165 MPH is the maximum structural cruising speed, the upper limit of the green arc.

16.
3265. (Refer to figure 4 below.) What is the full flap operating range for the airplane?

A—60 to 100 MPH.
B—60 to 208 MPH.
C—65 to 165 MPH.

Answer (A) is correct (3265). *(PHAK Chap 3)*
   The full flap operating range is indicated by the white arc on the airspeed indicator. The airspeed indicator in Fig. 4 indicates the full flap operating range is from 60 to 100 MPH.
   Answer (B) is incorrect because 60 to 208 MPH is the entire operating range of this airplane. Answer (C) is incorrect because 65 to 165 MPH is the normal operating range for this airplane (green arc).

17.
3268. (Refer to figure 4 below.) Which color identifies the never-exceed speed?

A—Lower limit of the yellow arc.
B—Upper limit of the white arc.
C—The red radial line.

Answer (C) is correct (3268). *(PHAK Chap 3)*
   The never-exceed speed is indicated by a red line and is found at the upper limit of the yellow arc. Operating above this speed may result in structural damage.
   Answer (A) is incorrect because the lower limit of the yellow arc is the beginning of the caution range. Answer (B) is incorrect because the upper limit of the white arc is the maximum speed at which flaps may be extended.

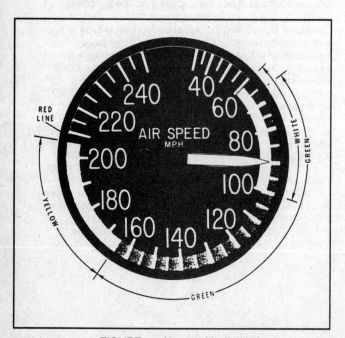

FIGURE 4.--Airspeed Indicator*

*NOTE: Figure 4 is in color in the FAA *Computer Testing Supplement for Recreational Pilot and Private Pilot*, which you will use during your test.

18.

3269. (Refer to figure 4 on page 42.) Which color identifies the power-off stalling speed in a specified configuration?

A—Upper limit of the green arc.
B—Upper limit of the white arc.
C—Lower limit of the green arc.

Answer (C) is correct (3269). *(PHAK Chap 3)*
The lower airspeed limit of the green arc indicates the power-off stalling speed in a specified configuration. "Specified configuration" refers to flaps up and landing gear retracted.
Answer (A) is incorrect because the upper limit of the green arc is the maximum structural cruising speed. Answer (B) is incorrect because the upper airspeed limit of the white arc is the maximum flaps-extended speed. Structural damage to the flaps could occur if the flaps are extended above this airspeed.

19.

3270. (Refer to figure 4 on page 42.) What is the maximum flaps-extended speed?

A—65 MPH.
B—100 MPH.
C—165 MPH.

Answer (B) is correct (3270). *(PHAK Chap 3)*
The maximum flaps-extended speed is indicated by the upper limit of the white arc. This is the highest airspeed at which a pilot should extend full flaps. At higher airspeeds, severe strain or structural failure could result. The upper limit of the white arc on the airspeed indicator shown in Fig. 4 indicates 100 MPH.
Answer (A) is incorrect because 65 MPH is the lower limit of the green arc, which is the power-off stall speed in a specified configuration. Answer (C) is incorrect because 165 MPH is the upper limit of the green arc, which is the maximum structural cruising speed.

20.

3271. (Refer to figure 4 on page 42.) Which color identifies the normal flap operating range?

A—The lower limit of the white arc to the upper limit of the green arc.
B—The green arc.
C—The white arc.

Answer (C) is correct (3271). *(PHAK Chap 3)*
The normal flap operating range is indicated by the white arc. The power-off stall speed with flaps extended is at the lower limit of the arc, and the maximum speed at which flaps can be extended without damage to them is the upper limit of the arc.
Answer (A) is incorrect because the upper limit of the green arc well exceeds the upper limit of the white arc, which is the maximum flap extended speed. Answer (B) is incorrect because the green arc represents the normal operating range.

21.

3272. (Refer to figure 4 on page 42.) Which color identifies the power-off stalling speed with wing flaps and landing gear in the landing configuration?

A—Upper limit of the green arc.
B—Upper limit of the white arc.
C—Lower limit of the white arc.

Answer (C) is correct (3272). *(PHAK Chap 3)*
The lower limit of the white arc indicates the power-off stalling speed with wing flaps and landing gear in the landing position.
Answer (A) is incorrect because the upper limit of the green arc is the maximum structural cruising speed. Answer (B) is incorrect because the upper limit of the white arc is the maximum flaps-extended speed.

22.

3273. (Refer to figure 4 on page 42.) What is the maximum structural cruising speed?

A—100 MPH.
B—165 MPH.
C—208 MPH.

Answer (B) is correct (3273). *(PHAK Chap 3)*
The maximum structural cruising speed is the maximum speed for normal operation and is indicated as the upper limit of the green arc on an airspeed indicator. The upper limit of the green arc on the airspeed indicator shown in Fig. 4 indicates 165 MPH.
Answer (A) is incorrect because 100 MPH is the upper limit of the white arc and is the maximum speed at which the flaps can be extended. Answer (C) is incorrect because 208 MPH is the speed that should never be exceeded. Beyond this speed, structural damage to the airplane may occur.

2.4 Altimeter

23.
3251. (Refer to figure 3 below.) Altimeter 2 indicates

A—1,500 feet.
B—4,500 feet.
C—14,500 feet.

Answer (C) is correct (3251). *(PHAK Chap 3)*
   Altimeter 2 indicates 14,500 ft. because the shortest needle is between the 1 and the 2, indicating about 15,000 ft; the middle needle is between 4 and 5, indicating 4,500 ft; and the long needle is on 5, indicating 500 ft., i.e., 14,500 ft.
   Answer (A) is incorrect because, for 1,500 ft., the middle needle would have to be between 1 and 2, and the shortest needle between 0 and 1. Answer (B) is incorrect because, for 4,500 ft., the shortest needle would have to be between 0 and 1.

FIGURE 3.—Altimeter.

24.
3250. (Refer to figure 3 above.) Altimeter 1 indicates

A—500 feet.
B—1,500 feet.
C—10,500 feet.

Answer (C) is correct (3250). *(PHAK Chap 3)*
   The altimeter has three needles. The short needle indicates 10,000-ft. intervals, the middle-length needle indicates 1,000-ft. intervals, and the long needle indicates 100-ft. intervals. In altimeter 1, the shortest needle is on 1, which indicates about 10,000 ft. The middle-length needle indicates half-way between zero and 1, which is 500 ft. This is confirmed by the longest needle on 5, indicating 500 ft., i.e., 10,500 ft.
   Answer (A) is incorrect because, if it were indicating just 500 ft., the short and medium needles would have to be on or near zero. Answer (B) is incorrect because, if it were 1,500 ft., the shortest needle would be near zero and the middle needle would be between the 1 and the 2.

25.
3252. (Refer to figure 3 above.) Altimeter 3 indicates

A—9,500 feet.
B—10,950 feet.
C—15,940 feet.

Answer (A) is correct (3252). *(PHAK Chap 3)*
   Altimeter 3 indicates 9,500 ft. because the shortest needle is near 9 (i.e., about 10,000 ft.), the middle needle is between 9 and the 0, indicating between 9,000 and 10,000 ft., and the long needle is on 5, indicating 500 ft.
   Answer (B) is incorrect because, for 10,950 ft., the middle needle would have to be near the 1 and the long needle would have to be between the 9 and 0.
Answer (C) is incorrect because, for 15,940 ft., the short needle would have to be between 1 and 2, the middle needle near the 6, and the large needle between the 9 and 0.

26.
3253. (Refer to figure 3 on page 44.) Which altimeter(s) indicate(s) more than 10,000 feet?

A—1, 2, and 3.
B—1 and 2 only.
C—1 only.

Answer (B) is correct (3253). *(PHAK Chap 3)*
Altimeters 1 and 2 indicate over 10,000 ft. because 1 indicates 10,500 ft. and 2 indicates 14,500 ft. The short needle on 3 points just below 1, i.e., below 10,000 ft.
Answer (A) is incorrect because altimeter 3 is indicating 9,500 ft., which is less than 10,000 ft. Answer (C) is incorrect because altimeter 2 is indicating 14,500 ft., which is also more than 10,000 ft.

2.5 Types of Altitude

27.
3257. What is absolute altitude?

A—The altitude read directly from the altimeter.
B—The vertical distance of the aircraft above the surface.
C—The height above the standard datum plane.

Answer (B) is correct (3257). *(PHAK Chap 3)*
Absolute altitude is altitude above the surface, i.e., AGL.
Answer (A) is incorrect because it is indicated altitude. Answer (C) is incorrect because it is pressure altitude.

28.
3256. What is true altitude?

A—The vertical distance of the aircraft above sea level.
B—The vertical distance of the aircraft above the surface.
C—The height above the standard datum plane.

Answer (A) is correct (3256). *(PHAK Chap 3)*
True altitude is the actual altitude above mean sea level, i.e., MSL.
Answer (B) is incorrect because it represents absolute altitude. Answer (C) is incorrect because it is pressure altitude.

29.
3258. What is density altitude?

A—The height above the standard datum plane.
B—The pressure altitude corrected for nonstandard temperature.
C—The altitude read directly from the altimeter.

Answer (B) is correct (3258). *(PHAK Chap 3)*
Density altitude is the pressure altitude corrected for nonstandard temperature.
Answer (A) is incorrect because it defines pressure altitude. Answer (C) is incorrect because it is indicated altitude.

30.
3389. Under what condition is pressure altitude and density altitude the same value?

A—At sea level, when the temperature is 0 °F.
B—When the altimeter has no installation error.
C—At standard temperature.

Answer (C) is correct (3389). *(PHAK Chap 3)*
Pressure altitude and density altitude are the same when temperature is standard.
Answer (A) is incorrect because standard temperature at sea level is 59°F, not 0°F. Answer (B) is incorrect because installation error refers to pitot tubes and airspeed, not altimeter and altitude.

31.
3260. Under what condition is indicated altitude the same as true altitude?

A—If the altimeter has no mechanical error.
B—When at sea level under standard conditions.
C—When at 18,000 feet MSL with the altimeter set at 29.92.

Answer (B) is correct (3260). *(PHAK Chap 3)*
Indicated altitude (what you read on your altimeter) approximates the true altitude (distance above mean sea level) when standard conditions exist and your altimeter is properly calibrated.
Answer (A) is incorrect because the indicated altitude must be adjusted for nonstandard temperature for true altitude. Answer (C) is incorrect because the altimeter reads pressure altitude when set to 29.92, and that is only true altitude under standard conditions.

32.
3388. Under which condition will pressure altitude be equal to true altitude?

A—When the atmospheric pressure is 29.92" Hg.
B—When standard atmospheric conditions exist.
C—When indicated altitude is equal to the pressure altitude.

Answer (B) is correct (3388). *(AvW Chap 3)*
Pressure altitude equals true altitude when standard atmospheric conditions (29.92" Hg and 15°C at sea level) exist.
Answer (A) is incorrect because standard temperature must also exist. Answer (C) is incorrect because indicated altitude does not necessarily relate to true or pressure altitudes.

33.
3259. What is pressure altitude?

A—The indicated altitude corrected for position and installation error.
B—The altitude indicated when the barometric pressure scale is set to 29.92.
C—The indicated altitude corrected for nonstandard temperature and pressure.

Answer (B) is correct (3259). *(PHAK Chap 3)*
Pressure altitude is the airplane's height above the standard datum plane of 29.92" Hg. If the altimeter is set to 29.92" Hg, the indicated altitude is the pressure altitude.
Answer (A) is incorrect because "corrected for position and installation error" is used to define calibrated airspeed, not a type of altitude. Answer (C) is incorrect because it describes density altitude.

34.
3254. Altimeter setting is the value to which the barometric pressure scale of the altimeter is set so the altimeter indicates

A—calibrated altitude at field elevation.
B—absolute altitude at field elevation.
C—true altitude at field elevation.

Answer (C) is correct (3254). *(PHAK Chap 3)*
Altimeter setting is the value to which the scale of the pressure altimeter is set so that the altimeter indicates true altitude at field elevation.
Answer (A) is incorrect because "calibrated" refers to airspeed and airspeed indicators, not altitude and altimeters. Answer (B) is incorrect because absolute altitude is the altitude above the surface, not above MSL.

2.6 Setting the Altimeter

35.
3261. If it is necessary to set the altimeter from 29.15 to 29.85, what change occurs?

A—70-foot increase in indicated altitude.
B—70-foot increase in density altitude.
C—700-foot increase in indicated altitude.

Answer (C) is correct (3261). *(PHAK Chap 3)*
When increasing the altimeter setting from 29.15 to 29.85, the indicated altitude increases by 700 ft. The altimeter-indicated altitude moves in the same direction as the altimeter setting and changes about 1,000 ft. for every change of 1" Hg in the altimeter setting.
Answer (A) is incorrect because .7" Hg change in pressure is equal to 700 ft., not 70 ft., of altitude. Answer (B) is incorrect because density altitude is not affected by changing the altimeter setting.

36.
3387. If a pilot changes the altimeter setting from 30.11 to 29.96, what is the approximate change in indication?

A—Altimeter will indicate .15" Hg higher.
B—Altimeter will indicate 150 feet higher.
C—Altimeter will indicate 150 feet lower.

Answer (C) is correct (3387). *(PHAK Chap 3)*
Atmospheric pressure decreases approximately 1" of mercury for every 1,000 ft. of altitude gained. As an altimeter setting is changed, the change in altitude indication changes the same way (i.e., approximately 1,000 ft. for every 1" change in altimeter setting) and in the same direction (i.e., lowering the altimeter setting lowers the altitude reading). Thus, changing from 30.11 to 29.96 is a decrease of .15 in., or 150 ft. (.15 x 1,000 ft.) lower.
Answer (A) is incorrect because the altimeter indicates feet, not inches of mercury. Answer (B) is incorrect because the altimeter will show 150 ft. lower, not higher.

2.7 Altimeter Errors

37.
3390. If a flight is made from an area of low pressure into an area of high pressure without the altimeter setting being adjusted, the altimeter will indicate

A—the actual altitude above sea level.
B—higher than the actual altitude above sea level.
C—lower than the actual altitude above sea level.

Answer (C) is correct (3390). *(AvW Chap 3)*
When an altimeter setting is at a lower value than the correct setting, the altimeter is indicating less than it should and thus would be showing lower than the actual altitude above sea level.
Answer (A) is incorrect because the altimeter will show actual altitude only when it is set correctly. Answer (B) is incorrect because the increase in pressure causes the altimeter to read lower, not higher, than actual altitude.

38.
3391. If a flight is made from an area of high pressure into an area of lower pressure without the altimeter setting being adjusted, the altimeter will indicate

A—lower than the actual altitude above sea level.
B—higher than the actual altitude above sea level.
C—the actual altitude above sea level.

Answer (B) is correct (3391). *(AvW Chap 3)*
When flying from higher pressure to lower pressure without adjusting your altimeter, the altimeter will indicate a higher than actual altitude. As you adjust an altimeter barometric setting lower, the altimeter indicates lower.
Answer (A) is incorrect because the decrease in pressure causes the altimeter to read higher, not lower, than actual altitude. Answer (C) is incorrect because the altimeter will show actual altitude only when it is set correctly.

39.
3393. Which condition would cause the altimeter to indicate a lower altitude than true altitude?

A—Air temperature lower than standard.
B—Atmospheric pressure lower than standard.
C—Air temperature warmer than standard.

Answer (C) is correct (3393). *(AvW Chap 3)*
In air that is warmer than standard temperature, the airplane will be higher than the altimeter indicates. Said another way, the altimeter will indicate a lower altitude than actually flown.
Answer (A) is incorrect because, when flying in air that is colder than standard temperature, the airplane will be lower than the altimeter indicates ("high to low, look out below"). Answer (B) is incorrect because the altimeter setting corrects the altimeter for nonstandard pressure.

40.
3392. Under what condition will true altitude be lower than indicated altitude?

A—In colder than standard air temperature.
B—In warmer than standard air temperature.
C—When density altitude is higher than indicated altitude.

Answer (A) is correct (3392). *(AvW Chap 3)*
The airplane will be lower than the altimeter indicates when flying in air that is colder than standard temperature. Remember that altimeter readings are adjusted for changes in barometric pressure but not for changes in temperature. When one flies from warmer to cold air and keeps a constant indicated altitude at a constant altimeter setting, the plane has actually descended.
Answer (B) is incorrect because the altimeter indicates lower than actual altitude in warmer than standard temperature. Answer (C) is incorrect because a higher density altitude is usually the result of warmer, not colder, than standard temperature.

41.
3255. How do variations in temperature affect the altimeter?

A—Pressure levels are raised on warm days and the indicated altitude is lower than true altitude.
B—Higher temperatures expand the pressure levels and the indicated altitude is higher than true altitude.
C—Lower temperatures lower the pressure levels and the indicated altitude is lower than true altitude.

Answer (A) is correct (3255). *(PHAK Chap 3)*
On warm days, the atmospheric pressure levels are higher than on cold days. Your altimeter will indicate a lower than true altitude. Remember, "low to high, clear the sky."
Answer (B) is incorrect because expanding (or raising) the pressure levels will cause indicated altitude to be lower (not higher) than true altitude. Answer (C) is incorrect because lower pressure levels will cause indicated altitude to be higher (not lower) than true altitude.

2.8 Gyroscopic Instruments

42.
3277. (Refer to figure 7 on page 49.) The proper adjustment to make on the attitude indicator during level flight is to align the

A—horizon bar to the level-flight indication.
B—horizon bar to the miniature airplane.
C—miniature airplane to the horizon bar.

Answer (C) is correct (3277). *(PHAK Chap 3)*
The horizon bar (marked as B) on Fig. 7 represents the true horizon. This bar is fixed to the gyro and remains on a horizontal plane as the airplane is pitched or banked about its lateral or longitudinal axis, indicating the attitude of the airplane relative to the true horizon. An adjustment knob is provided, with which the pilot may move the miniature airplane (marked as C) up or down to align the miniature airplane with the horizontal bar to suit the pilot's line of vision.
Answer (A) is incorrect because aligning the miniature airplane to the horizon bar provides a level-flight indication. Answer (B) is incorrect because the miniature airplane is adjustable, not the horizon bar.

43.
3278. (Refer to figure 7 on page 49.) How should a pilot determine the direction of bank from an attitude indicator such as the one illustrated?

A—By the direction of deflection of the banking scale (A).
B—By the direction of deflection of the horizon bar (B).
C—By the relationship of the miniature airplane (C) to the deflected horizon bar (B).

Answer (C) is correct (3278). *(PHAK Chap 3)*
The direction of bank on the attitude indicator (AI) is indicated by the relationship of the miniature airplane to the deflecting horizon bar. The miniature airplane's relative position to the horizon indicates its attitude: nose high, nose low, left bank, right bank. As you look at the attitude indicator, you see your airplane as it is positioned with respect to the actual horizon. The attitude indicator in Fig. 7 indicates a level right turn.
Answer (A) is incorrect because the banking scale (marked as A) may move in the opposite direction, which is confusing. Answer (B) is incorrect because the horizon bar (marked as B) moves in the direction opposite the turn.

44.
3275. (Refer to figure 5 on page 49.) A turn coordinator provides an indication of the

A—movement of the aircraft about the yaw and roll axes.
B—angle of bank up to but not exceeding 30°.
C—attitude of the aircraft with reference to the longitudinal axis.

Answer (A) is correct (3275). *(PHAK Chap 3)*
There really are no yaw and roll axes, i.e., an airplane yaws about its vertical axis and rolls about its longitudinal axis. However, this is the best answer since the turn coordinator does indicate the roll and yaw movement of the airplane. The movement of the miniature airplane is proportional to the roll rate of the airplane. When the roll rate is reduced to zero (i.e., when the bank is held constant) the instrument provides an indication of the rate of turn.
Answer (B) is incorrect because the turn coordinator shows the rate of turn rather than angle of bank. Answer (C) is incorrect because the turn coordinator does not show the attitude of the airplane (as does the attitude indicator); it shows the rate of the roll and turn.

45.
3276. (Refer to figure 6 on page 49.) To receive accurate indications during flight from a heading indicator, the instrument must be

A—set prior to flight on a known heading.
B—calibrated on a compass rose at regular intervals.
C—periodically realigned with the magnetic compass as the gyro precesses.

Answer (C) is correct (3276). *(PHAK Chap 3)*
Due to gyroscopic precession, directional gyros must be periodically realigned with a magnetic compass. Friction is the major cause of its drifting from the correct heading.
Answer (A) is incorrect because the instrument must be periodically reset, not just set initially. Answer (B) is incorrect because there is no calibration of the heading indicator; rather, it is reset.

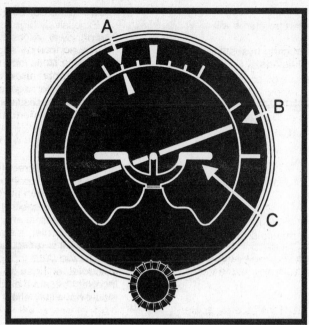

FIGURE 7.—Attitude Indicator.

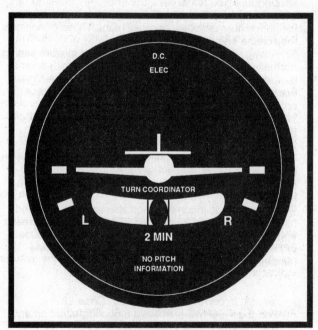

FIGURE 5.—Turn Coordinator.

FIGURE 6.—Heading Indicator.

2.9 Engine Temperature

46.

3245. An abnormally high engine oil temperature indication may be caused by

A—the oil level being too low.
B—operating with a too high viscosity oil.
C—operating with an excessively rich mixture.

Answer (A) is correct (3245). *(PHAK Chap 2)*

Operating with an excessively low oil level prevents the oil from being cooled adequately; i.e., an inadequate supply of oil will not be able to transfer engine heat to the engine's oil cooler (similar to a car engine's water radiator). Insufficient oil may also damage an engine from excessive friction within the cylinders and on other metal-to-metal contact parts.

Answer (B) is incorrect because the higher the viscosity, the better the lubricating and cooling capability of the oil. Answer (C) is incorrect because a rich fuel/air mixture usually decreases (not increases) engine temperature.

47.
3221. Excessively high engine temperatures will

A—cause damage to heat-conducting hoses and warping of the cylinder cooling fins.
B—cause loss of power, excessive oil consumption, and possible permanent internal engine damage.
C—not appreciably affect an aircraft engine.

Answer (B) is correct (3221). *(PHAK Chap 2)*
Excessively high engine temperatures will result in loss of power, excessive oil consumption, and possible permanent internal engine damage.
Answer (A) is incorrect because excessively high engine temperatures may cause internal engine damage, but external damage is less likely. Answer (C) is incorrect because an excessively high engine temperature can cause a loss of performance and possibly internal engine damage.

48.
3244. For internal cooling, reciprocating aircraft engines are especially dependent on

A—a properly functioning thermostat.
B—air flowing over the exhaust manifold.
C—the circulation of lubricating oil.

Answer (C) is correct (3244). *(PHAK Chap 2)*
An engine accomplishes much of its cooling by the flow of oil through the lubrication system. The lubrication system aids in cooling by reducing friction and absorbing heat from internal engine parts. Many airplane engines use an oil cooler, a small radiator device that will cool the oil before it is recirculated through the engine.
Answer (A) is incorrect because airplanes with air-cooled engines do not use thermostats. Answer (B) is incorrect because air flowing over the exhaust manifold would have little effect on internal engine parts cooling.

49.
3222. If the engine oil temperature and cylinder head temperature gauges have exceeded their normal operating range, the pilot may have been operating with

A—the mixture set too rich.
B—higher-than-normal oil pressure.
C—too much power and with the mixture set too lean.

Answer (C) is correct (3222). *(PHAK Chap 2)*
If the engine oil temperature and cylinder head temperature gauges exceed their normal operating range, it is possible that the power setting is too high and the fuel/air mixture is set excessively lean. These conditions may cause engine overheating.
Answer (A) is incorrect because a rich mixture setting normally causes lower (not higher-than-normal) engine temperature. Answer (B) is incorrect because a higher-than-normal oil pressure does not normally increase the engine temperature.

50.
3651. What action can a pilot take to aid in cooling an engine that is overheating during a climb?

A—Reduce rate of climb and increase airspeed.
B—Reduce climb speed and increase RPM.
C—Increase climb speed and increase RPM.

Answer (A) is correct (3651). *(PHAK Chap 2)*
If an airplane is overheating during a climb, the engine temperature will be decreased if the airspeed is increased. Airspeed will increase if the rate of climb is reduced.
Answer (B) is incorrect because reducing airspeed hinders cooling and increasing RPM will further increase engine temperature. Answer (C) is incorrect because increasing RPM will increase (not decrease) engine temperature.

51.
3652. What is one procedure to aid in cooling an engine that is overheating?

A—Enrich the fuel mixture.
B—Increase the RPM.
C—Reduce the airspeed.

Answer (A) is correct (3652). *(PHAK Chap 2)*
Enriched fuel mixtures have a cooling effect on an engine.
Answer (B) is incorrect because increasing the RPM increases the engine's internal heat. Answer (C) is incorrect because reducing the airspeed decreases the airflow needed for cooling, thus increasing the engine's temperature.

2.10 Constant-Speed Propeller

52.
3653. How is engine operation controlled on an engine equipped with a constant-speed propeller?

A—The throttle controls power output as registered on the manifold pressure gauge and the propeller control regulates engine RPM.
B—The throttle controls power output as registered on the manifold pressure gauge and the propeller control regulates a constant blade angle.
C—The throttle controls engine RPM as registered on the tachometer and the mixture control regulates the power output.

Answer (A) is correct (3653). *(PHAK Chap 2)*
Airplanes equipped with controllable-pitch propellers have both a throttle control and a propeller control. The throttle controls the power output of the engine, which is registered on the manifold pressure gauge. This is a simple barometer that measures the air pressure in the engine intake manifold in inches of mercury. The propeller control regulates the engine RPM, which is registered on a tachometer.
Answer (B) is incorrect because the propeller blade angle changes to control the RPM. Answer (C) is incorrect because the throttle controls power output (not RPM), and the mixture controls the fuel to air ratio (not power output).

53.
3655. A precaution for the operation of an engine equipped with a constant-speed propeller is to

A—avoid high RPM settings with high manifold pressure.
B—avoid high manifold pressure settings with low RPM.
C—always use a rich mixture with high RPM settings.

Answer (B) is correct (3655). *(PHAK Chap 2)*
For any given RPM, there is a manifold pressure that should not be exceeded. Manifold pressure is excessive for a given RPM when the cylinder design pressure is exceeded, placing undue stress on them. If repeated or extended, the stress would weaken the cylinder components and eventually cause engine failure.
Answer (A) is incorrect because it is the relationship of high manifold pressure with low RPM that is dangerous (not high RPM with high manifold pressure). Answer (C) is incorrect because the mixture control is related to engine cylinder temperature, not to RPM.

54.
3654. What is an advantage of a constant-speed propeller?

A—Permits the pilot to select and maintain a desired cruising speed.
B—Permits the pilot to select the blade angle for the most efficient performance.
C—Provides a smoother operation with stable RPM and eliminates vibrations.

Answer (B) is correct (3654). *(PHAK Chap 2)*
A controllable-pitch propeller (constant-speed) permits the pilot to select the blade angle that will result in the most efficient performance given the flight conditions. A low blade angle and a decreased pitch reduces the propeller drag and allows more engine RPM (power) for takeoffs. After airspeed is attained during cruising flight, the propeller blade is changed to a higher angle to increase pitch. The blade takes a larger bite of air at a lower RPM and consequently increases the efficiency of the flight. This process is similar to shifting gears in an automobile from low to high gear.
Answer (A) is incorrect because a desired cruising speed is possible with any airplane. Answer (C) is incorrect because vibrations are eliminated through propeller balancing, not a constant-speed propeller.

2.11 Engine Ignition Systems

55.
3223. One purpose of the dual ignition system on an aircraft engine is to provide for

A—improved engine performance.
B—uniform heat distribution.
C—balanced cylinder head pressure.

Answer (A) is correct (3223). *(PHAK Chap 2)*
Most airplane engines are equipped with dual ignition systems, which have two magnetos to supply the electrical current to two spark plugs for each combustion chamber. The main advantages of the dual system are increased safety and improved burning and combustion of the mixture, which results in improved performance.
Answer (B) is incorrect because the heat distribution within a cylinder is usually not uniform, even with dual ignition. Answer (C) is incorrect because balanced cylinder-head pressure is a nonsense phrase.

2.12 Carburetor Icing

56.
3236. With regard to carburetor ice, float-type carburetor systems in comparison to fuel injection systems are generally considered to be

A—more susceptible to icing.
B—equally susceptible to icing.
C—susceptible to icing only when visible moisture is present.

Answer (A) is correct (3236). *(PHAK Chap 2)*
Float-type carburetor systems are generally more susceptible to icing than fuel-injected engines. When there is visible moisture or high humidity and the temperature is between 20°F and 70°F, icing is possible, particularly at low power settings.
Answer (B) is incorrect because fuel injection systems are less susceptible to internal icing than a carburetor system, although air intake icing is equally possible in both systems. Answer (C) is incorrect because carburetor icing may occur in high humidity with no visible moisture.

57.
3225. The operating principle of float-type carburetors is based on the

A—automatic metering of air at the venturi as the aircraft gains altitude.
B—difference in air pressure at the venturi throat and the air inlet.
C—increase in air velocity in the throat of a venturi causing an increase in air pressure.

Answer (B) is correct (3225). *(PHAK Chap 2)*
In a float-type carburetor, air flows into the carburetor and through a venturi tube (a narrow throat in the carburetor). As the air flows more rapidly through the venturi, a low pressure area is created which draws the fuel from a main fuel jet located at the throat of the carburetor and into the airstream, where it is mixed with flowing air. It is called a float-type carburetor in that a ready supply of gasoline is kept in the float bowl by a float, which activates a fuel inlet valve.
Answer (A) is incorrect because the metering at the venturi is fuel, not air, and this is done manually with a mixture control. Answer (C) is incorrect because the increase in air velocity in the throat of a venturi causes a decrease (not increase) in air pressure (which draws the gas from the main fuel jet into the low-pressure air).

58.
3231. If an aircraft is equipped with a fixed-pitch propeller and a float-type carburetor, the first indication of carburetor ice would most likely be

A—a drop in oil temperature and cylinder head temperature.
B—engine roughness.
C—loss of RPM.

Answer (C) is correct (3231). *(PHAK Chap 2)*
In an airplane equipped with a fixed-pitch propeller and float-type carburetor, the first indication of carburetor ice would be a loss in RPM.
Answer (A) is incorrect because a carburetor icing condition does not cause a drop in oil temperature or cylinder head temperature. Answer (B) is incorrect because a loss in engine RPM should be evident before engine roughness became noticeable.

59.
3235. The presence of carburetor ice in an aircraft equipped with a fixed-pitch propeller can be verified by applying carburetor heat and noting

A—an increase in RPM and then a gradual decrease in RPM.
B—a decrease in RPM and then a constant RPM indication.
C—a decrease in RPM and then a gradual increase in RPM.

Answer (C) is correct (3235). *(PHAK Chap 2)*
The presence of carburetor ice in an airplane equipped with a fixed-pitch propeller can be verified by applying carburetor heat and noting a decrease in RPM and then a gradual increase. The decrease in RPM as heat is applied is caused by less dense hot air entering the engine and reducing power output. Also, if ice is present, melting water entering the engine may also cause a loss in performance. As the carburetor ice melts, however, the RPM gradually increases until it stabilizes when the ice is completely removed.
Answer (A) is incorrect because the warm air decreases engine power output and RPM. Ice melting further decreases RPM and then RPM increases slightly after the ice melts. Answer (B) is incorrect because after the ice melts, the RPM will increase gradually (not remain constant).

60.
3229. Which condition is most favorable to the development of carburetor icing?

A—Any temperature below freezing and a relative humidity of less than 50 percent.
B—Temperature between 32 and 50°F and low humidity.
C—Temperature between 20 and 70°F and high humidity.

Answer (C) is correct (3229). *(PHAK Chap 2)*
When the temperature is between 20°F and 70°F with visible moisture or high humidity, one should be on the alert for carburetor ice. During low or closed throttle settings, an engine is particularly susceptible to carburetor icing.
Answer (A) is incorrect because icing is possible at temperatures up to 70°F and only in high humidity or visible moisture. Answer (B) is incorrect because low humidity will generally preclude icing and the correct temperature range is 20°F to 70°F.

61.
3230. The possibility of carburetor icing exists even when the ambient air temperature is as

A—high as 70°F and the relative humidity is high.
B—high as 95°F and there is visible moisture.
C—low as 0°F and the relative humidity is high.

Answer (A) is correct (3230). *(PHAK Chap 2)*
When the temperature is between 20°F and 70°F with visible moisture or high humidity, one should be on the alert for carburetor ice. During low or closed throttle settings, an engine is particularly susceptible to carburetor icing.
Answer (B) is incorrect because icing is usually not a problem above 70°F. Answer (C) is incorrect because icing is usually not a problem below 20°F.

2.13 Carburetor Heat

62.
3234. Generally speaking, the use of carburetor heat tends to

A—decrease engine performance.
B—increase engine performance.
C—have no effect on engine performance.

Answer (A) is correct (3234). *(PHAK Chap 2)*
Use of carburetor heat tends to decrease the engine performance and also to increase the operating temperature. Warmer air is less dense, and engine performance decreases with density. Thus, carburetor heat should not be used when full power is required (as during takeoff) or during normal engine operation except as a check for the presence or removal of carburetor ice.
Answer (B) is incorrect because carburetor heat decreases (not increases) engine performance. Answer (C) is incorrect because carburetor heat does have an effect on performance.

63.
3232. Applying carburetor heat will

A—result in more air going through the carburetor.
B—enrich the fuel/air mixture.
C—not affect the fuel/air mixture.

Answer (B) is correct (3232). *(PHAK Chap 2)*
Applying carburetor heat will enrich the fuel/air mixture. Warm air is less dense than cold air, hence the application of heat increases the fuel-to-air ratio.
Answer (A) is incorrect because applying carburetor heat will not result in more air going into the carburetor. Answer (C) is incorrect because applying carburetor heat will enrich the fuel/air mixture.

64.
3233. What change occurs in the fuel/air mixture when carburetor heat is applied?

A—A decrease in RPM results from the lean mixture.
B—The fuel/air mixture becomes richer.
C—The fuel/air mixture becomes leaner.

Answer (B) is correct (3233). *(PHAK Chap 2)*
When carburetor heat is applied, hot air is introduced into the carburetor. Hot air is less dense than cold air; therefore, the decrease in air density with a constant amount of fuel makes a richer mixture.
Answer (A) is incorrect because a drop in RPM as carburetor heat is applied is due to the less dense air and melting ice, not a lean mixture. Answer (C) is incorrect because, when carburetor heat is applied, the fuel/air mixture becomes richer, not leaner.

2.14 Fuel/Air Mixture

65.
3227. During the run-up at a high-elevation airport, a pilot notes a slight engine roughness that is not affected by the magneto check but grows worse during the carburetor heat check. Under these circumstances, what would be the most logical initial action?

A—Check the results obtained with a leaner setting of the mixture.
B—Taxi back to the flight line for a maintenance check.
C—Reduce manifold pressure to control detonation.

Answer (A) is correct (3227). *(PHAK Chap 2)*
If, during a run-up at a high-elevation airport, you notice a slight roughness that is not affected by a magneto check but grows worse during the carburetor heat check, you should check the results obtained with a leaner setting of the mixture control. At a high-elevation field, the air is less dense and the application of carburetor heat increases the already too rich fuel-to-air mixture. By leaning the mixture during the run-up, the condition should improve.
Answer (B) is incorrect because this mixture condition is normal at a high-elevation field. However, if after leaning the mixture a satisfactory run-up cannot be obtained, the pilot should taxi back to the flight line for a maintenance check. Answer (C) is incorrect because the question describes a symptom of an excessively rich mixture, not detonation.

66.
3226. The basic purpose of adjusting the fuel/air mixture at altitude is to

A—decrease the amount of fuel in the mixture in order to compensate for increased air density.
B—decrease the fuel flow in order to compensate for decreased air density.
C—increase the amount of fuel in the mixture to compensate for the decrease in pressure and density of the air.

Answer (B) is correct (3226). *(PHAK Chap 2)*
At higher altitudes the air density is decreased. Thus the mixture control must be adjusted to decrease the fuel flow in order to maintain a constant fuel/air ratio.
Answer (A) is incorrect because air density decreases (not increases) at altitude. Answer (C) is incorrect because the mixture is decreased (not increased) in order to compensate for decreased air density.

67.
3228. While cruising at 9,500 feet MSL, the fuel/air mixture is properly adjusted. What will occur if a descent to 4,500 feet MSL is made without readjusting the mixture?

A—The fuel/air mixture may become excessively lean.
B—There will be more fuel in the cylinders than is needed for normal combustion, and the excess fuel will absorb heat and cool the engine.
C—The excessively rich mixture will create higher cylinder head temperatures and may cause detonation.

Answer (A) is correct (3228). *(PHAK Chap 2)*
At 9,500 ft., the mixture control is adjusted to provide the proper fuel/air ratio. As the airplane descends, the density of the air increases and there will be less fuel to air in the ratio, causing a leaner running engine. This excessively lean mixture will create higher cylinder temperature and may cause detonation.
Answer (B) is incorrect because, as air becomes more dense during the descent, there will be less (not more) fuel in the cylinders than is needed. Answer (C) is incorrect because the mixture will be excessively lean (not rich). Also, a rich mixture would create lower (not higher) cylinder head temperatures.

2.15 Abnormal Combustion

68.
3238. Detonation occurs in a reciprocating aircraft engine when

A—the spark plugs are fouled or shorted out or the wiring is defective.
B—hot spots in the combustion chamber ignite the fuel/air mixture in advance of normal ignition.
C—the unburned charge in the cylinders explodes instead of burning normally.

Answer (C) is correct (3238). *(PHAK Chap 2)*
Detonation occurs when the fuel/air mixture in the cylinders explodes instead of burning normally. This more rapid force slams the piston down instead of pushing it.
Answer (A) is incorrect because, if the spark plugs are "fouled" or the wiring is defective, the cylinders would not be firing; i.e., there would be no combustion. Answer (B) is incorrect because hot spots in the combustion chamber igniting the fuel/air mixture in advance of normal ignition is pre-ignition.

69.
3239. If a pilot suspects that the engine (with a fixed-pitch propeller) is detonating during climb-out after takeoff, the initial corrective action to take would be to

A—lean the mixture.
B—lower the nose slightly to increase airspeed.
C—apply carburetor heat.

Answer (B) is correct (3239). *(PHAK Chap 2)*
If you suspect engine detonation during climb-out after takeoff, you would normally decrease the pitch to increase airspeed (more cooling) and decrease the load on the engine. Detonation is usually caused by a poor grade of fuel or an excessive engine temperature.
Answer (A) is incorrect because leaning the mixture will increase engine temperature and increase detonation. Answer (C) is incorrect because, while carburetor heat will increase the fuel-to-air ratio, hot air flowing into the carburetor will not lower engine temperature. Also, the less dense air will decrease the engine power for climb-out.

70.
3237. If the grade of fuel used in an aircraft engine is lower than specified for the engine, it will most likely cause

A—a mixture of fuel and air that is not uniform in all cylinders.
B—lower cylinder head temperatures.
C—detonation.

Answer (C) is correct (3237). *(PHAK Chap 2)*
If the grade of fuel used in an airplane engine is lower than specified for the engine, it will probably cause detonation. Lower grades of fuel ignite at lower temperatures. A higher temperature engine (which should use a higher grade of fuel) may cause lower grade fuel to explode (detonate) rather than burn evenly.
Answer (A) is incorrect because the carburetor meters the lower-grade fuel quantity in the same manner as a higher grade of fuel. Answer (B) is incorrect because a lower grade of fuel will cause higher (not lower) cylinder head temperatures.

71.
3240. The uncontrolled firing of the fuel/air charge in advance of normal spark ignition is known as

A—combustion.
B—pre-ignition.
C—detonation.

Answer (B) is correct (3240). *(PHAK Chap 2)*
Pre-ignition is the ignition of the fuel prior to normal ignition or ignition before the electrical arcing occurs at the spark plug. Pre-ignition may be caused by excessively hot exhaust valves, carbon particles, or spark plugs and electrodes heated to an incandescent, or glowing, state. These hot spots are usually caused by high temperatures encountered during detonation. A significant difference between pre-ignition and detonation is that if the conditions for detonation exist in one cylinder they usually exist in all cylinders, but pre-ignition often takes place in only one or two cylinders.
Answer (A) is incorrect because combustion is the normal process which takes place inside the cylinders. Answer (C) is incorrect because detonation is an uncontrolled, explosive ignition of the fuel/air mixture within the cylinder's combustion chamber caused by a combination of excessively high temperature and pressure in the cylinder.

2.16 Aviation Fuel Practices

72.
3242. What type fuel can be substituted for an aircraft if the recommended octane is not available?

A—The next higher octane aviation gas.
B—The next lower octane aviation gas.
C—Unleaded automotive gas of the same octane rating.

Answer (A) is correct (3242). *(PHAK Chap 2)*
If the recommended octane is not available for an airplane, the next higher octane aviation gas should be used.
Answer (B) is incorrect because if the grade of fuel used in an airplane engine is lower than specified for the engine, it will probably cause detonation. Answer (C) is incorrect because, except for very special situations, only aviation gas should be used.

73.
3243. Filling the fuel tanks after the last flight of the day is considered a good operating procedure because this will

A—force any existing water to the top of the tank away from the fuel lines to the engine.
B—prevent expansion of the fuel by eliminating airspace in the tanks.
C—prevent moisture condensation by eliminating airspace in the tanks.

Answer (C) is correct (3243). *(PHAK Chap 2)*
Filling the fuel tanks after the last flight of the day is considered good operating practice because it prevents moisture condensation by eliminating airspace in the tanks. Humid air may result in condensation at night when the airplane cools.
Answer (A) is incorrect because water is heavier than fuel and will always settle to the bottom of the tank. Answer (B) is incorrect because filling the fuel tank will not prevent expansion of the fuel.

74.
3224. On aircraft equipped with fuel pumps, when is the auxiliary electric driven pump used?

A—All the time to aid the engine-driven fuel pump.
B—In the event engine-driven fuel pump fails.
C—Constantly except in starting the engine.

Answer (B) is correct (3224). *(PHAK Chap 2)*
In a fuel pump system, two fuel pumps are used on most airplanes. The main fuel pump is engine-driven and an auxiliary electric-driven pump is provided for use in the event the engine pump fails.
Answer (A) is incorrect because an auxiliary fuel pump is a backup system to the engine-driven fuel pump; it is not intended to aid the engine-driven fuel pump. Answer (C) is incorrect because the auxiliary electric fuel pump is normally used in starting the engine.

75.
3241. Which would most likely cause the cylinder head temperature and engine oil temperature gauges to exceed their normal operating ranges?

A—Using fuel that has a lower-than-specified fuel rating.
B—Using fuel that has a higher-than-specified fuel rating.
C—Operating with higher-than-normal oil pressure.

Answer (A) is correct (3241). *(PHAK Chap 2)*
Use of fuel with lower-than-specified fuel ratings, e.g., 80 octane instead of 100, can cause many problems, including higher operating temperatures, detonation, etc.
Answer (B) is incorrect because higher octane fuels usually result in lower cylinder head temperatures. Answer (C) is incorrect because higher-than-normal oil pressure provides better lubrication and cooling (although too high an oil pressure can break parts, lines, etc.).

2.17 Starting the Engine

76.
3656. What should be the first action after starting an aircraft engine?

A—Adjust for proper RPM and check for desired indications on the engine gauges.
B—Place the magneto or ignition switch momentarily in the OFF position to check for proper grounding.
C—Test each brake and the parking brake.

Answer (A) is correct (3656). *(PHAK Chap 2)*
After the engine starts, the engine speed should be adjusted to the proper RPM. Then the engine gauges should be reviewed, with the oil pressure being the most important gauge initially.
Answer (B) is incorrect because this check is normally done just prior to engine shutdown. Answer (C) is incorrect because this check is done during taxi.

77.
3657. Should it become necessary to handprop an airplane engine, it is extremely important that a competent pilot

A—call "contact" before touching the propeller.
B—be at the controls in the cockpit.
C—be in the cockpit and call out all commands.

Answer (B) is correct (3657). *(PHAK Chap 2)*
Because of the hazards involved in handstarting airplane engines, every precaution should be exercised. It is extremely important that a competent pilot be at the controls in the cockpit. Also, the person turning the propeller should be thoroughly familiar with the technique.
Answer (A) is incorrect because the person hand-propping the airplane yells "gas off, switch off, throttle closed, brakes set" before touching the propeller initially. Contact means the magnetos are on, i.e., "hot." This is not done until starting is attempted. Answer (C) is incorrect because the person handpropping the airplane (not the person in the cockpit) calls out the commands.

END OF CHAPTER

CHAPTER THREE
AIRPORTS, AIR TRAFFIC CONTROL, AND AIRSPACE

This chapter contains outlines of major concepts tested, all FAA test questions and answers regarding airports and Air Traffic Control, and an explanation of each answer. Each module, or subtopic, within this chapter is listed above with the number of questions from the FAA pilot knowledge test pertaining to that particular module. For each module, the first number following the parentheses is the page number on which the outline begins, and the next number is the page number on which the questions begin.

CAUTION: Recall that the **sole purpose** of this book is to expedite your passing the FAA pilot knowledge test for the private pilot certificate. Accordingly, all extraneous material (i.e., topics or regulations not directly tested on the FAA pilot knowledge test) is omitted, even though much more information and knowledge are necessary to fly safely. This additional material is presented in *Pilot Handbook* and *Private Pilot Flight Maneuvers and Practical Test Prep*, available from Gleim Publications, Inc. See the order form on page 326.

3.1 RUNWAY MARKINGS (Questions 1-5)

1. The number at the end of each runway indicates its magnetic alignment divided by 10°; e.g., runway 26 indicates 260° magnetic; runway 9 indicates 090° magnetic.

2. A displaced threshold is a threshold (marked as a broad solid line across the runway) that is not at the beginning of the full strength runway pavement. The remainder of the runway, following the displaced threshold, is the landing portion of the runway.

   a. The paved area before the displaced threshold (marked by arrows) is available for taxiing, the landing rollout, and takeoff of aircraft.

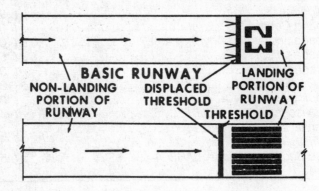

3. Chevrons mark any surface or area extending beyond the usable runway which appears usable but which, due to the nature of its structure, is unusable runway.

   a. This area is not available for any use, not even taxiing.

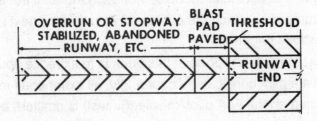

4. Closed runways are marked by an "X" on each runway end that is closed.

3.2 BEACONS AND TAXIWAY LIGHTS (Questions 6-11)

1. Operation of the green and white rotating beacon at an airport located in Class D airspace during the day indicates that the weather is not VFR, i.e.,

   a. The visibility is less than 3 SM, or
   b. The ceiling is less than 1,000 ft.

2. A lighted heliport may be identified by a green, yellow, and white rotating beacon.

3. Military airports are indicated by beacons with two white flashes between each green flash.

4. Airport taxiways are lighted with blue edge lights.

5. To operate pilot-controlled lighting (PCL), you should first click the mike seven times, which turns everything on. For high-intensity lights, leave it alone. For medium-intensity lights, key it five times. For low-intensity lights, key it three times.

3.3 AIRPORT TRAFFIC PATTERNS (Questions 12-19)

1. The segmented circle system provides traffic pattern information at airports without operating control towers. It consists of the

    a. Segmented circle -- located in a position affording maximum visibility to pilots in the air and on the ground, and providing a centralized point for the other elements of the system

    b. Landing strip indicators -- showing the alignment of landing runways (legs sticking out of the segmented circle)

    c. Traffic pattern indicators -- indicators at right angles to the landing strip indicator showing the direction of turn from base to final

        1) In the example below, runways 22 and 36 use left traffic, while runways 4 and 18 use right traffic.

        2) The "X" indicates that runways 4 and 22 are closed.

        3) The area behind the displaced thresholds of runways 18 and 36 (marked by arrows) can be used for taxiing and takeoff, but not for landing.

    d. Wind direction indicator -- a wind cone, wind sock, or wind tee installed near the runways to indicate wind direction

        1) The large end of the wind cone/wind sock points into the wind as does the large end (cross bar) of the wind tree.

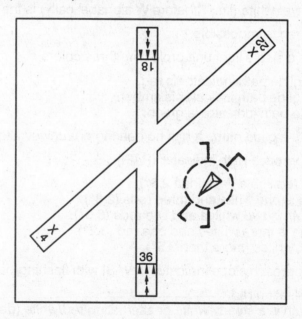

    e. Landing direction indicator -- a tetrahedron on a swivel installed when conditions at the airport warrant its use. It is used to indicate the direction of takeoffs and landings. It should be located at the center of a segmented circle and may be lighted for night operations.

        1) The small end points toward the direction in which a takeoff or landing should be made; i.e., the small end points into the wind.

2. If there is no segmented circle installed at the airport, traffic pattern indicators may be installed on or near the end of the runway.

3. Remember, you land

   a. In the same direction as the tip of the tetrahedron is pointing.

   b. As if you were flying out of the large (open) end of the wind cone or

   c. Toward the cross-bar end of a wind "T" (visualize the "T" as an airplane with no nose, with the top of the "T" being the wings).

4. If you are approaching an airport without an operating control tower,

   a. You must turn to the left when landing unless visual displays advise otherwise.
   b. You must comply with any FAA traffic pattern for that airport when departing.

3.4 VISUAL APPROACH SLOPE INDICATORS (VASI) (Questions 20-29)

1. Visual approach slope indicators (VASI) are a system of lights to provide visual descent information during an approach to landing.

2. The standard VASI consists of a two-barred tier of lights. You are

   a. Below the glide path if both light bars are red, i.e., "red means dead."

   b. On the glide path if the far (on top visually) lights are red and the near (on bottom visually) lights are white.

   c. Above the glide path if both light bars are white.

3. Remember, red over white (i.e., R before W alphabetically) is the desired sequence.

   a. White over red is impossible.

4. A tri-color VASI is a single light unit projecting three colors.

   a. The below glide path indicator is red.
   b. The above glide path indicator is amber.
   c. The on glide path indicator is green.

5. VASI only projects a glide path. It has no bearing on runway alignment.

6. On a precision approach path indicator (PAPI)

   a. Low is four red lights (less than 2.5°).
   b. Slightly low is one white and three reds (2.8°).
   c. On glide path is two whites and two reds (3.0°).
   d. Slightly high is three whites and one red (3.2°).
   e. High is four whites (more than 3.5°).

7. On a pulsating approach slope indicator (a VASI with flashing/pulsating signals)

   a. Low is a pulsating red.
   b. On glide path is a steady white or alternating red/white (depending on model).
   c. High is a pulsating white.

8. Each pilot of an airplane approaching to land on a runway served by a visual approach slope indicator shall maintain an altitude at or above the glide slope until a lower altitude is necessary for landing (FAR 91.129).

3.5 WAKE TURBULENCE (Questions 30-36)

1. Wingtip vortices (wake turbulence) are only created when airplanes develop lift.

2. The greatest vortex strength occurs when the generating aircraft is heavy, clean, and slow.

3. Wingtip vortex turbulence tends to sink into the flight path of airplanes operating below the airplane generating the turbulence.

   a. Thus, you should fly above the flight path of a large jet rather than below.

   b. You should also fly upwind rather than downwind of the flight path, since the vortices will drift with the wind.

4. The most dangerous wind, when taking off or landing behind a heavy aircraft, is the light quartering tailwind. It will push the vortices into your touchdown zone, even if you are executing proper procedures.

3.6 COLLISION AVOIDANCE (Questions 37-45)

1. Navigation lights on the aircraft consist of a red light on the left wing, a green light on the right wing, and a white light on the tail. In night flight,

   a. When an airplane is crossing in front of you from your right to left, you will observe a red light.

   b. When an airplane is crossing in front of you from your left to right, you will observe a green light.

   c. When an airplane is flying away from you, you will observe a steady white light.

   d. When an airplane is approaching you head-on, you will observe a red and green light but no white light.

   e. Note that the navigation lights on the wings cannot be seen from the rear.

2. A flashing red light on an aircraft is a rotating beacon and may be seen from any angle.

3. In daylight, the most effective way to scan for other aircraft is to use a series of short, regularly-spaced eye movements that bring successive areas of the sky into your central visual field.

   a. Each movement should not exceed 10°, and each area should be observed for at least one second to enable detection.

   b. Only a very small center area of the eye has the ability to send clear, sharply focused messages to the brain.

4. At night, collision avoidance scanning must use the off-center portions of the eyes. These portions are most effective at seeing objects at night.

   a. Accordingly, peripheral vision should be used, scanning small sectors and using off-center viewing.

5. Any aircraft that appears to have no relative motion with respect to your aircraft and stays in one scan quadrant is likely to be on a collision course.

   a. If it increases in size, you should take immediate evasive action.

6. Prior to each maneuver, a pilot should visually scan the entire area for collision avoidance.

   a. When climbing or descending VFR on an airway, you should execute gentle banks left and right to facilitate scanning for other aircraft.

7. All pilots are responsible for collision avoidance when operating in an alert area.

3.7 ATIS AND GROUND CONTROL (Questions 46-48)

1. Automatic Terminal Information Service (ATIS) is a continuous broadcast of recorded noncontrol information in selected high activity terminal areas (i.e., busy airports).

    a. The information is essential but routine.

2. The information included is the latest weather sequence, active runways, and other pertinent remarks.

    a. Ceilings are usually not broadcast if they are above 5,000 ft., and visibility is usually not mentioned if it is more than 5 SM.

3. After landing, you should contact ground control only when so instructed by the tower.

4. A clearance to taxi to the active runway is a clearance to taxi via taxiways and across intersecting runways, but not onto the active runway.

    a. When cleared to a runway, you are cleared to that runway's runup area, but not onto the active runway itself.

    b. "Taxi into position and hold" is the instruction to taxi onto the active runway and prepare for takeoff, but not to take off.

3.8 CLASS D AIRSPACE AND AIRPORT ADVISORY AREA (Questions 49-54)

1. Class D airspace is an area of controlled airspace surrounding an airport with an operating control tower, not associated with Class B or Class C airspace areas.

    a. Airspace at an airport with a part-time control tower is classified as Class D airspace only when the control tower is operating.

2. Class D airspace is depicted by a blue segmented (dashed) circle on a sectional chart.

3. When departing a non-tower satellite airport within Class D airspace, you must establish and maintain two-way radio communication with the primary airport's control tower.

    a. The primary airport is the airport for which the Class D airspace is designated.
    b. A satellite airport is any other airport within the Class D airspace area.

4. Class D airspace is normally the airspace up to 2,500 ft. above the surface of the airport.

    a. The actual lateral dimensions of Class D airspace are based on the instrument procedures for which the controlled airspace is established.

5. Two-way radio communication with the control tower is required for landings and takeoffs at all tower-controlled airports, regardless of weather conditions.

6. Airport Advisory Areas exist at noncontrolled airports that have a Flight Service Station (FSS) physically located on that airport.

    a. The FSS provides advisory (not control) information on traffic, weather, etc., to requesting aircraft.

3.9 CLASS C AIRSPACE (Questions 55-59)

1. Class C airspace consists of a surface area (formerly called the inner circle) and a shelf area (formerly called the outer circle).

    a. The surface area has a 5-NM radius from the primary airport

        1) Extending from the surface to 4,000 ft. above the airport elevation.

    b. The shelf area is an area from 5 to 10 NM from the primary airport

        1) Extending from 1,200 ft. to 4,000 ft. above the airport elevation.

2.   Surrounding the Class C airspace is the outer area. The outer area is not classified as Class C airspace.

   a.   ATC provides the same radar services as provided in Class C airspace.

   b.   The normal radius of the outer area of Class C airspace is 20 NM from the primary airport.

3.   The minimum equipment needed to operate in Class C airspace

   a.   4096 code transponder,
   b.   Mode C (altitude encoding) capability, and
   c.   Two-way radio communication capability.

4.   You must establish and maintain two-way radio communication with ATC prior to entering Class C airspace.

   a.   A clearance is not required because a clearance relates to IFR operations.

5.   When departing from a satellite airport without an operating control tower, you must contact ATC as soon as practicable after takeoff.

3.10 TERMINAL RADAR PROGRAMS (Questions 60-62)

1.   Terminal radar programs for VFR aircraft are classified as basic, TRSA, Class C, and Class B service.

   a.   Basic radar service provides safety alerts, traffic advisories, and limited vectoring on a workload- permitting basis.

   b.   TRSA service provides sequencing and separation for all participating VFR aircraft operating within a Terminal Radar Service Area (TRSA).

2.   Terminal radar program participation is voluntary for VFR traffic.

   a.   Contact approach control when inbound.

   b.   When departing, you should request radar traffic information from ground control on initial contact, along with your direction of flight.

3.11 TRANSPONDER CODES (Questions 63-65)

1.   Code 1200 is the standard VFR transponder code.

2.   The ident feature should not be engaged unless instructed by ATC.

3.   Certain special codes should never be engaged (except in an emergency), as they may cause problems at ATC centers:

   a.   7500 is the hijacking code.
   b.   7600 is the lost radio communication code.
   c.   7700 is the general emergency code.
   d.   7777 is the military interceptor code.

3.12 RADIO PHRASEOLOGY (Questions 66-68)

1.   When contacting a flight service station the proper call sign is the name of the FSS followed by "radio" (e.g., McAlester Radio).

2.   When contacting an En Route Flight Advisory Service (EFAS) the proper call sign is the name of the Air Route Traffic Control Center facility serving your area followed by "flight watch" (e.g., "Seattle Flight Watch").

3. Civilian aircraft should start their aircraft call sign with the make or model aircraft (e.g., Cessna 44WH or Baron 2DF).

    a. When a make or model is used the initial November is dropped from the call sign.

4. Pilots should state each digit of the call sign individually (e.g., 6449U = six, four, four, niner, uniform).

5. When calling out altitudes up to but not including 18,000 ft., state the separate digits of the thousands, plus the hundreds, if appropriate (e.g., 4,500 ft. = four thousand five hundred).

    a. Unless otherwise noted the altitudes are MSL.

3.13 ATC TRAFFIC ADVISORIES (Questions 69-72)

1. Radar traffic information services provide pilots with traffic advisories of nearby aircraft.

2. Traffic advisories provide information based on the position of other aircraft from your airplane in terms of clock direction in a no-wind condition (i.e., it is based on your ground track, not heading).

    a. 12 o'clock is straight ahead.
    b. 3 o'clock is directly off your right wing.
    c. 6 o'clock is directly behind you.
    d. 9 o'clock is directly off your left wing,
    e. Other positions are described accordingly, e.g., 2 o'clock, 10 o'clock.

3. Traffic advisories usually also include

    a. Distance away in miles.
    b. Direction of flight of other aircraft.
    c. Altitude of other aircraft.

3.14 ATC LIGHT SIGNALS (Questions 73-79)

1. In the absence of radio communications, the tower can communicate with you by light signals.

2. Light signal meanings depend on whether you are on the ground or in the air.

Light Signal	On the Ground	In the Air
Steady Green	Cleared for takeoff	Cleared to land
Flashing Green	Cleared to taxi	Return for landing *(to be followed by steady green at proper time)*
Steady Red	Stop	Give way to other aircraft and continue circling
Flashing Red	Taxi clear of landing area (runway) in use	Airport unsafe -- Do not land
Flashing White	Return to starting point on airport	Not applicable
Alternating Red and Green	General warning signal -- Exercise extreme caution	General warning signal -- Exercise extreme caution

3. Acknowledge light signals in the air by rocking wings in daylight and blinking lights at night.

4. If your radio fails and you wish to land at a tower-controlled airport, remain outside or above the airport's traffic pattern until the direction and flow of traffic has been determined, then join the traffic pattern and maintain visual contact with the tower to receive light signals.

3.15 ELTs AND VHF/DF (Questions 80-83)

1. ELTs transmit simultaneously on 121.5 and 243.0 MHz.

    a. You can monitor either frequency during flight and before shut down (after landing) to ensure your ELT has not been activated.

2. The VHF/Direction Finder facility is a ground operation that displays the magnetic direction of the airplane from the station each time the airplane transmits a signal to it.

3. In order to take advantage of VHF/DF radio reception for assistance in locating a position, an airplane must have both a VHF transmitter and a receiver. The transmitter and receiver are necessary to converse with a ground station having VHF/DF facilities.

    a. The transmitter is also needed to send the signal that the Direction Finder identifies in terms of magnetic heading from the facility.

3.16 LAND AND HOLD SHORT OPERATIONS (LAHSO) (Questions 84-88)

1. Land and hold short operations (LAHSO) take place at some airports with an operating control tower in order to increase airport capacity and improve the flow of traffic.

    a. LAHSO requires that you land and hold short of an intersecting runway, an intersecting taxiway, or some other designated point on a runway.

2. Before accepting a clearance to land and hold short, you must determine that you can safely land and stop within the available landing distance (ALD).

    a. ALD data are published in the special notices section of the *Airport/Facility Directory (A/FD)*.

    b. ATC will provide ALD data upon your request.

3. Student pilots should not participate in the LAHSO program.

4. The pilot in command has the final authority to accept or decline any land and hold short (LAHSO) clearance.

    a. You are expected to decline a LAHSO clearance if you determine it will compromise safety.

5. You should receive a LAHSO clearance only when there is a minimum ceiling of 1,000 ft. and visibility of 3 SM.

    a. The intent of having basic VFR weather conditions is to allow pilots to maintain visual contact with other aircraft and ground vehicle operations.

QUESTIONS AND ANSWER EXPLANATIONS

All the FAA questions from the pilot knowledge test for the private pilot certificate relating to airports and Air Traffic Control and the material outlined previously are reproduced on the following pages in the same modules as the outlines. To the immediate right of each question are the correct answer and answer explanation. You should cover these answers and answer explanations while responding to the questions. Refer to the general discussion in the Introduction on how to take the FAA pilot knowledge test.

Remember that the questions from the FAA pilot knowledge test bank have been reordered by topic, and the topics have been organized into a meaningful sequence. Accordingly, the first line of the answer explanation gives the FAA question number and the citation of the authoritative source for the answer.

3.1 Runway Markings

1.
3773. (Refer to figure 49 on page 67.) That portion of the runway identified by the letter A may be used for

A—landing.
B—taxiing and takeoff.
C—taxiing and landing.

Answer (B) is correct (3773). *(AIM Para 2-3-3)*
The portion of the runway identified by the letter A in Fig. 49 is a displaced threshold, as marked by arrows from the beginning of the runway pointing to the displaced threshold, which means it may be used for taxiing or takeoffs, but not for landings.
Answer (A) is incorrect because area A may be used for the landing rollout, but not the actual landing. Answer (C) is incorrect because area A may be used for the landing rollout, but not the actual landing.

2.
3774. (Refer to figure 49 on page 67.) According to the airport diagram, which statement is true?

A—Runway 30 is equipped at position E with emergency arresting gear to provide a means of stopping military aircraft.
B—Takeoffs may be started at position A on Runway 12, and the landing portion of this runway begins at position B.
C—The takeoff and landing portion of Runway 12 begins at position B.

Answer (B) is correct (3774). *(AIM Para 2-3-3)*
In Fig. 49, Runway 12 takeoffs may be started at position A, and the landing portion of this runway begins at position B. In this example, a displaced threshold exists at the beginning of Runway 12. The threshold is a heavy line across the runway, designating the beginning portion of a runway usable for landing. The paved area behind the displaced runway threshold is available for taxiing, the landing rollout, and the takeoff of aircraft.
Answer (A) is incorrect because arresting cables across the operational area of a runway are indicated by yellow circles 10 ft. in diameter painted across the runway at positions of the arresting cables. Area E has chevron markings, which indicates an overrun area. Answer (C) is incorrect because only the landing portion of RWY 12 begins at position B. The takeoff may be started in the paved area behind the displaced runway threshold (i.e., position A).

3.
3775. (Refer to figure 49 on page 67.) What is the difference between area A and area E on the airport depicted?

A—"A" may be used for taxi and takeoff; "E" may be used only as an overrun.
B—"A" may be used for all operations except heavy aircraft landings; "E" may be used only as an overrun.
C—"A" may be used only for taxiing; "E" may be used for all operations except landings.

Answer (A) is correct (3775). *(AIM Para 2-3-3)*
Area A in Fig. 49 is the paved area behind a displaced runway threshold, as identified by the arrows painted on the pavement. This area may be used for taxiing, the landing rollout, and the takeoff of aircraft. Area E is a stopway area, as identified by the chevrons. This area, due to the nature of its structure, is unusable except as an overrun.
Answer (B) is incorrect because area A cannot be used by any aircraft for landing. Answer (C) is incorrect because area A can also be used for takeoff and landing rollout. Area E cannot be used for any type of operation, except as an overrun.

4.
3776. (Refer to figure 49 on page 67.) Area C on the airport depicted is classified as a

A—stabilized area.
B—multiple heliport.
C—closed runway.

Answer (C) is correct (3776). *(AIM Para 2-3-6)*
The runway marked by the arrow C in Fig. 49 has Xs on the runway, indicating it is closed.
Answer (A) is incorrect because stabilized areas are designed to be load bearing but may be limited to emergency use only. Area E on the airport indicates a stabilized area. Answer (B) is incorrect because heliports are marked by Hs, not Xs.

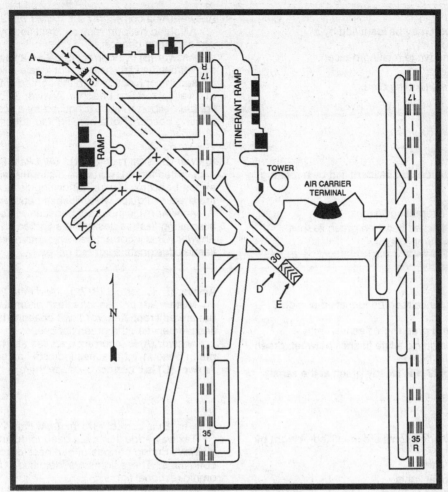

FIGURE 49.—Airport Diagram.

5.
3778. The numbers 9 and 27 on a runway indicate that the runway is oriented approximately

A—009° and 027° true.
B—090° and 270° true.
C—090° and 270° magnetic:

Answer (C) is correct (3778). *(AIM Para 2-3-3)*
Runway numbers are determined from the approach direction. The runway number is the whole number nearest one-tenth the magnetic direction of the centerline. Thus, the numbers 9 and 27 on a runway indicate that the runway is oriented approximately 090° and 270° magnetic.
Answer (A) is incorrect because the ending digit, not a leading zero, is dropped. Answer (B) is incorrect because runways are numbered based on magnetic (not true) direction.

3.2 Beacons and Taxiway Lights

6.
3769. An airport's rotating beacon operated during daylight hours indicates

A—there are obstructions on the airport.
B—that weather at the airport located in Class D airspace is below basic VFR weather minimums.
C—the Air Traffic Control tower is not in operation.

Answer (B) is correct (3769). *(AIM Para 2-1-8)*
Operation of the airport beacon during daylight hours often indicates that weather at the airport located in controlled airspace (e.g., Class D airspace) is below basic VFR weather minimums, i.e., less than 1,000 ft. ceiling or 3 SM visibility. Note that there is no regulatory requirement for daylight operation of an airport's rotating beacon.
Answer (A) is incorrect because the obstructions near or on airports are usually listed in NOTAMs or the Airport/Facility Directory as appropriate to their hazard. Answer (C) is incorrect because there is no visual signal of tower operation/non-operation.

7.
3770. A lighted heliport may be identified by a

A—green, yellow, and white rotating beacon.
B—flashing yellow light.
C—blue lighted square landing area.

Answer (A) is correct (3770). *(AIM Para 2-1-8)*
A lighted heliport may be identified by a green, yellow, and white rotating beacon.
Answer (B) is incorrect because a flashing yellow light is sometimes used to help a pilot locate a lighted water airport. It is used in conjunction with the lighted water airport's white and yellow rotating beacon. Answer (C) is incorrect because a lighted heliport may be identified by a green, yellow, and white rotating beacon, not a blue lighted square landing area.

8.
3771. A military air station can be identified by a rotating beacon that emits

A—white and green alternating flashes.
B—two quick, white flashes between green flashes.
C—green, yellow, and white flashes.

Answer (B) is correct (3771). *(AIM Para 2-1-8)*
Lighted land airports are distinguished by white and green airport beacons. To further distinguish it as a military airport, there are two quick white flashes between each green.
Answer (A) is incorrect because white and green alternating flashes designate a lighted civilian land airport. Answer (C) is incorrect because green, yellow, and white flashes designate a lighted heliport.

9.
3772. How can a military airport be identified at night?

A—Alternate white and green light flashes.
B—Dual peaked (two quick) white flashes between green flashes.
C—White flashing lights with steady green at the same location.

Answer (B) is correct (3772). *(AIM Para 2-1-8)*
Military airport beacons flash alternately white and green, but are differentiated from civil beacons by two quick white flashes between the green flashes.
Answer (A) is incorrect because alternating white and green beacon light flashes indicate lighted civil land airports. Answer (C) is incorrect because there is no such airport signal.

10.
3718. Airport taxiway edge lights are identified at night by

A—white directional lights.
B—blue omnidirectional lights.
C—alternate red and green lights.

Answer (B) is correct (3718). *(AIM Para 2-1-9)*
Taxiway edge lights are used to outline the edges of taxiways during periods of darkness or restricted visibility conditions. These lights are identified at night by blue omnidirectional lights.
Answer (A) is incorrect because white lights are standard runway edge lights. Answer (C) is incorrect because alternate red and green lights are a light gun signal which means exercise extreme caution to all aircraft.

11.
3768. To set the high intensity runway lights on medium intensity, the pilot should click the microphone seven times, then click it

A—one time.
B—three times.
C—five times.

Answer (C) is correct (3768). *(AIM Para 2-1-7)*
To turn on and set the runway lights on medium intensity, the recommended procedure is to key the mike 7 times; this assures that all the lights are on and at high intensity. Next key the mike 5 times to get the medium-intensity setting.
Answer (A) is incorrect because keying only one time will not adjust or turn the lights on at all. Answer (B) is incorrect because three additional microphone clicks will give the low-intensity setting.

3.3 Airport Traffic Patterns

12.
3123. Which is the correct traffic pattern departure procedure to use at a noncontrolled airport?

A—Depart in any direction consistent with safety, after crossing the airport boundary.
B—Make all turns to the left.
C—Comply with any FAA traffic pattern established for the airport.

Answer (C) is correct (3123). *(FAR 91.127)*
Each person operating an airplane to or from an airport without an operating control tower shall (1) in the case of an airplane approaching to land, make all turns of that airplane to the left unless the airport displays approved light signals or visual markings indicating that turns should be made to the right, in which case the pilot shall make all turns to the right, and (2) in the case of an airplane departing the airport, comply with any FAA traffic pattern for that airport.
Answer (A) is incorrect because the correct traffic pattern departure procedure at a noncontrolled airport is to comply with any FAA established traffic pattern, not to depart in any direction after crossing the airport boundary. Answer (B) is incorrect because the FAA may establish right- or left-hand traffic patterns, not only left-hand traffic.

13.
3807. (Refer to figure 51 below.) The segmented circle indicates that the airport traffic is

A—left-hand for Runway 36 and right-hand for Runway 18.
B—left-hand for Runway 18 and right-hand for Runway 36.
C—right-hand for Runway 9 and left-hand for Runway 27.

Answer (A) is correct (3807). *(AIM Para 4-3-3)*
A segmented circle (see Fig. 51) is installed at uncontrolled airports to provide traffic pattern information. The landing runway indicators are shown coming out of the segmented circle to show the alignment of landing runways. In Fig. 51 (given the answer choices), the available runways are 18-36 and 9-27.

The traffic pattern indicators are at the end of the landing runway indicators and are angled out at 90°. These indicate the direction of turn from base to final. Thus, the airport traffic is left-hand for Runway 36 and right-hand for Runway 18. It is also left-hand for Runway 9 and right-hand for Runway 27.

Answer (B) is incorrect because Runway 18 is right, not left, and Runway 36 is left, not right. Answer (C) is incorrect because Runway 9 is left, not right, and Runway 27 is right, not left.

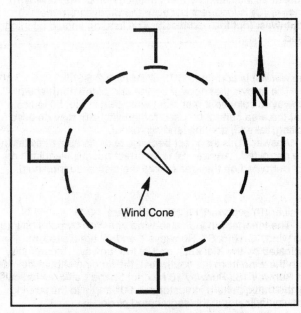

Wind Cone

FIGURE 51.—Airport Landing Indicator.

14.
3808. (Refer to figure 51 above.) The traffic patterns indicated in the segmented circle have been arranged to avoid flights over an area to the

A—south of the airport.
B—north of the airport.
C—southeast of the airport.

Answer (C) is correct (3808). *(AIM Para 4-3-3)*
The traffic patterns indicated in the segmented circle depicted in Fig. 51 have been arranged to avoid flights over an area to the southeast of the airport. All departures from the runways are to the north or west. All approaches to the airport indicate a pattern of arrival from 180° clockwise to 90°, leaving the southeastern quadrant free of flight.

Answer (A) is incorrect because arrivals on Runway 36 and departures on Runway 18 result in traffic to the south. Answer (B) is incorrect because Runway 9-27 produces traffic to the north in addition to Runway 36 departures and Runway 18 arrivals.

15.
3809. (Refer to figure 51 above.) The segmented circle indicates that a landing on Runway 26 will be with a

A—right-quartering headwind.
B—left-quartering headwind.
C—right-quartering tailwind.

Answer (A) is correct (3809). *(AIM Para 4-3-3)*
The wind cone at the center of the segmented circle depicted in Fig. 51 indicates that a landing on Runway 26 will be with a right-quartering headwind. The large end of the wind cone is pointing to the direction from which the wind is coming, i.e., a northwest headwind on the right quarter of an airplane landing from the east to the west.

Answer (B) is incorrect because a left-quartering headwind would be encountered landing on Runway 35. Answer (C) is incorrect because a right-quartering tailwind would be encountered landing on Runway 17.

16.
3810. (Refer to figure 51 on page 69.) Which runway and traffic pattern should be used as indicated by the wind cone in the segmented circle?

A—Right-hand traffic on Runway 9.
B—Right-hand traffic on Runway 18.
C—Left-hand traffic on Runway 36.

Answer (C) is correct (3810). *(AIM Para 4-3-3)*
The appropriate traffic pattern and runway, given a wind from the northwest (Fig. 51), is left-hand traffic on Runway 36, which would have a quartering headwind.
Answer (A) is incorrect because Runway 9 uses a left-hand pattern. Also, this would be a tailwind landing. Answer (B) is incorrect because, even though there is right traffic on Runway 18, this would be a tailwind landing.

17.
3806. (Refer to figure 50 below.) If the wind is as shown by the landing direction indicator, the pilot should land on

A—Runway 18 and expect a crosswind from the right.
B—Runway 22 directly into the wind.
C—Runway 36 and expect a crosswind from the right.

Answer (A) is correct (3806). *(AIM Para 4-3-3)*
Given a wind as shown by the landing direction indicator in Fig. 50, the pilot should land to the south on Runway 18 and expect a crosswind from the right. The tetrahedron points to the wind which is from the southwest.
Answer (B) is incorrect because Runways 4 and 22 are closed, as indicated by the X at each end of the runway. Answer (C) is incorrect because the wind is from the southwest (not the northeast). The landing should be into the wind.

18.
3777. (Refer to figure 50 below.) The arrows that appear on the end of the north/south runway indicate that the area

A—may be used only for taxiing.
B—is usable for taxiing, takeoff, and landing.
C—cannot be used for landing, but may be used for taxiing and takeoff.

Answer (C) is correct (3777). *(AIM Para 2-3-3)*
The arrows that appear on the end of the north/south runway (displaced thresholds) as shown in Fig. 50 indicate that the area cannot be used for landing, but may be used for taxiing, takeoff, and the landing rollout.
Answer (A) is incorrect because takeoffs as well as taxiing are permitted. Answer (B) is incorrect because landings are not permitted on the area before the displaced threshold.

19.
3805. (Refer to figure 50 below.) Select the proper traffic pattern and runway for landing.

A—Left-hand traffic and Runway 18.
B—Right-hand traffic and Runway 18.
C—Left-hand traffic and Runway 22.

Answer (B) is correct (3805). *(AIM Para 4-3-3)*
The tetrahedron indicates wind direction by pointing into the wind. On Fig. 50, Runways 4 and 22 are closed, as indicated by the X at each end of the runway. Accordingly, with the wind from the southwest, the landing should be made on Runway 18. Runway 18 has right-hand traffic, as indicated by the traffic pattern indicator at a 90° angle to the landing runway indicator in the segmented circle.
Answer (A) is incorrect because Runway 18 uses a right-hand (not left-hand) pattern. Answer (C) is incorrect because the X markings indicate that Runways 4 and 22 are closed.

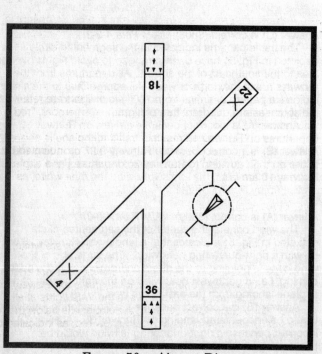

FIGURE 50.—Airport Diagram.

3.4 Visual Approach Slope Indicators (VASI)

20.
3763. An on glide slope indication from a tri-color VASI is

A—a white light signal.
B—a green light signal.
C—an amber light signal.

Answer (B) is correct (3763). *(AIM Para 2-1-2)*
Tri-color visual approach slope indicators normally consist of a single light unit projecting a 3-color visual approach path into the final approach area of the runway, upon which the indicator is installed. The below glide path indicator is red. The above glide path indicator is amber. The on glide path indicator is green. This type of indicator has a useful range of approximately ½ to 1 mi. in daytime and up to 5 mi. at night.
Answer (A) is incorrect because tri-color VASI does not emit a white light. Answer (C) is incorrect because amber indicates above (not on) the glide slope.

21.
3762. An above glide slope indication from a tri-color VASI is

A—a white light signal.
B—a green light signal.
C—an amber light signal.

Answer (C) is correct (3762). *(AIM Para 2-1-2)*
The tri-color VASI has three lights: amber for above the glide slope, green for on the glide slope, and red for below the glide slope.
Answer (A) is incorrect because tri-color VASI does not emit a white light. Answer (B) is incorrect because a green light means on (not above) the glide slope.

22.
3761. A below glide slope indication from a tri-color VASI is a

A—red light signal.
B—pink light signal.
C—green light signal.

Answer (A) is correct (3761). *(AIM Para 2-1-2)*
The tri-color VASI has three lights: amber for above the glide slope, green for on the glide slope, and red for below the glide slope.
Answer (B) is incorrect because a pink light may be seen on a pulsating (not tri-color) VASI when in the area of on, to slightly below, the glide slope. Answer (C) is incorrect because a green light means you are on the glide slope.

23.
3764. A below glide slope indication from a pulsating approach slope indicator is a

A—pulsating white light.
B—steady white light.
C—pulsating red light.

Answer (C) is correct (3764). *(AIM Para 2-1-2)*
A pulsating VASI indicator normally consists of a single light unit projecting a two-color visual approach path into the final approach area of the runway upon which the indicator is installed. The below glide slope indication is a pulsating red, the above glide slope is pulsating white, and the on glide slope is a steady white light. The useful range of this system is about 4 mi. during the day and up to 10 mi. at night.
Answer (A) is incorrect because a pulsating white light is an above glide slope indication. Answer (B) is incorrect because steady white is the on glide slope indication.

24.
3767. (Refer to figure 48 on page 72.) While on final approach to a runway equipped with a standard 2-bar VASI, the lights appear as shown by illustration D. This means that the aircraft is

A—above the glide slope.
B—below the glide slope.
C—on the glide slope.

Answer (B) is correct (3767). *(AIM Para 2-1-2)*
In illustration D of Fig. 48, both rows of lights are red. Thus, the aircraft is below the glide path. Remember, "red means dead."
Answer (A) is incorrect because, if the airplane is above the glide path, the lights would both show white, as indicated by illustration C. Answer (C) is incorrect because, if the airplane is on the glide path, the lights would be red over white, as indicated by illustration A.

25.
3766. (Refer to figure 48 on page 72.) VASI lights as shown by illustration C indicate that the airplane is

A—off course to the left.
B—above the glide slope.
C—below the glide slope.

Answer (B) is correct (3766). *(AIM Para 2-1-2)*
In illustration C of Fig. 48, both rows of lights are white, which means the airplane is above the glide path.
Answer (A) is incorrect because the VASI does not alert a pilot as to runway alignment, but a pilot who is excessively to the left or right may not be able to see the VASI lights at all. Answer (C) is incorrect because, if the airplane is below the glide path, both rows of lights would show red, as indicated by illustration D.

26.
3765. (Refer to figure 48 below.) Illustration A indicates that the aircraft is

A—below the glide slope.
B—on the glide slope.
C—above the glide slope.

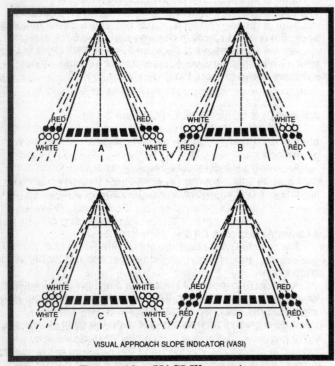

FIGURE 48.—VASI Illustrations.

Answer (B) is correct (3765). *(AIM Para 2-1-2)*
Illustration A indicates that the airplane is on the glide path (glide slope). The basic principle of the VASI is that of color differentiation between red and white. Each light unit projects a beam of light having a white segment in the upper part and a red segment in the lower part of the beam. Thus, to be on the glide slope you need to be on the lower part of the far light (red) and on the upper part of the near light (white).
Answer (A) is incorrect because, if the airplane is below the glide path, both rows of lights will be red, as indicated in D. Answer (C) is incorrect because, if the aircraft is above the glide path, both lights will be white, as indicated in C.

27.
3121. When approaching to land on a runway served by a visual approach slope indicator (VASI), the pilot shall

A—maintain an altitude that captures the glide slope at least 2 miles downwind from the runway threshold.
B—maintain an altitude at or above the glide slope.
C—remain on the glide slope and land between the two-light bar.

Answer (B) is correct (3121). *(FAR 91.129)*
An airplane approaching to land on a runway served by a VASI shall maintain an altitude at or above the glide slope until a lower altitude is necessary for a safe landing.
Answer (A) is incorrect because a VASI should not be used for descent until the airplane is visually lined up with the runway. Answer (C) is incorrect because it is unsafe to concentrate on the VASI after nearing the approach end of the runway; i.e., turn your attention to landing the airplane.

28.
3760. A slightly high glide slope indication from a precision approach path indicator is

A—four white lights.
B—three white lights and one red light.
C—two white lights and two red lights.

Answer (B) is correct (3760). *(AIM Para 2-1-2)*
A precision approach path indicator (PAPI) has a row of four lights, each of which is similar to a VASI, in that they emit a red or white light. Above the glide slope (more than 3.5°) is indicated by four white lights, a slightly above glide slope (3.2°) is indicated by three white lights and one red light, on glide slope (3°) is indicated by two white and two red lights, slightly below glide slope (2.8°) is indicated by one white and three red lights, and below (too low) the glide slope (less than 2.5°) is indicated by four red lights.
Answer (A) is incorrect because four white lights is a high or more than 3.5° glide slope. Answer (C) is incorrect because two white and two red lights is an on glide slope (3°).

29.
3120. Each pilot of an aircraft approaching to land on a runway served by a visual approach slope indicator (VASI) shall

A—maintain a 3° glide to the runway.
B—maintain an altitude at or above the glide slope.
C—stay high until the runway can be reached in a power-off landing.

Answer (B) is correct (3120). *(FAR 91.129)*
When approaching to land on a runway served by a VASI, each pilot of an airplane must fly at or above the VASI glide path until a lower altitude is necessary for a safe landing.
Answer (A) is incorrect because a VASI may be adjusted to provide a glide slope more or less than 3°. Answer (C) is incorrect because higher than the VASI glide path is not required.

3.5 Wake Turbulence

30.
3824. Wingtip vortices are created only when an aircraft is

A—operating at high airspeeds.
B—heavily loaded.
C—developing lift.

31.
3826. Wingtip vortices created by large aircraft tend to

A—sink below the aircraft generating turbulence.
B—rise into the traffic pattern.
C—rise into the takeoff or landing path of a crossing runway.

32.
3827. When taking off or landing at an airport where heavy aircraft are operating, one should be particularly alert to the hazards of wingtip vortices because this turbulence tends to

A—rise from a crossing runway into the takeoff or landing path.
B—rise into the traffic pattern area surrounding the airport.
C—sink into the flightpath of aircraft operating below the aircraft generating the turbulence.

33.
3825. The greatest vortex strength occurs when the generating aircraft is

A—light, dirty, and fast.
B—heavy, dirty, and fast.
C—heavy, clean, and slow.

34.
3828. The wind condition that requires maximum caution when avoiding wake turbulence on landing is a

A—light, quartering headwind.
B—light, quartering tailwind.
C—strong headwind.

Answer (C) is correct (3824). *(AIM Para 7-3-2)*
Wingtip vortices are the result of the pressure differential over and under a wing when that wing is producing lift. Wingtip vortices do not develop when an airplane is taxiing, although prop blast or jet thrust turbulence can be experienced near the rear of a large airplane which is taxiing.
Answer (A) is incorrect because the greatest turbulence is produced from an airplane operating at a slow airspeed. Answer (B) is incorrect because, even though a heavily loaded airplane may produce greater turbulence, an airplane does not have to be heavily loaded in order to produce wingtip vortices. Wingtip vortices are produced only when an airplane is developing lift.

Answer (A) is correct (3826). *(AIM Para 7-3-4)*
Wingtip vortices created by large airplanes tend to sink below the airplane generating the turbulence.
Answer (B) is incorrect because wingtip vortices sink, not rise. Answer (C) is incorrect because wingtip vortices do not rise or gain altitude, but sink toward the ground. However, they may move horizontally left or right depending on crosswind conditions.

Answer (C) is correct (3827). *(AIM Para 7-3-4)*
When taking off or landing at a busy airport where large, heavy airplanes are operating, you should be particularly alert to the hazards of wingtip vortices because this turbulence tends to sink into the flight paths of airplanes operating below the airplane generating the turbulence. Wingtip vortices are caused by a differential in high and low pressure at the wingtip of an airplane, creating a spiraling effect trailing behind the wingtip, similar to a horizontal tornado.
Answer (A) is incorrect because wingtip vortices always trail behind an airplane and descend toward the ground. However, they do drift with the wind and will not stay directly behind an airplane if there is a crosswind. Answer (B) is incorrect because wingtip vortices sink, not rise.

Answer (C) is correct (3825). *(AIM Para 7-3-3)*
Vortices are the greatest when the wingtips are at high angles of attack. This occurs at high gross weight, flaps up, and low airspeed (heavy, clean, and slow).
Answer (A) is incorrect because light aircraft produce less vortex turbulence than heavy aircraft. The use of flaps, spoilers, etc., (i.e., dirty) diminishes vortex turbulence. Answer (B) is incorrect because being dirty and/or fast causes the wingtip to be at a lower angle of attack, presenting less of a danger than when clean and/or slow.

Answer (B) is correct (3828). *(AIM Para 7-3-4)*
The most dangerous wind condition when avoiding wake turbulence on landing is a light, quartering tailwind. The tailwind can push the vortices forward which could put it in the touchdown zone of your aircraft even if you used proper procedures and landed beyond the touchdown point of the preceding aircraft. Also the quartering wind may push the upwind vortices to the middle of the runway.
Answer (A) is incorrect because headwinds push the vortices out of your touchdown zone if you land beyond the touchdown point of the preceding aircraft. Answer (C) is incorrect because strong winds help diffuse wake turbulence vortices.

35.
3830. When departing behind a heavy aircraft, the pilot should avoid wake turbulence by maneuvering the aircraft

A—below and downwind from the heavy aircraft.
B—above and upwind from the heavy aircraft.
C—below and upwind from the heavy aircraft.

Answer (B) is correct (3830). *(AIM Para 7-3-6)*
The proper procedure for departing behind a large aircraft is to rotate prior to the large aircraft's rotation point, then fly above and upwind of the large aircraft. Since vortices sink and drift downwind this should keep you clear.
Answer (A) is incorrect because you should remain above and upwind from the heavy aircraft. Answer (C) is incorrect because you should fly above the flight path of the large aircraft to avoid the sinking vortices.

36.
3829. When landing behind a large aircraft, the pilot should avoid wake turbulence by staying

A—above the large aircraft's final approach path and landing beyond the large aircraft's touchdown point.
B—below the large aircraft's final approach path and landing before the large aircraft's touchdown point.
C—above the large aircraft's final approach path and landing before the large aircraft's touchdown point.

Answer (A) is correct (3829). *(AIM Para 7-3-6)*
When landing behind a large aircraft your flight path should be above the other aircraft's flight path since the vortices sink. When the aircraft touches down, the vortices will stop, so you should thus touch down beyond where the large aircraft did.
Answer (B) is incorrect because below the flight path you will fly through the sinking vortices generated by the large aircraft. Answer (C) is incorrect because by landing before the large aircraft's touchdown point you will have to fly below the preceding aircraft's flight path.

3.6 Collision Avoidance

37.
3715. During a night flight, you observe a steady red light and a flashing red light ahead and at the same altitude. What is the general direction of movement of the other aircraft?

A—The other aircraft is crossing to the left.
B—The other aircraft is crossing to the right.
C—The other aircraft is approaching head-on.

Answer (A) is correct (3715). *(AFH Chap 10)*
Airplane position lights consist of a steady red light on the left wing (looking forward), a green light on the right wing, and a white light on the tail. Accordingly, if you observe a steady red light, you are looking at the tip of a left wing, which means the other plane is traveling from your right to left (crossing to the left). The red flashing light is the beacon.
Answer (B) is incorrect because, if the airplane were crossing to the right, you would see a steady green light. Answer (C) is incorrect because, if the airplane were approaching head-on, you would see both the red and the green lights.

38.
3716. During a night flight, you observe a steady white light and a flashing red light ahead and at the same altitude. What is the general direction of movement of the other aircraft?

A—The other aircraft is flying away from you.
B—The other aircraft is crossing to the left.
C—The other aircraft is crossing to the right.

Answer (A) is correct (3716). *(AFH Chap 10)*
A steady white light (the tail light) indicates the other airplane is moving away from you. The flashing red light is the beacon light.
Answer (B) is incorrect because you would observe a red light if another plane were crossing to your left. Answer (C) is incorrect because you would observe a green light if another airplane were crossing to your right.

39.
3717. During a night flight, you observe steady red and green lights ahead and at the same altitude. What is the general direction of movement of the other aircraft?

A—The other aircraft is crossing to the left.
B—The other aircraft is flying away from you.
C—The other aircraft is approaching head-on.

Answer (C) is correct (3717). *(AFH Chap 10)*
If you observe steady red and green lights at the same altitude, the other airplane is approaching head-on. You should take evasive action to the right.
Answer (A) is incorrect because, if the airplane were crossing to the left, you would observe only a red light. Answer (B) is incorrect because, if the other airplane were headed away from you, you would observe a white (tail) light.

40.
3834. The most effective method of scanning for other aircraft for collision avoidance during daylight hours is to use

A—regularly spaced concentration on the 3-, 9-, and 12-o'clock positions.
B—a series of short, regularly spaced eye movements to search each 10-degree sector.
C—peripheral vision by scanning small sectors and utilizing offcenter viewing.

Answer (B) is correct (3834). *(AC 90-48C)*
The most effective way to scan for other aircraft during daylight hours is to use a series of short, regularly spaced eye movements that bring successive areas of the sky into your central visual field. Each movement should not exceed 10°, and each area should be observed for at least one second to enable detection. Only a very small center area of the eye has the ability to send clear, sharply focused messages to the brain. All other areas provide less detail.
Answer (A) is incorrect because the spacing between the positions should be 10°, not 90°. Answer (C) is incorrect because this is the recommended nighttime scanning procedure.

41.
3714. The most effective method of scanning for other aircraft for collision avoidance during nighttime hours is to use

A—regularly spaced concentration on the 3-, 9-, and 12-o'clock positions.
B—a series of short, regularly spaced eye movements to search each 30-degree sector.
C—peripheral vision by scanning small sectors and utilizing offcenter viewing.

Answer (C) is correct (3714). *(AC 90-48C)*
At night, collision avoidance scanning must use the off-center portions of the eyes. These portions are most effective at seeing objects at night. Accordingly, peripheral vision should be used, scanning small sectors and using off-center viewing. This is in contrast to daytime searching for air traffic, when center viewing should be used.
Answer (A) is incorrect because all areas (up, below, and on all sides) should be scanned for other air traffic. Answer (B) is incorrect because smaller than 30° sectors should be scanned.

42.
3836. How can you determine if another aircraft is on a collision course with your aircraft?

A—The other aircraft will always appear to get larger and closer at a rapid rate.
B—The nose of each aircraft is pointed at the same point in space.
C—There will be no apparent relative motion between your aircraft and the other aircraft.

Answer (C) is correct (3836). *(AIM Para 8-1-8)*
Any aircraft that appears to have no relative motion and stays in one scan quadrant is likely to be on a collision course. Also, if a target shows no lateral or vertical motion, but increases in size, take evasive action.
Answer (A) is incorrect because aircraft on collision courses may not always appear to grow larger and/or to close at a rapid rate. Frequently, the degree of proximity cannot be detected. Answer (B) is incorrect because you may not be able to tell in exactly which direction the other airplane is pointed. Even if you could determine the direction of the other airplane, you may not be able to accurately project the flight paths of the two airplanes to determine if they indeed point to the same point in space and will arrive there at the same time (i.e., collide).

43.
3710. Prior to starting each maneuver, pilots should

A—check altitude, airspeed, and heading indications.
B—visually scan the entire area for collision avoidance.
C—announce their intentions on the nearest CTAF.

Answer (B) is correct (3710). *(AIM Para 4-4-14)*
Prior to each maneuver, a pilot should visually scan the entire area for collision avoidance. Many maneuvers require a clearing turn which should be used for this purpose.
Answer (A) is incorrect because altitude, speed, and heading may not all be critical to every maneuver. Collision avoidance is! Answer (C) is incorrect because CTAF is used for operations at an uncontrolled airport, not for pilots doing maneuvers away from an airport.

44.
3814. What procedure is recommended when climbing or descending VFR on an airway?

A—Execute gentle banks, left and right for continuous visual scanning of the airspace.
B—Advise the nearest FSS of the altitude changes.
C—Fly away from the centerline of the airway before changing altitude.

Answer (A) is correct (3814). *(AC 90-48C)*
When climbing (descending) VFR on an airway, you should execute gentle banks left and right to facilitate scanning for other aircraft. Collision avoidance is a constant priority and especially pertinent to climbs and descents on airways where other traffic is expected.
Answer (B) is incorrect because an FSS provides no en route traffic service. Answer (C) is incorrect because it is not necessary to leave the center of the airway, only to scan for other aircraft.

45.
3786. Responsibility for collision avoidance in an alert area rests with

A—the controlling agency.
B—all pilots.
C—Air Traffic Control.

Answer (B) is correct (3786). *(AIM Para 3-4-6)*
Alert areas may contain a high volume of pilot training or other unusual activity. Pilots using the area as well as pilots crossing the area are equally responsible for collision avoidance.
Answer (A) is incorrect because pilots are responsible for collision avoidance, not controlling agencies. Answer (C) is incorrect because pilots are responsible for collision avoidance, not ATC.

3.7 ATIS and Ground Control

46.
3811. After landing at a tower-controlled airport, when should the pilot contact ground control?

A—When advised by the tower to do so.
B—Prior to turning off the runway.
C—After reaching a taxiway that leads directly to the parking area.

Answer (A) is correct (3811). *(AIM Para 4-3-20)*
After landing at a tower-controlled airport, you should contact ground control on the appropriate frequency only when instructed by the tower.
Answer (B) is incorrect because a pilot should not change frequencies unless instructed to do so by the tower. Sometimes the tower controller will be handling both tower and ground frequencies. Switching without permission may be confusing to ATC. Answer (C) is incorrect because a pilot should not change frequencies unless instructed to do so by the tower. Sometimes the tower controller will be handling both tower and ground frequencies. Switching without permission may be confusing to ATC.

47.
3812. If instructed by ground control to taxi to Runway 9, the pilot may proceed

A—via taxiways and across runways to, but not onto, Runway 9.
B—to the next intersecting runway where further clearance is required.
C—via taxiways and across runways to Runway 9, where an immediate takeoff may be made.

Answer (A) is correct (3812). *(AIM Para 4-3-18)*
A clearance to taxi to the active runway means a pilot has been given permission to taxi via taxiways and across intersecting runways to, but not onto, the active runway.
Answer (B) is incorrect because such a clearance would indicate to hold short of the next intersecting runway. Answer (C) is incorrect because the clearance to taxi to a runway does not permit taxiing onto the active runway.

48.
3791. Automatic Terminal Information Service (ATIS) is the continuous broadcast of recorded information concerning

A—pilots of radar-identified aircraft whose aircraft is in dangerous proximity to terrain or to an obstruction.
B—nonessential information to reduce frequency congestion.
C—noncontrol information in selected high-activity terminal areas.

Answer (C) is correct (3791). *(AIM Para 4-1-13)*
The continuous broadcast of recorded noncontrol information is known as the Automatic Terminal Information Service (ATIS). ATIS includes weather, active runway, and other information that arriving and departing pilots need to know.
Answer (A) is incorrect because a controller who has a radar-identified aircraft under his/her control will issue a terrain or obstruction alert to an aircraft that is in dangerous proximity to terrain or to an obstruction. Answer (B) is incorrect because ATIS is considered essential (not nonessential) information, but routine, i.e., noncontrol.

3.8 Class D Airspace and Airport Advisory Area

49.
3117. A blue segmented circle on a Sectional Chart depicts which class airspace?

A—Class B.
B—Class C.
C—Class D.

Answer (C) is correct (3117). *(AIM Para 3-2-5)*
A blue segmented circle on a sectional chart depicts Class D airspace.
Answer (A) is incorrect because Class B airspace is depicted on a sectional chart by a solid, not segmented, blue circle. Answer (B) is incorrect because Class C airspace is depicted on a sectional chart by a solid magenta, not a blue segmented, circle.

50.
3118. Airspace at an airport with a part-time control tower is classified as Class D airspace only

A—when the weather minimums are below basic VFR.
B—when the associated control tower is in operation.
C—when the associated Flight Service Station is in operation.

Answer (B) is correct (3118). *(AIM Para 3-2-5)*
A Class D airspace area is automatically in effect when and only when the associated part-time control tower is in operation regardless of weather conditions, availability of radar services, or time of day. Airports with part-time operating towers only have a part-time Class D airspace area.
Answer (A) is incorrect because a Class D airspace area is automatically in effect when the tower is in operation, regardless of the weather conditions. Answer (C) is incorrect because a Class D airspace area is in effect when the associated control tower, not FSS, is in operation.

51.
3788. A non-tower satellite airport, within the same Class D airspace as that designated for the primary airport, requires radio communications be established and maintained with the

A—satellite airport's UNICOM.
B—associated Flight Service Station.
C—primary airport's control tower.

Answer (C) is correct (3788). *(AIM Para 3-2-5)*
Each pilot departing a non-tower satellite airport, within Class D airspace, must establish and maintain two-way radio communications with the primary airport's control tower as soon as practicable after departing.
Answer (A) is incorrect because, when departing a satellite airport without an operating control tower in Class D airspace, you must establish and maintain two-way radio communications with the primary airport's control tower, not the satellite airport's UNICOM. Answer (B) is incorrect because, when departing a satellite airport without an operating control tower in Class D airspace, you must establish and maintain two-way radio communications with the primary airport's control tower, not the associated FSS.

52.
3119. Unless otherwise authorized, two-way radio communications with Air Traffic Control are required for landings or takeoffs.

A—at all tower controlled airports regardless of weather conditions.
B—at all tower controlled airports only when weather conditions are less than VFR.
C—at all tower controlled airports within Class D airspace only when weather conditions are less than VFR.

Answer (A) is correct (3119). *(FAR 91.129)*
Two-way radio communications with air traffic control (ATC) are required for landing and taking off at all tower controlled airports, regardless of weather conditions. However, light signals from the tower may be used during radio failure.
Answer (B) is incorrect because radio communication is also required in VFR weather as well as IFR weather at all tower-controlled airports. Answer (C) is incorrect because radio communication is required in both VFR and IFR weather when landing at or taking off at all tower-controlled airports within Class D airspace.

53.
3787. The lateral dimensions of Class D airspace are based on

A—the number of airports that lie within the Class D airspace.
B—5 statute miles from the geographical center of the primary airport.
C—the instrument procedures for which the controlled airspace is established.

Answer (C) is correct (3787). *(AIM Para 3-2-5)*
The lateral dimensions of Class D airspace are based upon the instrument procedures for which the controlled airspace is established.
Answer (A) is incorrect because, while the FAA will attempt to exclude satellite airports as much as possible from Class D airspace, the major criteria for the lateral dimension will be based on the instrument procedures for which the controlled airspace is established. Answer (B) is incorrect because the lateral dimensions of Class D airspace are based on the instrument procedures for which the Class D airspace is established, not a specified radius from the primary airport.

54.
3789. Prior to entering an Airport Advisory Area, a pilot should

A—monitor ATIS for weather and traffic advisories.
B—contact approach control for vectors to the traffic pattern.
C—contact the local FSS for airport and traffic advisories.

Answer (C) is correct (3789). *(AIM Para 4-1-9)*
Airport Advisory Areas exist at noncontrolled airports that have a Flight Service Station (FSS) located on that airport. The FSS provides advisory (not control) information on traffic, weather, etc., to requesting aircraft. Accordingly, pilots should (not must) contact FSSs for advisory services.
Answer (A) is incorrect because ATIS (automatic terminal information service) provides prerecorded weather and airport data but not traffic advisories. Answer (B) is incorrect because approach control may provide vectors to the airport, but the controller will instruct you to switch to the advisory frequency for airport and traffic advisories.

3.9 Class C Airspace

55.
3780. The normal radius of the outer area of Class C airspace is

A—5 nautical miles.
B—15 nautical miles.
C—20 nautical miles.

Answer (C) is correct (3780). *(AIM Para 3-2-4)*
The outer area of Class C airspace has a normal radius of 20 NM with variations possible. This is in contrast to the Class C airspace area itself, which also has two circles: the first a 5-NM radius core surface area and the second a 10-NM radius shelf area.
Answer (A) is incorrect because 5 NM is the radius of the surface area of the Class C airspace. Answer (B) is incorrect because 15 NM is not a Class C airspace dimension.

56.
3781. All operations within Class C airspace must be in

A—accordance with instrument flight rules.
B—compliance with ATC clearances and instructions.
C—an aircraft equipped with a 4096-code transponder with Mode C encoding capability.

Answer (C) is correct (3781). *(AIM Para 3-2-4)*
To operate within Class C airspace, an aircraft must be equipped with a 4096-code transponder with Mode C (altitude encoding) capability.
Answer (A) is incorrect because IFR operations are not required within Class C airspace and there is no minimum pilot certification required, i.e., student pilots may operate within Class C airspace. Answer (B) is incorrect because clearances are not required to operate within Class C airspace areas; clearances relate to IFR operations.

57.
3779. The vertical limit of Class C airspace above the primary airport is normally

A—1,200 feet AGL.
B—3,000 feet AGL.
C—4,000 feet AGL.

Answer (C) is correct (3779). *(AIM Para 3-2-4)*
The vertical limit (ceiling) of Class C airspace is normally 4,000 ft. above the primary airport elevation.
Answer (A) is incorrect because 1,200 ft. AGL is the floor, not the vertical limit, of the Class C airspace shelf area (5 to 10 NM from primary airport). Answer (B) is incorrect because the vertical limit of Class C airspace is normally 4,000 ft. AGL, not 3,000 ft. AGL, above the elevation of the primary airport.

58.
3782. Under what condition may an aircraft operate from a satellite airport within Class C airspace?

A—The pilot must file a flight plan prior to departure.
B—The pilot must monitor ATC until clear of the Class C airspace.
C—The pilot must contact ATC as soon as practicable after takeoff.

Answer (C) is correct (3782). *(AIM Para 3-2-4)*
Aircraft departing from a satellite airport within Class C airspace with an operating control tower must establish and maintain two-way radio communication with the control tower and thereafter as instructed by ATC. When departing a satellite airport without an operating control tower, the pilot must contact and maintain two-way radio communication with ATC as soon as practicable after takeoff.
Answer (A) is incorrect because flight plans are not required in Class C airspace. Answer (B) is incorrect because the pilot must maintain communication with ATC, not just monitor ATC, in Class C airspace.

59.
3799. Which initial action should a pilot take prior to entering Class C airspace?

A—Contact approach control on the appropriate frequency.
B—Contact the tower and request permission to enter.
C—Contact the FSS for traffic advisories.

Answer (A) is correct (3799). *(AIM Para 3-2-4)*
Prior to entering Class C airspace, a pilot must contact and establish communication with approach control on the appropriate frequency.
Answer (B) is incorrect because the tower normally controls the air traffic in the traffic pattern, not the aircraft entering the Class C airspace area. Answer (C) is incorrect because the pilot should contact approach control, not FSS, prior to entering Class C airspace.

3.10 Terminal Radar Programs

60.
3798. TRSA Service in the terminal radar program provides

A—IFR separation (1,000 feet vertical and 3 miles lateral) between all aircraft.
B—warning to pilots when their aircraft are in unsafe proximity to terrain, obstructions, or other aircraft.
C—sequencing and separation for participating VFR aircraft.

Answer (C) is correct (3798). *(AIM Para 4-1-17)*
TRSA service in the terminal radar program provides sequencing and separation for all participating VFR aircraft within the airspace defined as a Terminal Radar Service Area (TRSA). Pilot participation is urged but is not mandatory.
Answer (A) is incorrect because TRSA service provides VFR aircraft with a 500-ft., not 1,000-ft., vertical clearance from other aircraft. Answer (B) is incorrect because TRSA service is for traffic advisories, separation between aircraft, and vectoring, not for obstruction clearance.

61.
3797. From whom should a departing VFR aircraft request radar traffic information during ground operations?

A—Clearance delivery.
B—Tower, just before takeoff.
C—Ground control, on initial contact.

Answer (C) is correct (3797). *(AIM Para 4-1-17)*
Pilots of departing VFR aircraft are encouraged to request radar traffic information by notifying ground control on initial contact with their request and proposed direction of flight.
Answer (A) is incorrect because clearance delivery is usually used at busier airports where radar traffic information may be provided without request. Answer (B) is incorrect because ground control rather than tower control is the appropriate place to make the request (giving ATC more time to coordinate your request).

62.
3796. Basic radar service in the terminal radar program is best described as

A—safety alerts, traffic advisories, and limited vectoring to VFR aircraft.
B—mandatory radar service provided by the Automated Radar Terminal System (ARTS) program.
C—wind-shear warning at participating airports.

Answer (A) is correct (3796). *(AIM Para 4-1-17)*
Basic radar service in the terminal radar program provides safety alerts, traffic advisories, and limited vectoring (on a workload-permitting basis) to VFR aircraft.
Answer (B) is incorrect because mandatory radar service is required only in Class B and Class C airspace. Answer (C) is incorrect because the Low-Level Wind Shear Alert System (LLWAS) is based on information gathered from various wind (speed and direction) sensors on and around the airport, not on radar.

3.11 Transponder Codes

63.
3803. If Air Traffic Control advises that radar service is terminated when the pilot is departing Class C airspace, the transponder should be set to code

A—0000.
B—1200.
C—4096.

Answer (B) is correct (3803). *(AIM Para 4-1-19)*
The code 1200 designates VFR operations when another number is not assigned by ATC.
Answer (A) is incorrect because 0000 is not a transponder code. Answer (C) is incorrect because the numbers only go up to 7, so a 9 is not possible.

64.
3800. When making routine transponder code changes, pilots should avoid inadvertent selection of which codes?

A—0700, 1700, 7000.
B—1200, 1500, 7000.
C—7500, 7600, 7700.

Answer (C) is correct (3800). *(AIM Para 4-1-19)*
Some special codes set aside for emergencies should be avoided during routine VFR flights. They are 7500 for hijacking, 7600 for lost radio communications, and 7700 for a general emergency. Additionally, you should know that code 7777 is reserved for military interceptors.
Answer (A) is incorrect because any of these may be assigned by ATC. Answer (B) is incorrect because 1200 is the standard VFR code.

65.
3801. When operating under VFR below 18,000 feet MSL, unless otherwise authorized, what transponder code should be selected?

A—1200.
B—7600.
C—7700.

Answer (A) is correct (3801). *(AIM Para 4-1-19)*
The standard VFR transponder code is 1200. Since all flight operations above 18,000 ft. MSL are to be IFR, code 1200 is not used above that height.
Answer (B) is incorrect because 7600 is the lost radio communications code. Answer (C) is incorrect because 7700 is the general emergency code.

3.12 Radio Phraseology

66.
3613. When flying HAWK N666CB, the proper phraseology for initial contact with McAlester AFSS is

A—"MC ALESTER RADIO, HAWK SIX SIX SIX CHARLIE BRAVO, RECEIVING ARDMORE VORTAC, OVER."
B—"MC ALESTER STATION, HAWK SIX SIX SIX CEE BEE, RECEIVING ARDMORE VORTAC, OVER."
C—"MC ALESTER FLIGHT SERVICE STATION, HAWK NOVEMBER SIX CHARLIE BRAVO, RECEIVING ARDMORE VORTAC, OVER."

Answer (A) is correct (3613). (AIM Para 4-2-3)
When calling a ground station, pilots should begin with the name of the facility and the type of facility. Any FSS is referred to as "Radio." When the aircraft manufacturer's name or model is stated, the prefix "N" is dropped. When transmitting and receiving on different frequencies, indicate the name of the VOR or frequency on which a reply is expected. Thus, the proper phraseology on initial contact with McAlester AFSS is McAlester Radio, Hawk Six Six Six Charlie Bravo, Receiving Ardmore VORTAC, Over. (NOTE: The word "over" has been dropped from common usage.)
Answer (B) is incorrect because it is McAlester radio, not station, and C is Charlie, B is Bravo, not cee bee. Answer (C) is incorrect because it is radio, not flight service station. November is dropped in favor of Hawk, also it is six, six, six Charlie Bravo (not six Charlie Bravo).

67.
3614. The correct method of stating 4,500 feet MSL to ATC is

A—"FOUR THOUSAND FIVE HUNDRED."
B—"FOUR POINT FIVE."
C—"FORTY-FIVE HUNDRED FEET MSL."

Answer (A) is correct (3614). (AIM Para 4-2-9)
The proper phraseology for altitudes up to but not including 18,000 ft. MSL is to state the separate digits of the thousands, plus the hundreds, if appropriate. It would be "four thousand, five hundred."
Answer (B) is incorrect because four point five is slang (not correct) phraseology. Answer (C) is incorrect because the thousand is spoken separately from the hundreds and not together. A stated altitude is understood to be MSL, unless otherwise stated.

68.
3615. The correct method of stating 10,500 feet MSL to ATC is

A—"TEN THOUSAND, FIVE HUNDRED FEET."
B—"TEN POINT FIVE."
C—"ONE ZERO THOUSAND, FIVE HUNDRED."

Answer (C) is correct (3615). (AIM Para 4-2-9)
The proper phraseology for altitudes up to but not including 18,000 ft. MSL is to state the separate digits of the thousands, plus the hundreds, if appropriate. It would be one zero thousand, five hundred.
Answer (A) is incorrect because it is one zero, not ten. Answer (B) is incorrect because ten point five is slang (not correct) phraseology.

3.13 ATC Traffic Advisories

69.
3792. An ATC radar facility issues the following advisory to a pilot flying on a heading of 090°:

"TRAFFIC 3 O'CLOCK, 2 MILES, WESTBOUND..."

Where should the pilot look for this traffic?

A—East.
B—South.
C—West.

Answer (B) is correct (3792). (AIM Para 4-1-14)
If you receive traffic information service from radar and are told you have traffic at the 3 o'clock position, traffic is in the direction of the right wingtip, or to the south.
Answer (A) is incorrect because east is the 12 o'clock position. Answer (C) is incorrect because west is the 6 o'clock position.

70.
3793. An ATC radar facility issues the following advisory to a pilot flying on a heading of 360°:

"TRAFFIC 10 O'CLOCK, 2 MILES, SOUTHBOUND..."

Where should the pilot look for this traffic?

A—Northwest.
B—Northeast.
C—Southwest.

Answer (A) is correct (3793). (AIM Para 4-1-14)
The controller is telling you that traffic is at 10 o'clock and 2 mi. 9 o'clock is the left wingtip, and 10 o'clock is 2/3 of the way from the nose of the airplane (12 o'clock) to the left wingtip. Thus, you are looking northwest.
Answer (B) is incorrect because northeast would be in the 1 to 2 o'clock position. Answer (C) is incorrect because southwest would be in the 7 to 8 o'clock position.

71.
3794. An ATC radar facility issues the following advisory to a pilot during a local flight:

"TRAFFIC 2 O'CLOCK, 5 MILES, NORTHBOUND..."

Where should the pilot look for this traffic?

A—Between directly ahead and 90° to the left.
B—Between directly behind and 90° to the right.
C—Between directly ahead and 90° to the right.

Answer (C) is correct (3794). *(AIM Para 4-1-14)*
The right wingtip is 3 o'clock, and the nose is 12 o'clock. A controller report of traffic 2 o'clock, 5 mi., northbound indicates that the traffic is to the right of the airplane's nose, just ahead of the right wingtip.
Answer (A) is incorrect because the area directly ahead to 90° left is the area from 12 o'clock to 9 o'clock. Answer (B) is incorrect because the area directly behind to 90° right is the area from 6 o'clock to 3 o'clock.

72.
3795. An ATC radar facility issues the following advisory to a pilot flying north in a calm wind:

"TRAFFIC 9 O'CLOCK, 2 MILES, SOUTHBOUND..."

Where should the pilot look for this traffic?

A—South.
B—North.
C—West.

Answer (C) is correct (3795). *(AIM Para 4-1-14)*
Traffic at 9 o'clock is off the left wingtip. The nose of the airplane is 12 o'clock, the left wingtip is 9 o'clock, the tail is 6 o'clock, and the right wingtip is 3 o'clock. With a north heading the aircraft at 9 o'clock would be west of you.
Answer (A) is incorrect because south would be the 6 o'clock position. Answer (B) is incorrect because north would be the 12 o'clock position.

3.14 ATC Light Signals

73.
3116. While on final approach for landing, an alternating green and red light followed by a flashing red light is received from the control tower. Under these circumstances, the pilot should

A—discontinue the approach, fly the same traffic pattern and approach again, and land.
B—exercise extreme caution and abandon the approach, realizing the airport is unsafe for landing.
C—abandon the approach, circle the airport to the right, and expect a flashing white light when the airport is safe for landing.

Answer (B) is correct (3116). *(FAR 91.125)*
An alternating red and green light signaled from a control tower means "exercise extreme caution" whether to an airplane on the ground or in the air. The flashing red light received while in the air indicates the airport is not safe and the pilot should not land.
Answer (A) is incorrect because a flashing green (not red) light means to return for a landing. Answer (C) is incorrect because a flashing green (not red) light means to return for a landing and a flashing white light does not have a meaning to aircraft in flight.

74.
3111. A steady green light signal directed from the control tower to an aircraft in flight is a signal that the pilot

A—is cleared to land.
B—should give way to other aircraft and continue circling.
C—should return for landing.

Answer (A) is correct (3111). *(FAR 91.125)*
A steady green light signal from the tower to an airplane in flight means cleared to land.
Answer (B) is incorrect because give way to other aircraft and continue circling is signaled by a steady red light to an airplane in the air. Answer (C) is incorrect because return for landing is signaled by a flashing green light to an airplane in the air.

75.
3114. A flashing white light signal from the control tower to a taxiing aircraft is an indication to

A—taxi at a faster speed.
B—taxi only on taxiways and not cross runways.
C—return to the starting point on the airport.

Answer (C) is correct (3114). *(FAR 91.125)*
A flashing white light given to an aircraft taxiing along the ground means to return to the aircraft's starting point.
Answer (A) is incorrect because there is no light signal which means to taxi at a faster speed. Answer (B) is incorrect because there is no light signal (by itself) which means to taxi only on taxiways and not cross runways.

76.
3113. If the control tower uses a light signal to direct a pilot to give way to other aircraft and continue circling, the light will be

A—flashing red.
B—steady red.
C—alternating red and green.

Answer (B) is correct (3113). *(FAR 91.125)*
A steady red light signal given to an aircraft in the air means to give way to other aircraft and continue circling.
Answer (A) is incorrect because when in the air a flashing red light means airport unsafe, do not land. Answer (C) is incorrect because alternating red and green light always means exercise extreme caution.

77.
3112. Which light signal from the control tower clears a pilot to taxi?

A—Flashing green.
B—Steady green.
C—Flashing white.

Answer (A) is correct (3112). *(FAR 91.125)*
A flashing green gives the pilot permission to taxi.
Answer (B) is incorrect because a steady green light means cleared to take off if on the ground or to land if in the air. Answer (C) is incorrect because a flashing white light means to return to the starting point on the airport for aircraft only on the ground.

78.
3115. An alternating red and green light signal directed from the control tower to an aircraft in flight is a signal to

A—hold position.
B—exercise extreme caution.
C—not land; the airport is unsafe.

Answer (B) is correct (3115). *(FAR 91.125)*
A flashing red and green light given anytime means exercise extreme caution.
Answer (A) is incorrect because a steady red when taxiing means hold your position. There is no light signal to tell you to hold your position when in flight, only to give way to other aircraft and continue circling. Answer (C) is incorrect because this is a flashing red which means do not land; airport unsafe.

79.
3804. If the aircraft's radio fails, what is the recommended procedure when landing at a controlled airport?

A—Observe the traffic flow, enter the pattern, and look for a light signal from the tower.
B—Enter a crosswind leg and rock the wings.
C—Flash the landing lights and cycle the landing gear while circling the airport.

Answer (A) is correct (3804). *(AIM Para 4-2-13)*
If your radio fails and you wish to land at a tower controlled airport, remain outside or above the airport's traffic pattern until the direction and flow of traffic has been determined, then join the airport traffic pattern and maintain visual contact with the tower to receive light signals.
Answer (B) is incorrect because crosswind entry is not required; also, you rock the wings to acknowledge light signals during daylight hours. Answer (C) is incorrect because flashing the landing light is a method of acknowledging light signals at night and cycling the landing gear is not an option available to fixed-gear aircraft.

3.15 ELTs and VHF/DF

80.
3819. When activated, an emergency locator transmitter (ELT) transmits on

A—118.0 and 118.8 MHz.
B—121.5 and 243.0 MHz.
C—123.0 and 119.0 MHz.

Answer (B) is correct (3819). *(AIM Para 6-2-5)*
When activated, an emergency locator transmitter (ELT) transmits simultaneously on the international distress frequencies of 121.5 and 243.0 MHz.
Answer (A) is incorrect because 118.0 and 118.8 MHz are not emergency frequencies. Answer (C) is incorrect because 123.0 and 119.0 MHz are not emergency frequencies.

81.
3822. Which procedure is recommended to ensure that the emergency locator transmitter (ELT) has not been activated?

A—Turn off the aircraft ELT after landing.
B—Ask the airport tower if they are receiving an ELT signal.
C—Monitor 121.5 before engine shutdown.

Answer (C) is correct (3822). *(AIM Para 6-2-5)*
To ensure that your ELT has not been activated, you can monitor 121.5 MHz or 243.0 MHz in flight when a receiver is available and prior to engine shut-down at the end of each flight.
Answer (A) is incorrect because, if you turn off the ELT, there is no way of telling whether it has been activated. Answer (B) is incorrect because the tower or ATC should not be bothered by questions about your ELT transmissions. If, however, you do receive signals on 121.5, IMMEDIATELY report it to ATC and/or FSS.

82.
3843. The letters VHF/DF appearing in the Airport/Facility Directory for a certain airport indicate that

A—this airport is designated as an airport of entry.
B—the Flight Service Station has equipment with which to determine your direction from the station.
C—this airport has a direct-line phone to the Flight Service Station.

Answer (B) is correct (3843). *(AIM Para 1-1-17)*
The VHF/Direction Finder (DF) facility is a ground operation that displays the magnetic direction of the airplane from the station each time the airplane communication radio transmits a signal to it. It is used by ATC and FSS to assist lost pilots by telling them which direction they are from the receiving station.
Answer (A) is incorrect because an airport of entry is indicated by the letters AOE. Answer (C) is incorrect because a direct phone line to FSS is indicated by the letters DL following the FSS identifier.

83.
3759. To use VHF/DF facilities for assistance in locating an aircraft's position, the aircraft must have a

A—VHF transmitter and receiver.
B—4096-code transponder.
C—VOR receiver and DME.

Answer (A) is correct (3759). *(AIM Para 1-1-17)*
The VHF/Direction Finder (DF) facility is a ground operation that displays the magnetic direction of the airplane from the station each time the airplane communication (VHF) radio transmits a signal to it. Thus, to use such facilities for assistance in locating an airplane position, the airplane must have both a VHF transmitter (to send the signal) and a receiver (to communicate with the operator, who reads out the displayed magnetic direction).
Answer (B) is incorrect because transponders are received by radar, not VHF/DF. Answer (C) is incorrect because VORs and DMEs relate to (rely on) VORTACs.

3.16 Land and Hold Short Operations (LAHSO)

84.
3951. Who should not participate in the Land and Hold Short Operations (LAHSO) program?

A—Recreational pilots only.
B—Military pilots.
C—Student pilots.

Answer (C) is correct (3951). *(AIM Para 4-3-11)*
Land and hold short operations (LAHSO) take place at some airports with an operating control tower in order to increase the total capacity and improve the flow of traffic. LAHSO requires that a pilot not use the full length of the runway but, rather, that (s)he stop and hold short before reaching an intersecting runway, taxiway, or other specified point on the landing runway. Student pilots or pilots who are not familiar with LAHSO should not participate in the program.
Answer (A) is incorrect because a recreational pilot cannot operate at an airport with an operating control tower (unless working on obtaining his/her private pilot certificate under the supervision of a CFI) and would not have a choice as to whether or not to participate. Answer (B) is incorrect because student pilots or pilots unfamiliar with LAHSO, not military pilots, should not participate in the program.

85.
3952. Who has final authority to accept or decline any land and hold short (LAHSO) clearance?

A—Pilot-in-command.
B—Owner/operator.
C—Second-in-command.

Answer (A) is correct (3952). *(AIM Para 4-3-11)*
Land and hold short operations (LAHSO) take place at some airports with an operating control tower in order to increase the total capacity and improve the flow of traffic. LAHSO requires that a pilot not use the full length of the runway but, rather, that (s)he stop and hold short before reaching an intersecting runway, taxiway, or other specified point on the landing runway. LAHSO requires familiarity with the available landing distance (ALD) for given LAHSO combinations and with the landing performance of the aircraft. The pilot in command has the final authority to accept or decline any land and hold short clearance.
Answer (B) is incorrect because the pilot in command, regardless of whether or not (s)he is the owner, has the final authority to accept or decline a LAHSO clearance. Answer (C) is incorrect because the pilot in command, not the second in command, has final authority to accept or decline a LAHSO clearance.

86.
3953. When should pilots decline a land and hold short (LAHSO) clearance?

A—When it will compromise safety.
B—Only when the tower operator concurs.
C—Pilots can not decline clearance.

Answer (A) is correct (3953).   *(AIM Para 4-3-11)*
Land and hold short operations (LAHSO) take place at some airports with an operating control tower in order to increase the total capacity and improve the flow of traffic. LAHSO requires that a pilot not use the full length of the runway but, rather, that (s)he stop and hold short before reaching an intersecting runway, taxiway, or other specified point on the landing runway. LAHSO requires familiarity with the available landing distance (ALD) for given LAHSO combinations and with the landing performance of the aircraft. Pilots are expected to decline a land and hold short clearance if they determine that it will compromise safety.
Answer (B) is incorrect because the pilot in command has the final authority to accept or decline a land and hold short clearance; agreement from the tower operator is not required. Answer (C) is incorrect because the pilot in command has the authority to decline a land and hold short clearance.

87.
3954. Where is the "Available Landing Distance" (ALD) data published for an airport that utilizes Land and Hold Short Operations (LAHSO) published?

A—Airport/Facility Directory (A/FD).
B—14 CFR Part 91, General Operating and Flight Rules.
C—Aeronautical Information Manual (AIM).

Answer (A) is correct (3954).   *(AIM Para 4-3-11)*
Land and hold short operations (LAHSO) take place at some airports with an operating control tower in order to increase the total capacity and improve the flow of traffic. LAHSO requires that a pilot not use the full length of the runway but, rather, that (s)he stop and hold short before reaching an intersecting runway, taxiway, or other specified point on the landing runway. LAHSO requires familiarity with the available landing distance (ALD) for given LAHSO combinations and with the landing performance of the aircraft. ALD data are published in the special notices section of the *Airport/Facility Directory*.
Answer (B) is incorrect because ALD data are published in the *A/FD*, not in 14 CFR Part 91. Answer (C) is incorrect because the ALD data are published in the *A/FD*, not in the *AIM*, which contains information on how LAHSO are to be conducted.

88.
3955. What is the minimum visibility for a pilot to receive a land and hold short (LAHSO) clearance?

A—3 nautical miles.
B—3 statute miles.
C—1 statute mile.

Answer (B) is correct (3955).   *(AIM Para 4-3-11)*
You should receive a land and hold short (LAHSO) clearance only when there is a minimum ceiling of 1,000 ft. and visibility of 3 SM. The intent of having basic VFR weather conditions is to allow pilots to maintain visual contact with other aircraft and ground vehicle operations.
Answer (A) is incorrect because the minimum visibility for a pilot to receive a land and hold short (LAHSO) clearance is 3 SM, not 3 NM. Remember, visibility is reported in statute miles, not nautical miles. Answer (C) is incorrect because the minimum visibility for a pilot to receive a special VFR clearance, not a land and hold short clearance, is 1 SM.

END OF CHAPTER

CHAPTER FOUR
FEDERAL AVIATION REGULATIONS

(continued)

This chapter contains outlines of major concepts tested, all FAA test questions and answers regarding Federal Aviation Regulations (FARs), and an explanation of each answer. Each module, or subtopic, within this chapter is listed above and on page 85 with the number of questions from the FAA pilot knowledge test pertaining to that particular module. For each module, the first number following the parentheses is the page number on which the outline begins, and the next number is the page number on which the questions begin.

CAUTION: Recall that the **sole purpose** of this book is to expedite your passing the FAA pilot knowledge test for the private pilot certificate. Accordingly, all extraneous material (i.e., topics or regulations not directly tested on the FAA pilot knowledge test) is omitted, even though much more information and knowledge are necessary to fly safely. This additional material is presented in *Pilot Handbook* and *Private Pilot Flight Maneuvers and Practical Test Prep*, available from Gleim Publications, Inc. See the order form on page 326.

The 25 questions beginning on page 112 specifically refer to recreational pilots. Recreational pilots are responsible for all applicable FARs. Subpart D of FAR Part 61, "Recreational Pilots," specifically applies. It is numbered 61.96 through 61.101.

61.96	Applicability and Eligibility Requirements: General
61.97	Aeronautical Knowledge
61.98	Flight Proficiency
61.99	Aeronautical Experience
61.100	Pilots Based on Small Islands
61.101	Recreational Pilot Privileges and Limitations

All of the 25 recreational pilot questions test FAR 61.101.

4.1 FAR PART 1
1.1 General Definitions (Questions 1-6)

1. **Night** means the time between the end of evening civil twilight and the beginning of morning civil twilight, as published in the American Air Almanac converted to local time.

    a. Note that for "recency of experience" (FAR 61.57), night is defined as from 1 hr. after sunset to 1 hr. before sunrise.

    b. Be careful; there are questions on both definitions.

2. **Aircraft categories** (for certification of airmen); broad classifications of aircraft

    a. Airplane   c. Glider
    b. Rotorcraft   d. Lighter-than-air

3. **Airplane classes** (for certification of airmen)

    a. Single-engine land   c. Single-engine sea
    b. Multiengine land   d. Multiengine sea

4. **Rotorcraft classes** (for certification of airmen)

    a. Helicopter
    b. Gyrocopter

5. **Lighter-than-air classes** (for certification of airmen)

    a. Airship   c. Hot air balloon
    b. Free balloon   d. Gas balloon

6. Note the above category and class definitions are for certification of airmen purposes. For certification of aircraft there are different definitions:

    a. **Category** (for certification of aircraft purposes) is based on intended use or operating limitations.

    1) Transport   5) Restricted
    2) Normal   6) Acrobatic
    3) Utility   7) Provisional
    4) Limited

    b. **Classes** as used for certification of aircraft are the same as, or very similar to, categories for certification of airmen, e.g., airplane, rotorcraft, glider, lighter-than-air.

7. **Air traffic control (ATC) clearance** means an authorization to proceed under specific traffic conditions in controlled airspace.

1.2 Abbreviations and Symbols (Questions 7-13)

1. V_{FE} means maximum flap extended speed.

2. V_{LE} means maximum landing gear extended speed.

3. V_{NO} means maximum structural cruising speed.

4. V_A means design maneuvering speed.

5. V_{SO} means the stalling speed or the minimum steady flight speed in the landing configuration.

6. V_X means speed for best angle of climb.

7. V_Y means speed for best rate of climb.

4.2 FAR PART 21
21.181 Duration of Airworthiness Certificates (Question 14)

1.   Airworthiness certificates remain in force as long as maintenance and alteration of the aircraft are performed per FARs.

4.2A FAR PART 39
39.1 Applicability (Question 15)

1.   Airworthiness Directives (ADs) are issued under FAR Part 39 by the FAA to require correction of unsafe conditions found in an airplane, an airplane engine, a propeller, or an appliance when such conditions exist and are likely to exist or develop in other products of the same design.

    a.   Since ADs are issued under FAR Part 39, they are regulatory and must be complied with, unless a specific exemption is granted.

39.3 General (Question 16)

1.   No person may operate a product to which an AD applies except in accordance with the requirements of that AD.

    a.   Thus, you may operate an airplane that is not in compliance with an AD, if such operation is allowed by the AD.

4.3 FAR PART 43
43.3 Persons Authorized to Perform Maintenance, Preventive Maintenance, Rebuilding, and Alterations (Question 17)

1.   A person who holds a pilot certificate (e.g., private pilot) may perform preventive maintenance on any airplane owned or operated by that pilot which is not used in air carrier services.

43.7 Persons Authorized to Approve Aircraft Airframes, Aircraft Engines, Propellers, Appliances, or Component Parts for Return to Service after Maintenance, Preventive Maintenance, Rebuilding, or Alteration (Question 18)

1.   To approve the airplane for return to service, after preventive maintenance was done by a pilot, the pilot must hold at least a private pilot certificate.

43.9 Maintenance Records (Question 19)

1.   After preventive maintenance has been performed, the signature, certificate number, and kind of certificate held by the person approving the work and a description of the work must be entered in the aircraft maintenance records.

Part 43, Appendix A. Major Alterations and Repairs and Preventive Maintenance
(Questions 20-21)

1.   Preventive maintenance means simple or minor preservation operations and the replacement of small standard parts not involving complex assembly operations. Examples include

    a.   Replenishing hydraulic fluid, and
    b.   Servicing landing gear wheel bearings.

4.4 FAR PART 61
61.3 Requirements for Certificates, Ratings, and Authorizations (Questions 22-25)

1.   When acting as a pilot in command or as a required pilot flight crewmember, you must have a valid pilot certificate and a current and appropriate medical certificate in your personal possession or readily accessible in the airplane.

2.   You must present your pilot certificate or medical certificate upon the request of the Administrator of the FAA or his/her representative, or the NTSB, or any federal, state, or local law enforcement officer.

61.23 Medical Certificates: Requirement and Duration (Questions 26-30)

1. For operations requiring a private, recreational, or student pilot certificate, a first-, second-, or third-class medical certificate issued

    a. Before September 16, 1996, expires at the end of the last day of the month, 2 years after the date of examination shown on the certificate.

    b. On or after September 16, 1996, expires at the end of the last day of the month either

        1) 3 years after the date of examination shown on the certificate, if you have not reached your 40th birthday on or before the date of examination or

        2) 2 years after the date of examination shown on the certificate, if you have reached your 40th birthday on or before the date of examination.

61.31 Type Rating Requirements, Additional Training, and Authorization Requirements (Questions 31-34)

1. To act as pilot in command of a complex airplane, you must receive and log ground and flight training and receive a logbook endorsement.

    a. A complex airplane is defined as an airplane with retractable landing gear, flaps, and a controllable pitch propeller.

2. To act as pilot in command of a high-performance airplane, you must receive and log ground and flight training and receive a logbook endorsement.

    a. A high-performance airplane is defined as an airplane with an engine of more than 200 horsepower.

3. A person may not act as pilot in command of any of the following aircraft unless (s)he holds a type rating for that aircraft:

    a. A large aircraft (i.e., over 12,500 lb. gross weight)
    b. A turbojet-powered airplane
    c. Other aircraft specified by the FAA through aircraft type certification procedures

61.56 Flight Review (Questions 35-38)

1. A flight review must have been satisfactorily completed within the previous 24 calendar months to act as pilot in command of an aircraft.

    a. A proficiency check or flight test for a pilot certificate, rating, or other operating privileges will also satisfy this requirement.

    b. Satisfactory completion of the review or flight test must be endorsed in the pilot's logbook by the reviewer.

2. The expiration of the 24-month period for the flight review falls on the last day of the 24th month after the month of the examination date (i.e., 24 calendar months).

61.57 Recent Flight Experience: Pilot in Command (Questions 39-44)

1. To carry passengers, you must have made three landings and three takeoffs within the preceding 90 days.

    a. All three landings must be made in aircraft of the same category, class, and, if a type rating is required, the same type as the one in which passengers are to be carried.

        1) The categories are airplane, rotorcraft, glider, and lighter-than-air.

        2) The classes are single-engine land, single-engine sea, multiengine land, and multiengine sea.

    b. The landings must be to a full stop if the airplane is tailwheel (conventional) rather than nosewheel.

2. To carry passengers at night, you must, within the last 90 days, have made three takeoffs and three landings to a full stop at night in an aircraft of the same category, class, and type, if required.

   a. Night in this case is defined as the period beginning 1 hr. after sunset and ending 1 hr. before sunrise.

61.60 Change of Address (Question 45)

1. You must notify the FAA Airman Certification Branch in writing of any change in your permanent mailing address.

2. You may not exercise the privileges of your pilot certificate after 30 days from moving unless you make this notification.

61.69 Glider Towing: Experience and Training Requirements (Questions 46-47)

1. Any person may tow a glider if that person has

   a. At least a private pilot certificate

   b. 100 hr. of pilot in command time in the aircraft category, class, and type, if required, that the pilot is using to tow a glider

   c. Within the preceding 12 months

      1) Made at least three actual or simulated glider tows while accompanied by a qualified pilot, or

      2) Made at least three flights as pilot in command of a glider towed by an aircraft

61.113 Private Pilot Privileges and Limitations: Pilot in Command (Questions 48-50)

1. Private pilots may not pay less than an equal (pro rata) share of the operating expenses of a flight with the passengers.

   a. These operating expenses may involve only fuel, oil, airport expenditures, or rental fees.

2. Private pilots may operate an aircraft carrying passengers on business only if the flight is incidental to that business or employment and the pilot is not paid as a pilot.

   a. For example, a CPA who is a private pilot might fly an aircraft carrying CPAs to a client. Such flight is incidental to the CPA's professional duties or business.

3. A pilot may act as a pilot in command of an aircraft used in a passenger-carrying airlift sponsored by a charitable organization for which passengers make donations to the organization if

   a. The local FSDO (FAA Flight Standards District Office) is notified at least 7 days before the flight,

   b. The flight is conducted from an adequate public airport,

   c. The pilot has logged at least 200 hr.,

   d. No acrobatic or formation flights are performed,

   e. The aircraft complies with the 100-hr. inspection rule, and

   f. The flight is day-VFR.

4.5 RECREATIONAL PILOT RELATED FARs

NOTE: This section is not tested on the private pilot knowledge test.

61.101 Recreational Pilot Privileges and Limitations (Questions 51-75)

1. A recreational pilot may carry only one passenger.

    a. A recreational pilot may not pay less than the pro rata (equal) share of the operating expenses of a flight with a passenger, provided the expenses involve only fuel, oil, airport expenses, or aircraft rental fees.

2. A recreational pilot may act as pilot in command of an airplane

    a. Only when the flight is within 50 NM of an airport at which the pilot has received ground and flight training from an authorized flight instructor

        1) The pilot must have in his/her personal possession while aboard the airplane a logbook endorsement that permits flight within 50 NM from the departure airport.

    b. When the flight exceeds 50 NM if (s)he receives ground and flight training on the cross-country training requirements for a private pilot and has his/her logbook endorsed certifying proficiency in cross-country flight by an authorized instructor

3. A recreational pilot may NOT act as pilot in command of an aircraft

    a. Certificated for more than four occupants, with more than one engine, with an engine of more than 180 horsepower, or with retractable landing gear

    b. Classified as a multiengine airplane, powered-lift, glider, airship, or balloon

    c. Carrying a passenger or property for compensation or hire

    d. For compensation or hire

    e. In furtherance of a business

    f. Between sunset and sunrise (e.g., night time)

    g. In airspace in which communication with ATC is required

    h. At an altitude of more than 10,000 ft. MSL or 2,000 ft. AGL, whichever is higher

    i. With flight or surface visibility of less than 3 SM

        1) In Class G airspace, the cloud clearance requirement is

            a) Clear of clouds when 1,200 ft. AGL or less

            b) 1,000 ft. above, 500 ft. below, and 2,000 ft. horizontally from clouds when more than 1,200 ft. AGL but less than 10,000 ft. MSL

    j. Without visual reference to the surface

    k. On a flight outside the U.S.

    l. For demonstration of that aircraft in flight to a prospective buyer

    m. Used in a passenger-carrying airlift and sponsored by a charitable organization

    n. Towing any object

4. A recreational pilot may NOT act as a required pilot flight crewmember on any aircraft for which more than one pilot is required.

5. A recreational pilot who has logged fewer than 400 flight hr. and who has not logged pilot-in-command time in an aircraft within the preceding 180 days may not act as pilot in command of an aircraft until the pilot has received flight training from an authorized flight instructor who certifies in the pilot's logbook that the pilot is competent to act as pilot in command.

6. The recreational pilot certificate states, "Holder does not meet ICAO requirements."

7. For the purpose of obtaining additional certificates or ratings, while under the supervision of an authorized flight instructor, a recreational pilot may fly as sole occupant of an aircraft

    a. For which the pilot does not hold an appropriate category or class rating
    b. Within airspace that requires communication with air traffic control
    c. Between sunset and sunrise, provided the flight or surface visibility is at least 5 SM
    d. In excess of 50 NM from an airport at which flight instruction is received

    NOTE: For any of these situations, the recreational pilot shall carry the logbook that has been properly endorsed for each flight by an authorized flight instructor.

8. When flying a transponder-equipped aircraft, a recreational pilot should set that transponder on code (squawk) 1200, which is the VFR code.

4.6 FAR PART 71
71.75 Extent of Federal Airways (Questions 76-77)

1. Federal airways include that Class E airspace

    a. Extending upward from 1,200 ft. AGL to and including 17,999 ft. MSL
    b. Within parallel boundary lines 4 NM each side of the airway's centerline

4.7 FAR PART 91
91.3 Responsibility and Authority of the Pilot in Command (Question 78)

1. In emergencies, a pilot may deviate from the FARs to the extent needed to maintain the safety of the airplane and passengers.

2. The pilot in command of an aircraft is directly responsible for, and is the final authority as to, the operation of that aircraft.

3. A written report of any deviations from FARs should be filed with the FAA upon request.

91.7 Civil Aircraft Airworthiness (Question 79)

1. The pilot in command is responsible for determining that the airplane is airworthy prior to every flight.

91.9 Civil Aircraft Flight Manual, Marking, and Placard Requirements (Question 80)

1. The airworthiness certificate, the FAA registration certificate, and the aircraft flight manual or operating limitations must be aboard.

2. The acronym ARROW can be used as a memory aid. The FCC (Federal Communications Commission), not the FAA, requires the radio station license. As of January 1, 1997, the radio station license is required only for international flights.

    A irworthiness certificate
    R egistration certificate
    R adio station license (FCC requirement for international flight)
    O perating limitations, including
    W eight and balance data

3. The operating limitations of an airplane may be found in the current FAA-approved flight manual, approved manual material, markings, and placards, or any combination thereof.

91.15 Dropping Objects (Question 81)

1. No pilot in command of a civil aircraft may allow any object to be dropped from that aircraft in flight that creates a hazard to persons or property.

   a. However, this section does not prohibit the dropping of any object if reasonable precautions are taken to avoid injury or damage to persons or property.

91.17 Alcohol or Drugs (Questions 82-84)

1. No person may act as a crewmember of a civil airplane while having .04 percent by weight or more alcohol in the blood or if any alcoholic beverages have been consumed within the preceding 8 hr.

2. No person may act as a crewmember of a civil airplane if using any drug that affects the person's faculties in any way contrary to safety.

3. Pilots may not allow a person who is obviously intoxicated or under the influence of drugs to be carried in a civil airplane

   a. Unless the person is a medical patient under proper care or in an emergency.

91.103 Preflight Action (Questions 85-87)

1. Pilots are required to familiarize themselves with all available information concerning the flight prior to every flight, and specifically to determine

   a. For any flight, runway lengths at airports of intended use and the airplane's takeoff and landing requirements, and

   b. For IFR flights or those not in the vicinity of an airport,

      1) Weather reports and forecasts,
      2) Fuel requirements,
      3) Alternatives available if the planned flight cannot be completed, and
      4) Any known traffic delays.

91.105 Flight Crewmembers at Stations (Questions 88-89)

1. During takeoff and landing, and while en route, each required flight crewmember shall keep his/her safety belt fastened while at his/her station.

   a. If shoulder harnesses are available they must be used for takeoff and landing.

91.107 Use of Safety Belts, Shoulder Harnesses, and Child Restraint Systems (Questions 90-92)

1. Pilots must ensure that each occupant is briefed on how to use the safety belts and, if installed, shoulder harness.

2. Pilots must notify all occupants to fasten their safety belts before taxiing, taking off, or landing.

3. All passengers of airplanes must wear their safety belts during taxi, takeoffs, and landings.

   a. A passenger who has not reached his/her second birthday may be held by an adult.

   b. Sport parachutists may use the floor of the aircraft as a seat (but still must use safety belts).

91.111 Operating near Other Aircraft (Question 93)

1. No person may operate an aircraft in formation flight except by prior arrangement with the pilot in command of each aircraft in the formation.

91.113 Right-of-Way Rules: Except Water Operations (Questions 94-100)

1. Aircraft in distress have the right-of-way over all other aircraft.

2. When two aircraft are approaching head on or nearly so, the pilot of each aircraft should turn to his/her right, regardless of category.

3. When two aircraft of different categories are converging, the right-of-way depends upon who has the least maneuverability. Thus, the right-of-way belongs to

   a. Balloons over
   b. Gliders over
   c. Airships over
   d. Airplanes or rotorcraft.

4. When aircraft of the same category are converging at approximately the same altitude, except head on or nearly so, the aircraft to the other's right has the right-of-way.

   a. If an airplane of the same category as yours is approaching from your right side, it has the right-of-way.

5. When two or more aircraft are approaching an airport for the purpose of landing, the aircraft at the lower altitude has the right-of-way.

   a. This rule shall not be abused by cutting in front of or overtaking another aircraft.

6. An aircraft towing or refueling another aircraft has the right-of-way over all engine-driven aircraft.

91.115 Right-of-Way Rules: Water Operations (Question 101)

1. When aircraft, or an aircraft and a vessel, are on crossing courses, the aircraft or vessel to the other's right has the right-of-way.

91.117 Aircraft Speed (Questions 102-105)

1. The speed limit is 250 kt. (288 MPH) when flying below 10,000 ft. MSL and in Class B airspace.

2. When flying under Class B airspace or in VFR corridors through Class B airspace, the speed limit is 200 kt. (230 MPH).

3. When at or below 2,500 ft. AGL and within 4 NM of the primary airport of Class C or Class D airspace, the speed limit is 200 kt. (230 MPH).

91.119 Minimum Safe Altitudes: General (Questions 106-109)

1. Over congested areas (cities, towns, settlements, or open-air assemblies), a pilot must maintain an altitude of 1,000 ft. above the highest obstacle within a horizontal radius of 2,000 ft. of the airplane.

2. The minimum altitude over other than congested areas is 500 ft. AGL.

   a. Over open water or sparsely populated areas, an airplane may not be operated closer than 500 ft. to any person, vessel, vehicle, or structure.

3. Altitude in all areas must be sufficient to permit an emergency landing without undue hazard to persons or property on the surface if a power unit fails.

91.121 Altimeter Settings (Questions 110-112)

1. Prior to takeoff, the altimeter should be set to the current local altimeter setting.

   a. If the current local altimeter setting is not available, use the departure airport elevation.

2. The altimeter of an airplane is required to be set to 29.92 at or above 18,000 ft. MSL,

   a. To guarantee vertical separation of airplanes above 18,000 ft. MSL.

91.123 Compliance with ATC Clearances and Instructions (Questions 113-117)

1. When an ATC clearance is obtained, no pilot may deviate from that clearance, except in an emergency, unless an amended clearance is obtained. If you feel a rule deviation will occur, you should immediately advise ATC.

2. If you receive priority from ATC in an emergency, you must, upon request, file a detailed report within 48 hr. to the chief of that ATC facility even if no rule has been violated.

3. During an in-flight emergency, the pilot in command may deviate from the FARs to the extent necessary to handle the emergency.

   a. The pilot should notify ATC about the deviation as soon as possible.
   b. If priority is given, a written report (if requested) must be submitted in 48 hr.

91.130 Operations in Class C Airspace (Question 118)

1. Class C airspace is controlled airspace which requires radio communication with ATC.

   a. A pilot must establish two-way radio communication prior to entering Class C airspace and maintain it while within Class C airspace, regardless of weather conditions.

91.131 Operations in Class B Airspace (Questions 119-121)

1. Class B airspace is controlled airspace usually found at larger airports with high volumes of traffic.

2. Requirements for operating within Class B airspace:

   a. A pilot must hold at least a private pilot certificate or a student pilot certificate with the appropriate logbook endorsements.

   b. Authorization must be received from ATC, regardless of weather conditions.

   c. The airplane must have a two-way communications radio and a transponder equipped with Mode C. Mode C permits ATC to obtain an altitude readout on its radar screen.

      1) A VOR receiver is required only when operating IFR.

3.   Student pilot operations in Class B airspace are only permitted with appropriate logbook endorsements.

    a.   For flight through Class B airspace, the student pilot must

        1)   Receive ground and flight instructions pertaining to that specific Class B airspace area.

        2)   Have a CFI logbook endorsement within 90 days for solo flight in that specific Class B airspace area.

    b.   For takeoffs and landings at an airport within Class B airspace, the student pilot must

        1)   Receive ground and flight instructions pertaining to that specific Class B airspace area.

        2)   Have a CFI logbook endorsement within 90 days for solo flight at that specific airport.

    c.   No student pilot may take off or land at the following airports:

Atlanta Hartsfield	Newark International
Boston Logan	New York Kennedy
Chicago O'Hare International	New York La Guardia
Dallas/Fort Worth International	San Francisco International
Los Angeles International	Washington National
Miami International	Andrews AFB

4.   With certain exceptions, all aircraft within a 30-NM radius of a Class B primary airport and from the surface up to 10,000 ft. MSL must have an operable transponder with Mode C.

91.133 Restricted and Prohibited Areas (Question 122)

1.   Restricted areas are a type of special use airspace within which your right to fly is limited.

    a.   Restricted areas have unusual and often invisible hazards to aircraft (i.e., balloons, military operations, etc.).

    b.   Although restricted areas are not always in use during the times posted in the legend of sectional charts, permission to fly in that airspace must be obtained from the controlling agency.

        1)   The controlling agency is listed for each restricted area at the bottom of sectional charts.

91.135 Operations in Class A Airspace (Question 123)

1.   Since Class A airspace requires operation under IFR at specific flight levels assigned by ATC, VFR flights are prohibited.

91.151 Fuel Requirements for Flight in VFR Conditions (Questions 124-125)

1.   During the day, FARs require fuel sufficient to fly to the first point of intended landing and then for an additional 30 min., assuming normal cruise speed.

2.   At night, sufficient fuel to fly an additional 45 min. is required.

91.155 Basic VFR Weather Minimums (Questions 126-140)

Cloud Clearance and Visibility Required for VFR

Airspace	Flight Visibility	Distance from Clouds		Airspace	Flight Visibility	Distance from Clouds
Class A	Not applicable	Not applicable		**Class G:** 1,200 ft. or less above the surface (regardless of MSL altitude)		
Class B	3 SM	Clear of clouds		Day	1 SM	Clear of clouds
Class C	3 SM	500 ft. below 1,000 ft. above 2,000 ft. horiz.		Night, except as provided in 1. below	3 SM	500 ft. below 1,000 ft. above 2,000 ft. horiz.
Class D	3 SM	500 ft. below 1,000 ft. above 2,000 ft. horiz.		More than 1,200 ft. above the surface but less than 10,000 ft. MSL		
Class E:				Day	1 SM	500 ft. below 1,000 ft. above 2,000 ft. horiz.
Less than 10,000 ft. MSL	3 SM	500 ft. below 1,000 ft. above 2,000 ft. horiz.		Night	3 SM	500 ft. below 1,000 ft. above 2,000 ft. horiz.
At or above 10,000 ft. MSL	5 SM	1,000 ft. below 1,000 ft. above 1 SM horiz.		More than 1,200 ft. above the surface and at or above 10,000 ft. MSL	5 SM	1,000 ft. below 1,000 ft. above 1 SM horiz.

1. An airplane may be operated clear of clouds in Class G airspace at night below 1,200 ft. AGL when the visibility is less than 3 SM but more than 1 SM in an airport traffic pattern and within ½ NM of the runway.

2. Except when operating under a special VFR clearance

   a. You may not operate your airplane beneath the ceiling under VFR within the lateral boundaries of the surface areas of Class B, Class C, Class D, or Class E airspace designated for an airport when the ceiling is less than 1,000 ft.

   b. You may not take off, land, or enter the traffic pattern of an airport in Class B, Class C, Class D, or Class E airspace unless the ground visibility is at least 3 SM. If ground visibility is not reported, flight visibility must be at least 3 SM.

91.157 Special VFR Weather Minimums (Questions 141-145)

1. With some exceptions, special VFR clearances can be requested in Class B, Class C, Class D, or Class E airspace areas.

   a. The flight requirements are to remain clear of clouds and have visibility of at least 1 SM.

2. Flight under special VFR clearance at night is only permitted if the pilot has an instrument rating and the aircraft is IFR equipped.

3. Special VFR is an ATC clearance obtained from the control tower. If there is no control tower, obtain the clearance from the appropriate air traffic control facility.

91.159 VFR Cruising Altitude or Flight Level (Questions 146-149)

1. Specified altitudes are required for VFR cruising flight at more than 3,000 ft. AGL and below 18,000 ft. MSL.

    a. The altitude prescribed is based upon the magnetic course (not magnetic heading).

    b. The altitude is prescribed in ft. above mean sea level (MSL).

    c. Use an odd thousand-foot MSL altitude plus 500 ft. for magnetic courses of 0° to 179°, e.g., 3,500, 5,500, 7,500 ft.

    d. Use an even thousand-foot MSL altitude plus 500 ft. for magnetic courses of 180° to 359°, e.g., 4,500, 6,500, or 8,500 ft.

    e. As a memory aid, the "e" in "even" does not indicate east; i.e., on east heading of 0° through 179°, use odd rather than even.

        1) "East is odd, west is even odder."

91.203 Civil Aircraft: Certifications Required (Question 150)

1. The aircraft's airworthiness certificate, registration certificate, and operating limitations must be aboard an aircraft during flight.

91.207 Emergency Locator Transmitters (Questions 151-154)

1. ELT batteries must be replaced (or recharged, if rechargeable) after 1 cumulative hr. of use or after 50% of their useful life expires.

2. ELTs may only be tested on the ground during the first 5 min. after the hour.

    a. No airborne checks are allowed.

91.209 Aircraft Lights (Question 155)

1. Airplanes operating (on the ground or in the air) between sunset and sunrise must display lighted position (navigation) lights, except in Alaska.

91.211 Supplemental Oxygen (Questions 156-157)

1. All occupants must be provided with oxygen in an airplane operated at cabin pressure altitudes above 15,000 ft. MSL.

    a. Pilots and crewmembers may not operate an airplane at cabin pressure altitudes above 12,500 ft. MSL up to and including 14,000 ft. MSL for more than 30 min. without supplemental oxygen.

    b. Pilots and crewmembers must use supplemental oxygen at cabin pressure altitudes above 14,000 ft. MSL.

91.215 ATC Transponder and Altitude Reporting Equipment and Use (Questions 158-159)

1. All aircraft must have and use an altitude encoding transponder when operating

    a. Within Class A airspace
    b. Within Class B airspace
    c. Within 30 NM of the Class B airspace primary airport
    d. Within and above Class C airspace
    e. Above 10,000 ft. MSL except at and below 2,500 ft. AGL

91.303 Aerobatic Flight (Questions 160-163)

1. Aerobatic flight includes all intentional maneuvers that

    a. Are not necessary for normal flight and
    b. Involve an abrupt change in the airplane's attitude.

2. Aerobatic flight is prohibited

    a. When visibility is less than 3 SM;

    b. When altitude is less than 1,500 ft. above the ground;

    c. Within the lateral boundaries of the surface areas of Class B, Class C, Class D, or Class E airspace designated for an airport;

    d. Within 4 NM of the centerline of any Federal airway; or

    e. Over any congested area or over an open-air assembly of people.

91.307 Parachutes and Parachuting (Questions 164-166)

1. With certain exceptions, each occupant of an aircraft must wear an approved parachute during any intentional maneuver exceeding

    a. 60° bank, or
    b. A nose-up or nose-down attitude of 30°.

2. A chair-type parachute must be packed by a certificated and appropriately rated parachute rigger within the preceding 120 days.

91.313 Restricted Category Civil Aircraft: Operating Limitations (Question 167)

1. Restricted category civil aircraft may not normally be operated

    a. Over densely populated areas,
    b. In congested airways, or
    c. Near a busy airport where passenger transport is conducted.

91.319 Aircraft Having Experimental Certificates: Operating Limitations (Question 168)

1. No person may operate an aircraft that has an experimental or restricted certificate over a densely populated area or in a congested airway unless authorized by the FAA.

91.403 General (Question 169-170)

1. The owner or operator of an aircraft is primarily responsible for maintaining that aircraft in an airworthy condition and for complying with all Airworthiness Directives (ADs).

2. An operator is a person who uses, or causes to use or authorizes to use, an aircraft for the purpose of air navigation, including the piloting of an aircraft, with or without the right of legal control (i.e., owner, lessee, or otherwise).

    a. Thus, the pilot in command is also responsible for ensuring that the aircraft is maintained in an airworthy condition and that there is compliance with all ADs.

91.405 Maintenance Required (Question 171-172)

1. Each owner or operator of an aircraft shall ensure that maintenance personnel make the appropriate entries in the aircraft maintenance records indicating the aircraft has been approved for return to service.

91.407 Operation after Maintenance, Preventive Maintenance, Rebuilding, or Alteration (Questions 173-174)

1. When aircraft alterations or repairs change the flight characteristics, the aircraft must be test flown and approved for return to service prior to carrying passengers.

    a. The pilot test flying the aircraft must be at least a private pilot and rated for the type of aircraft being tested.

91.409 Inspections (Questions 175-178)

1. Annual inspections expire on the last day of the 12th calendar month after the previous annual inspection.

2. All aircraft that are used for compensation or hire including flight instruction must be inspected on a 100-hr. basis in addition to the annual inspection.

    a. 100-hr. inspections are due every 100 hr. from the prior due time, regardless of when the inspection was actually performed.

91.413 ATC Transponder Tests and Inspections (Questions 179-180)

1. No person may use an ATC transponder unless it has been tested and inspected within the preceding 24 calendar months.

91.417 Maintenance Records (Questions 181-184)

1. An airplane may not be flown unless it has been given an annual inspection within the preceding 12 calendar months.

    a. The annual inspection expires after 1 year, on the last day of the month of issuance.

2. The completion of the annual inspection and the airplane's return to service should be appropriately documented in the airplane maintenance records.

    a. The documentation should include the current status of airworthiness directives and the method of compliance.

3. The airworthiness of an airplane can be determined by a preflight inspection and a review of the maintenance records.

4.8 NTSB PART 830
830.5 Immediate Notification (Questions 185-188)

1. Even when no injuries occur to occupants, an airplane accident resulting in substantial damage must be reported to the nearest National Transportation Safety Board (NTSB) field office immediately.

2. The following incidents must also be reported immediately to the NTSB:

    a. Inability of any required crewmember to perform normal flight duties because of in-flight injury or illness

    b. In-flight fire

    c. Flight control system malfunction or failure

    d. An overdue airplane that is believed to be involved in an accident

    e. An airplane collision in flight

    f. Turbine (jet) engine failures

830.10 Preservation of Aircraft Wreckage, Mail, Cargo, and Records (Question 189)

1. Prior to the time the Board or its authorized representative takes custody of aircraft wreckage, mail, or cargo, such wreckage, mail, or cargo may not be disturbed or moved except

   a. To remove persons injured or trapped,
   b. To protect the wreckage from further damage, or
   c. To protect the public from injury.

830.15 Reports and Statements to Be Filed (Questions 190-191)

1. The operator of an aircraft shall file a report on Board Form 6120.1/2 within 10 days after an accident.

   a. A report must be filed within 7 days if an overdue aircraft is still missing.

2. A report on an incident for which immediate notification is required (830.5) shall be filed only when requested by an authorized representative of the Board.

QUESTIONS AND ANSWER EXPLANATIONS

All the FAA questions from the pilot knowledge test for the private pilot certificate relating to FARs and the material outlined previously are reproduced on the following pages in the same modules as the outlines. To the immediate right of each question are the correct answer and answer explanation. You should cover these answers and answer explanations while responding to the questions. Refer to the general discussion in the Introduction on how to take the FAA pilot knowledge test.

Remember that the questions from the FAA pilot knowledge test bank have been reordered by topic, and the topics are organized into a meaningful sequence. Accordingly, the first line of the answer explanation gives the FAA question number and the citation of the authoritative source for the answer.

4.1 FAR PART 1
1.1 General Definitions

1.
3001. With respect to the certification of airmen, which is a category of aircraft?

A—Gyroplane, helicopter, airship, free balloon.
B—Airplane, rotorcraft, glider, lighter-than-air.
C—Single-engine land and sea, multiengine land and sea.

Answer (B) is correct (3001). *(FAR 1.1)*
Category of aircraft, as used with respect to the certification, ratings, privileges, and limitations of airmen, means a broad classification of aircraft. Examples include: airplane, rotorcraft, glider, and lighter-than-air.
Answer (A) is incorrect because gyroplane, helicopter, airship, and free balloon are classes (not categories) used with respect to the certification of airmen. Answer (C) is incorrect because single-engine land and sea, multiengine land and sea are classes (not categories) used with respect to the certification of airmen.

2.
3002. With respect to the certification of airmen, which is a class of aircraft?

A—Airplane, rotorcraft, glider, lighter-than-air.
B—Single-engine land and sea, multiengine land and sea.
C—Lighter-than-air, airship, hot air balloon, gas balloon.

Answer (B) is correct (3002). *(FAR 1.1)*
Class of aircraft, as used with respect to the certification, ratings, privileges, and limitations of airmen, means a classification of aircraft within a category having similar operating characteristics. Examples include single engine, multiengine, land, water, gyroplane, helicopter, airship, and free balloon.
Answer (A) is incorrect because airplane, rotorcraft, glider, and lighter-than-air are categories, not classes, used with respect to the certification of airmen. Answer (C) is incorrect because lighter-than-air is a category, not class, of aircraft used with respect to the certification of airmen.

3.

3003. With respect to the certification of aircraft, which is a category of aircraft?

A—Normal, utility, acrobatic.
B—Airplane, rotorcraft, glider.
C—Landplane, seaplane.

Answer (A) is correct (3003). *(FAR 1.1)*
Category of aircraft, as used with respect to the certification of aircraft, means a grouping of aircraft based upon intended use or operating limitations. Examples include transport, normal, utility, acrobatic, limited, restricted, and provisional.
Answer (B) is incorrect because airplane, rotorcraft, and glider are categories of aircraft used with respect to the certification of airmen, not aircraft. Answer (C) is incorrect because landplane and seaplane are classes, not categories, of aircraft used with respect to the certification of aircraft.

4.

3004. With respect to the certification of aircraft, which is a class of aircraft?

A—Airplane, rotorcraft, glider, balloon.
B—Normal, utility, acrobatic, limited.
C—Transport, restricted, provisional.

Answer (A) is correct (3004). *(FAR 1.1)*
Class of aircraft, as used with respect to the certification of aircraft, means a broad grouping of aircraft having similar characteristics of propulsion, flight, or landing. Examples include airplane, rotorcraft, glider, balloon, landplane, and seaplane.
Answer (B) is incorrect because normal, utility, acrobatic, and limited are categories, not classes, of aircraft used with respect to the certification of aircraft. Answer (C) is incorrect because transport, restricted, and provisional are categories, not classes, of aircraft used with respect to the certification of aircraft.

5.

3005. The definition of nighttime is

A—sunset to sunrise.
B—1 hour after sunset to 1 hour before sunrise.
C—the time between the end of evening civil twilight and the beginning of morning civil twilight.

Answer (C) is correct (3005). *(FAR 1.1)*
"Night" means the time between the end of evening civil twilight and the beginning of morning civil twilight, as published in the American Air Almanac, converted to local time.
Answer (A) is incorrect because "sunset to sunrise" is the time during which navigation lights must be used. Answer (B) is incorrect because 1 hr. after sunset to 1 hr. before sunrise is the definition for nighttime recency of experience requirements.

6.

3837. An ATC clearance provides

A—priority over all other traffic.
B—adequate separation from all traffic.
C—authorization to proceed under specified traffic conditions in controlled airspace.

Answer (C) is correct (3837). *(FAR 1.1)*
A clearance issued by ATC is predicated on known traffic and known physical airport conditions. An ATC clearance means an authorization by ATC, for the purpose of preventing collision between known airplanes, for an airplane to proceed under specified conditions within controlled airspace.
Answer (A) is incorrect because an ATC clearance does not necessarily give priority over other traffic (although it might in some instances). Answer (B) is incorrect because an ATC clearance only provides separation from other participating traffic.

1.2 Abbreviations and Symbols

7.

3007. Which V-speed represents maximum flap extended speed?

A—V_{FE}.
B—V_{LOF}.
C—V_{FC}.

Answer (A) is correct (3007). *(FAR 1.2)*
V_{FE} means the maximum flap extended speed.
Answer (B) is incorrect because V_{LOF} means liftoff (not maximum flap extended) speed. Answer (C) is incorrect because V_{FC} means maximum speed for stability characteristics, not maximum flap extended speed.

8.

3008. Which V-speed represents maximum landing gear extended speed?

A—V_{LE}.
B—V_{LO}.
C—V_{FE}.

Answer (A) is correct (3008). *(FAR 1.2)*
V_{LE} means the maximum landing gear extended speed.
Answer (B) is incorrect because V_{LO} is the maximum landing gear operating (not extended) speed. Answer (C) is incorrect because V_{FE} is the maximum flap (not landing gear) extended speed.

9.
3009. V_{NO} is defined as the

A—normal operating range.
B—never-exceed speed.
C—maximum structural cruising speed.

Answer (C) is correct (3009). *(FAR 1.2)*
V_{NO} is defined as the maximum structural cruising speed.
Answer (A) is incorrect because the normal airspeed operating range is indicated by the green arc on the airspeed indicator. There is no V-speed for this range. Answer (B) is incorrect because V_{NE} (not V_{NO}) is the never-exceed speed.

10.
3006. Which V-speed represents maneuvering speed?

A—V_A.
B—V_{LO}.
C—V_{NE}.

Answer (A) is correct (3006). *(FAR 1.2)*
V_A means design maneuvering speed.
Answer (B) is incorrect because V_{LO} is the maximum landing gear operating, not the maneuvering, speed. Answer (C) is incorrect because V_{NE} is the never-exceed, not the maneuvering, speed.

11.
3010. V_{S0} is defined as the

A—stalling speed or minimum steady flight speed in the landing configuration.
B—stalling speed or minimum steady flight speed in a specified configuration.
C—stalling speed or minimum takeoff safety speed.

Answer (A) is correct (3010). *(FAR 1.2)*
V_{S0} is defined as the stalling speed or minimum steady flight speed in the landing configuration.
Answer (B) is incorrect because V_{S1} (not V_{S0}) is the stalling speed or minimum steady flight speed in a specified configuration. Answer (C) is incorrect because V_S (not V_{S0}) is the stalling speed and V_2 min. (not V_{S0}) is the minimum takeoff safety speed.

12.
3011. Which would provide the greatest gain in altitude in the shortest distance during climb after takeoff?

A—V_Y.
B—V_A.
C—V_X.

Answer (C) is correct (3011). *(FAR 1.2 and AFH Chap 3)*
V_X means the best angle of climb airspeed (i.e., the airspeed which will provide the greatest gain in altitude in the shortest distance).
Answer (A) is incorrect because V_Y is the airspeed for the best rate (not angle) of climb. Answer (B) is incorrect because V_A is the design maneuvering airspeed, not the best angle of climb airspeed.

13.
3012a. After takeoff, which airspeed would the pilot use to gain the most altitude in a given period of time?

A—V_Y.
B—V_X.
C—V_A.

Answer (A) is correct (3012). *(FAR 1.2 and AFH Chap 3)*
V_Y means the airspeed for the best rate of climb (i.e., the airspeed that you use to gain the most altitude in a given period of time).
Answer (B) is incorrect because V_X is the airspeed for the best angle (not rate) of climb. Answer (C) is incorrect because V_A is the design maneuvering airspeed, not the best rate of climb airspeed.

4.2 FAR PART 21
21.181 Duration of Airworthiness Certificates

14.
3187. How long does the Airworthiness Certificate of an aircraft remain valid?

A—As long as the aircraft has a current Registration Certificate.
B—Indefinitely, unless the aircraft suffers major damage.
C—As long as the aircraft is maintained and operated as required by Federal Aviation Regulations.

Answer (C) is correct (3187). *(FAR 21.181)*
The airworthiness certificate of an airplane remains valid as long as the airplane is in an airworthy condition, i.e., operated and maintained as required by the FARs.
Answer (A) is incorrect because the registration certificate is the document evidencing ownership. A changed registration has no effect on the airworthiness certificate. Answer (B) is incorrect because the airplane must be maintained and operated according to the FARs, not indefinitely. Even if the aircraft suffers major damage, as long as all required repairs are made, the Airworthiness Certificate remains valid.

4.2A FAR PART 39
39.1 Applicability

15.
3012b. What should an owner or operator know about Airworthiness Directives (AD's)?

A—For informational purposes only.
B—They are mandatory.
C—They are voluntary.

Answer (B) is correct (3012b). *(FAR 39.1)*
Airworthiness Directives (ADs) are issued under FAR Part 39 by the FAA to require correction of unsafe conditions found in an airplane, an airplane engine, a propeller, or an appliance when such conditions exist and are likely to exist or develop in other products of the same design. Since ADs are issued under FAR Part 39, they are regulatory and must be complied with, unless a specific exemption is granted.
Answer (A) is incorrect because ADs outline required maintenance; they are not for informational purposes only. Answer (C) is incorrect because ADs are mandatory, not voluntary.

39.3 General

16.
3012c. May a pilot operate an aircraft that is not in compliance with an Airworthiness Directive (AD)?

A—Yes, under VFR conditions only.
B—Yes, AD's are only voluntary.
C—Yes, if allowed by the AD.

Answer (C) is correct (3012c). *(FAR 39.3)*
An AD is used to notify aircraft owners and other interested persons of unsafe conditions and prescribe the conditions under which the product (e.g., an aircraft) may continue to be operated. An AD may be one of an emergency nature requiring immediate compliance upon receipt or one of a less urgent nature requiring compliance within a relatively longer period of time. You may operate an airplane that is not in compliance with an AD, if such operation is allowed by the AD.
Answer (A) is incorrect because an AD, not the operating conditions, may allow an aircraft to be operated before compliance with the AD. Answer (B) is incorrect because ADs are mandatory, not voluntary.

4.3 FAR PART 43
43.3 Persons Authorized to Perform Maintenance, Preventive Maintenance, Rebuilding, and Alterations

17.
3013b. What regulation allows a private pilot to perform preventive maintenance?

A—14 CFR Part 91.403.
B—14 CFR Part 43.7.
C—14 CFR Part 61.113.

Answer (B) is correct (3013b). *(FAR 43.3)*
Preventive maintenance means simple or minor preservation operations and the replacement of small standard parts not involving complex assembly operations. Appendix A to Part 43 provides a list of work that is considered preventive maintenance. Part 43 allows a person who holds a pilot certificate to perform preventive maintenance on any aircraft owned or operated by that pilot which is not used in air carrier service.
Answer (A) is incorrect because FAR 91.403 provides the general operating rules relating to maintenance, not those relating to who can perform preventive maintenance. Answer (C) is incorrect because FAR 61.113 provides the limitations and privileges of a private pilot as pilot in command.

43.7 Persons Authorized to Approve Aircraft Airframes, Aircraft Engines, Propellers, Appliances, or Component Parts for Return to Service after Maintenance, Preventive Maintenance, Rebuilding, or Alteration

18.
3013c. Who may perform preventive maintenance on an aircraft and approve it for return to service?

A—Student or Recreational pilot.
B—Private or Commercial pilot.
C—None of the above.

Answer (B) is correct (3013c). *(FAR 43.7)*
A person who holds a pilot certificate issued under Part 61 may perform preventive maintenance on any airplane owned or operated by that pilot which is not used in air carrier service. To approve the airplane for return to service after preventive maintenance is performed by a pilot, the pilot must hold at least a private pilot certificate.
Answer (A) is incorrect because, while a student or recreational pilot may perform preventive maintenance on any airplane owned or operated by that pilot, the pilot must hold at least a private pilot certificate to approve the airplane's return to service. Answer (C) is incorrect because any pilot may perform preventive maintenance on an airplane owned or operated by that pilot, but the pilot must hold at least a private pilot certificate to approve the airplane's return to service.

43.9 Maintenance Records

19.

3013a. Preventive maintenance has been performed on an aircraft. What paperwork is required?

A—A full, detailed description of the work done must be entered in the airframe logbook.

B—The date the work was completed, and the name of the person who did the work must be entered in the airframe and engine logbook.

C—The signature, certificate number, and kind of certificate held by the person approving the work and a description of the work must be entered in the aircraft maintenance records.

Answer (C) is correct (3013a). *(FAR 43.9)*

After preventive maintenance has been performed, the signature, certificate number, and kind of certificate held by the person approving the work and a description of the work must be entered in the aircraft maintenance records.

Answer (A) is incorrect because the signature, certificate number, and kind of certificate, in addition to the description of work performed, must be entered into the maintenance records. Answer (B) is incorrect because a description of work completed, signature, certificate number, and kind of certificate held by the person approving the work (if different than the person who did the work) in addition to the date the work was completed, must be entered into the maintenance records.

Part 43, Appendix A. Major Alterations and Repairs and Preventive Maintenance

20.

3014. Which operation would be described as preventive maintenance?

A—Servicing landing gear wheel bearings.

B—Alteration of main seat support brackets.

C—Engine adjustments to allow automotive gas to be used.

Answer (A) is correct (3014). *(Appendix A to Part 43)*

Appendix A to Part 43 provides a list of work that is considered preventive maintenance. Preventive maintenance means simple or minor preservation operations and the replacement of small standard parts not involving complex assembly operations. Servicing landing gear wheel bearings, such as cleaning and greasing, is considered preventive maintenance.

Answer (B) is incorrect because the alteration of main seat support brackets is considered an airframe major repair, not preventative maintenance. Answer (C) is incorrect because engine adjustments to allow automotive gas to be used is considered a powerplant major alteration, not preventive maintenance.

21.

3015. Which operation would be described as preventive maintenance?

A—Repair of landing gear brace struts.

B—Replenishing hydraulic fluid.

C—Repair of portions of skin sheets by making additional seams.

Answer (B) is correct (3015). *(Appendix A to Part 43)*

Appendix A to Part 43 provides a list of work that is considered preventive maintenance. Preventive maintenance means simple or minor preservation operations and the replacement of small standard parts not involving complex assembly operations. An example of preventive maintenance is replenishing hydraulic fluid.

Answer (A) is incorrect because the repair of landing gear brace struts is considered an airframe major repair, not preventive maintenance. Answer (C) is incorrect because the repair of portions of skin sheets by making additional seams is considered an airframe major repair, not preventive maintenance.

4.4 FAR PART 61
61.3 Requirements for Certificates, Ratings, and Authorizations

22.

3017. When must a current pilot certificate be in the pilot's personal possession or readily accessible in the aircraft?

A—When acting as a crew chief during launch and recovery.

B—Only when passengers are carried.

C—Anytime when acting as pilot in command or as a required crewmember.

Answer (C) is correct (3017). *(FAR 61.3)*

Current and appropriate pilot and medical certificates must be in your personal possession or readily accessible in the aircraft when you act as pilot in command (PIC) or as a required pilot flight crewmember.

Answer (A) is incorrect because a current pilot certificate must be in your personal possession when acting as a PIC or as a required crewmember of an aircraft, not when acting as a crew chief during launch and recovery of an airship. Answer (B) is incorrect because anytime you fly as PIC or as a required crewmember, you must have a current pilot certificate in your personal possession regardless of whether passengers are carried or not.

23.
3018. A recreational or private pilot acting as pilot in command, or in any other capacity as a required pilot flight crewmember, must have in his or her personal possession or readily accessible in the aircraft a current

A—logbook endorsement to show that a flight review has been satisfactorily accomplished.
B—medical certificate if required and an appropriate pilot certificate.
C—endorsement on the pilot certificate to show that a flight review has been satisfactorily accomplished.

Answer (B) is correct (3018). *(FAR 61.3)*
Current and appropriate pilot and medical certificates must be in your personal possession or readily accessible in the aircraft when you act as pilot in command (PIC) or as a required pilot flight crewmember.
Answer (A) is incorrect because, as a private pilot, you need not have your logbook in your possession or readily accessible aboard the airplane. A recreational pilot must carry a logbook to show evidence of an endorsement that permits certain flights, not to show completion of a flight review. Answer (C) is incorrect because the endorsement after satisfactorily completing a flight review is made in your pilot logbook, not on your pilot certificate.

24.
3016. What document(s) must be in your personal possession or readily accessible in the aircraft while operating as pilot in command of an aircraft?

A—Certificates showing accomplishment of a checkout in the aircraft and a current biennial flight review.
B—A pilot certificate with an endorsement showing accomplishment of an annual flight review and a pilot logbook showing recency of experience.
C—An appropriate pilot certificate and an appropriate current medical certificate if required.

Answer (C) is correct (3016). *(FAR 61.3)*
Current and appropriate pilot and medical certificates must be in your personal possession or readily accessible in the aircraft when you act as pilot in command (PIC) or as a required pilot flight crewmember.
Answer (A) is incorrect because flight reviews and checkouts in aircraft are documented in your logbook rather than on separate certificates and need not be in your personal possession. Answer (B) is incorrect because the endorsement after satisfactorily completing a flight review is made in your logbook, not on your pilot certificate. You are not required to have your pilot logbook in your personal possession while acting as pilot in command.

25.
3019. Each person who holds a pilot certificate or a medical certificate shall present it for inspection upon the request of the Administrator, the National Transportation Safety Board, or any

A—authorized representative of the Department of Transportation.
B—person in a position of authority.
C—federal, state, or local law enforcement officer.

Answer (C) is correct (3019). *(FAR 61.3)*
Each person who holds a pilot certificate, flight instructor certificate, medical certificate, authorization, or license required by the FARs shall present it for inspection upon the request of the Administrator (of the FAA), an authorized representative of the National Transportation Safety Board, or any Federal, State, or local law enforcement officer.
Answer (A) is incorrect because it is just one example of those who can ask to inspect pilot and medical certificates. Answer (B) is incorrect because not just any person with any kind of authority, such as a foreman, can inspect your pilot certificate or medical certificate.

61.23 Duration of Medical Certificates

26.
3020. A Third-Class Medical Certificate is issued to a 36-year-old pilot on August 10, this year. To exercise the privileges of a Private Pilot Certificate, the medical certificate will be valid until midnight on

A—August 10, 2 years later.
B—August 31, 3 years later.
C—August 31, 2 years later.

Answer (B) is correct (3020). *(FAR 61.23)*
A pilot may exercise the privileges of a private pilot certificate under a third-class medical certificate until it expires at the end of the last day of the month 3 years after it was issued, for pilots less than 40 years old on the date of the medical examination. A third-class medical certificate issued to a 36-year-old pilot on Aug. 10 will be valid until midnight on Aug. 31, 3 years later.
Answer (A) is incorrect because medical certificates expire at the last day of the month. Thus, a medical certificate issued on Aug. 10 will expire on Aug. 31, not Aug. 10. Additionally, since the pilot is less than 40 years old, the third-class medical certificate is valid for 3 years, not 2 years. Answer (C) is incorrect because a pilot may exercise the privileges of a private pilot certificate under a third-class medical certificate until it expires at the end of the last day of the month 2 years later if the pilot was 40 years old or older, not less than 40 years old, on the date of the medical examination.

27.
3021. A Third-Class Medical Certificate is issued to a 51-year-old pilot on May 3, this year. To exercise the privileges of a Private Pilot Certificate, the medical certificate will be valid until midnight on

A—May 3, 1 year later.
B—May 31, 1 year later.
C—May 31, 2 years later.

Answer (C) is correct (3021). *(FAR 61.23)*
A pilot may exercise the privileges of a private pilot certificate under a third-class medical certificate until it expires at the end of the last day of the month 2 years after it was issued, for pilots 40 years old or older on the date of the medical examination. A third-class medical certificate issued to a 51-year-old pilot on May 3 will be valid until midnight on May 31, 2 years later.
Answer (A) is incorrect because medical certificates expire on the last day of the month. Thus, a medical certificate issued on May 3 will expire on May 31, not May 3. Additionally, a third-class medical certificate is valid for 2 years, not 1 year, if the pilot is over 40 years old. Answer (B) is incorrect because a pilot may exercise the privileges of a private pilot certificate under a third-class medical certificate until it expires at the end of the last day of the month, 2 years, not 1 year, later if the pilot was 40 years old or older on the date of the examination.

28.
3022. For private pilot operations, a Second-Class Medical Certificate issued to a 42-year-old pilot on July 15, this year, will expire at midnight on

A—July 15, 2 years later.
B—July 31, 1 year later.
C—July 31, 2 years later.

Answer (C) is correct (3022). *(FAR 61.23)*
For private pilot operations, a second-class medical certificate will expire at the end of the last day of the month, 2 years after it was issued, for pilots 40 years old or older on the date of the medical examination. For private pilot operations, a second-class medical certificate issued to a 42-year-old pilot on July 15 will be valid until midnight on July 31, 2 years later.
Answer (A) is incorrect because a medical certificate expires on the last day of the month. Thus, a medical certificate issued on July 15 will expire on July 31, not July 15. Answer (B) is incorrect because a second-class medical certificate is valid for 1 year for operations requiring a commercial pilot certificate.

29.
3023. For private pilot operations, a First-Class Medical Certificate issued to a 23-year-old pilot on October 21, this year, will expire at midnight on

A—October 21, 2 years later.
B—October 31, next year.
C—October 31, 3 years later.

Answer (C) is correct (3023). *(FAR 61.23)*
For private pilot operations, a first-class medical certificate will expire at the end of the last day of the month, 3 years after it was issued, for pilots less than 40 years old on the date of the medical examination. For private pilot operations, a first-class medical certificate issued to a 23-year-old pilot on Oct. 21 will be valid until midnight on Oct. 31, 3 years later.
Answer (A) is incorrect because a medical certificate expires on the last day of the month. Thus, a medical certificate issued on Oct. 21 will expire on Oct. 31, not Oct. 21. Additionally, for private pilot operations, the medical certificate is valid for 3 years, not 2 years, for a pilot less than 40 years old on the date of the medical examination. Answer (B) is incorrect because a first-class medical certificate is valid for 1 year for operations requiring a commercial pilot certificate.

30.
3039. A Third-Class Medical Certificate was issued to a 19-year-old pilot on August 10, this year. To exercise the privileges of a recreational or private pilot certificate, the medical certificate will expire at midnight on

A—August 10, 2 years later.
B—August 31, 3 years later.
C—August 31, 2 years later.

Answer (B) is correct (3039). *(FAR 61.23)*
A pilot may exercise the privileges of a recreational or private pilot certificate under a third-class medical certificate until it expires at the end of the last day of the month 3 years after it was issued, for pilots less than 40 years old at the time of the medical examination. A third-class medical certificate issued to a 19-year-old pilot on Aug. 10 will expire at midnight on Aug. 31, 3 years later.
Answer (A) is incorrect because medical certificates expire at the end of the month. A medical certificate issued on Aug. 10 will expire at midnight on Aug. 31, not Aug. 10. Answer (C) is incorrect because a pilot may exercise the privileges of a recreational or private pilot certificate under a third-class medical certificate until it expires at the end of the last day of the month 2 years later if the pilot was 40 years old or older, not less than 40 years old, on the date of the medical examination.

61.31 Type Rating Requirements, Additional Training, and Authorization Requirements

31.
3026. Before a person holding a private pilot certificate may act as pilot in command of a high-performance airplane, that person must have

A—passed a flight test in that airplane from an FAA inspector.
B—an endorsement in that person's logbook that he or she is competent to act as pilot in command.
C—received ground and flight instruction from an authorized flight instructor who then endorses that person's logbook.

Answer (C) is correct (3026). *(FAR 61.31)*
A private pilot may not act as pilot in command of a high-performance airplane (an airplane with an engine of more than 200 horsepower) unless (s)he has received and logged ground and flight training from an authorized instructor who has certified in his/her logbook that (s)he is proficient to operate a high-performance airplane.
Answer (A) is incorrect because no FAA flight test is required, only ground and flight training and an endorsement from an authorized flight instructor. Answer (B) is incorrect because the ground and flight training and endorsement must be by an authorized flight instructor.

32.
3025. What is the definition of a high-performance airplane?

A—An airplane with 180 horsepower, or retractable landing gear, flaps, and a fixed-pitch propeller.
B—An airplane with a normal cruise speed in excess of 200 knots.
C—An airplane with an engine of more than 200 horsepower.

Answer (C) is correct (3025). *(FAR 61.31)*
A high-performance airplane is defined as an airplane with an engine of more than 200 horsepower.
Answer (A) is incorrect because a high-performance airplane is an airplane with an engine of more than 200 horsepower, not an airplane with 180 horsepower, or retractable landing gear, flaps, and a fixed-pitch propeller. Answer (B) is incorrect because a high-performance airplane is an airplane with an engine of more than 200 horsepower, not an airplane with a normal cruise speed in excess of 200 kt.

33.
3024. The pilot in command is required to hold a type rating in which aircraft?

A—Aircraft operated under an authorization issued by the Administrator.
B—Aircraft having a gross weight of more than 12,500 pounds.
C—Aircraft involved in ferry flights, training flights, or test flights.

Answer (B) is correct (3024). *(FAR 61.31)*
A person may not act as pilot in command of any of the following aircraft unless he holds a type rating for that aircraft:
(1) A large aircraft (except lighter-than-air), i.e., over 12,500 lb. gross weight.
(2) A turbojet-powered airplane
(3) Other aircraft specified by the FAA through aircraft type certificate procedures
Answer (A) is incorrect because all aircraft, not only those requiring type ratings, are operated under an authorization issued by the Administrator of the FAA. Answer (C) is incorrect because any type of aircraft can be involved in ferry flights, training flights, or test flights and may not require a type rating (e.g., your single-engine trainer airplane on a training flight).

34.
3027. In order to act as pilot in command of a high-performance airplane, a pilot must have

A—made and logged three solo takeoffs and landings in a high-performance airplane.
B—received and logged ground and flight instruction in an airplane that has more than 200 horsepower.
C—passed a flight test in a high-performance airplane.

Answer (B) is correct (3027). *(FAR 61.31)*
Prior to acting as pilot in command of an airplane with an engine of more than 200 horsepower, a person is required to receive and log ground and flight training in such an airplane from an authorized flight instructor who has certified in the pilot's logbook that the individual is proficient to operate a high-performance airplane.
Answer (A) is incorrect because, in order to act as pilot in command of a high-performance airplane, you must have received and logged ground and flight training from an authorized flight instructor, not have made three solo takeoffs and landings. Answer (C) is incorrect because you must have received and logged ground and flight training, and a logbook endorsement from an authorized flight instructor, not a flight test, is required prior to acting as a pilot in command of a high-performance airplane.

61.56 Flight Review

35.
3028. To act as pilot in command of an aircraft carrying passengers, a pilot must show by logbook endorsement the satisfactory completion of a flight review or completion of a pilot proficiency check within the preceding

A—6 calendar months.
B—12 calendar months.
C—24 calendar months.

Answer (C) is correct (3028). *(FAR 61.56)*
    To act as pilot in command of an aircraft (whether carrying passengers or not), a pilot must show by logbook endorsement the satisfactory completion of a flight review or completion of a pilot proficiency check within the preceding 24 calendar months.
    Answer (A) is incorrect because a pilot must have satisfactorily completed a flight review or completion of a pilot proficiency check within the preceding 24 (not 6) calendar months. Answer (B) is incorrect because a pilot must have satisfactorily completed a flight review or completion of a pilot proficiency check within the preceding 24 (not 12) calendar months.

36.
3040. If a recreational or private pilot had a flight review on August 8, this year, when is the next flight review required?

A—August 8, 2 years later.
B—August 31, next year.
C—August 31, 2 years later.

Answer (C) is correct (3040). *(FAR 61.56)*
    A pilot is required to have a flight review within the preceding 24 calendar months before the month in which the pilot acts as pilot in command. Thus, a pilot who had a flight review on Aug. 8 of this year, must have a flight review completed by Aug. 31, 2 years later.
    Answer (A) is incorrect because flight reviews expire at the end of the month. Thus, a flight review on Aug. 8 will expire on Aug. 31, not Aug. 8. Answer (B) is incorrect because a flight review is valid for 2 years, not 1 year.

37.
3041. Each recreational or private pilot is required to have

A—a biennial flight review.
B—an annual flight review.
C—a semiannual flight review.

Answer (A) is correct (3041). *(FAR 61.56)*
    Each recreational or private pilot is required to have a biennial (every 2 years) flight review.
    Answer (B) is incorrect because each pilot is required to have a biennial, not annual, flight review. Answer (C) is incorrect because each pilot is required to have a biennial, not semiannual, flight review.

38.
3042. If a recreational or private pilot had a flight review on August 8, this year, when is the next flight review required?

A—August 8, next year.
B—August 31, 1 year later.
C—August 31, 2 years later.

Answer (C) is correct (3042). *(FAR 61.56)*
    A pilot is required to have a flight review within the preceding 24 calendar months before the month in which the pilot acts as pilot in command. Thus, a recreational or private pilot who had a flight review on Aug. 8 of this year, must have a flight review completed by Aug. 31, 2 years later.
    Answer (A) is incorrect because flight reviews expire at the end of the month. Thus, a flight review on Aug. 8 will expire on Aug. 31, not Aug. 8. Answer (B) is incorrect because a flight review is valid for 2 years, not 1 year.

61.57 Recent Flight Experience: Pilot in Command

39.
3030. To act as pilot in command of an aircraft carrying passengers, the pilot must have made at least three takeoffs and three landings in an aircraft of the same category, class, and if a type rating is required, of the same type, within the preceding

A—90 days.
B—12 calendar months.
C—24 calendar months.

Answer (A) is correct (3030). *(FAR 61.57)*
    To act as pilot in command of an airplane with passengers aboard, you must have made at least three takeoffs and three landings (to a full stop if in a tailwheel airplane) in an airplane of the same category, class, and, if a type rating is required, of the same type within the preceding 90 days. Category refers to airplane, rotorcraft, etc.; class refers to single or multiengine, land or sea.
    Answer (B) is incorrect because a flight review, not recency experience, is required every 24, not 12, calendar months. Answer (C) is incorrect because a flight review, not recency experience, is normally required of all pilots every 24 months.

40.
3029. If recency of experience requirements for night flight are not met and official sunset is 1830, the latest time passengers may be carried is

A—1829.
B—1859.
C—1929.

Answer (C) is correct (3029). *(FAR 61.57)*
For the purpose of night recency experience flight time, night is defined as the period beginning 1 hr. after sunset and ending 1 hr. before sunrise. If you have not met the night experience requirements, and official sunset is 1830, a landing must be accomplished at or before 1929 if passengers are carried.
Answer (A) is incorrect because 1829 is the time that night begins for the purpose of turning on aircraft position (navigation) lights. Answer (B) is incorrect because there is no regulation concerning the time 30 min. after official sunset.

41.
3031. To act as pilot in command of an aircraft carrying passengers, the pilot must have made three takeoffs and three landings within the preceding 90 days in an aircraft of the same

A—make and model.
B—category and class, but not type.
C—category, class, and type, if a type rating is required.

Answer (C) is correct (3031). *(FAR 61.57)*
No one may act as pilot in command of an airplane carrying passengers unless within the preceding 90 days (s)he has made three takeoffs and three landings as sole manipulator of the controls in an aircraft of the same category and class and, if a type rating is required, the same type. If the aircraft is a tailwheel airplane, the landings must have been to a full stop.
Answer (A) is incorrect because it must be the same category and class (not make and model) and, if a type rating is required, the same type. Answer (B) is incorrect because it must be the same type aircraft if a type rating is required for that aircraft.

42.
3033. The three takeoffs and landings that are required to act as pilot in command at night must be done during the time period from

A—sunset to sunrise.
B—1 hour after sunset to 1 hour before sunrise.
C—the end of evening civil twilight to the beginning of morning civil twilight.

Answer (B) is correct (3033). *(FAR 61.57)*
No one may act as pilot in command of an aircraft carrying passengers at night (i.e., the period from 1 hr. after sunset to 1 hr. before sunrise as published in the American Air Almanac) unless (s)he has made three takeoffs and three landings to a full stop within the preceding 90 days, at night, in the category and class of aircraft to be used.
Answer (A) is incorrect because the period from sunset to sunrise is the time that aircraft lights are required to be on, not the time period for night recency experience. Answer (C) is incorrect because the end of evening civil twilight to the beginning of morning civil twilight is the definition of night, not the time period for night recency experience.

43.
3034. To meet the recency of experience requirements to act as pilot in command carrying passengers at night, a pilot must have made at least three takeoffs and three landings to a full stop within the preceding 90 days in

A—the same category and class of aircraft to be used.
B—the same type of aircraft to be used.
C—any aircraft.

Answer (A) is correct (3034). *(FAR 61.57)*
No one may act as pilot in command of an aircraft carrying passengers at night (i.e., the period from 1 hr. after sunset to 1 hr. before sunrise) unless (s)he has made three takeoffs and three landings to a full stop within the preceding 90 days, at night, in the category and class of aircraft to be used.
Answer (B) is incorrect because unless a type-rating is required it does not have to be the same type of aircraft. ("Type" refers to a specific make and general model, e.g., Cessna 152/172.) Answer (C) is incorrect because it must be the same category and class (not any) of aircraft to be used.

44.
3032. The takeoffs and landings required to meet the recency of experience requirements for carrying passengers in a tailwheel airplane

A—may be touch and go or full stop.
B—must be touch and go.
C—must be to a full stop.

Answer (C) is correct (3032). *(FAR 61.57)*
To comply with recency requirements for carrying passengers in a tailwheel airplane, one must have made three takeoffs and landings to a full stop within the past 90 days.
Answer (A) is incorrect because in a tailwheel airplane the takeoffs and landings must be to a full stop only, not touch and go. Answer (B) is incorrect because in a tailwheel airplane the takeoffs and landings must be to a full stop, not touch and go.

61.60 Change of Address

45.
3035. If a certificated pilot changes permanent mailing address and fails to notify the FAA Airmen Certification Branch of the new address, the pilot is entitled to exercise the privileges of the pilot certificate for a period of only

A—30 days after the date of the move.
B—60 days after the date of the move.
C—90 days after the date of the move.

Answer (A) is correct (3035). *(FAR 61.60)*
If you have changed your permanent mailing address, you may not exercise the privileges of your pilot certificate after 30 days from the date of the address change unless you have notified the FAA in writing of the change. You are required to notify the Airman Certification Branch at Box 25082, Oklahoma City, OK, 73125.
Note: While you must notify the FAA if your address changes, you are not required to carry a certificate that shows your current address. The FAA will not issue a new certificate upon receipt of your new address unless you send a written request and $2 to the address shown above.
Answer (B) is incorrect because if you change your permanent mailing address you may exercise the privileges of your pilot certificate for a period of only 30 (not 60) days after the date you move unless you notify the FAA in writing of the change. Answer (C) is incorrect because if you change your permanent mailing address you may exercise the privileges of your pilot certificate for a period of only 30 (not 90) days after the date you move unless you notify the FAA in writing of the change.

61.69 Glider Towing: Experience and Training Requirements

46.
3036. A certificated private pilot may not act as pilot in command of an aircraft towing a glider unless there is entered in the pilot's logbook a minimum of

A—100 hours of pilot flight time in any aircraft, that the pilot is using to tow a glider.
B—100 hours of pilot-in-command time in the aircraft category, class, and type, if required, that the pilot is using to tow a glider.
C—200 hours of pilot-in-command time in the aircraft category, class, and type, if required, that the pilot is using to tow a glider.

Answer (B) is correct (3036). *(FAR 61.69(a)(2))*
As a private pilot, you may not act as pilot in command of an aircraft towing a glider unless you have had, and entered in your logbook, at least 100 hr. of pilot-in-command time in the aircraft category, class, and type, if required, that you are using to tow a glider.
Answer (A) is incorrect because you must have logged at least 100 hr. as pilot in command in the aircraft category, class, and type, if required, that you are using to tow a glider, not just any aircraft. Answer (C) is incorrect because you must have logged at least 100 hr., not 200 hr., as pilot in command.

47.
3037. To act as pilot in command of an aircraft towing a glider, a pilot is required to have made within the preceding 12 months

A—at least three flights as observer in a glider being towed by an aircraft.
B—at least three flights in a powered glider.
C—at least three actual or simulated glider tows while accompanied by a qualified pilot.

Answer (C) is correct (3037). *(FAR 61.69)*
To act as pilot in command of an aircraft towing a glider, you are required to have made, in the preceding 12 months,
(1) At least three actual or simulated glider tows while accompanied by a qualified pilot, or
(2) At least three flights as pilot in command of a glider towed by an aircraft.
Answer (A) is incorrect because you are required to have made within the preceding 12 months at least three flights as pilot in command, not as an observer, of a glider being towed by an aircraft. Answer (B) is incorrect because you are required to have made within the preceding 12 months at least three flights as pilot in command of a glider towed by an aircraft, not three flights in a powered glider.

61.113 Private Pilot Privileges and Limitations: Pilot in Command

48.
3064. In regard to privileges and limitations, a private pilot may

A—act as pilot in command of an aircraft carrying a passenger for compensation if the flight is in connection with a business or employment.
B—not pay less than the pro rata share of the operating expenses of a flight with passengers provided the expenses involve only fuel, oil, airport expenditures, or rental fees.
C—not be paid in any manner for the operating expenses of a flight.

Answer (B) is correct (3064). *(FAR 61.113)*
A private pilot may not pay less than an equal (pro rata) share of the operating expenses of a flight with passengers. These expenses may involve only fuel, oil, airport expenditures (e.g., landing fees, tie-down fees, etc.), or rental fees.
Answer (A) is incorrect because a private pilot cannot act as pilot in command of an aircraft carrying a passenger for compensation. Answer (C) is incorrect because a private pilot may equally share the operating expenses of a flight with his/her passengers.

49.
3065. According to regulations pertaining to privileges and limitations, a private pilot may

A—be paid for the operating expenses of a flight if at least three takeoffs and three landings were made by the pilot within the preceding 90 days.
B—not pay less than the pro rata share of the operating expenses of a flight with passengers provided the expenses involve only fuel, oil, airport expenditures, or rental fees.
C—not be paid in any manner for the operating expenses of a flight.

Answer (B) is correct (3065). *(FAR 61.113)*
A private pilot may not pay less than an equal (pro rata) share of the operating expenses of a flight with passengers. These expenses may involve only fuel, oil, airport expenditures (e.g., landing fees, tie-down fees, etc.), or rental fees.
Answer (A) is incorrect because a private pilot may be paid for the operating expenses of a flight in connection with any business or employment if the flight is only incidental to that business or employment and no passengers or property are carried for compensation or hire, not if the pilot has made three takeoffs and landings in the preceding 90 days. Answer (C) is incorrect because a private pilot may equally share the operating expenses of a flight with his/her passengers.

50.
3066. What exception, if any, permits a private pilot to act as pilot in command of an aircraft carrying passengers who pay for the flight?

A—If the passengers pay all the operating expenses.
B—If a donation is made to a charitable organization for the flight.
C—There is no exception.

Answer (B) is correct (3066). *(FAR 61.118)*
A private pilot may act as pilot in command of an airplane used in a passenger-carrying airlift sponsored by a charitable organization for which passengers make donations to the organization, provided the following requirements are met: the local FSDO is notified at least 7 days before the flight, the flight is conducted from an adequate public airport, the pilot has logged at least 200 hr., no acrobatic or formation flights are performed, the 100-hr. inspection of the airplane requirement is complied with, and the flight is day-VFR.
Answer (A) is incorrect because a private pilot may only share the operating costs, not have the passengers pay for all the operating costs. Answer (C) is incorrect because the exception is a passenger-carrying airlift sponsored by a charitable organization.

4.5 RECREATIONAL PILOT RELATED FARs
61.101 Recreational Pilot Privileges and Limitations

QUESTIONS 51-75 SPECIFICALLY REFER TO RECREATIONAL PILOTS
THESE QUESTIONS ARE NOT TESTED ON THE PRIVATE PILOT KNOWLEDGE TEST

51.
3038. A recreational pilot acting as pilot in command must have in his or her personal possession while aboard the aircraft

A—a current logbook endorsement to show that a flight review has been satisfactorily accomplished.
B—the pilot logbook to show recent experience requirements to serve as pilot in command have been met.
C—a current logbook endorsement that permits flight within 50 nautical miles from the departure airport.

Answer (C) is correct (3038). *(FAR 61.101)*
A recreational pilot acting as pilot in command must have in his/her personal possession while aboard the airplane a current logbook endorsement that permits flight within 50 NM from the departure airport.
Answer (A) is incorrect because, to act as pilot in command, a recreational pilot must have in his/her personal possession while aboard the aircraft a current logbook endorsement that permits flight within 50 NM from the departure airport, not an endorsement to show that a flight review has been satisfactorily completed. Answer (B) is incorrect because, to act as pilot in command, a recreational pilot must have in his/her personal possession while aboard the aircraft a logbook endorsement that permits flight within 50 NM from the departure airport, not a logbook showing that the recent experience requirements have been met.

52.
3043. How many passengers is a recreational pilot allowed to carry on board?

A—One.
B—Two.
C—Three.

Answer (A) is correct (3043). *(FAR 61.101)*
Recreational pilots may carry **not** more than one passenger.
Answer (B) is incorrect because a recreational pilot is allowed to carry only one passenger (not two). Answer (C) is incorrect because a recreational pilot is allowed to carry only one passenger (not three).

53.
3044. According to regulations pertaining to privileges and limitations, a recreational pilot may

A—be paid for the operating expenses of a flight.
B—not pay less than the pro rata share of the operating expenses of a flight with a passenger.
C—not be paid in any manner for the operating expenses of a flight.

Answer (B) is correct (3044). *(FAR 61.101)*
A recreational pilot may not pay less than an equal (pro rata) share of the operating expenses of the flight with a passenger. These expenses may involve only fuel, oil, airport expenditures (e.g., landing fees, tie-down fees, etc.), or rental fees.
Answer (A) is incorrect because operating expenses can only be shared by a passenger, not paid for by a passenger; i.e., a recreational pilot cannot carry a passenger or property for compensation or hire. Answer (C) is incorrect because a recreational pilot may equally share operating expenses of the flight with the passenger.

54.
3045. In regard to privileges and limitations, a recreational pilot may

A—fly for compensation or hire within 50 nautical miles from the departure airport with a logbook endorsement.
B—not pay less than the pro rata share of the operating expenses of a flight with a passenger.
C—not be paid in any manner for the operating expenses of a flight from a passenger.

Answer (B) is correct (3045). *(FAR 61.101)*
A recreational pilot may not pay less than an equal (pro rata) share of the operating expenses of the flight with a passenger. These expenses may involve only fuel, oil, airport expenditures (e.g., landing fees, tie-down fees, etc.), or rental fees.
Answer (A) is incorrect because recreational pilots may **not** fly for compensation or hire. Answer (C) is incorrect because a recreational pilot may equally share operating expenses of the flight with a passenger.

55.
3046. When may a recreational pilot act as pilot in command on a cross-country flight that exceeds 50 nautical miles from the departure airport?

A—After receiving ground and flight instructions on cross-country training and a logbook endorsement.
B—After attaining 100 hours of pilot-in-command time and a logbook endorsement.
C—12 calendar months after receiving his or her recreational pilot certificate and a logbook endorsement.

Answer (A) is correct (3046). *(FAR 61.101)*
A recreational pilot may act as pilot in command on a cross-country flight that exceeds 50 NM from the departure airport, provided that person has received ground and flight training from an authorized instructor on the cross-country training requirements for a private pilot certificate and has received a logbook endorsement, which is in the person's possession in the aircraft, certifying the person is proficient in cross-country flying.
Answer (B) is incorrect because a recreational pilot may act as pilot in command on a cross-country flight that exceeds 50 NM from the departure airport after receiving ground and flight training from an authorized instructor on the cross-country training requirements for a private pilot certificate and after receiving a logbook endorsement, not after attaining 100 hr. as pilot-in-command time and a logbook endorsement. Answer (C) is incorrect because a recreational pilot may act as pilot in command on a cross-country flight after receiving ground and flight training from an authorized instructor on the cross-country training requirements for a private pilot certificate and after receiving a logbook endorsement, not 12 months after receiving his/her recreational pilot certificate and a logbook endorsement.

56.
3047. A recreational pilot may act as pilot in command of an aircraft that is certificated for a maximum of how many occupants?

A—Two.
B—Three.
C—Four.

Answer (C) is correct (3047). *(FAR 61.101)*
Recreational pilots may **not** act as pilot in command of an aircraft that is certificated for more than four occupants. Note, however, that only two occupants are permitted, the recreational pilot and a passenger.
Answer (A) is incorrect because a recreational pilot can act as pilot in command of an aircraft that is certificated for up to four (not two) occupants. Answer (B) is incorrect because recreational pilots can act as pilot in command of an aircraft certificated for up to four (not three) occupants.

57.
3048. A recreational pilot may act as pilot in command of an aircraft with a maximum engine horsepower of

A—160.
B—180.
C—200.

Answer (B) is correct (3048). *(FAR 61.101)*
A recreational pilot may act as pilot in command of an aircraft with a maximum engine horsepower of 180.
Answer (A) is incorrect because a recreational pilot may act as pilot in command of an aircraft with a maximum horsepower of 180 (not 160). Answer (C) is incorrect because a recreational pilot may act as pilot in command of an aircraft with a maximum horsepower of 180 (not 200).

58.
3051. With respect to daylight hours, what is the earliest time a recreational pilot may take off?

A—One hour before sunrise.
B—At sunrise.
C—At the beginning of morning civil twilight.

Answer (B) is correct (3051). *(FAR 61.101)*
A recreational pilot may not act as pilot in command of an airplane between sunset and sunrise. Thus, the earliest time a recreational pilot may take off is at sunrise.
Answer (A) is incorrect because the earliest time a recreational pilot may take off is at sunrise, not 1 hr. before sunrise. Answer (C) is incorrect because the earliest time a recreational pilot may take off is at sunrise, not at the beginning of morning civil twilight.

59.
3049. What exception, if any, permits a recreational pilot to act as pilot in command of an aircraft carrying a passenger for hire?

A—If the passenger pays no more than the operating expenses.
B—If a donation is made to a charitable organization for the flight.
C—There is no exception.

Answer (C) is correct (3049). *(FAR 61.101)*
Recreational pilots may **not** act as pilot in command of an aircraft for compensation or hire. There is no exception.
Answer (A) is incorrect because a passenger may share expenses, but not pay for the flight. Answer (B) is incorrect because acting as pilot in command of an aircraft used in a passenger carrying airlift and sponsored by a charitable organization is specifically prohibited by FAR 61.101.

60.
3050. May a recreational pilot act as pilot in command of an aircraft in furtherance of a business?

A—Yes, if the flight is only incidental to that business.
B—Yes, providing the aircraft does not carry a person or property for compensation or hire.
C—No, it is not allowed.

Answer (C) is correct (3050). *(FAR 61.101)*
Recreational pilots may **not** act as pilot in command of an aircraft that is used in furtherance of a business. There is no exception.
Answer (A) is incorrect because there is no exception to permit recreational pilots to use aircraft in furtherance of a business. Answer (B) is incorrect because there is no exception to permit recreational pilots to use aircraft in furtherance of a business.

61.
3053. When may a recreational pilot operate to or from an airport that lies within Class C airspace?

A—Anytime the control tower is in operation.
B—When the ceiling is at least 1,000 feet and the surface visibility is at least 3 miles.
C—For the purpose of obtaining an additional certificate or rating while under the supervision of an authorized flight instructor.

Answer (C) is correct (3053). *(FAR 61.101)*
For the purpose of obtaining an additional certificate or rating while under the supervision of an authorized flight instructor, a recreational pilot may fly as sole occupant of an airplane within airspace that requires communication with ATC, such as Class C airspace. [Note that in this situation, (s)he is active as a student pilot, not a recreational pilot.]
Answer (A) is incorrect because a recreational pilot may only fly within airspace that requires communication with ATC (e.g., Class C airspace) when under the supervision of an authorized flight instructor for the purpose of obtaining an additional certificate or rating, regardless of whether the control tower is operating. Answer (B) is incorrect because a recreational pilot may only fly within airspace that requires communication with ATC (e.g., Class C airspace) when under the supervision of an authorized flight instructor for the purpose of obtaining an additional certificate or rating, not simply when the ceiling is at least 1,000 ft. and the surface visibility is at least 3 SM.

62.
3052. If sunset is 2021 and the end of evening civil twilight is 2043, when must a recreational pilot terminate the flight?

A—2021.
B—2043.
C—2121.

Answer (A) is correct (3052). *(FAR 61.101)*
A recreational pilot may not act as pilot in command of an airplane between sunset and sunrise. Thus, if sunset is 2021, the recreational pilot must terminate the flight at 2021.
Answer (B) is incorrect because the requirements regarding recreational pilots are in terms of sunset and sunrise, not evening civil twilight. Answer (C) is incorrect because a recreational pilot must stop flying at sunset, not 1 hr. after sunset.

63.

3054. Under what conditions may a recreational pilot operate at an airport that lies within Class D airspace and that has a part-time control tower in operation?

A—Between sunrise and sunset when the tower is in operation, the ceiling is at least 2,500 feet, and the visibility is at least 3 miles.

B—Any time when the tower is in operation, the ceiling is at least 3,000 feet, and the visibility is more than 1 mile.

C—Between sunrise and sunset when the tower is closed, the ceiling is at least 1,000 feet, and the visibility is at least 3 miles.

Answer (C) is correct (3054). *(FAR 61.101)*
A recreational pilot may not operate in airspace in which communication with ATC is required, e.g., Class D airspace. When a part-time control tower at an airport in Class D airspace is closed, the Class D airspace is classified as either Class E or Class G airspace, which does not require communication with ATC. A recreational pilot must maintain flight or surface visibility of 3 SM or greater, and the flight must be during the day. To operate at an airport in Class E airspace, the ceiling must be at least 1,000 ft. and the visibility at least 3 SM (FAR 91.155).
Answer (A) is incorrect because the condition to operate at an airport with a part-time control tower is that the control tower not be in operation. The ceiling must be at least 1,000 ft., not 2,500 ft., at an airport in Class E airspace. Answer (B) is incorrect because the condition to operate at an airport with a part-time control tower is that the control tower not be in operation. The ceiling must be at least 1,000 ft., not 3,000 ft., at an airport in Class E airspace, and visibility for a recreational pilot must be at least 3 SM, not 1 SM.

64.

3055. When may a recreational pilot fly above 10,000 feet MSL?

A—When 2,000 feet AGL or below.

B—When 2,500 feet AGL or below.

C—When outside of controlled airspace.

Answer (A) is correct (3055). *(FAR 61.101)*
Recreational pilots may **not** act as pilot in command of an aircraft at an altitude of more than 10,000 ft. MSL or 2,000 ft. AGL, whichever is higher. Thus, an airplane may fly above 10,000 ft. MSL only if below 2,000 ft. AGL.
Answer (B) is incorrect because a recreational pilot may fly above 10,000 ft. MSL when 2,000 (not 2,500) ft. AGL or below. Answer (C) is incorrect because the higher of 10,000 ft. MSL or 2,000 ft. AGL limitation on recreational pilots is both in and out of controlled airspace.

65.

3056. During daytime, what is the minimum flight or surface visibility required for recreational pilots in Class G airspace below 10,000 feet MSL?

A—1 mile.

B—3 miles.

C—5 miles.

Answer (B) is correct (3056). *(FAR 61.101)*
The minimum flight or surface visibility required for recreational pilots in Class G airspace below 10,000 ft. MSL during the day is 3 SM.
Answer (A) is incorrect because the minimum daytime flight or surface visibility for recreational pilots in Class G airspace below 10,000 ft. MSL is 3, not 1, SM. Answer (C) is incorrect because the minimum daytime flight or surface visibility for recreational pilots in Class G airspace below 10,000 ft. MSL is 3, not 5, SM.

66.

3620b. (Refer to figure 23, area 1, on page 254.) The visibility and cloud clearance requirements to operate over Sandpoint Airport at less than 700 feet AGL are

A—3 miles and clear of clouds.

B—3 miles and 1,000 feet above, 500 feet below, and 2,000 feet horizontally from each cloud.

C—1 mile and 1,000 feet above, 500 feet below, and 2,000 feet horizontally from each cloud.

Answer (A) is correct (3620b.). *(FAR 61.101 and 91.155)*
Sandpoint Airport is about 1 in. above the number 1 in Fig. 23. The airspace around Sandpoint Airport is Class G from the surface to 2,827 ft. MSL (700 ft. AGL). For a recreational pilot to operate over Sandpoint Airport at less than 700 ft. AGL, the visibility and cloud clearance requirements are 3 SM and clear of clouds.
Answer (B) is incorrect because the cloud clearance of 1,000 ft. above, 500 ft. below, and 2,000 ft. horizontally is the requirement in Class G airspace above 1,200 ft. AGL, not less than 700 ft. AGL. Answer (C) is incorrect because a recreational pilot must have a visibility of, at minimum, 3 SM, not 1 SM, and the cloud clearance of 1,000 ft. above, 500 ft. below, and 2,000 ft. horizontally is the requirement in Class G airspace above 1,200 ft. AGL, not less than 700 ft. AGL.

67.
3621b. (Refer to figure 27, area 2, on page 258.) The visibility and cloud clearance requirements to operate over the town of Cooperstown below 700 feet AGL are

A—1 mile and 1,000 feet above, 500 feet below, and 2,000 feet horizontally from clouds.
B—3 miles and clear of clouds.
C—1 mile and clear of clouds.

Answer (B) is correct (3621b.). *(FAR 61.101 and 91.155)*
The town of Cooperstown is about 3/4 in. above and to the right of the number 2 in Fig. 27. The airspace over the town of Cooperstown (yellow color) is Class G from the surface to 2,124 ft. MSL (700 ft. AGL) since the town lies inside the magenta shaded area. For a recreational pilot to operate over the town of Cooperstown below 700 ft. AGL, the minimum visibility is 3 SM and the cloud clearance requirement is to remain clear of clouds.
Answer (A) is incorrect because the minimum visibility requirement for a recreational pilot is 3 SM, not 1 SM. Additionally, the cloud clearance requirement in Class G airspace below 1,200 ft. AGL is to remain clear of clouds, not to remain 1,000 ft. above, 500 ft. below, and 2,000 ft. horizontally. Answer (C) is incorrect because the minimum visibility requirement for a recreational pilot is 3 SM, not 1 SM.

68.
3057. During daytime, what is the minimum flight visibility required for recreational pilots in controlled airspace below 10,000 feet MSL?

A—1 mile.
B—3 miles.
C—5 miles.

Answer (B) is correct (3057). *(FAR 61.101)*
The minimum flight visibility for recreational pilots in Class E airspace below 10,000 ft. MSL during the day is 3 SM.
Answer (A) is incorrect because the minimum daytime flight or surface visibility for recreational pilots in Class E airspace below 10,000 ft. MSL is 3 SM, not 1 SM. Answer (C) is incorrect because the minimum daytime flight or surface visibility for recreational pilots in Class E airspace below 10,000 ft. MSL is 3 SM, not 5 SM.

69.
3058. Under what conditions, if any, may a recreational pilot demonstrate an aircraft in flight to a prospective buyer?

A—The buyer pays all the operating expenses.
B—The flight is not outside the United States.
C—None.

Answer (C) is correct (3058). *(FAR 61.101)*
Recreational pilots may **not** act as pilot in command of an aircraft to demonstrate that aircraft in flight to a prospective buyer.
Answer (A) is incorrect because it is prohibited. A passenger may only share, not pay all of the operating expenses. Answer (B) is incorrect because recreational pilots may not act as pilot in command to demonstrate an aircraft to a prospective buyer.

70.
3060. When must a recreational pilot have a pilot-in-command flight check?

A—Every 400 hours.
B—Every 180 days.
C—If the pilot has less than 400 total flight hours and has not flown as pilot in command in an aircraft within the preceding 180 days.

Answer (C) is correct (3060). *(FAR 61.101)*
The recreational pilot who has logged fewer than 400 flight hr. and has not logged pilot in command time in an aircraft within the preceding 180 days may **not** act as pilot in command of an aircraft until the pilot has received flight instruction from an authorized flight instructor who certifies in the pilot's logbook that the pilot is competent to act as pilot in command of the aircraft.
Answer (A) is incorrect because a recreational pilot must have a pilot-in-command check if the pilot has less than 400 total flight hr. and has not flown as pilot in command in an aircraft within the preceding 180 days, not every 400 hr. Answer (B) is incorrect because the 180 days refers to the time interval from the most recent time the recreational pilot (with less than 400 flight hr.) acted as pilot in command.

71.
3059. When, if ever, may a recreational pilot act as pilot in command in an aircraft towing a banner?

A—If the pilot has logged 100 hours of flight time in powered aircraft.
B—If the pilot has an endorsement in his/her pilot logbook from an authorized flight instructor.
C—It is not allowed.

Answer (C) is correct (3059). *(FAR 61.101)*
Recreational pilots may **not** act as pilot in command of an aircraft that is towing any object.
Answer (A) is incorrect because a recreational pilot may not act as pilot in command of an airplane that is towing a banner regardless of the amount of flight time. Answer (B) is incorrect because a recreational pilot may not act as pilot in command of an airplane that is towing a banner.

72.
3061. A recreational pilot may fly as sole occupant of an aircraft at night while under the supervision of a flight instructor provided the flight or surface visibility is at least

A—3 miles.
B—4 miles.
C—5 miles.

Answer (C) is correct (3061). *(FAR 61.101)*
For the purposes of obtaining additional certificates or ratings, a recreational pilot may fly as sole occupant in the aircraft between sunset and sunrise while under the supervision of an authorized flight instructor, providing the flight or surface visibility is at least 5 SM.
Answer (A) is incorrect because a recreational pilot may fly as sole occupant of an airplane at night while under the supervision of a flight instructor provided the flight or surface visibility is at least 5 SM, not 3 SM. Answer (B) is incorrect because a recreational pilot may fly as sole occupant of an airplane at night while under the supervision of a flight instructor provided the flight or surface visibility is at least 5 SM, not 4 SM.

73.
3134. What minimum visibility and clearance from clouds are required for a recreational pilot in Class G airspace at 1,200 feet AGL or below during daylight hours?

A—1 mile visibility and clear of clouds.
B—3 miles visibility and clear of clouds.
C—3 miles visibility, 500 feet below the clouds.

Answer (B) is correct (3134). *(FAR 61.101 and 91.155)*
Recreational pilots may **not** act as pilot in command of an aircraft when the visibility is less than 3 SM. Additionally, FAR 91.155 specifies basic VFR weather minimums which permit pilots to fly in Class G airspace 1,200 ft. AGL or below at 1 SM clear of clouds. Thus, the 3-SM recreational pilot limitation and the clear of clouds situation apply.
Answer (A) is incorrect because recreational pilots may never fly when visibility is less than 3 SM. Answer (C) is incorrect because at 1,200 ft. AGL or below in Class G airspace there is no separation from cloud requirement. One must only remain clear of clouds.

74.
3135. Outside controlled airspace, the minimum flight visibility requirement for a recreational pilot flying VFR above 1,200 feet AGL and below 10,000 feet MSL during daylight hours is

A—1 mile.
B—3 miles.
C—5 miles.

Answer (B) is correct (3135). *(FAR 61.101 and 91.155)*
Recreational pilots may **not** act as pilot in command of an aircraft when the visibility is less than 3 SM.
Answer (A) is incorrect because the minimum flight visibility requirement for a recreational pilot is 3 SM, not 1 SM. Answer (C) is incorrect because the minimum flight visibility requirement for a recreational pilot is 3 SM, not 5 SM.

75.
3802. Unless otherwise authorized, if flying a transponder equipped aircraft, a recreational pilot should squawk which VFR code?

A—1200.
B—7600.
C—7700.

Answer (A) is correct (3802). *(AIM Para 4-1-19)*
A recreational pilot, flying a transponder-equipped aircraft, should set that transponder on code (squawk) 1200, which is the VFR code.
Answer (B) is incorrect because 7600 is the lost communication code. Answer (C) is incorrect because 7700 is the general emergency code.

4.6 FAR PART 71
71.75 Extent of Federal Airways

76.
3067. The width of a Federal Airway from either side of the centerline is

A—4 nautical miles.
B—6 nautical miles.
C—8 nautical miles.

Answer (A) is correct (3067). *(FAR 71.75)*
The width of a Federal Airway from either side of the centerline is 4 NM.
Answer (B) is incorrect because the width of a Federal Airway from either side of the centerline is 4 NM, not 6 NM. Answer (C) is incorrect because the width of a Federal Airway from either side of the centerline is 4 NM, not 8 NM.

77.
3068. Unless otherwise specified, Federal Airways include that Class E airspace extending upward from

A—700 feet above the surface up to and including 17,999 feet MSL.
B—1,200 feet above the surface up to and including 17,999 feet MSL.
C—the surface up to and including 18,000 feet MSL.

Answer (B) is correct (3068). *(FAR 71.75)*
Unless otherwise specified, Federal Airways include that Class E airspace extending from 1,200 ft. above the surface up to and including 17,999 ft.
Answer (A) is incorrect because Federal Airways extend from 1,200 (not 700) ft. above the surface up to and including 17,999 ft. MSL. Answer (C) is incorrect because Federal Airways extend from 1,200 ft. above the surface up to and including 17,999 ft. MSL, not 18,000 ft. MSL. The airspace which extends upward from 18,000 ft. MSL is Class A airspace.

4.7 FAR PART 91
91.3 Responsibility and Authority of the Pilot in Command

78.
3070. The final authority as to the operation of an aircraft is the

A—Federal Aviation Administration.
B—pilot in command.
C—aircraft manufacturer.

Answer (B) is correct (3070). *(FAR 91.3)*
The final authority as to the operation of an aircraft is the pilot in command.
Answer (A) is incorrect because the final authority as to the operation of an aircraft is the pilot in command, not the FAA. Answer (C) is incorrect because the final authority as to the operation of an aircraft is the pilot in command, not the aircraft manufacturer.

91.7 Civil Aircraft Airworthiness

79.
3074. Who is responsible for determining if an aircraft is in condition for safe flight?

A—A certificated aircraft mechanic.
B—The pilot in command.
C—The owner or operator.

Answer (B) is correct (3074). *(FAR 91.7)*
The pilot in command of an aircraft is directly responsible for, and is the final authority for, determining whether the airplane is in condition for safe flight.
Answer (A) is incorrect because the pilot in command (not a certificated aircraft mechanic) is responsible for determining if an aircraft is in condition for safe flight. Answer (C) is incorrect because the pilot in command (not the owner or operator) is responsible for determining if an aircraft is in condition for safe flight.

91.9 Civil Aircraft Flight Manual, Marking, and Placard Requirements

80.
3075. Where may an aircraft's operating limitations be found?

A—On the Airworthiness Certificate.
B—In the current, FAA-approved flight manual, approved manual material, markings, and placards, or any combination thereof.
C—In the aircraft airframe and engine logbooks.

Answer (B) is correct (3075). *(FAR 91.9)*
An aircraft's operating limitations may be found in the current, FAA-approved flight manual, approved manual material, markings, and placards, or any combination thereof.
Answer (A) is incorrect because the airworthiness certificate only indicates the airplane was in an airworthy condition when delivered from the factory, not its operating limitations. Answer (C) is incorrect because the airframe and engine logbooks contain the airplane's maintenance record, not its operating limitations.

91.15 Dropping Objects

81.
3076. Under what conditions may objects be dropped from an aircraft?

A—Only in an emergency.
B—If precautions are taken to avoid injury or damage to persons or property on the surface.
C—If prior permission is received from the Federal Aviation Administration.

Answer (B) is correct (3076). *(FAR 91.15)*
No pilot in command of a civil aircraft may allow any object to be dropped from that aircraft in flight that creates a hazard to persons or property. However, this section does not prohibit the dropping of any object if reasonable precautions are taken to avoid injury or damage to persons or property.
Answer (A) is incorrect because objects may be dropped from an aircraft if precautions are taken to avoid injury or damage to persons or property on the surface, not only in an emergency. Answer (C) is incorrect because objects may be dropped from an aircraft if precautions are taken to avoid injury or damage to persons or property on the surface. Prior permission from the FAA is not required.

91.17 Alcohol or Drugs

82.
3079. No person may attempt to act as a crewmember of a civil aircraft with

A—.008 percent by weight or more alcohol in the blood.
B—.004 percent by weight or more alcohol in the blood.
C—.04 percent by weight or more alcohol in the blood.

Answer (C) is correct (3079). *(FAR 91.17)*
No person may act or attempt to act as a crewmember of a civil aircraft, while having a .04% by weight or more alcohol in the blood.
Answer (A) is incorrect because no person may attempt to act as a crewmember of a civil aircraft with .04% (not .008%) by weight or more alcohol in the blood. Answer (B) is incorrect because no person may attempt to act as a crewmember of a civil aircraft with .04% (not .004%) by weight or more in the blood.

83.
3077. A person may not act as a crewmember of a civil aircraft if alcoholic beverages have been consumed by that person within the preceding

A—8 hours.
B—12 hours.
C—24 hours.

Answer (A) is correct (3077). *(FAR 91.17)*
No person may act as a crewmember of a civil aircraft if alcoholic beverages have been consumed by that person within the preceding 8 hr.
Answer (B) is incorrect because no person may act as a crewmember of a civil aircraft within 8 (not 12) hr. after the consumption of any alcoholic beverage. Answer (C) is incorrect because no person may act as a crewmember of a civil aircraft within 8 (not 24) hr. after the consumption of any alcoholic beverage.

84.
3078. Under what condition, if any, may a pilot allow a person who is obviously under the influence of drugs to be carried aboard an aircraft?

A—In an emergency or if the person is a medical patient under proper care.
B—Only if the person does not have access to the cockpit or pilot's compartment.
C—Under no condition.

Answer (A) is correct (3078). *(FAR 91.17)*
No pilot of a civil aircraft may allow a person who demonstrates by manner or physical indications that the individual is under the influence of drugs to be carried in that aircraft, except in an emergency or if the person is a medical patient under proper care.
Answer (B) is incorrect because no pilot may allow a person who is obviously under the influence of drugs to be carried aboard an aircraft except in an emergency or if the person is a medical patient under proper care, not if that person does not have access to the cockpit or pilot's compartment. Answer (C) is incorrect because a pilot may allow a person who is obviously under the influence of drugs to be carried aboard an aircraft in an emergency or if the person is a medical patient under proper care.

91.103 Preflight Action

85.
3081. Preflight action, as required for all flights away from the vicinity of an airport, shall include

A—the designation of an alternate airport.
B—a study of arrival procedures at airports/heliports of intended use.
C—an alternate course of action if the flight cannot be completed as planned.

Answer (C) is correct (3081). *(FAR 91.103)*
Preflight actions for flights not in the vicinity of an airport include checking weather reports and forecasts, fuel requirements, alternatives available if the planned flight cannot be completed, and any known traffic delays.
Answer (A) is incorrect because preflight action, as required for all flights away from the vicinity of an airport, shall include an alternate course of action if the flight cannot be completed as planned, not just the designation of an alternate airport. Answer (B) is incorrect because preflight action, as required for all flights away from the vicinity of an airport, shall include an alternate course of action if the flight cannot be completed as planned, not simply a study of arrival procedures at airports of intended use.

86.
3082. In addition to other preflight actions for a VFR flight away from the vicinity of the departure airport, regulations specifically require the pilot in command to

A—review traffic control light signal procedures.
B—check the accuracy of the navigation equipment and the emergency locator transmitter (ELT).
C—determine runway lengths at airports of intended use and the aircraft's takeoff and landing distance data.

Answer (C) is correct (3082). *(FAR 91.103)*
Preflight actions for a VFR flight away from the vicinity of the departure airport specifically require the pilot in command to determine runway lengths at airports of intended use and the aircraft's takeoff and landing distance data.
Answer (A) is incorrect because preflight actions for a VFR flight away from the vicinity of an airport require the pilot in command to determine runway lengths at airports of intended use and takeoff and landing distance data, not a review of traffic control light signal procedures. Answer (B) is incorrect because preflight actions for a VFR flight away from the vicinity of an airport require the pilot in command to determine runway lengths at airports of intended use and takeoff and landing distance data, not a check of navigation equipment accuracy and the ELT.

87.
3080. Which preflight action is specifically required of the pilot prior to each flight?

A—Check the aircraft logbooks for appropriate entries.
B—Become familiar with all available information concerning the flight.
C—Review wake turbulence avoidance procedures.

Answer (B) is correct (3080). *(FAR 91.103)*
Each pilot in command will, before beginning a flight, become familiar with all available information concerning that flight.
Answer (A) is incorrect because during preflight action the pilot is required to become familiar with all available information concerning the flight, not just to check the aircraft logbook for appropriate entries. Answer (C) is incorrect because during preflight action the pilot is required to become familiar with all available information concerning the flight, not simply review wake turbulence avoidance procedures.

91.105 Flight Crewmembers at Stations

88.
3083. Flight crewmembers are required to keep their safety belts and shoulder harnesses fastened during

A—takeoffs and landings.
B—all flight conditions.
C—flight in turbulent air.

Answer (A) is correct (3083). *(FAR 91.105)*
During takeoff and landing, and while en route, each required flight crewmember shall keep his/her safety belt fastened while at the crewmember station. If shoulder harnesses are available, they must be used by crew-members during takeoff and landing.
Answer (B) is incorrect because flight crewmembers are required to keep their shoulder harnesses fastened only during takeoffs and landings, not during all flight conditions. Answer (C) is incorrect because flight crew-members are required to keep their shoulder harnesses fastened only during takeoffs and landings, not during flight in turbulent air.

89.
3084. Which best describes the flight conditions under which flight crewmembers are specifically required to keep their safety belts and shoulder harnesses fastened?

A—Safety belts during takeoff and landing; shoulder harnesses during takeoff and landing.
B—Safety belts during takeoff and landing; shoulder harnesses during takeoff and landing and while en route.
C—Safety belts during takeoff and landing and while en route; shoulder harnesses during takeoff and landing.

Answer (C) is correct (3084). *(FAR 91.105)*
During takeoff and landing, and while en route, each required flight crewmember shall keep his/her safety belt fastened while at the crewmember station. If shoulder harnesses are available, they must be used by crewmembers during takeoff and landing.
Answer (A) is incorrect because safety belts must be worn while en route. Answer (B) is incorrect because safety belts (not shoulder harnesses) are required to be fastened while en route.

91.107 Use of Safety Belts, Shoulder Harnesses, and Child Restraint Systems

90.
3087. Safety belts are required to be properly secured about which persons in an aircraft and when?

A—Pilots only, during takeoffs and landings.
B—Passengers, during taxi, takeoffs, and landings only.
C—Each person on board the aircraft during the entire flight.

Answer (B) is correct (3087). *(FAR 91.107)*
Regulations require that safety belts in an airplane be properly secured about all passengers during taxi, takeoffs, and landings.
Answer (A) is incorrect because regulations require passengers as well as crewmembers to wear safety belts during takeoffs and landings. Answer (C) is incorrect because, although it is a good procedure, safety belts are required only for passengers during taxi, takeoffs, and landings.

91.
3085. With respect to passengers, what obligation, if any, does a pilot in command have concerning the use of safety belts?

A—The pilot in command must instruct the passengers to keep their safety belts fastened for the entire flight.
B—The pilot in command must brief the passengers on the use of safety belts and notify them to fasten their safety belts during taxi, takeoff, and landing.
C—The pilot in command has no obligation in regard to passengers' use of safety belts.

Answer (B) is correct (3085). *(FAR 91.107)*
The pilot in command is required to brief the pas-sengers on the use of safety belts and notify them to fasten their safety belts during taxi, takeoff, and landing.
Answer (A) is incorrect because the pilot in command is only required to notify the passengers to fasten their safety belts during taxi, takeoff, and landing, not during the entire flight. Answer (C) is incorrect because the pilot in command has the obligation both to instruct passengers on the use of safety belts and to require their use during taxi, takeoffs, and landings.

92.

3086. With certain exceptions, safety belts are required to be secured about passengers during

A—taxi, takeoffs, and landings.
B—all flight conditions.
C—flight in turbulent air.

Answer (A) is correct (3086). *(FAR 91.107)*
During the taxi, takeoff, and landing of U.S. registered civil aircraft, each person on board that aircraft must occupy a seat or berth with a safety belt and shoulder harness, if installed, properly secured about him/her. However, a person who has not reached his/her second birthday may be held by an adult who is occupying a seat or berth, and a person on board for the purpose of engaging in sport parachuting may use the floor of the aircraft as a seat (but is still required to use approved safety belts for takeoff).
Answer (B) is incorrect because safety belts are required to be secured about passengers only during taxi, takeoffs, and landings, not during all flight conditions. Answer (C) is incorrect because safety belts are required to be secured about passengers during taxi, takeoffs, and landings, not during flight in turbulent air.

91.111 Operating near Other Aircraft

93.

3088. No person may operate an aircraft in formation flight

A—over a densely populated area.
B—in Class D airspace under special VFR.
C—except by prior arrangement with the pilot in command of each aircraft.

Answer (C) is correct (3088). *(FAR 91.111)*
No person may operate in formation flight except by arrangement with the pilot in command of each aircraft in formation.
Answer (A) is incorrect because no person may operate an aircraft in formation flight except by prior arrangement with the pilot in command of each aircraft. There are no restrictions about formation flights over a densely populated area. Answer (B) is incorrect because no person may operate an aircraft in formation flight except by prior arrangement with the pilot in command of each aircraft. There are no restrictions about formation flight in Class D airspace under special VFR.

91.113 Right-of-Way Rules: Except Water Operations

94.

3092. An airplane and an airship are converging. If the airship is left of the airplane's position, which aircraft has the right-of-way?

A—The airship.
B—The airplane.
C—Each pilot should alter course to the right.

Answer (A) is correct (3092). *(FAR 91.113)*
When aircraft of different categories are converging, the less maneuverable aircraft has the right-of-way. Thus, the airship has the right-of-way in this question.
Answer (B) is incorrect because, when converging, the airship has the right-of-way over an airplane or rotorcraft. Answer (C) is incorrect because each pilot would alter course to the right if the airship and airplane were approaching head-on, or nearly so, not converging.

95.

3095. When two or more aircraft are approaching an airport for the purpose of landing, the right-of-way belongs to the aircraft

A—that has the other to its right.
B—that is the least maneuverable.
C—at the lower altitude, but it shall not take advantage of this rule to cut in front of or to overtake another.

Answer (C) is correct (3095). *(FAR 91.113)*
When two or more aircraft are approaching an airport for the purpose of landing, the aircraft at the lower altitude has the right-of-way, but it shall not take advantage of this rule to cut in front of or to overtake another aircraft.
Answer (A) is incorrect because when two or more aircraft are approaching an airport for the purpose of landing, the right-of-way belongs to the aircraft at the lower altitude, not the aircraft that has the other to the right. Answer (B) is incorrect because when two or more aircraft are approaching an airport for the purpose of landing, the right-of-way belongs to the aircraft at the lower altitude, not the aircraft that is the least maneuverable.

96.
3091. Which aircraft has the right-of-way over the other aircraft listed?

A—Glider.
B—Airship.
C—Aircraft refueling other aircraft.

Answer (A) is correct (3091). *(FAR 91.113)*
If aircraft of different categories are converging, the right-of-way depends upon who has the least maneuverability. A glider has right-of-way over an airship, airplane or rotorcraft.
Answer (B) is incorrect because an airship has the right-of-way over an airplane or rotorcraft, not a glider. Answer (C) is incorrect because aircraft refueling have right-of-way over all engine-driven aircraft. A glider has no engine.

97.
3094. What action should the pilots of a glider and an airplane take if on a head-on collision course?

A—The airplane pilot should give way to the left.
B—The glider pilot should give way to the right.
C—Both pilots should give way to the right.

Answer (C) is correct (3094). *(FAR 91.113)*
When aircraft are approaching head-on, or nearly so (regardless of category), each aircraft shall alter course to the right.
Answer (A) is incorrect because the glider has the right-of-way unless the two aircraft are approaching head-on, in which case both pilots should give way by turning to the right. Answer (B) is incorrect because both pilots of a glider and an airplane should give way to the right, not only the glider pilot.

98.
3090. What action is required when two aircraft of the same category converge, but not head-on?

A—The faster aircraft shall give way.
B—The aircraft on the left shall give way.
C—Each aircraft shall give way to the right.

Answer (B) is correct (3090). *(FAR 91.113)*
When two aircraft of the same category converge (but not head-on), the aircraft to the other's right has the right-of-way. Thus, an airplane on the left gives way to the airplane on the right.
Answer (A) is incorrect because when two aircraft of the same category converge (but not head-on), the aircraft on the left (not the faster aircraft) shall give way. Answer (C) is incorrect because the required action when two aircraft are approaching head-on or nearly so is for each aircraft to give way to the right.

99.
3093. Which aircraft has the right-of-way over the other aircraft listed?

A—Airship.
B—Aircraft towing other aircraft.
C—Gyroplane.

Answer (B) is correct (3093). *(FAR 91.113)*
An aircraft towing or refueling another aircraft has the right-of-way over all engine-driven aircraft. An airship is an engine-driven, lighter-than-air aircraft that can be steered.
Answer (A) is incorrect because an airship has the right-of-way over an airplane or rotorcraft, but not an aircraft towing other aircraft. Answer (C) is incorrect because a gyroplane (which is a rotorcraft) must give way to both an airship and aircraft towing other aircraft.

100.
3089. Which aircraft has the right-of-way over all other air traffic?

A—A balloon.
B—An aircraft in distress.
C—An aircraft on final approach to land.

Answer (B) is correct (3089). *(FAR 91.113)*
An aircraft in distress has the right-of-way over all other aircraft.
Answer (A) is incorrect because an aircraft in distress (not a balloon) has the right-of-way over all other air traffic. Answer (C) is incorrect because an aircraft in distress (not an aircraft on final approach to land) has the right-of-way over all other air traffic.

91.115 Right-of-Way Rules: Water Operations

101.
3096. A seaplane and a motorboat are on crossing courses. If the motorboat is to the left of the seaplane, which has the right-of-way?

A—The motorboat.
B—The seaplane.
C—Both should alter course to the right.

Answer (B) is correct (3096). *(FAR 91.115)*
When aircraft, or an aircraft and a vessel (e.g., a motorboat), are on crossing courses, the aircraft or vessel to the other's right has the right-of-way. Since the seaplane is to the motorboat's right, the seaplane has the right-of-way.
Answer (A) is incorrect because on crossing courses the aircraft or vessel to the other's right has the right-of-way. Since the seaplane is to the right of the motorboat, the seaplane (not the motorboat) has the right-of-way. Answer (C) is incorrect because both would alter course to the right only if they were approaching head-on, or nearly so.

91.117 Aircraft Speed

102.
3100. When flying in a VFR corridor designated through Class B airspace, the maximum speed authorized is

A—180 knots.
B—200 knots.
C—250 knots.

Answer (B) is correct (3100). *(FAR 91.117)*
No person may operate an airplane in a VFR corridor designated through Class B airspace at an indicated airspeed of more than 200 kt. (230 MPH).
Answer (A) is incorrect because when flying in a VFR corridor designated through Class B airspace, the maximum speed authorized is 200 (not 180) kt. Answer (C) is incorrect because 250 kt. is the maximum speed authorized below 10,000 ft. MSL, not when flying in a VFR corridor through Class B airspace.

103.
3097. Unless otherwise authorized, what is the maximum indicated airspeed at which a person may operate an aircraft below 10,000 feet MSL?

A—200 knots.
B—250 knots.
C—288 knots.

Answer (B) is correct (3097). *(FAR 91.117)*
Unless otherwise authorized by ATC, no person may operate an aircraft below 10,000 ft. MSL at an indicated airspeed of more than 250 kt. (288 MPH).
Answer (A) is incorrect because 200 kt. is the maximum indicated airspeed when at or below 2,500 ft. above the surface and within 4 NM of the primary airport of a Class C or Class D airspace area, not the maximum indicated airspeed for operations below 10,000 ft. MSL. Answer (C) is incorrect because the maximum indicated airspeed below 10,000 ft. MSL is 288 MPH, not 288 kt.

104.
3099. When flying in the airspace underlying Class B airspace, the maximum speed authorized is

A—200 knots.
B—230 knots.
C—250 knots.

Answer (A) is correct (3099). *(FAR 91.117)*
No person may operate an airplane in the airspace underlying Class B airspace at an indicated airspeed of more than 200 kt. (230 MPH).
Answer (B) is incorrect because the maximum indicated airspeed authorized in the airspace underlying Class B airspace is 230 MPH, not 230 kt. Answer (C) is incorrect because 250 kt. is the maximum indicated airspeed when operating an airplane below 10,000 ft. MSL, not in the airspace underlying Class B airspace.

105.
3098. Unless otherwise authorized, the maximum indicated airspeed at which aircraft may be flown when at or below 2,500 feet AGL and within 4 nautical miles of the primary airport of Class C airspace is

A—200 knots.
B—230 knots.
C—250 knots.

Answer (A) is correct (3098). *(FAR 91.117)*
Unless otherwise authorized, the maximum indicated airspeed at which an airplane may be flown when at or below 2,500 ft. AGL and within 4 NM of the primary airport of Class C airspace is 200 kt. (230 mph).
Answer (B) is incorrect because 230 mph, not 230 kt., is the maximum indicated airspeed at which an airplane may be flown when at or below 2,500 ft. AGL and within 4 NM of the primary airport of a Class C airspace area. Answer (C) is incorrect because 250 kt. is the maximum indicated airspeed at which an airplane may be flown below 10,000 ft. MSL or in Class B airspace, not when at or below 2,500 ft. AGL and within 4 NM of the primary airport of a Class C airspace area.

91.119 Minimum Safe Altitudes: General

106.
3104. Except when necessary for takeoff or landing, an aircraft may not be operated closer than what distance from any person, vessel, vehicle, or structure?

A—500 feet.
B—700 feet.
C—1,000 feet.

Answer (A) is correct (3104). *(FAR 91.119)*
Over other than congested areas, an altitude of 500 ft. above the surface is required. Over open water and sparsely populated areas, a distance of 500 ft. from any person, vessel, vehicle, or structure must be maintained.
Answer (B) is incorrect because an aircraft may not be operated closer than 500 (not 700) ft. from any person, vessel, vehicle, or structure. Answer (C) is incorrect because an aircraft may not be operated closer than 500 (not 1,000) ft. from any person, vessel, vehicle, or structure.

107.
3101. Except when necessary for takeoff or landing, what is the minimum safe altitude for a pilot to operate an aircraft anywhere?

A—An altitude allowing, if a power unit fails, an emergency landing without undue hazard to persons or property on the surface.
B—An altitude of 500 feet above the surface and no closer than 500 feet to any person, vessel, vehicle, or structure.
C—An altitude of 500 feet above the highest obstacle within a horizontal radius of 1,000 feet.

Answer (A) is correct (3101). *(FAR 91.119)*
Except when necessary for takeoff or landing, no person may operate an aircraft anywhere below an altitude allowing, if a power unit fails, an emergency landing without undue hazard to persons or property on the surface.
Answer (B) is incorrect because an altitude of 500 ft. above the surface is the minimum safe altitude over other than congested areas and no closer than 500 ft. to any person, vessel, vehicle, or structure is the minimum safe altitude over open water or sparsely populated areas. Answer (C) is incorrect because the minimum safe altitude anywhere is an altitude that allows an emergency landing to be made without undue hazards to persons or property on the surface, not 500 ft. above the highest obstacle within a horizontal radius of 1,000 ft.

108.
3102. Except when necessary for takeoff or landing, what is the minimum safe altitude required for a pilot to operate an aircraft over congested areas?

A—An altitude of 1,000 feet above any person, vessel, vehicle, or structure.
B—An altitude of 500 feet above the highest obstacle within a horizontal radius of 1,000 feet of the aircraft.
C—An altitude of 1,000 feet above the highest obstacle within a horizontal radius of 2,000 feet of the aircraft.

Answer (C) is correct (3102). *(FAR 91.119)*
When operating an aircraft over any congested area of a city, town, or settlement, or over an open air assembly of persons, a pilot must remain at an altitude of 1,000 ft. above the highest obstacle within a horizontal radius of 2,000 ft. of the aircraft.
Answer (A) is incorrect because the minimum safe altitude to operate an aircraft over a congested area is an altitude of 1,000 ft. above the highest obstacle (not above any person, vessel, vehicle, or structure) within a horizontal distance of 2,000 ft. Answer (B) is incorrect because the minimum safe altitude to operate an aircraft over a congested area is an altitude of 1,000 (not 500) ft. above the highest obstacle within a horizontal radius of 2,000 (not 1,000) ft. of the aircraft.

109.
3103. Except when necessary for takeoff or landing, what is the minimum safe altitude required for a pilot to operate an aircraft over other than a congested area?

A—An altitude allowing, if a power unit fails, an emergency landing without undue hazard to persons or property on the surface.
B—An altitude of 500 feet AGL, except over open water or a sparsely populated area, which requires 500 feet from any person, vessel, vehicle, or structure.
C—An altitude of 500 feet above the highest obstacle within a horizontal radius of 1,000 feet.

Answer (B) is correct (3103). *(FAR 91.119)*
Over other than congested areas, an altitude of 500 ft. above the surface is required. Over open water and sparsely populated areas, a distance of 500 ft. from any person, vessel, vehicle, or structure must be maintained.
Answer (A) is incorrect because an altitude allowing, if a power unit fails, an emergency landing without undue hazard to persons or property on the surface is the general minimum safe altitude for anywhere, not specifically for operation over other than a congested area. Answer (C) is incorrect because the minimum safe altitude over other than a congested area is an altitude of 500 ft. AGL (not above the highest obstacle within a horizontal radius of 1,000 ft.), except over open water or a sparsely populated area, which requires 500 ft. from any person, vessel, vehicle, or structure.

91.121 Altimeter Settings

110.
3106. Prior to takeoff, the altimeter should be set to which altitude or altimeter setting?

A—The current local altimeter setting, if available, or the departure airport elevation.
B—The corrected density altitude of the departure airport.
C—The corrected pressure altitude for the departure airport.

Answer (A) is correct (3106). *(FAR 91.121)*
Prior to takeoff, the altimeter should be set to the local altimeter setting, or to the departure airport elevation.
Answer (B) is incorrect because density altitude is pressure altitude corrected for nonstandard temperature variations and is determined from flight computers or graphs, not an altimeter. Answer (C) is incorrect because pressure altitude is only used at or above 18,000 ft. MSL.

111.
3105. If an altimeter setting is not available before flight, to which altitude should the pilot adjust the altimeter?

A—The elevation of the nearest airport corrected to mean sea level.
B—The elevation of the departure area.
C—Pressure altitude corrected for nonstandard temperature.

Answer (B) is correct (3105). *(FAR 91.121)*
When the local altimeter setting is not available at takeoff, the pilot should adjust the altimeter to the elevation of the departure area.
Answer (A) is incorrect because airport elevation is always expressed in true altitude, or feet above MSL. Answer (C) is incorrect because pressure altitude adjusted for nonstandard temperature is density altitude, not true altitude.

112.
3107. At what altitude shall the altimeter be set to 29.92, when climbing to cruising flight level?

A—14,500 feet MSL.
B—18,000 feet MSL.
C—24,000 feet MSL.

Answer (B) is correct (3107). *(FAR 91.121)*
Pressure altitude is the altitude used for all flights at and above 18,000 ft. MSL, i.e., in Class A airspace. When climbing to or above 18,000 ft. MSL, one does not use local altimeter settings, but rather 29.92" Hg after reaching 18,000 ft. MSL.
Answer (A) is incorrect because 14,500 ft. MSL is the base of Class E airspace, unless otherwise indicated. Answer (C) is incorrect because 24,000 ft. MSL is the altitude above which DME is required aboard the airplane.

91.123 Compliance with ATC Clearances and Instructions

113.
3073. When must a pilot who deviates from a regulation during an emergency send a written report of that deviation to the Administrator?

A—Within 7 days.
B—Within 10 days.
C—Upon request.

Answer (C) is correct (3073). *(FAR 91.3)*
A pilot who deviates from a regulation during an emergency must send a written report of that deviation to the Administrator of the FAA only upon request.
Answer (A) is incorrect because a written report of a deviation from a regulation during an emergency must be sent to the Administrator upon request, not within 7 days. Answer (B) is incorrect because a written report of a deviation from a regulation during an emergency must be sent to the Administrator upon request, not within 10 days.

114.
3109. When would a pilot be required to submit a detailed report of an emergency which caused the pilot to deviate from an ATC clearance?

A—When requested by ATC.
B—Immediately.
C—Within 7 days.

Answer (A) is correct (3109). *(FAR 91.123)*
Each pilot in command who is given priority by ATC in an emergency shall, if requested by ATC, submit a detailed report within 48 hrs. to the manager of that ATC facility.
Answer (B) is incorrect because a pilot would be required to submit a detailed report of an emergency which caused him/her to deviate from an ATC clearance when requested by ATC (not immediately). Answer (C) is incorrect because a pilot would be required to submit a detailed report of an emergency which caused him/her to deviate from an ATC clearance when requested by ATC (not within 7 days).

115.
3072. If an in-flight emergency requires immediate action, the pilot in command may

A—deviate from the FAR's to the extent required to meet the emergency, but must submit a written report to the Administrator within 24 hours.
B—deviate from the FAR's to the extent required to meet that emergency.
C—not deviate from the FAR's unless prior to the deviation approval is granted by the Administrator.

Answer (B) is correct (3072). *(FAR 91.3)*
In an in-flight emergency requiring immediate action, the pilot in command may deviate from the FARs to the extent required to meet that emergency. A written report of the deviation must be sent to the Administrator of the FAA only if requested.
Answer (A) is incorrect because a written report must be sent to the Administrator of the FAA only upon request. Answer (C) is incorrect because the pilot in command may deviate from the FARs to the extent required to meet that emergency without the approval of the Administrator of the FAA.

116.
3108. When an ATC clearance has been obtained, no pilot in command may deviate from that clearance, unless that pilot obtains an amended clearance. The one exception to this regulation is

A—when the clearance states "at pilot's discretion."
B—an emergency.
C—if the clearance contains a restriction.

Answer (B) is correct (3108). *(FAR 91.123)*
When an ATC clearance has been obtained, no pilot in command may deviate from that clearance, except in an emergency, unless an amended clearance is obtained.
Answer (A) is incorrect because the words, "at the pilot's discretion" are part of an ATC clearance, so this is not an exception. Answer (C) is incorrect because any restriction is still part of the clearance, so this is not an exception.

117.
3110. What action, if any, is appropriate if the pilot deviates from an ATC instruction during an emergency and is given priority?

A—Take no special action since you are pilot in command.
B—File a detailed report within 48 hours to the chief of the appropriate ATC facility, if requested.
C—File a report to the FAA Administrator, as soon as possible.

Answer (B) is correct (3110). *(FAR 91.123)*
Each pilot in command who is given priority by ATC in an emergency shall, if requested by ATC, submit a detailed report within 48 hrs. to the manager of that ATC facility.
Answer (A) is incorrect because as pilot in command you must file a detailed report within 48 hr. to the chief of the appropriate ATC facility, if requested. Answer (C) is incorrect because a detailed report must be filed to the chief of the appropriate ATC facility (not the FAA Administrator) if requested (not as soon as possible).

91.130 Operations in Class C Airspace

118.
3124. Two-way radio communication must be established with the Air Traffic Control facility having jurisdiction over the area prior to entering which class airspace?

A—Class C.
B—Class E.
C—Class G.

Answer (A) is correct (3124). *(FAR 91.130)*
No person may operate an aircraft in Class C airspace unless two-way radio communication is established with the ATC facility having jurisdiction over the airspace prior to entering that area.
Answer (B) is incorrect because, while a Class E airspace area is controlled airspace, two-way radio communication is not required to be established with ATC prior to entering VFR weather conditions. Answer (C) is incorrect because two-way radio communication with ATC is not required for any operations in Class G airspace.

91.131 Operations in Class B Airspace

119.
3126. What minimum pilot certification is required for operation within Class B airspace?

A—Recreational Pilot Certificate.
B—Private Pilot Certificate or Student Pilot Certificate with appropriate logbook endorsements.
C—Private Pilot Certificate with an instrument rating.

Answer (B) is correct (3126). *(FAR 91.131)*
No person may take off or land aircraft at an airport within Class B airspace or operate an aircraft within Class B airspace unless they are at least a private pilot or, if a student pilot, they have the appropriate logbook endorsement required by FAR 61.95.
Answer (A) is incorrect because a recreational pilot is restricted from operating in airspace (e.g., Class B airspace) which requires communication with ATC. Answer (C) is incorrect because an instrument rating is not required to operate in Class B airspace.

120.
3127. What minimum pilot certification is required for operation within Class B airspace?

A—Private Pilot Certificate or Student Pilot Certificate with appropriate logbook endorsements.
B—Commercial Pilot Certificate.
C—Private Pilot Certificate with an instrument rating.

Answer (A) is correct (3127). *(FAR 91.131)*
No person may take off or land aircraft at an airport within Class B airspace or operate an aircraft within Class B airspace unless they are at least a private pilot or, if a student pilot, they have the appropriate logbook endorsement required by FAR 61.95.
Answer (B) is incorrect because the minimum pilot certification to operate in Class B airspace is a private pilot certificate or student pilot certificate with appropriate logbook endorsements, not a commercial pilot certificate. Answer (C) is incorrect because an instrument rating is not required to operate in Class B airspace.

121.
3166. With certain exceptions, all aircraft within 30 miles of a Class B primary airport from the surface upward to 10,000 feet MSL must be equipped with

A—an operable VOR or TACAN receiver and an ADF receiver.
B—instruments and equipment required for IFR operations.
C—an operable transponder having either Mode S or 4096-code capability with Mode C automatic altitude reporting capability.

Answer (C) is correct (3166). *(FAR 91.131)*
All aircraft within 30 NM of a Class B primary airport must be equipped with an operable transponder having either Mode S or 4096-code capability with Mode C automatic altitude reporting capability. The exception is any aircraft which was not originally certificated with an engine-driven electrical system or which has not subsequently been certified with such a system installed, balloon, or glider may conduct operations in the airspace within 30 NM of a Class B airspace primary airport provided such operations are conducted (1) outside any Class A, Class B, or Class C airspace area; and (2) below the altitude of the ceiling of a Class B or Class C airspace area or 10,000 ft. MSL, whichever is lower.
Answer (A) is incorrect because an operable VOR or TACAN receiver and an ADF receiver are not required within 30 NM of a Class B primary airport, only an operable transponder having either Mode S or 4096-code capability with Mode C automatic altitude reporting capability. Answer (B) is incorrect because an operable transponder having either Mode S or 4096-code capability with Mode C automatic altitude reporting capability is required within 30 NM of a Class B primary airport, not instruments and equipment required for IFR operations.

91.133 Restricted and Prohibited Areas

122.
3783. Under what condition, if any, may pilots fly through a restricted area?

A—When flying on airways with an ATC clearance.
B—With the controlling agency's authorization.
C—Regulations do not allow this.

Answer (B) is correct (3783). *(FAR 91.133)*
An aircraft may not be operated within a restricted area unless permission has been obtained from the controlling agency. Frequently, the ATC within the area acts as the controlling agent's authorization; e.g., an approach control in a military restricted area can permit aircraft to enter it when the restricted area is not active.
Answer (A) is incorrect because airways do not penetrate restricted areas. Answer (C) is incorrect because restricted areas may be entered with proper authorization.

91.135 Operations in Class A Airspace

123.
3130. In which type of airspace are VFR flights prohibited?

A—Class A.
B—Class B.
C—Class C.

Answer (A) is correct (3130). *(FAR 91.135)*
Class A airspace (from 18,000 ft. MSL up to and including FL 600) require operation under IFR at specific flight levels assigned by ATC. Accordingly, VFR flights are prohibited.
Answer (B) is incorrect because VFR flights are prohibited in Class A, not Class B, airspace. Answer (C) is incorrect because VFR flights are prohibited in Class A, not Class C, airspace.

91.151 Fuel Requirements for Flight in VFR Conditions

124.
3132. What is the specific fuel requirement for flight under VFR at night in an airplane?

A—Enough to complete the flight at normal cruising speed with adverse wind conditions.
B—Enough to fly to the first point of intended landing and to fly after that for 30 minutes at normal cruising speed.
C—Enough to fly to the first point of intended landing and to fly after that for 45 minutes at normal cruising speed.

Answer (C) is correct (3132). *(FAR 91.151)*
    The night VFR requirement is enough fuel to fly to the first point of intended landing and to fly thereafter for 45 min. at normal cruising speed given forecast conditions.
    Answer (A) is incorrect because the fuel requirements are based upon the wind conditions existing that day plus the 45-min. reserve. Answer (B) is incorrect because a 30-min. reserve is the requirement for day flight.

125.
3131. What is the specific fuel requirement for flight under VFR during daylight hours in an airplane?

A—Enough to complete the flight at normal cruising speed with adverse wind conditions.
B—Enough to fly to the first point of intended landing and to fly after that for 30 minutes at normal cruising speed.
C—Enough to fly to the first point of intended landing and to fly after that for 45 minutes at normal cruising speed.

Answer (B) is correct (3131). *(FAR 91.151)*
    The day-VFR requirement is enough fuel to fly to the first point of intended landing and thereafter for 30 min. at normal cruising speed.
    Answer (A) is incorrect because the fuel requirements are based upon the wind conditions existing that day plus the 30-min. reserve. Answer (C) is incorrect because a 45-min. reserve is the requirement for night flight.

91.155 Basic VFR Weather Minimums

126.
3145. The minimum flight visibility required for VFR flights above 10,000 feet MSL and more than 1,200 feet AGL in controlled airspace is

A—1 mile.
B—3 miles.
C—5 miles.

Answer (C) is correct (3145). *(FAR 91.155)*
    Controlled airspace is the generic term for Class A, B, C, D, or E airspace. Of these, only in Class E airspace is the minimum flight visibility 5 SM for VFR flights at or above 10,000 ft. MSL.
    Note: AGL altitudes are not used in controlled airspace. In Class E airspace, the visibility and distance from clouds are given for (1) below 10,000 ft. MSL and (2) at or above 10,000 ft. MSL.
    Answer (A) is incorrect because 1 SM is the visibility in Class G, not Class E, airspace when more than 1,200 ft. AGL but less, not more, than 10,000 ft. MSL. Answer (B) is incorrect because 3 SM is the minimum visibility in Class E airspace when below, not at or above, 10,000 ft. MSL.

127.
3141. VFR flight in controlled airspace above 1,200 feet AGL and below 10,000 feet MSL requires a minimum visibility and vertical cloud clearance of

A—3 miles, and 500 feet below or 1,000 feet above the clouds in controlled airspace.
B—5 miles, and 1,000 feet below or 1,000 feet above the clouds at all altitudes.
C—5 miles, and 1,000 feet below or 1,000 feet above the clouds only in Class A airspace.

Answer (A) is correct (3141). *(FAR 91.155)*
    Controlled airspace is the generic term for Class A, B, C, D, or E airspace. Only in Class C, D, or below 10,000 ft. MSL in Class E airspace are the minimum flight visibility and vertical distance from cloud for VFR flight required to be 3 SM, and 500 ft. below or 1,000 ft. above the clouds.
    Note: AGL altitudes are not used in controlled airspace. In Class E airspace, the visibility and distance from clouds are given for (1) below 10,000 ft. MSL and (2) at or above 10,000 ft. MSL.
    Answer (B) is incorrect because 5 SM and 1,000 ft. above and below the clouds is the minimum visibility and vertical cloud clearance in Class E airspace at altitudes at or above, not below, 10,000 ft. MSL. Answer (C) is incorrect because VFR flight in Class A airspace is prohibited.

128.
3146. For VFR flight operations above 10,000 feet MSL and more than 1,200 feet AGL, the minimum horizontal distance from clouds required is

A—1,000 feet.
B—2,000 feet.
C—1 mile.

129.
3149. The basic VFR weather minimums for operating an aircraft within Class D airspace are

A—500-foot ceiling and 1 mile visibility.
B—1,000-foot ceiling and 3 miles visibility.
C—clear of clouds and 2 miles visibility.

130.
3139. The minimum distance from clouds required for VFR operations on an airway below 10,000 feet MSL is

A—remain clear of clouds.
B—500 feet below, 1,000 feet above, and 2,000 feet horizontally.
C—500 feet above, 1,000 feet below, and 2,000 feet horizontally.

131.
3137. What minimum visibility and clearance from clouds are required for VFR operations in Class G airspace at 700 feet AGL or below during daylight hours?

A—1 mile visibility and clear of clouds.
B—1 mile visibility, 500 feet below, 1,000 feet above, and 2,000 feet horizontal clearance from clouds.
C—3 miles visibility and clear of clouds.

Answer (C) is correct (3146). *(FAR 91.155)*
For VFR flight operations in Class G airspace at altitudes more than 1,200 ft. AGL and at or above 10,000 ft. MSL, the minimum horizontal distance from clouds required is 1 SM.
Note: The FAA question fails to specify what type of airspace. Since AGL altitudes are not used in controlled airspace (Class A, B, C, D, or E), that implies Class G airspace.
Answer (A) is incorrect because 1,000 ft. is the minimum vertical, not horizontal, distance from the clouds. Answer (B) is incorrect because 2,000 ft. is the minimum horizontal distance from clouds in Class G airspace at night below, not above, 10,000 ft. MSL and when at altitudes more than 1,200 ft. AGL but less, not more, than 10,000 ft. MSL.

Answer (B) is correct (3149). *(FAR 91.155)*
The basic VFR weather minimums for operating an aircraft within Class D airspace are 1,000-ft. ceiling and 3 SM visibility.
Answer (A) is incorrect because the basic VFR weather minimums for operating an aircraft in Class D airspace are 1,000-ft., not 500-ft., ceiling and 3, not 1, SM visibility. Answer (C) is incorrect because the basic VFR weather minimums for operating an aircraft in Class D airspace are 1,000-ft. ceiling, not clear of clouds, and 3, not 2, SM visibility.

Answer (B) is correct (3139). *(FAR 91.155)*
An airway includes that Class E airspace extending upward from 1,200 ft. AGL to, but not including, 18,000 ft. MSL. The minimum distance from clouds below 10,000 ft. MSL in Class E airspace is 500 ft. below, 1,000 ft. above, and 2,000 ft. horizontally.
Answer (A) is incorrect because clear of clouds is the minimum distance from clouds required in Class B, not Class E, airspace. Answer (C) is incorrect because the minimum distance from clouds required for VFR operations in Class E airspace below 10,000 ft. MSL is 500 ft. below, not above; 1,000 ft. above, not below; and 2,000 ft. horizontally.

Answer (A) is correct (3137). *(FAR 91.155)*
Below 1,200 ft. AGL in Class G airspace during daylight hours, the VFR weather minimum is 1 SM visibility and clear of clouds.
Answer (B) is incorrect because 1 SM visibility, 500 ft. below, 1,000 ft. above, and 2,000 ft. horizontal clearance from clouds is the minimum visibility and clearance from clouds in Class G airspace at more than 1,200 ft. AGL but less than 10,000 ft. MSL, not at 700 ft. AGL. At night the requirement is 3 SM and 500 ft. below, 1,000 ft. above, and 2,000 ft. horizontal from clouds. Answer (C) is incorrect because 3 SM visibility and clear of clouds are the visibility and clearance from clouds requirements in Class B, not Class G, airspace.

132.
3138. What minimum flight visibility is required for VFR flight operations on an airway below 10,000 feet MSL?

A—1 mile.
B—3 miles.
C—4 miles.

Answer (B) is correct (3138). *(FAR 91.155)*
An airway includes that Class E airspace extending upward from 1,200 ft. AGL to, but not including, 18,000 ft. MSL. The minimum flight visibility for VFR flight operations in Class E airspace less than 10,000 ft. MSL is 3 SM.
Answer (A) is incorrect because 1 SM is the minimum daytime visibility for a VFR flight below 10,000 ft. MSL in Class G, not Class E, airspace. Answer (C) is incorrect because the minimum flight visibility for VFR flight operations in Class E airspace below 10,000 ft. MSL is 3 SM, not 4 SM.

133.
3142. During operations outside controlled airspace at altitudes of more than 1,200 feet AGL, but less than 10,000 feet MSL, the minimum flight visibility for VFR flight at night is

A—1 mile.
B—3 miles.
C—5 miles.

Answer (B) is correct (3142). *(FAR 91.155)*
When operating outside controlled airspace (i.e., Class G airspace) at night at altitudes of more than 1,200 ft. AGL, but less than 10,000 ft. MSL, the minimum flight visibility is 3 SM.
Answer (A) is incorrect because 1 SM is the minimum day, not night, flight visibility in Class G airspace at altitudes of more than 1,200 ft. AGL, but less than 10,000 ft. MSL. Answer (C) is incorrect because 5 SM is for operations more than 1,200 ft. AGL and at or above, not below, 10,000 ft. MSL in Class G airspace.

134.
3140. During operations within controlled airspace at altitudes of more than 1,200 feet AGL, but less than 10,000 feet MSL, the minimum distance above clouds requirement for VFR flight is

A—500 feet.
B—1,000 feet.
C—1,500 feet.

Answer (B) is correct (3140). *(FAR 91.155)*
Controlled airspace is the generic term for Class A, B, C, D, or E airspace. Only in Class C, D, or below 10,000 ft. MSL in Class E airspace are the minimum flight visibility and vertical distance from cloud for VFR flight required to be 3 SM, and 500 ft. below or 1,000 ft. above the clouds.
Note: AGL altitudes are not used in controlled airspace. In Class E airspace, the visibility and distance from clouds are given for (1) below 10,000 ft. MSL and (2) at or above 10,000 ft. MSL.
Answer (A) is incorrect because 500 ft. is the minimum distance below, not above, clouds requirement for VFR flight in Class E airspace at altitudes of less than 10,000 ft. MSL. Answer (C) is incorrect because the minimum distance above clouds requirement for VFR flight in Class E airspace at altitudes of less than 10,000 ft. MSL is 1,000 ft., not 1,500 ft.

135.
3148. No person may take off or land an aircraft under basic VFR at an airport that lies within Class D airspace unless the

A—flight visibility at that airport is at least 1 mile.
B—ground visibility at that airport is at least 1 mile.
C—ground visibility at that airport is at least 3 miles.

Answer (C) is correct (3148). *(FAR 91.155)*
No person may take off or land an aircraft at any airport that lies within Class D airspace under basic VFR unless the ground visibility is 3 SM. If ground visibility is not reported, flight visibility during landing or takeoff, or while operating in the traffic pattern, must be at least 3 SM.
Answer (A) is incorrect because flight visibility during landing or takeoff under basic VFR must be at least 3, not 1, SM. Answer (B) is incorrect because ground visibility during landing or takeoff under basic VFR must be at least 3, not 1, SM.

136.
3147. During operations at altitudes of more than 1,200 feet AGL and at or above 10,000 feet MSL, the minimum distance above clouds requirement for VFR flight is

A—500 feet.
B—1,000 feet.
C—1,500 feet.

Answer (B) is correct (3147). *(FAR 91.155)*
    During operations in Class G airspace at altitudes of more than 1,200 ft. AGL and at or above 10,000 ft. MSL, the minimum distance above clouds requirement for VFR flight is 1,000 ft.
    Note: The FAA question fails to specify what type of airspace. Since AGL altitudes are not used in controlled airspace (Class A, B, C, D, and E), that implies Class G airspace.
    Answer (A) is incorrect because 500 ft. is the vertical distance below, not above, the clouds for VFR operations below, not at or above, 10,000 ft. MSL and above 1,200 ft. AGL in Class G airspace. Answer (C) is incorrect because 1,000 ft., not 1,500 ft., is the vertical distance required above the clouds for VFR operations above 1,200 ft. AGL and at or above 10,000 ft. MSL in Class G airspace.

137.
3143. Outside controlled airspace, the minimum flight visibility requirement for VFR flight above 1,200 feet AGL and below 10,000 feet MSL during daylight hours is

A—1 mile.
B—3 miles.
C—5 miles.

Answer (A) is correct (3143). *(FAR 91.155)*
    Outside controlled airspace (i.e., Class G airspace) at altitudes above 1,200 ft. AGL and below 10,000 ft. MSL, the minimum flight visibility requirement for VFR flight during the day is 1 SM.
    Answer (B) is incorrect because 3 SM is the minimum VFR flight visibility required at night, not day, for flights in Class G airspace at altitudes below 10,000 ft. MSL. Answer (C) is incorrect because 5 SM is the minimum VFR flight visibility required for flights in Class G airspace above 1,200 ft. AGL and at or above, not below, 10,000 ft. MSL.

138.
3144. During operations outside controlled airspace at altitudes of more than 1,200 feet AGL, but less than 10,000 feet MSL, the minimum distance below clouds requirement for VFR flight at night is

A—500 feet.
B—1,000 feet.
C—1,500 feet.

Answer (A) is correct (3144). *(FAR 91.155)*
    Outside controlled airspace (i.e., Class G airspace) at altitudes above 1,200 ft. AGL and less than 10,000 ft. MSL, the minimum distance below clouds requirement for VFR flight at night is 500 ft.
    Answer (B) is incorrect because 1,000 ft. is the minimum distance above, not below, the clouds. Answer (C) is incorrect because the minimum distance below the clouds is 500 ft., not 1,500 ft.

139.
3136. During operations within controlled airspace at altitudes of less than 1,200 feet AGL, the minimum horizontal distance from clouds requirement for VFR flight is

A—1,000 feet.
B—1,500 feet.
C—2,000 feet.

Answer (C) is correct (3136). *(FAR 91.155)*
    Controlled airspace is the generic term for Class A, B, C, D, or E airspace. Only in Class C, D, or below 10,000 ft. MSL in Class E airspace is the minimum horizontal distance from clouds for VFR flight required to be 2,000 ft.
    Note: AGL altitudes are not used in controlled airspace. In Class E airspace, the visibility and distance from clouds are given for (1) below 10,000 ft. MSL and (2) at or above 10,000 ft. MSL.
    Answer (A) is incorrect because 1,000 ft. is the minimum vertical, not horizontal, distance above the clouds in Class E airspace below 10,000 ft. MSL. Answer (B) is incorrect because the minimum horizontal distance is 2,000 ft., not 1,500 ft.

140.
3069. Normal VFR operations in Class D airspace with an operating control tower require the visibility and ceiling to be at least

A—1,000 feet and 1 mile.
B—1,000 feet and 3 miles.
C—2,500 feet and 3 miles.

Answer (B) is correct (3069). *(FAR 91.155)*
    The basic VFR weather minimums for operating an aircraft within Class D airspace are a 1,000-ft. ceiling and 3 SM visibility.
    Answer (A) is incorrect because the basic VFR weather minimums for operating an aircraft in Class D airspace are a 1,000-ft. ceiling and 3 SM, not 1 SM, visibility. Answer (C) is incorrect because the basic VFR weather minimums for operating an aircraft in Class D airspace are a 1,000-ft., not 2,500-ft., ceiling and 3 SM visibility.

91.157 Special VFR Weather Minimums

141.
3813. What ATC facility should the pilot contact to receive a special VFR departure clearance in Class D airspace?

A—Automated Flight Service Station.
B—Air Traffic Control Tower.
C—Air Route Traffic Control Center.

Answer (B) is correct (3813). *(FAR 91.157)*
When special VFR is needed, the pilot should contact the Air Traffic Control Tower to receive a departure clearance in Class D airspace.
Answer (A) is incorrect because a pilot may request a clearance through an FSS for a special VFR clearance in Class E, not Class D, airspace. The FSS would only act as a relay point between the pilot and the ATC facility responsible for the Class E airspace (i.e., FSS personnel cannot issue a clearance). Answer (C) is incorrect because an Air Route Traffic Control Center can issue a clearance for a special VFR for an airport in Class E, not Class D, airspace.

142.
3150. A special VFR clearance authorizes the pilot of an aircraft to operate VFR while within Class D airspace when the visibility is

A—less than 1 mile and the ceiling is less than 1,000 feet.
B—at least 1 mile and the aircraft can remain clear of clouds.
C—at least 3 miles and the aircraft can remain clear of clouds.

Answer (B) is correct (3150). *(FAR 91.157)*
To operate within Class D airspace under special VFR clearance, visibility must be at least 1 SM. There is no ceiling requirement, but the aircraft must remain clear of clouds.
Answer (A) is incorrect because a special VFR clearance authorizes the pilot to operate VFR within Class D airspace if the visibility is at least, not below, 1 SM. Answer (C) is incorrect because a special VFR clearance requires the pilot to maintain at least 1 SM, not 3 SM, visibility and remain clear of clouds.

143.
3154. No person may operate an airplane within Class D airspace at night under special VFR unless the

A—flight can be conducted 500 feet below the clouds.
B—airplane is equipped for instrument flight.
C—flight visibility is at least 3 miles.

Answer (B) is correct (3154). *(FAR 91.157)*
To operate under special VFR within Class D airspace at night, the pilot must be instrument rated and the airplane equipped for instrument flight.
Answer (A) is incorrect because the only additional requirement at night for special VFR in Class D airspace is that the airplane be IFR equipped and the pilot be instrument rated, not conduct the flight 500 ft. below the clouds. Answer (C) is incorrect because, for special VFR at night in Class D airspace, the flight visibility must be at least 1 SM, not 3 SM.

144.
3153. What are the minimum requirements for airplane operations under special VFR in Class D airspace at night?

A—The airplane must be under radar surveillance at all times while in Class D airspace.
B—The airplane must be equipped for IFR with an altitude reporting transponder.
C—The pilot must be instrument rated, and the airplane must be IFR equipped.

Answer (C) is correct (3153). *(FAR 91.157)*
To operate under special VFR within Class D airspace at night, the pilot must be instrument rated and the airplane must be IFR equipped.
Answer (A) is incorrect because, to operate an airplane under special VFR at night in Class D airspace, there is no requirement that the airplane be under radar surveillance. Answer (B) is incorrect because there is no requirement for an altitude reporting transponder for special VFR at night in Class D airspace, but the pilot must be instrument rated.

145.
3151. What is the minimum weather condition required for airplanes operating under special VFR in Class D airspace?

A—1 mile flight visibility.
B—1 mile flight visibility and 1,000-foot ceiling.
C—3 miles flight visibility and 1,000-foot ceiling.

Answer (A) is correct (3151). *(FAR 91.157)*
To operate within Class D airspace under special VFR clearance, visibility must be at least 1 SM. There is no ceiling requirement, but the aircraft must remain clear of clouds.
Answer (B) is incorrect because, to operate within Class D airspace under a special VFR clearance, there is no (not 1,000-ft.) ceiling requirement other than to remain clear of clouds. Answer (C) is incorrect because 3 SM flight visibility and 1,000-ft. ceiling are basic (not special) VFR weather minimums to operate an airplane in Class D airspace.

91.159 VFR Cruising Altitude or Flight Level

146.
3156. Which VFR cruising altitude is acceptable for a flight on a Victor Airway with a magnetic course of 175°? The terrain is less than 1,000 feet.

A—4,500 feet.
B—5,000 feet.
C—5,500 feet.

Answer (C) is correct (3156). *(FAR 91.159)*
When operating a VFR flight above 3,000 ft. AGL on a magnetic course of 0° through 179°, fly any odd thousand-ft. MSL altitude plus 500 ft. Thus, on a magnetic course of 175°, an appropriate VFR cruising altitude is 5,500 ft.
Answer (A) is incorrect because 4,500 ft. would be an acceptable VFR cruising altitude if you were on a magnetic course of 180° to 359°, not 175°. Answer (B) is incorrect because, on a magnetic course of 175°, the acceptable VFR cruising altitude is an odd thousand plus 500 ft. (5,500 ft., not 5,000 ft.).

147.
3155. Which cruising altitude is appropriate for a VFR flight on a magnetic course of 135°?

A—Even thousand.
B—Even thousand plus 500 feet.
C—Odd thousand plus 500 feet.

Answer (C) is correct (3155). *(FAR 91.159)*
When operating a VFR flight above 3,000 ft. AGL on a magnetic course of 0° through 179°, fly any odd thousand-ft. MSL altitude plus 500 ft. Thus, on a magnetic course of 135°, an appropriate VFR cruising altitude is an odd thousand plus 500 ft.
Answer (A) is incorrect because a VFR flight on a magnetic course of 135° will use an odd (not even) thousand, plus 500 ft. altitude. Answer (B) is incorrect because a VFR flight on a magnetic course of 135° will use an odd (not even) thousand plus 500 ft. altitude.

148.
3157. Which VFR cruising altitude is appropriate when flying above 3,000 feet AGL on a magnetic course of 185°?

A—4,000 feet.
B—4,500 feet.
C—5,000 feet.

Answer (B) is correct (3157). *(FAR 91.159)*
When operating a VFR flight above 3,000 ft. AGL on a magnetic course of 180° through 359°, fly any even thousand-ft. MSL altitude, plus 500 ft. Thus, on a magnetic course of 185°, an appropriate VFR cruising altitude is 4,500 ft.
Answer (A) is incorrect because on a magnetic course of 185° the appropriate VFR cruising altitude is an even thousand-ft. plus 500 ft. altitude (4,500 ft., not 4,000 ft.). Answer (C) is incorrect because on a magnetic course of 185° the appropriate VFR cruising altitude is an even (not odd) thousand-ft., plus 500 ft. (4,500 ft., not 5,000 ft.).

149.
3158. Each person operating an aircraft at a VFR cruising altitude shall maintain an odd-thousand plus 500-foot altitude while on a

A—magnetic heading of 0° through 179°.
B—magnetic course of 0° through 179°.
C—true course of 0° through 179°.

Answer (B) is correct (3158). *(FAR 91.159)*
When operating above 3,000 ft. AGL but less than 18,000 ft. MSL on a magnetic course of 0° to 179°, fly at an odd thousand-ft. MSL altitude plus 500 ft.
Answer (A) is incorrect because a magnetic heading includes wind correction, and VFR cruising altitudes are based on magnetic course, i.e., without wind correction. Answer (C) is incorrect because true course does not include an adjustment for magnetic variation.

91.203 Civil Aircraft: Certifications Required

150.
3159. In addition to a valid Airworthiness Certificate, what documents or records must be aboard an aircraft during flight?

A—Aircraft engine and airframe logbooks, and owner's manual.
B—Radio operator's permit, and repair and alteration forms.
C—Operating limitations and Registration Certificate.

Answer (C) is correct (3159). *(FAR 91.203 and 91.9)*
FAR 91.203 requires both an Airworthiness Certificate and a Registration Certificate to be aboard aircraft during flight. FAR 91.9 requires that operating limitations be available in the aircraft in an approved Airplane Flight Manual, approved manual material, markings, and placards, or any combination thereof.
Answer (A) is incorrect because the airframe and engine logbooks are usually maintained and stored on the ground. Answer (B) is incorrect because repair and alteration forms are handled in the maintenance shop. Also, the Radio Operator's permit, although carried by the pilot, is an FCC requirement. A pilot may still fly without it as long as (s)he does not use any radio equipment that transmits a signal (e.g., communication, DME, or transponder).

91.207 Emergency Locator Transmitters

151.
3160. When must batteries in an emergency locator transmitter (ELT) be replaced or recharged, if rechargeable?

A—After any inadvertent activation of the ELT.
B—When the ELT has been in use for more than 1 cumulative hour.
C—When the ELT can no longer be heard over the airplane's communication radio receiver.

Answer (B) is correct (3160). *(FAR 91.207)*
ELT batteries must be replaced or recharged (if rechargeable) when the transmitter has been in use for more than 1 cumulative hr. or when 50% of their useful life (or useful life of charge) has expired.
Answer (A) is incorrect because the batteries in an ELT must be replaced (or recharged, if rechargeable) only after the transmitter has been used for more than 1 cumulative hr., not after any inadvertent activation of the transmitter. Answer (C) is incorrect because ELT batteries are replaced (or recharged, if rechargeable) based on use or useful life, not when an ELT can no longer be heard over the airplane's communication radio receiver.

152.
3821. When may an emergency locator transmitter (ELT) be tested?

A—Anytime.
B—At 15 and 45 minutes past the hour.
C—During the first 5 minutes after the hour.

Answer (C) is correct (3821). *(AIM Para 6-2-5)*
Emergency locator transmitters (ELT) may only be tested on the ground during the first 5 min. after the hour. Other times it is only allowed with prior arrangement with the nearest FAA Control Tower or FSS. No airborne checks are allowed.
Answer (A) is incorrect because an ELT should only be tested during the first 5 min. after the hour, not anytime. Answer (B) is incorrect because an ELT should only be tested during the first 5 min. after the hour, not at 15 and 45 min. past the hour.

153.
3161. When are non-rechargeable batteries of an emergency locator transmitter (ELT) required to be replaced?

A—Every 24 months.
B—When 50 percent of their useful life expires.
C—At the time of each 100-hour or annual inspection.

Answer (B) is correct (3161). *(FAR 91.207)*
Non-rechargeable batteries of an ELT must be replaced when 50% of their useful life expires or after the transmitter has been in use for more than 1 cumulative hr.
Answer (A) is incorrect because every 24 months is the requirement for the transponder to be tested and inspected, not when non-rechargeable ELT batteries are to be replaced. Answer (C) is incorrect because non-rechargeable ELT batteries are replaced when 50% of their useful life expires or after 1 cumulative hr. of use, not necessarily at the time of each 100-hr. or annual inspection.

154.
3820. When must the battery in an emergency locator transmitter (ELT) be replaced (or recharged if the battery is rechargeable)?

A—After one-half the battery's useful life.
B—During each annual and 100-hour inspection.
C—Every 24 calendar months.

Answer (A) is correct (3820). *(FAR 91.207)*
Emergency locator transmitter (ELT) batteries must be replaced or recharged after 50% of their useful life has expired or when the transmitter has been in use for more than 1 cumulative hr.
Answer (B) is incorrect because ELT batteries must be replaced (or recharged) after one-half the battery's useful life has expired, not during each annual and 100-hr. inspection. Answer (C) is incorrect because a transponder (not an ELT battery) must be tested and inspected every 24 calendar months.

91.209 Aircraft Lights

155.
3162. Except in Alaska, during what time period should lighted position lights be displayed on an aircraft?

A—End of evening civil twilight to the beginning of morning civil twilight.
B—1 hour after sunset to 1 hour before sunrise.
C—Sunset to sunrise.

Answer (C) is correct (3162). *(FAR 91.209)*
Except in Alaska, no person may operate an aircraft during the period from sunset to sunrise unless the aircraft's lighted position lights are on.
Answer (A) is incorrect because end of evening civil twilight to the beginning of morning civil twilight is the definition of night, not the time period in which lighted position lights be displayed on an aircraft. Answer (B) is incorrect because the period from 1 hr. after sunset to 1 hr. before sunrise is the time used to meet night recency requirements, not when the aircraft position lights should be on.

91.211 Supplemental Oxygen

156.
3164. Unless each occupant is provided with supplemental oxygen, no person may operate a civil aircraft of U.S. registry above a maximum cabin pressure altitude of

A—12,500 feet MSL.
B—14,000 feet MSL.
C—15,000 feet MSL.

Answer (C) is correct (3164). *(FAR 91.211)*
No person may operate a civil aircraft of U.S. registry at cabin pressure altitudes above 15,000 ft. MSL unless each occupant is provided with supplemental oxygen.
Answer (A) is incorrect because at cabin pressure altitudes above 12,500 ft. MSL, up to and including 14,000 ft. MSL, only the minimum required flight crew, not each occupant, must be provided with and use supplemental oxygen after 30 min. at those altitudes. Answer (B) is incorrect because at cabin pressure altitudes above 14,000 ft. MSL, only the minimum required flight crew, not each occupant, must be provided with and continuously use supplemental oxygen at those altitudes.

157.
3163. When operating an aircraft at cabin pressure altitudes above 12,500 feet MSL up to and including 14,000 feet MSL, supplemental oxygen shall be used during

A—the entire flight time at those altitudes.
B—that flight time in excess of 10 minutes at those altitudes.
C—that flight time in excess of 30 minutes at those altitudes.

Answer (C) is correct (3163). *(FAR 91.211)*
At cabin pressure altitudes above 12,500 ft. MSL, up to and including 14,000 ft. MSL, the required minimum flight crew must use supplemental oxygen only after 30 min. at those altitudes.
Answer (A) is incorrect because, at cabin pressure altitudes above 12,500 ft. MSL up to and including 14,000 ft. MSL, supplemental oxygen shall be used during that time in excess of 30 min. (not the entire flight time) at those altitudes. Answer (B) is incorrect because, at cabin pressure altitudes above 12,500 ft. MSL up to and including 14,000 ft. MSL, supplemental oxygen shall be used during that time in excess of 30 (not 10) min. at those altitudes.

91.215 ATC Transponder and Altitude Reporting Equipment and Use

158.
3165. An operable 4096-code transponder with an encoding altimeter is required in which airspace?

A—Class A, Class B (and within 30 miles of the Class B primary airport), and Class C.
B—Class D and Class E (below 10,000 feet MSL).
C—Class D and Class G (below 10,000 feet MSL).

Answer (A) is correct (3165). *(FAR 91.215)*
An operable transponder with an encoding altimeter (Mode C) is required in Class A, Class B (and within 30 NM of the Class B primary airport), and Class C airspace, and at or above 10,000 ft. MSL excluding that airspace below 2,500 ft. AGL.
Answer (B) is incorrect because an operable 4096-code transponder with an encoding altimeter is not required to operate in Class D or Class E (below 10,000 ft. MSL) airspace. Answer (C) is incorrect because an operable 4096-code transponder with an encoding altimeter is not required to operate in Class D or Class G (below 10,000 ft. MSL) airspace.

159.
3129. An operable 4096-code transponder and Mode C encoding altimeter are required in

A—Class B airspace and within 30 miles of the Class B primary airport.
B—Class D airspace.
C—Class E airspace below 10,000 feet MSL.

Answer (A) is correct (3129). *(FAR 91.215)*
An operable 4096-code transponder and Mode C encoding altimeter are required in Class B airspace and within 30 NM of the Class B primary airport.
Answer (B) is incorrect because an operable 4096-code transponder and Mode C encoding altimeter are required in Class B airspace and within 30 NM of the Class B primary airport, not Class D airspace. Answer (C) is incorrect because an operable 4096-code transponder and Mode C encoding altimeter are required in Class B airspace and within 30 NM of the Class B primary airport, not Class E airspace below 10,000 ft. MSL.

91.303 Aerobatic Flight

160.
3168. In which class of airspace is acrobatic flight prohibited?

A—Class E airspace not designated for Federal Airways above 1,500 feet AGL.
B—Class E airspace below 1,500 feet AGL.
C—Class G airspace above 1,500 feet AGL.

Answer (B) is correct (3168). *(FAR 91.303)*
No person may operate an aircraft in acrobatic flight below an altitude of 1,500 ft. AGL.
Answer (A) is incorrect because acrobatic flight is prohibited in Class E airspace within 4 NM of the centerline of a Federal Airway, not in all Class E airspace. Answer (C) is incorrect because acrobatic flight is only prohibited below 1,500 ft. AGL.

161.
3170. No person may operate an aircraft in acrobatic flight when the flight visibility is less than

A—3 miles.
B—5 miles.
C—7 miles.

Answer (A) is correct (3170). *(FAR 91.303)*
No person may operate an aircraft in acrobatic flight when the flight visibility is less than 3 SM.
Answer (B) is incorrect because the minimum flight visibility for acrobatic flight is 3 SM, not 5 SM. Answer (C) is incorrect because the minimum flight visibility for acrobatic flight is 3 SM, not 7 SM.

162.
3169. What is the lowest altitude permitted for acrobatic flight?

A—1,000 feet AGL.
B—1,500 feet AGL.
C—2,000 feet AGL.

Answer (B) is correct (3169). *(FAR 91.303)*
No person may operate an aircraft in acrobatic flight below 1,500 ft. AGL.
Answer (A) is incorrect because 1,500 ft. AGL, not 1,000 ft. AGL, is the lowest altitude permitted for acrobatic flight. Answer (C) is incorrect because 1,500 ft. AGL, not 2,000 ft. AGL, is the lowest altitude permitted for acrobatic flight.

163.
3167. No person may operate an aircraft in acrobatic flight when

A—flight visibility is less than 5 miles.
B—over any congested area of a city, town, or settlement.
C—less than 2,500 feet AGL.

Answer (B) is correct (3167). *(FAR 91.303)*
No person may operate an aircraft in acrobatic flight over any congested area of a city, town, or settlement.
Answer (A) is incorrect because the flight visibility limitation for acrobatic flight is 3 SM, not 5 SM. Answer (C) is incorrect because the minimum altitude for acrobatic flight is 1,500 ft. AGL, not 2,500 ft. AGL.

91.307 Parachutes and Parachuting

164.
3173. With certain exceptions, when must each occupant of an aircraft wear an approved parachute?

A—When a door is removed from the aircraft to facilitate parachute jumpers.
B—When intentionally pitching the nose of the aircraft up or down 30° or more.
C—When intentionally banking in excess of 30°.

Answer (B) is correct (3173). *(FAR 91.307)*
Unless each occupant of an airplane is wearing an approved parachute, no pilot carrying any other person (other than a crewmember) may execute any intentional maneuver that exceeds a bank of 60° or a nose-up or nose-down attitude of 30° relative to the horizon.
Answer (A) is incorrect because pilots of airplanes that are carrying parachute jumpers are not required to use a parachute. Answer (C) is incorrect because a parachute is required when an intentional bank that exceeds 60°, not 30°, is to be made.

165.
3171. A chair-type parachute must have been packed by a certificated and appropriately rated parachute rigger within the preceding

A—60 days.
B—90 days.
C—120 days.

Answer (C) is correct (3171). *(FAR 91.307)*
No pilot of a civil aircraft may allow a parachute that is available for emergency use to be carried in that aircraft unless it is an approved type and, if a chair type, it has been packed by a certificated and appropriately rated parachute rigger within the preceding 120 days.
Answer (A) is incorrect because a chair-type parachute must have been packed by a certificated and appropriately rated parachute rigger within the preceding 120 days, not 60 days. Answer (B) is incorrect because a chair-type parachute must have been packed by a certificated and appropriately rated parachute rigger within the preceding 120 days, not 90 days.

166.
3172. An approved chair-type parachute may be carried in an aircraft for emergency use if it has been packed by an appropriately rated parachute rigger within the preceding

A—120 days.
B—180 days.
C—365 days.

Answer (A) is correct (3172). *(FAR 91.307)*
No pilot of a civil aircraft may allow a parachute that is available for emergency use to be carried in that aircraft unless it is an approved type and, if a chair type, it has been packed by a certificated and appropriately rated parachute rigger within the preceding 120 days.
Answer (B) is incorrect because a chair-type parachute must have been packed by an appropriately rated parachute rigger within the preceding 120 (not 180) days. Answer (C) is incorrect because a chair-type parachute must have been packed by an appropriately rated parachute rigger within the preceding 120 (not 365) days.

91.313 Restricted Category Civil Aircraft: Operating Limitations

167.
3178. Which is normally prohibited when operating a restricted category civil aircraft?

A—Flight under instrument flight rules.
B—Flight over a densely populated area.
C—Flight within Class D airspace.

Answer (B) is correct (3178). *(FAR 91.313)*
Normally, no person may operate a restricted category civil aircraft over a densely populated area.
Answer (A) is incorrect because flight over a densely populated area, not IFR flight, is normally prohibited when operating a restricted category civil aircraft. Answer (C) is incorrect because flight over a densely populated area, not within Class D airspace, is normally prohibited when operating a restricted category civil aircraft.

91.319 Aircraft Having Experimental Certificates: Operating Limitations

168.
3179. Unless otherwise specifically authorized, no person may operate an aircraft that has an experimental certificate

A—beneath the floor of Class B airspace.
B—over a densely populated area or in a congested airway.
C—from the primary airport within Class D airspace.

Answer (B) is correct (3179). *(FAR 91.319)*
Unless otherwise specifically authorized, no person may operate an aircraft that has an experimental certificate over a densely populated area or along a congested airway.
Answer (A) is incorrect because normally no person may operate an aircraft that has an experimental certificate along a congested airway, not beneath the floor of Class B airspace. Answer (C) is incorrect because a person can operate an aircraft that has an experimental certificate from the primary airport within Class D airspace as long as ATC is notified of the experimental nature of the aircraft.

91.403 General

169.
3180a. The responsibility for ensuring that an aircraft is maintained in an airworthy condition is primarily that of the

A—pilot in command.
B—owner or operator.
C—mechanic who performs the work.

Answer (B) is correct (3180). *(FAR 91.403)*
The owner or operator of an aircraft is primarily responsible for maintaining that aircraft in an airworthy condition. The term "operator" includes the pilot in command.
Answer (A) is incorrect because the owner or operator, not only the pilot in command, of an aircraft is responsible for assuring the airworthiness of the aircraft. Answer (C) is incorrect because, although a mechanic will perform inspections and maintenance, the primary responsibility for an aircraft's airworthiness lies with its owner or operator.

170.
3181c. Who is responsible for ensuring Airworthiness Directives (AD's) are complied with?

A—Owner or operator.
B—Repair station.
C—Mechanic with inspection authorization (IA).

Answer (A) is correct (3181c). *(FAR 91.403)*
Airworthiness Directives (ADs) are regulatory and must be complied with, unless a specific exemption is granted. It is the responsibility of the owner or operator to assure compliance with all pertinent ADs, including those ADs that require recurrent or continuing action.
Answer (B) is incorrect because the owner or operator, not a repair station, is responsible for ensuring ADs are complied with. Answer (C) is incorrect because the owner or operator, not a mechanic with inspection authorization, is responsible for ensuring ADs are complied with.

91.405 Maintenance Required

171.
3181a. The responsibility for ensuring that maintenance personnel make the appropriate entries in the aircraft maintenance records indicating the aircraft has been approved for return to service lies with the

A—owner or operator.
B—pilot in command.
C—mechanic who performed the work.

Answer (A) is correct (3181). *(FAR 91.405)*
Each owner or operator of an aircraft shall ensure that maintenance personnel make the appropriate entries in the aircraft maintenance records indicating the aircraft has been approved for return to service.
Answer (B) is incorrect because the owner or operator, not only the pilot in command, is responsible for ensuring that maintenance personnel make the proper entries in the aircraft's maintenance records. Answer (C) is incorrect because the owner or operator, not the mechanic who performed the work, is responsible for ensuring that proper entries are made in the aircraft's maintenance records.

172.
3181b. Who is responsible for ensuring appropriate entries are made in maintenance records indicating the aircraft has been approved for return to service?

A—Owner or operator.
B—Certified mechanic.
C—Repair station.

Answer (A) is correct (3181b). *(FAR 91.405)*.
It is the responsibility of the owner or operator of an aircraft to ensure that appropriate entries are made in maintenance records by maintenance personnel indicating the aircraft has been approved for return to service.
Answer (B) is incorrect because the certified mechanic performing the work must make the entries, but it is the responsibility of the owner or operator to ensure that the entries have been made. Answer (C) is incorrect because it is the responsibility of the owner or operator, not a repair station, to ensure appropriate entries have been made.

91.407 Operation after Maintenance, Preventive Maintenance, Rebuilding, or Alteration

173.
3183. If an alteration or repair substantially affects an aircraft's operation in flight, that aircraft must be test flown by an appropriately-rated pilot and approved for return to service prior to being operated

A—by any private pilot.
B—with passengers aboard.
C—for compensation or hire.

Answer (B) is correct (3183). *(FAR 91.407)*
If an alteration or repair has been made that substantially affects the airplane's flight characteristics, the airplane must be test flown and approved for return to service by an appropriately rated pilot prior to being operated with passengers aboard. The test pilot must be at least a private pilot and appropriately rated for the airplane being tested and must make an operational check of the alteration or repair made, and log the flight in the aircraft records.
Answer (A) is incorrect because, if an alteration or repair substantially affects an aircraft's operation in flight, a private pilot may only test fly that airplane if (s)he is appropriately rated to fly that airplane. Answer (C) is incorrect because, after any alteration or repair that substantially affects an aircraft's operation in flight, that aircraft must be test flown and approved for return to service prior to being operated with any passengers aboard, not for compensation or hire.

174.
3184. Before passengers can be carried in an aircraft that has been altered in a manner that may have appreciably changed its flight characteristics, it must be flight tested by an appropriately-rated pilot who holds at least a

A—Commercial Pilot Certificate with an instrument rating.
B—Private Pilot Certificate.
C—Commercial Pilot Certificate and a mechanic's certificate.

Answer (B) is correct (3184). *(FAR 91.407)*
If an alteration or repair has been made that may have changed an airplane's flight characteristics, the airplane must be test flown and approved for return to service by an appropriately rated pilot prior to being operated with passengers aboard. The test pilot must be at least a private pilot and appropriately rated for the airplane being tested.
Answer (A) is incorrect because the test flight must be made by an appropriately rated pilot who holds at least a private (not commercial) pilot certificate. An instrument rating is not required. Answer (C) is incorrect because the test flight must be made by an appropriately rated pilot who holds at least a private (not commercial) pilot certificate. A mechanic's certificate is not required for the test pilot.

91.409 Inspections

175.
3190. A 100-hour inspection was due at 3302.5 hours. The 100-hour inspection was actually done at 3309.5 hours. When is the next 100-hour inspection due?

A — 3312.5 hours.
B — 3402.5 hours.
C — 3409.5 hours.

Answer (B) is correct (3190). *(FAR 91.409)*
Since the 100-hr. inspection was due at 3302.5 hr., the next 100-hr. inspection is due at 3402.5 (3302.5 + 100). The excess time used before the 100-hr. inspection was done must be included in computing the next 100 hr. of time in service.
Answer (A) is incorrect because 3312.5 hr. is the latest time on the tachometer the last 100-hr. inspection could have been completed, not when the next 100-hr. inspection is due. Answer (C) is incorrect because 3409.5 hr. is 100 hr. from the actual completion time of the last inspection, but the excess time is computed into the next 100 hr. of time in service, or 100 hr. from the last due time.

176.
3185. An aircraft's annual inspection was performed on July 12, this year. The next annual inspection will be due no later than

A — July 1, next year.
B — July 13, next year.
C — July 31, next year.

Answer (C) is correct (3185). *(FAR 91.409)*
Annual inspections expire on the last day of the 12th calendar month after the previous annual inspection. If an annual inspection is performed on July 12 of this year, it will expire at midnight on July 31 next year.
Answer (A) is incorrect because annual inspections are due on the last day of the month. Thus, if an annual inspection is performed July 12, this year the next annual inspection is due July 31 (not July 1), next year.
Answer (B) is incorrect because annual inspections are due on the last day of the month. Thus, if an annual inspection is performed July 12, this year the next annual inspection is due July 31 (not July 13), next year.

177.
3188. What aircraft inspections are required for rental aircraft that are also used for flight instruction?

A — Annual and 100-hour inspections.
B — Biannual and 100-hour inspections.
C — Annual and 50-hour inspections.

Answer (A) is correct (3188). *(FAR 91.409)*
All aircraft that are used for hire (e.g., rental) and flight instruction must be inspected on a 100-hr. basis. Also an annual inspection must be completed.
Answer (B) is incorrect because an annual, not biannual, inspection is required for all aircraft. A 100-hr. inspection is also required for aircraft rented for flight instruction. Answer (C) is incorrect because besides an annual inspection, aircraft rented for flight instruction purposes are also required to have a 100- (not 50-) hr. inspection.

178.
3189. An aircraft had a 100-hour inspection when the tachometer read 1259.6. When is the next 100-hour inspection due?

A — 1349.6 hours.
B — 1359.6 hours.
C — 1369.6 hours.

Answer (B) is correct (3189). *(FAR 91.409)*
The next 100-hr. inspection is due within 100 hr. of time in service. The 100-hr. may be exceeded by 10 hr. in order to get to a place where the work can be done. Add 100 hr. to 1259.6 to get the next inspection, due at 1359.6.
Answer (A) is incorrect because the 100-hr. inspection is due when the tachometer indicates 1359.6 hr (1259.6 + 100), not 1349.6 hr. Answer (C) is incorrect because 1369.6 hr. is 10 hr. over the 100-hr. limitation which is allowed if the aircraft is en route to reach a place where the inspection can be done. The 100-hr. inspection is due at 1359.6 hr. (1259.6 + 100), not 1369.6 hr.

91.413 ATC Transponder Tests and Inspections

179.
3191. No person may use an ATC transponder unless it has been tested and inspected within at least the preceding

A — 6 calendar months.
B — 12 calendar months.
C — 24 calendar months.

Answer (C) is correct (3191). *(FAR 91.413)*
No person may use an ATC transponder that is specified in the regulations unless within the preceding 24 calendar months it has been tested and found to comply with its operating specifications.
Answer (A) is incorrect because an ATC transponder must be tested and inspected every 24 (not 6) calendar months. Answer (B) is incorrect because an ATC transponder must be tested and inspected every 24 (not 12) calendar months.

180.
3192. Maintenance records show the last transponder inspection was performed on September 1, 1993. The next inspection will be due no later than

A—September 30, 1994.
B—September 1, 1995.
C—September 30, 1995.

Answer (C) is correct (3192). *(FAR 91.413)*
No person may use an ATC transponder that is specified in the regulations unless within the preceding 24 calendar months it has been tested and found to comply with its operating specifications. Thus, if the last inspection was performed on September 1, 1993, the next inspection will be due no later than September 30, 1995.
Answer (A) is incorrect because the requirement is within the preceding 24 (not 12) calendar months. Answer (B) is incorrect because the "preceding 24 calendar months" for the next inspection begins October 1, 1993 and ends September 30, 1995, not September 1, 1995.

91.417 Maintenance Records

181.
3182. Completion of an annual inspection and the return of the aircraft to service should always be indicated by

A—the relicensing date on the Registration Certificate.
B—an appropriate notation in the aircraft maintenance records.
C—an inspection sticker placed on the instrument panel that lists the annual inspection completion date.

Answer (B) is correct (3182). *(FAR 91.417)*
Completion of an annual inspection and the return of the aircraft to service should always be indicated by an appropriate notation in the aircraft's maintenance records.
Answer (A) is incorrect because the registration certificate shows ownership, not completion of an annual inspection. Answer (C) is incorrect because maintenance information is found in the airplane logbooks, not on inspection stickers.

182.
3186. To determine the expiration date of the last annual aircraft inspection, a person should refer to the

A—Airworthiness Certificate.
B—Registration Certificate.
C—aircraft maintenance records.

Answer (C) is correct (3186). *(FAR 91.417)*
After maintenance inspections have been completed, maintenance personnel should make the appropriate entries in the aircraft maintenance records or logbooks. This is where the date of the last annual inspection can be found.
Answer (A) is incorrect because to determine the expiration date of the last annual inspection, a person should refer to the aircraft maintenance records, not the Airworthiness Certificate. Answer (B) is incorrect because to determine the expiration date of the last annual inspection, a person should refer to the aircraft maintenance records, not the Registration Certificate.

183.
3193. Which records or documents shall the owner or operator of an aircraft keep to show compliance with an applicable Airworthiness Directive?

A—Aircraft maintenance records.
B—Airworthiness Certificate and Pilot's Operating Handbook.
C—Airworthiness and Registration Certificates.

Answer (A) is correct (3193). *(FAR 91.417)*
Aircraft maintenance records must show the current status of applicable airworthiness directives (ADs) including, for each, the method of compliance, the AD number, and revision date. If the AD involves recurring action, the time and date when the next action is required.
Answer (B) is incorrect because compliance with an AD is found in aircraft maintenance records, not the Airworthiness Certificate and *Pilot's Operating Handbook*. Answer (C) is incorrect because compliance with an AD is found in aircraft maintenance records, not in the Airworthiness and Registration Certificates.

184.
3180b. The airworthiness of an aircraft can be determined by a preflight inspection and a

A—statement from the owner or operator that the aircraft is airworthy.
B—log book endorsement from a flight instructor.
C—review of the maintenance records.

Answer (C) is correct (3180b). *(FAR 91.417)*
As pilot in command, you are responsible for determining whether your aircraft is in condition for safe flight. Only by conducting a preflight inspection and a review of the maintenance records can you determine whether all required maintenance has been performed and, thus, whether the aircraft is airworthy.
Answer (A) is incorrect because a statement from the owner or operator that the aircraft is airworthy does not assure that all required maintenance has been performed. Answer (B) is incorrect because a log book endorsement from a flight instructor does not give any assurance that the aircraft has received required maintenance, and it is not required for determining airworthiness.

4.8 NTSB PART 830
830.5 Immediate Notification

185.
3194. If an aircraft is involved in an accident which results in substantial damage to the aircraft, the nearest NTSB field office should be notified

A—immediately.
B—within 48 hours.
C—within 7 days.

Answer (A) is correct (3194). *(NTSB 830.5)*
The NTSB must be notified immediately and by the most expeditious means possible when an aircraft accident or any of various listed incidents occurs or when an aircraft is overdue and is believed to have been in an accident. Answer (B) is incorrect because an aircraft involved in an accident must be reported immediately (not within 48 hr.) to the NTSB office. Answer (C) is incorrect because an aircraft accident must be reported immediately (not within 7 days) to the nearest NTSB office.

186.
3196. Which incident would necessitate an immediate notification to the nearest NTSB field office?

A—An in-flight generator/alternator failure.
B—An in-flight fire.
C—An in-flight loss of VOR receiver capability.

Answer (B) is correct (3196). *(NTSB 830.5)*
The NTSB must be notified immediately and by the most expeditious means possible when an aircraft accident or any of various listed incidents occurs or when an aircraft is overdue and believed to have been in an accident. The following are considered incidents:

1. Flight control system malfunction or failure;
2. Inability of any required flight crewmember to perform normal flight duties as a result of injury or illness;
3. Failure of structural components of a turbine engine, excluding compressor and turbine blades and vanes;
4. In-flight fire; or
5. Aircraft collision in flight.

Answer (A) is incorrect because an in-flight generator/alternator failure does not require immediate notification. Answer (C) is incorrect because an in-flight loss of VOR receiver capability does not require any type of notification to the NTSB.

187.
3195. Which incident requires an immediate notification to the nearest NTSB field office?

A—A forced landing due to engine failure.
B—Landing gear damage, due to a hard landing.
C—Flight control system malfunction or failure.

Answer (C) is correct (3195). *(NTSB 830.5)*
The NTSB must be notified immediately and by the most expeditious means possible when an aircraft accident or any of various listed incidents occurs or when an aircraft is overdue and believed to have been in an accident. The following are considered incidents:

1. Flight control system malfunction or failure;
2. Inability of any required flight crewmember to perform normal flight duties as a result of injury or illness;
3. Failure of structural components of a turbine engine, excluding compressor and turbine blades and vanes;
4. In-flight fire; or
5. Aircraft collision in flight.

Answer (A) is incorrect because only failure of structural components of a turbine engine (not a forced landing due to engine failure) must be reported immediately to the nearest NTSB office. Answer (B) is incorrect because landing gear damage due to a hard landing is not considered an incident that requires immediate notification to the NTSB.

END OF CHAPTER

188.
3197. Which incident requires an immediate notification be made to the nearest NTSB field office?

A—An overdue aircraft that is believed to be involved in an accident.
B—An in-flight radio communications failure.
C—An in-flight generator or alternator failure.

Answer (A) is correct (3197). *(NTSB 830.5)*
    The NTSB must be notified immediately and by the most expeditious means possible when an aircraft is overdue and is believed to have been involved in an accident.
    Answer (B) is incorrect because an in-flight radio communications failure does not require notification to the NTSB at any time. Answer (C) is incorrect because an in-flight generator or alternator failure does not require notification to the NTSB at any time.

830.10 Preservation of Aircraft Wreckage, Mail, Cargo, and Records

189.
3198. May aircraft wreckage be moved prior to the time the NTSB takes custody?

A—Yes, but only if moved by a federal, state, or local law enforcement officer.
B—Yes, but only to protect the wreckage from further damage.
C—No, it may not be moved under any circumstances.

Answer (B) is correct (3198). *(NTSB 830.10)*
    Prior to the time the Board or its authorized representative takes custody of aircraft wreckage, mail, or cargo, such wreckage, mail, or cargo may not be disturbed or moved except to the extent necessary:
1. To remove persons injured or trapped;
2. To protect the wreckage from further damage; or
3. To protect the public from injury.

    Answer (A) is incorrect because aircraft wreckage can only be moved to protect the wreckage from further damage, protect the public from injury, or to remove persons injured or trapped, not by any federal, state, or local law enforcement officer. Answer (C) is incorrect because aircraft wreckage may be moved in certain circumstances, such as to remove persons injured or trapped, to protect the wreckage from further damage, or to protect the public from injury.

830.15 Reports and Statements to Be Filed

190.
3199. The operator of an aircraft that has been involved in an accident is required to file an accident report within how many days?

A—5.
B—7.
C—10.

Answer (C) is correct (3199). *(NTSB 830.15)*
    The operator of an aircraft shall file a report on NTSB Form 6120.1/2 within 10 days after an accident, or after 7 days if an overdue aircraft is still missing. A report on an incident for which notification is required shall be filed only as required.
    Answer (A) is incorrect because NTSB Form 6120.1/2 is required within 10 (not 5) days after an accident.
Answer (B) is incorrect because NTSB Form 6120.1/2 is required within 10 (not 7) days after an accident.

191.
3200. The operator of an aircraft that has been involved in an incident is required to submit a report to the nearest field office of the NTSB

A—within 7 days.
B—within 10 days.
C—when requested.

Answer (C) is correct (3200). *(NTSB 830.15)*
    The operator of an aircraft shall file a report on NTSB Form 6120.1/2 only when requested. A report is required within 10 days of an accident, or after 7 days if an overdue aircraft is still missing.
    Answer (A) is incorrect because 7 days is the time allowed to file a written report on an overdue aircraft that is still missing; an incident requires a report only when requested. Answer (B) is incorrect because a report must be filed within 10 days of an accident; an incident requires a report only when requested.

END OF CHAPTER

CHAPTER FIVE
AIRPLANE PERFORMANCE AND WEIGHT AND BALANCE

This chapter contains outlines of major concepts tested, all FAA test questions and answers regarding airplane performance and weight and balance and an explanation of each answer. Each module, or subtopic, within this chapter is listed above with the number of questions from the FAA pilot knowledge test pertaining to that particular module. For each module, the first number following the parentheses is the page number on which the outline begins, and the next number is the page number on which the questions begin.

CAUTION: Recall that the **sole purpose** of this book is to expedite your passing the FAA pilot knowledge test for the private pilot certificate. Accordingly, all extraneous material (i.e., topics or regulations not directly tested on the FAA pilot knowledge test) is omitted, even though much more information and knowledge are necessary to fly safely. This additional material is presented in *Pilot Handbook* and *Private Pilot Flight Maneuvers and Practical Test Prep*, available from Gleim Publications, Inc. See the order form on page 326.

Many of the topics in this chapter require interpretation of graphs and charts. Graphs and charts pictorially describe the relationship between two or more variables. Thus, they are a substitute for solving one or more equations. Each time you must interpret (i.e., get an answer from) a graph or chart, you should

1. Understand clearly what is required, e.g., landing roll distance, weight, etc.
2. Analyze the chart or graph to determine the variables involved, including

   a. Labelled sides (axes) of the graph or chart
   b. Labelled lines within the graph or chart

3. Plug the data given in the question into the graph or chart.
4. Finally, determine the value of the item required in the question.

5.1 DENSITY ALTITUDE (Questions 1-7)

1.   Density altitude is a measurement of the density of the air expressed in terms of altitude.

   a.   Air density varies inversely with altitude; i.e., air is very dense at low altitudes and less dense at high altitudes.

   b.   Temperature, humidity, and barometric pressure also affect air density.

   1)   A scale of air density to altitude has been established using a standard temperature and pressure for each altitude. At sea level, standard is 15°C and 29.92" Hg.

   2)   When temperature and pressure are not at standard (which is almost always), density altitude will not be the same as true altitude.

2.   You are required to know how barometric pressure, temperature, and humidity affect density altitude. Visualize the following:

   a.   As barometric pressure increases, the air becomes more compressed and compact. This is an increase in density. Air density is higher if the pressure is high, so the density altitude is said to be lower.

   1)   Density altitude is increased by a decrease in pressure.
   2)   Density altitude is decreased by an increase in pressure.

   b.   As temperature increases, the air expands and therefore becomes less dense. This decrease in density means a higher density altitude. Remember, air is normally less dense at higher altitudes.

   1)   Density altitude is increased by an increase in temperature.
   2)   Density altitude is decreased by a decrease in temperature.

   c.   As relative humidity increases, the air becomes less dense. A given volume of moist air weighs less than the same volume of dry air. This decrease in density means a higher density altitude.

   1)   Density altitude is increased by an increase in humidity.
   2)   Density altitude is decreased by a decrease in humidity.

3.   Said another way, density altitude varies directly with temperature and humidity, and inversely with barometric pressure:

   a.   Cold, dry air and higher barometric pressure = low density altitude.
   b.   Hot, humid air and lower barometric pressure = high density altitude.

4.   Pressure altitude is based on standard temperature. Therefore, density altitude will exceed pressure altitude if the temperature is above standard.

5.   The primary reason for computing density altitude is to determine airplane performance.

   a.   High density altitude reduces an airplane's overall performance.

   b.   For example, climb performance is less and takeoff distance is longer.

   c.   Propellers have less efficiency because there is less air for the propeller to get a grip on.

   d.   However, the same indicated airspeed is used for takeoffs and landings regardless of altitude or air density because the airspeed indicator is also directly affected by air density.

5.2 DENSITY ALTITUDE COMPUTATIONS (Questions 8-15)

1. Density altitude is determined most easily by finding the pressure altitude (indicated altitude when your altimeter is set to 29.92) and adjusting for the temperature.

   a. The adjustment may be made using your flight computer or a density altitude chart. This part of the FAA test requires you to use a density altitude chart.

2. When using a density altitude chart (see Figure 8 on page 152),

   a. Adjust the airport elevation to pressure altitude by adding or subtracting the conversion factor for the current altimeter setting.

   b. To adjust the pressure altitude for nonstandard temperature, plot the intersection of the actual air temperature (listed on the horizontal axis of the chart) with the pressure altitude lines that slope diagonally upward. Move left horizontally from the intersection to read density altitude on the vertical axis of the chart.

   c. EXAMPLE: Outside air temperature   90°F
                   Altimeter setting   30.20" Hg
                   Airport elevation   4,725 ft.

   Referring to Figure 8 on page 152, you determine the density altitude to be approximately 7,400 ft. This is found as follows:

   1) The altimeter setting of 30.20 requires a –257 altitude correction factor.

   2) Subtract 257 from field elevation of 4,725 ft. to obtain pressure altitude of 4,468 ft.

   3) Locate 90°F on the bottom axis of the chart and move up to intersect the diagonal pressure altitude line of 4,468 ft.

   4) Move horizontally to the left axis of the chart to obtain the density altitude of about 7,400 ft.

   5) Note that while true altitude (i.e., airport elevation) is 4,725 ft., density altitude is about 7,400 ft.!

   6) Finally, note that you may determine the effects of temperature changes on density altitude simply by following the above chart procedure and substituting different temperatures.

5.3 TAKEOFF DISTANCE (Questions 16-19)

1. Conditions that reduce airplane takeoff and climb performance are

    a. High altitude
    b. High temperature
    c. High humidity

2. Takeoff distance performance is displayed in the airplane operating manual either

    a. In chart form or
    b. On a graph

3. If a graph, it is usually presented in terms of density altitude. Thus, one must first adjust the airport elevation for nonstandard pressure and temperature.

    a. In the graph used on this exam (see Figure 41 on page 156), the first section on the left uses outside air temperature and pressure altitude to obtain density altitude.

        1) The curved line on the left portion is standard atmosphere, which you use when the question calls for standard temperature.

    b. The second section of the graph, to the right of the first reference line, takes the weight in pounds into account.

    c. The third section of the graph, to the right of the second reference line, takes the headwind or tailwind into account.

    d. The fourth section of the graph, at the right margin, takes obstacles into account.

    e. EXAMPLE: Given an outside air temperature of 15°C, a pressure altitude of 5,650 ft., a takeoff weight of 2,950 lb., and a headwind component of 9 kt., find the ground roll and the total takeoff distance over a 50-ft. obstacle. Use Figure 41 on page 156.

    f. The solution to the example problem is marked with the dotted arrows on the graph. Move straight up from 15°C (which is also where the standard temperature line begins) to the pressure altitude of 5,650 ft. and then horizontally to the right to the first reference line. It is not necessary to adjust for weight because the airplane is at maximum weight of 2,950 lb. Continuing to the next reference line, the headwind component of 9 kt. means an adjustment downward in the wind component section (parallel to the guidelines). Finally, moving straight to the right gives the ground roll of 1,375 ft. The total takeoff distance over a 50-ft. obstacle, following parallel to the guideline up and to the right, is 2,300 ft.

5.4 CRUISE POWER SETTINGS (Questions 20-24)

1. Cruise power settings are found by use of a table (see Figure 36 on page 158).

    a. It is based on 65% power.

    b. It consists of three sections to adjust for varying temperatures:

        1) Standard temperature (in middle)
        2) ISA −20°C (on left)
        3) ISA +20°C (on right)

    c. Values found on the table based on various pressure altitudes and temperatures include

        1) Engine RPM

        2) Manifold pressure (in. Hg)

        3) Fuel flow in gal. per hr. (with the expected fuel pressure gauge indication in pounds per square inch)

        4) True airspeed (kt. and MPH)

2. The FAA test questions gauge your ability to find values on the chart and interpolate between lines (see Figure 36 on page 158).

   a. EXAMPLE: A value for 9,500 ft. would be 75% of the distance between the number for 8,000 ft. and the number for 10,000 ft.

   b. EXAMPLE: At a pressure altitude of 6,000 ft. and a temperature of 26°C and with no wind, a 1,000-NM trip would take 71.42 gal. of fuel (1,000 ÷ 161 kt. = 6.21 hr.) (6.21 hr. x 11.5 gph = 71.42 gal.).

5.5 CROSSWIND COMPONENTS (Questions 25-30)

1. Airplanes have a limit to the amount of direct crosswind in which they can land. When the wind is not directly across the runway (i.e., quartering), a crosswind component chart may be used to determine the amount of direct crosswind. Variables on the crosswind component charts are

   a. Angle between wind and runway
   b. Wind velocity

   NOTE: The coordinates on the vertical and horizontal axes of the graph will indicate the headwind and crosswind components of a quartering wind.

2. Refer to the crosswind component graph, which is Figure 37 on page 160.

   a. Note the example on the chart of a 40-kt. wind at a 30° angle.

   b. Find the 30° wind angle line. This is the angle between the wind direction and runway direction, e.g., runway 18 and wind from 210°.

   c. Find the 40-kt. wind velocity arc. Note the intersection of the wind arc and the 30° angle line.

      1) Drop straight down to determine the crosswind component of 20 kt.; i.e., landing in this situation would be like having a direct crosswind of 20 kt.

      2) Move horizontally to the left to determine the headwind component of 35 kt.; i.e., landing in this situation would be like having a headwind of 35 kt.

      3) EXAMPLE: You have been given 20 kt. as the maximum crosswind component for the airplane, and the angle between the runway and the wind is 30°. What is the maximum wind velocity without exceeding the 20-kt. crosswind component? Find where the 20-kt. crosswind line from the bottom of the chart crosses the 30° angle line, and note that it intersects the 40-kt. wind velocity line. This means you can land an airplane with a 20-kt. maximum crosswind component in a 40-kt. wind from a 30° angle to the runway.

5.6 LANDING DISTANCE (Questions 31-40)

1. Required landing distances differ at various altitudes and temperatures due to changes in air density.

   a. However, indicated airspeed for landing is the same at all altitudes.

2. Landing distance information is given in airplane operating manuals in chart or graph form to adjust for headwind, temperature, and dry grass runways.

3. It is imperative that you distinguish between distances for clearing a 50-ft. obstacle and distances without a 50-ft. obstacle at the beginning of the runway (the latter is described as the ground roll).

4. See Figure 38 on page 162 for an example landing distance graph. It is used in the same manner as the takeoff distance graph discussed on page 146 and printed on page 156.

5. Refer to Figure 39 on page 164, which is a landing distance table.

    a. It has been computed for landing with no wind, at standard temperature, and at pressure altitude.

    b. The bottom "notes" tell you how to adjust for wind, nonstandard temperature, and a grass runway.

        1) Note 1 says to decrease the distance for a headwind. Note that tailwind hurts much more than headwind helps, so you cannot use the headwind formula in reverse.

    c. EXAMPLE: Given standard air temperature, 8-kt. headwind, and pressure altitude of 2,500 ft., find both the ground roll and the landing distance to clear a 50-ft. obstacle.

        1) On the table (Figure 39) for 2,500 ft., at standard temperature with no wind, the ground roll is 470 ft. and the distance to clear a 50-ft. obstacle is 1,135 ft. These amounts must be decreased by 20% because of the headwind (8 kt./4 x 10% = 20%). Therefore, the ground roll is 376 ft. (470 x 80%) and the distance to clear a 50-ft. obstacle is 908 ft. (1,135 x 80%).

5.7 WEIGHT AND BALANCE DEFINITIONS (Questions 41-44)

1. **Empty weight** consists of the airframe, engine, and all items of operating equipment permanently installed in the airplane, including optional special equipment, fixed ballast, hydraulic fluid, unusable fuel, and undrainable (or, in some aircraft, all) oil.

2. Standard weights have been established for numerous items involved in weight and balance computations.

    a. The standard weight for aviation gasoline (AVGAS) is 6 lb./gal.

        1) EXAMPLE: 90 lb. of gasoline is equal to 15 gal. (90 ÷ 6)

3. The **center of gravity** (CG) is the point of balance along the airplane's longitudinal axis. By multiplying the weight of each component of the airplane by its arm (distance from an arbitrary reference point, called the reference datum), that component's moment is determined. The CG of the airplane is the sum of all the moments divided by the total weight.

5.8 CENTER OF GRAVITY GRAPHS (Questions 45-49)

1. The **loading graph** may be used to determine the load moment. (See top graph in Fig. 35 on page 168.)

    a. On most graphs, the load weight in pounds is listed on the vertical axis. Diagonal lines represent various items such as fuel, baggage, pilot and front seat passengers, and back seat passengers.

        1) Move horizontally to the right across the chart from the amount of weight to intersect the line which represents the particular item.

        2) From the point of intersection of the weight with the appropriate diagonal line, drop straight down to the bottom of the chart to the moments displayed on the horizontal axis. Note that each moment shown on the graph is actually a moment index, or moment/1,000. This reduces the moments to smaller, more manageable numbers.

    b. Then total the weights and moments for all items being loaded.

c.   EXAMPLE: Determine the load (total) moment/1,000 in the following situation:

	Weight (lb.)	Moment/1,000 (lb.-in.)
Empty weight	1,350	51.5
Pilot & front seat passenger	400	?
Baggage	120	?
Usable fuel (38 gal. x 6 lb./gal.)	228	?
Oil (8 qt.)	15	−0.2

1)   Compute the moment of the pilot and front seat passenger by referring to the loading graph, and locate 400 on the weight scale. Move horizontally across the graph to intersect the diagonal line representing the pilot and front passenger, and then to the bottom scale which indicates a moment of approximately 15.0.

2)   Locate 120 on the weight scale for the baggage. Move horizontally across the graph to intersect the diagonal line that represents baggage, then down vertically to the bottom which indicates a moment of approximately 11.5.

3)   Locate 228 on the weight scale for the usable fuel. Move horizontally across the graph to intersect the diagonal line representing fuel, then down vertically to the bottom scale which indicates a moment of 11.0.

4)   Notice a −0.2 moment for the engine oil (see note 2 on Fig. 35 on page 168). Add all moments except this negative moment, and obtain a total of 89.0. Then subtract the negative moment to obtain a total aircraft moment of 88.8.

d.   Now add all the weights to determine that the airplane's maximum gross weight is not exceeded.

	Weight (lb.)	Moment/1,000 (lb.-in.)
Empty weight	1,350	51.5
Pilot & passengers	400	15.0
Baggage	120	11.5
Fuel	228	11.0
Oil	15	−0.2
	2,113	88.8

2.   The **center of gravity moment envelope chart** (see bottom graph in Fig. 35 on page 168) is a graph showing CG moment limits for various gross weights. Acceptable limits are established as an area on the graph. This area is called the envelope. Weight is on the vertical axis and moments on the horizontal axis.

a.   Identify the center of gravity point on the center of gravity moment envelope graph by plotting the total loaded aircraft weight across to the right.

b.   Plot the total moment upward from the bottom.

c.   The intersection will be within the CG moment envelope if the airplane has been loaded within limits.

d.   EXAMPLE: Using the data above, locate the weight of 2,113 lb. on the vertical axis, and then move across the chart to the moment line of 88.8. The point of intersection will indicate that the aircraft is within both CG (i.e., normal category) and gross weight (i.e., less than 2,300 lb.) limits.

5.9 CENTER OF GRAVITY TABLES (Questions 50-57)

1. Another approach to determining weight and CG limits is to use tables.
2. First, determine the total moment from the Useful Load Weights and Moments Table (Fig. 33 on page 172).
    a. Moments can be read directly from the table for a specific weight.
    b. If weight is between values, you can use the basic formula to determine the moment:

$$Weight \times Arm = Moment$$

        1) Then divide by 100 to determine moment/100.

3. Then use the Moment Limits vs. Weight Table (Fig. 34 on page 173) to see if the total moment is within maximum and minimum limits for the gross weight.

QUESTIONS AND ANSWER EXPLANATIONS

All the FAA questions from the pilot knowledge test for the private pilot certificate relating to airplane performance and the material outlined previously are reproduced on the following pages in the same modules as the outlines. To the immediate right of each question are the correct answer and answer explanation. You should cover these answers and answer explanations while responding to the questions. Refer to the general discussion in the Introduction on how to take the FAA pilot knowledge test.

Remember that the questions from the FAA pilot knowledge test bank have been reordered by topic, and the topics have been organized into a meaningful sequence. Accordingly, the first line of the answer explanation gives the FAA question number and the citation of the authoritative source for the answer.

5.1 Density Altitude

1.
3386. What are the standard temperature and pressure values for sea level?

A—15 °C and 29.92" Hg.
B—59 °C and 1013.2 millibars.
C—59 °F and 29.92 millibars.

Answer (A) is correct (3386). *(AvW Chap 3)*
The standard temperature and pressure values for sea level are 15°C and 29.92" Hg. This is equivalent to 59°F and 1013.2 millibars of mercury.
Answer (B) is incorrect because standard temperature is 59°F (not 59°C). Answer (C) is incorrect because standard pressure is 29.92" Hg (not 29.92 millibars).

2.
3300. What effect, if any, does high humidity have on aircraft performance?

A—It increases performance.
B—It decreases performance.
C—It has no effect on performance.

Answer (B) is correct (3300). *(PHAK Chap 4)*
As the air becomes more humid, it becomes less dense. This is because a given volume of moist air weighs less than the same volume of dry air. Less dense air reduces aircraft performance.
Answer (A) is incorrect because high humidity reduces (not increases) performance. Answer (C) is incorrect because the three factors which affect aircraft performance are pressure, temperature, and humidity.

3.

3394. Which factor would tend to increase the density altitude at a given airport?

A—An increase in barometric pressure.
B—An increase in ambient temperature.
C—A decrease in relative humidity.

Answer (B) is correct (3394). *(AvW Chap 3)*
When air temperature increases, density altitude increases because, at a higher temperature, the air is less dense.
Answer (A) is incorrect because density altitude decreases as barometric pressure increases. Answer (C) is incorrect because density altitude decreases as relative humidity decreases.

4.

3246. What effect does high density altitude, as compared to low density altitude, have on propeller efficiency and why?

A—Efficiency is increased due to less friction on the propeller blades.
B—Efficiency is reduced because the propeller exerts less force at high density altitudes than at low density altitudes.
C—Efficiency is reduced due to the increased force of the propeller in the thinner air.

Answer (B) is correct (3246). *(AvW Chap 3)*
The propeller produces thrust in proportion to the mass of air being accelerated through the rotating propeller. If the air is less dense, the propeller efficiency is decreased. Remember, higher density altitude refers to less dense air.
Answer (A) is incorrect because there is decreased, not increased, efficiency. Answer (C) is incorrect because the propeller exerts less (not more) force on the air when the air is thinner, i.e., at higher density altitudes.

5.

3291. What effect does high density altitude have on aircraft performance?

A—It increases engine performance.
B—It reduces climb performance.
C—It increases takeoff performance.

Answer (B) is correct (3291). *(PHAK Chap 4)*
High density altitude reduces all aspects of an airplane's performance, including takeoff and climb performance.
Answer (A) is incorrect because engine performance is decreased (not increased). Answer (C) is incorrect because takeoff runway length is increased, i.e., reduces takeoff performance.

6.

3290. Which combination of atmospheric conditions will reduce aircraft takeoff and climb performance?

A—Low temperature, low relative humidity, and low density altitude.
B—High temperature, low relative humidity, and low density altitude.
C—High temperature, high relative humidity, and high density altitude.

Answer (C) is correct (3290). *(PHAK Chap 4)*
Takeoff and climb performance are reduced by high density altitude. High density altitude is a result of high temperatures and high relative humidity.
Answer (A) is incorrect because low temperature, low relative humidity, and low density altitude all improve airplane performance. Answer (B) is incorrect because low relative humidity and low density altitude both improve airplane performance.

7.

3289. If the outside air temperature (OAT) at a given altitude is warmer than standard, the density altitude is

A—equal to pressure altitude.
B—lower than pressure altitude.
C—higher than pressure altitude.

Answer (C) is correct (3289). *(PHAK Chap 3)*
When temperature increases, the air expands and therefore becomes less dense. This decrease in density means a higher density altitude. Pressure altitude is based on standard temperature. Thus, density altitude exceeds pressure altitude when the temperature is warmer than standard.
Answer (A) is incorrect because density altitude equals pressure altitude only when temperature is standard. Answer (B) is incorrect because density altitude is lower than pressure altitude when the temperature is below standard.

DENSITY ALTITUDE CHART

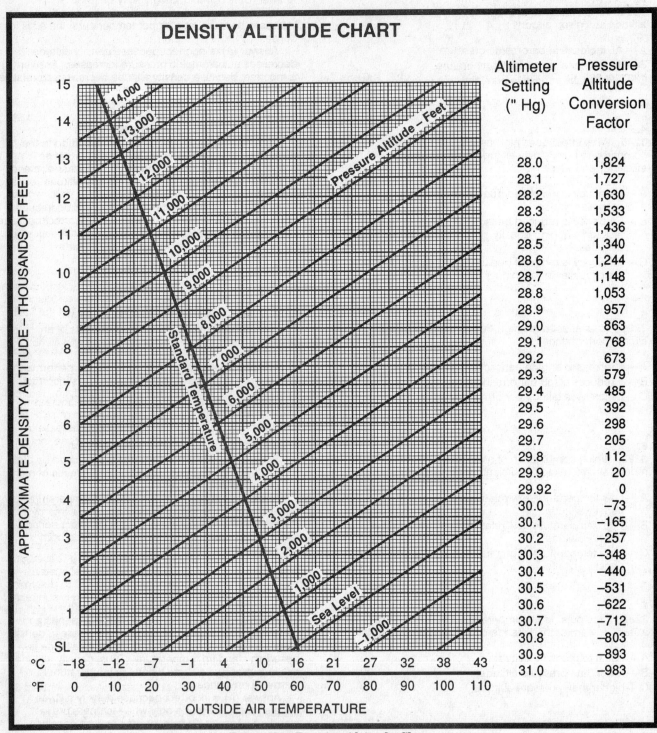

Altimeter Setting (" Hg)	Pressure Altitude Conversion Factor
28.0	1,824
28.1	1,727
28.2	1,630
28.3	1,533
28.4	1,436
28.5	1,340
28.6	1,244
28.7	1,148
28.8	1,053
28.9	957
29.0	863
29.1	768
29.2	673
29.3	579
29.4	485
29.5	392
29.6	298
29.7	205
29.8	112
29.9	20
29.92	0
30.0	−73
30.1	−165
30.2	−257
30.3	−348
30.4	−440
30.5	−531
30.6	−622
30.7	−712
30.8	−803
30.9	−893
31.0	−983

FIGURE 8.—Density Altitude Chart.

5.2 Density Altitude Computations

8.
3298. (Refer to figure 8 on page 152.) Determine the density altitude for these conditions:

Altimeter setting 30.35
Runway temperature . . . . +25 °F
Airport elevation . . . . 3,894 ft MSL

A—2,000 feet MSL.
B—2,900 feet MSL.
C—3,500 feet MSL.

Answer (A) is correct (3298). *(PHAK Chap 4)*
With an altimeter setting of 30.35" Hg, 394 ft. must be subtracted from a field elevation of 3,894 to obtain a pressure altitude of 3,500 ft. Note that the higher-than-normal pressure of 30.35 means the pressure altitude will be less than true altitude. The 394 ft. was found by interpolation: 30.3 on the graph is –348, and 30.4 was –440 ft. Adding one-half the –92 ft. difference (–46 ft.) to –348 ft. results in –394 ft. Once you have found the pressure altitude, use the chart to plot 3,500 ft. pressure altitude at 25°F, to reach 2,000 ft. density altitude. Note that since the temperature is lower than standard, the density altitude is lower than the pressure altitude.
Answer (B) is incorrect because 2,900 ft. MSL would be the density altitude if you added (not subtracted) 394 ft. to 3,894 ft. Answer (C) is incorrect because 3,500 ft. MSL is pressure (not density) altitude.

9.
3296. (Refer to figure 8 on page 152.) What is the effect of a temperature increase from 30 to 50 °F on the density altitude if the pressure altitude remains at 3,000 feet MSL?

A—900-foot increase.
B—1,100-foot decrease.
C—1,300-foot increase.

Answer (C) is correct (3296). *(PHAK Chap 4)*
Increasing the temperature from 30°F to 50°F, given a constant pressure altitude of 3,000 ft., requires you to find the 3,000-ft. line on the density altitude chart at the 30°F level. At this point, the density altitude is approximately 1,650 ft. Then move up the 3,000-ft. line to 50°F, where the density altitude is approximately 2,950 ft. There is an approximate 1,300-ft. increase (2,950 – 1,650 ft.). Note that 50°F is just about standard and pressure altitude is very close to density altitude.
Answer (A) is incorrect because a 900-ft. increase would be caused by a temperature increase of 14°F (not 20°F). Answer (B) is incorrect because a decrease in density altitude would be caused by a decrease, not an increase, in temperature.

10.
3295. (Refer to figure 8 on page 152.) Determine the pressure altitude at an airport that is 3,563 feet MSL with an altimeter setting of 29.96.

A—3,527 feet MSL.
B—3,556 feet MSL.
C—3,639 feet MSL.

Answer (A) is correct (3295). *(PHAK Chap 4)*
Note that the question asks only for pressure altitude, not density altitude. Pressure altitude is determined by adjusting the altimeter setting to 29.92" Hg, i.e., adjusting for nonstandard pressure. This is the true altitude plus or minus the pressure altitude conversion factor (based on current altimeter setting). On the chart, an altimeter setting of 30.0 requires you to subtract 73 ft. to determine pressure altitude (note that at 29.92, nothing is subtracted because that is pressure altitude). Since 29.96 is half way between 29.92 and 30.0, you need only subtract 36 (–73/2) from 3,563 ft. to obtain a pressure altitude of 3,527 ft. (3,563 – 36). Note that a higher-than-standard barometric pressure means pressure altitude is lower than true altitude.
Answer (B) is incorrect because you must subtract 36 (not 7) from 3,563 ft. to obtain the correct pressure altitude. Answer (C) is incorrect because you must subtract 36 (not add 76) from 3,563 ft. to obtain the correct pressure altitude.

11.
3299. (Refer to figure 8 on page 152.) What is the effect of a temperature decrease and a pressure altitude increase on the density altitude from 90°F and 1,250 feet pressure altitude to 55°F and 1,750 feet pressure altitude?

A—1,700-foot increase.
B—1,300-foot decrease.
C—1,700-foot decrease.

Answer (C) is correct (3299). *(PHAK Chap 4)*
     The requirement is the effect of a temperature decrease and a pressure altitude increase on density altitude. First, find the density altitude at 90°F and 1,250 ft. (approximately 3,600 ft.). Then find the density altitude at 55°F and 1,750 ft. pressure altitude (approximately 1,900 ft.). Next, subtract the two numbers. 3,600 ft. minus 1,900 ft. equals a 1,700-ft. decrease in density altitude.
     Answer (A) is incorrect because such a large decrease in temperature would decrease, not increase, density altitude. Answer (B) is incorrect because density altitude would decrease 1,300 ft. if the temperature decreased to 60°F, not 55°F.

12.
3297. (Refer to figure 8 on page 152.) Determine the pressure altitude at an airport that is 1,386 feet MSL with an altimeter setting of 29.97.

A—1,341 feet MSL.
B—1,451 feet MSL.
C—1,562 feet MSL.

Answer (A) is correct (3297). *(PHAK Chap 4)*
     Pressure altitude is determined by adjusting the altimeter setting to 29.92" Hg. This is the true altitude plus or minus the pressure altitude conversion factor (based on current altimeter setting). Since 29.97 is not a number given on the conversion chart, you must interpolate. Compute 5/8 of –73 (since 29.97 is 5/8 of the way between 29.92 and 30.0), which is 45. Subtract 45 ft. from 1,386 ft. to obtain a pressure altitude of 1,341 ft. Note if the altimeter setting is greater than standard (e.g., 29.97), the pressure altitude (i.e., altimeter set to 29.92) will be less than true altitude.
     Answer (B) is incorrect because you must subtract 45 ft. (not add 65) from 1,386 ft. to obtain the correct pressure altitude. Answer (C) is incorrect because you must subtract 45 ft. (not add 176) from 1,386 ft. to obtain the correct pressure altitude.

13.
3292. (Refer to figure 8 on page 152.) What is the effect of a temperature increase from 25 to 50 °F on the density altitude if the pressure altitude remains at 5,000 feet?

A—1,200-foot increase.
B—1,400-foot increase.
C—1,650-foot increase.

Answer (C) is correct (3292). *(PHAK Chap 4)*
     Increasing the temperature from 25°F to 50°F, given a pressure altitude of 5,000 ft., requires you to find the 5,000-ft. line on the density altitude chart at the 25°F level. At this point, the density altitude is approximately 3,850 ft. Then move up the 5,000-ft. line to 50°F, where the density altitude is approximately 5,500 ft. There is about a 1,650-ft. increase (5,500 – 3,850 ft.). As temperature increases, so does density altitude; i.e., the atmosphere becomes thinner (less dense).
     Answer (A) is incorrect because a 1,200-ft. increase would result from a temperature increase of 18°F (not 25°F). Answer (B) is incorrect because a 1,400-ft. increase would result from a temperature increase of 20°F (not 25°F).

14.

3293. (Refer to figure 8 on page 152.) Determine the pressure altitude with an indicated altitude of 1,380 feet MSL with an altimeter setting of 28.22 at standard temperature.

A—3,010 feet MSL.
B—2,991 feet MSL.
C—2,913 feet MSL.

Answer (B) is correct (3293). *(PHAK Chap 4)*
   Pressure altitude is determined by adjusting the altimeter setting to 29.92" Hg, i.e., adjusting for nonstandard pressure. This is the indicated altitude of 1,380 ft. plus or minus the pressure altitude conversion factor (based on the current altimeter setting).
   On the right side of Fig. 8 is a pressure altitude conversion factor schedule. Add 1,533 ft. for an altimeter setting of 28.30 and 1,630 ft. for an altimeter setting of 28.20. Using interpolation, you must subtract 20% of the difference between 28.3 and 28.2 from 1,630 ft. (1,630 – 1,533 = 97 x .2 = 19). Then, 1,630 – 19 = 1,611 and add 1,611 ft. to 1,380 ft. to get the pressure altitude of 2,991 ft.
   Answer (A) is incorrect because 3,010 ft. MSL is obtained by adding the conversion factor for an altimeter setting of 28.20, not an altimeter setting of 28.22, to the indicated altitude. Answer (C) is incorrect because 2,913 ft. MSL is obtained by adding the conversion factor for an altimeter setting of 28.30, not an altimeter setting of 28.22, to the indicated altitude.

15.

3294. (Refer to figure 8 on page 152.) Determine the density altitude for these conditions:

Altimeter setting 29.25
Runway temperature . . . . +81 °F
Airport elevation . . . . 5,250 ft MSL

A—4,600 feet MSL.
B—5,877 feet MSL.
C—8,500 feet MSL.

Answer (C) is correct (3294). *(PHAK Chap 4)*
   With an altimeter setting of 29.25" Hg, about 626 ft. (579 plus ½ the 94-ft. pressure altitude conversion factor difference between 29.2 and 29.3) must be added to the field elevation of 5,250 ft. to obtain the pressure altitude, or 5,876 ft. Note barometric pressure is less than standard and pressure altitude is greater than true altitude. Next convert pressure altitude to density altitude. On the chart, find the point at which the pressure altitude line for 5,876 ft. crosses the 81°F line. The density altitude at that spot shows somewhere in the mid-8,000s ft. The closest answer choice is 8,500 ft. Note that, when temperature is higher than standard, density altitude exceeds pressure altitude.
   Answer (A) is incorrect because 4,600 ft. MSL would be pressure altitude if 650 ft. were subtracted from, not added to, 5,250 ft. MSL. Answer (B) is incorrect because 5,877 ft. MSL is pressure altitude, not density altitude.

5.3 Takeoff Distance

16.
3705. (Refer to figure 41 below.) Determine the total distance required for takeoff to clear a 50-foot obstacle.

OAT .... Std
Pressure altitude .... 4,000 ft
Takeoff weight .... 2,800 lb
Headwind component .... Calm

A—1,500 feet.
B—1,750 feet.
C—2,000 feet.

Answer (B) is correct (3705). *(PHAK Chap 4)*
   The takeoff distance to clear a 50-ft. obstacle is required. Begin on the left side of the graph at standard temperature (as represented by the curved line labeled "ISA"). From the intersection of the standard temperature line and the 4,000-ft. pressure altitude, proceed horizontally to the right to the first reference line, and then move parallel to the closest guideline to 2,800 lb. From there, proceed horizontally to the right to the third reference line (skip the second reference line because there is no wind), and move parallel to the closest guideline all the way to the far right. You are at 1,750 ft., which is the takeoff distance to clear a 50-ft. obstacle.
   Answer (A) is incorrect because 1,500 ft. would be the total distance required with a 10-kt. headwind.
   Answer (C) is incorrect because 2,000 ft. would be the total distance required at maximum takeoff weight.

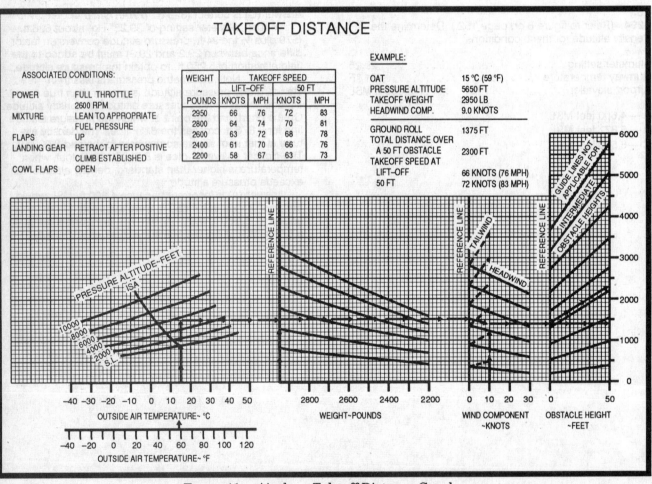

FIGURE 41.—Airplane Takeoff Distance Graph.

17.
3707. (Refer to figure 41 on page 156.) Determine the approximate ground roll distance required for takeoff.

OAT .... 100 °F
Pressure altitude .... 2,000 ft
Takeoff weight .... 2,750 lb
Headwind component .... Calm

A—1,150 feet.
B—1,300 feet.
C—1,800 feet.

Answer (A) is correct (3707). *(PHAK Chap 4)*
Begin on the left section of Fig. 41 at 100°F (see outside air temperature at the bottom). Move up vertically to the pressure altitude of 2,000 ft. Then proceed horizontally to the first reference line. Since takeoff weight is 2,750, move parallel to the closest guideline to 2,750 lb. Then proceed horizontally to the second reference line. Since the wind is calm, proceed again horizontally to the right-hand margin of the diagram (ignore the third reference line because there is no obstacle, i.e., ground roll is desired), which will be at 1,150 ft.
Answer (B) is incorrect because 1,300 ft. would be the ground roll distance required at maximum takeoff weight. Answer (C) is incorrect because 1,800 ft. would be the total distance required to clear a 50-ft. obstacle.

18.
3706. (Refer to figure 41 on page 156.) Determine the total distance required for takeoff to clear a 50-foot obstacle.

OAT .... Std
Pressure altitude .... Sea level
Takeoff weight .... 2,700 lb
Headwind component .... Calm

A—1,000 feet.
B—1,400 feet.
C—1,700 feet.

Answer (B) is correct (3706). *(PHAK Chap 4)*
Begin in the left section of Fig. 41 by finding the intersection of the sea level pressure altitude and standard temperature (59°F) and proceed horizontally to the right to the first reference line. Then proceed parallel to the closest guideline, to 2,700 lb. From there, proceed horizontally to the right to the third reference line. You skip the second reference line because the wind is calm. Then proceed upward parallel to the closest guideline to the far right side. To clear the 50-ft. obstacle, you need a takeoff distance of about 1,400 ft.
Answer (A) is incorrect because 1,000 ft. would be the total distance required at 2,200 lb. takeoff weight. Answer (C) is incorrect because 1,700 ft. would be the total distance required at maximum takeoff weight.

19.
3708. (Refer to figure 41 on page 156.) Determine the approximate ground roll distance required for takeoff.

OAT .... 90 °F
Pressure altitude .... 2,000 ft
Takeoff weight .... 2,500 lb
Headwind component .... 20 kts

A—650 feet.
B—850 feet.
C—1,000 feet.

Answer (A) is correct (3708). *(PHAK Chap 4)*
Begin with the intersection of the 2,000-ft. pressure altitude curve and 90°F in the left section of Fig. 41. Move horizontally to the right to the first reference line, and then parallel to the closest guideline to 2,500 lb. Then move horizontally to the right to the second reference line, and then parallel to the closest guideline to the right to 20 kt. Then move horizontally to the right, directly to the right margin because there is no obstacle clearance. You should end up at about 650 ft., which is the required ground roll when there is no obstacle to clear.
Answer (B) is incorrect because 850 ft. would be the ground roll distance required if the wind were calm. Answer (C) is incorrect because 1,000 ft. would be the ground roll distance required at maximum takeoff weight.

5.4 Cruise Power Settings

20.
3681. (Refer to figure 36 below.) What fuel flow should a pilot expect at 11,000 feet on a standard day with 65 percent maximum continuous power?

A—10.6 gallons per hour.
B—11.2 gallons per hour.
C—11.8 gallons per hour.

Answer (B) is correct (3681). *(PHAK Chap 4)*
Note that the entire chart applies to 65% maximum continuous power (regardless of the throttle), so use the middle section of the chart which is labeled a standard day.
The fuel flow at 11,000 ft. on a standard day would be 1/2 of the way between the fuel flow at 10,000 ft. (11.5 GPH) and the fuel flow at 12,000 ft. (10.9 GPH). Thus, the fuel flow at 11,000 ft. would be 11.5 – 0.3, or 11.2 GPH.
Answer (A) is incorrect because you must add (not subtract) 0.3 to 10.9 to obtain the correct fuel flow.
Answer (C) is incorrect because you must subtract (not add) 0.3 from 11.5 to obtain the correct fuel flow.

CRUISE POWER SETTINGS
65% MAXIMUM CONTINUOUS POWER (OR FULL THROTTLE)
2800 POUNDS

PRESS ALT.	ISA –20 °C (–36 °F)								STANDARD DAY (ISA)								ISA +20 °C (+36 °F)							
	IOAT		ENGINE SPEED	MAN. PRESS	FUEL FLOW PER ENGINE		TAS		IOAT		ENGINE SPEED	MAN. PRESS	FUEL FLOW PER ENGINE		TAS		IOAT		ENGINE SPEED	MAN. PRESS	FUEL FLOW PER ENGINE		TAS	
FEET	°F	°C	RPM	IN HG	PSI	GPH	KTS	MPH	°F	°C	RPM	IN HG	PSI	GPH	KTS	MPH	°F	°C	RPM	IN HG	PSI	GPH	KTS	MPH
SL	27	-3	2450	20.7	6.6	11.5	147	169	63	17	2450	21.2	6.6	11.5	150	173	99	37	2450	21.8	6.6	11.5	153	176
2000	19	-7	2450	20.4	6.6	11.5	149	171	55	13	2450	21.0	6.6	11.5	153	176	91	33	2450	21.5	6.6	11.5	156	180
4000	12	-11	2450	20.1	6.6	11.5	152	175	48	9	2450	20.7	6.6	11.5	156	180	84	29	2450	21.3	6.6	11.5	159	183
6000	5	-15	2450	19.8	6.6	11.5	155	178	41	5	2450	20.4	6.6	11.5	158	182	79	26	2450	21.0	6.6	11.5	161	185
8000	-2	-19	2450	19.5	6.6	11.5	157	181	36	2	2450	20.2	6.6	11.5	161	185	72	22	2450	20.8	6.6	11.5	164	189
10000	-8	-22	2450	19.2	6.6	11.5	160	184	28	-2	2450	19.9	6.6	11.5	163	188	64	18	2450	20.3	6.5	11.4	166	191
12000	-15	-26	2450	18.8	6.4	11.3	162	186	21	-6	2450	18.8	6.1	10.9	163	188	57	14	2450	18.8	5.9	10.6	163	188
14000	-22	-30	2450	17.4	5.8	10.5	159	183	14	-10	2450	17.4	5.6	10.1	160	184	50	10	2450	17.4	5.4	9.8	160	184
16000	-29	-34	2450	16.1	5.3	9.7	156	180	7	-14	2450	16.1	5.1	9.4	156	180	43	6	2450	16.1	4.9	9.1	155	178

NOTES: 1. Full throttle manifold pressure settings are approximate.
2. Shaded area represents operation with full throttle.

FIGURE 36.—Airplane Power Setting Table.

21.
3679. (Refer to figure 36 on page 158.) What is the expected fuel consumption for a 1,000-nautical mile flight under the following conditions?

Pressure altitude . . . . 8,000 ft
Temperature . . . . 22 °C
Manifold pressure . . . . 20.8" Hg
Wind . . . . Calm

A—60.2 gallons.
B—70.1 gallons.
C—73.2 gallons.

Answer (B) is correct (3679). (PHAK Chap 4)
To determine the fuel consumption, you need to know the number of hours the flight will last and the gallons per hour the airplane will use. The chart is divided into three sections. They differ based on air temperature. Use the right section of the chart as the temperature at 8,000 ft. is 22°C.
At a pressure altitude of 8,000 ft., 20.8" Hg manifold pressure, and 22°C, the fuel flow is 11.5 GPH and the true airspeed is 164 kt. Given a calm wind, the 1,000-NM trip will take 6.09 hr. (1,000 NM ÷ 164 kt).

6.09 hr. x 11.5 GPH = 70.1 gal.

Answer (A) is incorrect because 60.2 gal. is the expected fuel consumption for a 1,000-NM flight with a true airspeed of 189 (not 164) kt. Answer (C) is incorrect because 73.2 gal. is the expected fuel consumption for a 1,000-NM flight with a true airspeed of 157 (not 164) kt.

22.
3680. (Refer to figure 36 on page 158.) What is the expected fuel consumption for a 500-nautical mile flight under the following conditions?

Pressure altitude . . . . 4,000 ft
Temperature . . . . +29 °C
Manifold pressure . . . . 21.3" Hg
Wind . . . . Calm

A—31.4 gallons.
B—36.1 gallons.
C—40.1 gallons.

Answer (B) is correct (3680). (PHAK Chap 4)
At 4,000 ft., 21.3" Hg manifold pressure, and 29°C (use the section on the right), the fuel flow will be 11.5 GPH, and the true airspeed will be 159 kt. The 500-NM trip will take 3.14 hr. (500 NM ÷ 159 kt).

3.14 hr. x 11.5 GPH = 36.1 gal.

Answer (A) is incorrect because 31.4 gal. is the expected fuel consumption for a 500-NM flight with a true airspeed of 183 (not 159) kt. Answer (C) is incorrect because 40.1 gal. is the expected fuel consumption for a 500-NM flight with a true airspeed of 143 (not 159) kt.

23.
3682. (Refer to figure 36 on page 158.) Determine the approximate manifold pressure setting with 2,450 RPM to achieve 65 percent maximum continuous power at 6,500 feet with a temperature of 36 °F higher than standard.

A—19.8" Hg.
B—20.8" Hg.
C—21.0" Hg.

Answer (C) is correct (3682). (PHAK Chap 4)
The part of the chart on the right is for temperatures 36°F greater than standard. At 6,500 ft. with a temperature of 36°F higher than standard, the required manifold pressure change is 1/4 of the difference between the 21.0" Hg at 6,000 ft. and the 20.8" Hg at 8,000 ft., or slightly less than 21.0. Thus, 21.0 is the best answer given. The manifold pressure is closer to 21.0 than 20.8.
Answer (A) is incorrect because 19.8" Hg would achieve 65% power at 36°F below (not above) standard temperature. Answer (B) is incorrect because the manifold pressure at 6,500 ft. is closer to 21.0 than 20.8.

24.
3678. (Refer to figure 36 on page 158.) Approximately what true airspeed should a pilot expect with 65 percent maximum continuous power at 9,500 feet with a temperature of 36 °F below standard?

A—178 MPH.
B—181 MPH.
C—183 MPH.

Answer (C) is correct (3678). (PHAK Chap 4)
The left part of the chart applies to 36°F below standard. At 8,000 ft., TAS is 181 MPH. At 10,000 ft., TAS is 184 MPH. At 9,500 ft., with a temperature 36°F below standard, the expected true airspeed is 75% above the 181 MPH at 8,000 ft. toward the 184 MPH at 10,000 ft., i.e., approximately 183 MPH.
Answer (A) is incorrect because 178 MPH is the expected TAS at 6,000 ft. Answer (B) is incorrect because 181 MPH is the expected TAS at 8,000 ft.

5.5 Crosswind Components

25.
3688. (Refer to figure 37 below.) What is the crosswind component for a landing on Runway 18 if the tower reports the wind as 220° at 30 knots?

A—19 knots.
B—23 knots.
C—30 knots.

Answer (A) is correct (3688). *(PHAK Chap 4)*
The requirement is the crosswind component, which is found on the horizontal axis of the graph. You are given a 30-kt. wind speed (the wind speed is shown on the circular lines or arcs). First, calculate the angle between the wind and the runway (220° – 180° = 40°). Next, find the intersection of the 40° line and the 30-kt. headwind arc. Then, proceed downward to determine a crosswind component of 19 kt.
Note the crosswind component is on the horizontal axis and the headwind component is on the vertical axis.
Answer (B) is incorrect because 23 kt. is the headwind (not crosswind) component. Answer (C) is incorrect because 30 kt. is the total wind (not crosswind component).

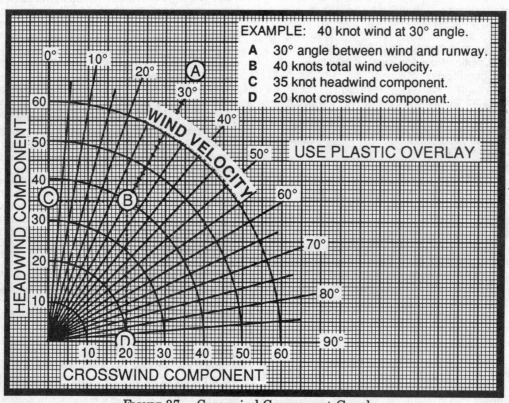

FIGURE 37.—Crosswind Component Graph.

26.
3683. (Refer to figure 37 above.) What is the headwind component for a landing on Runway 18 if the tower reports the wind as 220° at 30 knots?

A—19 knots.
B—23 knots.
C—26 knots.

Answer (B) is correct (3683). *(PHAK Chap 4)*
The headwind component is on the vertical axis (left-hand side of the graph). Find the same intersection as in the preceding question, i.e., the 30-kt. wind speed arc, and the 40° angle between wind direction and flight path (220° – 180°). Then move horizontally to the left and read approximately 23 kt.
Answer (A) is incorrect because 19 kt. is the crosswind (not headwind) component. Answer (C) is incorrect because 26 kt. would be the headwind component if the wind were 30° (not 40°) off the runway.

27.
3684. (Refer to figure 37 on page 160.) Determine the maximum wind velocity for a 45° crosswind if the maximum crosswind component for the airplane is 25 knots.

A—25 knots.
B—29 knots.
C—35 knots.

28.
3686. (Refer to figure 37 on page 160.) With a reported wind of north at 20 knots, which runway (6, 29, or 32) is acceptable for use for an airplane with a 13-knot maximum crosswind component?

A—Runway 6.
B—Runway 29.
C—Runway 32.

29.
3685. (Refer to figure 37 on page 160.) What is the maximum wind velocity for a 30° crosswind if the maximum crosswind component for the airplane is 12 knots?

A—16 knots.
B—20 knots.
C—24 knots.

30.
3687. (Refer to figure 37 on page 160.) With a reported wind of south at 20 knots, which runway (10, 14, or 24) is appropriate for an airplane with a 13-knot maximum crosswind component?

A—Runway 10.
B—Runway 14.
C—Runway 24.

Answer (C) is correct (3684). *(PHAK Chap 4)*
Start on the bottom of the graph's horizontal axis at 25 kt. and move straight upward to the 45° angle between wind direction and flight path line (half-way between the 40° and 50° lines). Note that you are half-way between the 30 and 40 arc-shaped wind speed lines, which means that the maximum wind velocity for a 45° crosswind is 35 kt. if the airplane is limited to a 25-kt. crosswind component.
Answer (A) is incorrect because 25 kt. would be the maximum wind velocity for a 90° (not 45°) crosswind. Answer (B) is incorrect because 29 kt. would be the maximum wind velocity for a 60° (not 45°) crosswind.

Answer (C) is correct (3686). *(PHAK Chap 4)*
If the wind is from the north (i.e., either 360° or 0°) at 20 kt., runway 32, i.e., 320°, would provide a 40° crosswind component (360° − 320°). Given a 20-kt. wind, find the intersection between the 20-kt. arc and the angle between wind direction and the flight path of 40°. Dropping straight downward to the horizontal axis gives 13 kt., which is the maximum crosswind component of the example airplane.
Answer (A) is incorrect because runway 6 would have a crosswind component of approximately 17 kt. Answer (B) is incorrect because runway 29 would have a crosswind component of 19 kt.

Answer (C) is correct (3685). *(PHAK Chap 4)*
Start on the graph's horizontal axis at 12 kt. and move upward to the 30° angle between wind direction and flight path line. Note that you are almost half-way between the 20 and 30 arc-shaped wind speed lines, which means that the maximum wind velocity for a 30° crosswind is approximately 24 kt. if the airplane is limited to a 12-kt. crosswind component.
Answer (A) is incorrect because 16 kt. would be the maximum wind velocity for a 50° (not 30°) crosswind. Answer (B) is incorrect because 20 kt. would be the maximum wind velocity for a 40° (not 30°) crosswind.

Answer (B) is correct (3687). *(PHAK Chap 4)*
If the wind is from the south at 20 kt., runway 14, i.e., 140°, would provide a 40° crosswind component (180° − 140°). Given a 20-kt. wind, find the intersection between the 20-kt. arc and the angle between wind direction and the flight path of 40°. Dropping straight downward to the horizontal axis gives 13 kt., which is the maximum crosswind component of the example airplane.
Answer (A) is incorrect because runway 10 would have a crosswind component of 20 kt. Answer (C) is incorrect because runway 24 would have a crosswind component of approximately 17 kt.

5.6 Landing Distance

31.
3690. (Refer to figure 38 below.) Determine the total distance required to land.

OAT	Std
Pressure altitude	10,000 ft
Weight	2,400 lb
Wind component	Calm
Obstacle	50 ft..

A—750 feet.
B—1,925 feet.
C—1,450 feet.

Answer (B) is correct (3690). *(PHAK Chap 4)*

The landing distance graphs are very similar to the takeoff distance graphs. Begin with the pressure altitude line of 10,000 ft. and the intersection with the standard temperature line which begins at 20°C and slopes up and to the left; i.e., standard temperature decreases as pressure altitude increases. Then move horizontally to the right to the first reference line. Proceed parallel to the closest guideline to 2,400 lb. Proceed horizontally to the right to the second reference line. Since the wind is calm, proceed horizontally to the third reference line. Given a 50-ft. obstacle, proceed parallel to the closest guideline to the right margin to determine a distance of approximately 1,900 ft.

Answer (A) is incorrect because 750 ft. is the total distance required to land with a 30-kt. headwind, not a calm wind, and without an obstacle, not with a 50-ft. obstacle. Answer (C) is incorrect because 1,450 ft. is the approximate total distance required to land at a pressure altitude of 2,000 ft., not 10,000 ft., and a weight of 2,300 lb., not 2,400 lb.

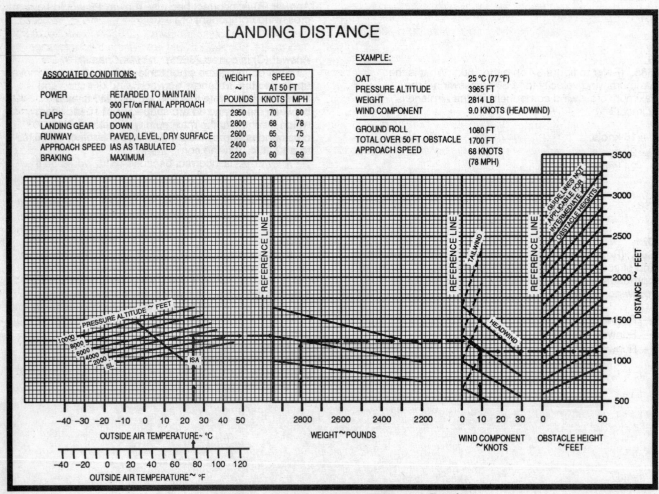

FIGURE 38.—Airplane Landing Distance Graph.

32.

3692. (Refer to figure 38 on page 162.) Determine the approximate total distance required to land over a 50-ft. obstacle.

OAT . . . . 90°F
Pressure altitude . . . . 4,000 ft
Weight . . . . 2,800 lb
Headwind component . . . . 10 kts

A—1,525 feet.
B—1,775 feet.
C—1,950 feet.

Answer (B) is correct (3692). *(PHAK Chap 4)*
To determine the total landing distance, begin at the left side of Fig. 38 on the 4,000-ft. pressure altitude line at the intersection of 90°F. Proceed horizontally to the right to the first reference line. Proceed parallel to the closest guideline to 2,800 lb., and then straight across to the second reference line. Since the headwind component is 10 kt., proceed parallel to the closest headwind guideline to the 10-kt. line. Then move directly to the right, to the third reference line. Given a 50-ft. obstacle, proceed parallel to the closest guideline for obstacles to find the total distance of approximately 1,775 ft.
Answer (A) is incorrect because a distance of 1,525 ft. would be the total distance required with an 18-kt. headwind, not a 10-kt. headwind. Answer (C) is incorrect because a distance of 1,950 ft. would be the total distance required with calm wind conditions, not with a 10-kt. headwind.

33.

3691. (Refer to figure 38 on page 162.) Determine the total distance required to land.

OAT . . . . 90°F
Pressure altitude . . . . 3,000 ft
Weight . . . . 2,900 lb
Headwind component . . . . 10 kts
Obstacle . . . . 50 ft

A—1,450 feet.
B—1,550 feet.
C—1,725 feet.

Answer (C) is correct (3691). *(PHAK Chap 4)*
To determine the total landing distance, begin with pressure altitude of 3,000 ft. (between the 2,000- and 4,000-ft. lines) at its intersection with 90°F. Proceed horizontally to the right to the first reference line, and then parallel to the closest guideline to 2,900 lb. From that point, proceed horizontally to the second reference line. Since there is a headwind component of 10 kt., proceed parallel to the closest headwind guideline down to 10 kt. and then horizontally to the right to the third reference line. Given a 50-ft. obstacle, proceed parallel to the closest guideline for obstacles to find the landing distance of approximately 1,725 ft.
Answer (A) is incorrect because 1,450 ft. would be the total distance required with a 20-kt., not 10-kt., headwind. Answer (B) is incorrect because 1,550 ft. would be the total distance required at a pressure altitude of 2,000 ft., not 3,000 ft.

34.

3689. (Refer to figure 38 on page 162.) Determine the total distance required to land.

OAT . . . . 32°F
Pressure altitude . . . . 8,000 ft
Weight . . . . 2,600 lb
Headwind component . . . . 20 kts
Obstacle . . . . 50 ft

A—850 feet.
B—1,400 feet.
C—1,750 feet.

Answer (B) is correct (3689). *(PHAK Chap 4)*
To determine the total landing distance, begin with the pressure altitude of 8,000 ft. at its intersection with 32°F (0°C). Proceed horizontally to the first reference line, and then parallel to the closest guideline to 2,600 lb. From that point, proceed horizontally to the second reference line. Since there is a headwind component of 20 kt., follow parallel to the closest headwind guideline down to 20 kt., and then horizontally to the right to the third reference line. Given a 50-ft. obstacle, proceed parallel to the closest guideline for obstacles to find the landing distance of approximately 1,400 ft.
Answer (A) is incorrect because 850 ft. would be the ground roll with no obstacle. Answer (C) is incorrect because 1,750 ft. would be the total distance required at maximum landing weight.

35.
3693. (Refer to figure 39 below.) Determine the approximate landing ground roll distance.

Pressure altitude . . . . Sea level
Headwind . . . . 4 kts
Temperature . . . . Std

A—356 feet.
B—401 feet.
C—490 feet.

36.
3697. (Refer to figure 39 below.) Determine the total distance required to land over a 50-ft. obstacle.

Pressure altitude . . . . 3,750 ft
Headwind . . . . 12 kts
Temperature . . . . Std

A—794 feet.
B—836 feet.
C—816 feet.

37.
3696. (Refer to figure 39 below.) Determine the approximate landing ground roll distance.

Pressure altitude . . . . 5,000 ft
Headwind . . . . Calm
Temperature . . . . 101°F

A—495 feet.
B—545 feet.
C—445 feet.

Answer (B) is correct (3693). (PHAK Chap 4)
At sea level, the ground roll is 445 ft. The standard temperature needs no adjustment. According to Note 1 in Fig. 39, the distance should be decreased 10% for each 4 kt. of headwind, so the headwind of 4 kt. means that the landing distance is reduced by 10%. The result is 401 ft. (445 ft. x 90%).
Answer (A) is incorrect because 356 ft. would be the ground roll with an 8-kt., not a 4-kt., headwind. Answer (C) is incorrect because ground roll is reduced, not increased, to account for headwind.

Answer (C) is correct (3697). (PHAK Chap 4)
The total distance to clear a 50-ft. obstacle for a 3,750-ft. pressure altitude is required. Note that this altitude lies halfway between 2,500 ft. and 5,000 ft. Halfway between the total distance at 2,500 ft. of 1,135 ft. and the total distance at 5,000 ft. of 1,195 ft. is 1,165 ft. Since the headwind is 12 kt., the total distance must be reduced by 30% (10% for each 4 kt.).

$$70\% \times 1,165 = 816 \text{ ft.}$$

Answer (A) is incorrect because 794 ft. would be the total distance to land at a pressure altitude of 2,500 ft., not 3,750 ft., with a 12-kt. headwind and standard temperature. Answer (B) is incorrect because 836 ft. would be the total distance to land at a pressure altitude of 5,000 ft., not 3,750 ft., with a 12-kt. headwind and standard temperature.

Answer (B) is correct (3696). (PHAK Chap 4)
The ground roll distance at 5,000 ft. is 495 ft. According to Note 2 in Fig. 39, since the temperature is 60°F above standard, the distance should be increased by 10%.

$$495 \text{ ft.} \times 110\% = 545 \text{ ft.}$$

Answer (A) is incorrect because 495 ft. would be ground roll if the temperature were 41°F, not 101°F. Answer (C) is incorrect because 445 ft. is obtained by decreasing, not increasing, the distance for a temperature 60°F above standard.

LANDING DISTANCE

FLAPS LOWERED TO 40° - POWER OFF
HARD SURFACE RUNWAY - ZERO WIND

GROSS WEIGHT LB	APPROACH SPEED, IAS, MPH	AT SEA LEVEL & 59 °F		AT 2500 FT & 50 °F		AT 5000 FT & 41 °F		AT 7500 FT & 32 °F	
		GROUND ROLL	TOTAL TO CLEAR 50 FT OBS	GROUND ROLL	TOTAL TO CLEAR 50 FT OBS	GROUND ROLL	TOTAL TO CLEAR 50 FT OBS	GROUND ROLL	TOTAL TO CLEAR 50 FT OBS
1600	60	445	1075	470	1135	495	1195	520	1255

NOTES: 1. Decrease the distances shown by 10% for each 4 knots of headwind.
2. Increase the distance by 10% for each 60 °F temperature increase above standard.
3. For operation on a dry, grass runway, increase distances (both "ground roll" and "total to clear 50 ft obstacle") by 20% of the "total to clear 50 ft obstacle" figure.

FIGURE 39.—Airplane Landing Distance Table.

38.
3698. (Refer to figure 39 on page 164.) Determine the approximate landing ground roll distance.

Pressure altitude . . . . 1,250 ft
Headwind . . . . 8 kts
Temperature . . . . Std

A—275 feet.
B—366 feet.
C—470 feet.

Answer (B) is correct (3698). *(PHAK Chap 4)*
The landing ground roll at a pressure altitude of 1,250 ft. is required. The difference between landing distance at sea level and 2,500 ft. is 25 ft. (470 – 445). One-half of this distance (12) plus the 445 ft. at sea level is 457 ft. The temperature is standard, requiring no adjustment. The headwind of 8 kt. requires the distance to be decreased by 20%. Thus, the distance required will be 366 ft. (457 x 80%).
Answer (A) is incorrect because the distance should be decreased by 20% (not 40%). Answer (C) is incorrect because 470 ft. is the distance required at 2,500 ft. in a calm wind.

39.
3694. (Refer to figure 39 on page 164.) Determine the total distance required to land over a 50-foot obstacle.

Pressure altitude . . . . 7,500 ft
Headwind . . . . 8 kts
Temperature . . . . 32°F
Runway . . . . Hard surface

A—1,004 feet.
B—1,205 feet.
C—1,506 feet.

Answer (A) is correct (3694). *(PHAK Chap 4)*
Under normal conditions, the total landing distance required to clear a 50-ft. obstacle is 1,255 ft. The temperature is standard (32°F), requiring no adjustment. The headwind of 8 kt. reduces the 1,255 by 20% (10% for each 4 kt.). Thus, the total distance required will be 1,004 ft. (1,255 x 80%).
Answer (B) is incorrect because 1,205 ft. results from incorrectly assuming that an adjustment for a dry grass runway is necessary and then applying that adjustment (an increase of 20%) to 1,004 ft. rather than to the total landing distance required to clear a 50-ft. obstacle as stated in Note 3, which is 1,255 ft. Answer (C) is incorrect because 1,506 ft. is obtained by increasing, not decreasing, the distance for the headwind.

40.
3695. (Refer to figure 39 on page 164.) Determine the total distance required to land over a 50-foot obstacle.

Pressure altitude . . . . 5,000 ft
Headwind . . . . 8 kts
Temperature . . . . 41°F
Runway . . . . Hard surface

A—837 feet.
B—956 feet.
C—1,076 feet.

Answer (B) is correct (3695). *(PHAK Chap 4)*
Under standard conditions, the distance to land over a 50-ft. obstacle at 5,000 ft. is 1,195 ft. The temperature is standard, requiring no adjustment. The headwind of 8 kt., however, requires that the distance be decreased by 20% (10% for each 4 kt. headwind). Thus, the landing ground roll will be 956 ft. (80% of 1,195).
Answer (A) is incorrect because the distance should be decreased by 20% (not 30%). Answer (C) is incorrect because the distance should be decreased by 20% (not 10%).

5.7 Weight and Balance Definitions

41.
3661. Which items are included in the empty weight of an aircraft?

A—Unusable fuel and undrainable oil.
B—Only the airframe, powerplant, and optional equipment.
C—Full fuel tanks and engine oil to capacity.

Answer (A) is correct (3661). *(PHAK Chap 4)*
The empty weight of an airplane includes airframe, engines, and all items of operating equipment that have fixed locations and are permanently installed. It includes optional and special equipment, fixed ballast, hydraulic fluid, unusable fuel, and undrainable oil.
Answer (B) is incorrect because unusable and undrainable fuel and oil and permanently installed optional equipment are also included in empty weight. Answer (C) is incorrect because usable fuel (included in full fuel) and full engine oil are not components of basic empty weight.

42.
3662. An aircraft is loaded 110 pounds over maximum certificated gross weight. If fuel (gasoline) is drained to bring the aircraft weight within limits, how much fuel should be drained?

A—15.7 gallons.
B—16.2 gallons.
C—18.4 gallons.

Answer (C) is correct (3662). *(PHAK Chap 4)*
Fuel weighs 6 lb./gal. If an airplane is 110 lb. over maximum gross weight, 18.4 gal. (110 lb./6) must be drained to bring the airplane weight within limits.
Answer (A) is incorrect because fuel weighs 6 (not 7) lb./gal. Answer (B) is incorrect because fuel weighs 6 (not 6.8) lb./gal.

43.
3663. If an aircraft is loaded 90 pounds over maximum certificated gross weight and fuel (gasoline) is drained to bring the aircraft weight within limits, how much fuel should be drained?

A—10 gallons.
B—12 gallons.
C—15 gallons.

Answer (C) is correct (3663). *(PHAK Chap 4)*
Since fuel weighs 6 lb./gal., draining 15 gal. (90 lb./6) will reduce the weight of an airplane that is 90 lb. over maximum gross weight to the acceptable amount.
Answer (A) is incorrect because fuel weighs 6 (not 9) lb./gal. Answer (B) is incorrect because fuel weighs 6 (not 7.5) lb./gal.

44.
3664. GIVEN:

	WEIGHT (LB)	ARM (IN)	MOMENT (LB-IN)
Empty weight	1,495.0	101.4	151,593.0
Pilot and passengers	380.0	64.0	---
Fuel (30 gal usable no reserve)	---	96.0	---

The CG is located how far aft of datum?

A—CG 92.44.
B—CG 94.01.
C—CG 119.8.

Answer (B) is correct (3664). *(PHAK Chap 4)*
To compute the CG you must first multiply each weight by the arm to get the moment. Note that the fuel is given as 30 gal. To get the weight multiply the 30 by 6 lb. per gal. (30 x 6) = 180 lb.

	Weight (lb.)	Arm (in.)	Moment (lb.-in.)
Empty weight	1,495.0	101.4	151,593.0
Pilot and passengers	380.0	64.0	24,320.0
Fuel (30 x 6)	180.0	96.0	17,280.0
	2,055.0		193,193.0

Now add the weights and moments. To get CG, you divide total moment by total weight (193,193 ÷ 2,055.0) = a CG of 94.01 in.
Answer (A) is incorrect because the total moment must be divided by the total weight to obtain the correct CG. Answer (C) is incorrect because the total moment must be divided by the total weight to obtain the correct CG.

5.8 Center of Gravity Graphs

45.
3669. (Refer to figure 35 on page 168.) What is the maximum amount of baggage that may be loaded aboard the airplane for the CG to remain within the moment envelope?

	WEIGHT (LB)	MOM/1000
Empty weight	1,350	51.5
Pilot and front passenger	250	---
Rear passengers	400	---
Baggage	---	---
Fuel, 30 gal.	---	---
Oil, 8 qt.	---	−0.2

A — 105 pounds.
B — 110 pounds.
C — 120 pounds.

Answer (A) is correct (3669). *(PHAK Chap 4)*

To compute the amount of weight left for baggage, compute each individual moment by using the loading graph and add them up. First, compute the moment for the pilot and front seat passenger with a weight of 250 lb. Refer to the loading graph and the vertical scale at the left side and find the value of 250. From this position, move to the right horizontally across the graph until you intersect the diagonal line that represents pilot and front passenger. From this point, move vertically down to the bottom scale, which indicates a moment of about 9.2.

To compute rear passenger moment, measure up the vertical scale of the loading graph to a value of 400, horizontally across to intersect the rear passenger diagonal line, and down vertically to the moment scale, which indicates approximately 29.0.

To compute the moment of the fuel, you must recall that fuel weighs 6 lb. per gal. The question gives 30 gal., for a total fuel weight of 180 lb. Now move up the weight scale on the loading graph to 180, then horizontally across to intersect the diagonal line that represents fuel, then vertically down to the moment scale, which indicates approximately 8.7.

To get the weight of the oil, see Note (2) at the bottom of the loading graph section of Fig. 35. It gives 15 lb. as the weight with a moment of −.2.

Now total the weights (2,195 lb. including 15 lb. of engine oil). Also total the moments (98.2 including engine oil with a negative 0.2 moment).

With this information, refer to the center of gravity moment envelope chart. Note that the maximum weight in the envelope is 2,300 lb. 2,300 lb. − 2,195 lb. already totaled leaves a maximum possible 105 lb. for baggage. However, you must be sure 105 lb. of baggage does not exceed the 109 moments allowed at the top of the envelope. On the loading graph, 105 lb. of baggage indicates approximately 10 moments.

Thus, a total of 108.2 moments (98.2 + 10) is within the 109 moments allowed on the envelope for 2,300 lb. of weight. Therefore, baggage of 105 lb. can be loaded.

	Weight	Moment/1000 lb.-in.
Empty weight	1,350	51.5
Pilot and front seat passenger	250	9.2
Rear passengers	400	29.0
Baggage	?	?
Fuel (30 gal. x 6 lb./gal.)	180	8.7
Oil	15	−0.2
	2,195	98.2
		(without baggage)

Answer (B) is incorrect because 110 lb. of baggage would exceed the airplane's maximum gross weight. Answer (C) is incorrect because 120 lb. of baggage would exceed the airplane's maximum gross weight.

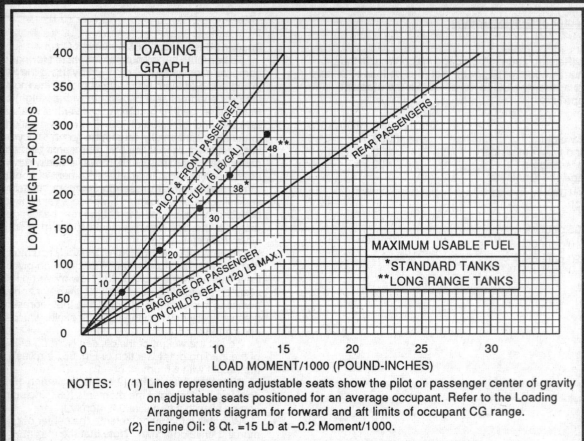

NOTES: (1) Lines representing adjustable seats show the pilot or passenger center of gravity on adjustable seats positioned for an average occupant. Refer to the Loading Arrangements diagram for forward and aft limits of occupant CG range.

(2) Engine Oil: 8 Qt. =15 Lb at −0.2 Moment/1000.

NOTE: The empty weight of this airplane does not include the weight of the oil.

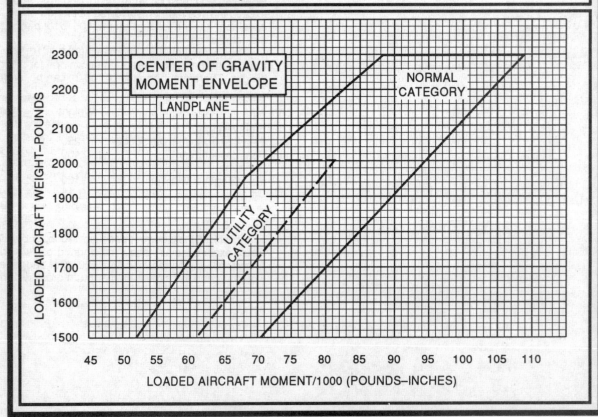

FIGURE 35.—Airplane Weight and Balance Graphs.

46.

3670. (Refer to figure 35 on page 168.) Calculate the moment of the airplane and determine which category is applicable.

	WEIGHT (LB)	MOM/1000
Empty weight	1,350	51.5
Pilot and front passenger	310	---
Rear passengers	96	---
Fuel, 38 gal	---	---
Oil, 8 qt	---	−0.2

A—79.2, utility category.

B—80.8, utility category.

C—81.2, normal category.

47.

3671. (Refer to figure 35 on page 168.) What is the maximum amount of fuel that may be aboard the airplane on takeoff if loaded as follows?

	WEIGHT (LB)	MOM/1000
Empty weight	1,350	51.5
Pilot and front passenger	340	---
Rear passengers	310	---
Baggage	45	---
Oil, 8 qt	---	---

A—24 gallons.

B—32 gallons.

C—40 gallons.

Answer (B) is correct (3670). *(PHAK Chap 4)*

First, total the weight and get 1,999 lb. Note that the 38 gal. of fuel weighs 228 lb. (38 gal. x 6 lb./gal.).

Find the moments for the pilot and front seat passengers, rear passengers, and fuel by using the loading graph in Fig. 35. Find the oil weight and moment by consulting Note (2) on Fig. 35. It is 15 lb. and −0.2 moments. Total the moments as shown in the schedule below.

Now refer to the center of gravity moment envelope. Find the gross weight of 1,999 on the vertical scale, and move horizontally across the chart until intersecting the vertical line that represents the 80.8 moment. Note that a moment of 80.8 lb.-in. falls into the utility category envelope.

	Weight	Moment/1000 lb.-in.
Empty weight	1,350	51.5
Pilot and front seat passenger	310	11.5
Rear passengers	96	7.0
Fuel (38 gal. x 6 lb./gal.)	228	11.0
Oil (8 qt.)	15	−0.2
	1,999	80.8

Answer (A) is incorrect because 79.2 is 1.6 less than the correct moment of 80.8 lb.-in. Answer (C) is incorrect because the moment of the oil must be subtracted, not added.

Answer (C) is correct (3671). *(PHAK Chap 4)*

To find the maximum amount of fuel this airplane can carry, add the empty weight (1,350), pilot and front passenger weight (340), rear passengers (310), baggage (45), and oil (15), for a total of 2,060 lb. (Find the oil weight and moment by consulting Note (2) on Fig. 35. It is 15 lb. and −0.2 moments.) Gross weight maximum on the center of gravity moment envelope chart is 2,300. Thus, 240 lb. of weight (2,300 − 2,060) is available for fuel. Since each gallon of fuel weighs 6 lb., this airplane can carry 40 gal. of fuel (240/6 lb. per gal.) if its center of gravity moments do not exceed the limit. Note that long-range tanks were not mentioned; assume they exist.

Compute the moments for each item. The empty weight moment is given as 51.5. Calculate the moment for the pilot and front passenger as 12.5, the rear passengers as 22.5, the fuel as 11.5, the baggage as 4.0, and the oil as −0.2. These total to 101.8, which is within the envelope, so 40 gal. of fuel may be carried.

	Weight	Moment/1000 lb.-in.
Empty weight	1,350	51.5
Pilot and front seat passenger	340	12.5
Rear passengers	310	22.5
Baggage	45	4.0
Fuel (40 gal. x 6 lb./gal.)	240	11.5
Oil	15	−0.2
	2,300	101.8

Answer (A) is incorrect because more than 24 gal. of fuel may be carried. Answer (B) is incorrect because more than 32 gal. of fuel may be carried.

48.
3672. (Refer to figure 35 on page 168.) Determine the moment with the following data:

	WEIGHT (LB)	MOM/1000
Empty weight	1,350	51.5
Pilot and front passenger	340	---
Fuel (std tanks)	Capacity	---
Oil, 8 qt	---	---

A—69.9 pound-inches.
B—74.9 pound-inches.
C—77.6 pound-inches.

Answer (B) is correct (3672). *(PHAK Chap 4)*
To find the CG moment/1000, find the moments for each item and total the moments as shown in the schedule below. For the fuel, the loading graph shows the maximum as 38 gal. for standard tanks (38 gal. x 6 lb. = 228 lb.). (Find the oil weight and moment by consulting Note (2) on Fig. 35; it is 15 lb. and –0.2. moments.) These total 74.9, so answer (B) is correct.

	Weight	Moment/1000 lb.-in.
Empty weight	1,350	51.5
Pilot and front seat passenger	340	12.6
Fuel	228	11.0
Oil	15	–0.2
	1,933	74.9

Answer (A) is incorrect because this would be the moment with only 20 gal. (not full capacity) of fuel on board. Answer (C) is incorrect because this would be the moment with full long-range (not standard) tanks on board.

49.
3673. (Refer to figure 35 on page 168.) Determine the aircraft loaded moment and the aircraft category.

	WEIGHT (LB)	MOM/1000
Empty weight	1,350	51.5
Pilot and front passenger	380	---
Fuel, 48 gal	288	---
Oil, 8 qt	---	---

A—78.2, normal category.
B—79.2, normal category.
C—80.4, utility category.

Answer (B) is correct (3673). *(PHAK Chap 4)*
The moments for the pilot, front passenger, fuel, and oil must be found on the loading graph in Fig. 35. Total all the moments and the weight as shown in the schedule below.
Now refer to the center of gravity moment envelope graph. Find the gross weight of 2,033 on the vertical scale, and move horizontally across the graph until intersecting the vertical line that represents the 79.2 moment. A moment of 79.2 lb.-in. falls into the normal category envelope.

	Weight	Moment/1000 lb.-in.
Empty weight	1,350	51.5
Pilot and front seat passenger	380	14.2
Fuel (capacity)	288	13.7
Oil	15	–0.2
	2,033	79.2

Answer (A) is incorrect because 78.2 lb.-in. is 1.0 less than the correct moment of 79.2 lb.-in. Answer (C) is incorrect because 80.4 lb.-in. is 1.2 more than the correct moment of 79.2 lb.-in.

5.9 Center of Gravity Tables

50.

3665. (Refer to figures 33 and 34 on pages 172 and 173.) Determine if the airplane weight and balance is within limits.

Front seat occupants .... 340 lb
Rear seat occupants .... 295 lb
Fuel (main wing tanks) .... 44 gal
Baggage .... 56 lb

A—20 pounds overweight, CG aft of aft limits.
B—20 pounds overweight, CG within limits.
C—20 pounds overweight, CG forward of forward limits.

Answer (B) is correct (3665). *(PHAK Chap 4)*
Both the total weight and the total moment must be calculated. As in most weight and balance problems, you should begin by setting up a schedule as below. Note that the empty weight in Fig. 33 is given as 2,015 with a moment/100 in. of 1,554 (note the change to moment/100 on this chart), and that empty weight includes the oil.

The next step is to compute the moment/100 for each item. The front seat occupants' moment/100 is 289 (340 x 85 ÷ 100). The rear seat occupants' moment/100 is 357 (295 x 121 ÷ 100). The fuel (main tanks) weight of 264 lb. and moment/100 of 198 is read directly from the table. The baggage moment/100 is 78 (56 x 140 ÷ 100).

The last step is to go to the Moment Limits versus Weight chart (Fig. 34), and note that the maximum weight allowed is 2,950, which means that the plane is 20 lb. over. At a moment/100 of 2,476, the plane is within the CG limits because the moments/100 may be from 2,422 to 2,499 at 2,950 lb.

	Weight	Moment/100 lb.-in.
Empty weight w/oil	2,015	1,554
Front seat	340	289
Rear seat	295	357
Fuel (44 gal. x 6 lb./gal.)	264	198
Baggage	56	78
	2,970	2,476

Answer (A) is incorrect because the total moment of 2,476 lb.-in. is less (not more) than the aft limit of 2,499 lb.-in. at 2,950 lb. Answer (C) is incorrect because the total moment of 2,476 lb.-in. is more (not less) than the forward limit of 2,422 lb.-in. at 2,900 lb.

51.

3667. (Refer to figures 33 and 34 on pages 172 and 173.) Calculate the weight and balance and determine if the CG and the weight of the airplane are within limits.

Front seat occupants .... 350 lb
Rear seat occupants .... 325 lb
Baggage .... 27 lb
Fuel .... 35 gal

A—CG 81.7, out of limits forward.
B—CG 83.4, within limits.
C—CG 84.1, within limits.

Answer (B) is correct (3667). *(PHAK Chap 4)*
Total weight, total moment, and CG must all be calculated. As in most weight and balance problems, you should begin by setting up the schedule as shown below.

Next, go to the Moment Limits vs. Weight chart (Fig. 34), and note that the maximum weight allowed is 2,950, which means that this airplane is 23 lb. under maximum weight. At a total moment of 2,441, it is also within the CG limits (2,399 to 2,483) at that weight.

Finally, compute the CG. Recall that Fig. 33 gives moment per 100 in. The total moment is therefore 244,100 (2,441 x 100). The CG is 244,100/2,927 = 83.4.

	Weight	Moment/100 lb.-in.
Empty weight w/oil	2,015	1,554
Front seat	350	298
Rear seat	325	393
Fuel, main (35 gal.)	210	158
Baggage	27	38
	2,927	2,441

Answer (A) is incorrect because the correct moment of 2,441 lb.-in./100 is within CG limits. Answer (C) is incorrect because you must divide the total moment by the total weight to arrive at the correct CG of 83.4 in.

USEFUL LOAD WEIGHTS AND MOMENTS

OCCUPANTS

FRONT SEATS ARM 85		REAR SEATS ARM 121	
Weight	Moment 100	Weight	Moment 100
120	102	120	145
130	110	130	157
140	119	140	169
150	128	150	182
160	136	160	194
170	144	170	206
180	153	180	218
190	162	190	230
200	170	200	242

USABLE FUEL

MAIN WING TANKS ARM 75

Gallons	Weight	Moment 100
5	30	22
10	60	45
15	90	68
20	120	90
25	150	112
30	180	135
35	210	158
40	240	180
44	264	198

BAGGAGE OR 5TH SEAT OCCUPANT ARM 140

Weight	Moment 100
10	14
20	28
30	42
40	56
50	70
60	84
70	98
80	112
90	126
100	140
110	154
120	168
130	182
140	196
150	210
160	224
170	238
180	252
190	266
200	280
210	294
220	308
230	322
240	336
250	350
260	364
270	378

AUXILIARY WING TANKS ARM 94

Gallons	Weight	Moment 100
5	30	28
10	60	56
15	90	85
19	114	107

*OIL

Quarts	Weight	Moment 100
10	19	5

*Included in basic Empty Weight

Empty Weight ~ 2015

MOM / 100 ~ 1554

MOMENT LIMITS vs WEIGHT

Moment limits are based on the following weight and center of gravity limit data (landing gear down).

WEIGHT CONDITION	FORWARD CG LIMIT	AFT CG LIMIT
2950 lb (takeoff or landing)	82.1	84.7
2525 lb	77.5	85.7
2475 lb or less	77.0	85.7

FIGURE 33.—Airplane Weight and Balance Tables.

MOMENT LIMITS vs WEIGHT (Continued)

Weight	Minimum Moment 100	Maximum Moment 100	Weight	Minimum Moment 100	Maximum Moment 100
2100	1617	1800	2600	2037	2224
2110	1625	1808	2610	2048	2232
2120	1632	1817	2620	2058	2239
2130	1640	1825	2630	2069	2247
2140	1648	1834	2640	2080	2255
2150	1656	1843	2650	2090	2263
2160	1663	1851	2660	2101	2271
2170	1671	1860	2670	2112	2279
2180	1679	1868	2680	2123	2287
2190	1686	1877	2690	2133	2295
2200	1694	1885	2700	2144	2303
2210	1702	1894	2710	2155	2311
2220	1709	1903	2720	2166	2319
2230	1717	1911	2730	2177	2326
2240	1725	1920	2740	2188	2334
2250	1733	1928	2750	2199	2342
2260	1740	1937	2760	2210	2350
2270	1748	1945	2770	2221	2358
2280	1756	1954	2780	2232	2366
2290	1763	1963	2790	2243	2374
2300	1771	1971			
2310	1779	1980	2800	2254	2381
2320	1786	1988	2810	2265	2389
2330	1794	1997	2820	2276	2397
2340	1802	2005	2830	2287	2405
2350	1810	2014	2840	2298	2413
2360	1817	2023	2850	2309	2421
2370	1825	2031	2860	2320	2428
2380	1833	2040	2870	2332	2436
2390	1840	2048	2880	2343	2444
			2890	2354	2452
2400	1848	2057	2900	2365	2460
2410	1856	2065	2910	2377	2468
2420	1863	2074	2920	2388	2475
2430	1871	2083	2930	2399	2483
2440	1879	2091	2940	2411	2491
2450	1887	2100	2950	2422	2499
2460	1894	2108			
2470	1902	2117			
2480	1911	2125			
2490	1921	2134			
2500	1932	2143			
2510	1942	2151			
2520	1953	2160			
2530	1963	2168			
2540	1974	2176			
2550	1984	2184			
2560	1995	2192			
2570	2005	2200			
2580	2016	2208			
2590	2026	2216			

FIGURE 34.—Airplane Weight and Balance Tables.

52.
3666. (Refer to figures 33 and 34 on pages 172 and 173.) What is the maximum amount of baggage that can be carried when the airplane is loaded as follows?

Front seat occupants	387 lb
Rear seat occupants	293 lb
Fuel	35 gal

A—45 pounds.
B—63 pounds.
C—220 pounds.

Answer (A) is correct (3666). *(PHAK Chap 4)*
The maximum allowable weight on the Moment Limits vs. Weight chart (Fig. 34) is 2,950 lb. The total of the given weights is 2,905 lb. (including the empty weight of the airplane at 2,015 lb. and the fuel at 6 lb./gal.), so baggage cannot weigh more than 45 lb.

It is still necessary to compute total moments to verify that the position of these weights does not move the CG out of CG limits.

The total moment of 2,460 lies safely between the moment limits of 2,422 and 2,499 on Fig. 34, at the maximum weight, so this airplane can carry as much as 45 lb. of baggage when loaded in this manner.

	Weight	Moment/100 lb.-in.
Empty weight w/oil	2,015	1,554
Front seat	387	330
Rear seat	293	355
Fuel, main (35 gal.)	210	158
Baggage	45	63
	2,950	2,460

Answer (B) is incorrect because 63 lb. of baggage would load the airplane above its maximum gross weight. Answer (C) is incorrect because 220 lb. of baggage would load the airplane above its maximum gross weight.

53.
3668. (Refer to figures 33 and 34 on pages 172 and 173.) Determine if the airplane weight and balance is within limits.

Front seat occupants	415 lb
Rear seat occupants	110 lb
Fuel, main tanks	44 gal
Fuel, aux. tanks	19 gal
Baggage	32 lb

A—19 pounds overweight, CG within limits.
B—19 pounds overweight, CG out of limits forward.
C—Weight within limits, CG out of limits.

Answer (C) is correct (3668). *(PHAK Chap 4)*
Both the weight and the total moment must be calculated. Begin by setting up the schedule shown below. The fuel must be separated into main and auxiliary tanks, but weights and moments for both tanks are provided in Fig. 33.

Since 415 lb. is not shown on the front seat table, simply multiply the weight by the arm shown at the top of the table (415 lb. x 85 in. = 35,275 lb.-in.) and divide by 100 for moment/100 of 353 (35,275 ÷ 100 = 352.75). The rear seat moment must also be multiplied (110 lb. x 121 in. = 13,310 lb.-in.). Divide by 100 to get 133.1, or 133 lb.-in./100. The last step is to go to the Moment Limits vs. Weight chart (Fig. 34). The maximum weight allowed is 2,950, which means that the airplane weight is within the limits. However, the CG is out of limits because the minimum moment/100 for a weight of 2,950 lb. is 2,422.

	Weight	Moment/100 lb.-in.
Empty weight w/oil	2,015	1,554
Front seat	415	353
Rear seat	110	133
Fuel, main	264	198
Fuel, aux.	114	107
Baggage	32	45
	2,950	2,390

Answer (A) is incorrect because the airplane's weight of 2,950 lb. is within limits. Answer (B) is incorrect because the airplane's weight of 2,950 lb. is within limits.

54.
3675. (Refer to figures 33 and 34 on pages 172 and 173.) Which action can adjust the airplane's weight to maximum gross weight and the CG within limits for takeoff?

Front seat occupants .... 425 lb
Rear seat occupants .... 300 lb
Fuel, main tanks .... 44 gal

A—Drain 12 gallons of fuel.
B—Drain 9 gallons of fuel.
C—Transfer 12 gallons of fuel from the main tanks to the auxiliary tanks.

Answer (B) is correct (3675). *(PHAK Chap 4)*
First, determine the total weight to see how much must be reduced. As shown below, this original weight is 3,004 lb. Fig. 34 shows the maximum weight as 2,950 lb. Thus, you must adjust the total weight by removing 54 lb. (3,004 – 2,950). Since fuel weighs 6 lb./gal., you must drain at least 9 gal.
To check for CG, recompute the total moment using a new fuel moment of 158 (from the chart) for 210 lb. The plane now weighs 2,950 lb. with a total moment of 2,437, which falls within the moment limits on Fig. 34.

	Original Weight	Adjusted Weight	Moment/100 lb.-in.
Empty weight with oil	2,015	2,015	1,554
Front seat	425	425	362
Rear seat	300	300	363
Fuel	264	210	158
	3,004	2,950	2,437

Answer (A) is incorrect because it is not necessary to drain 12 gal., only 9 gal. Answer (C) is incorrect because transferring fuel to auxiliary tanks will only affect the moment, not the total weight.

55.
3677. (Refer to figures 33 and 34 on pages 172 and 173.) With the airplane loaded as follows, what action can be taken to balance the airplane?

Front seat occupants .... 411 lb
Rear seat occupants .... 100 lb
Main wing tanks .... 44 gal

A—Fill the auxiliary wing tanks.
B—Add a 100-pound weight to the baggage compartment.
C—Transfer 10 gallons of fuel from the main tanks to the auxiliary tanks.

Answer (B) is correct (3677). *(PHAK Chap 4)*
You need to calculate the weight and moment. The weight of the empty plane including oil is 2,015, with a moment of 1,554. The 411 lb. in the front seats has a total moment of 349.35 [411 x 85 (ARM) = 34,935/100 = 349.35]. The rear seat occupants have a weight of 100 lb. and a moment of 121.0 [100 x 121 (ARM) = 12,100/100 = 121.0]. The fuel weight is given on the chart as 264 lb. with a moment of 198.

	Weight	Moment/100 lb.-in.
Empty weight	2,015	1,554
Front seat	411	349.35
Rear seat	100	121.0
Fuel	264	198.0
	2,790	2,222.35

On the Fig. 34 chart, the minimum moment for 2,790 lb. is 2,243. Thus, the CG of 2,222.35 is forward. Evaluate A, B, and C to see which puts the CG within limits.

	Weight	Moment/100
A	+114	+107
B	+100	+140
C	+60	+56
	−60	−45
	0	+11

Answer (B) is correct because at 2,890 lb. (2,790 + 100), moment/100 of 2,362.35 (2,222.35 + 140) is over the minimum moment/100 of 2,354.
Answer (A) is incorrect because at 2,904 lb. (2,790 + 114), the calculated moment/100 of 2,329.35 (2,222.35 + 107) does not reach the minimum required moment/100 of 2,370 for that weight. Answer (C) is incorrect because at 2,790 lb. an increase of 11 moment/100 does not reach the minimum of 2,243.

56.
3674. (Refer to figures 33 and 34 on pages 172 and 173.) Upon landing, the front passenger (180 pounds) departs the airplane. A rear passenger (204 pounds) moves to the front passenger position. What effect does this have on the CG if the airplane weighed 2,690 pounds and the MOM/100 was 2,260 just prior to the passenger transfer?

A—The CG moves forward approximately 3 inches.
B—The weight changes, but the CG is not affected.
C—The CG moves forward approximately 0.1 inch.

Answer (A) is correct (3674). *(AWBH Chap 2)*
The requirement is the effect of a change in loading. Look at Fig. 33 for occupants. Losing the 180-lb. passenger from the front seat reduces the MOM/100 by 153. Moving the 204-lb. passenger from the rear seat to the front reduces the MOM/100 by about 74 (247 – 173). The total moment reduction is thus about 227 (153 + 74). As calculated below, the CG moves forward from 84.01 to 81.00 in.

$$Old\ CG = \frac{226,000\ lb.\text{-}in.}{2,690\ lb.} = 84.01\ in.$$

$$New\ CG = \frac{203,300\ lb.\text{-}in.}{2,510\ lb.} = 81.00\ in.$$

Answer (B) is incorrect because intuitively one can see that the CG will be affected. Answer (C) is incorrect because intuitively one can see that the CG will move forward more than only 0.1 in.

57.
3676. (Refer to figures 33 and 34 on pages 172 and 173.) What effect does a 35-gallon fuel burn (main tanks) have on the weight and balance if the airplane weighed 2,890 pounds and the MOM/100 was 2,452 at takeoff?

A—Weight is reduced by 210 pounds and the CG is aft of limits.
B—Weight is reduced by 210 pounds and the CG is unaffected.
C—Weight is reduced to 2,680 pounds and the CG moves forward.

Answer (A) is correct (3676). *(AWBH Chap 2)*
The effect of a 35-gal. fuel burn on weight balance is required. Burning 35 gal. of fuel will reduce weight by 210 lb. and moment by 158. At 2,680 lb. (2,890 – 210), the 2,294 MOM/100 (2,452 – 158) is above the maximum moment of 2,287; i.e., CG is aft of limits. This is why weight and balance should always be computed for the beginning and end of each flight.
Answer (B) is incorrect because intuitively one can see that the CG would be affected. Answer (C) is incorrect because although the moment has decreased, the CG (moment divided by weight) has moved aft.

END OF CHAPTER

CHAPTER SIX
AEROMEDICAL FACTORS AND
AERONAUTICAL DECISION MAKING (ADM)

This chapter contains outlines of major concepts tested, all FAA test questions and answers regarding aeromedical factors and aeronautical decision making (ADM), and an explanation of each answer. Each module, or subtopic, within this chapter is listed above with the number of questions from the FAA pilot knowledge test pertaining to that particular module. For each module, the first number following the parentheses is the page number on which the outline begins, and the next number is the page number on which the questions begin.

CAUTION: Recall that the **sole purpose** of this book is to expedite your passing the FAA pilot knowledge test for the private pilot certificate. Accordingly, all extraneous material (i.e., topics or regulations not directly tested on the FAA pilot knowledge test) is omitted, even though much more information and knowledge are necessary to fly safely. This additional material is presented in *Pilot Handbook* and *Private Pilot Flight Maneuvers and Practical Test Prep*, available from Gleim Publications, Inc. See the order form on page 326.

6.1 HYPOXIA (Question 1)

1. Hypoxia is oxygen deficiency in the bloodstream and may cause lack of clear thinking, fatigue, euphoria, and, shortly thereafter, unconsciousness.

6.2 HYPERVENTILATION (Questions 2-4)

1. Hyperventilation occurs when an excessive amount of air is breathed out of the lungs, e.g., when one becomes excited or undergoes stress, tension, fear, or anxiety.

    a. This results in an excessive amount of carbon dioxide passed out of the body and too much oxygen retained.

    b. The symptoms are dizziness, hot and cold sensations, nausea, etc.

2. Overcome hyperventilation symptoms by slowing the breathing rate, breathing into a bag, or talking aloud.

6.3 SPATIAL DISORIENTATION (Questions 5-8)

1. Spatial disorientation, e.g., not knowing whether you are going up or down, is a state of temporary confusion resulting from misleading information being sent to the brain by various sensory organs.

2. If you lose outside visual references and become disoriented, you are experiencing spatial disorientation. This occurs when you rely on the sensations of muscles and inner ear to tell you what the airplane's attitude is.

    a. This might occur during a night flight, in clouds, or in dust.

3. The best way to overcome the effects of spatial disorientation is to rely on the airplane instruments.

6.4 VISION (Questions 9-13)

1. Pilots should adapt their eyes for night flying by avoiding bright white lights for 30 min. prior to flight.

2. Due to the eye's physiology, off-center eyesight is better than direct at night. Pilots should scan slowly at night to permit off-center viewing.

3.   Scanning for traffic is best accomplished by bringing small portions of the sky into the central field of vision slowly in succession.

4.   Haze can create the illusion of traffic or terrain being farther away than they actually are.

6.5 CARBON MONOXIDE (Questions 14-15)

1.   Blurred (hazy) thinking, uneasiness, dizziness, and tightness across the forehead are early symptoms of carbon monoxide poisoning. They are followed by a headache and, with large accumulations of carbon monoxide, a loss of muscle power.

2.   Increases in altitude increase susceptibility to carbon monoxide poisoning because of decreased oxygen availability.

6.6 AERONAUTICAL DECISION MAKING (ADM) (Questions 16-25)

1.   **Aeronautical decision making (ADM)** is a systematic approach to the mental process used by pilots to consistently determine the best course of action in response to a given set of circumstances.

2.   Most pilots have fallen prey to dangerous tendencies or behavioral problems at some time. Scud running, continuing visual flight into instrument conditions, and neglecting checklists are three examples of these dangerous tendencies or behavioral problems that must be identified and eliminated.

   a.   In scud running, a pilot pushes his/her capabilities and the airplane to the limits by trying to maintain visual contact with the terrain while trying to avoid contact with it during low visibility and ceilings.

   b.   Continuing visual flight into instrument conditions often leads to spatial disorientation or collision with the ground or obstacles.

   c.   Neglect of checklists is an example of a pilot's unjustified reliance on his/her short- and long-term memory for repetitive tasks.

3.   ADM addresses five hazardous attitudes that contribute to poor pilot judgment.

   a.   Recognition of hazardous attitudes (thoughts) is the first step in neutralizing them in the ADM process.

   b.   When you recognize a hazardous attitude, you should label it as hazardous and then correct it by stating the corresponding antidote, as shown below.

Hazardous Attitude	Antidote
Antiauthority: *Don't tell me!*	Follow the rules. They are usually right.
Impulsivity: *Do something quickly!*	Not so fast. Think first.
Invulnerability: *It won't happen to me.*	It could happen to me.
Macho: *I can do it.*	Taking chances is foolish.
Resignation: *What's the use?*	I'm not helpless. I can make a difference.

4.   You are responsible for determining whether or not you are fit to fly for a particular flight.

   a.   You should ask, "Could I pass my medical examination right now?" If you cannot answer with an absolute yes, you should not fly.

5.   Human error is the one common factor that affects most preventable accidents.

   a.   A pilot who is involved in an accident usually knows what went wrong and was aware of the possible hazards when (s)he was making the decision that led to the wrong course of action.

6.1 Hypoxia

1.
3844. Which statement best defines hypoxia?

A—A state of oxygen deficiency in the body.
B—An abnormal increase in the volume of air breathed.
C—A condition of gas bubble formation around the joints or muscles.

Answer (A) is correct (3844). *(AIM Para 8-1-2)*
Hypoxia is oxygen deficiency in the bloodstream and may cause lack of clear thinking, fatigue, euphoria and, shortly thereafter, unconsciousness.
Answer (B) is incorrect because it describes a cause of hyperventilation. Answer (C) is incorrect because it describes decompression sickness after scuba diving.

6.2 Hyperventilation

2.
3845. Rapid or extra deep breathing while using oxygen can cause a condition known as

A—hyperventilation.
B—aerosinusitis.
C—aerotitis.

Answer (A) is correct (3845). *(AIM Para 8-1-3)*
Hyperventilation occurs when an excessive amount of carbon dioxide is passed out of the body and too much oxygen is retained. This occurs when breathing rapidly, and especially when using oxygen.
Answer (B) is incorrect because aerosinusitis is an inflammation of the sinuses caused by changes in atmospheric pressure. Answer (C) is incorrect because aerotitis is an inflammation of the inner ear caused by changes in atmospheric pressure.

3.
3846. Which would most likely result in hyperventilation?

A—Emotional tension, anxiety, or fear.
B—The excessive consumption of alcohol.
C—An extremely slow rate of breathing and insufficient oxygen.

Answer (A) is correct (3846). *(AIM Para 8-1-3)*
Hyperventilation usually occurs when one becomes excited or undergoes stress, which results in an increase in one's rate of breathing.
Answer (B) is incorrect because hyperventilation is usually caused by some type of stress, not by alcohol. Answer (C) is incorrect because the opposite is true: hyperventilation is an extremely fast rate of breathing and excessive oxygen.

4.
3847. A pilot should be able to overcome the symptoms or avoid future occurrences of hyperventilation by

A—closely monitoring the flight instruments to control the airplane.
B—slowing the breathing rate, breathing into a bag, or talking aloud.
C—increasing the breathing rate in order to increase lung ventilation.

Answer (B) is correct (3847). *(AIM Para 8-1-3)*
To recover from hyperventilation, the pilot should slow the breathing rate, breathe into a bag, or talk aloud.
Answer (A) is incorrect because closely monitoring the flight instruments is used to overcome vertigo (spatial disorientation). Answer (C) is incorrect because increased breathing aggravates hyperventilation.

6.3 Spatial Disorientation

5.
3852. Pilots are more subject to spatial disorientation
if

A—they ignore the sensations of muscles and inner ear.
B—body signals are used to interpret flight attitude.
C—eyes are moved often in the process of cross-checking the flight instruments.

Answer (B) is correct (3852). *(AIM Para 8-1-5)*
Spatial disorientation is a state of temporary confusion resulting from misleading information being sent to the brain by various sensory organs. Thus the pilot should ignore sensations of muscles and inner ear and kinesthetic senses (those which sense motion).
Answer (A) is incorrect because ignoring the sensations of muscles and inner ear will help overcome spatial disorientation. Answer (C) is incorrect because cross-checking the flight instruments will help prevent spatial disorientation.

6.
3853. If a pilot experiences spatial disorientation during flight in a restricted visibility condition, the best way to overcome the effect is to

A—rely upon the aircraft instrument indications.
B—concentrate on yaw, pitch, and roll sensations.
C—consciously slow the breathing rate until symptoms clear and then resume normal breathing rate.

Answer (A) is correct (3853). *(AIM Para 8-1-5)*
The best way to overcome the effects of spatial disorientation is to rely entirely on the aircraft's instrument indications and not upon body sensations. Sight of the horizon also overrides inner ear sensations. Thus, in areas of poor visibility, especially, such bodily signals should be ignored.
Answer (B) is incorrect because yaw, pitch, and roll sensations should be ignored. Answer (C) is incorrect because a decrease in breathing rate is proper treatment for hyperventilation, not spatial disorientation.

7.

3850. The danger of spatial disorientation during flight in poor visual conditions may be reduced by

A—shifting the eyes quickly between the exterior visual field and the instrument panel.

B—having faith in the instruments rather than taking a chance on the sensory organs.

C—leaning the body in the opposite direction of the motion of the aircraft.

Answer (B) is correct (3850). *(AIM Para 8-1-5)*

Various complex motions and forces and certain visual scenes encountered in flight can create illusions of motion and position. Spatial disorientation from these illusions can be prevented only by visual reference to reliable fixed points on the ground and horizon or to flight instruments.

Answer (A) is incorrect because in poor visual conditions, reliable exterior references are not available. Answer (C) is incorrect because to avoid spatial disorientation, the pilot should avoid undue head and body movements and rely totally on the flight instruments. By moving the body in response to perceived motion, the conflicting signals reaching the brain will cause spatial disorientation.

8.

3851. A state of temporary confusion resulting from misleading information being sent to the brain by various sensory organs is defined as

A—spatial disorientation.

B—hyperventilation.

C—hypoxia.

Answer (A) is correct (3851). *(AIM Para 8-1-5)*

A state of temporary confusion resulting from misleading information being sent to the brain by various sensory organs is defined as vertigo (spatial disorientation). Put simply, the pilot cannot determine his/her relationship to the earth's horizon.

Answer (B) is incorrect because hyperventilation causes excessive oxygen and/or a decrease in carbon dioxide in the bloodstream. Answer (C) is incorrect because hypoxia occurs when there is insufficient oxygen in the bloodstream.

6.4 Vision

9.

3835. Which technique should a pilot use to scan for traffic to the right and left during straight-and-level flight?

A—Systematically focus on different segments of the sky for short intervals.

B—Concentrate on relative movement detected in the peripheral vision area.

C—Continuous sweeping of the windshield from right to left.

Answer (A) is correct (3835). *(AIM Para 8-1-6)*

Due to the fact that eyes can focus only on a narrow viewing area, effective scanning is accomplished with a series of short, regularly spaced eye movements that bring successive areas of the sky into the central vision field.

Answer (B) is incorrect because it concerns scanning for traffic at night. Answer (C) is incorrect because you must continually scan successive small portions of the sky. The eyes can focus only on a narrow viewing area, and require at least 1 sec. to detect a faraway object.

10.

3833. What effect does haze have on the ability to see traffic or terrain features during flight?

A—Haze causes the eyes to focus at infinity.

B—The eyes tend to overwork in haze and do not detect relative movement easily.

C—All traffic or terrain features appear to be farther away than their actual distance.

Answer (C) is correct (3833). *(AIM Para 8-1-5)*

Atmospheric haze can create the illusion of being at a greater distance from traffic or terrain than you actually are. This is especially prevalent on landings.

Answer (A) is incorrect because in haze the eyes focus at a comfortable distance which may be only 10 to 30 ft. outside of the cockpit. Answer (B) is incorrect because in haze the eyes relax and tend to stare outside without focusing or looking for common visual cues.

11.

3849. What preparation should a pilot make to adapt the eyes for night flying?

A—Wear sunglasses after sunset until ready for flight.

B—Avoid red lights at least 30 minutes before the flight.

C—Avoid bright white lights at least 30 minutes before the flight.

Answer (C) is correct (3849). *(AFH Chap 10)*

Prepare for night flying by letting your eyes adapt to darkness, including avoiding bright white light for at least 30 min. prior to night flight.

Answer (A) is incorrect because it is not the type of glasses to wear but rather the avoidance of bright white lights. Answer (B) is incorrect because white, not red lights, impair night vision.

12.

3712. What is the most effective way to use the eyes during night flight?

A—Look only at far away, dim lights.

B—Scan slowly to permit offcenter viewing.

C—Concentrate directly on each object for a few seconds.

Answer (B) is correct (3712). *(AFH Chap 10)*

Physiologically, the eyes are most effective at seeing objects off-center at night. Accordingly, pilots should scan slowly to permit off-center viewing.

Answer (A) is incorrect because pilots must look at their gauges and instruments which are 2 ft. in front of them. Answer (C) is incorrect because one's peripheral (off-center) vision is more effective at night.

13.

3713. The best method to use when looking for other traffic at night is to

A—look to the side of the object and scan slowly.

B—scan the visual field very rapidly.

C—look to the side of the object and scan rapidly.

Answer (A) is correct (3713). *(AFH Chap 10)*

Physiologically, the eyes are most effective at seeing objects off-center at night. Accordingly, pilots should scan slowly to permit off-center viewing.

Answer (B) is incorrect because scanning should always be done slowly and methodically. Answer (C) is incorrect because scanning should always be done slowly and methodically.

6.5 Carbon Monoxide

14.
3832. Large accumulations of carbon monoxide in the human body result in

A—tightness across the forehead.
B—loss of muscular power.
C—an increased sense of well-being.

Answer (B) is correct (3832). *(AC 20-328)*
Carbon monoxide reduces the ability of the blood to carry oxygen. Large accumulations result in loss of muscular power.
Answer (A) is incorrect because it describes an early symptom, not the effect of large accumulations. Answer (C) is incorrect because euphoria is a result of the lack of sufficient oxygen, not specifically an accumulation of carbon monoxide.

15.
3848. Susceptibility to carbon monoxide poisoning increases as

A—altitude increases.
B—altitude decreases.
C—air pressure increases.

Answer (A) is correct (3848). *(AIM Para 8-1-4)*
Carbon monoxide poisoning results in an oxygen deficiency. Since there is less oxygen available at higher altitudes, carbon monoxide poisoning can occur with lesser amounts of carbon monoxide as altitude increases.
Answer (B) is incorrect because there is more available oxygen at lower altitudes. Answer (C) is incorrect because there is more available oxygen at higher air pressures.

6.6 Aeronautical Decision Making (ADM)

16.
3931. What is it often called when a pilot pushes his or her capabilities and the aircraft's limits by trying to maintain visual contact with the terrain in low visibility and ceiling?

A—Scud running.
B—Mind set.
C—Peer pressure.

Answer (A) is correct (3931). *(AC 60-22)*
Scud running refers to a pilot's pushing his/her capabilities and the aircraft's limits by trying to maintain visual contact with the terrain while flying with a low visibility or ceiling. Scud running is a dangerous (and often illegal) practice that may lead to a mishap. This dangerous tendency must be identified and eliminated.
Answer (B) is incorrect because mind-set may produce an inability to recognize and cope with changes in the situation requiring actions different from those anticipated or planned. Answer (C) is incorrect because peer pressure may produce poor decision making based upon an emotional response to peers rather than an objective evaluation of a situation.

17.
3939. What often leads to spatial disorientation or collision with ground/obstacles when flying under Visual Flight Rules (VFR)?

A—Continual flight into instrument conditions.
B—Getting behind the aircraft.
C—Duck-under syndrome.

Answer (A) is correct (3939). *(AC 60-22)*
Continuing VFR flight into instrument conditions often leads to spatial disorientation or collision with ground/obstacles due to the loss of outside visual references. It is even more dangerous if the pilot is not instrument qualified or current.
Answer (B) is incorrect because getting behind the aircraft results in allowing events or the situation to control your actions, rather than the other way around. Answer (C) is incorrect because duck-under syndrome is the tendency to descend below minimums during an approach based on the belief that there is always a fudge factor built in; it occurs during IFR, not VFR, flight.

18.
3940. What is one of the neglected items when a pilot relies on short and long term memory for repetitive tasks?

A—Checklists.
B—Situation awareness.
C—Flying outside the envelope.

Answer (A) is correct (3940). *(AC 60-22)*
Neglect of checklists, flight planning, preflight inspections, etc., is an indication of a pilot's unjustified reliance on his/her short- and long-term memory for repetitive flying tasks.
Answer (B) is incorrect because situation awareness suffers when a pilot gets behind the airplane, which results in an inability to recognize deteriorating circumstances and/or misjudgment on the rate of deterioration. Answer (C) is incorrect because flying outside the envelope occurs when the pilot believes (often in error) that the aircraft's high-performance capability meets the demands imposed by the pilot's (often overestimated) flying skills.

19.
3932. What is the antidote when a pilot has a hazardous attitude, such as "Antiauthority"?

A—Rules do not apply in this situation.
B—I know what I am doing.
C—Follow the rules.

Answer (C) is correct (3932). *(AC 60-22)*
When you recognize a hazardous thought, you should correct it by stating the corresponding antidote. The antidote for the antiauthority ("Do not tell me!") hazardous attitude is "Follow the rules; they are usually right."
Answer (A) is incorrect because "Rules do not apply in this situation" is an example of the antiauthority hazardous attitude, not its antidote. Answer (B) is incorrect because "I know what I'm doing" is an example of the macho hazardous attitude, not an antidote to the antiauthority attitude.

20.
3933. What is the antidote when a pilot has a hazardous attitude, such as "Impulsivity"?

A—It could happen to me.
B—Do it quickly to get it over with.
C—Not so fast, think first.

Answer (C) is correct (3933). *(AC 60-22)*
When you recognize a hazardous thought, you should correct it by stating the corresponding antidote. The antidote for the impulsivity ("Do something quickly!") hazardous attitude is "Not so fast, think first."
Answer (A) is incorrect because "It could happen to me" is the antidote for the invulnerability, not impulsivity, hazardous attitude. Answer (B) is incorrect because "Do it quickly and get it over with" is an example of the impulsivity hazardous attitude, not its antidote.

21.
3934. What is the antidote when a pilot has a hazardous attitude, such as "Invulnerability"?

A—It will not happen to me.
B—It can not be that bad.
C—It could happen to me.

Answer (C) is correct (3934). *(AC 60-22)*
When you recognize a hazardous thought, you should correct it by stating the corresponding antidote. The antidote for the invulnerability ("It will not happen to me") hazardous attitude is "It could happen to me."
Answer (A) is incorrect because "It will not happen to me" is an example of the invulnerability hazardous attitude, not its antidote. Answer (B) is incorrect because "It cannot be that bad" is an example of the invulnerability hazardous attitude, not its antidote.

22.
3935. What is the antidote when a pilot has a hazardous attitude, such as "Macho"?

A—I can do it.
B—Taking chances is foolish.
C—Nothing will happen.

Answer (B) is correct (3935). *(AC 60-22)*
When you recognize a hazardous thought, you should correct it by stating the corresponding antidote. The antidote for the macho ("I can do it") hazardous attitude is "Taking chances is foolish."
Answer (A) is incorrect because "I can do it" is an example of the macho hazardous attitude, not its antidote. Answer (C) is incorrect because "Nothing will happen" is an example of the invulnerability hazardous attitude, not an antidote to the macho attitude.

23.
3936. What is the antidote when a pilot has a hazardous attitude, such as "Resignation"?

A—What is the use.
B—Someone else is responsible.
C—I am not helpless.

Answer (C) is correct (3936). *(AC 60-22)*
When you recognize a hazardous thought, you should correct it by stating the corresponding antidote. The antidote for the resignation ("What is the use?") hazardous attitude is "I am not helpless. I can make a difference."
Answer (A) is incorrect because "What is the use?" is an example of the resignation hazardous attitude, not its antidote. Answer (B) is incorrect because "Someone else is responsible" is an example of the resignation hazardous attitude, not its antidote.

24.
3937. Who is responsible for determining whether a pilot is fit to fly for a particular flight, even though he or she holds a current medical certificate?

A—The FAA.
B—The medical examiner.
C—The pilot.

Answer (C) is correct (3937). *(AC 60-22)*
A number of factors, from lack of sleep to an illness, can reduce a pilot's fitness to make a particular flight. It is the responsibility of the pilot to determine whether (s)he is fit to make a particular flight, even though (s)he holds a current medical certificate. Additionally, FAR 61.53 prohibits a pilot who possesses a current medical certificate from acting as pilot in command, or in any other capacity as a required pilot flight crewmember, while the pilot has a known medical condition or an aggravation of a known medical condition that would make the pilot unable to meet the standards for a medical certificate.
Answer (A) is incorrect because the pilot, not the FAA, is responsible for determining whether (s)he is fit for a particular flight. Answer (B) is incorrect because the pilot, not the medical examiner, is responsible for determining whether (s)he is fit for a particular flight.

25.
3938. What is the one common factor which affects most preventable accidents?

A—Structural failure.
B—Mechanical malfunction.
C—Human error.

Answer (C) is correct (3938). *(AC 60-22)*
Most preventable accidents, such as fuel starvation or exhaustion, VFR flight into IFR conditions leading to disorientation, and flight into known icing, have one common factor: human error. Pilots who are involved in accidents usually know what went wrong. In the interest of expediency, cost savings, or other often irrelevant factors, the wrong course of action (decision) was chosen.
Answer (A) is incorrect because most preventable accidents have human error, not structural failure, as a common factor. Answer (B) is incorrect because most preventable accidents have human error, not mechanical malfunction, as a common factor.

END OF CHAPTER

CHAPTER SEVEN
AVIATION WEATHER

This chapter contains outlines of major concepts tested, all FAA test questions and answers regarding weather, and an explanation of each answer. Each module, or subtopic, within this chapter is listed above with the number of questions from the FAA pilot knowledge test pertaining to that particular module. For each module, the first number following the parentheses is the page number on which the outline begins, and the next number is the page number on which the questions begin.

CAUTION: Recall that the **sole purpose** of this book is to expedite your passing the FAA pilot knowledge test for the private pilot certificate. Accordingly, all extraneous material (i.e., topics or regulations not directly tested on the FAA pilot knowledge test) is omitted, even though much more information and knowledge are necessary to fly safely. This additional material is presented in *Pilot Handbook* and *Private Pilot Flight Maneuvers and Practical Test Prep*, available from Gleim Publications, Inc. See the order form on page 326.

7.1 CAUSES OF WEATHER (Questions 1-3)

1. Every physical process of weather is accompanied by, or is the result of, heat exchanges.

2. Unequal heating of the Earth's surface causes differences in pressure and altimeter settings.

3. The Coriolis force deflects winds to the right in the Northern Hemisphere. It is caused by the Earth's rotation.

    a. The deflections caused by Coriolis force are less at the surface due to the slower wind speed.

    b. The wind speed is slower at the surface due to friction between wind and the Earth's surface.

7.2 CONVECTIVE CURRENTS (Questions 4-5)

1. Sea breezes are caused by cool and more dense air moving inland off the water. Once inland, over the warmer land, the air heats up and rises. Currents push the air over the water where it cools and descends, starting the process over again.

2. The development of thermals depends upon solar heating.

7.3 FRONTS (Questions 6-8)

1. A front is the zone of transition (boundary) between two air masses of different density, e.g., the area separating a high pressure system and a low pressure system.

2. There is always a change in wind when flying across a front.

3. The most easily recognizable change when crossing a front is the change in temperature.

7.4 THUNDERSTORMS (Questions 9-17)

1. Thunderstorms have three phases in their life cycle:

    a. Cumulus: The building stage of a thunderstorm when there are continuous updrafts.

    b. Mature: The time of greatest intensity when there are both updrafts and downdrafts (causing severe wind shear and turbulence).

        1) The commencing of rain on the Earth's surface indicates the beginning of the mature stage of a thunderstorm.

    c. Dissipating: When there are only downdrafts; i.e., the storm is raining itself out.

2. Thunderstorms are produced by cumulonimbus clouds. They form when there is

    a. Sufficient water vapor,
    b. An unstable lapse rate, and
    c. An initial upward boost to start the process.

3. Thunderstorms produce wind shear turbulence, a hazardous and invisible phenomenon particularly for airplanes landing and taking off.

    a. Hazardous wind shear near the ground can also be present during periods of strong temperature inversion.

4. The most severe thunderstorm conditions (heavy hail, destructive winds, tornadoes, etc.) are generally associated with squall line thunderstorms.

    a. A squall line is a nonfrontal narrow band of thunderstorms usually ahead of a cold front.

5. A thunderstorm, by definition, has lightning because that is what causes thunder.

6. Embedded thunderstorms are obscured (i.e., pilots cannot see them) because they occur in very cloudy conditions.

7.5 ICING (Questions 18-20)

1. Structural icing requires two conditions:

    a. Flight through visible moisture, and
    b. The temperature at freezing or below.

2. Freezing rain usually causes the greatest accumulation of structural ice.

3. Ice pellets are caused when rain droplets freeze at a higher altitude, i.e., freezing rain exists above.

7.6 MOUNTAIN WAVE (Questions 21-23)

1. Lenticular clouds are almond or lens-shaped clouds, usually found on the leeward side of a mountain range.

    a. They may contain winds of 50 kt. or more.
    b. They appear stationary as the wind blows through them.

2. Expect mountain wave turbulence when the air is stable and winds of 40 kt. or greater blow across a mountain or ridge.

7.7 WIND SHEAR (Questions 24-26)

1. Wind shear can occur at any altitude and be horizontal and/or vertical, i.e., whenever adjacent air is flowing in different directions or speeds.

2. Expect wind shear in a temperature inversion whenever wind speed at 2,000 to 4,000 ft. AGL is 25 kt. or more.

3. Hazardous wind shear may be expected in areas of low-level temperature inversions, frontal zones, and clear air turbulence.

7.8 TEMPERATURE/DEW POINT AND FOG (Questions 27-36)

1. When the air temperature is within 5° of the dew point and the spread is decreasing, you should expect fog and/or low clouds.

    a. Dew point is the temperature at which the air will have 100% humidity, i.e., be saturated.

    b. Thus, air temperature determines how much water vapor can be held by the air.

    c. Frost forms when both the collecting surface is below the dew point of the adjacent air AND the dew point is below freezing. Frost is the direct sublimation of water vapor to ice crystals.

2. Water vapor becomes visible as it condenses into clouds, fog, or dew.

3. Evaporation is the conversion of liquid to water vapor.

4. Sublimation is the conversion of solids (e.g., ice) to water vapor or water vapor to solids (e.g., frost).

5. Radiation fog (shallow fog) is most likely to occur when there is a clear sky, little or no wind, and a small temperature/dew point spread.

6. Advection fog forms as a result of moist air condensing as it moves over a cooler surface.

7. Upslope fog results from warm, moist air being cooled as it is forced up sloping terrain.

8. Precipitation-induced fog occurs when warm rain or drizzle falls through cool air and evaporation from the precipitation saturates the cool air and forms fog.

    a. Precipitation-induced fog is usually associated with fronts.
    b. Because of this, it is in the proximity of icing, turbulence, and thunderstorms.

9. Steam fog forms in winter when cold, dry air passes from land areas over comparatively warm ocean waters and is composed entirely of water droplets that often freeze quickly.

    a. Low-level turbulence can occur and icing can become hazardous in steam fog.

7.9 CLOUDS (Questions 37-43)

1. Clouds are divided into four families based on their height:

    a. High clouds
    b. Middle clouds
    c. Low clouds
    d. Clouds with extensive vertical development

2. The greatest turbulence is in cumulonimbus clouds.

3. Towering cumulus are early stages of cumulonimbus; they usually indicate convective turbulence.

4. Lifting action, unstable air, and moisture are the ingredients for the formation of cumulonimbus clouds.

5. Nimbus means rain cloud.

6. When air rises in a convective current, it cools at the rate of 5.4°F/1,000 ft., and its dew point decreases 1°F/1,000 ft. The temperature and dew point then are converging at 4.4°F/1,000 ft.

    a. Since clouds form when the temperature/dew point spread is 0°, we can use this to estimate the bases of cumulus clouds.

    b. The surface temperature/dew point spread divided by 4.4°F equals the bases of cumulus clouds in thousands of feet above ground level (AGL).

    c. EXAMPLE: A surface dew point of 56°F and a surface temperature of 69°F results in an estimate of cumulus cloud bases at 3,000 ft. AGL: 69°F – 56°F = 13°F temperature/dew point spread; 13°F/4.4°F = approximately 3,000 ft. AGL.

7.10 STABILITY OF AIR MASSES (Questions 44-52)

1. Stable air characteristics

    a. Stratiform clouds
    b. Smooth air
    c. Fair-to-poor visibility in haze and smoke
    d. Continuous precipitation

2. Unstable air characteristics

    a. Cumuliform clouds
    b. Turbulent air
    c. Good visibility
    d. Showery precipitation

3. When air is warmed from below, it rises and causes instability.

4. The lapse rate is the decrease in temperature with increase in altitude. As the lapse rate increases (i.e., air cools more with increases in altitude), air is more unstable.

    a. The lapse rate can be used to determine the stability of air masses.

5. Moist, stable air moving up a mountain slope produces stratus type clouds as it cools.

6. Turbulence and clouds with extensive vertical development result when unstable air rises.

7. Steady precipitation preceding a front is usually an indication of a warm front, which results from warm air being cooled from the bottom by colder air.

    a. This results in stable air with stratiform clouds and little or no turbulence.

7.11 TEMPERATURE INVERSIONS (Questions 53-56)

1. Normally, temperature decreases as altitude increases. A temperature inversion occurs when temperature increases as altitude increases.

2. Temperature inversions usually result in a stable layer of air.

3. A temperature inversion often develops near the ground on clear, cool nights when the wind is light.

    a. It is caused by terrestrial radiation.

4. Smooth air with restricted visibility is usually found beneath a low level temperature inversion.

QUESTIONS AND ANSWER EXPLANATIONS

All the FAA questions from the pilot knowledge test for the private pilot certificate relating to airplanes and the weather material outlined previously are reproduced on the following pages in the same modules as the outlines. To the immediate right of each question are the correct answer and answer explanation. You should cover these answers and answer explanations while responding to the questions. Refer to the general discussion in the Introduction on how to take the FAA pilot knowledge test.

Remember that the questions from the FAA pilot knowledge test bank have been reordered by topic, and the topics have been organized into a meaningful sequence. Accordingly, the first line of the answer explanation gives the FAA question number and the citation of the authoritative source for the answer.

7.1 Causes of Weather

1.
3381. Every physical process of weather is accompanied by, or is the result of, a

A—movement of air.
B—pressure differential.
C—heat exchange.

Answer (C) is correct (3381). *(AvW Chap 2)*
   Every physical process of weather is accompanied by, or is the result of, a heat exchange. A heat differential (difference between the temperatures of two air masses) causes a differential in pressure, which in turn causes movement of air. Heat exchanges occur constantly, e.g., melting, cooling, updrafts, downdrafts, wind, etc.
   Answer (A) is incorrect because movement of air is a result of heat exchange. Answer (B) is incorrect because pressure differential is a result of heat exchange.

2.
3382. What causes variations in altimeter settings between weather reporting points?

A—Unequal heating of the Earth's surface.
B—Variation of terrain elevation.
C—Coriolis force.

Answer (A) is correct (3382). *(AvW Chap 3)*
   Unequal heating of the Earth's surface causes differences in air pressure, which is reflected in differences in altimeter settings between weather reporting points.
   Answer (B) is incorrect because variations in altimeter settings between stations is a result of unequal heating of the Earth's surface, not variations of terrain elevations. Answer (C) is incorrect because variations in altimeter settings between stations is a result of unequal heating of the Earth's surface, not the Coriolis force.

3.
3395. The wind at 5,000 feet AGL is southwesterly while the surface wind is southerly. This difference in direction is primarily due to

A— stronger pressure gradient at higher altitudes.
B— friction between the wind and the surface.
C— stronger Coriolis force at the surface.

Answer (B) is correct (3395). (AvW Chap 4)
Winds aloft at 5,000 ft. are largely affected by Coriolis force, which deflects wind to the right, in the Northern Hemisphere. But at the surface, the winds will be more southerly (they were southwesterly aloft) because Coriolis force has less effect at the surface where the wind speed is slower. The wind speed is slower at the surface due to the friction between the wind and the surface.
Answer (A) is incorrect because pressure gradient is a force which causes wind, not the reason for wind direction differences. Answer (C) is incorrect because the Coriolis force at the surface is weaker (not stronger) with slower wind speed.

7.2 Convective Currents

4.
3450. Convective circulation patterns associated with sea breezes are caused by

A— warm, dense air moving inland from over the water.
B— water absorbing and radiating heat faster than the land.
C— cool, dense air moving inland from over the water.

Answer (C) is correct (3450). (AvW Chap 4)
Sea breezes are caused by cool and more dense air moving inland off the water. Once over the warmer land, the air heats up and rises. Thus the cooler, more dense air from the sea forces the warmer air up. Currents push the hot air over the water where it cools and descends, starting the cycle over again. This process is caused by land heating faster than water.
Answer (A) is incorrect because the air over the water is cooler (not warmer). Answer (B) is incorrect because water absorbs and radiates heat slower (not faster) than land.

5.
3448. The development of thermals depends upon

A— a counterclockwise circulation of air.
B— temperature inversions.
C— solar heating.

Answer (C) is correct (3448). (AvW Chap 4)
Thermals are updrafts in small scale convective currents. Convective currents are caused by uneven heating of the earth's surface. Solar heating is the means of heating the earth's surface.
Answer (A) is incorrect because a counterclockwise circulation describes an area of low pressure in the Northern Hemisphere. Answer (B) is incorrect because a temperature inversion is an increase in temperature with height, which hinders the development of thermals.

7.3 Fronts

6.
3421. The boundary between two different air masses is referred to as a

A— frontolysis.
B— frontogenesis.
C— front.

Answer (C) is correct (3421). (AvW Chap 8)
A front is a surface, interface, or transition zone of discontinuity between two adjacent air masses of different densities. It is the boundary between two different air masses.
Answer (A) is incorrect because frontolysis is the dissipation of a front. Answer (B) is incorrect because frontogenesis is the initial formation of a front or frontal zone.

7.
3423. One weather phenomenon which will always occur when flying across a front is a change in the

A— wind direction.
B— type of precipitation.
C— stability of the air mass.

Answer (A) is correct (3423). (AvW Chap 8)
The definition of a front is the zone of transition between two air masses of different air pressure or density, e.g., the area separating high and low pressure systems. Due to the difference in changes in pressure systems, there will be a change in wind.
Answer (B) is incorrect because frequently precipitation will exist or not exist for both sides of the front: rain showers before and after or no precipitation before or after a dry front. Answer (C) is incorrect because fronts separate air masses with different pressures, not stabilities, e.g., both air masses could be either stable or unstable.

8.
3422. One of the most easily recognized discontinuities across a front is

A—a change in temperature.
B—an increase in cloud coverage.
C—an increase in relative humidity.

Answer (A) is correct (3422). *(AvW Chap 8)*
Of the many changes which take place across a front the most easily recognized is the change in temperature. When flying through a front you will notice a significant change in temperature, especially at low altitudes.
Answer (B) is incorrect because, although cloud formations may indicate a frontal system, they may not be present or easily recognized across the front. Answer (C) is incorrect because precipitation is not always associated with a front.

7.4 Thunderstorms

9.
3441. If there is thunderstorm activity in the vicinity of an airport at which you plan to land, which hazardous atmospheric phenomenon might be expected on the landing approach?

A—Precipitation static.
B—Wind-shear turbulence.
C—Steady rain.

Answer (B) is correct (3441). *(AvW Chap 11)*
The most hazardous atmospheric phenomenon near thunderstorms is wind shear turbulence.
Answer (A) is incorrect because precipitation static is a steady, high level of noise in radio receivers which is caused by intense corona discharges from sharp metallic points and edges of flying aircraft. This discharge may be seen at night and is also called St. Elmo's fire. Answer (C) is incorrect because thunderstorms are usually associated with unstable air, which would produce rain showers (not steady rain).

10.
3440. A nonfrontal, narrow band of active thunderstorms that often develop ahead of a cold front is known as a

A—prefrontal system.
B—squall line.
C—dry line.

Answer (B) is correct (3440). *(AvW Chap 11)*
A nonfrontal, narrow band of active thunderstorms that often develop ahead of a cold front is known as a squall line.
Answer (A) is incorrect because a prefrontal system is a term that has no meaning. Answer (C) is incorrect because a dry line is a front that seldom has any significant air mass contrast, except for moisture.

11.
3436. What conditions are necessary for the formation of thunderstorms?

A—High humidity, lifting force, and unstable conditions.
B—High humidity, high temperature, and cumulus clouds.
C—Lifting force, moist air, and extensive cloud cover.

Answer (A) is correct (3436). *(AvW Chap 11)*
Thunderstorms form when there is sufficient water vapor, an unstable lapse rate, and an initial upward boost (lifting) to start the storm process.
Answer (B) is incorrect because a high temperature is not required for the formation of thunderstorms. Answer (C) is incorrect because extensive cloud cover is not necessary for the formation of thunderstorms.

12.
3437. During the life cycle of a thunderstorm, which stage is characterized predominately by downdrafts?

A—Cumulus.
B—Dissipating.
C—Mature.

Answer (B) is correct (3437). *(AvW Chap 11)*
Thunderstorms have three life cycles: cumulus, mature, and dissipating. It is in the dissipating stage that the storm is characterized by downdrafts as the storm rains itself out.
Answer (A) is incorrect because cumulus is the building stage when there are updrafts. Answer (C) is incorrect because the mature stage is when there are both updrafts and downdrafts, which create dangerous wind shears.

13.
3438. Thunderstorms reach their greatest intensity during the

A—mature stage.
B—downdraft stage.
C—cumulus stage.

Answer (A) is correct (3438). *(AvW Chap 11)*
Thunderstorms reach their greatest intensity during the mature stage, where updrafts and downdrafts cause a high level of wind shear.
Answer (B) is incorrect because the downdraft stage is known as the dissipating stage, which is when the thunderstorm rains itself out. Answer (C) is incorrect because the cumulus stage is characterized by continuous updrafts and is not the most intense stage of a thunderstorm.

14.
3434. What feature is normally associated with the cumulus stage of a thunderstorm?

A— Roll cloud.
B— Continuous updraft.
C— Frequent lightning.

Answer (B) is correct (3434). *(AvW Chap 11)*
The cumulus stage of a thunderstorm has continuous updrafts which build the storm. The water droplets are carried up until they become too heavy. Once they begin falling and creating downdrafts, the storm changes from the cumulus to the mature stage.
Answer (A) is incorrect because the roll cloud is the cloud on the ground which is formed by the downrushing cold air pushing out from underneath the bottom of the thunderstorm. Answer (C) is incorrect because frequent lightning is associated with the mature stage where there is a considerable amount of wind shear and static electricity.

15.
3435. Which weather phenomenon signals the beginning of the mature stage of a thunderstorm?

A— The appearance of an anvil top.
B— Precipitation beginning to fall.
C— Maximum growth rate of the clouds.

Answer (B) is correct (3435). *(AvW Chap 11)*
The mature stage of a thunderstorm begins when rain begins falling. This means that the downdrafts are occurring sufficiently to carry water all the way through the thunderstorm.
Answer (A) is incorrect because the appearance of an anvil top normally occurs during the dissipating stage when the upper winds blow the top of the cloud down-wind. Answer (C) is incorrect because the maximum growth rate of clouds is later in the mature stage, and does not necessarily mark the start of the mature stage.

16.
3439. Thunderstorms which generally produce the most intense hazard to aircraft are

A— squall line thunderstorms.
B— steady-state thunderstorms.
C— warm front thunderstorms.

Answer (A) is correct (3439). *(AvW Chap 11)*
A squall line is a nonfrontal narrow band of active thunderstorms. It often contains severe, steady-state thunderstorms and presents the single most intense weather hazard to airplanes.
Answer (B) is incorrect because steady-state thunderstorms are normally associated with weather systems and often form into squall lines. Answer (C) is incorrect because squall line (not warm front) thunderstorms generally produce the most intense hazard to aircraft.

17.
3452. Which weather phenomenon is always associated with a thunderstorm?

A— Lightning.
B— Heavy rain.
C— Hail.

Answer (A) is correct (3452). *(AvW Chap 11)*
A thunderstorm, by definition, has lightning, because lightning causes the thunder.
Answer (B) is incorrect because, while heavy rain showers usually occur, hail may occur instead.
Answer (C) is incorrect because hail is produced only when the lifting action extends above the freezing level and the supercooled water begins to freeze.

7.5 Icing

18.
3429. One in-flight condition necessary for structural icing to form is

A— small temperature/dewpoint spread.
B— stratiform clouds.
C— visible moisture.

Answer (C) is correct (3429). *(AvW Chap 10)*
Two conditions are necessary for structural icing while in flight. First, the airplane must be flying through visible moisture, such as rain or cloud droplets. Second, the temperature at the point where the moisture strikes the airplane must be freezing or below.
Answer (A) is incorrect because the temperature dew point spread is not a factor in icing as it is in the formation of fog or clouds. Answer (B) is incorrect because no special cloud formation is necessary for icing as long as visible moisture is present.

19.
3430. In which environment is aircraft structural ice most likely to have the highest accumulation rate?

A— Cumulus clouds with below freezing temperatures.
B— Freezing drizzle.
C— Freezing rain.

Answer (C) is correct (3430). *(AvW Chap 10)*
Freezing rain usually causes the highest accumulation rate of structural icing because of the nature of the supercooled water striking the airplane.
Answer (A) is incorrect because, while icing potential is great in cumulus clouds with below freezing temperatures, the highest accumulation rate is in an area with large, supercooled water drops (i.e., freezing rain). Answer (B) is incorrect because freezing drizzle will not build up ice as quickly as freezing rain will.

20.
3402. The presence of ice pellets at the surface is evidence that there

A— are thunderstorms in the area.
B— has been cold frontal passage.
C— is a temperature inversion with freezing rain at a higher altitude.

Answer (C) is correct (3402). *(AvW Chap 5)*
Rain falling through colder air may freeze during its descent, falling as ice pellets. Ice pellets always indicate freezing rain at a higher altitude.
Answer (A) is incorrect because ice pellets form when rain freezes during its descent which may or may not be as a result of a thunderstorm. Answer (B) is incorrect because ice pellets only indicate that rain is freezing at a higher altitude, not that a cold front has passed through an area.

7.6 Mountain Wave

21.
3417. An almond or lens-shaped cloud which appears stationary, but which may contain winds of 50 knots or more, is referred to as

A— an inactive frontal cloud.
B— a funnel cloud.
C— a lenticular cloud.

Answer (C) is correct (3417). *(AvW Chap 9)*
Lenticular clouds are lens-shaped clouds which indicate the crests of standing mountain waves. They form in the updraft and dissipate in the downdraft, so they do not move as the wind blows through them. Lenticular clouds may contain winds of 50 kt. or more and are extremely dangerous.
Answer (A) is incorrect because frontal clouds usually do not contain winds of 50 kt. or more, and if they do, they do not appear stationary. Answer (B) is incorrect because a funnel cloud is not stationary.

22.
3418. Crests of standing mountain waves may be marked by stationary, lens-shaped clouds known as

A— mammatocumulus clouds.
B— standing lenticular clouds.
C— roll clouds.

Answer (B) is correct (3418). *(AvW Chap 9)*
Lens-shaped clouds, which indicate crests of standing mountain waves, are called standing lenticular clouds. They form in the updraft and dissipate in the downdraft so that they do not move as the wind blows through them.
Answer (A) is incorrect because cumulonimbus mamma clouds (also mammatocumulus) are cumulonimbus clouds with pods or circular domes on the bottom that indicate severe turbulence. Answer (C) is incorrect because roll clouds are low-level, turbulent areas in the shear zone between the plow wind surrounding the outrushing air from a thunderstorm and the surrounding air.

23.
3425. Possible mountain wave turbulence could be anticipated when winds of 40 knots or greater blow

A— across a mountain ridge, and the air is stable.
B— down a mountain valley, and the air is unstable.
C— parallel to a mountain peak, and the air is stable.

Answer (A) is correct (3425). *(AvW Chap 9)*
Always anticipate possible mountain wave turbulence when the air is stable and winds of 40 kt. or greater blow across a mountain or ridge.
Answer (B) is incorrect because the wind must blow across the mountain or ridge before it flows down a valley. The air must also be stable. If the air is unstable and produces convective turbulence, it will rise and disrupt the "wave." Answer (C) is incorrect because any time the winds are 40 kt. or more and blowing across (not parallel) to the mountains, you should anticipate mountain wave turbulence.

7.7 Wind Shear

24.
3426. Where does wind shear occur?

A— Only at higher altitudes.
B— Only at lower altitudes.
C— At all altitudes, in all directions.

Answer (C) is correct (3426). *(AvW Chap 9)*
Wind shear is the eddies in between two wind currents of differing velocities, direction, or both. Wind shear may be associated with either a wind shift or a wind speed gradient at any level in the atmosphere.
Answer (A) is incorrect because a wind shear may occur at any (not only higher) altitudes. Answer (B) is incorrect because a wind shear may occur at any (not only lower) altitudes.

25.
3428. A pilot can expect a wind-shear zone in a temperature inversion whenever the windspeed at 2,000 to 4,000 feet above the surface is at least

A— 10 knots.
B— 15 knots.
C— 25 knots.

Answer (C) is correct (3428). *(AvW Chap 9)*
When taking off or landing in calm wind under clear skies within a few hours before or after sunset, prepare for a temperature inversion near the ground. You can be relatively certain of a shear zone in the inversion if you know the wind is 25 kt. or more at 2,000 to 4,000 ft. Allow a margin of airspeed above normal climb or approach speed to alleviate the danger of stall in the event of turbulence or sudden change in wind velocity.
Answer (A) is incorrect because a wind shear zone can be expected in a temperature inversion at 2,000 to 4,000 ft. AGL if the wind speed is at least 25 (not 10) kt. Answer (B) is incorrect because a wind shear zone can be expected in a temperature inversion at 2,000 to 4,000 ft. AGL if the wind speed is at least 25 (not 15) kt.

26.
3427. When may hazardous wind shear be expected?

A— When stable air crosses a mountain barrier where it tends to flow in layers forming lenticular clouds.
B— In areas of low-level temperature inversion, frontal zones, and clear air turbulence.
C— Following frontal passage when stratocumulus clouds form indicating mechanical mixing.

Answer (B) is correct (3427). *(AvW Chap 9)*
Wind shear is the abrupt rate of change of wind velocity (direction and/or speed) per unit of distance and is normally expressed as vertical or horizontal wind shear. Hazardous wind shear may be expected in areas of low-level temperature inversion, frontal zones, and clear air turbulence.
Answer (A) is incorrect because a mountain wave forms when stable air crosses a mountain barrier where it tends to flow in layers forming lenticular clouds. Turbulence, not wind shear, is expected in this area. Answer (C) is incorrect because mechanical turbulence (not wind shear) may be expected following frontal passage when clouds form, indicating mechanical mixing.

7.8 Temperature/Dew Point and Fog

27.
3444. If the temperature/dewpoint spread is small and decreasing, and the temperature is 62 °F, what type weather is most likely to develop?

A— Freezing precipitation.
B— Thunderstorms.
C— Fog or low clouds.

Answer (C) is correct (3444). *(AvW Chap 5)*
The difference between the air temperature and dew point is the temperature/dew point spread. As the temperature/dew point spread decreases, fog or low clouds tend to develop.
Answer (A) is incorrect because there cannot be freezing precipitation if the temperature is 62°F.
Answer (B) is incorrect because thunderstorms have to do with unstable lapse rates, not temperature/dew point spreads.

28.
3397. What is meant by the term "dewpoint"?

A— The temperature at which condensation and evaporation are equal.
B— The temperature at which dew will always form.
C— The temperature to which air must be cooled to become saturated.

Answer (C) is correct (3397). *(AvW Chap 5)*
Dew point is the temperature to which air must be cooled to become saturated, or have 100% humidity.
Answer (A) is incorrect because evaporation is the change from water to water vapor and is not directly related to the dew point. Answer (B) is incorrect because dew forms only when heat radiates from an object whose temperature lowers below the dew point of the adjacent air.

29.
3398. The amount of water vapor which air can hold depends on the

A— dewpoint.
B— air temperature.
C— stability of the air.

30.
3400. What are the processes by which moisture is added to unsaturated air?

A— Evaporation and sublimation.
B— Heating and condensation.
C— Supersaturation and evaporation.

31.
3401. Which conditions result in the formation of frost?

A— The temperature of the collecting surface is at or below freezing when small droplets of moisture fall on the surface.
B— The temperature of the collecting surface is at or below the dewpoint of the adjacent air and the dewpoint is below freezing.
C— The temperature of the surrounding air is at or below freezing when small drops of moisture fall on the collecting surface.

32.
3399. Clouds, fog, or dew will always form when

A— water vapor condenses.
B— water vapor is present.
C— relative humidity reaches 100 percent.

33.
3447. Low-level turbulence can occur and icing can become hazardous in which type of fog?

A— Rain-induced fog.
B— Upslope fog.
C— Steam fog.

Answer (B) is correct (3398). *(AvW Chap 5)*
Air temperature largely determines how much water vapor can be held by the air. Warm air can hold more water vapor than cool air.
Answer (A) is incorrect because dew point is the temperature at which air must be cooled to become saturated by the water vapor already present in the air. Answer (C) is incorrect because air stability is the state of the atmosphere at which vertical distribution of temperature is such that air particles will resist displacement from their initial level.

Answer (A) is correct (3400). *(AvW Chap 5)*
Evaporation is the process of converting a liquid to water vapor, and sublimation is the process of converting ice to water vapor.
Answer (B) is incorrect because heating alone does not add moisture. Condensation is the change of water vapor to liquid water. Answer (C) is incorrect because supersaturation is a nonsense term in this context.

Answer (B) is correct (3401). *(AvW Chap 5)*
Frost forms when both the collecting surface is below the dew point of the adjacent air AND the dew point is below freezing. Frost is the direct sublimation of water vapor to ice crystals.
Answer (A) is incorrect because if small droplets of water fall on the collecting surface which is at or below freezing, ice (not frost) will form. Answer (C) is incorrect because if small droplets of water fall while the surrounding air is at or below freezing, ice (not frost) will form.

Answer (A) is correct (3399). *(AvW Chap 5)*
As water vapor condenses, it becomes visible as clouds, fog, or dew.
Answer (B) is incorrect because water vapor is usually always present but does not form clouds, fog, or dew without condensation. Answer (C) is incorrect because even at 100% humidity water vapor may not condense, e.g., sufficient condensation nuclei may not be present.

Answer (C) is correct (3447). *(AvW Chap 14)*
Steam fog forms in winter when cold, dry air passes from land areas over comparatively warm ocean waters, and is composed entirely of water droplets that often freeze quickly. Low-level turbulence can occur and icing can become hazardous.
Answer (A) is incorrect because precipitation- (rain-) induced fog is formed when relatively warm rain or drizzle falls through cool air, and evaporation from the precipitation saturates the cool air and forms fog. While the hazards of turbulence and icing may occur in the proximity of rain-induced fog, these hazards occur as a result of the steam fog formation process. Answer (B) is incorrect because upslope fog forms when moist, stable air is cooled as it moves up sloping terrain.

34.

3445. In which situation is advection fog most likely to form?

A— A warm, moist air mass on the windward side of mountains.

B— An air mass moving inland from the coast in winter.

C— A light breeze blowing colder air out to sea.

35.

3443. What situation is most conducive to the formation of radiation fog?

A— Warm, moist air over low, flatland areas on clear, calm nights.

B— Moist, tropical air moving over cold, offshore water.

C— The movement of cold air over much warmer water.

36.

3446. What types of fog depend upon wind in order to exist?

A— Radiation fog and ice fog.

B— Steam fog and ground fog.

C— Advection fog and upslope fog.

7.9 Clouds

37.

3416. Clouds are divided into four families according to their

A— outward shape.

B— height range.

C— composition.

38.

3415. The suffix "nimbus," used in naming clouds, means

A— a cloud with extensive vertical development.

B— a rain cloud.

C— a middle cloud containing ice pellets.

39.

3433. The conditions necessary for the formation of cumulonimbus clouds are a lifting action and

A— unstable air containing an excess of condensation nuclei.

B— unstable, moist air.

C— either stable or unstable air.

Answer (B) is correct (3445). *(AvW Chap 12)*

Advection fog forms when moist air moves over colder ground or water. It is most common in coastal areas.

Answer (A) is incorrect because a warm, moist air mass on the windward side of mountains produces rain or upslope fog as it blows upward and cools. Answer (C) is incorrect because a light breeze blowing colder air out to sea causes steam fog.

Answer (A) is correct (3443). *(AvW Chap 12)*

Radiation fog is shallow fog of which ground fog is one form. It occurs under conditions of clear skies, little or no wind, and a small temperature/dew point spread. The fog forms almost exclusively at night or near dawn as a result of terrestrial radiation cooling the ground and the ground cooling the air on contact with it.

Answer (B) is incorrect because moist, tropical air moving over cold, offshore water causes advection fog, not radiation fog. Answer (C) is incorrect because movement of cold dry air over much warmer water results in steam fog.

Answer (C) is correct (3446). *(AvW Chap 14)*

Advection fog forms when moist air moves over colder ground or water. It is most common in coastal areas. Upslope fog forms when wind blows moist air upward over rising terrain and the air cools below its dew point. Both advection fog and upslope fog require wind to move air masses.

Answer (A) is incorrect because no wind is required for the formation of either radiation or ice fog. Answer (B) is incorrect because no wind is required for the formation of ground (radiation) fog.

Answer (B) is correct (3416). *(AvW Chap 7)*

The four families of clouds are high clouds, middle clouds, low clouds, and clouds with extensive vertical development. Thus, they are based upon their height range.

Answer (A) is incorrect because clouds are divided by their height range, not outward shape. Answer (C) is incorrect because clouds are divided by their height range, not by their composition.

Answer (B) is correct (3415). *(AvW Chap 7)*

The suffix nimbus or the prefix nimbo means a rain cloud.

Answer (A) is incorrect because clouds with extensive vertical development are called either towering cumulus or cumulonimbus. Answer (C) is incorrect because a middle cloud has the prefix alto.

Answer (B) is correct (3433). *(AvW Chap 11)*

Unstable moist air in addition to a lifting action, i.e., convective activity, are needed to form cumulonimbus clouds.

Answer (A) is incorrect because there must be moisture available to produce the clouds and rain; i.e., in a hot, dry dust storm, there would be no thunderstorm. Answer (C) is incorrect because the air must be unstable or there will be no lifting action.

40.
3419. What clouds have the greatest turbulence?

A— Towering cumulus.
B— Cumulonimbus.
C— Nimbostratus.

41.
3420. What cloud types would indicate convective turbulence?

A— Cirrus clouds.
B— Nimbostratus clouds.
C— Towering cumulus clouds.

42.
3410. At approximately what altitude above the surface would the pilot expect the base of cumuliform clouds if the surface air temperature is 82 °F and the dewpoint is 38 °F?

A— 9,000 feet AGL.
B— 10,000 feet AGL.
C— 11,000 feet AGL.

43.
3409. What is the approximate base of the cumulus clouds if the surface air temperature at 1,000 feet MSL is 70 °F and the dewpoint is 48 °F?

A— 4,000 feet MSL.
B— 5,000 feet MSL.
C— 6,000 feet MSL.

Answer (B) is correct (3419). *(AvW Chap 7)*
The greatest turbulence occurs in cumulonimbus clouds, which are thunderstorm clouds.
Answer (A) is incorrect because towering cumulus are an earlier stage of cumulonimbus clouds. Answer (C) is incorrect because nimbostratus is a gray or dark, massive cloud layer diffused by more or less continuous rain or ice pellets. It is a middle cloud with very little turbulence but may pose serious icing problems.

Answer (C) is correct (3420). *(AvW Chap 7)*
Towering cumulus clouds are an early stage of cumulonimbus clouds, or thunderstorms, which are based on convective turbulence, i.e., an unstable lapse rate.
Answer (A) is incorrect because cirrus clouds are high, thin, featherlike ice crystal clouds in patches and narrow bands which are not based on any convective activity. Answer (B) is incorrect because nimbostratus are gray or dark, massive clouds diffused by more or less continuous rain or ice pellets with very little turbulence.

Answer (B) is correct (3410). *(AvW Chap 6)*
The height of cumuliform cloud bases can be estimated using surface temperature/dew point spread. Unsaturated air in a convective current cools at about 5.4°F/1,000 ft., and dew point decreases about 1°F/1,000 ft. In a convective current, temperature and dew point converge at about 4.4°F/1,000 ft. Thus, if the temperature/dew point spread is 44° (82° – 38°), divide 44 by 4.4 to obtain 10,000 ft. AGL.
Answer (A) is incorrect because 9,000 ft. AGL is the approximate height of the base of cumuliform clouds if the temperature/dew point spread is 40°F. Answer (C) is incorrect because 11,000 ft. AGL is the approximate height of the base of cumuliform clouds if the temperature/dew point spread is 48°F.

Answer (C) is the best answer (3409). *(AvW Chap 6)*
The height of cumuliform cloud bases can be estimated using surface temperature/dew point spread. Unsaturated air in a convective current cools at about 5.4°F/1,000 ft., and dew point decreases about 1°F/1,000 ft. In a convective current, temperature and dew point converge at about 4.4°F/1,000 ft. Thus, if the temperature and dew point are 70°F and 48°F, respectively, at 1,000 ft. MSL, there would be a 22° spread which, divided by the lapse rate of 4.4, is approximately 5,000 ft. AGL, or 6,000 ft. MSL (5,000 + 1,000).
Answer (A) is incorrect because 4,000 ft. MSL is the approximate base of the cumulus clouds if the temperature at 1,000 ft. MSL is 61°F, not 70°F. Answer (B) is incorrect because 5,000 ft. AGL, not MSL, is the approximate base of the cumulus clouds.

7.10 Stability of Air Masses

44.
3405. What is a characteristic of stable air?

A— Stratiform clouds.
B— Unlimited visibility.
C— Cumulus clouds.

Answer (A) is correct (3405). *(AvW Chap 8)*
Characteristics of a stable air mass include stratiform clouds, continuous precipitation, smooth air, and fair to poor visibility in haze and smoke.
Answer (B) is incorrect because restricted, not unlimited, visibility is an indication of stable air.
Answer (C) is incorrect because fair weather cumulus clouds indicate unstable conditions, not stable conditions.

45.
3406. Moist, stable air flowing upslope can be expected to

A— produce stratus type clouds.
B— cause showers and thunderstorms.
C— develop convective turbulence.

Answer (A) is correct (3406). *(AvW Chap 6)*
Moist, stable air flowing upslope can be expected to produce stratus type clouds as the air cools adiabatically as it moves up sloping terrain.
Answer (B) is incorrect because showers and thunderstorms are characteristics of unstable (not stable) air. Answer (C) is incorrect because convective turbulence is a characteristic of unstable (not stable) air.

46.
3407. If an unstable air mass is forced upward, what type clouds can be expected?

A— Stratus clouds with little vertical development.
B— Stratus clouds with considerable associated turbulence.
C— Clouds with considerable vertical development and associated turbulence.

Answer (C) is correct (3407). *(AvW Chap 6)*
When unstable air is lifted, it usually results in considerable vertical development and associated turbulence, i.e., convective activity.
Answer (A) is incorrect because stable rather than unstable air creates stratus clouds with little vertical development. Answer (B) is incorrect because stratus (layer-type) clouds usually have little turbulence unless they are lenticular clouds created by mountain waves or other high-altitude clouds associated with high winds near or in the jet stream.

47.
3413. What are characteristics of unstable air?

A— Turbulence and good surface visibility.
B— Turbulence and poor surface visibility.
C— Nimbostratus clouds and good surface visibility.

Answer (A) is correct (3413). *(AvW Chap 8)*
Characteristics of an unstable air mass include cumuliform clouds, showery precipitation, turbulence, and good visibility, except in blowing obstructions.
Answer (B) is incorrect because poor surface visibility is a characteristic of stable (not unstable) air. Answer (C) is incorrect because stratus clouds are characteristic of stable (not unstable) air.

48.
3414. A stable air mass is most likely to have which characteristic?

A— Showery precipitation.
B— Turbulent air.
C— Smooth air.

Answer (C) is correct (3414). *(AvW Chap 8)*
Characteristics of a stable air mass include stratiform clouds and fog, continuous precipitation, smooth air, and fair to poor visibility in haze and smoke.
Answer (A) is incorrect because showery precipitation is a characteristic of an unstable (not stable) air mass. Answer (B) is incorrect because turbulent air is a characteristic of an unstable (not stable) air mass.

49.
3424. Steady precipitation preceding a front is an indication of

A— stratiform clouds with moderate turbulence.
B— cumuliform clouds with little or no turbulence.
C— stratiform clouds with little or no turbulence.

Answer (C) is correct (3424). *(AvW Chap 8)*
Steady precipitation preceding a front is usually an indication of a warm front, which results from warm air being cooled from the bottom by colder air. This results in stratiform clouds with little or no turbulence.
Answer (A) is incorrect because stratiform clouds usually are not turbulent. Answer (B) is incorrect because cumuliform clouds have showery rather than steady precipitation.

50.
3412. What are characteristics of a moist, unstable air mass?

A—Cumuliform clouds and showery precipitation.
B—Poor visibility and smooth air.
C—Stratiform clouds and showery precipitation.

Answer (A) is correct (3412). *(AvW Chap 8)*
Characteristics of an unstable air mass include cumuliform clouds, showery precipitation, turbulence, and good visibility, except in blowing obstructions.
Answer (B) is incorrect because poor visibility and smooth air are characteristics of stable (not unstable) air. Answer (C) is incorrect because stratiform clouds and continuous precipitation are characteristics of stable (not unstable) air.

51.
3403. What measurement can be used to determine the stability of the atmosphere?

A—Atmospheric pressure.
B—Actual lapse rate.
C—Surface temperature.

Answer (B) is correct (3403). *(AvW Chap 6)*
The stability of the atmosphere is determined by vertical movements of air. Warm air rises when the air above is cooler. The actual lapse rate, which is the decrease of temperature with altitude, is therefore a measure of stability.
Answer (A) is incorrect because atmospheric pressure is the pressure exerted by the atmosphere as a consequence of gravitational attraction exerted upon the "column" of air lying directly above the point in question. It cannot be used to determine stability. Answer (C) is incorrect because, while the surface temperature may have some effect on temperature changes and air movements, it is the actual lapse rate that determines the stability of the atmosphere.

52.
3404. What would decrease the stability of an air mass?

A—Warming from below.
B—Cooling from below.
C—Decrease in water vapor.

Answer (A) is correct (3404). *(AvW Chap 6)*
When air is warmed from below, even though cooling adiabatically, it remains warmer than the surrounding air. The colder, more dense surrounding air forces the warmer air upward and an unstable condition develops.
Answer (B) is incorrect because cooling from below means the surrounding air is warmer, which would increase (not decrease) the stability of an air mass. Answer (C) is incorrect because, as water vapor in air decreases, the air mass tends to increase (not decrease) stability.

7.11 Temperature Inversions

53.
3408. What feature is associated with a temperature inversion?

A—A stable layer of air.
B—An unstable layer of air.
C—Chinook winds on mountain slopes.

Answer (A) is correct (3408). *(AvW Chap 6)*
A temperature inversion is associated with an increase in temperature with height, a reversal of normal decrease in temperature with height. Thus, any warm air rises to where it is the same temperature and forms a stable layer of air.
Answer (B) is incorrect because instability is a result of rising air remaining warmer than the surrounding air aloft, which would not occur with a temperature inversion. Answer (C) is incorrect because a Chinook wind is a warm, dry downslope wind blowing down the eastern slopes of the Rocky Mountains over the adjacent plains in the U.S. and Canada.

54.
3384. The most frequent type of ground or surface-based temperature inversion is that which is produced by

A— terrestrial radiation on a clear, relatively still night.
B— warm air being lifted rapidly aloft in the vicinity of mountainous terrain.
C— the movement of colder air under warm air, or the movement of warm air over cold air.

55.
3383. A temperature inversion would most likely result in which weather condition?

A— Clouds with extensive vertical development above an inversion aloft.
B— Good visibility in the lower levels of the atmosphere and poor visibility above an inversion aloft.
C— An increase in temperature as altitude is increased.

56.
3385. Which weather conditions should be expected beneath a low-level temperature inversion layer when the relative humidity is high?

A— Smooth air, poor visibility, fog, haze, or low clouds.
B— Light wind shear, poor visibility, haze, and light rain.
C— Turbulent air, poor visibility, fog, low stratus type clouds, and showery precipitation.

Answer (A) is correct (3384). *(AvW Chap 2)*
An inversion often develops near the ground on clear, cool nights when wind is light. The ground loses heat and cools the air near the ground while the temperature a few hundred feet above changes very little. Thus, temperature increases in height, which is an inversion.
Answer (B) is incorrect because warm air being lifted rapidly aloft in the vicinity of mountainous terrain describes convective activity. Answer (C) is incorrect because the movement of colder air under warm air, which causes an inversion, is caused by a cold front, not terrestrial radiation (warm air moving over cold air is a warm front).

Answer (C) is correct (3383). *(AvW Chap 2)*
By definition, a temperature inversion is a situation in which the temperature increases as altitude increases. The normal situation is that the temperature decreases as altitude increases.
Answer (A) is incorrect because vertical development does not occur in an inversion situation because the warm air cannot rise when the air above is warmer. Answer (B) is incorrect because the inversion traps dust, smoke, and other nuclei beneath the inversion, which reduces visibility.

Answer (A) is correct (3385). *(AvW Chap 12)*
Beneath temperature inversions, there is usually smooth air because there is little vertical movement due to the inversion. There is also poor visibility due to fog, haze, and low clouds (when there is high relative humidity).
Answer (B) is incorrect because wind shears usually do not occur below a low-level temperature inversion. They occur at or just above the inversion. Answer (C) is incorrect because turbulent air and showery precipitation are not present with low-level temperature inversions.

END OF CHAPTER

CHAPTER EIGHT
AVIATION WEATHER SERVICES

This chapter contains outlines of major concepts tested, all FAA test questions and answers regarding weather, and an explanation of each answer. Each module, or subtopic, within this chapter is listed above with the number of questions from the FAA pilot knowledge test pertaining to that particular module. For each module, the first number following the parentheses is the page number on which the outline begins, and the next number is the page number on which the questions begin.

CAUTION: Recall that the **sole purpose** of this book is to expedite your passing the FAA pilot knowledge test for the private pilot certificate. Accordingly, all extraneous material (i.e., topics or regulations not directly tested on the FAA pilot knowledge test) is omitted, even though much more information and knowledge are necessary to fly safely. This additional material is presented in *Pilot Handbook* and *Private Pilot Flight Maneuvers and Practical Test Prep*, available from Gleim Publications, Inc. See the order form on page 326.

8.1 WEATHER BRIEFINGS (Questions 1-10)

1. When requesting a telephone weather briefing, you should identify

   a. Yourself as a pilot
   b. Your intended route
   c. Your intended destination
   d. Whether you are flying VFR or IFR
   e. Type of aircraft
   f. Proposed departure time and time en route

2. A standard briefing should be obtained before every flight. This briefing will provide all the necessary information for a safe flight.

3. An outlook briefing is provided when it is 6 or more hours before proposed departure time.

4. An abbreviated briefing will be provided when the user requests information to

   a. Supplement mass disseminated data,
   b. Update a previous briefing, or
   c. Be limited to specific information.

8.2 AVIATION ROUTINE WEATHER REPORT (METAR) (Questions 11-16)

1. Aviation routine weather reports (METARs) are actual weather observations at the time indicated on the report. There are two types of reports.

    a. **METAR** is a routine weather report.
    b. **SPECI** is a nonroutine weather report.

2. Following the type of report are the elements listed below:

    a. The four-letter ICAO station identifier

        1) In the contiguous 48 states, the three-letter domestic identifier is prefixed with a "K."

    b. Date and time of report. It is appended with a "Z" to denote Coordinated Universal Time (UTC).

    c. Modifier (if required)

    d. Wind. Wind is reported as a five-digit group (six digits if the wind speed is greater than 99 kt.). It is appended with the abbreviation KT to denote the use of knots for wind speed.

        1) If the wind is gusty, it is reported as a "G" after the speed, followed by the highest gust reported.

        2) EXAMPLE: **11012G18KT** means wind from 110° true at 12 kt. with gusts to 18 kt.

    e. Visibility. Prevailing visibility is reported in statute miles with "SM" appended to it.

        1) EXAMPLE: **1 1/2SM** means visibility 1½ SM.

    f. Runway visual range

    g. Weather phenomena

        1) **RA** is used to indicate rain.

    h. Sky conditions

        1) The ceiling is the lowest broken or overcast layer, or vertical visibility into an obscuration.

        2) Cloud bases are reported with three digits in hundreds of feet AGL.

            a) EXAMPLE: **OVC007** means overcast cloud layer at 700 ft. AGL.

    i. Temperature/dew point. They are reported in a two-digit form in whole degrees Celsius separated by a solidus, "/."

    j. Altimeter

    k. Remarks (RMK)

        1) **RAB35** means rain began at 35 min. past the hour.

3. EXAMPLE: METAR KAUS 301651Z 12008KT 4SM −RA HZ BKN010 OVC023 21/17 A3005 RMK RAB25

    a. **METAR** is a routine weather observation.
    b. **KAUS** is Austin, TX.
    c. **301651Z** means the observation was taken on the 30th day at 1651 UTC (or Z).
    d. **12008KT** means the wind is from 120° true at 8 kt.
    e. **4SM** means the visibility is 4 statute miles.
    f. **−RA HZ** means light rain and haze.
    g. **BKN010 OVC023** means ceiling 1,000 ft. broken, 2,300 ft. overcast.
    h. **21/17** means the temperature is 21°C and the dew point is 17°C.
    i. **A3005** means the altimeter setting is 30.05 in. of Hg.
    j. **RMK RAB25** means remarks, rain began at 25 min. past the hour., i.e., 1625 UTC.

8.3 PILOT WEATHER REPORT (PIREP) (Questions 17-21)

1. No observation is more timely or needed than the one you make from the cockpit.
2. PIREPs are transmitted in a format illustrated below.

UUA/UA	Type of report: URGENT (UUA) - Any PIREP that contains any of the following weather phenomena: tornadoes, funnel clouds, or waterspouts; severe or extreme turbulence, including clear air turbulence (CAT); severe icing; hail; low-level wind shear (LLWS) (pilot reports air speed fluctuations of 10 knots or more within 2,000 feet of the surface); any other weather phenomena reported which are considered by the controller to be hazardous, or potentially hazardous, to flight operations. ROUTINE (UA) - Any PIREP that contains weather phenomena not listed above, including low-level wind shear reports with air speed fluctuations of less than 10 knots.
/OV	Location: Use VHF NAVAID(s) or an airport using the three- or four-letter location identifier. Position can be over a site, at some location relative to a site, or along a route. Ex: /OV KABC; /OV KABC090025; /OV KABC045020-DEF; /OV KABC-KDEF
/TM	Time: Four digits in UTC. Ex: /TM 0915
/FL	Altitude/Flight level: Three digits for hundreds of feet with no space between FL and altitude. If not known, use UNKN. Ex: /FL095; /FL310; /FLUNKN
/TP	Aircraft type: Four digits maximum; if not known, use UNKN. Ex: /TP L329; /TP B737; /TP UNKN
/SK	Sky cover: Describes cloud amount, height of cloud bases, and height of cloud tops. If unknown, use UNKN. Ex: /SK SCT040-TOP080; /SK BKNUNKN-TOP075; /SK BKN-OVC050-TOPUNKN; /SK OVCUNKN-TOP085
/WX	Flight visibility and weather: Flight visibility (FV) reported first and use standard METAR weather symbols. Intensity (– for light, no qualifier for moderate, and + for heavy) shall be coded for all precipitation types except ice crystals and hail. Ex: /WX FV05SM – RA; /WX FV01 SN BR; /WX RA
/TA	Temperature (Celsius): If below zero, prefix with an "M." Temperature should also be reported if icing is reported. Ex: /TA 15; /TA M06
/WV	Wind: Direction from which the wind is blowing coded in tens of degrees using three digits. Directions of less than 100 degrees shall be preceded by a zero. The wind speed shall be entered as a two- or three-digit group immediately following the direction, coded in whole knots using the hundreds, tens, and units digits. Ex: /WV 27045KT; /WV 280110KT
/TB	Turbulence: Use standard contractions for intensity and type (CAT or CHOP when appropriate). Include altitude only if different from FL. Ex: /TB EXTRM; /TB OCNL LGT-MDT BLO 090; /TB MOD-SEV CHOP 080-110
/IC	Icing: Describe using standard intensity and type contractions. Include altitude only if different from FL. Ex: /IC LGT-MDT RIME; /IC SEV CLR 028-045
/RM	Remarks: Use free form to clarify the report putting hazardous elements first Ex: /RM LLWS –15 KT SFC-030 DURGC RY 22 JFK

3. All heights are given as MSL. To determine AGL, subtract the field height from the given height.

4. Turbulence is reported as

    a. Light = LGT
    b. Moderate = MDT
    c. Severe = SVR

5. Icing is reported as

    a. Clear = CLR
    b. Rime = RIME

6. Cloud layers are reported with heights for bases, tops, and layer type if available. "No entry" means that information was not given.

    a. EXAMPLE: SK 024 BKN 032/042 BKN-OVC decoded means a broken layer 2,400 ft. MSL to 3,200 ft. MSL. A second layer is broken to overcast starting at 4,200 ft. MSL.

7. Wind direction and velocity are given as a five- or six-digit code (e.g., /**WV 27045** means 270° at 45 kt.).

8. Air temperature is expressed in degrees Celsius (°C).

8.4 AVIATION AREA FORECAST (Questions 22-29)

1. Aviation area forecasts (FA) are forecasts of visual meteorological conditions (VMC), clouds, and general weather conditions for several states and/or portions of states. They can be used to interpolate conditions at airports which have no terminal forecasts. FAs are issued three times a day and consist of

    a. A 12-hr. forecast
    b. An additional 6-hr. categorical outlook

2. FA weather format. An example is presented on page 214 for questions 26 through 29. It is presented in abbreviations. You will see this same FA utilizing abbreviations on your pilot knowledge test.

3. There are four sections in an FA:

    a. Communication and product header section
    b. Precautionary Statements section
    c. Synopsis section (for the purposes of the test, this section is not considered a forecast)
    d. VFR clouds/weather section (VFR CLDS/WX); this section is referred to as the forecast section

        1)   Included in the VFR CLDS/WX section is a categorical outlook that is valid for an additional 6 hr. For the purposes of the test, the categorical outlook is not considered a forecast.

4. In order to get a complete weather picture, including icing, turbulence, and IFR conditions, an FA must be supplemented by In-Flight Aviation Weather Advisories (AIRMETs Zulu, Tango, and Sierra).

    a. A pilot should refer to the In-Flight Aviation Weather Advisories to determine the freezing level and areas of probable icing aloft.

8.5 TERMINAL AERODROME FORECAST (TAF) (Questions 30-37)

1. Terminal aerodrome forecasts (TAFs) are weather forecasts for selected airports throughout the country.

2. The elements of a TAF are listed below:

    a. Type of report

        1)   **TAF** is a routine forecast.
        2)   **TAF AMD** is an amended forecast.

    b. ICAO station identifier

    c. Date and time the forecast is actually prepared

    d. Valid period of the forecast

    e. Forecast meteorological conditions. This is the body of the forecast and includes the following:

        1)   Wind
        2)   Visibility
        3)   Weather
        4)   Sky condition

            a)   Cumulonimbus clouds (CB) are the only cloud type forecast in TAFs.

3.   EXAMPLE:

TAF
KBRO 300545Z 300606 VRB04KT 3SM SCT040 OVC150 TEMPO 2124 SHRA
        FM0200 10010KT P6SM OVC020 BECMG0306 NSW BKN020=

a. **TAF** is a routine forecast.

b. **KBRO** is Brownsville, TX.

c. **300545Z** means the forecast was prepared on the 30th day at 0545 UTC.

d. **300606** means the forecast is valid from the 30th day at 0600 UTC until 0600 UTC the following day.

e. **VRB04KT 3SM SCT040 OVC150 TEMPO 2124 SHRA** means the forecast from 0600 until 0200 UTC is wind variable in direction at 4 kt., visibility 3 SM, scattered cloud layer at 4,000 ft., ceiling 15,000 ft. overcast, with occasional rain showers between 2100 and 2400 UTC.

f. **FM0200 10010KT P6SM OVC020 BECMG0306 NSW BKN020=** means the forecast from 0200 until 0300 is wind 100° true at 10 kt., visibility greater than 6 SM, ceiling 2,000 ft. overcast then becoming no significant weather, ceiling 2,000 ft. broken between 0300 to 0600 UTC.

   1)   Note that, since the becoming group (BECMG) did not forecast wind and visibility, they are the same as the previous forecast group, i.e., wind 100° true at 10 kt., visibility greater than 6 SM.

8.6 WEATHER DEPICTION CHARTS (Questions 38-43)

1. A weather depiction chart is an outline of the United States depicting sky conditions at the time stated on the chart based on METAR reports.

a. Reporting stations are marked with a little circle.

   1)   If the sky is clear, the circle is open; if overcast, the circle is solid; if scattered, the circle is 1/4 solid; if broken, the circle is 3/4 solid. If the sky is obscured, there is an "X" in the circle.

   2)   The height of clouds is expressed in hundreds of feet above ground level, e.g., 120 means 12,000 ft. AGL.

2. Areas with ceilings below 1,000 ft. and/or visibility less than 3 SM, i.e., below VFR, are bracketed with solid black contour lines and are shaded.

a. Visibility is indicated next to the circle; e.g., 2 stands for 2 SM visibility.

   1)   If the visibility is greater than 6 SM, it is not reported.

b. Areas of marginal VFR with ceilings of 1,000 to 3,000 ft. and/or visibility at 3 to 5 SM are bracketed by solid black contour lines and are unshaded.

c. Ceilings greater than 3,000 ft. and visibility greater than 5 SM are not indicated by contour lines on weather depiction charts.

3. Significant weather is indicated by the following symbols:

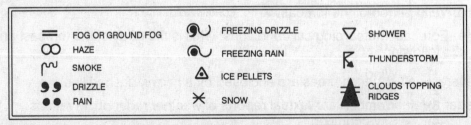

4. The weather depiction chart quickly shows pilots where weather conditions reported are above or below VFR minimums.

5. The weather depiction chart displays recent positions of frontal systems and indicates the type of front by symbols.

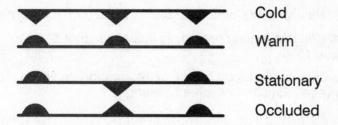

Cold

Warm

Stationary

Occluded

8.7 RADAR SUMMARY CHARTS AND RADAR WEATHER REPORTS (Questions 44-50)

1. Radar summary charts graphically display a collection of radar reports concerning the type, intensity, and movement of precipitation, e.g., squall lines, specific thunderstorm cells, and other areas of hazardous precipitation.

   a. Lines and cells of hazardous thunderstorms can be seen on radar summary charts and are not shown on other weather charts.

2. The following symbols are used on radar summary charts.

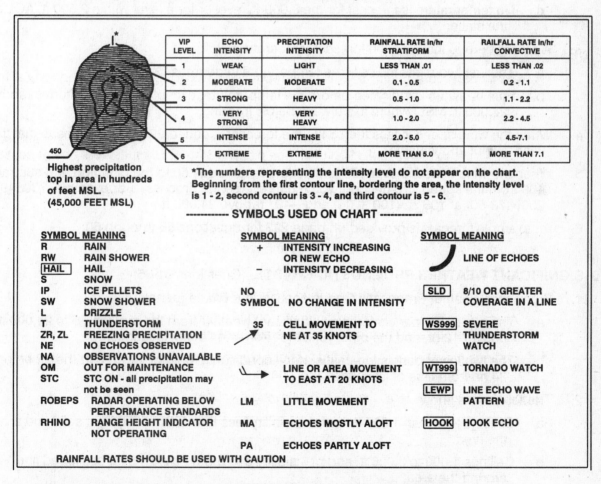

3. Severe weather watch areas are enclosed by a heavy, dashed line.

4. Radar weather reports are textual reports of weather radar observations.

   a. They include the type, intensity, location, and cell movement of precipitation.

      1) Intensity trend information is no longer included.

8.8 EN ROUTE FLIGHT ADVISORY SERVICE (EFAS) (Questions 51-53)

1. En Route Flight Advisory Service (EFAS) provides weather advisories on 122.0 MHz below FL 180. It is called Flight Watch.

    a. Generally, service is available from 6 a.m. to 10 p.m. local time.

    b. EFAS provides information regarding actual weather and thunderstorm activity along a proposed route.

2. It is designed to be a continual exchange of information on winds, turbulence, visibility, icing, etc., between pilots and weather briefers.

8.9 WINDS AND TEMPERATURES ALOFT FORECASTS (FD) (Questions 54-60)

1. Forecast winds and temperatures are provided at specified altitudes for specific locations in the United States.

2. A four-digit group (used when temperatures are not forecast) shows wind direction with reference to **true** north and the wind speed in **knots**.

    a. The first two digits indicate the wind direction after a zero is added.

    b. The next two digits indicate the wind speed.

    c. No temperature is forecast for the 3,000-ft. level or for a level within 2,500 ft. AGL of the station.

3. A six-digit group includes the forecast temperature aloft.

    a. The last two digits indicate the temperature in degrees Celsius.

    b. Plus or minus is indicated before the temperature, except at higher altitudes (above 24,000 ft. MSL) where it is always below freezing.

4. When the wind speed is less than 5 kt., the forecast is coded 9900, which means that the wind is light and variable.

5. When the wind speed is over 100 kt., the forecaster adds 50 to the direction and subtracts 100 from the speed. To decode, you must reverse the process. For example, 730649 = 230° (73-50) at 106 kt. (100 + 06) and −49° (above 24,000 ft.).

6. An example forecast is provided on page 223 for questions 56 through 60.

8.10 SIGNIFICANT WEATHER PROGNOSTIC CHARTS (Questions 61-65)

1. Significant Weather Prognostic Charts contain four charts (panels).

    a. The two upper panels forecast significant weather from the surface up to 24,000 ft: one for 12 hr. and the other for 24 hr. from the time of issuance.

    b. The two lower panels forecast surface conditions: one for 12 hr. and the other for 24 hr. from time of issuance.

2. The top panels show

    a. Ceilings less than 1,000 ft. and/or visibility less than 3 SM (IFR) by a solid line around the area;

    b. Ceilings 1,000 to 3,000 ft. and/or visibility 3 to 5 SM (MVFR) by a scalloped line around the area;

    c. Moderate or greater turbulence by a broken line around the area;

       1) A peaked hat _⋀_ indicates moderate turbulence.
       2) Altitudes are indicated on the chart; e.g., <u>180</u> means from surface to 18,000 ft.

      d.   Freezing levels, given by a dashed line corresponding to the height of the freezing level.

3.   The bottom panels show the location of

      a.   Highs, lows, fronts

      b.   Other areas of significant weather

          1)   Unshaded outlined areas indicate precipitation covering half or less of the area.

          2)   Shaded outlined areas indicate precipitation covering more than half of the area.

          3)   Precipitation type and intensity is reported with standard symbols. Some examples include:

              a)   thunderstorms embedded in a larger area of continuous moderate rain

              b)   thunderstorms embedded in a larger area of intermittent moderate rain

              c)   continuous light to moderate snow

              d)   intermittent light to moderate snow

          4)   Precipitation symbols may be connected to an area of precipitation by an arrow if there is not sufficient room to place them in that area.

4.   These charts are used to determine areas to avoid (freezing levels and turbulence).

8.11 TRANSCRIBED WEATHER BROADCASTS (Questions 66-68)

1.   TWEBs are continuous recordings of meteorological and aeronautical information broadcast on certain NDB and VOR facilities.

      a.   Generally, they are based on specific routes of flight.

8.12 AIRMETs AND SIGMETs (Questions 69-73)

1.   SIGMETs and AIRMETs are issued to notify pilots en route of the possibility of encountering hazardous flying conditions.

2.   SIGMET advisories include weather phenomena which are potentially hazardous to all aircraft.

      a.   Convective SIGMETs include

          1)   Tornadoes

          2)   Lines of thunderstorms

          3)   Embedded thunderstorms

          4)   Thunderstorm areas greater than or equal to thunderstorm intensity level 4 with an area coverage of 40% or more

          5)   Hail greater than or equal to 3/4 in. diameter

      b.   SIGMETs include

          1)   Severe or extreme turbulence or clear air turbulence (CAT) not associated with thunderstorms

          2)   Severe icing not associated with thunderstorms

          3)   Duststorms, sandstorms, or volcanic ash lowering visibility to less than 3 SM

          4)   Volcanic eruption

3.   AIRMETs apply to light (e.g., small single-engine) aircraft to notify of

    a.   Moderate icing
    b.   Moderate turbulence
    c.   Visibility less than 3 SM or ceilings less than 1,000 ft.
    d.   Sustained winds of 30 kt. or more at the surface
    e.   Extensive mountain obscurement

QUESTIONS AND ANSWER EXPLANATIONS

All the FAA questions from the pilot knowledge test for the private pilot certificate relating to airplanes and the weather material outlined previously are reproduced on the following pages in the same modules as the outlines. To the immediate right of each question are the correct answer and answer explanation. You should cover these answers and answer explanations while responding to the questions. Refer to the general discussion in the Introduction on how to take the FAA pilot knowledge test.

Remember that the questions from the FAA pilot knowledge test bank have been reordered by topic, and the topics have been organized into a meaningful sequence. Accordingly, the first line of the answer explanation gives the FAA question number and the citation of the authoritative source for the answer.

8.1 Weather Briefings

1.
3456. To get a complete weather briefing for the planned flight, the pilot should request

A—a general briefing.
B—an abbreviated briefing.
C—a standard briefing.

Answer (C) is correct (3456). *(AWS Sect 1)*
To get a complete briefing before a planned flight, the pilot should request a standard briefing. This will include all pertinent information needed for a safe flight.
Answer (A) is incorrect because a general briefing is not standard terminology for any type of weather briefing. Answer (B) is incorrect because an abbreviated briefing is only provided as a supplement to mass disseminated data, a previous briefing, or is to be limited to specific information.

2.
3457. Which type weather briefing should a pilot request, when departing within the hour, if no preliminary weather information has been received?

A—Outlook briefing.
B—Abbreviated briefing.
C—Standard briefing.

Answer (C) is correct (3457). *(AWS Sect 1)*
A pilot should request a standard briefing anytime (s)he is planning a flight and has not received a previous briefing or has not received preliminary information through mass dissemination media (e.g., TWEB, PATWAS, etc.).
Answer (A) is incorrect because outlook briefings are for flights 6 hr. or more in the future. Answer (B) is incorrect because abbreviated briefings are to update previous briefings, supplement other data, or to answer a specific inquiry.

3.
3458. Which type of weather briefing should a pilot request to supplement mass disseminated data?

A—An outlook briefing.
B—A supplemental briefing.
C—An abbreviated briefing.

Answer (C) is correct (3458). *(AWS Sect 1)*
An abbreviated briefing will be provided when the user requests information to supplement mass disseminated data, update a previous briefing, or to be limited to specific information.
Answer (A) is incorrect because an outlook briefing should be requested if the proposed departure time is 6 hr. or more in the future. Answer (B) is incorrect because a supplemental briefing is not a standard type of briefing.

4.
3460. A weather briefing that is provided when the information requested is 6 or more hours in advance of the proposed departure time is

A—an outlook briefing.
B—a forecast briefing.
C—a prognostic briefing.

Answer (A) is correct (3460). *(AWS Sect 1)*
 An outlook briefing is given when the briefing is 6 or more hours before the proposed departure time.
 Answer (B) is incorrect because a forecast briefing is not a type of weather briefing. Answer (C) is incorrect because a prognostic briefing is not a type of weather briefing.

5.
3526. What should pilots state initially when telephoning a weather briefing facility for preflight weather information?

A—Tell the number of occupants on board.
B—State their total flight time.
C—Identify themselves as pilots.

Answer (C) is correct (3526). *(AWS Sect 1)*
 When telephoning for a weather briefing, you should identify yourself as a pilot so the person can give you an aviation-oriented briefing. Many nonpilots call weather briefing facilities to get the weather for other activities.
 Answer (A) is incorrect because the number of occupants on board is information needed for a flight plan, not for a weather briefing. Answer (B) is incorrect because total flight time is a question asked by insurance companies, not information needed for a weather briefing.

6.
3527. What should pilots state initially when telephoning a weather briefing facility for preflight weather information?

A—The intended route of flight radio frequencies.
B—The intended route of flight and destination.
C—The address of the pilot in command.

Answer (B) is correct (3527). *(AWS Sect 1)*
 By telling the briefer your intended route and destination, the briefer will be able to provide you a more relevant briefing.
 Answer (A) is incorrect because the radio frequencies to be used are the pilot's preflight responsibility, not the weather briefer's. Answer (C) is incorrect because the address of the pilot in command is information needed for a flight plan, not for a weather briefing.

7.
3455. When telephoning a weather briefing facility for preflight weather information, pilots should state

A—the aircraft identification or the pilot's name.
B—true airspeed.
C—fuel on board.

Answer (A) is correct (3455). *(AWS Sect 1)*
 When requesting a briefing you should provide the briefer with the following information: VFR or IFR, aircraft identification or the pilot's name, aircraft type, departure point, route of flight, destination, altitude, estimated time of departure, and time en route or estimated time of arrival.
 Answer (B) is incorrect because true airspeed is information provided on a flight plan. Answer (C) is incorrect because fuel on board is information provided on a flight plan.

8.
3528. When telephoning a weather briefing facility for preflight weather information, pilots should state

A—the full name and address of the formation commander.
B—that they possess a current pilot certificate.
C—whether they intend to fly VFR only.

Answer (C) is correct (3528). *(AWS Sect 1)*
 When telephoning for a weather briefing, one should identify oneself as a pilot, the route, destination, type of airplane, and whether one intends to fly VFR or IFR to permit the weather briefer to give you the most complete briefing.
 Answer (A) is incorrect because the full name and address of the formation commander is information provided on a flight plan. Answer (B) is incorrect because you should state that you are a pilot, not that you possess a current pilot certificate.

9.
3459. To update a previous weather briefing, a pilot should request

A— an abbreviated briefing.
B— a standard briefing.
C— an outlook briefing.

Answer (A) is correct (3459). *(AWS Sect 1)*
An abbreviated briefing will be provided when the user requests information (1) to supplement mass disseminated data, (2) to update a previous briefing, or (3) to be limited to specific information.
Answer (B) is incorrect because a standard briefing is a complete preflight briefing to include all (not update) information pertinent to a safe flight. Answer (C) is incorrect because an outlook briefing is for a flight at least 6 hr. in the future.

10.
3461. When requesting weather information for the following morning, a pilot should request

A— an outlook briefing.
B— a standard briefing.
C— an abbreviated briefing.

Answer (A) is correct (3461). *(AWS Sect 1)*
An outlook briefing should be requested when the briefing is 6 or more hr. in advance of the proposed departure.
Answer (B) is incorrect because a standard briefing should be requested if the proposed departure time is less than 6 hr. in the future and you have not received a previous briefing or have received information through mass dissemination media. Answer (C) is incorrect because an abbreviated briefing is requested to supplement mass disseminated data, to update a previous briefing, or to be limited to specific information.

8.2 Aviation Routine Weather Report (METAR)

11.
3463. For aviation purposes, ceiling is defined as the height above the Earth's surface of the

A— lowest reported obscuration and the highest layer of clouds reported as overcast.
B— lowest broken or overcast layer or vertical visibility into an obscuration.
C— lowest layer of clouds reported as scattered, broken, or thin.

Answer (B) is correct (3463). *(AWS Sect 2)*
A ceiling layer is not designated in the METAR code. For aviation purposes, the ceiling is the lowest broken or overcast layer, or vertical visibility into an obscuration.
Answer (A) is incorrect because a ceiling is the lowest, not highest, broken or overcast layer, or the vertical visibility into an obscuration, not the lowest obscuration. Answer (C) is incorrect because a ceiling is the lowest broken or overcast, not scattered, layer. Also, there is no provision for reporting thin layers in the METAR code.

12.
3467. (Refer to figure 12 below.) What are the current conditions depicted for Chicago Midway Airport (KMDW)?

A— Sky 700 feet overcast, visibility 1-1/2SM, rain.
B— Sky 7000 feet overcast, visibility 1-1/2SM, heavy rain.
C— Sky 700 feet overcast, visibility 11, occasionally 2SM, with rain.

Answer (A) is correct (3467). *(AWS Sect 2)*
At KMDW a special METAR (SPECI) was taken at 1856Z and reported wind 320° at 5 kt., visibility 1½ SM in moderate rain, overcast clouds at 700 ft., temperature 17°C, dew point 16°C, altimeter 29.80 in. Hg, remarks follow, rain began at 35 min. past the hour.
Answer (B) is incorrect because the intensity of the rain is moderate, not heavy. Heavy rain would be coded +RA. Answer (C) is incorrect because visibility is 1½ SM, not 11 SM with an occasional 2 SM.

METAR KINK 121845Z 11012G18KT 15SM SKC 25/17 A3000

METAR KBOI 121854Z 13004KT 30SM SCT150 17/6 A3015

METAR KLAX 121852Z 25004KT 6SM BR SCT007 SCT250 16/15 A2991

SPECI KMDW 121856Z 32005KT 1 1/2SM RA OVC007 17/16 A2980 RMK RAB35

SPECI KJFK 121853Z 18004KT 1/2SM FG R04/2200 OVC005 20/18 A3006

FIGURE 12.—**Aviation Routine Weather Reports (METAR).**

13.
3462. (Refer to figure 12 on page 210.) Which of the reporting stations have VFR weather?

A—All.
B—KINK, KBOI, and KJFK.
C—KINK, KBOI, and KLAX.

Answer (C) is correct (3462). *(AWS Sect 2)*
KINK is reporting visibility of 15 SM and sky clear (15SM SKC); KBOI is reporting visibility of 30 SM and a scattered cloud layer base at 15,000 ft. (30SM SCT150); and KLAX is reporting visibility of 6SM in mist (fog) with a scattered cloud layer at 700 ft. and another one at 25,000 ft. (6SM BR SCT007 SCT250). All of these conditions are above VFR weather minimums of 1,000-ft. ceiling and/or 3-SM visibility.
Answer (A) is incorrect because KMDW is reporting a visibility of 1½ SM in rain and a ceiling of 700 ft. overcast (1 1/2SM RA OVC007), and KJFK is reporting a visibility of 1/2SM in fog and a ceiling of 500 ft. overcast (1/2SM FG OVC005). Both of these are below VFR weather minimums of 1,000-ft. ceiling and/or 3-SM visibility. Answer (B) is incorrect because KJFK is reporting a visibility of ½ SM in fog and a ceiling of 500 ft. overcast (1/2SM FG OVC005), which is below the VFR weather minimums of 1,000-ft. ceiling and/or 3-SM visibility.

14.
3464. (Refer to figure 12 on page 210.) The wind direction and velocity at KJFK is from

A—180° true at 4 knots.
B—180° magnetic at 4 knots.
C—040° true at 18 knots.

Answer (A) is correct (3464). *(AWS Sect 2)*
The wind group at KJFK is coded as 18004KT. The first three digits are the direction the wind is blowing from referenced to true north. The next two digits are the speed in knots. Thus, the wind direction and speed at KJFK are 180° true at 4 kt.
Answer (B) is incorrect because wind direction is referenced to true, not magnetic, north. Answer (C) is incorrect because the wind direction is 180° true, not 040° true, at 4 kt., not 18 kt.

15.
3465. (Refer to figure 12 on page 210.) What are the wind conditions at Wink, Texas (KINK)?

A—Calm.
B—110° at 12 knots, gusts 18 knots.
C—111° at 2 knots, gusts 18 knots.

Answer (B) is correct (3465). *(AWS Sect 2)*
The wind group at KINK is coded as 11012G18KT. The first three digits are the direction the wind is blowing from referenced to true north. The next two digits are the wind speed in knots. If the wind is gusty, it is reported as a "G" after the speed followed by the highest (or peak) gust reported. Thus, the wind conditions at KINK are 110° true at 12 kt., peak gust at 18 kt.
Answer (A) is incorrect because a calm wind would be reported as 00000KT, not 11012G18KT. Answer (C) is incorrect because the wind conditions at KINK are 110°, not 111°, at 12 kt., not 2 kt.

16.
3466. (Refer to figure 12 on page 210.) The remarks section for KMDW has RAB35 listed. This entry means

A—blowing mist has reduced the visibility to 1-1/2 SM.
B—rain began at 1835Z.
C—the barometer has risen .35" Hg.

Answer (B) is correct (3466). *(AWS Sect 2)*
In the remarks (RMK) section for KMDW, RAB35 means that rain began at 35 min. past the hour. Since the report was taken at 1856Z, rain began at 35 min. past the hour, or 1835Z.
Answer (A) is incorrect because RAB35 means that rain began at 35 min. past the hour, not that blowing mist has reduced the visibility to 1½ SM. Answer (C) is incorrect because RAB35 means that rain began at 35 min. past the hour, not that the barometer has risen .35 in. Hg.

8.3 Pilot Weather Report (PIREP)

17.
3474. (Refer to figure 14 below.) If the terrain elevation is 1,295 feet MSL, what is the height above ground level of the base of the ceiling?

A—505 feet AGL.
B—1,295 feet AGL.
C—6,586 feet AGL.

Answer (A) is correct (3474). *(AWS Sect 3)*
Refer to the PIREP (identified by the letters UA) in Fig. 14. The base of the ceiling is reported in the sky cover (SK) section. The first layer is considered a ceiling (i.e., broken) and the base is 1,800 ft. MSL. The height above ground of the broken base is 505 ft. AGL (1,800 – 1,295).
Answer (B) is incorrect because 1,295 ft. MSL (not AGL) is the terrain elevation. Answer (C) is incorrect because the ceiling base is 505 ft. (not 6,586 ft.) AGL.

18.
3472. (Refer to figure 14 below.) The base and tops of the overcast layer reported by a pilot are

A—1,800 feet MSL and 5,500 feet MSL.
B—5,500 feet AGL and 7,200 feet MSL.
C—7,200 feet MSL and 8,900 feet MSL.

Answer (C) is correct (3472). *(AWS Sect 3)*
Refer to the PIREP (identified by the letters UA) in Fig. 14. The base and tops of the overcast layer are reported in the sky conditions (identified by the letters SK). This pilot has reported the base of the overcast layer at 7,200 ft. and the top of the overcast layer at 8,900 ft. (072 OVC 089). All altitudes are stated in MSL unless otherwise noted. Thus, the base and top of the overcast layer are reported as 7,200 ft. MSL and 8,900 ft. MSL, respectively.
Answer (A) is incorrect because 1,800 ft. MSL and 5,500 ft. MSL are the base and top of the broken (BKN), not overcast (OVC), layer. Answer (B) is incorrect because 5,500 ft. MSL (not AGL) is the top of the broken (BKN) layer, not the base of the overcast (OVC) layer.

19.
3473. (Refer to figure 14 below.) The wind and temperature at 12,000 feet MSL as reported by a pilot are

A—080° at 21 knots and -7 °C.
B—090° at 21 MPH and –9 °F.
C—090° at 21 knots and –9 °C.

Answer (A) is correct (3473). *(AWS Sect 3)*
Refer to the PIREP (identified by the letters UA) in Fig. 14. The wind is reported in the section identified by the letters WV and is presented in five or six digits. The temperature is reported in the section identified by the letters TA in °C, and if below 0°C, prefixed with an "M." The wind is reported as 080° at 21 kt. with a temperature of –7°C.
Answer (B) is incorrect because speed is given in kt., not MPH. Temperature is given in degrees Celsius (not Fahrenheit) and is reported as -7, not -9. Answer (C) is incorrect because the wind is reported as being from 080°, not 090°, and temperature is reported as –9°C, not –9°F.

20.
3475. (Refer to figure 14 below.) The intensity of the turbulence reported at a specific altitude is

A—moderate at 5,500 feet and at 7,200 feet.
B—moderate from 5,500 feet to 7,200 feet.
C—light from 5,500 feet to 7,200 feet.

Answer (C) is correct (3475). *(AWS Sect 3)*
Refer to the PIREP (identified by the letters UA) in Fig. 14. The turbulence is reported in the section identified by the letters TB. In the PIREP the turbulence is reported as light from 5,500 ft. to 7,200 ft. (TB LGT 055-072).
Answer (A) is incorrect because turbulence is reported from 5,500 to 7,200 ft. MSL, not only at 5,500 ft. and 7,200 ft. Answer (B) is incorrect because rime ice (not turbulence) is reported as light to moderate from 7,200 to 8,900 ft. MSL (not 5,500 to 7,200 ft. MSL).

UA/OV KOKC-KTUL/TM 1800/FL120/TP BE90//SK BKN018-TOP055/OVC072-
TOP089/CLR ABV/TA M7/WV 08021/TB LGT 055-072/IC LGT-MOD RIME 072-089

FIGURE 14.—Pilot Weather Report.

21.

3476. (Refer to figure 14 on page 212.) The intensity and type of icing reported by a pilot is

A—light to moderate.
B—light to moderate clear.
C—light to moderate rime.

Answer (C) is correct (3476). *(AWS Sect 3)*
Refer to the PIREP (identified by the letters UA) in Fig. 14. The icing conditions are reported following the letters IC. In this report, icing is reported as light to moderate rime (LGT–MDT RIME) between 7,200 to 8,900 ft. MSL (072–089).
Answer (A) is incorrect because the question asks not only for the intensity of the icing (light to moderate) but also the type, which is rime (RIME) ice. Answer (B) is incorrect because the type is rime (not clear) ice.

8.4 Aviation Area Forecast

22.

3487. To best determine general forecast weather conditions over several states, the pilot should refer to

A—Aviation Area Forecasts.
B—Weather Depiction Charts.
C—Satellite Maps.

Answer (A) is correct (3487). *(AWS Sect 4)*
An aviation area forecast is a prediction of general weather conditions over an area consisting of several states or portions of states. It is used to obtain expected en route weather conditions and also to provide an insight to weather conditions that might be expected at airports where weather reports or forecasts are not issued.
Answer (B) is incorrect because weather depiction charts are compiled from METAR reports of observed, not forecast, areas. Answer (C) is incorrect because satellite pictures (maps) are observed pictures used to determine the presence and types of clouds, not forecast conditions.

23.

3489. To determine the freezing level and areas of probable icing aloft, the pilot should refer to the

A—Inflight Aviation Weather Advisories.
B—Weather Depiction Chart.
C—Area Forecast.

Answer (A) is correct (3489). *(AWS Sect 4)*
To determine the freezing level and areas of probable icing aloft, you should refer to the In-Flight Aviation Weather Advisories (AIRMET Zulu for icing and freezing level; AIRMET Tango for turbulence, strong winds/low-level wind shear; and AIRMET Sierra for IFR conditions and mountain obscuration.) In-Flight Aviation Weather Advisories supplement the area forecast.
Answer (B) is incorrect because the Weather Depiction Chart does not include any icing information. Answer (C) is incorrect because the Area Forecast alone contains no icing information; it must be supplemented by In-Flight Aviation Weather Advisories.

24.

3490. The section of the Area Forecast entitled "VFR CLDS/WX" contains a general description of

A—cloudiness and weather significant to flight operations broken down by states or other geographical areas.
B—forecast sky cover, cloud tops, visibility, and obstructions to vision along specific routes.
C—weather advisories still in effect at the time of issue.

Answer (A) is correct (3490). *(AWS Sect 4)*
The VFR CLDS/WX is the clouds and weather plus categorical outlook section, which contains a summary of cloudiness and weather significant to VFR flight operations broken down by states or other geographical areas.
Answer (B) is incorrect because a summary of forecast sky cover, cloud tops, visibility, and obstructions to vision along specific routes is contained in a TWEB route forecast. Answer (C) is incorrect because AIRMETs and SIGMETs are listed in in-flight weather advisories, not an FA.

25.

3478. From which primary source should information be obtained regarding expected weather at the estimated time of arrival if your destination has no Terminal Forecast?

A—Low-Level Prognostic Chart.
B—Weather Depiction Chart.
C—Area Forecast.

Answer (C) is correct (3478). *(AWS Sect 4)*
An area forecast (FA) is a forecast of general weather conditions over an area the size of several states. It is used to determine forecast en route weather and to interpolate conditions at airports which do not have a TAF issued.
Answer (A) is incorrect because a Low-Level Prognostic Chart forecasts weather conditions expected to exist 12 hr. and 24 hr. in the future for the entire U.S. Answer (B) is incorrect because a Weather Depiction Chart is a national map prepared from METAR reports that give a broad overview of observed weather conditions as of the time on the chart. It is not a forecast.

```
BOSC FA 241845
SYNOPSIS AND VFR CLDS/WX
SYNOPSIS VALID UNTIL 251300
CLDS/WX VALID UNTIL 250700...OTLK VALID 250700-251300
ME NH VT MA RI CT NY LO NJ PA OH LE WV MD DC DE VA AND CSTL WTRS

SEE AIRMET SIERRA FOR IFR CONDS AND MTN OBSCN.
TS IMPLY SEV OR GTR TURB SEV ICE LLWS AND IFR CONDS.
NON MSL HGTS DENOTED BY AGL OR CIG.

SYNOPSIS...19Z CDFNT ALG A 160NE ACK-ENE LN...CONTG AS A QSTNRY
FNT ALG AN END-50SW MSS LN. BY 13Z...CDFNT ALG A 140ESE ACK-HTO
LN...CONTG AS A QSTNRY FNT ALG A HTO-SYR-YYZ LN. TROF ACRS CNTRL
PA INTO NRN VA.  ...REYNOLDS...

OH LE
NRN HLF OH LE...SCT-BKN025 OVC045. CLDS LYRD 150. SCT SHRA. WDLY
     SCT TSRA. CB TOPS FL350. 23-01Z OVC020-030. VIS 3SM BR. OCNL -
     RA. OTLK...IFR CIG BR FG.
SWRN QTR OH...BKN050-060 TOPS 100. OTLK...MVFR BR.
SERN QTR OH...SCT-BKN040 BKN070 TOPS 120. WDLY SCT -TSRA. 00Z
     SCT-BKN030 OVC050. WDLY SCT -TSRA. CB TOPS FL350. OTLK...VFR
     SHRA.

CHIC FA 241945
SYNOPSIS AND VFR CLDS/WX
SYNOPSIS VALID UNTIL 251400
CLDS/WX VALID UNTIL 250800...OTLK VALID 250800-251400
ND SD NE KS MN IA MO WI LM LS MI LH IL IN KY

SEE AIRMET SIERRA FOR IFR CONDS AND MTN OBSCN.
TS IMPLY SEV OR GTR TURB SEV ICE LLWS AND IFR CONDS.
NON MSL HGTS DENOTED BY AGL OR CIG.

SYNOPSIS...LOW PRES AREA 20Z CNTRD OVR SERN WI FCST MOV NEWD INTO
LH BY 12Z AND WKN. LOW PRES FCST DEEPEN OVR ERN CO DURG PD AND
MOV NR WRN KS BORDER BY 14Z. DVLPG CDFNT WL MOV EWD INTO S CNTRL
NE-CNTRL KS BY 14Z.  ..SMITH..

UPR MI LS
WRN PTNS...AGL SCT030 SCT-BKN050. TOPS 080. 02-05Z BECMG CIG
     OVC010 VIS 3-5SM BR. OTLK...IFR CIG BR.
ERN PTNS...CIG BKN020 OVC040. OCNL VIS 3-5SM -RA BR. TOPS FL200.
     23Z CIG OVC010 VIS 3-5SM -RA BR. OTLK...IFR CIG BR.

LWR MI LM LH
CNTRL/NRN PTNS...CIG OVC010 VIS 3-5SM -RA BR. TOPS FL200.
     OTLK...IFR CIG BR.

SRN THIRD...CIG OVC015-025. SCT -SHRA. TOPS 150. 00-02Z BECMG CIG
     OVC010 VIS 3-5SM BR. TOPS 060. OTLK...IFR CIG BR.

IN
NRN HALF...CIG BKN035 BKN080. TOPS FL200. SCT -SHRA. 00Z CIG
     BKN-SCT040  BKN-SCT080. TOPS 120. 06Z AGL SCT-BKN030. TOPS 080.
     OCNL VIS 3-5SM BR. OTLK...MVFR CIG BR.
SRN HALF...AGL SCT050 SCT-BKN100. TOPS 120. 07Z AGL SCT 030
     SCT100. OTLK...VFR.
```

FIGURE 16.—Area Forecast.

26.
3492. (Refer to figure 16 on page 214.) The Chicago FA forecast section is valid until the twenty-fifth at

A—1945Z.
B—0800Z.
C—1400Z.

Answer (B) is correct (3492). *(AWS Sect 4)*
The Chicago area forecast (FA) is the second of two FAs depicted in Fig. 16. There is a note in the communication and product header section that says "CLDS/WX VALID UNTIL 250800," which means that the VFR clouds and weather section of the FA (the forecast section) is valid until 0800Z on the 25th.
Answer (A) is incorrect because the note, "CHIC FA 241945," in the communication and product header section means that the FA was issued at 1945Z on the 24th, not that it is valid until 1945Z on the 25th. Answer (C) is incorrect because the synopsis and categorical outlook (which are not considered to be forecasts), not the forecast section, are valid until 1400Z on the 25th, as indicated by the notes "SYNOPSIS VALID UNTIL 251400" and "OTLK VALID 250800-251400."

27.
3491. (Refer to figure 16 on page 214.) What sky condition and visibility are forecast for upper Michigan in the eastern portions after 2300Z?

A—Ceiling 100 feet overcast and 3 to 5 statute miles visibility.
B—Ceiling 1,000 feet overcast and 3 to 5 nautical miles visibility.
C—Ceiling 1,000 feet overcast and 3 to 5 statute miles visibility.

Answer (C) is correct (3491). *(AWS Sect 4)*
The Chicago area forecast (FA) is the second of two FAs depicted in Fig. 16. It contains an entry labeled "UPR MI LS," meaning "upper Michigan and Lake Superior." Under this heading is a section labeled "ERN PTNS," meaning "eastern portions." The entry, "23Z CIG OVC010 VIS 3-5SM -RA BR," means that from 2300Z, the forecast weather is an overcast ceiling at 1,000 ft. AGL, with 3 to 5 statute miles visibility in light rain and mist.
Answer (A) is incorrect because the ceiling is forecast to be overcast at 1,000 ft., not 100 ft., which would be coded as "OVC001." Answer (B) is incorrect because visibilities are always given in statute, not nautical, miles.

28.
3488. (Refer to figure 16 on page 214.) What is the outlook for the southern half of Indiana after 0700Z?

A—VFR.
B—Scattered clouds at 3,000 feet AGL.
C—Scattered clouds at 10,000 feet.

Answer (A) is correct (3488). *(AWS Sect 4)*
The question asks for the outlook for the southern half of Indiana after 0700Z. Indiana (IN) is covered by the Chicago area forecast (FA), which is the second of two FAs depicted in Fig. 16. There is a heading under "IN" labeled "SRN HALF," meaning "southern half." Under this heading is an entry, "OTLK...VFR," meaning that the categorical outlook is for VFR conditions. Note in the communication and product header section that there is a note, "OTLK VALID 250800-251400," meaning that the categorical outlook is valid from 0800Z to 1400Z on the 25th. Therefore, the outlook does not become valid until one hour after 0700Z. You should still select "VFR" as the answer for this question because it specifically asks for the outlook after 0700Z, not at 0700Z; 0800Z is after 0700Z.
Answer (B) is incorrect because scattered clouds at 3,000 ft. AGL is a forecast sky condition from 0700Z to 0800Z (when the VFR CLDS/WX section becomes invalid); it is not an outlook, which would simply indicate whether VFR, MVFR, or IFR conditions are expected. Answer (C) is incorrect because scattered clouds at 10,000 ft. is a forecast sky condition from 0700Z to 0800Z (when the VFR CLDS/WX section becomes invalid); it is not an outlook, which would simply indicate whether VFR, MVFR, or IFR conditions are expected.

29.
3493. (Refer to figure 16 on page 214.) What sky condition and type obstructions to vision are forecast for upper Michigan in the Western portions from 0200Z until 0500Z?

A—Ceiling becoming 1,000 feet overcast with visibility 3 to 5 statute miles in mist.
B—Ceiling becoming 100 feet overcast with visibility 3 to 5 statute miles in mist.
C—Ceiling becoming 1,000 feet overcast with visibility 3 to 5 nautical miles in mist.

8.5 Terminal Aerodrome Forecast (TAF)

30.
3480. (Refer to figure 15 on page 217.) In the TAF for KMEM, what does "SHRA" stand for?

A—Rain showers.
B—A shift in wind direction is expected.
C—A significant change in precipitation is possible.

31.
3485. (Refer to figure 15 on page 217.) During the time period from 0600Z to 0800Z, what visibility is forecast for KOKC?

A—Greater than 6 statute miles.
B—Possibly 6 statute miles.
C—Not forecasted.

32.
3484. (Refer to figure 15 on page 217.) In the TAF from KOKC, the clear sky becomes

A—overcast at 2,000 feet during the forecast period between 2200Z and 2400Z.
B—overcast at 200 feet with a 40% probability of becoming overcast at 600 feet during the forecast period between 2200Z and 2400Z.
C—overcast at 200 feet with the probability of becoming overcast at 400 feet during the forecast period between 2200Z and 2400Z.

33.
3479. (Refer to figure 15 on page 217.) What is the valid period for the TAF for KMEM?

A—1200Z to 1200Z.
B—1200Z to 1800Z.
C—1800Z to 1800Z.

Answer (A) is correct (3493). *(AWS Sect 4)*
The Chicago area forecast (FA) is the second of two FAs depicted in figure 16. It contains an entry labeled "UPR MI LS," meaning "upper Michigan and Lake Superior." Under this heading is a section labeled "WRN PTNS," meaning "western portions." The entry, "02-05Z BECMG CIG OVC 010 VIS 3-5SM BR," means that between 0200Z and 0500Z, the weather conditions are forecast to become an overcast ceiling at 1,000 ft., with 3-5 statute miles visibility in mist.
Answer (B) is incorrect because the ceiling is forecast to become overcast at 1,000 ft., not 100 ft., which would be coded as "OVC001." Answer (C) is incorrect because visibilities are always given in statute, not nautical, miles.

Answer (A) is correct (3480). *(AWS Sect 4)*
SHRA is a coded group of forecast weather. SH is a descriptor which means showers. RA is a type of precipitation which means rain. Thus, SHRA means rain showers.
Answer (B) is incorrect because SHRA means rain showers, not that a shift in wind direction is expected. A change in wind direction would be reflected by a forecast wind. Answer (C) is incorrect because SHRA means rain showers, not that a significant change in precipitation is possible.

Answer (A) is correct (3485). *(AWS Sect 4)*
At KOKC, between 0600Z and 0800Z, conditions are forecast to become wind 210° at 15 kt., visibility greater than 6 SM (P6SM), scattered clouds at 4,000 ft. with conditions continuing until the end of the forecast (1200Z).
Answer (B) is incorrect because, between 0600Z and 0800Z, the visibility is forecast to be greater than, not possibly, 6 SM. Answer (C) is incorrect because, between 0600Z and 0800Z, the visibility is forecast to be greater than 6 statute miles (P6SM).

Answer (A) is correct (3484). *(AWS Sect 4)*
In the TAF for KOKC, from 2200Z to 2400Z, the conditions are forecast to gradually become wind 200° at 13 kt. with gusts to 20 kt., visibility 4 SM in moderate rain showers, overcast clouds at 2,000 ft. Between the hours of 0000Z and 0600Z, a chance (40%) exists of visibility 2 SM in thunderstorm with moderate rain, and 800 ft. overcast, cumulus clouds.
Answer (B) is incorrect because, between 2200Z and 2400Z, the coded sky condition of OVC020 means overcast clouds at 2,000 ft., not 200 ft. Answer (C) is incorrect because, between 2200Z and 2400Z, the coded sky condition of OVC020 means overcast clouds at 2,000 ft., not 200 ft.

Answer (C) is correct (3479). *(AWS Sect 4)*
The valid period of a TAF follows the four-letter location identifier and the six-digit issuance date/time. The valid period group is a two-digit date followed by the two-digit beginning hour and the two-digit ending hour. The valid period of the TAF for KMEM is 121818, which means the forecast is valid from the 12th day at 1800Z until the 13th at 1800Z.
Answer (A) is incorrect because the valid period of the TAF for KOKC, not KMEM, is from 1200Z to 1200Z. Answer (B) is incorrect because the valid period of the TAF for KMEM is from the 12th day, not 1200Z, at 1800Z until the 13th at 1800Z.

34.
3481. (Refer to figure 15 below.) Between 1000Z and 1200Z the visibility at KMEM is forecast to be?

A—1/2 statute mile.
B—3 statute miles.
C—6 statute miles.

35.
3482. (Refer to figure 15 below.) What is the forecast wind for KMEM from 1600Z until the end of the forecast?

A—No significant wind.
B—Variable in direction at 6 knots.
C—Variable in direction at 4 knots.

36.
3483. (Refer to figure 15 below.) In the TAF from KOKC, the "FM (FROM) Group" is forecast for the hours from 1600Z to 2200Z with the wind from

A—160° at 10 knots.
B—180° at 10 knots.
C—180° at 10 knots, becoming 200° at 13 knots.

37.
3486. (Refer to figure 15 below.) The only cloud type forecast in TAF reports is

A—Nimbostratus.
B—Cumulonimbus.
C—Scattered cumulus.

Answer (B) is correct (3481). *(AWS Sect 4)*
Between 1000Z and 1200Z, the conditions at KMEM are forecast to gradually become wind calm, visibility 3 SM in mist, sky clear with temporary (occasional) visibility 1/2 SM in fog between 1200Z and 1400Z. Conditions are expected to continue until 1600Z.
Answer (A) is incorrect because, between the hours of 1200Z and 1400Z, not between 1000Z and 1200Z, the forecast is for temporary (occasional) visibility of 1/2 SM in fog. Answer (C) is incorrect because, between 1000Z and 1200Z, the forecast visibility for KMEM is 3 SM, not 6 SM.

Answer (B) is correct (3482). *(AWS Sect 4)*
The forecast for KMEM from 1600Z until the end of the forecast (1800Z) is wind direction variable at 6 kt. (VRB06KT), visibility greater than 6 SM, and sky clear.
Answer (A) is incorrect because the wind is forecast to be variable in direction at 6 kt. Answer (C) is incorrect because the wind is forecast to be variable in direction at 6 kt., not 4 kt. KMEM of 020° at 8 kt. is for 0600Z until 0800Z, not from 1600Z until the end of the forecast.

Answer (B) is correct (3483). *(AWS Sect 4)*
The **FM** group states that, from 1600Z until 2200Z (time of next change group), the forecast wind is 180° at 10 kt.
Answer (A) is incorrect because the forecast wind is 180°, not 160°, at 10 kt. Answer (C) is incorrect because the **BECMG** (becoming) group is a change group and is not part of the **FM** forecast group. The wind will gradually become 200° at 13 kt. with gusts to 20 kt., between 2200Z and 2400Z.

Answer (B) is correct (3486). *(AWS Sect 4)*
Cumulonimbus clouds are the only cloud type forecast in TAFs. If cumulonimbus clouds are expected at the airport, the contraction **CB** is appended to the cloud layer which represents the base of the cumulonimbus cloud(s).
Answer (A) is incorrect because the only cloud type forecast in TAFs is cumulonimbus, not nimbostratus, clouds. Answer (C) is incorrect because the only cloud type forecast in TAFs is cumulonimbus, not scattered cumulus, clouds.

```
TAF

KMEM   121720Z 121818 20012KT 5SM HZ BKN030 PROB40 2022 1SM TSRA OVC008CB
       FM2200 33015G20KT P6SM BKN015 OVC025 PROB40 2202 3SM SHRA
       FM0200 35012KT OVC008 PROB40 0205 2SM -RASN BECMG 0608 02008KT BKN012
        BECMG 1012 00000KT 3SM BR SKC TEMPO 1214 1/2SM FG
       FM1600 VRB06KT P6SM SKC=

KOKC   051130Z 051212 14008KT 5SM BR BKN030 TEMPO 1316 1 1/2SM BR
       FM1600 18010KT P6SM SKC BECMG 2224 20013G20KT 4SM SHRA OVC020
        PROB40 0006 2SM TSRA OVC008CB BECMG 0608 21015KT P6SM SCT040=
```

FIGURE 15.—Terminal Aerodrome Forecasts (TAF).

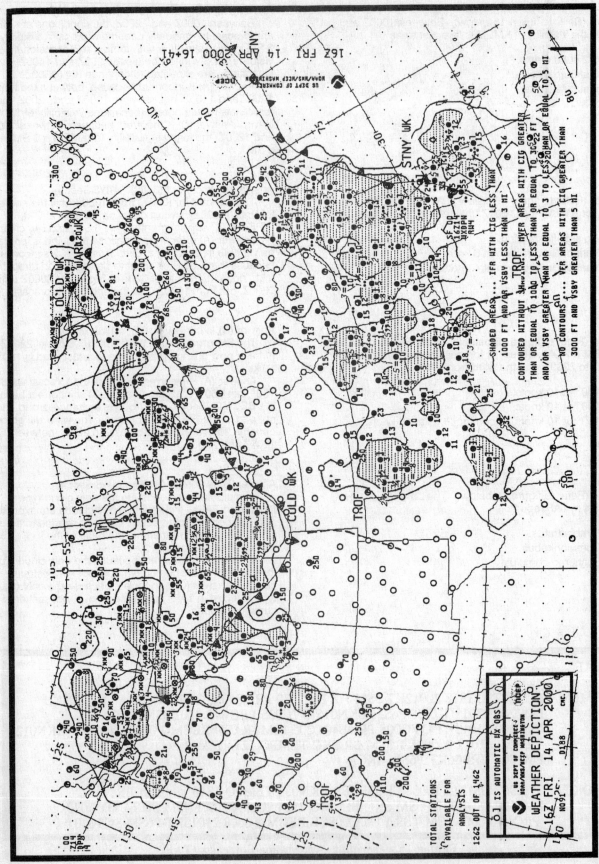

FIGURE 18.—Weather Depiction Chart.

8.6 Weather Depiction Charts

38.
3509. (Refer to figure 18 on page 218.) Of what value is the Weather Depiction Chart to the pilot?

A—For determining general weather conditions on which to base flight planning.
B—For a forecast of cloud coverage, visibilities, and frontal activity.
C—For determining frontal trends and air mass characteristics.

Answer (A) is correct (3509). *(AWS Sect 6)*
The weather depiction chart is prepared from surface aviation weather reports giving a quick picture of weather conditions as of the time stated on the chart. Thus, it presents general weather conditions on which to base flight planning.
Answer (B) is incorrect because a significant weather prognostic chart can provide a forecast of cloud coverage, visibilities, and frontal activity. A weather depiction chart shows actual, not forecast, conditions. Answer (C) is incorrect because a composite moisture stability chart would be used to determine the characteristics of an air mass.

39.
3508. (Refer to figure 18 on page 218.) The IFR weather in northern Texas is due to

A—intermittent rain.
B—low ceilings.
C—dust devils.

Answer (B) is correct (3508). *(AWS Sect 6)*
Refer to the Weather Depiction Chart in Fig. 18. The shaded area around northern Texas and central Oklahoma indicates that IFR conditions exist. The symbols "3=⚬̇" and "3=₈" mean that the visibility is 3 SM in fog (3=), and the sky is overcast at 600 ft. (⚬̇) to 800 ft. (₈) AGL. Thus, low ceilings between 600-800 ft. are the source of IFR weather conditions.
Answer (A) is incorrect because a solid round dot (•) indicates intermittent rain. Answer (C) is incorrect because ₈ indicates dust devils, which are small vigorous whirlwinds, usually of short duration, made visible by dust, sand, or debris picked up from the ground.

40.
3511. (Refer to figure 18 on page 218.) What weather phenomenon is causing IFR conditions in central Oklahoma?

A—Low visibility only.
B—Low ceilings and visibility.
C—Heavy rain showers.

Answer (B) is correct (3511). *(AWS Sect 6)*
Refer to the Weather Depiction Chart in Fig. 18. In central Oklahoma, the IFR conditions are caused by low ceilings and visibility. In the shaded area over central Oklahoma and northern Texas, there are six darkened circles with numbers ranging from one to eight below them, signifying overcast skies with ceilings at 100 to 800 ft. The circles also have numbers ranging from 3/4 to 3 beside them, signifying visibilities between 3/4 and 3 statute miles. The IFR conditions are therefore due to low ceilings and visibility.
Answer (A) is incorrect because there are also low ceilings in the area from 100 to 800 ft. Answer (C) is incorrect because heavy rain showers are shown by the symbol ▽̇ .

41.
3507. (Refer to figure 18 on page 218.) What is the status of the front that extends from Nebraska through the upper peninsula of Michigan?

A—Cold.
B—Stationary.
C—Warm.

Answer (A) is correct (3507). *(AWS Sect 6)*
Refer to the Weather Depiction Chart in Fig. 18. The front that extends from Nebraska through the upper peninsula of Michigan is a cold front, as shown by the pointed scallops on the southern side of the frontal line.
Answer (B) is incorrect because a stationary front has pointed scallops on one side of the frontal line and rounded scallops on the other. Answer (C) is incorrect because a warm front has rounded scallops, not pointed scallops.

42.
3512. (Refer to figure 18 on page 218.) According to the Weather Depiction Chart, the weather for a flight from southern Michigan to north Indiana is ceilings

A—1,000 to 3,000 feet and/or visibility 3 to 5 miles.
B—less than 1,000 feet and/or visibility less than 3 miles.
C—greater than 3,000 feet and visibility greater than 5 miles.

Answer (C) is correct (3512). *(AWS Sect 6)*
Refer to the Weather Depiction Chart in Fig. 18. The weather from southern Michigan to north Indiana is shown by the lack of shading or contours to have ceilings greater than 3,000 ft. and visibilities greater than 5 miles.
Answer (A) is incorrect because 1,000 to 3,000 feet ceilings and/or visibilities between 3 and 5 statute miles (MVFR conditions) are indicated on Weather Depiction Charts by an unshaded area surrounded by a contour. Answer (B) is incorrect because ceilings less than 1,000 ft. and/or visibilities less than 3 statute miles (IFR conditions) are indicated on Weather Depiction Charts by a shaded area surrounded by a contour.

43.
3510. (Refer to figure 18 on page 218.) The marginal weather in central Kentucky is due to low

A—ceiling.
B—ceiling and visibility.
C—visibility.

Answer (A) is correct (3510). *(AWS Sect 6)*
Refer to the Weather Depiction Chart in Fig. 18. The MVFR weather in central Kentucky is indicated by the contour line without shading. The station symbol indicates an overcast ceiling at 3,000 ft. MVFR is ceiling 1,000 ft. to 3,000 ft. and/or visibility 3 to 5 SM. Thus, the marginal weather is due to a low ceiling.
Answer (B) is incorrect because the marginal weather is caused by low ceilings only. Answer (C) is incorrect because the visibility is greater than 6 SM (indicated by the lack of a report). Therefore, the visibility is not a cause of the marginal conditions.

8.7 Radar Summary Charts and Radar Weather Reports

44.
3515. (Refer to figure 19, area B, on page 221.) What is the top for precipitation of the radar return?

A—24,000 feet AGL.
B—2,400 feet MSL.
C—24,000 feet MSL.

Answer (C) is correct (3515). *(AWS Sect 7)*
Refer to the Radar Summary Chart in Fig. 19. The radar return at B (northern Nevada) has a "240" with a line under it. This means the maximum top of the precipitation is 24,000 ft. MSL.
Answer (A) is incorrect because the height of precipitation returns is given in MSL, not AGL.
Answer (B) is incorrect because the height of precipitation returns is given in hundreds, not tens, of feet MSL. "240" means 24,000, not 2,400.

45.
3519. What does the heavy dashed line that forms a large rectangular box on a radar summary chart refer to?

A—Areas of heavy rain.
B—Severe weather watch area.
C—Areas of hail 1/4 inch in diameter.

Answer (B) is correct (3519). *(AWS Sect 7)*
On a Radar Summary Chart, severe weather watch areas are outlined by heavy dashed lines.
Answer (A) is incorrect because areas of heavy rain would be labeled with "R" for rain and "+" for heavy or increasing in intensity. Answer (C) is incorrect because hail is denoted by a box with hail printed inside (HAIL).

46.
3516. (Refer to figure 19, area B, on page 221.) What type of weather is occurring in the radar return?

A—Continuous rain.
B—Light to moderate rain showers.
C—Rain showers increasing in intensity.

Answer (A) is correct (3516). *(AWS Sect 7)*
Refer to the Radar Summary Chart in Fig. 19. The radar return around point B is labeled with an "R." This means rain (R) that is light to moderate due to the single contour, and is steady or continuous, due to the lack of an intensity symbol (+ or –).
Answer (B) is incorrect because rain showers would be indicated by the symbol "RW." Answer (C) is incorrect because rain showers increasing in intensity would be indicated by the symbol "RW+."

47.
3517. (Refer to figure 19, area D, on page 221.) What is the direction and speed of movement of the cell?

A—North at 17 knots.
B—South at 17 knots.
C—North at 17 MPH.

Answer (A) is correct (3517). *(AWS Sect 7)*
Refer to the Radar Summary Chart in Fig. 19. The radar return at D (Virginia) has an arrow pointing north with "17" at the point. The movement is thus north at 17 kt.
Answer (B) is incorrect because the arrow above the cell at point D points north, not south. This arrow indicates the direction of the cell's movement.
Answer (C) is incorrect because the speed of cell movement is given in knots, not MPH.

48.

3518. (Refer to figure 19, area E, below.) The top of the precipitation of the cell is

A—16,000 feet AGL.
B—25,000 feet MSL.
C—16,000 feet MSL.

Answer (C) is correct (3518). *(AWS Sect 7)*

Refer to the Radar Summary Chart in Fig. 19. The cell ½ in. below point E (Virginia/North Carolina) has a "160" with a line under it. This means the maximum top of the precipitation is 16,000 ft. MSL.

Answer (A) is incorrect because the height of precipitation returns is given in MSL, not AGL.
Answer (B) is incorrect because the "250" with a line under it (indicating 25,000 ft. MSL) extends from the large cell covering Florida, Alabama, and Georgia. This cell is associated with area G, not area E.

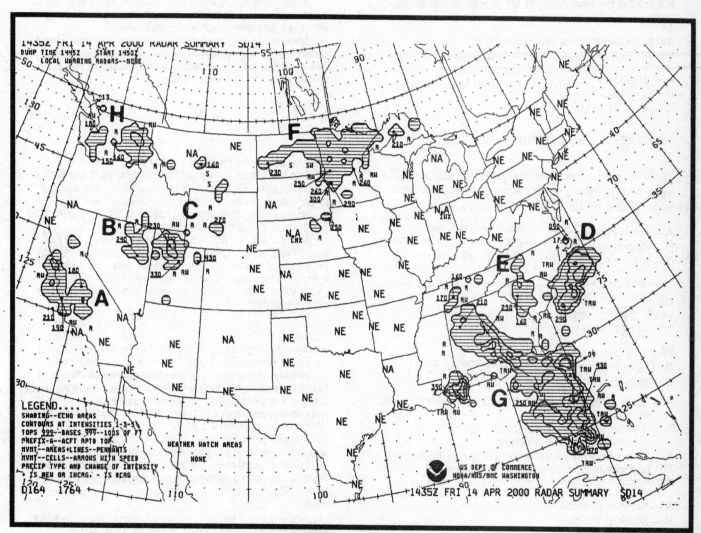

FIGURE 19.—Radar Summary Chart.

49.
3514. What information is provided by the Radar Summary Chart that is not shown on other weather charts?

A—Lines and cells of hazardous thunderstorms.
B—Ceilings and precipitation between reporting stations.
C—Types of clouds between reporting stations.

Answer (A) is correct (3514). *(AWS Sect 7)*
The Radar Summary Charts show lines of thunderstorms and hazardous cells that are not shown on other weather charts.
Answer (B) is incorrect because weather radar primarily detects particles of precipitation size within a cloud or falling from a cloud, it does not detect clouds and fog. Thus, it cannot determine ceilings. Answer (C) is incorrect because the Radar Summary Chart can provide the type of precipitation (not clouds) between reporting stations.

50.
3513. Radar weather reports are of special interest to pilots because they indicate

A—large areas of low ceilings and fog.
B—location of precipitation along with type, intensity, and cell movement of precipitation.
C—location of precipitation along with type, intensity, and trend.

Answer (B) is correct (3513). *(AWS Sect 7)*
Radar weather reports are of special interest to pilots because they report the location of precipitation along with type, intensity, and cell movement.
Answer (A) is incorrect because weather radar cannot detect clouds or fog, only precipitation size particles. Answer (C) is incorrect because radar weather reports no longer include trend information.

8.8 En Route Flight Advisory Service (EFAS)

51.
3616. How should contact be established with an En Route Flight Advisory Service (EFAS) station, and what service would be expected?

A—Call EFAS on 122.2 for routine weather, current reports on hazardous weather, and altimeter settings.
B—Call flight assistance on 122.5 for advisory service pertaining to severe weather.
C—Call Flight Watch on 122.0 for information regarding actual weather and thunderstorm activity along proposed route.

Answer (C) is correct (3616). *(AIM Para 7-1-4)*
The frequency designed for en route flight advisory stations calling Flight Watch is 122.0 MHz. It is designed to provide en route aircraft with timely and meaningful weather advisories during the route. It is not for complete briefings or random weather reports.
Answer (A) is incorrect because you would call FSS (not EFAS) on 122.2 for routine weather, current reports on hazardous weather, and altimeter settings. Answer (B) is incorrect because you would possibly call FSS (not Flight Watch) on 122.5 for advisory service pertaining to severe weather.

52.
3617. What service should a pilot normally expect from an En Route Flight Advisory Service (EFAS) station?

A—Actual weather information and thunderstorm activity along the route.
B—Preferential routing and radar vectoring to circumnavigate severe weather.
C—Severe weather information, changes to flight plans, and receipt of routine position reports.

Answer (A) is correct (3617). *(AIM Para 7-1-4)*
Flight Watch is designed to provide en route traffic with timely and meaningful weather advisories pertinent to the type of flight intended. It is designed to be a continuous exchange of information on winds, turbulence, visibility, icing, etc., between pilots and Flight Watch specialists on the ground.
Answer (B) is incorrect because preferential routing and radar vectoring is provided by approach control and ATC center. Answer (C) is incorrect because changes to flight plans and routine position reports should be given to an FSS.

53.
3823. Below FL180, en route weather advisories should be obtained from an FSS on

A—122.0 MHz.
B—122.1 MHz.
C—123.6 MHz.

Answer (A) is correct (3823). *(AIM Para 7-1-4)*
Below FL 180, to receive weather advisories along your route, you should contact Flight Watch on 122.0 MHz.
Answer (B) is incorrect because 122.1 MHz is the pilot-to-FSS frequency used on duplex remote communication facilities. Answer (C) is incorrect because 123.6 MHz is the common FSS frequency for airport advisory service.

8.9 Winds and Temperatures Aloft Forecasts (FD)

54.
3506. When the term "light and variable" is used in reference to a Winds Aloft Forecast, the coded group and windspeed is

A—0000 and less than 7 knots.
B—9900 and less than 5 knots.
C—9999 and less than 10 knots.

Answer (B) is correct (3506). *(AWS Sect 4)*
When winds are light and variable on a Winds Aloft Forecast (FD), it is coded 9900 and wind speed is less than 5 kt.
Answer (A) is incorrect because when winds are light and variable, it is coded 9900 (not 0000) and the wind speed is less than 5 (not 7) kt. Answer (C) is incorrect because when winds are light and variable, it is coded 9900 (not 9999) and the wind speed is less than 5 (not 10) kt.

55.
3505. What values are used for Winds Aloft Forecasts?

A—Magnetic direction and knots.
B—Magnetic direction and miles per hour.
C—True direction and knots.

Answer (C) is correct (3505). *(AWS Sect 4)*
For Winds Aloft Forecasts, the wind direction is given in true direction and the wind speed is in knots.
Answer (A) is incorrect because ATC (not Winds Aloft Forecasts) will provide winds in magnetic direction and kt. Answer (B) is incorrect because Winds Aloft Forecast will provide winds based on true (not magnetic) direction and speed in kt. (not MPH).

56.
3501. (Refer to figure 17 below.) What wind is forecast for STL at 12,000 feet?

A—230° true at 39 knots.
B—230° true at 56 knots.
C—230° magnetic at 56 knots.

Answer (A) is correct (3501). *(AWS Sect 4)*
Refer to the FD forecast in Fig. 17. Locate STL and move right to the 12,000-ft. column. The wind forecast (first four digits) is coded as 2339, which means the wind is 230° true at 39 kt.
Answer (B) is incorrect because 230° true at 56 kt. is the forecast wind direction and speed for 18,000 ft., not 12,000 ft. Answer (C) is incorrect because the first two digits are direction referenced to true (not magnetic) north. Thus, 2356 is 230° true (not magnetic) at 56 kt., which is the forecast wind direction and speed for 18,000 ft., not 12,000 ft.

FD WBC 151745
DATA BASED ON 151200Z
VALID 1600Z FOR USE 1800-0300Z. TEMPS NEG ABV 24000

FT	3000	6000	9000	12000	18000	24000	30000	34000	39000
ALS			2420	2635-08	2535-18	2444-30	245945	246755	246862
AMA		2714	2725+00	2625-04	2531-15	2542-27	265842	256352	256762
DEN			2321-04	2532-08	2434-19	2441-31	235347	236056	236262
HLC		1707-01	2113-03	2219-07	2330-17	2435-30	244145	244854	245561
MKC	0507	2006+03	2215-01	2322-06	2338-17	2348-29	236143	237252	238160
STL	2113	2325+07	2332+02	2339-04	2356-16	2373-27	239440	730649	731960

FIGURE 17.—Winds and Temperatures Aloft Forecast.

57.
3502. (Refer to figure 17 above.) Determine the wind and temperature aloft forecast for DEN at 9,000 feet.

A—230° magnetic at 53 knots, temperature 47 °C.
B—230° true at 53 knots, temperature −47 °C.
C—230° true at 21 knots, temperature −4 °C.

Answer (C) is correct (3502). *(AWS Sect 4)*
Refer to the FD forecast in Fig. 17. Locate DEN on the left side of the chart and move to the right to the 9,000-ft. column. The wind and temperature forecast is coded as 2321-04. The forecast is decoded as 230° true at 21 kt., temperature −4°C.
Answer (A) is incorrect because 23 is 230° true (not magnetic) and the temperature is −4°C, not 47°C. Answer (B) is incorrect because the temperature is −4°C, not −47°C, which is the temperature for DEN at 30,000 ft., not 9,000 ft.

58.
3504. (Refer to figure 17 on page 223.) What wind is forecast for STL at 12,000 feet?

A—230° magnetic at 39 knots.
B—230° true at 39 knots.
C—230° true at 106 knots.

Answer (B) is correct (3504). *(AWS Sect 4)*
Refer to the FD forecast in Fig. 17. Locate STL on the left side of the chart and move to the right to the 12,000 ft. column. The wind forecast (first four digits) is coded as 2339. The forecast is decoded as 230° true at 39 kt.
Answer (A) is incorrect because the wind is from 230° true, not magnetic. Answer (B) is incorrect because 230° true at 106 kt. is the forecast wind speed and direction for 34,000 ft., not 12,000 ft. (coded as 7306).

59.
3503. (Refer to figure 17 on page 223.) Determine the wind and temperature aloft forecast for MKC at 6,000 ft.

A—050° true at 7 knots, temperature missing.
B—200° magnetic at 6 knots, temperature +3°C.
C—200° true at 6 knots, temperature +3 °C.

Answer (C) is correct (3503). *(AWS Sect 4)*
Refer to the FD forecast in Fig. 17. Locate MKC on the left side of the chart and move to the right to the 6,000-ft. column. The wind and temperature forecast is coded as 2006+03, which translates as the forecast wind at 200° true at 6 kt. and a temperature of 3°C.
Answer (A) is incorrect because 050° true at 7 kt. with no forecast temperature is the forecast for MKC at 3,000 ft., not 6,000 ft. Answer (B) is incorrect because wind direction is given in true degrees, not magnetic degrees.

60.
3500. (Refer to figure 17 on page 223.) What wind is forecast for STL at 9,000 feet?

A—230° magnetic at 25 knots.
B—230° true at 32 knots.
C—230° true at 25 knots.

Answer (B) is correct (3500). *(AWS Sect 4)*
Refer to the FD forecast in Fig. 17. Locate STL on the left side of the chart and move right to the 9,000-ft. column. The coded wind forecast (first four digits) is 2332. Thus, the forecast wind is 230° true at 32 kt.
Answer (A) is incorrect because wind direction is forecast in true (not magnetic) direction. Wind forecast of 230° true at 25 kt. is for STL at 6,000 ft., not 9,000 ft. Answer (C) is incorrect because 230° at 25 kt. is the wind forecast for STL at 6,000 ft., not 9,000 ft.

8.10 Significant Weather Prognostic Charts

61.
3522. (Refer to figure 20 on page 225.) What weather is forecast for the Florida area just ahead of the stationary front during the first 12 hours?

A—Ceiling 1,000 to 3,000 feet and/or visibility 3 to 5 miles with intermittent precipitation.
B—Ceiling 1,000 to 3,000 feet and/or visibility 3 to 5 miles with continuous precipitation.
C—Ceiling less than 1,000 feet and/or visibility less than 3 miles with continuous precipitation.

Answer (B) is correct (3522). *(AWS Sect 11)*
Refer to the Significant Weather Prognostic Chart in Fig. 20. During the first 12 hr. (bottom and top left panels), the weather just ahead of the stationary front which extends from coastal Virginia into the Gulf of Mexico is forecast to have ceilings from 1,000 to 3,000 ft. and/or visibility 3 to 5 SM (as indicated by the scalloped lines) with continuous light to moderate rain covering more than half the area (as indicated by the shading).
Answer (A) is incorrect because thunderstorms embedded in an area of moderate continuous, not intermittent, precipitation are forecast just ahead of the stationary front, as indicated by the following symbol: ⚡. Thunderstorms embedded in an area of intermittent rain would be indicated with this symbol: ⚡. Answer (C) is incorrect because marginal VFR conditions (ceilings from 1,000 to 3,000 ft. and/or visibility from 3 to 5 SM), not IFR conditions (ceilings less than 1,000 ft. and/or visibility less than 3 miles) are forecast, as indicated by the scalloped line surrounding the southeastern states on the top left panel.

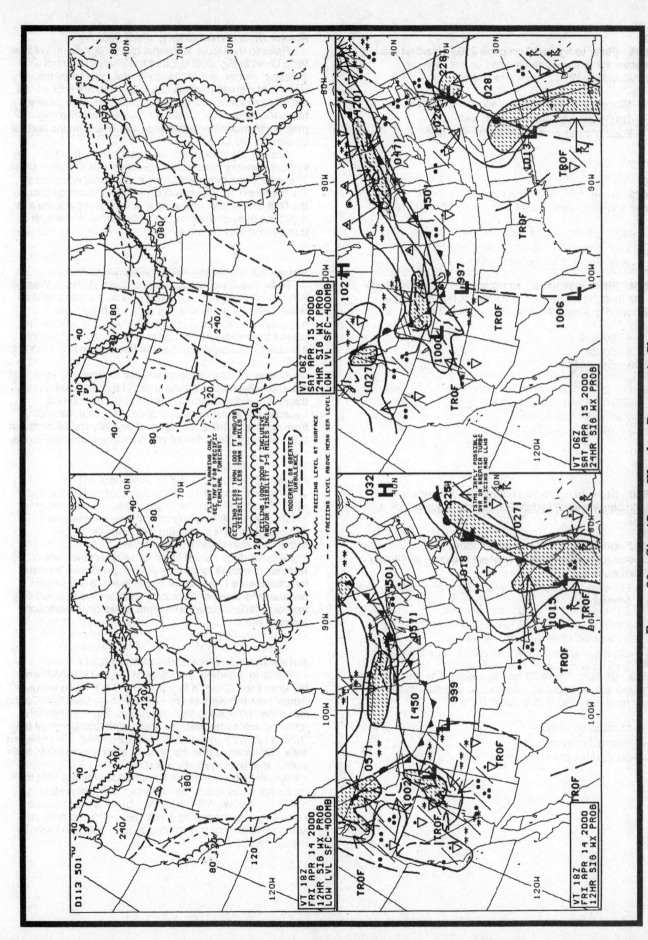

FIGURE 20.—Significant Weather Prognostic Chart.

62.
3521. (Refer to figure 20 on page 225.) Interpret the weather symbol depicted in Utah on the 12-hour Significant Weather Prognostic Chart.

A—Moderate turbulence, surface to 18,000 feet.
B—Thunderstorm tops at 18,000 feet.
C—Base of clear air turbulence, 18,000 feet.

Answer (A) is correct (3521). *(AWS Sect 11)*
Refer to the upper left panel of the Significant Weather Prog Chart in Fig. 20. In Utah, the weather symbol indicates moderate turbulence as designated by the symbol of a small peaked hat. Note that the broken line indicates moderate or greater turbulence. The peaked hat is the symbol for moderate turbulence. The <u>180</u> means the moderate turbulence extends from the surface upward to 18,000 ft.
Answer (B) is incorrect because the peaked hat symbol denotes moderate turbulence, not thunderstorms. The symbol for thunderstorms is shown by what looks like the letter "R," as shown on the 12-hr. surface prog in the Gulf of Mexico. Answer (C) is incorrect because this is not the base of the clear air turbulence. A line over a number indicates a base.

63.
3524. (Refer to figure 20 on page 225.) At what altitude is the freezing level over the middle of Florida on the 12-hour Significant Weather Prognostic Chart?

A—4,000 feet.
B—8,000 feet.
C—12,000 feet.

Answer (C) is correct (3524). *(AWS Sect 11)*
Refer to the upper left panel of the Significant Weather Prog Chart in Fig. 20. On prog charts, the freezing level is indicated by a dashed line, with the height given in hundreds of feet MSL. In Fig. 20, there is a dashed line across the middle of Florida, marked with "120" just off the coast. This signifies that the freezing level is 12,000 ft. MSL.
Answer (A) is incorrect because the freezing level is at 4,000 ft. MSL across the northern U.S. and Canada, not over the middle of Florida. Answer (B) is incorrect because the freezing level is at 8,000 ft. MSL extending from southern California, upward and across the northern U.S., and into New Jersey, not over the middle of Florida.

64.
3520. (Refer to figure 20 on page 225.) How are Significant Weather Prognostic Charts best used by a pilot?

A—For overall planning at all altitudes.
B—For determining areas to avoid (freezing levels and turbulence).
C—For analyzing current frontal activity and cloud coverage.

Answer (B) is correct (3520). *(AWS Sect 11)*
Weather prognostic charts forecast conditions that exist 12 and 24 hr. in the future. They include two types of forecasts: low level significant weather such as IFR and marginal VFR areas and moderate or greater turbulence areas and freezing levels.
Answer (A) is incorrect because a complete set of weather forecasts for overall planning includes terminal forecasts, area forecasts, etc. Answer (C) is incorrect because the weather depiction chart shows analysis of frontal activities, cloud coverage, areas of precipitation, ceilings, etc.

65.
3523. (Refer to figure 20 on page 225.) The enclosed shaded area associated with the low pressure system over northern Utah is forecast to have

A—continuous snow.
B—intermittent snow.
C—continuous snow showers.

Answer (A) is correct (3523). *(AWS Sect 11)*
Refer to the lower left panel of the 24-hr. Significant Weather Prog Chart in Fig. 20. There is a low pressure center over northern Utah, indicated by a bold "L." To the left of the "L" is a shaded area, indicating precipitation covering more than half the area. Just to the right of the "L" is a symbol, ٭⁄٭ , with an arrow pointing to the shaded area. This means that the shaded area is forecast to have continuous light to moderate snow.
Answer (B) is incorrect because intermittent light to moderate snow would be indicated with the symbol, ٭⁄٭ , not ٭⁄٭ . Answer (C) is incorrect because continuous snow showers are indicated for the unshaded area in southern Utah, not the shaded area in northern Utah, by the symbol ٭⁄٭ .

8.11 Transcribed Weather Broadcasts

66.
3494. To obtain a continuous transcribed weather briefing, including winds aloft and route forecasts for a cross-country flight, a pilot should monitor a

A—Transcribed Weather Broadcast (TWEB) on an NDB or a VOR facility.
B—VHF radio receiver tuned to an Automatic Terminal Information Service (ATIS) frequency.
C—regularly scheduled weather broadcast on a VOR frequency.

Answer (A) is correct (3494). *(AIM Para 7-1-8)*
  To obtain a continuous transcribed weather briefing, including winds aloft and route forecasts for a cross-country flight, a pilot should monitor a TWEB on the ADF (low-frequency) radio receiver and/or the VOR.
  Answer (B) is incorrect because ATIS frequency gives transcribed information about an airport's operations and only its immediate weather conditions. Answer (C) is incorrect because TWEB and HIWAS (Hazardous In-Flight Weather Advisory Service), the two weather broadcasts transmitted over VORs, are recordings that are played continuously and are updated as needed. They are not regularly scheduled.

67.
3454. Transcribed Weather Broadcasts (TWEB's) may be monitored by tuning the appropriate radio receiver to certain

A—airport advisory frequencies.
B—VOR and NDB frequencies.
C—ATIS frequencies.

Answer (B) is correct (3454). *(AIM Para 7-1-8)*
  Transcribed Weather Broadcasts (TWEBs) are broadcast on selected VOR and NDB frequencies.
  Answer (A) is incorrect because airport advisory frequencies are used for obtaining traffic information at noncontrolled airports. Answer (C) is incorrect because ATIS provides weather and noncontrol information for a particular airport.

68.
3453. Individual forecasts for specific routes of flight can be obtained from which weather source?

A—Transcribed Weather Broadcasts (TWEB's).
B—Terminal Aerodrome Forecasts.
C—Area Forecasts.

Answer (A) is correct (3453). *(AIM Para 7-1-8)*
  Forecasts for specific routes of flight should be obtained from Transcribed Weather Broadcasts (TWEBs) which are based upon specific routes.
  Answer (B) is incorrect because Terminal Aerodrome Forecasts deal only with specific terminal areas. Answer (C) is incorrect because area forecasts cover broad areas including several states and parts of states, and do not address specific routes.

8.12 AIRMETs and SIGMETs

69.
3497. SIGMET's are issued as a warning of weather conditions hazardous to which aircraft?

A—Small aircraft only.
B—Large aircraft only.
C—All aircraft.

Answer (C) is correct (3497). *(AWS Sect 4)*
  SIGMETs (significant meteorological information) warn of weather considered potentially hazardous to all aircraft. SIGMET advisories cover severe and extreme turbulence; severe icing; and widespread duststorms, sandstorms, or volcanic ash that reduce visibility to less than 3 SM.
  Answer (A) is incorrect because SIGMETs apply to all aircraft, not just to small aircraft. Answer (B) is incorrect because SIGMETs apply to all aircraft, not just to large aircraft.

70.
3499. AIRMETs are advisories of significant weather phenomena but of lower intensities than SIGMETs and are intended for dissemination to

A — only IFR pilots.
B — all pilots.
C — only VFR pilots.

Answer (B) is correct (3499). *(AWS Sect 4)*
AIRMETs are advisories of significant weather phenomena that describe conditions at intensities lower than those which require the issuance of SIGMETs. They are intended for dissemination to all pilots.
Answer (A) is incorrect because AIRMETs are intended for dissemination to all pilots, not just IFR pilots. Answer (C) is incorrect because AIRMETs are intended for dissemination to all pilots, not just VFR pilots.

71.
3498. Which in-flight advisory would contain information on severe icing not associated with thunderstorms?

A — Convective SIGMET.
B — SIGMET.
C — AIRMET.

Answer (B) is correct (3498). *(AWS Sect 4)*
SIGMET advisories cover severe icing not associated with thunderstorms; severe or extreme turbulence or clear air turbulence not associated with thunderstorms; dust-storms, sandstorms, or volcanic ash that reduce visibility to less than 3 SM; and volcanic eruption.
Answer (A) is incorrect because a convective SIGMET is issued concerning convective activity such as tornadoes and severe thunderstorms. Any convective SIGMET implies severe icing, which is associated with thunderstorms. Answer (C) is incorrect because AIRMETs are issued for moderate, not severe, icing.

72.
3496. What information is contained in a CONVECTIVE SIGMET?

A — Tornadoes, embedded thunderstorms, and hail 3/4 inch or greater in diameter.
B — Severe icing, severe turbulence, or widespread dust storms lowering visibility to less than 3 miles.
C — Surface winds greater than 40 knots or thunderstorms equal to or greater than video integrator processor (VIP) level 4.

Answer (A) is correct (3496). *(AWS Sect 4)*
Convective SIGMETs are issued for tornadoes, lines of thunderstorms, embedded thunderstorms of any intensity level, areas of thunderstorms greater than or equal to VIP level 4 with an area coverage of 40% or more, and hail ¾ in. or greater.
Answer (B) is incorrect because a SIGMET, not a convective SIGMET, is issued for severe icing, severe turbulence, or widespread duststorms lowering visibility to less than 3 SM. Answer (C) is incorrect because a severe thunderstorm having surface winds of 50 kt. or greater, not 40 kt., will be contained in a convective SIGMET.

73.
3495. What is indicated when a current CONVECTIVE SIGMET forecasts thunderstorms?

A — Moderate thunderstorms covering 30 percent of the area.
B — Moderate or severe turbulence.
C — Thunderstorms obscured by massive cloud layers.

Answer (C) is correct (3495). *(AWS Sect 4)*
Convective SIGMETs are issued for tornadoes, lines of thunderstorms, embedded (i.e., obscured by massive cloud layers) thunderstorms of any intensity level, areas of thunderstorms greater than or equal to VIP level 4 with an area coverage of 40% or more, and hail ¾ in. or greater.
Answer (A) is incorrect because thunderstorms would be very strong (VIP level 4) or greater, not moderate, and cover 40%, not 30%, of the area for a convective SIGMET. Answer (B) is incorrect because a convective SIGMET that is issued for thunderstorms implies severe or greater, not moderate, turbulence.

END OF CHAPTER

CHAPTER NINE
NAVIGATION: CHARTS,
PUBLICATIONS, FLIGHT COMPUTERS

This chapter contains outlines of major concepts tested, all FAA test questions and answers regarding navigation charts, and an explanation of each answer. Each module, or subtopic, within this chapter is listed above with the number of questions from the FAA pilot knowledge test pertaining to that particular module. For each module, the first number following the parentheses is the page number on which the outline begins, and the next number is the page number on which the questions begin.

Many of the questions in this chapter ask about the sectional (aeronautical) charts, which appear as Legend 1 and Figures 21 through 27. The acronym ACL is the question source code used to refer to this aeronautical chart legend. To produce the legend and these charts economically, we have put them on pages 251 through 258. As you will need to turn to these pages frequently, mark them with "dog ears"; i.e., fold their corners, or paper clip them. Also, the second module, Airspace and Altitudes, is long (29 questions) and covers a number of diverse topics regarding interpretation of sectional charts. Be prepared.

Note that a number of questions in Chapter 11, Cross-Country Flight Planning, will refer you to these same figures. Those questions require you to compute magnetic heading, true course, time en route, etc.

CAUTION: Recall that the **sole purpose** of this book is to expedite your passing the FAA pilot knowledge test for the private pilot certificate. Accordingly, all extraneous material (i.e., topics or regulations not directly tested on the FAA pilot knowledge test) is omitted, even though much more information and knowledge are necessary to fly safely. This additional material is presented in *Pilot Handbook* and *Private Pilot Flight Maneuvers and Practical Test Prep*, available from Gleim Publications, Inc. See the order form on page 326.

9.1 LONGITUDE AND LATITUDE (Questions 1-5)

1. The location of an airport can be determined by the intersection of lines of latitude and longitude.

    a. Lines of latitude are parallel to the equator, and those north of the equator are numbered from 0° to 90° north latitude.

    b. Lines of longitude are lines which extend from the north pole to the south pole. The prime meridian (which passes through Greenwich, England) is 0° longitude with 180° on both the east and west sides of the prime meridian.

2. The lines of latitude and longitude are printed on aeronautical charts (e.g., sectional) with each degree subdivided into 60 equal segments called minutes, i.e., ½° is 30′ (the min. symbol is " ′ ").

9.2 AIRSPACE AND ALTITUDES (Questions 6-34)

Cloud Clearance and Visibility Required for VFR

Airspace	Flight Visibility	Distance from Clouds		Airspace	Flight Visibility	Distance from Clouds
Class A	Not applicable	Not applicable		**Class G:** 1,200 ft. or less above the surface (regardless of MSL altitude)		
Class B	3 SM	Clear of clouds		Day	1 SM	Clear of clouds
Class C	3 SM	500 ft. below 1,000 ft. above 2,000 ft. horiz.		Night, except as provided in 1. below	3 SM	500 ft. below 1,000 ft. above 2,000 ft. horiz.
Class D	3 SM	500 ft. below 1,000 ft. above 2,000 ft. horiz.		More than 1,200 ft. above the surface but less than 10,000 ft. MSL		
Class E: Less than 10,000 ft. MSL	3 SM	500 ft. below 1,000 ft. above 2,000 ft. horiz.		Day	1 SM	500 ft. below 1,000 ft. above 2,000 ft. horiz.
At or above 10,000 ft. MSL	5 SM	1,000 ft. below 1,000 ft. above 1 SM horiz.		Night	3 SM	500 ft. below 1,000 ft. above 2,000 ft. horiz.
				More than 1,200 ft. above the surface and at or above 10,000 ft. MSL	5 SM	1,000 ft. below 1,000 ft. above 1 SM horiz.

1. An airplane may be operated clear of clouds in Class G airspace at night below 1,200 ft. AGL when the visibility is less than 3 SM but more than 1 SM in an airport traffic pattern and within ½ NM of the runway.

2. Class G airspace is all navigable airspace that is not classified as Class A, Class B, Class C, Class D, or Class E airspace.

3.   The lower limits of Class E airspace

    a.   Surface around airports marked by segmented (dashed) magenta (red) lines

    b.   700 ft. AGL in areas marked by magenta shading

    c.   1,200 ft. AGL for areas designated as federal airways and other areas marked by blue shading

        1)   In much of the contiguous U.S., the floor of Class E airspace is no higher than 1,200 ft. AGL anywhere.

            a)   Therefore, the blue shading is not shown because it would extend beyond the edge of the chart.

            b)   In these areas, unless the floor of Class E airspace is indicated by chart symbols to be below 1,200 ft. AGL, it is understood to be at 1,200 ft. AGL.

        2)   Airways are depicted as light blue lines between VOR facilities and are labeled with the letter "V" followed by numbers, i.e., V-120.

        3)   Federal airways extend up to 17,999 ft. MSL and are 8 NM wide.

    d.   If none of the above apply, the floor of Class E airspace begins at 14,500 ft. MSL.

4.   Class D airspace is an area of controlled airspace surrounding an airport with an operating control tower, not associated with Class B or Class C airspace areas.

    a.   Class D airspace is depicted by a segmented (dashed) blue line on sectional charts.

    b.   The height of the Class D airspace is shown in a broken box and is expressed in hundreds of feet MSL.

        1)   EXAMPLE: $\lceil _{29} \rceil$ means the height of the Class D airspace is 2,900 ft. MSL.

5.   Class C airspace areas are depicted by solid magenta lines on sectional charts.

    a.   The surface area (formerly called the inner circle) of Class C airspace, the area within 5 NM from the primary airport, begins at the surface and goes up to 4,000 ft. above the airport. The shelf area (formerly called the outer circle) of a Class C airspace area, the area from 5 NM to 10 NM from the primary airport, begins at about 1,200 ft. AGL and extends to the same altitude as the surface area.

    b.   The vertical limits are indicated on the chart within each circle and are expressed in hundreds of feet MSL. The top limit is shown above a straight line and the bottom limit beneath the line.

        1)   EXAMPLE: See Fig. 24 on page 255. At the bottom right (area 3) is the Savannah Class C airspace.

            a) $\dfrac{41}{SFC}$ in the surface area means Class C airspace extends from the surface (SFC) to 4,100 ft. MSL.

            b) $\dfrac{41}{13}$ in the shelf area means Class C airspace extends from 1,300 ft. MSL to 4,100 ft. MSL.

    c.   The minimum equipment needed to operate in Class C airspace

        1)   4096-code transponder
        2)   Mode C (altitude encoding) capability
        3)   Two-way radio communication capability

    d.   You must establish and maintain two-way radio communication with ATC prior to entering Class C airspace.

6. Class B airspace areas are depicted by heavy blue lines on sectional charts.

   a. The vertical limits are shown on the chart in the same manner as the vertical limits for Class C airspace discussed in item 5.b. on the previous page.

   b. The minimum equipment needed is

      1) A 4096-code transponder
      2) Mode C capability
      3) Two-way radio communication capability

7. When overlapping airspace designations apply to the same airspace, the more restrictive designation applies. Remember that Class A airspace is the most restrictive, and Class G is the least restrictive.

   a. EXAMPLE: The primary airport of a Class D airspace area underlies Class B airspace. The ceiling of the Class D airspace is 3,100 ft. MSL, and the floor of the Class B airspace is 3,000 ft. MSL. Since Class B is more restrictive than Class D, the overlapping airspace between 3,000 ft. and 3,100 ft. MSL is considered to be Class B airspace.

8. Special use airspace includes prohibited, restricted, warning, military operations, alert, national security, and controlled firing areas.

   a. **Restricted areas** denote the existence of unusual, often invisible hazards to aircraft such as military firing, aerial gunnery, or guided missiles.

   b. **Warning areas** contain activity that may be hazardous to nonparticipating aircraft, e.g., aerial gunnery, guided missiles, etc.

      1) Warning areas extend from 3 NM outward from the U.S. coast.
      2) A warning area may be located over domestic air or international waters or both.

   c. **Military operations areas (MOAs)** denote areas of military training activities.

      1) Pilots should contact any FSS within 100 NM to determine the MOA hours of operation.

      2) If it is active, the pilot should contact the controlling agency prior to entering the MOA for traffic advisories because of high-density military training.

      3) When operating in an MOA, exercise extreme caution when military activity is being conducted.

9. **Military training routes (MTR)** are established below 10,000 ft. MSL for operations at speeds in excess of 250 kt.

   a. IR means the routes are made in accordance with IFRs.

      1) VR means the routes are made in accordance with VFRs.

   b. MTRs that include one or more segments above 1,500 ft. AGL are identified by a three-digit number.

      1) MTRs with no segment above 1,500 ft. AGL are identified by a four-digit number.

10. Information about parachute jumping areas and glider operations is contained in the *Airport/Facility Directory (A/FD)*. Parachute jumping areas are marked on sectional charts with a parachute symbol.

11. Over national wildlife refuges, pilots are requested to maintain a minimum altitude of 2,000 ft. AGL.

12. Airport data on sectional charts include the following information:

    a. The name of the airport

    b. The elevation of the airport, followed by the length of the longest hard-surfaced runway. An L between the altitude and length indicates lighting.

       1) EXAMPLE: 1008 L 70 means 1,008 ft. MSL airport elevation, L is for lighting sunset to sunrise, and the length of the longest hard-surfaced runway is 7,000 ft.

       2) If the L has an asterisk beside it, airport lighting limitations exist, and you should refer to the *A/FD* for information.

    c. The UNICOM frequency if one has been assigned (e.g., 122.8) is shown after or underneath the runway length.

    d. At controlled airports, the tower frequency is usually under the airport name and above the runway information. It is preceded by CT.

       1) If not a federal control tower, NFCT precedes the CT frequency.

    e. A small, star-shaped symbol immediately above the airport symbol indicates a rotating beacon from sunset to sunrise.

    f. The notation "NO SVFR" above the airport name means that fixed-wing special VFR operations are prohibited.

13. Obstructions on sectional charts

    a. Obstructions of a height less than 1,000 ft. AGL have the symbol **A**.

       1) A group of such obstructions has the symbol **M**.

    b. Obstructions of a height of 1,000 ft. or more AGL have the symbol **⅄**.

       1) A group of such obstructions has the symbol **⅏**.

    c. Obstructions with high-intensity lights have arrows, or lightning bolts, projecting from the top of the obstruction symbol.

    d. The actual height of the top of obstructions is listed near the obstruction by two numbers: one in bold print over another in light print with parentheses around it.

       1) The bold number is the elevation of the top of the obstruction in feet above MSL.

       2) The light number in parentheses is the height of the obstruction in feet AGL.

       3) The elevation (MSL) at the base of the obstruction is the bold figures minus the light figures.

         a) Use this computation to compute terrain elevation.

         b) Terrain elevation is also given in the airport identifier for each airport and by the contour lines and color shading on the chart.

    e. You must maintain at least 1,000 ft. above obstructions in congested areas and 500 ft. above obstructions in other areas.

14. Navigational facilities are depicted on sectional charts with various symbols depending on type and services available. These symbols are shown in Legend 1 on page 251.

    a. A VORTAC is depicted as a hexagon with a dot in the center and a small solid rectangle attached to three of the six sides.

    b. A VOR/DME is depicted as a hexagon within a square.

    c. A VOR is depicted as a hexagon with a dot in the center.

9.3 IDENTIFYING LANDMARKS (Questions 35-38)

1.   On aeronautical charts, magenta (red) flags denote prominent landmarks which may be used as visual reporting checkpoints for VFR traffic when contacting ATC.

2.   The word "CAUTION" on aeronautical charts usually has an accompanying explanation of the hazard.

3.   Airports with a rotating beacon will have a star at the top of the airport symbol on sectional charts.

4.   Airports attended during normal business hours and having fuel service are indicated on airport symbols by the presence of small solid squares at the top and bottom and on both sides (9 o'clock and 3 o'clock) on the airport symbol.

9.4 RADIO FREQUENCIES (Questions 39-49)

1.   At airports without operating control towers, you should use the Common Traffic Advisory Frequency (CTAF), marked with a letter C in the airport data on the sectional chart.

   a.   The control tower (CT) frequency is usually used for CTAF when the control tower is closed.

   b.   At airports without control towers but with FSS at the airport, the FSS airport advisory frequency is usually the CTAF.

   c.   At airports without a tower or FSS, the UNICOM frequency is the CTAF.

   d.   At airports without a tower, FSS, or UNICOM, the CTAF is MULTICOM, i.e., 122.9.

   e.   Inbound and outbound traffic should communicate position and monitor CTAF within a 10-NM radius of the airport and give position reports when in the traffic pattern.

   f.   At airports with operating control towers the UNICOM frequency listed on the sectional chart and A/FD can be used to request services such as fuel, phone calls, and catering.

2.   Flight Watch is the common term for En Route Flight Advisory Service (EFAS). It specifically provides en route aircraft with current weather along their route of flight.

   a.   Flight Watch is available throughout the country on 122.0 between 5,000 ft. MSL and 18,000 ft. MSL.

   b.   The name of the nearest Flight Watch facility is sometimes indicated in communications boxes.

3.   Hazardous Inflight Weather Advisory Service (HIWAS) is available from navigation facilities that have a small square inside the lower right corner of the navigation aid identifier box.

9.5 FAA ADVISORY CIRCULARS (Questions 50-53)

1.   The FAA issues advisory circulars to provide a systematic means for the issuance of nonregulatory material of interest to the aviation public.

2.   The circulars are issued in a numbered system of general subject matter areas to correspond with the subject areas in Federal Aviation Regulations (e.g., 60 Airmen, 70 Airspace, 90 Air Traffic Control and General Operation).

3.   FAA Advisory Circulars are available from the FAA and the U.S. Government Printing Office.

   a.   An Advisory Circular Checklist (AC 00-2) is available by writing the U.S. Department of Transportation, Subsequent Distribution Office, SVC-121.23, Ardmore East Business Center, 3341 Q 75th Ave., Landover, MD, 20785.

9.6 AIRPORT/FACILITY DIRECTORY (Questions 54-58)

1. *Airport/Facility Directories (A/FDs)* are published by the U.S. Department of Commerce every 56 days for each of seven geographical districts of the United States.

   a. *A/FDs* provide information on services available, runways, special conditions at the airport, communications, navigation aids, etc.

2. The airport name comes first.

3. The third item on the first line is the number of miles and direction of the airport from the city.

   a. EXAMPLE: **4 NW** means 4 NM northwest of the city.

4. Right-turn traffic is indicated by "Rgt tfc" following a runway number.

5. When a control tower is not in operation, the CTAF frequency (found in the section titled **Communications**) should be used for traffic advisories.

6. Initial communication should be with Approach Control if available where you are landing. The frequency is listed following "APP/DEP CON."

   a. It may be different for approaches from different headings.
   b. It may be operational only for certain hours of the day.

7. In Class C airspace, VFR aircraft are provided the following radar services:

   a. Sequencing to the primary Class C airport
   b. Approved separation between IFR and VFR aircraft
   c. Basic radar services, including safety alerts, limited vectoring, and traffic advisories

8. A sample *A/FD* legend and explanations are reproduced on pages 236 to 243 from Appendix 2 of the FAA's *Computerized Testing Supplement for Recreational Pilot and Private Pilot*. That is, you will have access to them during the examination.

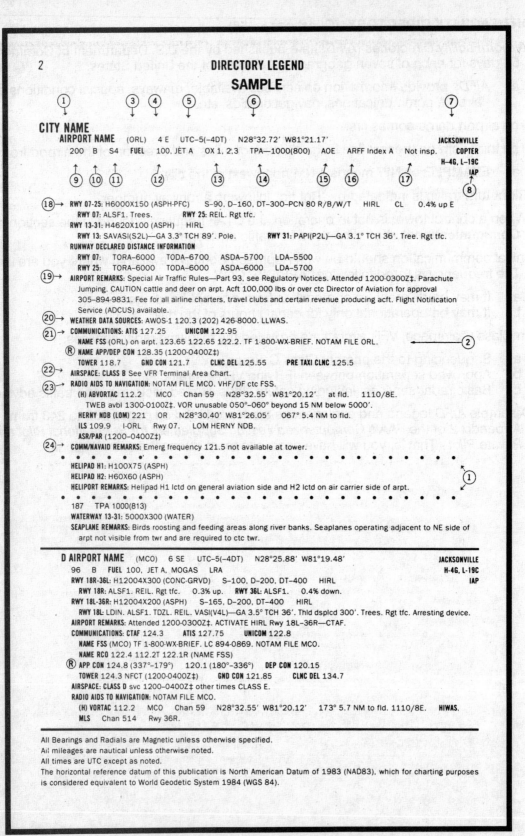

LEGEND 2.—Airport/Facility Directory.

DIRECTORY LEGEND 3

LEGEND

This Directory is an alphabetical listing of data on record with the FAA on all airports that are open to the public, associated terminal control facilities, air route traffic control centers and radio aids to navigation within the conterminous United States, Puerto Rico and the Virgin Islands. Airports are listed alphabetically by associated city name and cross referenced by airport name. Facilities associated with an airport, but with a different name, are listed individually under their own name, as well as under the airport with which they are associated.

The listing of an airport in this directory merely indicates the airport operator's willingness to accommodate transient aircraft, and does not represent that the facility conforms with any Federal or local standards, or that it has been approved for use on the part of the general public.

The information on obstructions is taken from reports submitted to the FAA. It has not been verified in all cases. Pilots are cautioned that objects not indicated in this tabulation (or on charts) may exist which can create a hazard to flight operation.

Detailed specifics concerning services and facilities tabulated within this directory are contained in Aeronautical Information Manual, Basic Flight Information and ATC Procedures.

The legend items that follow explain in detail the contents of this Directory and are keyed to the circled numbers on the sample on the preceding page.

① CITY/AIRPORT NAME

Airports and facilities in this directory are listed alphabetically by associated city and state. Where the city name is different from the airport name the city name will appear on the line above the airport name. Airports with the same associated city name will be listed alphabetically by airport name and will be separated by a dashed rule line. All others will be separated by a solid rule line. (Designated Helipads and Seaplane Landing Areas (Water) associated with a land airport will be separated by a dotted line.)

② NOTAM SERVICE

All public use landing areas are provided NOTAM ''D'' (distant dissemination) and NOTAM ''L'' (local dissemination) service. Airport NOTAM file identifier is shown following the associated FSS data for individual airports, e.g. ''NOTAM FILE IAD''. See AIM, Basic Flight Information and ATC Procedures for detailed description of NOTAM's.

③ LOCATION IDENTIFIER

A three or four character code assigned to airports. These identifiers are used by ATC in lieu of the airport name in flight plans, flight strips and other written records and computer operations.

④ AIRPORT LOCATION

Airport location is expressed as distance and direction from the center of the associated city in nautical miles and cardinal points, i.e., 4 NE.

⑤ TIME CONVERSION

Hours of operation of all facilities are expressed in Coordinated Universal Time (UTC) and shown as ''Z'' time. The directory indicates the number of hours to be subtracted from UTC to obtain local standard time and local daylight saving time UTC–5(–4DT). The symbol ‡ indicates that during periods of Daylight Saving Time effective hours will be one hour earlier than shown. In those areas where daylight saving time is not observed that (–4DT) and ‡ will not be shown. All states observe daylight savings time except Arizona, Hawaii and that portion of Indiana in the Eastern Time Zone and Puerto Rico and the Virgin Islands.

⑥ GEOGRAPHIC POSITION OF AIRPORT

Positions are shown in degrees, minutes and hundredths of a minute and represent the approximate center of mass of all usable runways.

⑦ CHARTS

The Sectional Chart and Low and High Altitude Enroute Chart and panel on which the airport or facility is located. Helicopter Chart locations will be indicated as, i.e., COPTER.

⑧ INSTRUMENT APPROACH PROCEDURES

IAP indicates an airport for which a prescribed (Public Use) FAA Instrument Approach Procedure has been published.

⑨ ELEVATION

The highest point of an airport's usable runways measured in feet from mean sea level. When elevation is sea level it will be indicated as (00). When elevation is below sea level a minus (–) sign will precede the figure.

⑩ ROTATING LIGHT BEACON

B indicates rotating beacon is available. Rotating beacons operate dusk to dawn unless otherwise indicated in AIRPORT REMARKS.

⑪ SERVICING

S1: Minor airframe repairs.	S3: Major airframe and minor powerplant repairs.
S2: Minor airframe and minor powerplant repairs.	S4: Major airframe and major powerplant repairs.

LEGEND 3.—Airport/Facility Directory.

4   **DIRECTORY LEGEND**

⑫ FUEL

CODE	FUEL	CODE	FUEL
80	Grade 80 gasoline (Red)	B	Jet B—Wide-cut turbine fuel, freeze point–50° C.
100	Grade 100 gasoline (Green)		
100LL	100LL gasoline (low lead) (Blue)	B+	Jet B—Wide-cut turbine fuel with icing inhibitor, freeze point–50° C.
115	Grade 115 gasoline		
A	Jet A—Kerosene freeze point–40° C.	MOGAS	Automobile gasoline which is to be used as aircraft fuel.
A1	Jet A-1—Kerosene freeze point–50°C.		
A1+	Jet A-1—Kerosene with icing inhibitor, freeze point–50° C.		

NOTE: Automobile Gasoline. Certain automobile gasoline may be used in specific aircraft engines if a FAA supplemental type cetificate has been obtained. Automobile gasoline which is to be used in aircraft engines will be identified as ''MOGAS'', however, the grade/type and other octane rating will not be published.

Data shown on fuel availability represents the most recent information the publisher has been able to acquire. Because of a variety of factors, the fuel listed may not always be obtainable by transient civil pilots. Confirmation of availability of fuel should be made directly with fuel dispensers at locations where refueling is planned.

⑬ OXYGEN

OX 1	High Pressure	OX 3	High Pressure—Replacement Bottles
OX 2	Low Pressure	OX 4	Low Pressure—Replacement Bottles

⑭ TRAFFIC PATTERN ALTITUDE

Traffic Pattern Altitude (TPA)—The first figure shown is TPA above mean sea level. The second figure in parentheses is TPA above airport elevation.

⑮ AIRPORT OF ENTRY, LANDING RIGHTS, AND CUSTOMS USER FEE AIRPORTS

U.S. CUSTOMS USER FEE AIRPORT—Private Aircraft operators are frequently required to pay the costs associated with customs processing.

AOE—Airport of Entry—A customs Airport of Entry where permission from U.S. Customs is not required, however, at least one hour advance notice of arrival must be furnished.

LRA—Landing Rights Airport—Application for permission to land must be submitted in advance to U.S. Customs. At least one hour advance notice of arrival must be furnished.

NOTE: Advance notice of arrival at both an AOE and LRA airport may be included in the flight plan when filed in Canada or Mexico, where Flight Notification Service (ADCUS) is available the airport remark will indicate this service. This notice will also be treated as an application for permission to land in the case of an LRA. Although advance notice of arrival may be relayed to Customs through Mexico, Canadian, and U.S. Communications facilities by flight plan, the aircraft operator is solely responsible for insuring that Customs receives the notification. (See Customs, Immigration and Naturalization, Public Health and Agriculture Department requirements in the International Flight Information Manual for further details.)

⑯ CERTIFICATED AIRPORT (FAR 139)

Airports serving Department of Transportation certified carriers and certified under FAR, Part 139, are indicated by the ARFF index; i.e., ARFF Index A, which relates to the availability of crash, fire, rescue equipment.

FAR—PART 139 CERTIFICATED AIRPORTS
INDICES AND AIRCRAFT RESCUE AND FIRE FIGHTING EQUIPMENT REQUIREMENTS

Airport Index	Required No. Vehicles	Aircraft Length	Scheduled Departures	Agent + Water for Foam
A	1	<90'	≥1	500#DC or HALON 1211 or 450#DC + 100 gal H₂O
B	1 or 2	≥90', <126'	≥5	Index A + 1500 gal H₂O
		≥126', <159'	<5	
C	2 or 3	≥126', <159'	≥5	Index A + 3000 gal H₂O
		≥159', <200'	<5	
D	3	≥159', <200'	≥5	Index A + 4000 gal H₂O
		>200'	<5	
E	3	≥200'	≥5	Index A + 6000 gal H₂O

> Greater Than; < Less Than; ≥ Equal or Greater Than; ≤ Equal or Less Than;   H₂O—Water; DC—Dry Chemical.

NOTE: The listing of ARFF index does not necessarily assure coverage for non-air carrier operations or at other than prescribed times for air carrier. ARFF Index Ltd.—indicates ARFF coverage may or may not be available, for information contact airport manager prior to flight.

LEGEND 4.—Airport/Facility Directory.

DIRECTORY LEGEND 5

⑰ FAA INSPECTION

All airports not inspected by FAA will be identified by the note: Not insp. This indicates that the airport information has been provided by the owner or operator of the field.

⑱ RUNWAY DATA

Runway information is shown on two lines. That information common to the entire runway is shown on the first line while information concerning the runway ends are shown on the second or following line. Lengthy information will be placed in the Airport Remarks.

Runway direction, surface, length, width, weight bearing capacity, lighting, slope and appropriate remarks are shown for each runway. Direction, length, width, lighting and remarks are shown for sealanes. The full dimensions of helipads are shown, i.e., 50X150.

RUNWAY SURFACE AND LENGTH

Runway lengths prefixed by the letter "H" indicate that the runways are hard surfaced (concrete, asphalt). If the runway length is not prefixed, the surface is sod, clay, etc. The runway surface composition is indicated in parentheses after runway length as follows:

(AFSC)—Aggregate friction seal coat	(GRVD)—Grooved	(RFSC)—Rubberized friction seal coat
(ASPH)—Asphalt	(GRVL)—Gravel, or cinders	(TURF)—Turf
(CONC)—Concrete	(PFC)—Porous friction courses	(TRTD)—Treated
(DIRT)—Dirt	(PSP)—Pierced steel plank	(WC)—Wire combed

RUNWAY WEIGHT BEARING CAPACITY

Runway strength data shown in this publication is derived from available information and is a realistic estimate of capability at an average level of activity. It is not intended as a maximum allowable weight or as an operating limitation. Many airport pavements are capable of supporting limited operations with gross weights of 25-50% in excess of the published figures. Permissible operating weights, insofar as runway strengths are concerned, are a matter of agreement between the owner and user. When desiring to operate into any airport at weights in excess of those published in the publication, users should contact the airport management for permission. Add 000 to figure following S, D, DT, DDT, AUW, etc., for gross weight capacity:

- S—Single–wheel type landing gear. (DC-3), (C-47), (F-15), etc.
- D—Dual–wheel type landing gear. (DC-6), etc.
- T—Twin–wheel type landing gear. (DC-6), (C-9A), etc.
- ST—Single–tandem type landing gear. (C-130).
- SBTT—Single–belly twin tandem landing gear (KC-10).
- DT—Dual–tandem type landing gear, (707), etc.
- TT—Twin–tandem type (includes quadricycle) landing gear (707), (B-52), (C-135), etc.
- TRT—Triple–tandem landing gear, (C-17)
- DDT—Double dual–tandem landing gear. (E4A/747).
- TDT—Twin delta–tandem landing gear. (C-5, Concorde).
- AUW—All up weight. Maximum weight bearing capacity for any aircraft irrespective of landing gear configuration.
- SWL—Single Wheel Loading. (This includes information submitted in terms of Equivalent Single Wheel Loading (ESWL) and Single Isolated Wheel Loading). SWL figures are shown in thousands of pounds with the last three figures being omitted.
- PSI—Pounds per square inch. PSI is the actual figure expressing maximum pounds per square inch runway will support, e.g., (SWL 000/PSI 535).

Quadricycle and dual-tandem are considered virtually equal for runway weight bearing consideration, as are single-tandem and dual-wheel. Omission of weight bearing capacity indicates information unknown.

The ACN/PCN System is the ICAO method of reporting pavement strength for pavements with bearing strengths greater than 12,500 pounds. The Pavement Classification Number (PCN) is established by an engineering assessment of the runway. The PCN is for use in conjunction with an Aircraft Classification Number (ACN). Consult the Aircraft Flight Manual or other appropriate source for ACN tables or charts. Currently, ACN data may not be available for all aircraft. If an ACN table or chart is available, the ACN can be calculated by taking into account the aircraft weight, the pavement type, and the subgrade category. For runways that have been evaluated under the ACN/PCN system, the PCN will be shown as a five part code (e.g. PCN 80 R/B/W/T). Details of the coded format are as follows:

(1) The PCN NUMBER—The reported PCN indicates that an aircraft with an ACN equal or less than the reported PCN can operate on the pavement subject to any limitation on the tire pressure.

(2) The type of pavement:
  R — Rigid
  F — Flexible

(3) The pavement subgrade category:
  A — High
  B — Medium
  C — Low
  D — Ultra-low

(4) The maximum tire pressure authorized for the pavement:
  W — High, no limit
  X — Medium, limited to 217 psi
  Y — Low, limited to 145 psi
  Z — Very low, limited to 73 psi

(5) Pavement evaluation method:
  T — Technical evaluation
  U — By experience of aircraft using the pavement

NOTE: Prior permission from the airport controlling authority is required when the ACN of the aircraft exceeds the published PCN or aircraft tire pressure exceeds the published limits.

LEGEND 5.—Airport/Facility Directory.

6   DIRECTORY LEGEND

RUNWAY LIGHTING

Lights are in operation sunset to sunrise. Lighting available by prior arrangement only or operating part of the night only and/or pilot controlled and with specific operating hours are indicated under airport remarks. Since obstructions are usually lighted, obstruction lighting is not included in this code. Unlighted obstructions on or surrounding an airport will be noted in airport remarks. Runway lights nonstandard (NSTD) are systems for which the light fixtures are not FAA approved L-800 series: color, intensity, or spacing does not meet FAA standards. Nonstandard runway lights, VASI, or any other system not listed below will be shown in airport remarks.

Temporary, emergency or limited runway edge lighting such as flares, smudge pots, lanterns or portable runway lights will also be shown in airport remarks. Types of lighting are shown with the runway or runway end they serve.

NSTD—Light system fails to meet FAA standards.
LIRL—Low Intensity Runway Lights
MIRL—Medium Intensity Runway Lights
HIRL—High Intensity Runway Lights
RAIL—Runway Alignment Indicator Lights
REIL—Runway End Identifier Lights
CL—Centerline Lights
TDZL—Touchdown Zone Lights
ODALS—Omni Directional Approach Lighting System.
AF OVRN—Air Force Overrun 1000' Standard Approach Lighting System.
LDIN—Lead-In Lighting System.
MALS—Medium Intensity Approach Lighting System.
MALSF—Medium Intensity Approach Lighting System with Sequenced Flashing Lights.
MALSR—Medium Intensity Approach Lighting System with Runway Alignment Indicator Lights.

SALS—Short Approach Lighting System.
SALSF—Short Approach Lighting System with Sequenced Flashing Lights.
SSALS—Simplified Short Approach Lighting System.
SSALF—Simplified Short Approach Lighting System with Sequenced Flashing Lights.
SSALR—Simplified Short Approach Lighting System with Runway Alignment Indicator Lights.
ALSAF—High Intensity Approach Lighting System with Sequenced Flashing Lights
ALSF1—High Intensity Approach Lighting System with Sequenced Flashing Lights, Category I, Configuration.
ALSF2—High Intensity Approach Lighting System with Sequenced Flashing Lights, Category II, Configuration.
VASI—Visual Approach Slope Indicator System.

NOTE: Civil ALSF-2 may be operated as SSALR during favorable weather conditions.

VISUAL GLIDESLOPE INDICATORS

APAP—A system of panels, which may or may not be lighted, used for alignment of approach path.

PNIL   APAP on left side of runway

PAPI—Precision Approach Path Indicator
P2L   2-identical light units placed on left side of runway
P2R   2-identical light units placed on right side of runway

PVASI—Pulsating/steady burning visual approach slope indicator, normally a single light unit projecting two colors.
PSIL·   PVASI on left side of runway

SAVASI—Simplified Abbreviated Visual Approach Slope Indicator
S2L   2-box SAVASI on left side of runway

TRCV—Tri-color visual approach slope indicator, normally a single light unit projecting three colors.
TRIL   TRCV on left side of runway

VASI—Visual Approach Slope Indicator
V2L   2-box VASI on left side of runway
V2R   2-box VASI on right side of runway
V4L   4-box VASI on left side of runway
V4R   4-box VASI on right side of runway

PNIR   APAP on right side of runway

P4L   4-identical light units placed on left side of runway
P4R   4-identical light units placed on right side of runway

PSIR·   PVASI on right-side of runway

S2R   2-box SAVASI on right side of runway

TRIR   TRCV on right side of runway

V6L   6-box VASI on left side of runway
V6R   6-box VASI on right side of runway
V12   12-box VASI on both sides of runway
V16   16-box VASI on both sides of runway

NOTE: Approach slope angle and threshold crossing height will be shown when available; i.e., –GA 3.5° TCH 37'.

PILOT CONTROL OF AIRPORT LIGHTING

Key Mike	Function
7 times within 5 seconds	Highest intensity available
5 times within 5 seconds	Medium or lower intensity (Lower REIL or REIL-Off)
3 times within 5 seconds	Lowest intensity available (Lower REIL or REIL-Off)

Available systems will be indicated in the Airport Remarks, as follows:

ACTIVATE MALSR Rwy 07, HIRL Rwy 07–25–122.8 (or CTAF).
or
ACTIVATE MIRL Rwy 18–36–122.8 (or CTAF).
or
ACTIVATE VASI and REIL, Rwy 07–122.8 (or CTAF).

Where the airport is not served by an instrument approach procedure and/or has an independent type system of different specification installed by the airport sponsor, descriptions of the type lights, method of control, and operating frequency will be explained in clear text. See AIM, "Basic Flight Information and ATC Procedures," for detailed description of pilot control of airport lighting.

RUNWAY SLOPE

Runway slope will be shown only when it is 0.3 percent or more. On runways less than 8000 feet: When available the direction of the slope upward will be indicated, ie., 0.3% up NW. On runways 8000 feet or greater: When available the slope will be shown on the runway end line, ie., RWY 13: 0.3% up., RWY 21: Pole. Rgt tfc. 0.4% down.

RUNWAY END DATA

Lighting systems such as VASI, MALSR, REIL; obstructions; displaced thresholds will be shown on the specific runway end. "Rgt tfc"—Right traffic indicates right turns should be made on landing and takeoff for specified runway end.

LEGEND 6.—Airport/Facility Directory.

DIRECTORY LEGEND   7

RUNWAY DECLARED DISTANCE INFORMATION

TORA—Take-off Run Available
TODA—Take-off Distance Available
ASDA—Accelerate-Stop Distance Available
LDA—Landing Distance Available

⑲ AIRPORT REMARKS

Landing Fee indicates landing charges for private or non-revenue producing aircraft, in addition, fees may be charged for planes that remain over a couple of hours and buy no services, or at major airline terminals for all aircraft.
Remarks—Data is confined to operational items affecting the status and usability of the airport.
Parachute Jumping.—See ''PARACHUTE'' tabulation for details.
Unless otherwise stated, remarks including runway ends refer to the runway's approach end.

⑳ WEATHER DATA SOURCES

ASOS—Automated Surface Observing System. Reports the same as an AWOS-3 plus precipitation identification and intensity, and freezing rain occurrence (future enhancement).
AWOS—Automated Weather Observing System

  AWOS-A—reports altimeter setting.
  AWOS-1—reports altimeter setting, wind data and usually temperature, dewpoint and density altitude.
  AWOS-2—reports the same as AWOS-1 plus visibility.
  AWOS-3—reports the same as AWOS-1 plus visibility and cloud/ceiling data.
  See AIM, Basic Flight Information and ATC Procedures for detailed description of AWOS.

HIWAS—See RADIO AIDS TO NAVIGATION
LAWRS—Limited Aviation Weather Reporting Station where observers report cloud height, weather, obstructions to vision, temperature and dewpoint (in most cases), surface wind, altimeter and pertinent remarks.
LLWAS—indicates a Low Level Wind Shear Alert System consisting of a center field and several field perimeter anemometers.
SAWRS—identifies airports that have a Supplemental Aviation Weather Reporting Station available to pilots for current weather information.
SWSL—Supplemental Weather Service Location providing current local weather information via radio and telephone.

㉑ COMMUNICATIONS

Communications will be listed in sequence in the order shown below:
Common Traffic Advisory Frequency (CTAF), Automatic Terminal Information Service (ATIS) and Aeronautical Advisory Stations (UNICOM) along with their frequency is shown, where available, on the line following the heading ''COMMUNICATIONS.'' When the CTAF and UNICOM is the same frequency, the frequency will be shown as CTAF/UNICOM freq.
Flight Service Station (FSS) information. The associated FSS will be shown followed by the identifier and information concerning availability of telephone service, e.g., Direct Line (DL), Local Call (LC-384-2341), Toll free call, dial (TF 800—852-7036 or TF 1–800–227–7160), Long Distance (LD 202-426-8800 or LD 1-202-555-1212) etc. The airport NOTAM file identifier will be shown as ''NOTAM FILE IAD.'' Where the FSS is located on the field it will be indicated as ''on arpt'' following the identifier. Frequencies available will follow. The FSS telephone number will follow along with any significant operational information. FSS's whose name is not the same as the airport on which located will also be listed in the normal alphabetical name listing for the state in which located. Remote Communications Outlet (RCO) providing service to the airport followed by the frequency and name of the Controlling FSS.
FSS's provide information on airport conditions, radio aids and other facilities, and process flight plans. Local Airport Advisory Service is provided on the CTAF by FSS's located at non-tower airports or airports where the tower is not in operation.
(See AIM, Par. 157/158 Traffic Advisory Practices at airports where a tower is not in operation or AC 90 - 42C.)
Aviation weather briefing service is provided by FSS specialists. Flight and weather briefing services are also available by calling the telephone numbers listed.
Remote Communications Outlet (RCO)—An unmanned air/ground communications facility, remotely controlled and providing UHF or VHF communications capability to extend the service range of an FSS.
Civil Communications Frequencies—Civil communications frequencies used in the FSS air/ground system are now operated simplex on 122.0, 122.2, 122.3, 122.4, 122.6, 123.6; emergency 121.5; plus receive-only on 122.05, 122.1, 122.15, and 123.6.

  a. 122.0 is assigned as the Enroute Flight Advisory Service channel at selected FSS's.
  b. 122.2 is assigned to most FSS's as a common enroute simplex service.
  c. 123.6 is assigned as the airport advisory channel at non-tower FSS locations, however, it is still in commission at some FSS's collocated with towers to provide part time Local Airport Advisory Service.
  d. 122.1 is the primary receive-only frequency at VOR's. 122.05, 122.15 and 123.6 are assigned at selected VOR's meeting certain criteria.
  e. Some FSS's are assigned 50 kHz channels for simplex operation in the 122-123 MHz band (e.g. 122.35). Pilots using the FSS A/G system should refer to this directory or appropriate charts to determine frequencies available at the FSS or remoted facility through which they wish to communicate.

Part time FSS hours of operation are shown in remarks under facility name.

  Emergency frequency 121.5 is available at all Flight Service Stations, Towers, Approach Control and RADAR facilities, unless indicated as not available.
Frequencies published followed by the letter ''T'' or ''R'', indicate that the facility will only transmit or receive respectively on that frequency. All radio aids to navigation frequencies are transmit only.

LEGEND 7.—Airport/Facility Directory.

8   DIRECTORY LEGEND

TERMINAL SERVICES

CTAF—A program designed to get all vehicles and aircraft at uncontrolled airports on a common frequency.

ATIS—A continuous broadcast of recorded non-control information in selected areas of high activity.

UNICOM—A non-government air/ground radio communications facility utilized to provide general airport advisory service.

APP CON —Approach Control. The symbol Ⓡ indicates radar approach control.

TOWER—Control tower

GND CON—Ground Control

DEP CON—Departure Control. The symbol Ⓡ indicates radar departure control.

CLNC DEL—Clearance Delivery.

PRE TAXI CLNC—Pre taxi clearance

VFR ADVSY SVC—VFR Advisory Service. Service provided by Non-Radar Approach Control.

   Advisory Service for VFR aircraft (upon a workload basis) ctc APP CON.

TOWER, APP CON and DEP CON RADIO CALL will be the same as the airport name unless indicated otherwise.

㉒ AIRSPACE

CLASS B—Radar Sequencing and Separation Service for all aircraft in CLASS B airspace

TRSA—Radar Sequencing and Separation Service for participating VFR Aircraft within a Terminal Radar Service Area

Class C, D, and E airspace described in this publication is that airspace usually consisting of a 5 NM radius core surface area that begins at the surface and extends upward to an altitude above the airport elevation (charted in MSL for Class C and Class D).

When CLASS C airspace defaults to CLASS E, the core surface area becomes CLASS E. This will be formatted as: **AIRSPACE: CLASS C** svc "times" ctc **APP CON** other times CLASS E.

When Class C airspace defaults to Class G, the core surface area becomes Class G up to but not including the overlying controlled airspace. There are Class E airspace areas beginning at either 700' or 1200' AGL used to transition to/from the terminal or enroute environment. This will be formatted as: **AIRSPACE: CLASS C** svc "times" ctc **APP CON** other times CLASS G. CLASS E 700' (or 1200') AGL & abv.

NOTE: AIRSPACE SVC EFF "TIMES" INCLUDE ALL ASSOCIATED EXTENSIONS. Arrival extensions for instrument approach procedures become part of the primary core surface area. These extensions may be either Class D or Class E airspace and are effective concurrent with the times of the primary core surface area.

(See CLASS AIRSPACE in the Aeronautical Information Manual for further details)

㉓ RADIO AIDS TO NAVIGATION

The Airport Facility Directory lists by facility name all Radio Aids to Navigation, except Military TACANS, that appear on National Ocean Service Visual or IFR Aeronautical Charts and those upon which the FAA has approved an Instrument Approach Procedure. All VOR, VORTAC ILS and MLS equipment in the National Airspace System has an automatic monitoring and shutdown feature in the event of malfunction. Unmonitored, as used in this publication for any navigational aid, means that FSS or tower personnel cannot observe the malfunction or shutdown signal. The NAVAID NOTAM file identifier will be shown as "NOTAM FILE IAD" and will be listed on the Radio Aids to Navigation line. When two or more NAVAIDS are listed and the NOTAM file identifier is different than shown on the Radio Aids to Navigation line, then it will be shown with the NAVAID listing. NOTAM file identifiers for ILS's and their components (e.g., NDB (LOM) are the same as the identifiers for the associated airports and are not repeated. Hazardous Inflight Weather Advisory Service (HIWAS) will be shown where this service is broadcast over selected VOR's.

NAVAID information is tabulated as indicated in the following sample:

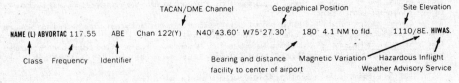

VOR unusable 020 -060 beyond 26 NM below 3500'

Restriction within the normal altitude/range of the navigational aid (See primary alphabetical listing for restrictions on VORTAC and VOR/DME).

   Note: Those DME channel numbers with a (Y) suffix require TACAN to be placed in the "Y" mode to receive distance information.

HIWAS—Hazardous Inflight Weather Advisory Service is a continuous broadcast of inflight weather advisories including summarized SIGMETs, convective SIGMETs, AIRMETs and urgent PIREPs. HIWAS is presently broadcast over selected VOR's and will be implemented throughout the conterminous U.S.

ASR/PAR—Indicates that Surveillance (ASR) or Precision (PAR) radar instrument approach minimums are published in the U.S. Terminal Procedures. Only part-time hours of operation will be shown.

LEGEND 8.—Airport/Facility Directory.

DIRECTORY LEGEND 9

RADIO CLASS DESIGNATIONS

VOR/DME/TACAN Standard Service Volume (SSV) Classifications

SSV Class	Altitudes	Distance (NM)
(T) Terminal	1000' to 12,000'	25
(L) Low Altitude	1000' to 18,000'	40
(H) High Altitude	1000' to 14,500'	40
	14,500' to 18,000'	100
	18,000' to 45,000'	130
	45,000' to 60,000'	100

NOTE: Additionally, (H) facilities provide (L) and (T) service volume and (L) facilities provide (T) service. Altitudes are with respect to the station's site elevation. Coverage is not available in a cone of airspace directly above the facility.

The term VOR is, operationally, a general term covering the VHF omnidirectional bearing type of facility without regard to the fact that the power, the frequency protected service volume, the equipment configuration, and operational requirements may vary between facilities at different locations.

AB	Automatic Weather Broadcast
DF	Direction Finding Service.
DME	UHF standard (TACAN compatible) distance measuring equipment.
DME(Y)	UHF standard (TACAN compatible) distance measuring equipment that require TACAN to be placed in the "Y" mode to receive DME.
H	Non-directional radio beacon (homing), power 50 watts to less than 2,000 watts (50 NM at all altitudes).
HH	Non-directional radio beacon (homing), power 2,000 watts or more (75 NM at all altitudes).
H-SAB	Non-directional radio beacons providing automatic transcribed weather service.
ILS	Instrument Landing System (voice, where available, on localizer channel).
ISMLS	Interim Standard Microwave Landing System.
LDA	Localizer Directional Aid.
LMM	Compass locator station when installed at middle marker site (15 NM at all altitudes).
LOM	Compass locator station when installed at outer marker site (15 NM at all altitudes).
MH	Non-directional radio beacon (homing) power less than 50 watts (25 NM at all altitudes).
MLS	Microwave Landing System
S	Simultaneous range homing signal and/or voice.
SABH	Non-directional radio beacon not authorized for IFR or ATC. Provides automatic weather broadcasts.
SDF	Simplified Direction Facility.
TACAN	UHF navigational facility-omnidirectional course and distance information.
VOR	VHF navigational facility-omnidirectional course only.
VOR/DME	Collocated VOR navigational facility and UHF standard distance measuring equipment.
VORTAC	Collocated VOR and TACAN navigational facilities.
W	Without voice on radio facility frequency.
Z	VHF station location marker at a LF radio facility.

LEGEND 9.—Airport/Facility Directory.

9.1 Longitude and Latitude

1.
3530. (Refer to figure 21, area 3, on page 252.) Determine the approximate latitude and longitude of Currituck County Airport.

A—36°24'N – 76°01'W.
B—36°48'N – 76°01'W.
C—47°24'N – 75°58'W.

Answer (A) is correct (3530). *(PHAK Chap 8)*
On Fig. 21, find the Currituck County Airport, which is northeast of area 3. Note that the airport symbol is just to the west of 76° longitude (find 76° just north of Virginia Beach and at the bottom of the chart). There are 60 min. between the 76° and 77° lines of longitude, with each tick mark depicting 1 min. The airport is one tick to the west of the 76° line, or 76°01'W.
The latitude is below the 30-min. latitude line across the center of the chart. See the numbered latitude lines at the top (37°) and bottom (36°) of the chart. Since each tick mark represents 1 min. of latitude, and the airport is approximately six ticks south of the 36°30'N latitude, the airport is at 36°24'N latitude. Thus, Currituck County Airport is located at approximately 36°24'N – 76°01'W.
Answer (B) is incorrect because Currituck County Airport is south of the 36°30'N (not 37°00'N) line of latitude. Answer (C) is incorrect because Currituck County Airport is west (not east) of the 76°W line of longitude and 47°24'N is 11°N of the airport.

2.
3535. (Refer to figure 22, area 2, on page 253.) Which airport is located at approximately 47°39'30"N latitude and 100°53'00"W longitude?

A—Linrud.
B—Crooked Lake.
C—Johnson.

Answer (B) is correct (3535). *(PHAK Chap 8)*
On Fig. 22, you are asked to locate an airport at 47°39'30"N latitude and 100°53' longitude. Note that the 101° longitude line runs down the middle of the page. Accordingly, the airport you are seeking is 7 min. to the east of that line.
Each crossline is 1 min. on the latitude and longitude lines. The 48° latitude line is approximately two-thirds of the way up the chart. The 47°30' latitude line is about one-fourth of the way up. One-third up from 47°30' to 48° latitude would be 47°39'. At this spot is Crooked Lake Airport.
Answer (A) is incorrect because Linrud is north of the 48° latitude line. Answer (C) is incorrect because both Johnson airports are south of 47°30' latitude line.

3.
3536. (Refer to figure 22, area 3, on page 253.) Which airport is located at approximately 47°21'N latitude and 101°01'W longitude?

A—Underwood.
B—Evenson.
C—Washburn.

Answer (C) is correct (3536). *(PHAK Chap 8)*
See Fig. 22. Find the 48° line of latitude (2/3 up the page). Start at the 47°30' line of latitude (the line below the 48° line) and count down nine ticks to the 47°21' mark and draw a horizontal line on the chart. Next find the 101° line of longitude and go left one tick and draw a vertical line. The closest airport is Washburn.
Answer (A) is incorrect because Underwood is a city (not an airport) northwest of Washburn by about 1 in. Answer (B) is incorrect because Evenson is north of the 47°36' latitude line.

4.
3543. (Refer to figure 23, area 3, on page 254.) Determine the approximate latitude and longitude of Shoshone County Airport.

A—47°02′N – 116°11′W.
B—47°33′N – 116°11′W.
C—47°32′N – 116°41′W.

5.
3567. (Refer to figure 27, area 2, on page 258.) What is the approximate latitude and longitude of Cooperstown Airport?

A—47°25′N – 98°06′W.
B—47°25′N – 99°54′W.
C—47°55′N – 98°06′W.

9.2 Airspace and Altitudes

6.
3623. (Refer to figure 27, area 6, on page 258.) The airspace overlying and within 5 miles of Barnes County Airport is

A—Class D airspace from the surface to the floor of the overlying Class E airspace.
B—Class E airspace from the surface to 1,200 feet MSL.
C—Class G airspace from the surface to 700 feet AGL.

7.
3622. (Refer to figure 27, area 1, on page 258.) Identify the airspace over Lowe Airport.

A—Class G airspace -- surface up to but not including 1,200 feet AGL, Class E airspace -- 1,200 feet AGL up to but not including 18,000 feet MSL.
B—Class G airspace -- surface up to but not including 18,000 feet MSL.
C—Class G airspace -- surface up to but not including 700 feet MSL; Class E airspace -- 700 feet to 14,500 feet MSL.

Answer (B) is correct (3543). *(PHAK Chap 8)*
See Fig. 23, just below 3. Shoshone County Airport is just west of the 116° line of longitude (find 116° in the 8,000 MSL northwest of Shoshone). There are 60 min. between the 116° line and the 117° line. These are depicted in 1-min. ticks. Shoshone is 11 ticks or 11 min. past the 116° line.
Note that the 48° line of latitude is labeled. Find 48° just northeast of the 116°. The latitude and longitude lines are presented each 30 min. Since lines of latitude are also divided into 1-min. ticks the airport is three ticks above the 47°30′ line or 47°33′. The correct latitude and longitude is thus 47°33′N – 116°11′W.
Answer (A) is incorrect because Shoshone Airport is just north of the 47°30′ line of latitude (not 47°00′). Answer (C) is incorrect because Shoshone Airport is 11 ticks past the 116°00′ line of longitude (not 116°30′).

Answer (A) is correct (3567). *(PHAK Chap 8)*
First locate the Cooperstown Airport on Fig. 27. It is just above 2, middle right of chart. Note that it is to the left (west) of the 98° line of longitude. The line of longitude on the left side of the chart is 99°. Thus, the longitude is a little bit more than 98°, but not near 99°.
With respect to latitude, note that Cooperstown Airport is just below a line of latitude that is not marked in terms of degrees. However, the next line of latitude below is 47° (see the left side of the chart, northwest of the Jamestown Airport). As with longitude, there are two lines of latitude for every degree of latitude; i.e., each line is 30 min. Thus, latitude of the Cooperstown Airport is almost 47°30′, but not quite. Accordingly, answer (A) is correct. Cooperstown Airport's latitude is 47°25′N and longitude is 98°06′W.
Answer (B) is incorrect because Cooperstown is just west of the 98° line of longitude (not just east of 99°). Answer (C) is incorrect because Cooperstown is just south of the 47°30′ line of latitude (not the 48°00′ line).

Answer (C) is correct (3623). *(ACL)*
The requirement is the type of airspace overlying and within 5 SM from Barnes County Airport (Fig. 27). Note at 6 that Barnes County Airport is in the lower right and is surrounded by a shaded magenta (reddish) band, which means the floor of the controlled airspace is 700 ft. Thus, Class G airspace extends from the surface to 700 ft. AGL.
Answer (A) is incorrect because Class D airspace requires a control tower. The Barnes County Airport does not have a control tower, since the airport identifier is magenta, not blue. Answer (B) is incorrect because an airport located in Class E airspace would be marked by magenta dashed lines such as the ones surrounding Jamestown Airport to the left. Barnes has no such lines.

Answer (A) is correct (3622). *(ACL)*
The requirement is the type of airspace above Lowe Airport, which is located 2 inches left of 1 on Fig. 27. Because there is no blue shading depicted on the chart, Class E airspace is understood to begin at 1,200 ft. AGL unless otherwise indicated. There are no airspace symbols surrounding Lowe Airport, so Class G airspace exists from the surface to 1,200 ft. AGL, and Class E airspace exists from 1,200 ft. AGL up to, but not including, 18,000 ft. MSL.
Answer (B) is incorrect because the Class G airspace above Lowe Airport ends at 1,200 ft. AGL (the beginning of Class E airspace), not 18,000 ft. MSL. Answer (C) is incorrect because Class G airspace above Lowe Airport extends to 1,200 ft. AGL, indicated by the lack of any airspace symbols surrounding the airport (without which, Class G airspace is understood to begin at 1,200 ft. AGL). Class G airspace up to 700 ft. AGL (not MSL) would be indicated by magenta shading surrounding Lowe Airport. Additionally, Class E airspace above Lowe Airport extends to 18,000 ft. MSL, not 14,500 ft. MSL.

8.
3621a. (Refer to figure 27, area 2, on page 258.) The visibility and cloud clearance requirements to operate VFR during daylight hours over the town of Cooperstown between 1,200 feet AGL and 10,000 feet MSL are

A—1 mile and clear of clouds.
B—1 mile and 1,000 feet above, 500 feet below, and 2,000 feet horizontally from clouds.
C—3 miles and 1,000 feet above, 500 feet below, and 2,000 feet horizontally from clouds.

Answer (C) is correct (3621a). *(FAR 91.155)*
The airspace over the town of Cooperstown (Fig. 27, north of 2) is Class G airspace up to 700 ft. AGL, and Class E airspace from 700 ft. AGL up to but not including 18,000 ft. MSL (indicated by the magenta shading). Therefore, the visibility and cloud clearance requirements for daylight VFR operation over the town of Cooperstown between 1,200 ft. AGL and 10,000 ft. MSL are 3 miles and 1,000 ft. above, 500 ft. below, and 2,000 ft. horizontally.
Answer (A) is incorrect because 1 mile and clear of clouds are the visibility and cloud clearance requirements for daylight VFR operation over the town of Cooperstown up to, but no above, 700 ft. AGL (i.e., the visibility and cloud clearance requirements for Class G airspace below 1,200 ft. AGL). Answer (B) is incorrect because 1 mile and a distance from clouds of 1,000 ft. above, 500 ft. below, and 2,000 ft. horizontally are the visibility and cloud clearance requirements for daylight VFR operations at or above 1,200 ft. AGL, but below 10,000 ft. MSL, in Class G airspace. The airspace above Cooperstown in Class E above 700 ft. AGL.

9.
3602. (Refer to figure 27 on page 258.) What hazards to aircraft may exist in areas such as Devils Lake East MOA?

A—Unusual, often invisible, hazards to aircraft such as artillery firing, aerial gunnery, or guided missiles.
B—Military training activities that necessitate acrobatic or abrupt flight maneuvers.
C—High volume of pilot training or an unusual type of aerial activity.

Answer (B) is correct (3602). *(AIM Para 3-4-5)*
Military Operations Areas (MOAs) such as Devils Lake East in Fig. 27 consist of defined lateral and vertical limits that are designated for the purpose of separating military training activities from IFR traffic. Most training activities necessitate acrobatic or abrupt flight maneuvers. Therefore, the likelihood of a collision is increased inside an MOA. VFR traffic is permitted, but extra vigilance should be exercised in seeing and avoiding military aircraft.
Answer (A) is incorrect because unusual, often invisible, hazards to aircraft, such as artillery firing, aerial gunnery, or guided missiles, are characteristic of restricted areas, not MOAs. Answer (C) is incorrect because a high volume of pilot training or an unusual type of aerial activity is characteristic of alert areas, not MOAs.

10.
3785. What action should a pilot take when operating under VFR in a Military Operations Area (MOA)?

A—Obtain a clearance from the controlling agency prior to entering the MOA.
B—Operate only on the airways that transverse the MOA.
C—Exercise extreme caution when military activity is being conducted.

Answer (C) is correct (3785). *(AIM Para 3-4-5)*
Military operations areas consist of airspace established for separating military training activities from IFR traffic. VFR traffic should exercise extreme caution when flying within an MOA. Information regarding MOA activity can be obtained from flight service stations (FSSs) within 100 mi. of the MOA.
Answer (A) is incorrect because a clearance is not required to enter an MOA. Answer (B) is incorrect because VFR flights may fly anywhere in the MOA.

11.
3618. (Refer to figure 27, area 3, on page 258.) When flying over Arrowwood National Wildlife Refuge, a pilot should fly no lower than

A—2,000 feet AGL.
B—2,500 feet AGL.
C—3,000 feet AGL.

Answer (A) is correct (3618). *(AIM Para 7-4-6)*
See Fig. 27, which is about 2 in. to the left and slightly below 3. All aircraft are requested to maintain a minimum altitude of 2,000 ft. above the surface of a national wildlife refuge except if forced to land by emergency, landing at a designated site, or on official government business.
Answer (B) is incorrect because 2,500 ft. AGL has no significance to wildlife refuges. Answer (C) is incorrect because 3,000 ft. AGL has no significance to wildlife refuges.

12.
3831. Pilots flying over a national wildlife refuge are requested to fly no lower than

A—1,000 feet AGL.
B—2,000 feet AGL.
C—3,000 feet AGL.

Answer (B) is correct (3831). *(AIM Para 7-4-6)*
The Fish and Wildlife Service requests that pilots maintain a minimum altitude of 2,000 ft. above the terrain of national wildlife refuge areas.
Answer (A) is incorrect because 1,000 ft. AGL is the required distance above obstructions over congested areas. Answer (C) is incorrect because 3,000 ft. AGL has no significance to wildlife refuges.

13.
3601. (Refer to figure 21 on page 252.) What hazards to aircraft may exist in restricted areas such as R-5302B?

A—Unusual, often invisible, hazards such as aerial gunnery or guided missiles.
B—High volume of pilot training or an unusual type of aerial activity.
C—Military training activities that necessitate acrobatic or abrupt flight maneuvers.

Answer (A) is correct (3601). *(AIM Para 3-4-4)*
The question asks what may exist in restricted areas such as R-5302B (Fig. 21). Restricted areas denote the existence of unusual, often invisible hazards to aircraft such as military firing, aerial gunnery, or guided missiles.
Answer (B) is incorrect because a high volume of pilot training or an unusual type of aerial activity describes an alert, not a warning, area. Answer (C) is incorrect because military training activities that necessitate acrobatic or abrupt flight maneuvers are characteristic of MOAs, not restricted areas.

14.
3627. (Refer to figure 21, area 1, on page 252.) What minimum radio equipment is required to land and take off at Norfolk International?

A—Mode C transponder and omnireceiver.
B—Mode C transponder and two-way radio.
C—Mode C transponder, omnireceiver, and DME.

Answer (B) is correct (3627). *(AIM Para 3-2-4)*
The minimum equipment to land and take off at Norfolk International (Fig. 21) is a Mode C transponder and a two-way radio. Norfolk International is located within Class C airspace. Unless otherwise authorized, a pilot must establish and maintain radio communication with ATC prior to and while operating in the Class C airspace area. Mode C transponders are also required in and above all Class C airspace areas.
Answer (A) is incorrect because an omnireceiver (VOR) is not required in Class C airspace. Answer (C) is incorrect because neither an omnireceiver (VOR) nor a DME is required in Class C airspace.

15.
3633. (Refer to figure 21, area 2, on page 252.) The elevation of the Chesapeake Regional Airport is

A—20 feet.
B—36 feet.
C—360 feet.

Answer (A) is correct (3633). *(ACL)*
The requirement is the elevation of the Chesapeake Regional Airport (Fig. 21). East of 2, note that the second line of the airport identifier for Chesapeake Regional reads, "20 L 55 123.05." The first number, in bold type, is the altitude of the airport above MSL. It is followed by the L for lighted runway(s), 55 for the length of the longest runway (5,500 ft.), and the CTAF frequency (123.05).
Answer (B) is incorrect because 36 ft. is not listed as the elevation of anything near Chesapeake airport. Answer (C) is incorrect because 360 ft. is the height above ground of the group obstructions approximately 6 NM southeast of Chesapeake airport, not the elevation of the airport.

16.
3620a. (Refer to figure 23, area 1, on page 254.) The visibility and cloud clearance requirements to operate VFR during daylight hours over Sandpoint Airport at 1,200 feet AGL are

A—1 mile and clear of clouds.
B—1 mile and 1,000 feet above, 500 feet below, and 2,000 feet horizontally from each cloud.
C—3 miles and 1,000 feet above, 500 feet below, and 2,000 feet horizontally from each cloud.

Answer (C) is correct (3620a). *(FAR 91.155)*
The airspace around Sandpoint Airport is Class G airspace from the surface to 700 ft. AGL, and Class E airspace from 700 ft. AGL up to, but not including, 18,000 ft. MSL (indicated by the magenta shading). Therefore, 1,200 ft. AGL is within Class E airspace. The VFR visibility and cloud clearance requirements for operations in Class E airspace below 10,000 ft. MSL are 3 miles and a distance of 1,000 ft. above, 500 ft. below, and 2,000 ft. horizontally from each cloud.
Answer (A) is incorrect because 1 mile and clear of clouds are the visibility and cloud clearance requirements for VFR operations in Class G, not Class E, airspace at or below 1,200 ft. AGL. Answer (B) is incorrect because 1 mile and 1,000 ft. above, 500 ft. below, and 2,000 ft. horizontally are the visibility and cloud clearance requirements for VFR operations in Class G, not Class E, airspace at more than, not at, 1,200 ft. AGL but less than 10,000 ft. MSL.

17.
3629. (Refer to figure 23, area 3, on page 254.) The vertical limits of that portion of Class E airspace designated as a Federal Airway over Magee Airport are

A — 1,200 feet AGL to 17,999 feet MSL.
B — 700 feet MSL to 12,500 feet MSL.
C — 7,500 feet MSL to 17,999 feet MSL.

Answer (A) is correct (3629). *(ACL)*
Magee Airport on Fig. 23 is northwest of 3. The question asks for the vertical limits of the Class E airspace over the airport. Class E airspace areas extend upwards but do not include 18,000 ft. MSL (base of Class A airspace). The floor of a Class E airspace designated as an airway is 1,200 ft. AGL unless otherwise indicated.
Answer (B) is incorrect because this airway begins at 1,200 ft. AGL and extends upward to 17,999 ft. MSL, not 12,500 ft. MSL. Answer (C) is incorrect because Class E airspace designated as a Federal Airway begins at 1,200 ft. AGL, not 7,500 ft. MSL, unless otherwise indicated.

18.
3619. (Refer to figure 23, area 2, on page 254 and Legend 1 on page 251.) For information about the parachute jumping and glider operations at Silverwood Airport, refer to

A — notes on the border of the chart.
B — the Airport/Facility Directory.
C — the Notices to Airmen (NOTAM) publication.

Answer (B) is correct (3619). *(ACL)*
The miniature parachute near the Silverwood Airport (at 2 on Fig. 23) indicates a parachute jumping area. In Legend 1, the symbol for a parachute jumping area instructs you to see the *Airport/Facility Directory (A/FD)* for more information. The *A/FD* will also have information on the glider operations at Silverwood Airport.
Answer (A) is incorrect because the sectional chart legend identifies symbols only. Answer (C) is incorrect because NOTAMs are issued only for hazards to flight.

19.
3626. (Refer to figure 24, area 3, on page 255.) What is the floor of the Savannah Class C airspace at the shelf area (outer circle)?

A — 1,200 feet AGL.
B — 1,300 feet MSL.
C — 1,700 feet MSL.

Answer (B) is correct (3626). *(ACL)*
Class C airspace consists of a surface area and a shelf area. The floor of the shelf area is 1,200 ft. above the airport elevation. The Savannah Class C airspace (Fig. 24, area 3) is depicted by solid magenta circles. For each circle there is a number over a number or SFC. The numbers are in hundreds of feet MSL. The lower number represents the floor of the airspace. Thus, the floor of the shelf area of the Class C airspace is 1,300 ft. MSL ($\frac{41}{13}$).

Answer (A) is incorrect because the floor of the outer circle of Class C airspace does not vary with the ground elevation. The FAA specifies a fixed MSL altitude, rounded to the nearest 100 ft., which is about 1,200 ft. above the airport elevation. Answer (C) is incorrect because 1,700 ft. is the maximum elevation figure (MEF) of the quadrant encompassing Savannah Class C airspace, not the floor of the shelf area.

20.
3637. (Refer to figure 24, area 3, on page 255.) What is the height of the lighted obstacle approximately 6 nautical miles southwest of Savannah International?

A — 1,500 feet MSL.
B — 1,531 feet AGL.
C — 1,549 feet MSL.

Answer (C) is correct (3637). *(ACL)*
On Fig. 24, find the lighted obstacle noted by its proximity to Savannah International by being outside the surface area of the Class C airspace, which has a 5-NM radius. It is indicated by the obstacle symbol with arrows or lightning flashes extending from the tip. According to the numbers to the northeast of the symbol, the height of the obstacle is 1,549 ft. MSL or 1,534 ft. AGL.
Answer (A) is incorrect because the unlighted tower 8 NM, not 6 NM, southwest of the airport has a height of 1,500 ft. MSL. Answer (B) is incorrect because an unlighted, not lighted, tower 9 NM, not 6 NM, southwest of the airport has a height of 1,531 ft. AGL.

21.
3638. (Refer to figure 24, area 3, on page 255.) The top of the group obstruction approximately 11 nautical miles from the Savannah VORTAC on the 340° radial is

A — 455 feet MSL.
B — 400 feet AGL.
C — 432 feet MSL.

Answer (A) is correct (3638). *(ACL)*
To determine the height of the lighted stack, first find it on Fig. 24. Locate the compass rose and look along the 340 radial, knowing that the compass rose has a 10-NM radius. Just outside the compass rose is a group obstruction (stacks). Its height is 455 ft. MSL; AGL height is not shown.
Answer (B) is incorrect because 400 ft. AGL is the height of an obstruction to the northeast of the group obstruction. Answer (C) is incorrect because 432 ft. MSL is the height of a group obstruction on the 320, not 340, radial.

22.

3639. (Refer to figure 25, area 1, on page 256.) What minimum altitude is necessary to vertically clear the obstacle on the northeast side of Airpark East Airport by 500 feet?

A—1,010 feet MSL.
B—1,273 feet MSL.
C—1,283 feet MSL.

Answer (B) is correct (3639). *(ACL and FAR 91.119)*
Find Airpark East, which is near 1 in Fig. 25. Remember to locate the actual airport symbol, not just the name of the airport. It is 1 in. southwest of 1. The elevation of the top of the obstacle on the northeast side of the airport is marked in bold as 773 ft. MSL. Minimum altitude to clear the 773-ft. obstacle by 500 ft. is 1,273 ft. MSL.

Answer (A) is incorrect because the airport elevation, not the obstacle, is 510 ft. Answer (C) is incorrect because 283 appears as an AGL altitude of a tower 1 in. west of Caddo Mills Airport.

23.

3640. (Refer to figure 25, area 2, on page 256.) What minimum altitude is necessary to vertically clear the obstacle on the southeast side of Winnsboro Airport by 500 feet?

A—823 feet MSL.
B—1,013 feet MSL.
C—1,403 feet MSL.

Answer (C) is correct (3640). *(ACL)*
The first step is to find the obstacle on the southeast side of Winnsboro Airport on Fig. 25, near 2. The elevation numbers to the right of the obstruction symbol indicate that its top is 903 ft. MSL or a height of 323 ft. AGL. Thus, the clearance altitude is 1,403 ft. MSL (903 ft. MSL + 500 ft. of clearance).

Answer (A) is incorrect because, since the obstacle height is 323 ft. AGL (number in parentheses), the minimum altitude to clear the obstacle by 500 ft. is 823 ft. AGL, not 823 ft. MSL. Answer (B) is incorrect because 1,013 ft. MSL is 500 ft. above the airport elevation (513 ft. MSL), not 500 ft. above the top of the obstacle height of 903 ft.

24.

3628. (Refer to figure 26 on page 257.) At which airports is fixed-wing Special VFR not authorized?

A—Fort Worth Meacham and Fort Worth Spinks.
B—Dallas-Fort Worth International and Dallas Love Field.
C—Addison and Redbird.

Answer (B) is correct (3628). *(ACL)*
The first (top) line of the airport data for Dallas-Ft. Worth Int'l. and Dallas Love Field (Fig. 26, areas 5 and 6) indicates NO SVFR, which means no special VFR permitted for fixed-wing aircraft.

Answer (A) is incorrect because Ft. Worth Meacham permits special VFR operations since it is not indicated otherwise. Ft. Worth Spinks is a nontower airport; thus ATC does not grant or deny special VFR clearances. Answer (C) is incorrect because Addison and Redbird permit special VFR operations since it is not indicated otherwise.

25.

3624. (Refer to figure 26, area 7, on page 257.) The airspace overlying Mc Kinney (TKI) is controlled from the surface to

A—700 feet AGL.
B—2,900 feet MSL.
C—2,500 feet MSL.

Answer (B) is correct (3624). *(ACL)*
The airspace overlying Mc Kinney airport (TKI) (Fig. 26, northeast of 7) is Class D airspace as denoted by the segmented blue lines. The upper limit is depicted in a broken box in hundreds of feet MSL to the left of the airport symbol. The box contains the number "29," meaning that the vertical limit of the Class D airspace is 2,900 feet MSL.

Answer (A) is incorrect because 700 feet AGL is normally the vertical limit of uncontrolled, not controlled, airspace in the vicinity of non-towered airports with an authorized instrument approach. Answer (C) is incorrect because 2,500 feet AGL, not MSL, is normally the upper limit of Class D airspace. This is not the case here, where the upper limit is somewhat lower, at about 2,300 feet AGL (2,900 feet MSL – 586 feet AGL (field elevation) = 2,314 feet AGL).

26.
3625. (Refer to figure 26, area 4, on page 257.) The airspace directly overlying Fort Worth Meacham is

A—Class B airspace to 10,000 feet MSL.
B—Class C airspace to 5,000 feet MSL.
C—Class D airspace to 3,200 feet MSL.

Answer (C) is correct (3625). *(ACL)*
The airspace overlying Fort Worth Meacham (Fig. 26, southeast of 4) is Class D airspace as denoted by the segmented blue lines. The upper limit is depicted in a broken box in hundreds of feet MSL northeast of the airport. Thus, the Class D airspace extends from the surface to 3,200 ft. MSL.
Answer (A) is incorrect because Class D, not Class B, airspace extends from the surface of Ft. Worth Meacham. Class B airspace overlies the airport from 4,000 ft. MSL to 10,000 ft. MSL. Answer (B) is incorrect because Class D, not Class C, airspace directly overlies Ft. Worth Meacham from the surface to 3,200 ft. MSL, not 5,000 ft. MSL.

27.
3600. (Refer to figure 26, area 2, on page 257.) The floor of Class B airspace at Addison Airport is

A—at the surface.
B—3,000 feet MSL.
C—3,100 feet MSL.

Answer (B) is correct (3600). *(ACL, FAR 71.9)*
Addison Airport (Fig. 26, area 2) has a segmented blue circle around it depicting Class D airspace. Addison Airport also underlies Class B airspace as depicted by solid blue lines. The altitudes of the Class B airspace are shown as $\frac{110}{30}$, to the east of the airport. The bottom number denotes the floor of the Class B airspace to be 3,000 ft. MSL.
Answer (A) is incorrect because the floor of Class D, not Class B, airspace is at the surface. Answer (C) is incorrect because 3,100 ft. MSL is not a defined limit of any airspace over Addison airport.

28.
3599. (Refer to figure 26, area 4, on page 257.) The floor of Class B airspace overlying Hicks Airport (T67) north-northwest of Fort Worth Meacham Field is

A—at the surface.
B—3,200 feet MSL.
C—4,000 feet MSL.

Answer (C) is correct (3599). *(ACL)*
Hicks Airport (T67) on Fig. 26 is northeast of 4. Class B airspace is depicted by a solid blue line, as shown just west of the airport. Follow the blue line toward the bottom of the chart until you find a number over a number in blue, $\frac{110}{40}$. The bottom number denotes the floor of the Class B airspace as 4,000 ft. MSL.
Answer (A) is incorrect because the floor of the Class B airspace would be at the surface if SFC, not 40, was below the 100, as depicted just south of Dallas-Ft. Worth International Airport. Answer (B) is incorrect because 3,200 ft. is the upper limit of the Class D airspace for the Ft. Worth/Meacham Airport, not the floor of Class B airspace overlying Hicks Airport.

29.
3125. What minimum radio equipment is required for operation within Class C airspace?

A—Two-way radio communications equipment and a 4096-code transponder.
B—Two-way radio communications equipment, a 4096-code transponder, and DME.
C—Two-way radio communications equipment, a 4096-code transponder, and an encoding altimeter.

Answer (C) is correct (3125). *(AIM Para 3-2-4)*
To operate within Class C airspace, the aircraft must have

1. Two-way radio communications equipment,
2. A 4096-code transponder, and
3. An encoding altimeter.

Answer (A) is incorrect because an encoding altimeter (Mode C) is required in Class C airspace. Answer (B) is incorrect because DME is not required in Class C airspace.

30.
3128. What minimum radio equipment is required for VFR operation within Class B airspace?

A—Two-way radio communications equipment and a 4096-code transponder.
B—Two-way radio communications equipment, a 4096-code transponder, and an encoding altimeter.
C—Two-way radio communications equipment, a 4096-code transponder, an encoding altimeter, and a VOR or TACAN receiver.

Answer (B) is correct (3128). *(AIM Para 3-2-3)*
To operate within Class B airspace, the aircraft must have

1. Two-way radio communications equipment,
2. A 4096-code transponder, and
3. An encoding altimeter.

Answer (A) is incorrect because an encoding altimeter (Mode C) is also required in Class B airspace. Answer (C) is incorrect because a VOR or TACAN receiver is required for IFR, not VFR, operation within Class B airspace.

31.
3642. (Refer to figure 26, area 8, on page 257.) What minimum altitude is required to fly over the Cedar Hill TV towers in the congested area south of NAS Dallas?

A—2,555 feet MSL.
B—3,449 feet MSL.
C—3,349 feet MSL.

Answer (B) is correct (3642). *(FAR 91.119)*
The Cedar Hill TV towers (Fig. 26, west of 8) have an elevation of 2,449 ft. MSL. The minimum safe altitude over a congested area is 1,000 ft. above the highest obstacle within a horizontal radius of 2,000 ft. of the aircraft. Thus, to vertically clear the towers, the minimum altitude is 3,449 ft. MSL (2,449 + 1,000).
Answer (A) is incorrect because 2,555 ft. AGL, not 2,555 ft. MSL, is the minimum height to fly over the shortest, not the tallest, of the obstructions in the group. Answer (C) is incorrect because 3,349 ft. MSL is only 900 ft., not 1,000 ft., above the tallest structure.

32.
3634. (Refer to figure 22 on page 253.) The terrain elevation of the light tan area between Minot (area 1) and Audubon Lake (area 2) varies from

A—sea level to 2,000 feet MSL.
B—2,000 feet to 2,500 feet MSL.
C—2,000 feet to 2,700 feet MSL.

Answer (B) is correct (3634). *(ACL)*
The requirement is the terrain elevation in the tan area between 1 and 2 in Fig. 22. The tan area indicates terrain between 2,000 ft. and 3,000 ft. The elevation contours on sectionals vary by 500 ft. increments. The 2,000-ft. contour line is located where the color changes from light green to light tan. Since there is no other contour line in the light tan area, the terrain elevation is between 2,000 ft. and 2,500 ft. MSL. Also, Poleschook Airport (halfway between 1 and 2) indicates an elevation above MSL of 2,245.
Answer (A) is incorrect because the light tan area indicates terrain elevation from 2,000 ft. to 3,000 ft. MSL, not from sea level to 2,000 ft. MSL. Answer (C) is incorrect because elevation contours vary by 500 ft., not 700 ft.

33.
3643. (Refer to figure 26, area 5, on page 257.) The navigation facility at Dallas-Ft. Worth International (DFW) is a

A—VOR.
B—VORTAC.
C—VOR/DME.

Answer (C) is correct (3643). *(ACL)*
On Fig. 26, DFW is located at the center of the chart and the navigation facility is 1 NM south of the right set of parallel runways. The symbol is a hexagon with a dot in the center within a square. This is the symbol for a VOR/DME navigation facility.
Answer (A) is incorrect because a VOR facility symbol is a hexagon with a dot in the center, but is not located within a square. Answer (B) is incorrect because a VORTAC symbol is a hexagon with a dot in the center and a small rectangle attached to three of the six sides. The Ranger VORTAC is depicted approximately 7 NM to the west of DFW airport.

34.
3603. (Refer to figure 22, area 3, on page 253.) What type military flight operations should a pilot expect along IR 644?

A—IFR training flights above 1,500 feet AGL at speeds in excess of 250 knots.

B—VFR training flights above 1,500 feet AGL at speeds less than 250 knots.

C—Instrument training flights below 1,500 feet AGL at speeds in excess of 150 knots.

Answer (A) is correct (3603). *(AIM Para 3-5-2)*
In Fig. 22, IR 644 is below area 3. Military training flights are established to promote proficiency of military pilots in the interest of national defense. Military flight routes below 1,500 ft. are charted with four-digit numbers; those above 1,500 ft. have three-digit numbers. IR means the flights are made in accordance with IFR. (VR would mean they use VFR.) Thus, IR 644, a three-digit number, is above 1,500 ft., and flights will be flown under IFR rules.
Answer (B) is incorrect because VFR flights are coded VR (not IR), and the speeds are in excess of (not less than) 250 kt. Answer (C) is incorrect because military training flights below 1,500 ft. AGL have four-digit (not three-digit) identifier numbers, and the airspeed is in excess of 250 kt. (not 150 kt.).

9.3 Identifying Landmarks

35.
3632. (Refer to figure 21, area 2, on page 252.) The flag symbol at Lake Drummond represents a

A—compulsory reporting point for Norfolk Class C airspace.

B—compulsory reporting point for Hampton Roads Airport.

C—visual checkpoint used to identify position for initial callup to Norfolk Approach Control.

Answer (C) is correct (3632). *(ACL)*
The magenta (reddish) flag (Fig. 21, north of 2) at Lake Drummond signifies that the lake is a visual checkpoint that can be used to identify the position for initial callup to the Norfolk approach control.
Answer (A) is incorrect because compulsory reporting points are on IFR, not sectional, charts. They are used on IFR flights. Answer (B) is incorrect because compulsory reporting points are on IFR, not sectional, charts. They are used on IFR flights.

36.
3631. (Refer to figure 21, area 5, on page 252.) The CAUTION box denotes what hazard to aircraft?

A—Unmarked blimp hangars at 300 feet MSL.

B—Unmarked balloon on cable to 3,000 feet AGL.

C—Unmarked balloon on cable to 3,000 feet MSL.

Answer (C) is correct (3631). *(ACL)*
On Fig. 21, northwest of 5, find "CAUTION: UNMARKED BALLOON ON CABLE TO 3,000 MSL." This is self-explanatory.
Answer (A) is incorrect because the box clearly says that there is an unmarked balloon, not blimp hangars, to 3,000 ft. MSL, not 300 ft. MSL. Answer (B) is incorrect because the balloon extends to 3,000 ft. MSL, not AGL.

37.
3635. (Refer to figure 22 on page 253.) Which public use airports depicted are indicated as having fuel?

A—Minot Int'l (area 1) and Mercer County Regional Airport (area 3).

B—Minot Int'l (area 1) and Garrison (area 2).

C—Mercer County Regional Airport (area 3) and Garrison (area 2).

Answer (A) is correct (3635). *(ACL)*
On Fig. 22, the requirement is to identify the airports having fuel available. Airports having fuel available are designated by small squares extending from the top, bottom, and both sides of the airport symbol. Only Minot (area 1) and Mercer County Regional Airport (area 3) have such symbols.
Answer (B) is incorrect because Garrison (2 inches left of 2) does not indicate that fuel is available. Answer (C) is incorrect because Garrison (2 inches left of 2) does not indicate that fuel is available.

38.
3636. (Refer to figure 24 on page 255.) The flag symbols at Statesboro Bullock County Airport, Claxton-Evans County Airport, and Ridgeland Airport are

A—outer boundaries of Savannah Class C airspace.

B—airports with special traffic patterns.

C—visual checkpoints to identify position for initial callup prior to entering Savannah Class C airspace.

Answer (C) is correct (3636). *(ACL)*
On Fig. 24, note the flag symbols at Claxton-Evans County Airport (1 in. to the left of 2), at Statesboro Bullock County Airport (2 in. above 2), and at Ridgeland Airport (2 in. above 3). These airports are visual checkpoints to identify position for initial callup prior to entering the Savannah Class C airspace.
Answer (A) is incorrect because they do not indicate outer boundaries of the Class C airspace. The flags are outside the Class C airspace area, the boundaries of which are marked by solid magenta lines. Answer (B) is incorrect because airports with special traffic patterns are noted in the *Airport/Facility Directory* and also by markings at the airport around the wind sock or tetrahedron.

9.4 Radio Frequencies

39.
3611. (Refer to figure 27, area 4, on page 258.) The CTAF/UNICOM frequency at Jamestown Airport is

A—122.0 MHz.
B—123.0 MHz.
C—123.6 MHz.

Answer (B) is correct (3611). *(ACL)*
The UNICOM frequency is printed in bold italics in the airport identifier. At Jamestown it is 123.0 MHz. The C next to it indicates it as the CTAF.
Answer (A) is incorrect because 122.0 is the Flight Watch frequency, not UNICOM. Answer (C) is incorrect because 123.6 is an FSS frequency, not UNICOM.

40.
3610. (Refer to figure 27, area 2, on page 258.) What is the recommended communication procedure when inbound to land at Cooperstown Airport?

A—Broadcast intentions when 10 miles out on the CTAF/MULTICOM frequency, 122.9 MHz.
B—Contact UNICOM when 10 miles out on 122.8 MHz.
C—Circle the airport in a left turn prior to entering traffic.

Answer (A) is correct (3610). *(AIM Para 4-1-9)*
Find Cooperstown Airport, which is at the top of Fig. 27, just north of 2. You should broadcast your intentions when 10 NM out on the CTAF/MULTICOM frequency, 122.9 MHz.
Answer (B) is incorrect because there is no UNICOM indicated at Cooperstown, and the CTAF is 122.9, not 122.8. Answer (C) is incorrect because a left turn is not a communication procedure.

41.
3612. (Refer to figure 27, area 6, on page 258.) What is the CTAF/UNICOM frequency at Barnes County Airport?

A—122.0 MHz.
B—122.8 MHz.
C—123.6 MHz.

Answer (B) is correct (3612). *(ACL)*
In Fig. 27, Barnes County Airport is 1 in. below 6. The CTAF at Barnes County Airport is marked as the UNICOM frequency for the airport, i.e., 122.8.
Answer (A) is incorrect because 122.0 is Flight Watch. Answer (C) is incorrect because 123.6 is an FSS frequency.

42.
3604. (Refer to figure 21, area 3, on page 252.) What is the recommended communications procedure for a landing at Currituck County Airport?

A—Transmit intentions on 122.9 MHz when 10 miles out and give position reports in the traffic pattern.
B—Contact Elizabeth City FSS for airport advisory service.
C—Contact New Bern FSS for area traffic information.

Answer (A) is correct (3604). *(AIM Para 4-1-9)*
Find the symbol for Currituck County Airport, ½ in. northeast of 3 in Fig. 21. Incoming flights should use MULTICOM, 122.9, as the CTAF, because it is marked with a C. The recommended procedure is to report 10 NM out and then give position reports in the airport traffic pattern.
Answer (B) is incorrect because there is no Elizabeth City FSS. Elizabeth City is serviced by the Raleigh FSS, as indicated by "Raleigh" just below the identifier box for Elizabeth City VOR. Answer (C) is incorrect because the controlling FSS is Raleigh, not New Bern, and Raleigh FSS does not monitor 122.9, which is marked as the CTAF at Currituck County Airport.

43.
3630. (Refer to figure 22 on page 253.) On what frequency can a pilot receive Hazardous Inflight Weather Advisory Service (HIWAS) in the vicinity of area 1?

A—117.1 MHz.
B—118.0 MHz.
C—122.0 MHz.

Answer (A) is correct (3630). *(ACL)*
On Fig. 22, 1 is on the upper left and the Minot VORTAC information box is 1 in. below 1. Availability of Hazardous Inflight Weather Advisory Service (HIWAS) will be indicated by a circle which contains an "H," found in the upper right corner of a navigation frequency box. Note that the Minot VORTAC information box has such a symbol. Accordingly, a HIWAS can be obtained on the VOR frequency of 117.1.
Answer (B) is incorrect because "Ch 118" in the Minot VORTAC information box refers to the TACAN channel (the military equivalent of VOR/DME). Answer (C) is incorrect because 122.0 is the universal frequency for Flight Watch.

44.
3605. (Refer to figure 22, area 2, on page 253.) The CTAF/MULTICOM frequency for Garrison Airport is

A—122.8 MHz.
B—122.9 MHz.
C—123.0 MHz.

Answer (B) is correct (3605). *(ACL)*
The CTAF for Garrison Municipal Airport (2 inches left of 2 in Fig. 22) is 122.9, because that frequency is marked with a C.
Answer (A) is incorrect because there is no indication of 122.8 at Garrison. Answer (C) is incorrect because there is no indication of 123.0 at Garrison.

45.
3608. (Refer to figure 23, area 2, on page 254 and figure 32 below.) What is the correct UNICOM frequency to be used at Coeur D'Alene to request fuel?

A—135.075 MHz.
B—122.1/108.8 MHz.
C—122.8 MHz.

Answer (C) is correct (3608). *(ACL)*
The correct frequency to request fuel at the Coeur D'Alene Airport is the UNICOM frequency 122.8. It is given in Fig. 23, after "L74" in the airport information on the sectional chart. Radio frequencies are also given in Fig. 32, the *Airport/Facility Directory (A/FD)*, under "Communications."
Answer (A) is incorrect because 135.075 is the AWOS frequency for Coeur D'Alene Airport. Answer (B) is incorrect because 108.8 is the COE VOR/DME frequency, not the UNICOM, and 122.1 is not a frequency associated with Coeur D'Alene airport.

46.
3607. (Refer to figure 23, area 2, on page 254 and figure 32 below.) At Coeur D'Alene, which frequency should be used as a Common Traffic Advisory Frequency (CTAF) to monitor airport traffic?

A—122.05 MHz.
B—135.075 MHz.
C—122.8 MHz.

Answer (C) is correct (3607). *(A/FD)*
Fig. 32 is the *A/FD* excerpt for Coeur D'Alene Air Terminal. Look for the section titled **Communications**. On that same line, it states that the CTAF (and UNICOM) frequency is 122.8. The CTAF can also be found in the airport information on the sectional chart.
Answer (A) is incorrect because 122.05 is the remote communication outlet (RCO) frequency to contact Boise FSS in the vicinity of Coeur D'Alene, not the CTAF. Answer (B) is incorrect because 135.075 is the AWOS frequency, not the CTAF.

```
18                              IDAHO                                    

COEUR D'ALENE AIR TERMINAL    (COE)   9 NW   UTC−8(−7DT)   N47°46.46' W116°49.17'      GREAT FALLS
   2318   B   S4   FUEL 80, 100, JET A   OX 1, 2                                        H−1B, L−9A
   RWY 05−23: H7400X140 (ASPH−GRVD)   S−57, D−95, DT−165   HIRL   0.7%up NE              IAP
      RWY 05: MALSR.        RWY 23: REIL VASI(V4L)—GA 3.0° TCH 39'.
   RWY 01−19: H5400X75 (ASPH)   S−50, D−83, DT−150   MIRL
      RWY 01: REIL. Rgt tfc.
   AIRPORT REMARKS: Attended Mon−Fri 1500−0100Z‡. Rwy 05−23 potential standing water and/or ice on center 3000'
      of rwy. Arpt conditions avbl on UNICOM. Rwy 19 is designated calm wind rwy. ACTIVATE MIRL Rwy 01−19, HIRL
      Rwy 05−23 and MALSR Rwy 05—CTAF. REIL Rwy 23 opr only when HIRL on high ints.
   WEATHER DATA SOURCES: AWOS−3 135.075 (208) 772−8215.
   COMMUNICATIONS: CTAF/UNICOM 122.8
      BOISE FSS (BOI) TF 1−800−WX−BRIEF. NOTAM FILE COE.
      RCO 122.05 (BOISE FSS)
   ® SPOKANE APP/DEP CON 132.1
   RADIO AIDS TO NAVIGATION: NOTAM FILE COE.
      (T) VORW/DME 108.8   COE   Chan 25   N47°46.42' W116°49.24'   at fld. 2290/19E.
         DME portion unusable 280°−350° byd 15 NM blo 11000' 220°−240° byd 15 NM.
      LEENY NDB (LOM) 347   CO   N47°44.57' W116°57.66'   053° 6.0 NM to fld.
      ILS 110.7   I−COE   Rwy 05   LOM LEENY NDB. ILS localizer/glide slope unmonitored.
```

FIGURE 32.—Airport/Facility Directory Excerpt.

47.
3606. (Refer to figure 23, area 2, on page 254 and figure 32 on page 262.) At Coeur D'Alene, which frequency should be used as a Common Traffic Advisory Frequency (CTAF) to self-announce position and intentions?

A—122.05 MHz.
B—122.1/108.8 MHz.
C—122.8 MHz.

Answer (C) is correct (3606). *(A/FD)*
Fig. 32 is the *A/FD* excerpt for Coeur D'Alene Air Terminal. Look for the section titled **Communications**. On that same line, it states the CTAF (and UNICOM) frequency is 122.8.
Answer (A) is incorrect because 122.05 is the remote communications outlet (RCO) frequency to contact Boise FSS in the vicinity of Coeur D'Alene, not the CTAF. Answer (B) is incorrect because 108.8 is the COE VOR/DME frequency, not the CTAF.

48.
3609. (Refer to figure 26, area 3, on page 257.) If Redbird Tower is not in operation, which frequency should be used as a Common Traffic Advisory Frequency (CTAF) to monitor airport traffic?

A—120.3 MHz.
B—122.95 MHz.
C—126.35 MHz.

Answer (A) is correct (3609). *(ACL)*
In Fig. 26, find the Redbird Airport just above 3. When the Redbird tower is not in operation, the CTAF is 120.3 because that frequency is marked with a C.
Answer (B) is incorrect because 122.95 is the UNICOM frequency. Answer (C) is incorrect because 126.35 is the ATIS frequency.

49.
3641. (Refer to figure 26, area 2, on page 257.) The control tower frequency for Addison Airport is

A—122.95 MHz.
B—126.0 MHz.
C—133.4 MHz.

Answer (B) is correct (3641). *(ACL)*
Addison Airport (Fig. 26, area 2) control tower frequency is given as the first item in the second line of the airport data to the right of the airport symbol. The control tower (CT) frequency is 126.0 MHz.
Answer (A) is incorrect because 122.95 MHz is the UNICOM, not control tower, frequency for Addison Airport. Answer (C) is incorrect because 133.4 MHz is the ATIS, not control tower, frequency for Addison Airport.

9.5 FAA Advisory Circulars

50.
3709. FAA advisory circulars (some free, others at cost) are available to all pilots and are obtained by

A—distribution from the nearest FAA district office.
B—ordering those desired from the Government Printing Office.
C—subscribing to the Federal Register.

Answer (B) is correct (3709). *(AC 00-2)*
FAA Advisory Circulars are issued with the purpose of informing the public of nonregulatory material of interest. Free advisory circulars can be ordered from the FAA, while those at cost can be ordered from the Government Printing Office.
Answer (A) is incorrect because FAA offices have their own copies but none for distribution to the public. Answer (C) is incorrect because the *Federal Register* contains Notices of Proposed Rulemaking (NPRM) and final rules. It is a federal government publication.

51.
3856. FAA advisory circulars containing subject matter specifically related to Air Traffic Control and General Operations are issued under which subject number?

A—60.
B—70.
C—90.

Answer (C) is correct (3856). *(AC 00-2)*
FAA advisory circulars are numbered based on the numbering system used in the FARs

60 Airmen
70 Airspace
90 Air Traffic Control and General Operation

Answer (A) is incorrect because 60 refers to Airmen, not Air Traffic Control. Answer (B) is incorrect because 70 refers to Airspace, not Air Traffic Control.

52.
3854. FAA advisory circulars containing subject matter specifically related to Airmen are issued under which subject number?

A—60.
B—70.
C—90.

53.
3855. FAA advisory circulars containing subject matter specifically related to Airspace are issued under which subject number?

A—60.
B—70.
C—90.

9.6 Airport/Facility Directory

54.
3838. (Refer to figure 53 on page 265.) When approaching Lincoln Municipal from the west at noon for the purpose of landing, initial communications should be with

A—Lincoln Approach Control on 124.0 MHz.
B—Minneapolis Center on 128.75 MHz.
C—Lincoln Tower on 118.5 MHz.

55.
3839. (Refer to figure 53 on page 265.) Which type radar service is provided to VFR aircraft at Lincoln Municipal?

A—Sequencing to the primary Class C airport and standard separation.
B—Sequencing to the primary Class C airport and conflict resolution so that radar targets do not touch, or 1,000 feet vertical separation.
C—Sequencing to the primary Class C airport, traffic advisories, conflict resolution, and safety alerts.

Answer (A) is correct (3854). *(AC 00-2)*
FAA advisory circulars are numbered based on the numbering system used in the FARs

60 Airmen
70 Airspace
90 Air Traffic Control and General Operation

Answer (B) is incorrect because 70 relates to Airspace, not Airmen. Answer (C) is incorrect because 90 relates to Air Traffic Control and General Operation (not Airmen).

Answer (B) is correct (3855). *(AC 00-2)*
FAA advisory circulars are numbered based on the numbering system used in the FARs

60 Airmen
70 Airspace
90 Air Traffic Control and General Operation

Answer (A) is incorrect because 60 relates to Airmen, not Airspace. Answer (C) is incorrect because 90 relates to Air Traffic Control and General Operation, not Airspace.

Answer (A) is correct (3838). *(A/FD)*
Fig. 53 contains the *A/FD* excerpt for Lincoln Municipal. Locate the section titled **Airspace** and note that Lincoln Municipal is located in Class C airspace. The Class C airspace is in effect from 0530-0030 local time (1130-0630Z). You should contact approach control (app con) during that time before entering. Move up three lines to **App/Dep Con** and note that aircraft arriving from the west of Lincoln (i.e., 170° - 349°) at noon should initially contact Lincoln Approach Control on 124.0.

Answer (B) is incorrect because you would contact Minneapolis Center for basic radar services (i.e., flight following, assistance, etc.) between 0030 and 0530 local time, not at noon. Answer (C) is incorrect because, when approaching Lincoln Municipal at noon, your initial contact should be with approach control, not the tower.

Answer (C) is correct (3839). *(A/FD and AIM Para 4-1-17)*
Fig. 53 contains the *A/FD* excerpt for Lincoln Municipal. Locate the section titled **Airspace** to determine that Lincoln Municipal is located in Class C airspace. Once communications and radar contact are established, VFR aircraft are provided the following services:

1. Sequencing to the primary airport
2. Approved separation between IFR and VFR aircraft
3. Basic radar services, i.e., safety alerts, limited vectoring, and traffic advisories.

The FAA should change "conflict resolution" to "limited vectoring" in the future.

Answer (A) is incorrect because, in addition to sequencing to the primary Class C airport and standard separation, Class C radar service also includes basic radar services, i.e., traffic advisories and safety alerts. Answer (B) is incorrect because one radar service provided to VFR aircraft in Class C airspace provides for traffic advisories and conflict resolution so that radar targets do not touch, or 500 ft., not 1,000 ft., vertical separation.

180 **NEBRASKA**

LINCOLN MUNI (LNK) 4 NW UTC-6(-5DT) N40°51.05′ W96°45.55′   **OMAHA**
  1218 B S4 **FUEL** 100LL, JET A TPA—2218(1000) ARFF Index B   H-1E, 3F, 4F, L-11B
  RWY 17R-35L: H12901X200 (ASPH-CONC-GRVD) S-100, D-200, DT-400 HIRL   IAP
    RWY 17R: MALSR. VASI(V4L)—GA 3.0° TCH 55′. Rgt tfc. 0.4% down.
    RWY 35L: MALSR. VASI(V4L)—GA 3.0° TCH 55′.
  RWY 14-32: H8620X150 (ASPH-CONC-GRVD) S-80, D-170, DT-280 MIRL
    RWY 14: REIL. VASI(V4L)—GA 3.0° TCH 48′.
    RWY 32: VASI(V4L)—GA 3.0° TCH 53′. Thld dsplcd 431′. Pole. 0.3% up.
  RWY 17L-35R: H5400X100 (ASPH-CONC-AFSC) S-49, D-60 HIRL 0.8% up N
    RWY 17L: PAPI(P4L)—GA 3.0° TCH 33′.   **RWY 35R:** PAPI(P4L)—GA 3.0° TCH 40′. Pole. Rgt tfc.
  AIRPORT REMARKS: Attended continuously. Birds in vicinity of arpt. Twy D clsd between taxiways S and H indef. For
    MALSR Rwy 17R and Rwy 35L ctc twr. When twr clsd MALSR Rwy 17R and Rwy 35L preset on med ints, and REIL
    Rwy 14 left on when wind favor. NOTE: See Land and Hold Short Operations Section.
  WEATHER DATA SOURCES: ASOS (402) 474-9214. LLWAS
  COMMUNICATIONS: CTAF 118.5   **ATIS** 118.05   **UNICOM** 122.95
    COLUMBUS FSS (OLU) TF 1-800-WX-BRIEF. NOTAM FILE LNK.
    RCO 122.65 (COLUMBUS FSS)
   Ⓡ **APP/DEP CON** 124.0 (170°-349°) 124.8 (350°-169°) (1130-0630Z‡)
   Ⓡ **MINNEAPOLIS CENTER APP/DEP CON** 128.75 (0630-1130Z‡)
    TOWER 118.5 125.7 (1130-0630Z‡)   **GND CON** 121.9   **CLNC DEL** 120.7
  AIRSPACE: CLASS C svc 1130-0630Z‡ ctc **APP CON** other times **CLASS E.**
  RADIO AIDS TO NAVIGATION: NOTAM FILE LNK. VHF/DF ctc FSS.
    (H) VORTACW 116.1   LNK   Chan 108   N40°55.43′ W96°44.52′   181° 4.5 NM to fld. 1370/9E
    POTTS NDB (MHW/LOM) 385   LN   N40°44.83′ W96°45.75′   355° 6.2 NM to fld. Unmonitored when twr clsd.
    ILS 111.1   I-OCZ   Rwy 17R.   MM and OM unmonitored.
    ILS 109.9   I-LNK   Rwy 35L   LOM POTTS NDB. MM unmonitored. LOM unmonitored when twr clsd.
  COMM/NAVAID REMARKS: Emerg frequency 121.5 not available at tower.

LOUP CITY MUNI (NE03) 1 NW UTC-6(-5DT) N41°17.42′ W98°59.44′   **OMAHA**
  2070 B **FUEL** 100LL   L-11B
  RWY 15-33: H3200X50 (ASPH) S-8 LIRL
    RWY 33: Trees.
  RWY 04-22: 2100X100 (TURF)
    RWY 04: Tree.   **RWY 22:** Road.
  AIRPORT REMARKS: Unattended. For svc call 308-745-0328/1244/0664.
  COMMUNICATIONS: CTAF 122.9
    COLUMBUS FSS (OLU) TF 1-800-WX-BRIEF. NOTAM FILE OLU.
  RADIO AIDS TO NAVIGATION: NOTAM FILE OLU.
    WOLBACH (H) VORTAC 114.8   OBH   Chan 95   N41°22.54′ W98°21.22′   253° 29.3 NM to fld. 2010/7E.

MARTIN FLD (See SO SIOUX CITY)

MC COOK MUNI (MCK) 2 E UTC-6(-5DT) N40°12.36′ W100°35.51′   **OMAHA**
  2579 B S4 **FUEL** 100LL, JET A ARFF Index Ltd.   H-2D, L-11A
  RWY 12-30: H5999X100 (CONC) S-30, D-38 MIRL 0.6% up NW   IAP
    RWY 12: MALS. VASI(V4L)—GA 3.0° TCH 33′. Tree.   **RWY 30:** REIL. VASI(V4L)—GA 3.0° TCH 42′.
  RWY 03-21: H3999X75 (CONC) S-30, D-38 MIRL
    RWY 03: VASI(V2L)—GA 3.0° TCH 26′. Rgt tfc.   **RWY 21:** VASI(V2L)—GA 3.0° TCH 26′.
  RWY 17-35: 1350X200 (TURF)
  AIRPORT REMARKS: Attended daylight hours. Parachute Jumping. Deer on and in vicinity of arpt. Numerous
    waterfowl/migratory birds invof arpt. Arpt closed to air carrier operations with more than 30 passengers except
    24 hour PPR, call arpt manager 308-345-2022. Avoid McCook State (abandoned) arpt 7 miles NW on the MCK
    VOR/DME 313° radial at 8.3 DME. ACTIVATE VASI Rwys 12 and 30 and MALS Rwy 12—CTAF.
  COMMUNICATIONS: CTAF/UNICOM 122.8
    COLUMBUS FSS (OLU) TF 1-800-WX-BRIEF. NOTAM FILE MCK.
    RCO 122.6 (COLUMBUS FSS)
    DENVER CENTER APP/DEP CON 132.7
  AIRSPACE: CLASS E svc effective 1100-0500Z‡ except holidays other times **CLASS G.**
  RADIO AIDS TO NAVIGATION: NOTAM FILE MCK.
    (H) VORW/DME 115.3   MCK   Chan 100   N40°12.23′ W100°35.65′   at fld. 2570/8E.

FIGURE 53.—Airport/Facility Directory Excerpt.

56.
3842. (Refer to figure 53 on page 265.) Traffic patterns in effect at Lincoln Municipal are

A—to the right on Runway 17L and Runway 35L; to the left on Runway 17R and Runway 35R.

B—to the left on Runway 17L and Runway 35L; to the right on Runway 17R and Runway 35R.

C—to the right on Runways 14 - 32.

Answer (B) is correct (3842). (A/FD)
   Fig. 53 contains the A/FD excerpt for Lincoln Municipal. For this question, you need to locate the runway end data elements, i.e., **Rwy 17R**, **Rwy 35L**, **Rwy 14**, **Rwy 32**, **Rwy 17L**, and **Rwy 35R**. Traffic patterns are to the left unless right traffic is noted by the contraction **Rgt tfc**. The only runways with right traffic are Rwy 17R and Rwy 35R.
   Answer (A) is incorrect because traffic patterns are to the left, not right, for Rwy 17L and Rwy 35L. Traffic patterns are to the right, not left, on Rwy 17R and Rwy 35R. Answer (C) is incorrect because the traffic pattern for Rwy 14 and Rwy 32 is to the left, not right.

57.
3841. (Refer to figure 53 on page 265.) Where is Loup City Municipal located with relation to the city?

A—Northeast approximately 3 miles.

B—Northwest approximately 1 mile.

C—East approximately 10 miles.

Answer (B) is correct (3841). (A/FD)
   Fig. 53 contains the A/FD excerpt for Loup City Municipal. On the first line, the third item listed, **1 NW**, means that Loup City Municipal is located approximately 1 NM northwest of the city.
   Answer (A) is incorrect because **(NE03)** is the airport identifier, not an indication that the airport is 3 NM northeast of the city. Answer (C) is incorrect because the airport is approximately 1 NM northwest, not 10 NM east, of the city.

58.
3840. (Refer to figure 53 on page 265.) What is the recommended communications procedure for landing at Lincoln Municipal during the hours when the tower is not in operation?

A—Monitor airport traffic and announce your position and intentions on 118.5 MHz.

B—Contact UNICOM on 122.95 MHz for traffic advisories.

C—Monitor ATIS for airport conditions, then announce your position on 122.95 MHz.

Answer (A) is correct (3840). (A/FD)
   When the Lincoln Municipal tower is closed, you should monitor airport traffic and announce your position and intentions on the CTAF. Fig. 53 contains the A/FD excerpt for Lincoln Municipal. Locate the section titled **Communications** and note that on that same line the CTAF frequency is 118.5.
   Answer (B) is incorrect because, when the tower is not in operation, you should monitor other traffic and announce your position and intentions on the specified CTAF. At Lincoln Municipal, the CTAF is the tower frequency of 118.5, not the UNICOM frequency of 122.95. Answer (C) is incorrect because, when the tower is not in operation, you should monitor other traffic and announce your position and intentions on the specified CTAF. At Lincoln Municipal, the CTAF is the tower frequency of 118.5, not the UNICOM frequency of 122.95.

END OF CHAPTER

CHAPTER TEN
NAVIGATION SYSTEMS

This chapter contains outlines of major concepts tested, all FAA test questions and answers regarding navigation systems, and an explanation of each answer. Each module, or subtopic, within this chapter is listed above with the number of questions from the FAA pilot knowledge test pertaining to that particular module. For each module, the first number following the parentheses is the page number on which the outline begins, and the next number is the page number on which the questions begin.

Many of the questions in this chapter ask about the sectional charts, which appear as Figures 21 through 27. To produce them in color economically, we have put them together in Chapter 9, pages 251 to 258. As you will need to turn frequently to these seven pages, mark them with "dog ears" (fold their corners) or paper clip.

CAUTION: Recall that the **sole purpose** of this book is to expedite your passing the FAA pilot knowledge test for the private pilot certificate. Accordingly, all extraneous material (i.e., topics or regulations not directly tested on the FAA pilot knowledge test) is omitted, even though much more information and knowledge are necessary to fly safely. This additional material is presented in *Pilot Handbook* and *Private Pilot Flight Maneuvers and Practical Test Prep,* available from Gleim Publications, Inc. See the order form on page 326.

10.1 VOR TEST FACILITY (VOT) (Question 1)

1. VOR Test Facilities (VOTs) are available on a specific frequency at certain airports. The facility permits you to check the accuracy of your VOR receiver while you are on the ground.

2. Tune the navigation radio to the specified VOT frequency, and center the course deviation indicator.

   a. The OBS should read either 0° or 180°, regardless of your position at the airport.
   b. If 0°, the TO/FROM indicator should indicate FROM.
   c. If 180°, the TO/FROM indicator should indicate TO.
   d. Accuracy of the VOR should be ±4°.

10.2 DETERMINING POSITION (Questions 2-11)

1.   Several FAA exam questions require you to identify your position based on the intersection of given radials of two VORs.

    a.   To locate a position based on VOR radials, draw the radials on your chart or on the plastic overlay during the FAA knowledge test.

    b.   Remember that radials are from the VOR, or leaving the VOR.

    c.   Make sure you have located the correct radial on the compass rose before drawing your line.

    d.   Recheck yourself by counting in 10° or 5° intervals from each of the closest 30° intervals that are numbered and marked with an arrow.

2.   Other FAA exam questions require you to identify your position based upon the indications of a single VOR.

    a.   You must compare the OBS setting and the TO/FROM indicator with the aircraft heading. To indicate correctly, the OBS (top) setting must correspond roughly with the aircraft heading (e.g., 180° OBS (top) setting, 180° aircraft heading).

    b.   The TO/FROM indicator must correspond to the aircraft's flight path in relation to the VOR. Flying TO a VOR with a FROM indication and flying FROM a VOR with a TO indication will result in reverse sensing.

    c.   When flying directly from a station, the heading and the radial being flown will correspond (i.e., 360° heading FROM will be the 360° radial).

    d.   When flying directly TO a station, the heading flown and the radial being flown will be reciprocals (i.e., 180° heading TO will be on the 360° radial).

    e.   With regard to CDI deflection, you must pretend your airplane has the same heading as the OBS setting. A left deviation means you are right of course, and a right deviation means you are left of course.

        1)   If your heading and the OBS setting are not roughly the same, the CDI **will not** indicate correctly.

    f.   If no TO or FROM flag indication appears, the aircraft is in the area of ambiguity, i.e., 90° away from the radial dialed up on the OBS. To know the side of the station on which the aircraft is located, consult the CDI. The needle points toward the station.

10.3 AUTOMATIC DIRECTION FINDER (ADF) (Questions 12-29)

1.   The ADF indicator always has its needle pointing toward the NDB station (nondirectional beacon, also known as a radio beacon).

    a.   If the NDB is directly in front of the airplane, the needle will point straight up.

    b.   If the NDB is directly off the right wing, i.e., 3 o'clock, the needle will point directly to the right.

    c.   If the NDB is directly behind the aircraft, the needle will point straight down, etc.

    d.   The figure on the opposite page illustrates the terms that are used with the ADF.

2.   Relative bearing (RB) to the station is the number of degrees you would have to turn to the right to fly directly to the NDB. On a fixed card ADF, the

    a.   Relative bearing TO the station is shown by the head of the needle.

        1)   In the figure on the opposite page, the RB to the station is 220°.

    b.   Relative bearing FROM is given by the tail of the needle.

1) In the figure below, the RB from the station is 40° (220 − 180).

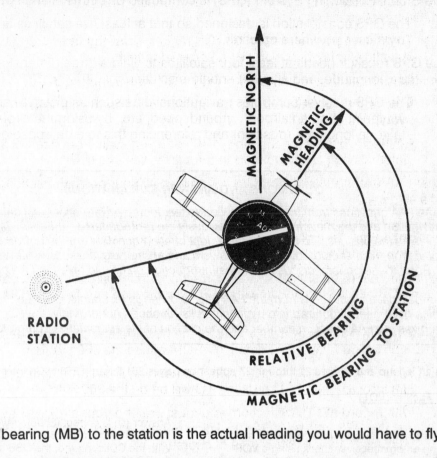

3. Magnetic bearing (MB) to the station is the actual heading you would have to fly to the station.

   a. If you turn right from your present heading to fly to the station, you are adding the number of degrees of turn to your heading.

   b. Thus, magnetic heading + relative bearing = magnetic bearing to the station, or MH + RB = MB (TO).

      1) For MB (FROM), subtract or add 180°.

      2) EXAMPLE: If the airplane shown above has an MH of 40° and an RB of 220°, the MB (TO) is 260° (40 + 220). The MB (FROM) is 80° (260 − 180).

4. A fixed card ADF always shows 0° at the top.

   a. Thus, RB may be read directly from the card and MB must be calculated using the above formula.

   b. If the MB is given, the MH may be calculated as follows: MB − RB = MH.

5. A movable card ADF always shows magnetic heading (MH) at the top.

   a. Thus, MB (TO) may be read directly from the card under the head of the needle.
   b. MB (FROM) is indicated by the tail of the needle.
   c. RB may be calculated as follows: MB − MH = RB.

6. When working ADF problems, it is often helpful to draw the information given (as illustrated above) to provide a picture of the airplane's position relative to the NDB station.

10.4 GLOBAL POSITIONING SYSTEM (GPS) (Questions 30-32)

1. The Global Positioning System (GPS) is composed of a constellation of 24 satellites.

    a. The GPS constellation is designed so that at least five satellites are always observable by a user anywhere on earth.

2. The GPS receiver needs at least four satellites to yield a three-dimensional position (latitude, longitude, and altitude) and time solution

    a. The GPS receiver computes navigational data such as distance and bearing to a waypoint (e.g., an airport), groundspeed, etc., by using the airplane's known latitude/longitude (position) and referencing this to a database built into the receiver.

QUESTIONS AND ANSWER EXPLANATIONS

All of the FAA questions from the pilot knowledge test for the private pilot certificate relating to the basics of navigation and the material outlined previously are reproduced on the following pages in the same modules as the outlines. To the immediate right of each question are the correct answer and answer explanation. You should cover these answers and answer explanations while responding to the questions. Refer to the general discussion in the Introduction on how to take the FAA pilot knowledge test.

Remember that the questions from the FAA pilot knowledge test bank have been reordered by topic, and the topics have been organized into a meaningful sequence. Accordingly, the first line of the answer explanation gives the FAA question number and the citation of the authoritative source for the answer.

The sectional chart legend and Figures 21 through 27 appear on pages 251 through 258 in Chapter 9.

10.1 VOR Test Facility (VOT)

1.
3598a. When the course deviation indicator (CDI) needle is centered during an omnireceiver check using a VOR test signal (VOT), the omnibearing selector (OBS) and the TO/FROM indicator should read

A—180° FROM, only if the pilot is due north of the VOT.

B—0° TO or 180° FROM, regardless of the pilot's position from the VOT.

C—0° FROM or 180° TO, regardless of the pilot's position from the VOT.

Answer (C) is correct (3598). *(AIM Para 1-1-4)*
A VOT transmits a 360° (0°) radial in all directions. With the CDI centered, the OBS should indicate 0° with the TO-FROM indicator showing FROM, or 180° TO, regardless of your position from the VOT. A good way to remember the VOT rule is to associate it with the Cessna 182, i.e., 180 TO.
Answer (A) is incorrect because with the OBS set at 180°, CDI centered, you should have a TO (not FROM) indication, regardless of your position from the VOT. Answer (B) is incorrect because the VOT transmits a 360° radial in all directions; thus, with the CDI centered and the OBS on 0°, you should have a FROM (not TO) indication and 180° TO (not FROM).

10.2 Determining Position

2.
3532. (Refer to figure 21 on page 252.) What is your approximate position on low altitude airway Victor 1, southwest of Norfolk (area 1), if the VOR receiver indicates you are on the 340° radial of Elizabeth City VOR (area 3)?

A—15 nautical miles from Norfolk VORTAC.

B—18 nautical miles from Norfolk VORTAC.

C—23 nautical miles from Norfolk VORTAC.

Answer (B) is correct (3532). *(PHAK Chap 8)*
First find V1 extending SW on the 233° radial from Norfolk VORTAC on Fig. 21. The V1 label appears just above 2. Then, draw along the 340° radial from Elizabeth City VOR (southwest of 3). If you are confused where the exact VOR is (center of compass rose), draw a line through the entire compass rose so your line coincides with both your radial (here 340°) and its reciprocal (here 160°). Note that the intersection with V1 is 18 NM from the Norfolk VORTAC.
Answer (A) is incorrect because 15 NM from Norfolk would be on the 345° radial. Answer (C) is incorrect because 23 NM from Norfolk would be on the 330° radial.

The sectional chart legend and Figures 21 through 27 appear on pages 251 through 258 in Chapter 9.

3.
3552. (Refer to figure 24 on page 255.) What is the approximate position of the aircraft if the VOR receivers indicate the 320° radial of Savannah VORTAC (area 3) and the 184° radial of Allendale VOR (area 1)?

A—Town of Guyton.
B—Town of Springfield.
C—3 miles east of Marlow.

Answer (B) is correct (3552). *(PHAK Chap 8)*
To locate a position based on VOR radials, draw the radials on your map or on the plastic overlay during the FAA pilot knowledge test. Remember that radials are from the VOR, or leaving the VOR. On Fig. 24, the 320° radial from Savannah extends northwest, and the 184° radial from Allendale extends south. They intersect over the town of Springfield.
Answer (A) is incorrect because Guyton is on the 308° radial, not 320° radial of Savannah VORTAC and the 188° radial, not 184° radial of Allendale VOR. Answer (C) is incorrect because 3 NM east of Marlow is on the 300° radial, not 320° radial of Savannah VORTAC and the 184° radial of Allendale VOR.

4.
3559. (Refer to figure 25 on page 256.) What is the approximate position of the aircraft if the VOR receivers indicate the 245° radial of Sulphur Springs VOR-DME (area 5) and the 140° radial of Bonham VORTAC (area 3)?

A—Glenmar Airport.
B—Meadowview Airport.
C—Majors Airport.

Answer (A) is correct (3559). *(PHAK Chap 8)*
To locate a position based on VOR radials, draw the radials on your map or on the plastic overlay during the FAA knowledge test. Remember that radials are from the VOR, or leaving the VOR.
On Fig. 25, the 245° radial from Sulphur Springs VOR-DME extends southwest, and the 140° radial from Bonham VORTAC extends southeast. They intersect about 1 mi. east of Glenmar Airport.
Answer (B) is incorrect because Meadowview Airport is on the 246°, not 245°, radial of Sulphur Springs VOR-DME and the 163°, not 140°, radial of Bonham VORTAC. Answer (C) is incorrect because Majors Airport is on the 157°, not 140°, radial of Bonham VORTAC.

5.
3566. (Refer to figure 26, area 5, on page 257.) The VOR is tuned to the Dallas/Fort Worth VORTAC. The omnibearing selector (OBS) is set on 253°, with a TO indication, and a right course deviation indicator (CDI) deflection. What is the aircraft's position from the VORTAC?

A—East-northeast.
B—North-northeast.
C—West-southwest.

Answer (A) is correct (3566). *(PHAK Chap 8)*
It is not necessary to refer to Fig. 26 to solve this problem. Write the word VOR on a piece of paper. Now draw a line through it, representing the 253° radial and its reciprocal. Now imagine you are flying along this line on a heading of 253°. With a TO indication and a right CDI deflection, you are northeast of the VOR, but south of the course.
Note: The FAA previously changed the figure to which this question refers without changing the question. Figure 26 depicts the Dallas-Ft. Worth VOR/DME, not a VORTAC.
Answer (B) is incorrect because you are south, not north, of the course. Answer (C) is incorrect because you have a TO, not FROM, indication.

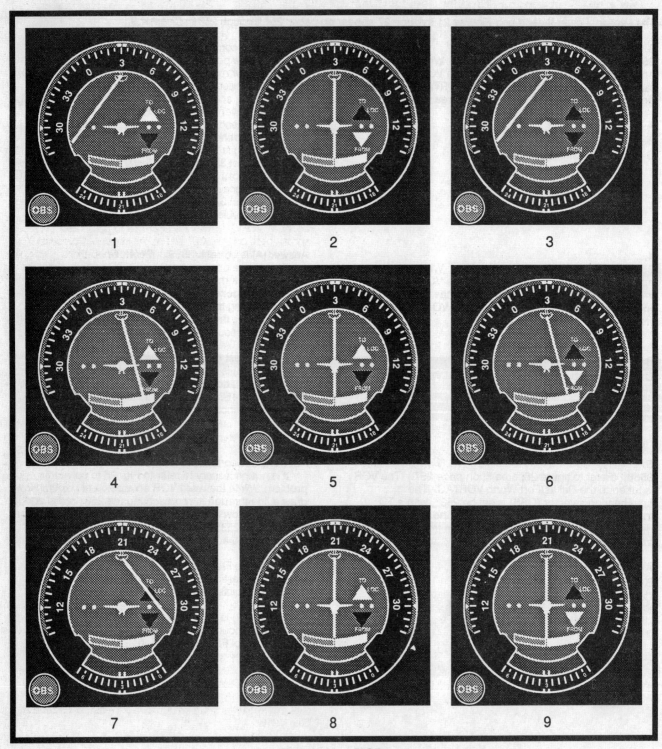

FIGURE 29.—VOR.

6.
3579. (Refer to figure 29, illustration 8, above.) The VOR receiver has the indications shown. What radial is the aircraft crossing?

A—030°.
B—210°.
C—300°.

Answer (A) is correct (3579). *(PHAK Chap 8)*
The OBS is set on 210° with the needle centered. The important factor is the (TO) indication showing. You are thus crossing the 210° inbound bearing but with a (TO) indication it is the 030° radial. If it was a (FROM) indication it would be the 210° radial.
Answer (B) is incorrect because if you were crossing the 210° radial, you would have a FROM (not TO) indication. Answer (C) is incorrect because the 3 at the bottom of the dial means 030° (not 300°).

The sectional chart legend and Figures 21 through 27 appear on pages 251 through 258 in Chapter 9.

7.
3570. (Refer to figure 27, areas 4 and 3, on page 258 and figure 29 on page 272.) The VOR is tuned to Jamestown VOR, and the aircraft is positioned over Cooperstown Airport. Which VOR indication is correct?

A—9.
B—2.
C—6.

Answer (C) is correct (3570). *(PHAK Chap 8)*
Cooperstown Airport (northeast of 2 in Fig. 27) is located on the 028° radial of the Jamestown VOR (south of 4). With a centered needle, you could have an OBS setting of 028° and a FROM indication or an OBS setting of 208° and a TO indication. VOR 6 fits the aircraft's location over Cooperstown Airport. You have a FROM indication with an OBS setting of 030° and a half-scale deflection of the CDI to the right (because Cooperstown Airport is north of your selected course). You are thus on approximately the 028° radial.
Answer (A) is incorrect because VOR 9 shows the aircraft's location as southwest of the Jamestown VOR, not over Cooperstown Airport. Answer (B) is incorrect because VOR 2 shows the aircraft's location as somewhere on the 030° radial, which would place it slightly south of, not over, Cooperstown Airport.

8.
3577. (Refer to figure 29, illustration 1, on page 272.) The VOR receiver has the indications shown. What is the aircraft's position relative to the station?

A—North.
B—East.
C—South.

Answer (C) is correct (3577). *(PHAK Chap 8)*
The OBS is set to 030°. If the needle were centered the airplane would be southwest of the station. The CDI is deflected full scale left so you are right of course. You are thus south of the VORTAC.
Answer (A) is incorrect because to be north would require a right CDI deflection and a FROM indication. Answer (B) is incorrect because to be east would require a left CDI deflection and a FROM indication.

9.
3578. (Refer to figure 29, illustration 3, on page 272.) The VOR receiver has the indications shown. What is the aircraft's position relative to the station?

A—East.
B—Southeast.
C—West.

Answer (B) is correct (3578). *(PHAK Chap 8)*
With no (TO) or (FROM) indications showing on VOR 3, Fig. 29, you must be flying in the zone of ambiguity from the VOR which is perpendicular to the OBS setting, i.e, on the 120° or 300° radials. Since you have a left deflection, you would be on the 120° radial, or southeast of the VOR.
Answer (A) is incorrect because if you were east, you would have a FROM indication. Answer (C) is incorrect because the 120° radial is southeast, not west.

10.
3533. (Refer to figure 21, area 3, on page 252 and figure 29 on page 272.) The VOR is tuned to Elizabeth City VOR, and the aircraft is positioned over Shawboro. Which VOR indication is correct?

A—5.
B—9.
C—2.

Answer (C) is correct (3533). *(PHAK Chap 8)*
See Fig. 21, northeast of 3 along the compass rose.
Shawboro is northeast of the Elizabeth City VOR on the 030° radial. To be over it, the needle should be centered with either an OBS setting of 210° and a TO indication, or with an OBS setting of 030° and a FROM indication. VOR 2 matches the latter description.
Answer (A) is incorrect because VOR 5 indicates that the aircraft is southwest, not northeast, of Elizabeth City VOR. Answer (B) is incorrect because VOR 9 indicates that the aircraft is southwest, not northeast, of Elizabeth City VOR.

11.
3561. (Refer to figure 25 on page 256 and figure 29 on page 272.) The VOR is tuned to Bonham VORTAC (area 3) and the aircraft is positioned over the town of Sulphur Springs (area 5). Which VOR indication is correct?

A—1.
B—8.
C—7.

Answer (C) is correct (3561). *(PHAK Chap 8)*
The town of Sulpher Springs (south-southwest of 5) is on the 120° radial of Bonham VORTAC. Illustration 7 shows the VOR receiver tuned to the 210° radial, which is perpendicular to (90° away from) the 120° radial. This places the aircraft in the zone of ambiguity, which results in neither a TO nor a FROM indication and an unstable CDI, which can be deflected left or right.
Answer (A) is incorrect because, with indication 1, the aircraft would have to be west of Sulphur Springs. Answer (B) is incorrect because it shows the aircraft on the 030° radial, which is well to the north of Sulphur Springs.

10.3 Automatic Direction Finder (ADF)

12.
3580. (Refer to figure 30, illustration 1, on page 275.) Determine the magnetic bearing TO the station.

A—030°.
B—180°.
C—210°.

Answer (C) is correct (3580). *(PHAK Chap 8)*
Fig. 30 shows movable card ADFs. In these, the airplane's magnetic heading is always on top and the needle always indicates the magnetic bearing TO the station. Thus, the magnetic bearing TO the station in ADF 1 is 210°.
Answer (A) is incorrect because the head (not the tail) indicates the magnetic bearing TO the station.
Answer (B) is incorrect because the magnetic bearing TO the station is 210° (not 180°).

13.
3581. (Refer to figure 30, illustration 2, on page 275.) What magnetic bearing should the pilot use to fly TO the station?

A—010°.
B—145°.
C—190°.

Answer (C) is correct (3581). *(PHAK Chap 8)*
Fig. 30, illustration 2, is a movable card ADF. This ADF displays the airplane's magnetic heading at the top, and the needle always points to the magnetic bearing TO the station. Thus, the magnetic bearing TO the station in ADF 2 is 190°.
Answer (A) is incorrect because 010° is the bearing FROM the station. Answer (B) is incorrect because 145° might be an appropriate heading to intercept the 190° bearing TO the station.

14.
3582. (Refer to figure 30, illustration 2, on page 275.) Determine the approximate heading to intercept the 180° bearing TO the station.

A—040°.
B—160°.
C—220°.

Answer (C) is correct (3582). *(PHAK Chap 8)*
A 180° bearing to the station would put us directly north of the station assuming no wind. Currently, we are northeast of the station (190° bearing), proceeding in a northwest direction (magnetic heading of 315°). If we want to intercept the 180° bearing to the station, we should turn to the southwest, or 220°.
Answer (A) is incorrect because 040° would take us in the opposite direction of the station. Answer (B) is incorrect because we are already east of the station and 160° would put us farther east.

15.
3583. (Refer to figure 30, illustration 3, on page 275.) What is the magnetic bearing FROM the station?

A—025°.
B—115°.
C—295°.

Answer (B) is correct (3583). *(PHAK Chap 8)*
The tail of the needle of an ADF indicates the magnetic bearing FROM the station on a movable card ADF. ADF 3 shows a magnetic bearing of 115° FROM.
Answer (A) is incorrect because 025° is the relative bearing TO (not the magnetic bearing FROM) the station. Answer (C) is incorrect because 295° is the magnetic bearing TO (not FROM) the station.

16.
3584. (Refer to figure 30 on page 275.) Which ADF indication represents the aircraft tracking TO the station with a right crosswind?

A—1.
B—2.
C—4.

Answer (C) is correct (3584). *(PHAK Chap 8)*
If you have a crosswind from the right, you must adjust your heading (crab) to the right to compensate for the wind. In that case, the needle would point to the left of the nose, as in ADF 4.
Answer (A) is incorrect because ADF 1 indicates the airplane tracking away from the station. Answer (B) is incorrect because ADF 2 indicates the airplane tracking away from the station.

17.
3585. (Refer to figure 30, illustration 1, on page 275.) What outbound bearing is the aircraft crossing?

A—030°.
B—150°.
C—180°.

Answer (A) is correct (3585). *(PHAK Chap 8)*
The outbound (magnetic) bearing is the bearing FROM the station, which is represented by the tail of the needle in a movable card ADF. The airplane in ADF 1 is crossing the 030° outbound bearing (radial) since the tail of the needle is pointing to 030°.
Answer (B) is incorrect because 150° is the reciprocal of the magnetic heading (not bearing). Answer (C) is incorrect because the needle does not point to 180°.

18.
3586. (Refer to figure 30, illustration 1, below.) What is the relative bearing TO the station?

A—030°.
B—210°.
C—240°.

Answer (C) is correct (3586). *(PHAK Chap 8)*
The relative bearing is measured clockwise from the nose of the airplane to the head of the needle. From ADF 1, the magnetic heading (MH) is 330° and the magnetic bearing (MB) TO the station is 210°. Use the following standard formula to solve for the relative bearing (RB) TO the station:

$$MH + RB = MB \text{ (TO)}$$
$$330° + RB = 210°$$
$$RB = -120° \ (210 - 330)$$

Since it is less than 0°, add 360° to determine the RB of 240° (−120 + 360).

Answer (A) is incorrect because 30° is the magnetic bearing FROM the station. Answer (B) is incorrect because 210° is the magnetic bearing TO the station.

19.
3587. (Refer to figure 30, illustration 2, below.) What is the relative bearing TO the station?

A—190°.
B—235°.
C—315°.

Answer (B) is correct (3587). *(PHAK Chap 8)*
The relative bearing is measured clockwise from the nose of the airplane to the head of the needle. Use the following standard formula from ADF 2 in the formula to determine the RB:

$$MH + RB = MB \text{ (TO)}$$
$$315° + RB = 190°$$
$$RB = -125° \ (190 - 315)$$

Since it is less than 0°, add 360° to determine the RB of 235° (−125 + 360) TO the station.

Answer (A) is incorrect because 190° is the magnetic (not relative) bearing TO the station. Answer (C) is incorrect because 315° is the magnetic heading of the aircraft.

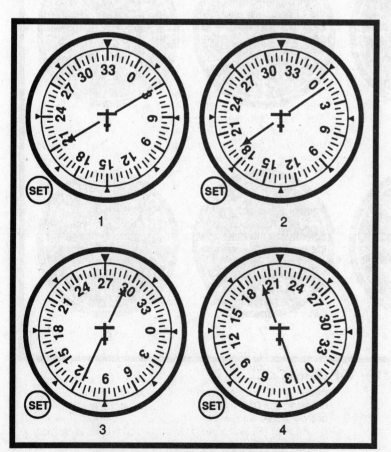

FIGURE 30.—ADF (Movable Card).

20.
3588. (Refer to figure 30, illustration 4, on page 275.) What is the relative bearing TO the station?

A—020°.
B—060°.
C—340°.

Answer (C) is correct (3588). *(PHAK Chap 8)*
The relative bearing (RB) is measured clockwise from the nose of the airplane to the head of the needle. Use the information from ADF 4 in the formula to determine the RB:

$$MH + RB = MB \text{ (TO)}$$
$$220° + RB = 200°$$
$$RB = -20° \text{ (200 - 220)}$$

Since it is less than 0°, add 360° to determine the RB of 340° (–20 + 360) TO the station.
Answer (A) is incorrect because 020° is the magnetic bearing FROM the station. Answer (B) is incorrect because 060° has no relevance to this problem.

21.
3591. (Refer to figure 31, illustration 3, below.) The relative bearing TO the station is

A—090°.
B—180°.
C—270°.

Answer (B) is correct (3591). *(PHAK Chap 8)*
The relative bearing (RB) is measured clockwise from the nose of the airplane to the head of the needle. Since this is a fixed card ADF, the needle points to the relative bearing TO the station. ADF 3 in Fig. 31 shows a relative bearing of 180°.
Answer (A) is incorrect because the needle does not point to the right wing. Answer (C) is incorrect because the needle does not point to the left wing.

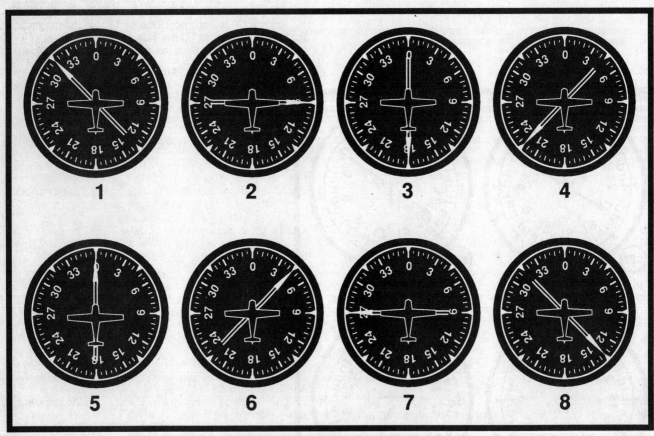

FIGURE 31.—ADF (Fixed Card).

22.
3589. (Refer to figure 31, illustration 1, on page 276.) The relative bearing TO the station is

A—045°.
B—180°.
C—315°.

Answer (C) is correct (3589). *(PHAK Chap 8)*
On a fixed card ADF, the needle points to the relative bearing TO the station. ADF 1 in Fig. 31 shows a relative bearing of 315°.
Answer (A) is incorrect because the needle does not point 45° to the right of the nose. Answer (B) is incorrect because the needle does not point to the tail.

23.
3590. (Refer to figure 31, illustration 2, on page 276.) The relative bearing TO the station is

A—090°.
B—180°.
C—270°.

Answer (A) is correct (3590). *(PHAK Chap 8)*
On a fixed card ADF, the needle points to the relative bearing TO the station. ADF 2 in Fig. 31 shows a relative bearing of 090° TO the station.
Answer (B) is incorrect because the needle does not point to the tail. Answer (C) is incorrect because the head (not the tail) of the needle indicates relative bearing.

24.
3592. (Refer to figure 31, illustration 4, on page 276.) On a magnetic heading of 320°, the magnetic bearing TO the station is

A—005°.
B—185°.
C—225°.

Answer (B) is correct (3592). *(PHAK Chap 8)*
The magnetic bearing TO the station is required. Use the standard ADF formula.

$$MH + RB = MB \text{ (TO)}$$
$$320° + 225° = MB \text{ (TO)}$$
$$545° = MB \text{ (TO)}$$

Since it is greater than 360°, subtract 360° to determine the MB (TO) is 185° (545 − 360).
Answer (A) is incorrect because 005° is not a relevant direction in this problem. Answer (C) is incorrect because 225° is the relative bearing.

25.
3593. (Refer to figure 31, illustration 5, on page 276.) On a magnetic heading of 035°, the magnetic bearing TO the station is

A—035°.
B—180°.
C—215°.

Answer (A) is correct (3593). *(PHAK Chap 8)*
The magnetic bearing TO the station is required. Use the standard ADF formula.

$$MH + RB = MB \text{ (TO)}$$
$$035° + 0° = MB \text{ (TO)}$$
$$035° = MB \text{ (TO)}$$

Answer (B) is incorrect because 180° is the relative bearing FROM the station. Answer (C) is incorrect because 215° is the magnetic bearing FROM the station.

26.
3594. (Refer to figure 31, illustration 6, on page 276.) On a magnetic heading of 120°, the magnetic bearing TO the station is

A—045°.
B—165°.
C—270°.

Answer (B) is correct (3594). *(PHAK Chap 8)*
The magnetic bearing TO the station is required. Use the standard ADF formula.

$$MH + RB = MB \text{ (TO)}$$
$$120° + 045° = MB \text{ (TO)}$$
$$165° = MB \text{ (TO)}$$

Answer (A) is incorrect because 045° is the relative bearing TO the station. Answer (C) is incorrect because 270° is not a relevant heading in this problem.

27.
3595. (Refer to figure 31, illustration 6, on page 276.) If the magnetic bearing TO the station is 240°, the magnetic heading is

A—045°.
B—105°.
C—195°.

Answer (C) is correct (3595). *(PHAK Chap 8)*
The magnetic heading is required. Use the standard ADF formula.

$$MH + RB = MB \text{ (TO)}$$
$$MH + 045° = 240°$$
$$MH = 240° − 045°$$
$$MH = 195°$$

Answer (A) is incorrect because 045° is the relative bearing TO the station. Answer (B) is incorrect because 105° is not a relevant heading in this problem.

28.
3596. (Refer to figure 31, illustration 7, on page 276.) If the magnetic bearing TO the station is 030°, the magnetic heading is

A—060°.
B—120°.
C—270°.

Answer (B) is correct (3596). *(PHAK Chap 8)*
The magnetic heading is required. Use the standard ADF formula.

$$MH + RB = MB \text{ (TO)}$$
$$MH + 270° = 030°$$
$$MH = 030° - 270°$$
$$MH = -240° \text{ (add 360°)}$$
$$MH = 120°$$

Answer (A) is incorrect because 060° is not a relevant heading in this problem. Answer (C) is incorrect because 270° is the relative bearing TO the station.

29.
3597. (Refer to figure 31, illustration 8, on page 276.) If the magnetic bearing TO the station is 135°, the magnetic heading is

A—135°.
B—270°.
C—360°.

Answer (C) is correct (3597). *(PHAK Chap 8)*
The magnetic heading is required. Use the standard ADF formula.

$$MH + RB = MB \text{ (TO)}$$
$$MH + 135° = 135°$$
$$MH = 0° = (360°)$$

Answer (A) is incorrect because 135° is both the relative and magnetic bearing TO the station. Answer (B) is incorrect because 270° is not a relevant heading in this problem.

10.4 Global Positioning System (GPS)

30.
3598b. How many satellites make up the Global Positioning System (GPS)?

A—25.
B—22.
C—24.

Answer (C) is correct (3598b). *(AIM Para 1-1-21)*
The Global Positioning System (GPS) is composed of a constellation of 24 satellites that broadcast signals decoded by a receiver in order to determine a three-dimensional position.
Answer (A) is incorrect because the GPS is composed of 24, not 25, satellites. Answer (B) is incorrect because the GPS is composed of 24, not 22, satellites.

31.
3598c. What is the minimum number of Global Positioning System (GPS) satellites that are observable by a user anywhere on earth?

A—6.
B—5.
C—4.

Answer (B) is correct (3598c). *(AIM Para 1-1-21)*
The Global Positioning System is composed of 24 satellites, at least five of which are observable at any given time anywhere on earth.
Answer (A) is incorrect because at least five, not six, satellites are visible anywhere on earth. Answer (C) is incorrect because at least five, not four, satellites are visible anywhere on earth.

32.
3598d. How many Global Positioning System (GPS) satellites are required to yield a three dimensional position (latitude, longitude, and altitude) and time solution?

A—5.
B—6.
C—4.

Answer (C) is correct (3598d). *(AIM Para 1-1-21)*
GPS satellites broadcast radio signals that are decoded by a receiver in order to triangulate a three-dimensional position by calculating distances based on the amount of time it takes the radio signals to reach the receiver. At least four GPS satellites are required to yield a three-dimensional position (latitude, longitude, and altitude) and time solution.
Answer (A) is incorrect because four, not five, satellites are required for a three-dimensional position and time solution. Answer (B) is incorrect because four, not six, satellites are required for a three-dimensional position and time solution.

END OF CHAPTER

CHAPTER ELEVEN
CROSS-COUNTRY FLIGHT PLANNING

This chapter contains outlines of major concepts tested, all FAA test questions and answers regarding cross-country flying, and an explanation of each answer. Each module, or subtopic, within this chapter is listed above with the number of questions from the FAA pilot knowledge test pertaining to that particular module. For each module, the first number following the parentheses is the page number on which the outline begins, and the next number is the page number on which the questions begin.

This book assumes that you are familiar with the standard flight computer. Full discussion with examples can be found in *Pilot Handbook*, Chapter 11.

CAUTION: Recall that the **sole purpose** of this book is to expedite passing the FAA pilot knowledge test for the private pilot certificate. Accordingly, all extraneous material (i.e., topics or regulations not directly tested) is omitted, even though much more information and knowledge are necessary to fly safely. This additional material is presented in *Pilot Handbook* and *Private Pilot Flight Maneuvers and Practical Test Prep*, available from Gleim Publications, Inc. See the order form on page 326.

11.1 VFR FLIGHT PLAN (Questions 1-4)

1. A VFR flight plan is a form (see Figure 52 on page 285) that contains 17 blocks of information. Only the following blocks are tested on the private pilot knowledge test:

    a. Block 7: "Cruising Altitude." Use only your initial requested altitude on your VFR flight plan.

    b. Block 9: "Destination (Name of airport and city)" should include the airport or place at which you plan to make your last landing for this flight.

        1) Unless you plan a stopover of more than 1 hr. elsewhere en route

    c. Block 12: "Fuel on Board" (in hours and minutes) requires the amount of usable fuel in the airplane at the time of departure, expressed in hours of flying time.

2. You should close your flight plan with the nearest FSS, or if one is not available, you may request any ATC facility to relay your cancellation to the FSS.

    a. Control towers (and ground control) do not automatically close VFR or DVFR flight plans since they do not know if a particular VFR aircraft is on a flight plan.

11.2 PREFLIGHT INSPECTION (Questions 5-7)

1. During the preflight inspection, the pilot in command is responsible for determining that the airplane is safe for flight.

2. The owner or operator is responsible for maintaining the airplane in an airworthy condition.

3. For the first flight of the day, the preflight inspection should be accomplished by a thorough and systematic means recommended by the manufacturer.

11.3 TAXIING TECHNIQUE (Questions 8-14)

1. When taxiing in strong quartering headwinds, the aileron should be up on the side from which the wind is blowing.

   a. The elevator should be in the neutral position for tricycle-geared airplanes.
   b. The elevator should be in the up position for tailwheel airplanes.

2. When taxiing during strong quartering tailwinds, the aileron should be down on the side from which the wind is blowing.

   a. The elevator should be in the down position (for both tricycle and tailwheel airplanes).

3. When taxiing high-wing, nosewheel-equipped airplanes, the most critical wind condition is a quartering tailwind.

11.4 MISCELLANEOUS AIRSPEED QUESTIONS (Questions 15-17)

1. When turbulence is encountered, the airplane's airspeed should be reduced to maneuvering speed (V_A).

   a. The pilot should attempt to maintain a level flight attitude.
   b. Constant altitude and constant airspeed are usually impossible and result in additional control pressure, which adds stress to the airplane.

2. Approaches and landings at night should be the same as in daylight (i.e., at same airspeeds and altitudes).

3. In the event of a power failure after becoming airborne, the most important thing to do is to immediately establish and maintain the best glide airspeed.

   a. Do not maintain altitude at the expense of airspeed or a stall/spin will result.

11.5 MAGNETIC COURSE (Questions 18-23)

1. To determine the magnetic course (MC) from one airport to another, correct the true course (TC) only for magnetic variation, i.e., make no allowance for wind correction angle.

   a. Determine the TC by placing the straight edge of a navigational plotter or protractor along the route, with the hole in the plotter on the intersection of the route and a meridian, or line of longitude (the vertical line with little crosslines).

      1) The TC is measured by the numbers on the protractor portion of the plotter (semi-circle) at the meridian.

      2) Note that up to four numbers (90° apart) are provided on the plotter. You must determine which is the direction of the flight, using a common sense approximation of your direction.

b.   Alternatively, you can use a line of latitude (horizontal line with little crosslines) if your course is in a north or south direction.

   1)   This is why there are four numbers on the plotter. You may be using either a meridian or line of latitude to measure your course and be going in either direction along the course line.

c.   Determine the MC by adjusting the TC for magnetic variation (angle between true north and magnetic north).

   1)   On sectional charts, a long dashed line provides the number of degrees of magnetic variation. The variation is either east or west and is signified by "E" or "W," e.g., 3°E or 5°W.

   2)   If the variation is east, subtract; if west, add. (Memory aid: east is least and west is best). This is from TC to MC.

2.   If your course is to or from a VOR, use the compass rose to determine the MC, i.e., no adjustment is needed from TC to MC.

a.   Compass roses have about a 3-in. diameter on sectional charts.
b.   Every 30° is labeled, as well as marked with an arrow inside the rose pointing out.
c.   Use the reciprocal to radials when flying toward the VOR.

   1)   EXAMPLE: If your course is toward an airport on the 180° radial rather than from the airport, your MC is 360°, not 180°.

11.6 MAGNETIC HEADING (Questions 24-29)

1.   To compute magnetic heading (MH) from MC, you must adjust for the wind.

a.   To compute wind effect, use the wind side of the computer.

   1)   Align the magnetic wind direction on the inner scale under the true index (top of the computer).

      a)   Wind direction is normally given in true, not magnetic, direction. Thus, you must first adjust the wind direction from true to magnetic.

      b)   Find the magnetic variation on the navigation chart. As with course corrections, add westerly variation and subtract easterly variation.

      c)   See the discussion of magnetic variation under Magnetic Course, 1.c. above.

      d)   EXAMPLE: Given wind of 330° and a 20°E variation, the magnetic direction of the wind is 310° (330° − 20°).

   2)   Slide the grid through the computer until the grommet (the hole in the center) is on the 100-kt. wind line. Measure up the vertical line the amount of wind speed in knots and put a pencil mark on the plastic.

   3)   Rotate the inner scale so the MC lies under the true index.

   4)   Slide the grid so that your pencil dot is superimposed over the true airspeed (TAS). The location of the grommet will indicate the groundspeed. This is needed for time en route calculations.

   5)   The pencil mark will indicate the wind correction angle (WCA). If to the left, it is a negative wind correction. If to the right, it is a positive wind correction.

b.   MH is found by adjusting the MC for the wind correction.

   1)   Add the number of degrees the pencil mark is to the right of the centerline or subtract the number of degrees to the left.

2. Author's Note: We suggest converting TC to MC and winds to magnetic before using the wind side of your computer. Then you do not have to convert your final answer from the wind side to magnetic.

    a. Many courses are to or from VORs, which allow you to use the compass rose to determine MC directly. That is, you can skip the plotter routine for TC.

Alternative: E6-B Computer Approach to Magnetic Heading

1. In the previous module, before computing the WCA and groundspeed (GS) on the wind side of the E6-B computer, we converted

    a. TC to MC
    b. Winds (true) to winds (magnetic)

2. The ALTERNATIVE METHOD suggested on your E6-B is to use TC and winds (true) on the wind side of your E6-B to compute your true heading (TH) and then convert TH to MH. The advantages of this method are

    a. You convert only one true direction to magnetic, not two.
    b. This is the way it has always been taught.

3. We suggest converting TC and wind (true) to magnetic because pilot activities are in terms of magnetic headings, courses, runways, radials, bearings, and final approach courses. When flying, you should always think magnetic, not true.

    a. While doing magnetic heading problems, you should visualize yourself flying each problem, e.g., a 270° course with a 300° wind will require a right (270° +) heading and have a headwind component.

4. On your E6-B, you will find directions such as

    a. Set Wind Direction opposite True Index.
    b. Mark Wind Dot up from Grommet.
    c. Place TC under True Index.
    d. Slide TAS under Wind Dot.
    e. Read GS under Grommet.
    f. Read WCA under Wind Dot.
    g. Complete the problem by use of the formulas.

5. The formulas given are

    > TH = TC ± WCA (wind correction angle)
    > MH = TH ± magnetic variation (E−, W+)
    > CH = MH ± compass deviation

6. We understand this ALTERNATIVE approach is widely used. It was developed prior to the VOR system, compass roses, airways, etc., which are all identified in magnetic direction, NOT true direction. Thus you may use it for textbook exercises, but when flying, think magnetic.

    a. Please use page 337 to comment favorably or unfavorably on our emphasis on magnetic. Thank you.

11.7 COMPASS HEADING (Question 30)

1. If a question asks for a compass heading (CH), the MH is converted to a CH by adding or subtracting deviation (installation error), which is indicated on a compass correction card usually mounted on the compass.

    a. Compass correction cards are needed because the metal, electric motors, and other instruments in each airplane affect the compass causing compass deviation.

b. Compass correction cards usually indicate corrections for every 30°.

1) For each 30°, you are given the corresponding MH and the heading you should follow, i.e., the CH.

2) The difference between these two headings is the amount to add or subtract.

FOR (MAGNETIC)	N	30	60	E	120	150
STEER (COMPASS)	0	28	57	85	117	148
FOR (MAGNETIC)	S	210	240	W	300	330
STEER (COMPASS)	180	212	243	274	303	332

Typical Compass Correction Card

3) EXAMPLE: Using the compass correction card to the right, your CH would be 085° if your MH were due east, and 332° if your MH were 330°.

4) If your MH does not coincide with a heading on the correction card, use the nearest one, i.e., interpolate.

11.8 TIME EN ROUTE (Questions 31-40)

1. A number of FAA questions require you to determine the time of arrival at some specified point on a sectional chart given the times that two other points on the chart were crossed. You must

   a. Compute your groundspeed based upon the distance already traveled (i.e., between the two given points) in the given time.

   b. Measure the additional distance to go.

   c. Compute the time required to travel to the next point.

2. First, measure the distances (1) already gone, and (2) remaining to go with a navigational plotter or a ruler.

   a. Remember that the scale at the bottom of sectional charts is 1:500,000.

   b. Because the questions give data in NM instead of SM (e.g., wind speed is given in knots), use NM.

3. To compute speed, place the distance already gone on the outer scale of the flight computer adjacent to the number of minutes it took on the inner scale.

   a. Read the number on the outer scale adjacent to the solid triangular pointer (i.e., at 60 min.). This is your groundspeed in knots.

   b. For numbers less than 10 on either scale, add a zero.

   c. EXAMPLE: If you travel 3 NM in 3 min., you are going 60 kt. Place 30 on the outer scale adjacent to 30 on the inner scale. Then the outer scale shows 60 kt. above the solid triangular pointer.

4. To compute the time required to fly to the next point, start with the speed on the outer scale adjacent to 60 min. on the inner scale (just as you had it in the preceding step). Find the remaining NM to go on the outer scale. The adjacent number on the inner scale is the number of minutes to go.

   a. EXAMPLE: Place 12 (for 120 kt.) on the outer scale over the solid triangular pointer (i.e., at 60 min.). Look along the outer scale and find 4 (for 40 NM). It should be directly above 2 (for 20 min.) on the inner scale.

5. Another type of time en route question has you compute the magnetic course, heading, and groundspeed.

   a. Determine the groundspeed as explained under Magnetic Heading on page 281.

   b. Recall that groundspeed appears under the grommet when you slide the grid on the wind side of your flight computer such that your pencil mark is on the TAS arc.

   c. Once you determine groundspeed, put it over 60 min. on the inner scale. Find the distance to go on the outer scale, and read the time en route on the inner scale.

11.9 TIME ZONE CORRECTIONS (Questions 41-46)

1. To correct for time zones, remember that there is a 1-hr. difference between each time zone, i.e., from the Eastern Time Zone to the Central Time Zone, from the Central Time Zone to the Mountain Time Zone, from the Mountain Time Zone to the Pacific Time Zone.

   a. Subtract 1 hr. for each time zone when traveling east to west, and add 1 hr. for each time zone when traveling west to east.

   b. Additionally, there may be daylight savings time (in the summer) or standard time in effect.

2. The number of hours to adjust to or from Coordinated Universal Time (UTC) are 4-5-6-7 in the summer, and 5-6-7-8 in the winter (for the four zones from east to west).

   a. EXAMPLE: To compute UTC, add 4 hr. to Eastern Daylight Savings Time and 5 hr. to Eastern Standard Time.

      1) Add 5 and 6 hr. respectively to Central Time.
      2) Add 6 and 7 hr. respectively to Mountain Time.
      3) Add 7 and 8 hr. respectively to Pacific Time.

   b. Remember, there is always a longer lag in standard than in daylight savings time.

3. For questions requiring the time of arrival at a destination airport, you should

   a. First add the hours en route to the time of departure and determine the time of arrival based on the time zone of departure.

   b. Then adjust the time to the time zone requested, i.e., UTC or time zone of arrival.

   c. Alternatively, convert the departure time to UTC, add hours en route, and convert to local time.

QUESTIONS AND ANSWER EXPLANATIONS

All the FAA questions from the pilot knowledge test for the private pilot certificate relating to cross-country flying and the material outlined previously are reproduced on the following pages in the same modules as the outlines. To the immediate right of each question are the correct answer and answer explanation. You should cover these answers and answer explanations while responding to the questions. Refer to the general discussion in the Introduction on how to take the FAA pilot knowledge test.

Remember that the questions from the FAA pilot knowledge test bank have been reordered by topic, and the topics have been organized into a meaningful sequence. Accordingly, the first line of the answer explanation gives the FAA question number and the citation of the authoritative source for the answer.

11.1 VFR Flight Plan

1.
3815. (Refer to figure 52 below.) If more than one cruising altitude is intended, which should be entered in block 7 of the flight plan?

A—Initial cruising altitude.
B—Highest cruising altitude.
C—Lowest cruising altitude.

Answer (A) is correct (3815). *(AIM Para 5-1-4)*
Use only your initial requested altitude on your VFR flight plan to assist briefers in providing weather and wind information.
Answer (B) is incorrect because the initial, not highest, altitude should be filed on your VFR flight plan. Answer (C) is incorrect because the initial, not lowest, altitude should be filed on your VFR flight plan.

2.
3816. (Refer to figure 52 below.) What information should be entered in block 9 for a VFR day flight?

A—The name of the airport of first intended landing.
B—The name of destination airport if no stopover for more than 1 hour is anticipated.
C—The name of the airport where the aircraft is based.

Answer (B) is correct (3816). *(AIM Para 5-1-4)*
In Block 9 of the flight plan form in Fig. 52, enter the name of the airport of last intended landing for that flight, as long as no stopover exceeds 1 hr.
Answer (A) is incorrect because the first intended landing, i.e., the end of the first leg of the flight, is included in the route of flight (Block 8). Answer (C) is incorrect because the name of the airport where the airplane is based is entered in block 14.

3.
3817. (Refer to figure 52 below.) What information should be entered in block 12 for a VFR day flight?

A—The estimated time en route plus 30 minutes.
B—The estimated time en route plus 45 minutes.
C—The amount of usable fuel on board expressed in time.

Answer (C) is correct (3817). *(AIM Para 5-1-4)*
Block 12 of the flight plan requires the amount of usable fuel in the airplane at the time of departure. It should be expressed in hours and minutes of flying time.
Answer (A) is incorrect because it states the VFR fuel requirement for day flight. Answer (B) is incorrect because it states the VFR fuel requirement for night flight.

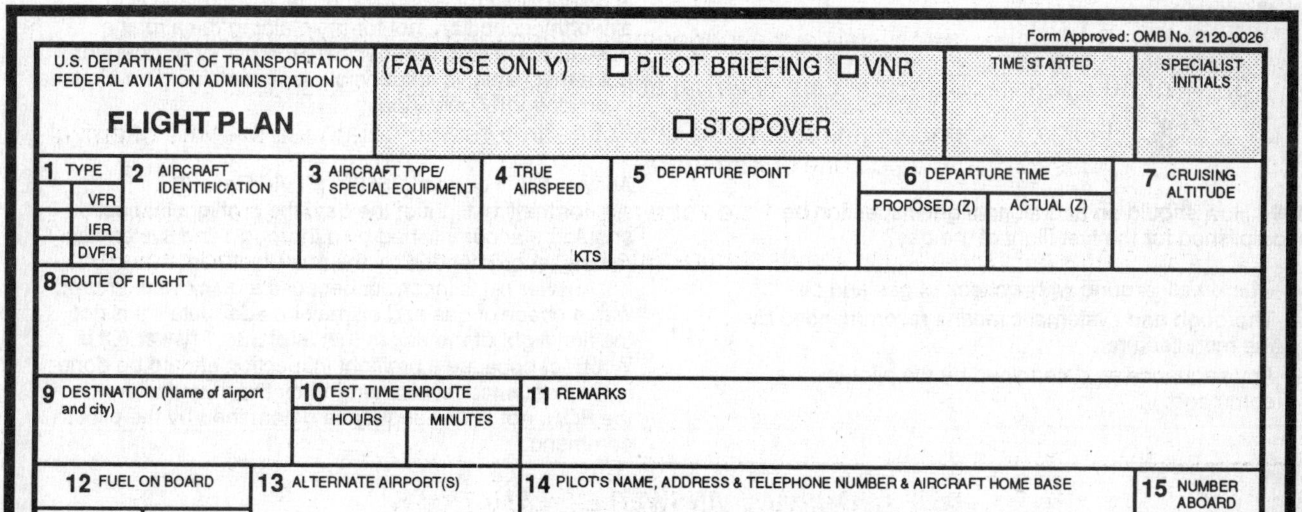
Form Approved: OMB No. 2120-0026
U.S. DEPARTMENT OF TRANSPORTATION
FEDERAL AVIATION ADMINISTRATION
FLIGHT PLAN
(FAA USE ONLY) ☐ PILOT BRIEFING ☐ VNR ☐ STOPOVER
TIME STARTED
SPECIALIST INITIALS
1 TYPE: VFR, IFR, DVFR
2 AIRCRAFT IDENTIFICATION
3 AIRCRAFT TYPE/ SPECIAL EQUIPMENT
4 TRUE AIRSPEED KTS
5 DEPARTURE POINT
6 DEPARTURE TIME: PROPOSED (Z), ACTUAL (Z)
7 CRUISING ALTITUDE
8 ROUTE OF FLIGHT
9 DESTINATION (Name of airport and city)
10 EST. TIME ENROUTE: HOURS, MINUTES
11 REMARKS
12 FUEL ON BOARD: HOURS, MINUTES
13 ALTERNATE AIRPORT(S)
14 PILOT'S NAME, ADDRESS & TELEPHONE NUMBER & AIRCRAFT HOME BASE
15 NUMBER ABOARD
17 DESTINATION CONTACT/TELEPHONE (OPTIONAL)
16 COLOR OF AIRCRAFT
CIVIL AIRCRAFT PILOTS. FAR Part 91 requires you file an IFR flight plan to operate under instrument flight rules in controlled airspace. Failure to file could result in a civil penalty not to exceed $1,000 for each violation (Section 901 of the Federal Aviation Act of 1958, as amended). Filing of a VFR flight plan is recommended as a good operating practice. See also Part 99 for requirements concerning DVFR flight plans.
FAA Form 7233-1 (8-82) CLOSE VFR FLIGHT PLAN WITH ____________ FSS ON ARRIVAL

FIGURE 52.—Flight Plan Form.

4.
3818. How should a VFR flight plan be closed at the completion of the flight at a controlled airport?

A—The tower will automatically close the flight plan when the aircraft turns off the runway.
B—The pilot must close the flight plan with the nearest FSS or other FAA facility upon landing.
C—The tower will relay the instructions to the nearest FSS when the aircraft contacts the tower for landing.

Answer (B) is correct (3818). *(AIM Para 5-1-12)*
A pilot is responsible for ensuring that the VFR or DVFR flight plan is canceled (FAR 91.153). You should close your flight plan with the nearest FSS or, if one is not available, you may request any ATC facility to relay your cancellation to the FSS.
Answer (A) is incorrect because the tower will automatically close an IFR (not VFR) flight plan. Answer (C) is incorrect because the tower will relay to the nearest FSS only if requested.

11.2 Preflight Inspection

5.
3658. During the preflight inspection who is responsible for determining the aircraft as safe for flight?

A—The pilot in command.
B—The owner or operator.
C—The certificated mechanic who performed the annual inspection.

Answer (A) is correct (3658). *(FAR 91.7)*
During the preflight inspection, the pilot in command is responsible for determining whether the airplane is in condition for safe flight.
Answer (B) is incorrect because the owner or operator is responsible for maintaining the airplane in an airworthy condition, not for determining whether the airplane is safe for flight during the preflight inspection. Answer (C) is incorrect because the pilot in command, not the mechanic who performed the annual inspection, is responsible for determining whether the airplane is safe for flight.

6.
3660. Who is primarily responsible for maintaining an aircraft in airworthy condition?

A—Pilot-in-command.
B—Owner or operator.
C—Mechanic.

Answer (B) is correct (3660). *(PHAK Chap 2)*
The owner or operator of an airplane is primarily responsible for maintaining an airplane in an airworthy condition, including compliance with all applicable Airworthiness Directives (ADs).
Answer (A) is incorrect because the pilot in command is responsible for determining that the airplane is in airworthy condition, not for maintaining the airplane. Answer (C) is incorrect because the owner or operator, not a mechanic, is responsible for maintaining an airplane in an airworthy condition.

7.
3659. How should an aircraft preflight inspection be accomplished for the first flight of the day?

A—Quick walk around with a check of gas and oil.
B—Thorough and systematic means recommended by the manufacturer.
C—Any sequence as determined by the pilot-in-command.

Answer (B) is correct (3659). *(PHAK Chap 2)*
For the first flight of the day, the preflight inspection should be accomplished by a thorough and systematic means recommended by the manufacturer.
Answer (A) is incorrect because a quick walk around with a check of gas and oil may be adequate if it is not the first flight of the day in that airplane. Answer (C) is incorrect because a preflight inspection should be done in the sequence recommended by the manufacturer in the *POH*, not in any sequence determined by the pilot in command.

11.3 Taxiing Technique

8.
3302. When taxiing with strong quartering tailwinds, which aileron positions should be used?

A—Aileron down on the downwind side.
B—Ailerons neutral.
C—Aileron down on the side from which the wind is blowing.

Answer (C) is correct (3302). *(AFH Chap 2)*
When there is a strong quartering tailwind, the aileron should be down on the side from which the wind is blowing (when taxiing away from the wind, turn away from the wind) to help keep the wind from getting under that wing and flipping the airplane over.
Answer (A) is incorrect because the aileron should be down on the upwind (not downwind) side. Answer (B) is incorrect because the aileron positions help control the airplane while taxiing in windy conditions.

9.
3303. Which aileron positions should a pilot generally use when taxiing in strong quartering headwinds?

A—Aileron up on the side from which the wind is blowing.
B—Aileron down on the side from which the wind is blowing.
C—Ailerons neutral.

Answer (A) is correct (3303). *(AFH Chap 2)*
When there is a strong quartering headwind, the aileron should be up on the side from which the wind is blowing to help keep the wind from getting under that wing and blowing the aircraft over. (When taxiing into the wind, turn into the wind.)
Answer (B) is incorrect because the aileron should be up (not down) on the side from which the wind is blowing (i.e., upwind). Answer (C) is incorrect because the aileron positions help control the airplane while taxiing in windy conditions.

10.
3304. Which wind condition would be most critical when taxiing a nosewheel equipped high-wing airplane?

A—Quartering tailwind.
B—Direct crosswind.
C—Quartering headwind.

Answer (A) is correct (3304). *(AFH Chap 2)*
The most critical wind condition when taxiing a nosewheel-equipped high-wing airplane is a quartering tailwind, which can flip a high-wing airplane over on its top. This should be prevented by holding the elevator in the down position, i.e., controls forward, and the aileron down on the side from which the wind is coming.
Answer (B) is incorrect because a direct crosswind will probably not flip an airplane over. However, it may weathervane the airplane into the wind. Answer (C) is incorrect because a headwind is aerodynamically the condition an airplane is designed for, i.e., wind from the front.

11.
3305. (Refer to figure 9, area A, below.) How should the flight controls be held while taxiing a tricycle-gear equipped airplane into a left quartering headwind?

A—Left aileron up, elevator neutral.
B—Left aileron down, elevator neutral.
C—Left aileron up, elevator down.

Answer (A) is correct (3305). *(AFH Chap 2)*
Given a left quartering headwind, the left aileron should be kept up to spoil the excess lift on the left wing that the crosswind is creating. The elevator should be neutral to keep from putting too much or too little weight on the nosewheel.
Answer (B) is incorrect because lowering the left aileron will increase the lift on the left wing. Answer (C) is incorrect because it describes the control setting for a right tailwind in a tailwheel airplane.

12.
3308. (Refer to figure 9, area C, below.) How should the flight controls be held while taxiing a tricycle-gear equipped airplane with a left quartering tailwind?

A—Left aileron up, elevator neutral.
B—Left aileron down, elevator down.
C—Left aileron up, elevator down.

Answer (B) is correct (3308). *(AFH Chap 2)*
With a left quartering tailwind, the left aileron should be down so the wind does not get under the left wing and flip the airplane over. Also, the elevator should be down, i.e., controls forward, so the wind does not get under the tail and blow the airplane tail over front.
Answer (A) is incorrect because it describes the control setting for a left headwind. Answer (C) is incorrect because it describes the control setting for a right tailwind.

13.
3306. (Refer to figure 9, area B, below.) How should the flight controls be held while taxiing a tailwheel airplane into a right quartering headwind?

A—Right aileron up, elevator up.
B—Right aileron down, elevator neutral.
C—Right aileron up, elevator down.

Answer (A) is correct (3306). *(AFH Chap 2)*
When there is a right quartering headwind, the right aileron should be up to spoil the excess lift on the right wing that the crosswind is creating. The elevator should be up to keep weight on the tailwheel to help maintain maneuverability.
Answer (B) is incorrect because the elevator should be up (not neutral) and the right aileron up (not down) when taxiing a tailwheel airplane in a right quartering headwind. Answer (C) is incorrect because the elevator should be up (not down) when taxiing in a right quartering headwind.

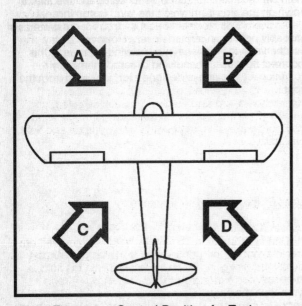

Figure 9.—Control Position for Taxi.

14.
3307. (Refer to figure 9, area C, above.) How should the flight controls be held while taxiing a tailwheel airplane with a left quartering tailwind?

A—Left aileron up, elevator neutral.
B—Left aileron down, elevator neutral.
C—Left aileron down, elevator down.

Answer (C) is correct (3307). *(AFH Chap 2)*
When there is a left quartering tailwind, the left aileron should be held down so the wind does not get under the left wing and flip the airplane over. Also, the elevator should be down, i.e., controls forward, so the wind does not get under the tail and blow the airplane tail over front.
Answer (A) is incorrect because the left aileron should be down (not up) and the elevator down (not neutral). Answer (B) is incorrect because the elevator should be down when taxiing with a tailwind.

11.4 Miscellaneous Airspeed Questions

15.
3442. Upon encountering severe turbulence, which flight condition should the pilot attempt to maintain?

A—Constant altitude and airspeed.
B—Constant angle of attack.
C—Level flight attitude.

Answer (C) is correct (3442). *(AC 00-24B)*
Attempting to hold altitude and airspeed in severe turbulence can lead to overstressing the airplane. Rather, you should set power to what normally will maintain V_A, and simply attempt to maintain a level flight attitude.
Answer (A) is incorrect because maintaining a constant altitude will require additional control movements, adding stress to the airplane. Answer (B) is incorrect because, in severe turbulence, the angle of attack will fluctuate due to the wind shears and wind shifts that cause the turbulence.

16.
3719. VFR approaches to land at night should be accomplished

A—at a higher airspeed.
B—with a steeper descent.
C—the same as during daytime.

Answer (C) is correct (3719). *(AFH Chap 10)*
Every effort should be made to execute approaches and landings at night in the same manner as they are made in the day. Inexperienced pilots often have a tendency to make approaches and landings at night with excessive airspeed.
Answer (A) is incorrect because approaching at a higher airspeed could result in floating into unseen obstacles at the far end of the runway. Answer (B) is incorrect because a steeper descent is not necessary. You should use the visual glide slope indicators at night whenever they are available.

17.
3711. The most important rule to remember in the event of a power failure after becoming airborne is to

A—immediately establish the proper gliding attitude and airspeed.
B—quickly check the fuel supply for possible fuel exhaustion.
C—determine the wind direction to plan for the forced landing.

Answer (A) is correct (3711). *(AFH Chap 12)*
In the event of a power failure after becoming airborne, the most important rule to remember is to maintain best glide airspeed. This will usually require a pitch attitude slightly higher than level flight. Invariably, with a power failure, one returns to ground, but emphasis should be put on a controlled return rather than a crash return. Many pilots attempt to maintain altitude at the expense of airspeed, resulting in a stall or stall/spin.
Answer (B) is incorrect because checking the fuel supply should only be done after a glide has been established and a landing site has been selected. Answer (C) is incorrect because landing into the wind may not be possible, depending upon altitude and field availability.

11.5 Magnetic Course

The sectional chart legend and Figures 21 through 27 appear on pages 251 through 258 in Chapter 9.

18.
3568. (Refer to figure 27 on page 258.) Determine the magnetic course from Breckheimer (Pvt) Airport (area 1) to Jamestown Airport (area 4).

A—360°.
B—188°.
C—180°.

Answer (C) is correct (3568). *(PHAK Chap 8)*
On Fig. 27, you are to find the magnetic course from Breckheimer Airport (top center) to Jamestown Airport (below 4). Since Jamestown has a VOR on the field, a compass rose exists around the Jamestown Airport symbol on the chart. Compass roses are based on magnetic courses. Thus, a straight line from Jamestown Airport to Breckheimer Airport coincides with the compass rose at 359°. Since the route is south to Jamestown, not north from Jamestown, compute the reciprocal direction as 179° (359° − 180°). The course, then, is approximately 180°.
Answer (A) is incorrect because the course from Breckheimer to Jamestown is southerly (not northerly). Answer (B) is incorrect because 188° is the true course, not the magnetic course.

The sectional chart legend and Figures 21 through 27 appear on pages 251 through 258 in Chapter 9.

19.
3531. (Refer to figure 21 on page 252.) Determine the magnetic course from First Flight Airport (area 5) to Hampton Roads Airport (area 2).

A—141°.
B—321°.
C—331°.

Answer (C) is correct (3531). *(PHAK Chap 8)*
You are to find the magnetic course from First Flight Airport (lower right corner) to Hampton Roads Airport (above 2 on Fig. 21). True course is the degrees clockwise from true north. Determine the true course by placing the straight edge of your plotter along the given route with the grommet at the intersection of your route and a meridian (the north/south line with crosslines). Here, TC is 321°. To convert this to a magnetic course, add the 10° westerly variation (indicated by the slanted dashed line across the upper right of the sectional), and find the magnetic course of 331°. Remember to subtract easterly variation and add westerly variation.
Answer (A) is incorrect because 141° is the true, not magnetic, course for a flight from Hampton Roads Airport to First Flight Airport, not for a flight from First Flight to Hampton Roads. Answer (B) is incorrect because 321° is the true, not magnetic, course.

20.
3539. (Refer to figure 22 on page 253.) What course should be selected on the omnibearing selector (OBS) to make a direct flight from Mercer County Regional Airport (area 3) to the Minot VORTAC (area 1) with a TO indication?

A—359°.
B—179°.
C—001°.

Answer (A) is correct (3539). *(PHAK Chap 8)*
Use Fig. 22 to find the course (omnibearing selector with a "TO" indication) from Mercer County Regional Airport (lower left corner) to the Minot VORTAC (right of 1). Note the compass rose (based on magnetic courses) which indicates the Minot VORTAC. A straight line from Mercer to Minot Airport coincides the compass rose at 179°. Since the route is north TO Minot, not south from Minot, compute the reciprocal direction as 359° (179° + 180°).
Answer (B) is incorrect because 179° is the radial on which a direct flight from Mercer County Regional Airport to the Minot VORTAC would be flown. If 179° is selected on the OBS, it will result in a FROM indication and reverse sensing. Answer (C) is incorrect because 001° would be the proper OBS setting for a flight originating 5 NM west of Mercer County Regional Airport, rather than directly from it.

21.
3553. (Refer to figure 24 on page 255.) On what course should the VOR receiver (OBS) be set to navigate direct from Hampton Varnville Airport (area 1) to Savannah VORTAC (area 3)?

A—003°.
B—183°.
C—200°.

Answer (B) is correct (3553). *(PHAK Chap 8)*
You are to find the OBS course setting from Hampton Varnville Airport (right of 1) to Savannah VORTAC (below 3 on Fig. 24). Since compass roses are based on magnetic courses, you can find that a straight line from Hampton Varnville Airport to Savannah VORTAC coincides the Savannah VORTAC compass rose at 003°. Since the route is south to (not north from) Savannah, compute the reciprocal direction as 183° magnetic (003° + 180°). To use the VOR properly when flying to a VOR station, the course you select with the OBS should be the reciprocal of the radial you will be tracking. If this is not done, reverse sensing occurs.
Answer (A) is incorrect because 003° would be the course north from, not south to, Savannah. Answer (C) is incorrect because 200° would be the course from Ridgeland Airport, not Hampton Varnville Airport, to Savannah VORTAC.

The sectional chart legend and Figures 21 through 27 appear on pages 251 through 258 in Chapter 9.

22.
3556. (Refer to figure 25 on page 256.) Determine the magnetic course from Airpark East Airport (area 1) to Winnsboro Airport (area 2). Magnetic variation is 6°30'E.

A—075°.
B—082°.
C—091°.

Answer (A) is correct (3556). *(PHAK Chap 8)*
To find the magnetic course from Airpark East Airport (lower left of chart) to Winnsboro Airport (right of 2 on Fig. 25), you must find true course and correct it for magnetic variation. Determine the true course by placing the straight edge of your plotter along the given route such that the grommet (center hole) is on a meridian (the north/south line with crosslines). True course of 82° is the number of degrees clockwise from true north. It is read on the protractor portion of your plotter at the intersection of the meridian. To convert this to a magnetic course, subtract the 6°30'E (or round up to 7°E) easterly variation and find that the magnetic course is 075°. Remember to subtract easterly variation and add westerly variation.
Answer (B) is incorrect because 082° is the true, not magnetic, course. Answer (C) is incorrect because you must subtract, not add, an easterly variation.

23.
3560. (Refer to figure 25 on page 256.) On what course should the VOR receiver (OBS) be set in order to navigate direct from Majors Airport (area 1) to Quitman VORTAC (area 2)?

A—101°.
B—108°.
C—281°.

Answer (A) is correct (3560). *(PHAK Chap 8)*
You are to find the radial to navigate direct from Majors Airport (less than 2 in. north and east of 1) to Quitman VORTAC (southeast of 2 on Fig. 25). A compass rose, based on magnetic course, exists around the Quitman VORTAC. A straight line from Majors Airport to Quitman VORTAC coincides with this compass rose at 281°. Since the route is east to (not west from) Quitman, compute the reciprocal direction as 101° magnetic (281° − 180°).
Answer (B) is incorrect because 108° is the true, not magnetic, course from Majors to Quitman VORTAC. A VORTAC always uses magnetic direction. Answer (C) is incorrect because 281° is the course west from, not east to, Quitman VORTAC.

11.6 Magnetic Heading

24.
3538. (Refer to figure 22 on page 253.) Determine the magnetic heading for a flight from Mercer County Regional Airport (area 3) to Minot International (area 1). The wind is from 330° at 25 knots, the true airspeed is 100 knots, and the magnetic variation is 10° east.

A—002°.
B—012°.
C—352°.

Answer (C) is correct (3538). *(PHAK Chap 8)*
On Fig. 22, begin by computing the true course (TC) from Mercer Co. Reg. (lower left corner) to Minot Int'l. (upper left center) by drawing a line between the two airports. Next, determine the TC by placing the grommet on the plotter at the intersection of the course line and a meridian (vertical line with cross-hatchings) and the top of the plotter aligned with the course line. Note the 012° TC on the edge of the protractor.
Next, subtract the 10° east magnetic variation from the TC to obtain a magnetic course (MC) of 002°. Since the wind is given true, subtract the 10° east magnetic variation to obtain a magnetic wind direction of 320° (330 − 10).
Now use the wind side of your computer to plot the wind direction and velocity. Place the magnetic wind direction of 320° on the inner scale on the true index. Mark 25 kt. up from the grommet with a pencil. Turn the inner scale to the magnetic course of 002°. Slide the grid up until the pencil mark lies over the line for true airspeed (TAS) of 100 kt. Correct for the 10° left wind angle by subtracting from the magnetic course of 002° to obtain a magnetic heading of 352°. This is intuitively correct because, given the magnetic course of 002° and a northwesterly wind, you must turn to the left (crab into the wind) to correct for it.
Answer (A) is incorrect because 002° is the magnetic course, not heading; i.e., you must still correct for wind drift. Answer (B) is incorrect because 012° is the true course, not magnetic heading.

The sectional chart legend and Figures 21 through 27 appear on pages 251 through 258 in Chapter 9.

25.
3546. (Refer to figure 23 on page 254.) What is the magnetic heading for a flight from Priest River Airport (area 1) to Shoshone County Airport (area 3)? The wind is from 030° at 12 knots and the true airspeed is 95 knots.

A—118°.
B—143°.
C—136°.

Answer (A) is correct (3546). (PHAK Chap 8)

On Fig. 23, begin by computing the true course from Priest River Airport (upper left corner) to Shoshone County Airport (just below 3) by laying a flight plotter between the two airports. The grommet should coincide with the meridian (vertical line with cross-hatchings). Note the 143° true course on the edge of the protractor.

Next, find the magnetic variation which is given by the dashed line marked 18°E, slanting in a northeasterly fashion just south of Carlin Bay private airport. Subtract the 18°E variation from TC to obtain a magnetic course of 125°. Since the wind is given true, reduce the true wind direction of 30° by the magnetic variation of 18°E to a magnetic wind direction of 12°.

Now use the wind side of your computer. Turning the inner circle to 12° under the true index, mark 12 kt. above the grommet. Set the magnetic course of 125° under the true index. Slide the grid so the pencil mark is on 95 kt. TAS. Note that the pencil mark is 7° left of the center line, requiring you to adjust the magnetic course to a 118° magnetic heading (125° − 7°). Subtract left, add right. That is, if you are on an easterly flight and the wind is from the north, you will want to correct to the left.

Answer (B) is incorrect because 143° is the true course, not the magnetic heading. Answer (C) is incorrect because 136° would be the magnetic heading if the wind was from 215° at 19 kt., not 030° at 12 kt.

26.
3547. (Refer to figure 23 on page 254.) Determine the magnetic heading for a flight from St. Maries Airport (area 4) to Priest River Airport (area 1). The wind is from 340° at 10 knots and the true airspeed is 90 knots.

A—327°.
B—320°.
C—345°.

Answer (A) is correct (3547). (PHAK Chap 8)

1. This flight is from St. Maries (just below 4) to Priest River (upper left corner) on Fig. 23.
2. TC is 346°.
3. MC = 346° − 18°E variation = 328°.
4. Wind magnetic = 340° − 18° = 322°.
5. Mark 10 kt. up when 322° under true index.
6. Put MC 328° under true index.
7. Slide grid so pencil mark is on 90 kt. TAS.
8. Note that the pencil mark is 1° left.
9. Subtract 1° from 328° MC for 327° MH.

Answer (B) is incorrect because 320° would be the magnetic heading if the wind was from 300° at 14 kt., not 340° at 10 kt. Answer (C) is incorrect because 345° is the approximate true course, not magnetic heading.

27.
3545. (Refer to figure 23 on page 254.) Determine the magnetic heading for a flight from Sandpoint Airport (area 1) to St. Maries Airport (area 4). The wind is from 215° at 25 knots and the true airspeed is 125 knots.

A—349°.
B—169°.
C—187°.

Answer (B) is correct (3545). (PHAK Chap 8)

1. This flight is from Sandpoint Airport (above 1), to St. Maries (below 4) on Fig. 23.
2. TC = 181°.
3. MC = 181° − 18°E variation = 163°.
4. Wind magnetic = 215° − 18°E variation = 197°.
5. Mark up 25 kt. with 197° under true index.
6. Put MC 163° under true index.
7. Slide grid so pencil mark is on 125 kt. TAS.
8. Note that the pencil mark is 6° right.
9. Add 6° to 163° MC for 169° MH.

Answer (A) is incorrect because 349° would be the magnetic heading for a flight from St. Maries Airport to Sandpoint Airport, not from Sandpoint to St. Maries, with the wind from 145°, not 215°, at 25 kt. Answer (C) is incorrect because 187° is the true heading, not the magnetic heading. Correction for 18° of easterly magnetic variation has not been applied.

The sectional chart legend and Figures 21 through 27 appear on pages 251 through 258 in Chapter 9.

28.
3565. (Refer to figure 26 on page 257.) Determine the magnetic heading for a flight from Fort Worth Meacham (area 4) to Denton Muni (area 1). The wind is from 330° at 25 knots, the true airspeed is 110 knots, and the magnetic variation is 7° east.

A—003°.
B—017°.
C—023°.

Answer (A) is correct (3565). *(PHAK Chap 8)*

1. The flight is from Fort Worth Meacham (southeast of 4) to Denton Muni (southwest of 1) on Fig. 26.
2. TC = 021°.
3. MC = 021° – 7°E variation = 014°.
4. Wind magnetic = 330° – 7°E variation = 323°.
5. Mark up 25 kt. with 323° under true index.
6. Put MC 014° under true index.
7. Slide grid so pencil mark is on 110 kt. TAS.
8. Note that the pencil mark is 11° left.
9. Subtract 11° from 014° MC for 003° MH.

    Answer (B) is incorrect because you must subtract (not add) an easterly variation. Answer (C) is incorrect because you must subtract (not add) a left wind correction.

29.
3550. (Refer to figure 24 on page 255.) Determine the heading for a flight from Allendale County Airport (area 1) to Claxton-Evans County Airport (area 2). The wind is from 090° at 16 knots and the true airspeed is 90 knots.

A—230°.
B—212°.
C—208°.

Answer (C) is correct (3550). *(PHAK Chap 8)*

1. This flight is from Allendale County (above 1) to Claxton-Evans County Airport (left of 2) on Fig. 24.
2. TC = 212°.
3. MC = 212° TC + 5°W variation = 217°.
4. Wind magnetic = 090° + 5°W variation = 095°.
5. Mark up 16 kt. with 095° under true index.
6. Place MC 217° under true index.
7. Move wind mark to 90 kt. TAS arc.
8. Note the pencil mark is 9° left.
9. Subtract 9° from 217° for 208° MH.

    Answer (A) is incorrect because 230° would be the approximate magnetic heading if the wind was out of 330° at 23 kt., not 090° at 16 kt. Answer (B) is incorrect because 212° is the true heading, not the magnetic heading.

11.7 Compass Heading

30.
3551. (Refer to figure 24 on page 255 and figure 59 on page 300.) Determine the compass heading for a flight from Claxton-Evans County Airport (area 2) to Hampton Varnville Airport (area 1). The wind is from 280° at 8 knots, and the true airspeed is 85 knots.

A—033°.
B—042°.
C—038°.

Answer (B) is correct (3551). *(PHAK Chap 8)*

1. This flight is from Claxton-Evans (left of 2) to Hampton Varnville (right of 1) on Fig. 24.
2. TC = 045°.
3. MC = 045° TC + 5°W variation = 050°.
4. Wind magnetic = 280° + 5°W variation = 285°.
5. Mark up 8 kt. with 285° under true index.
6. Place MC 050° under true index.
7. Move wind mark to 85 kt. TAS arc.
8. Note the pencil mark is 5° left.
9. Subtract 5° from 050° MC for 045° MH.
10. Subtract 3° compass variation (obtained from Fig. 59) from 045° to find the compass heading of 042°.

    Answer (A) is incorrect because 033° would be the approximate compass heading if the wind was out of 295° at 22 kt., not 280° at 8 kt. Answer (C) is incorrect because 038° would be the approximate compass heading if the wind was out of 295° at 12 kt.

The sectional chart legend and Figures 21 through 27 appear on pages 251 through 258 in Chapter 9.

11.8 Time En Route

31.
3529. (Refer to figure 21 on page 252.) En route to First Flight Airport (area 5), your flight passes over Hampton Roads Airport (area 2) at 1456 and then over Chesapeake Municipal at 1501. At what time should your flight arrive at First Flight?

A—1516.
B—1521.
C—1526.

Answer (C) is correct (3529). (PHAK Chap 8)
The distance between Hampton Roads Airport (about 2 in. north of 2) and Chesapeake Municipal (northeast of 2 on Fig. 21) is 10 NM. It took 5 min. (1501 – 1456) to go 10 NM, so the airplane is traveling at 2 NM per minute. The distance from Chesapeake Municipal to First Flight (right of 5) is 50 NM. At 2 NM per minute, it will take 25 min. 25 min. added to the time you passed Chesapeake Municipal (1501) is 1526.
Note: There is a discrepancy between this question and the figure. "Chesapeake Municipal" is labeled "Chesapeake Regional" on the chart.
Answer (A) is incorrect because at 2 NM per min., it will take 25 min., not 15 min, to reach first flight.
Answer (B) is incorrect because the 25 min. must be added to 1501, not 1456.

32.
3534. (Refer to figure 22 on page 253.) What is the estimated time en route from Mercer County Regional Airport (area 3) to Minot International (area 1)? The wind is from 330° at 25 knots and the true airspeed is 100 knots. Add 3-1/2 minutes for departure and climb-out.

A—44 minutes.
B—48 minutes.
C—52 minutes.

Answer (B) is correct (3534). (PHAK Chap 8)
The requirement is time en route and not magnetic heading, so there is no need to convert TC to MC.
Using Fig. 22, the time en route from Mercer Co. Reg. Airport (lower left corner) to Minot (right of 1) is determined by measuring the distance (60 NM measured with a plotter), determining the time based on ground-speed, and adding 3.5 min. for takeoff and climb. The TC is 012° as measured with a plotter. The wind is from 330° at 25 kt.
On the wind side of your flight computer, place the wind direction 330° under the true index and mark 25 kt. up. Rotate TC of 012° under the true index. Slide the grid so the pencil mark is on the arc for TAS of 100 kt. Read 80 kt. groundspeed under the grommet.
Turn to the calculator side and place the groundspeed of 80 kt. on the outer scale over 60 min. Find 60 NM on outer scale and note 45 min. on the inner scale. Add 3.5 min. to 45 min. for climb for en route time of approximately 48 min.
Answer (A) is incorrect because you must add 3.5 min. for departure and climbout. Answer (C) is incorrect because the time en route is 48 min. (not 52 min.).

The sectional chart legend and Figures 21 through 27 appear on pages 251 through 258 in Chapter 9.

33.
3541. (Refer to figure 23 on page 254.) Determine the estimated time en route for a flight from Priest River Airport (area 1) to Shoshone County Airport (area 3). The wind is from 030 at 12 knots and the true airspeed is 95 knots. Add 2 minutes for climb-out.

A — 29 minutes.
B — 27 minutes.
C — 31 minutes.

Answer (C) is correct (3541). *(PHAK Chap 8)*
The requirement is time en route and not magnetic heading, so there is no need to convert TC to MC.

1. To find the en route time from Priest River (upper left corner) to Shoshone County (southwest of 3), use Fig. 23.
2. Measure the distance with plotter to be 49 NM.
3. TC = 143°.
4. Mark up 12 kt. with 030° under true index.
5. Put TC of 143° under true index.
6. Slide the grid so the pencil mark is on TAS of 95 kt.
7. Read the groundspeed of 99 kt. under the grommet.
8. On the calculator side, place 99 kt. on the outer scale over 60 min.
9. Read 29-1/2 min. on the inner scale below 49 NM on the outer scale.
10. Add 2 min. for climb-out and the en route time is approximately 31 min.

Answer (A) is incorrect because 29 minutes would be the approximate time en route if you forgot to add 2 min. for climb-out. Answer (B) is incorrect because you must add, not subtract, the 2 min. for climb-out.

34.
3540. (Refer to figure 23 on page 254.) What is the estimated time en route from Sandpoint Airport (area 1) to St. Maries Airport (area 4)? The wind is from 215° at 25 knots, and the true airspeed is 125 knots.

A — 38 minutes.
B — 30 minutes.
C — 34 minutes.

Answer (C) is correct (3540). *(PHAK Chap 8)*
The requirement is time en route and not magnetic heading, so there is no need to convert TC to MC.

1. You are to find the time en route from Sandpoint Airport (north of 1) to St. Maries Airport (southeast of 4) on Fig. 23.
2. Measure the distance with plotter to be 59 NM.
3. TC = 181°.
4. Mark up 25 kt. with 215° under true index.
5. Put TC of 181° under true index.
6. Slide the grid so pencil mark is on TAS of 125 kt.
7. Read groundspeed of 104 kt. under the grommet.
8. On the calculator side, place 104 kt. on the outer scale over 60 min.
9. Find 59 NM on the outer scale and read 34 min. on the inner scale.

Answer (A) is incorrect because to make the trip in 38 min. would require a groundspeed of 93 kt., not 104 kt. Answer (B) is incorrect because to make the trip in 30 min. would require a groundspeed of 118 kt., not 104 kt.

The sectional chart legend and Figures 21 through 27 appear on pages 251 through 258 in Chapter 9.

35.
3542. (Refer to figure 23 on page 254.) What is the estimated time en route for a flight from St. Maries Airport (area 4) to Priest River Airport (area 1)? The wind is from 300° at 14 knots and the true airspeed is 90 knots. Add 3 minutes for climb-out.

A—38 minutes.
B—43 minutes.
C—48 minutes.

Answer (B) is correct (3542). *(PHAK Chap 8)*
The requirement is time en route and not magnetic heading, so there is no need to convert TC to MC.

1. Time en route from St. Maries Airport (southeast of 4) to Priest River Airport (upper left corner) on Fig. 23.
2. Measure the distance with plotter to be 54 NM.
3. TC = 346°.
4. Mark up 14 kt. with 300° under true index.
5. Put TC of 346° under true index.
6. Slide the grid so pencil mark is on TAS of 90 kt.
7. Read groundspeed of 80 kt. under the grommet.
8. On the calculator side, place 80 kt. on the outer scale over 60 min.
9. Find 54 NM on the outer scale and read 40 min. on the inner scale.
10. Add 3 min. for climb-out to get time en route of 43 min.

Answer (A) is incorrect because to make the trip in 38 min. would require a groundspeed of 92 kt. (not 80 kt.). Answer (C) is incorrect because to make the trip in 48 min. would require a groundspeed of 72 kt. (not 80 kt.).

36.
3554. (Refer to figure 24 on page 255.) While en route on Victor 185, a flight crosses the 248° radial of Allendale VOR at 0953 and then crosses the 216° radial of Allendale VOR at 1000. What is the estimated time of arrival at Savannah VORTAC?

A—1023.
B—1028.
C—1036.

Answer (B) is correct (3554). *(PHAK Chap 8)*
The first step is to find the three points involved. V185 runs southeast from the top left of Fig. 24. The first intersection (V70 and V185) is about 1 in. from the top of the chart. The second intersection (V157 and V185) is about 1½ in. farther along V185. The Savannah VORTAC is about 6 in. farther down V185.

Use the sectional scale 1:500,000. From the first intersection (V70 and V185), it is about 10 NM to the intersection of V185 and V157. From there it is 40 NM to Savannah VORTAC.

On your flight computer, place the 7 min. the first leg took (1000 − 0953) on the inner scale under 10 NM on the outer scale. Then find 40 NM on the outer scale. Read 28 min. on the inner scale, which is the time en route from the V185 and V157 intersection to the Savannah VORTAC. Arrival time over Savannah VORTAC is therefore 1028.

Answer (A) is incorrect because you must add 28 min. to 1000 to obtain the correct ETA of 1028. Answer (C) is incorrect because you must add 28 min. to 1000 to obtain the correct ETA of 1028.

The sectional chart legend and Figures 21 through 27 appear on pages 251 through 258 in Chapter 9.

37.
3549. (Refer to figure 24 on page 255.) What is the estimated time en route for a flight from Claxton-Evans County Airport (area 2) to Hampton Varnville Airport (area 1)? The wind is from 290° at 18 knots and the true airspeed is 85 knots. Add 2 minutes for climb-out.

A—35 minutes.
B—39 minutes.
C—44 minutes.

Answer (B) is correct (3549). *(PHAK Chap 8)*
The distance en route from Claxton-Evans (southwest of 2) to Hampton Varnville (east of 1 on Fig. 24) is approximately 57 NM. Also use your plotter to determine that the TC is 45°. The requirement is time en route and not magnetic heading, so there is no need to convert TC to MC.

Using the wind side of your computer, turn your true index to the wind direction of 290° and mark 18 kt. above the grommet with your pencil. Then turn the inner scale so that the true index is above the TC of 45°. Place the pencil mark on the TAS of 85 kt. and note the ground-speed of 91 kt. Turn your flight computer over and set the speed of 91 kt. above the 60-min. index on the inner scale. Then find the distance of 57 NM on the outer scale to determine a time en route of 37 min. Add 2 min. for climb-out, and the en route time is 39 min.

Answer (A) is incorrect because you must add (not subtract) 2 min. for climb-out to the time en route. Answer (C) is incorrect because the groundspeed is 91 kt. (not 81 kt.).

38.
3548. (Refer to figure 24 on page 255.) What is the estimated time en route for a flight from Allendale County Airport (area 1) to Claxton-Evans County Airport (area 2)? The wind is from 100° at 18 knots and the true airspeed is 115 knots. Add 2 minutes for climb-out.

A—33 minutes.
B—27 minutes.
C—30 minutes.

Answer (C) is correct (3548). *(PHAK Chap 8)*
The requirement is time en route and not magnetic heading, so there is no need to convert TC to MC.

1. To find the en route time from Allendale County (northeast of 1) to Claxton-Evans (southeast of 2), use Fig. 24.
2. Measure the distance with plotter to be 55 NM.
3. TC = 212°.
4. Mark up 18 kt. with 100° under true index.
5. Put TC of 212° under true index.
6. Slide the grid so the pencil mark is on TAS of 115 kt.
7. Read groundspeed of 120 kt. under the grommet.
8. On the calculator side, place 120 kt. on the outer scale over 60 min.
9. Read 28 min. on the inner scale below 55 NM on the outer scale.
10. Add 2 min. for climb-out and the en route time is 30 min.

Answer (A) is incorrect because the groundspeed is 120 kt., not 105 kt. Answer (B) is incorrect because the groundspeed is 120 kt., not 130 kt.

The sectional chart legend and Figures 21 through 27 appear on pages 251 through 258 in Chapter 9.

39.
3562. (Refer to figure 26 on page 257.) What is the estimated time en route for a flight from Denton Muni (area 1) to Addison (area 2)? The wind is from 200° at 20 knots, the true airspeed is 110 knots, and the magnetic variation is 7° east.

A—13 minutes.
B—16 minutes.
C—19 minutes.

Answer (A) is correct (3562). *(PHAK Chap 8)*
The requirement is time en route and not magnetic heading, so there is no need to convert TC to MC.

1. To find the en route time from Denton Muni (southwest of 1) to Addison (southwest of 2), use Fig. 26.
2. Measure the distance with plotter to be 23 NM.
3. TC = 128°.
4. Mark up 20 kt. with 200° under true index.
5. Put TC of 128° under true index.
6. Slide the grid so the pencil mark is on TAS of 110 kt.
7. Read groundspeed of 102 kt. under the grommet.
8. On the calculator side, place 102 kt. on the outer scale over 60 min.
9. Read 13 min. on the inner scale below 23 NM on the outer scale.

Answer (B) is incorrect because the groundspeed is 102 kt. (not 86 kt.). Answer (C) is incorrect because the groundspeed is 102 kt. (not 73 kt.).

40.
3563. (Refer to figure 26 on page 257.) Estimate the time en route from Addison (area 2) to Redbird (area 3). The wind is from 300° at 15 knots, the true airspeed is 120 knots, and the magnetic variation is 7° east.

A—8 minutes.
B—11 minutes.
C—14 minutes.

Answer (A) is correct (3563). *(PHAK Chap 8)*
The requirement is time en route and not magnetic heading, so there is no need to convert TC to MC.

1. To find the en route time from Addison (southwest of 2) to Redbird (above 3), use Fig. 26.
2. Measure the distance with plotter to be 18 NM.
3. TC = 186°.
4. Mark up 15 kt. with 300° under true index.
5. Put TC of 186° under true index.
6. Slide the grid so the pencil mark is on TAS of 120 kt.
7. Read groundspeed of 125 kt. under the grommet.
8. On the calculator side, place 125 kt. on the outer scale over 60 min.
9. Read 8.5 min. on the inner scale below 18 NM on the outer scale.

Answer (B) is incorrect because the groundspeed is 125 kt. (not 98 kt.). Answer (C) is incorrect because the groundspeed is 125 kt. (not 77 kt.).

11.9 Time Zone Corrections

41.
3571. (Refer to figure 28 on page 299.) An aircraft departs an airport in the eastern daylight time zone at 0945 EDT for a 2-hour flight to an airport located in the central daylight time zone. The landing should be at what coordinated universal time?

A—1345Z.
B—1445Z.
C—1545Z.

Answer (C) is correct (3571). *(Figure 28)*
First convert the departure time to coordinated universal time (Z) by using the time conversion table in Fig. 28. To convert from eastern daylight time (EDT), add 4 hr. to get 1345Z (0945 + 4 hr). A 2-hr. flight would have you arriving at your destination airport at 1545Z.

Answer (A) is incorrect because 1345Z (0945 EDT) is the departure time. Answer (B) is incorrect because you would arrive at an airport at 1445Z if the flight were 1 (not 2) hr.

42.
3572. (Refer to figure 28 on page 299.) An aircraft departs an airport in the central standard time zone at 0930 CST for a 2-hour flight to an airport located in the mountain standard time zone. The landing should be at what time?

A—0930 MST.
B—1030 MST.
C—1130 MST.

Answer (B) is correct (3572). *(Figure 28)*
Flying from the Central Standard Time Zone to the Mountain Standard Time Zone results in a 1-hr. gain due to time zone changes. A 2-hr. flight leaving at 0930 CST will arrive in the Mountain Standard Time Zone at 1130 CST, which is 1030 MST.

Answer (A) is incorrect because the aircraft departed at 0930 CST (not MST). Answer (C) is incorrect because a landing at 1130 MST would be correct for a 3-hr. (not 2-hr.) flight departing from the CST zone at 0930 CST to the MST zone.

43.

3573. (Refer to figure 28 below.) An aircraft departs an airport in the central standard time zone at 0845 CST for a 2-hour flight to an airport located in the mountain standard time zone. The landing should be at what coordinated universal time?

A—1345Z.
B—1445Z.
C—1645Z.

44.

3574. (Refer to figure 28 below.) An aircraft departs an airport in the mountain standard time zone at 1615 MST for a 2-hour 15-minute flight to an airport located in the Pacific standard time zone. The estimated time of arrival at the destination airport should be

A—1630 PST.
B—1730 PST.
C—1830 PST.

Answer (C) is correct (3573). *(Figure 28)*
First convert the departure time to coordinated universal time (Z) by using the time conversion table in Fig. 28. To convert from CST to Z, you must add 6 hr., thus 0845 CST is 1445Z (0845 + 6 hr.). A 2-hr. flight would make the estimated landing time at 1645Z (1445 + 2 hr.).
Answer (A) is incorrect because 1345Z is the departure time at 0845 CDT, not CST. Answer (B) is incorrect because 1445Z is the departure (not landing) time.

Answer (B) is correct (3574). *(Figure 28)*
Departing the Mountain Standard Time Zone at 1615 MST for a 2-hr. 15-min. flight would result in arrival in the Pacific Standard Time Zone at 1830 MST. Because there is a 1-hr. difference between Mountain Standard Time and Pacific Standard Time, 1 hr. must be subtracted from the 1830 MST arrival to determine the 1730 PST arrival.
Answer (A) is incorrect because an arrival time of 1630 PST would be for a 1-hr. 15-min. (not a 2-hr. 15-min.) flight. Answer (C) is incorrect because 1830 MST (not PST) is the estimated time of arrival at the destination airport.

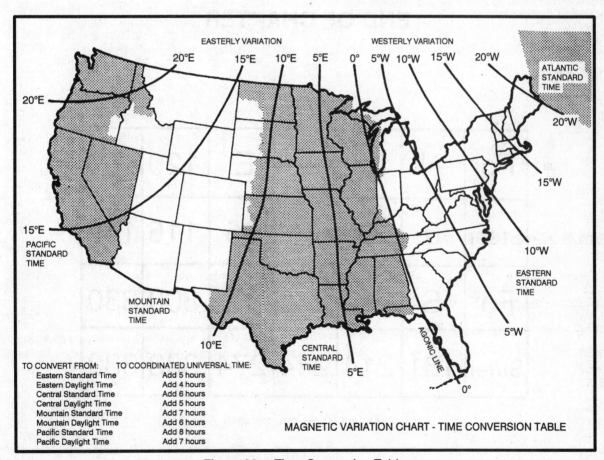

Figure 28.—Time Conversion Table.

45.
3575. (Refer to figure 28 on page 299.) An aircraft departs an airport in the Pacific standard time zone at 1030 PST for a 4-hour flight to an airport located in the central standard time zone. The landing should be at what coordinated universal time?

A—2030Z.
B—2130Z.
C—2230Z.

Answer (C) is correct (3575). *(Figure 28)*
    First, convert the departure time to coordinated universal time (Z) by using the time conversion table in Fig. 28. To convert from PST to Z, you must add 8 hr., thus 1030 PST is 1830Z (1030 + 8 hr.). A 4-hr. flight would make the proposed landing time at 2230Z (1830 + 4 hr.).
    Answer (A) is incorrect because 2030Z is for a flight of 2 (not 4) hr. Answer (B) is incorrect because 2130 is the proposed landing time if the departure time was 1030 PDT, not PST.

46.
3576. (Refer to figure 28 on page 299.) An aircraft departs an airport in the mountain standard time zone at 1515 MST for a 2-hour 30-minute flight to an airport located in the Pacific standard time zone. What is the estimated time of arrival at the destination airport?

A—1645 PST.
B—1745 PST.
C—1845 PST.

Answer (A) is correct (3576). *(Figure 28)*
    Departing the Mountain Standard Time (MST) Zone at 1515 MST for a 2-hr. 30-min. flight would result in arrival in the Pacific Standard Time (PST) Zone at 1745 MST. Because there is a 1-hr. difference between MST and PST, 1 hr. must be subtracted from the 1745 MST arrival to determine the 1645 PST estimated time of arrival at the destination airport.
    Answer (B) is incorrect because the estimated time of arrival at the destination airport is 1745 MST, not PST. Answer (C) is incorrect because 1845 PST would be the estimated arrival time for a 3-hr. 30-min. (not 2-hr. 30-min.) flight from the MST zone.

END OF CHAPTER

For	N	30	60	E	120	150
Steer	0	27	56	85	116	148
For	S	210	240	W	300	330
Steer	181	214	244	274	303	332

FIGURE 59.—Compass card.

APPENDIX A
PRIVATE PILOT PRACTICE TEST

The following 60 questions have been randomly selected from the 736 airplane questions in the FAA's private pilot test bank. You will be referred to figures (charts, tables, etc.) throughout this book. Be careful not to consult the answers or answer explanations when you look for and at the figures. Topical coverage in this practice test is similar to that of the FAA pilot knowledge test. Use the correct answer listing on page 306 to grade your practice test.

NOTE: Our *FAA Test Prep* software provides you with unlimited study and test sessions for your personal use. See the discussion on pages 14 through 19 in the Introduction of this book.

1.
3001. With respect to the certification of airmen, which is a category of aircraft?

A—Gyroplane, helicopter, airship, free balloon.
B—Airplane, rotorcraft, glider, lighter-than-air.
C—Single-engine land and sea, multiengine land and sea.

2.
3017. When must a current pilot certificate be in the pilot's personal possession or readily accessible in the aircraft?

A—When acting as a crew chief during launch and recovery.
B—Only when passengers are carried.
C—Anytime when acting as pilot in command or as a required crewmember.

3.
3033. The three takeoffs and landings that are required to act as pilot in command at night must be done during the time period from

A—sunset to sunrise.
B—1 hour after sunset to 1 hour before sunrise.
C—the end of evening civil twilight to the beginning of morning civil twilight.

4.
3064. In regard to privileges and limitations, a private pilot may

A—act as pilot in command of an aircraft carrying a passenger for compensation if the flight is in connection with a business or employment.
B—not pay less than the pro rata share of the operating expenses of a flight with passengers provided the expenses involve only fuel, oil, airport expenditures, or rental fees.
C—not be paid in any manner for the operating expenses of a flight.

5.
3078. Under what condition, if any, may a pilot allow a person who is obviously under the influence of drugs to be carried aboard an aircraft?

A—In an emergency or if the person is a medical patient under proper care.
B—Only if the person does not have access to the cockpit or pilot's compartment.
C—Under no condition.

6.
3092. An airplane and an airship are converging. If the airship is left of the airplane's position, which aircraft has the right-of-way?

A—The airship.
B—The airplane.
C—Each pilot should alter course to the right.

7.
3106. Prior to takeoff, the altimeter should be set to which altitude or altimeter setting?

A—The current local altimeter setting, if available, or the departure airport elevation.
B—The corrected density altitude of the departure airport.
C—The corrected pressure altitude for the departure airport.

8.
3120. Each pilot of an aircraft approaching to land on a runway served by a visual approach slope indicator (VASI) shall

A—maintain a 3° glide to the runway.
B—maintain an altitude at or above the glide slope.
C—stay high until the runway can be reached in a power-off landing.

9.
3136. During operations within controlled airspace at altitudes of less than 1,200 feet AGL, the minimum horizontal distance from clouds requirement for VFR flight is

A—1,000 feet.
B—1,500 feet.
C—2,000 feet.

10.
3164. Unless each occupant is provided with supplemental oxygen, no person may operate a civil aircraft of U.S. registry above a maximum cabin pressure altitude of

A—12,500 feet MSL.
B—14,000 feet MSL.
C—15,000 feet MSL.

11.
3190. A 100-hour inspection was due at 3302.5 hours. The 100-hour inspection was actually done at 3309.5 hours. When is the next 100-hour inspection due?

A—3312.5 hours.
B—3402.5 hours.
C—3409.5 hours.

12.
3197. Which incident requires an immediate notification be made to the nearest NTSB field office?

A—An overdue aircraft that is believed to be involved in an accident.
B—An in-flight radio communications failure.
C—An in-flight generator or alternator failure.

13.
3202. When are the four forces that act on an airplane in equilibrium?

A—During unaccelerated flight.
B—When the aircraft is accelerating.
C—When the aircraft is at rest on the ground.

14.
3211. What determines the longitudinal stability of an airplane?

A—The location of the CG with respect to the center of lift.
B—The effectiveness of the horizontal stabilizer, rudder, and rudder trim tab.
C—The relationship of thrust and lift to weight and drag.

15.
3220. What is one purpose of wing flaps?

A—To enable the pilot to make steeper approaches to a landing without increasing the airspeed.
B—To relieve the pilot of maintaining continuous pressure on the controls.
C—To decrease wing area to vary the lift.

16.
3229. Which condition is most favorable to the development of carburetor icing?

A—Any temperature below freezing and a relative humidity of less than 50 percent.
B—Temperature between 32 and 50 °F and low humidity.
C—Temperature between 20 and 70 °F and high humidity.

17.
3238. Detonation occurs in a reciprocating aircraft engine when

A—the spark plugs are fouled or shorted out or the wiring is defective.
B—hot spots in the combustion chamber ignite the fuel/air mixture in advance of normal ignition.
C—the unburned charge in the cylinders explodes instead of burning normally.

18.
3247. If the pitot tube and outside static vents become clogged, which instruments would be affected?

A—The altimeter, airspeed indicator, and turn-and-slip indicator.
B—The altimeter, airspeed indicator, and vertical speed indicator.
C—The altimeter, attitude indicator, and turn-and-slip indicator.

19.
3256. What is true altitude?

A—The vertical distance of the aircraft above sea level.
B—The vertical distance of the aircraft above the surface.
C—The height above the standard datum plane.

20.
3265. (Refer to figure 4 on page 42.) What is the full flap operating range for the airplane?

A—60 to 100 MPH.
B—60 to 208 MPH.
C—65 to 165 MPH.

21.
3274. What is an important airspeed limitation that is not color coded on airspeed indicators?

A— Never-exceed speed.
B— Maximum structural cruising speed.
C— Maneuvering speed.

22.
3283. In the Northern Hemisphere, the magnetic compass will normally indicate a turn toward the south when

A— a left turn is entered from an east heading.
B— a right turn is entered from a west heading.
C— the aircraft is decelerated while on a west heading.

23.
3292. (Refer to figure 8 on page 152.) What is the effect of a temperature increase from 25 to 50 °F on the density altitude if the pressure altitude remains at 5,000 feet?

A— 1,200-foot increase.
B— 1,400-foot increase.
C— 1,650-foot increase.

24.
3307. (Refer to figure 9, area C, on page 288.) How should the flight controls be held while taxiing a tailwheel airplane with a left quartering tailwind?

A— Left aileron up, elevator neutral.
B— Left aileron down, elevator neutral.
C— Left aileron down, elevator down.

25.
3381. Every physical process of weather is accompanied by, or is the result of, a

A— movement of air.
B— pressure differential.
C— heat exchange.

26.
3393. Which condition would cause the altimeter to indicate a lower altitude than true altitude?

A— Air temperature lower than standard.
B— Atmospheric pressure lower than standard.
C— Air temperature warmer than standard.

27.
3402. The presence of ice pellets at the surface is evidence that there

A— are thunderstorms in the area.
B— has been cold frontal passage.
C— is a temperature inversion with freezing rain at a higher altitude.

28.
3414. A stable air mass is most likely to have which characteristic?

A— Showery precipitation.
B— Turbulent air.
C— Smooth air.

29.
3426. Where does wind shear occur?

A— Only at higher altitudes.
B— Only at lower altitudes.
C— At all altitudes, in all directions.

30.
3438. Thunderstorms reach their greatest intensity during the

A— mature stage.
B— downdraft stage.
C— cumulus stage.

31.
3450. Convective circulation patterns associated with sea breezes are caused by

A— warm, dense air moving inland from over the water.
B— water absorbing and radiating heat faster than the land.
C— cool, dense air moving inland from over the water.

32.
3462. (Refer to figure 12 on page 210.) Which of the reporting stations have VFR weather?

A— All.
B— KINK, KBOI, and KJFK.
C— KINK, KBOI, and KLAX.

33.
3474. (Refer to figure 14 on page 212.) If the terrain elevation is 1,295 feet MSL, what is the height above ground level of the base of the ceiling?

A— 505 feet AGL.
B— 1,295 feet AGL.
C— 6,586 feet AGL.

34.
3486. (Refer to figure 15 on page 217.) The only cloud type forecast in TAF reports is

A— Nimbostratus.
B— Cumulonimbus.
C— Scattered cumulus.

35.
3498. Which in-flight advisory would contain information on severe icing not associated with thunderstorms?

A—Convective SIGMET.
B—SIGMET.
C—AIRMET.

36.
3514. What information is provided by the Radar Summary Chart that is not shown on other weather charts?

A—Lines and cells of hazardous thunderstorms.
B—Ceilings and precipitation between reporting stations.
C—Types of clouds between reporting stations.

37.
3530. (Refer to figure 21, area 3, on page 252.) Determine the approximate latitude and longitude of Currituck County Airport.

A—36°24′N – 76°01′W.
B—36°48′N – 76°01′W.
C—47°24′N – 75°58′W.

38.
3556. (Refer to figure 25 on page 256.) Determine the magnetic course from Airpark East Airport (area 1) to Winnsboro Airport (area 2). Magnetic variation is 6°30′E.

A—075°.
B—082°.
C—091°.

39.
3549. (Refer to figure 24 on page 255.) What is the estimated time en route for a flight from Claxton-Evans County Airport (area 2) to Hampton Varnville Airport (area 1)? The wind is from 290° at 18 knots and the true airspeed is 85 knots. Add 2 minutes for climb-out.

A—35 minutes.
B—39 minutes.
C—44 minutes.

40.
3559. (Refer to figure 25 on page 256.) What is the approximate position of the aircraft if the VOR receivers indicate the 245° radial of Sulphur Springs VOR-DME (area 5) and the 140° radial of Bonham VORTAC (area 3)?

A—Glenmar Airport.
B—Meadowview Airport.
C—Majors Airport.

41.
3565. (Refer to figure 26 on page 257.) Determine the magnetic heading for a flight from Fort Worth Meacham (area 4) to Denton Muni (area 1). The wind is from 330° at 25 knots, the true airspeed is 110 knots, and the magnetic variation is 7° east.

A—003°.
B—017°.
C—023°.

42.
3578. (Refer to figure 29, illustration 3, on page 272.) The VOR receiver has the indications shown. What is the aircraft's position relative to the station?

A—East.
B—Southeast.
C—West.

43.
3589. (Refer to figure 31, illustration 1, on page 276.) The relative bearing TO the station is

A—045°.
B—180°.
C—315°.

44.
3600. (Refer to figure 26, area 2, on page 257.) The floor of Class B airspace at Addison Airport is

A—at the surface.
B—3,000 feet MSL.
C—3,100 feet MSL.

45.
3610. (Refer to figure 27, area 2, on page 258.) What is the recommended communication procedure when inbound to land at Cooperstown Airport?

A—Broadcast intentions when 10 miles out on the CTAF/MULTICOM frequency, 122.9 MHz.
B—Contact UNICOM when 10 miles out on 122.8 MHz.
C—Circle the airport in a left turn prior to entering traffic.

46.
3625. (Refer to figure 26, area 4, on page 257.) The airspace directly overlying Fort Worth Meacham is

A—Class B airspace to 10,000 feet MSL.
B—Class C airspace to 5,000 feet MSL.
C—Class D airspace to 3,200 feet MSL.

47.
3637. (Refer to figure 24, area 3, on page 255.) What is the height of the lighted obstacle approximately 6 nautical miles southwest of Savannah International?

A—1,500 feet MSL.
B—1,531 feet AGL.
C—1,549 feet MSL.

48.
3641. (Refer to figure 26, area 2, on page 257.) The control tower frequency for Addison Airport is

A — 122.95 MHz.
B — 126.0 MHz.
C — 133.4 MHz.

49.
3651. What action can a pilot take to aid in cooling an engine that is overheating during a climb?

A — Reduce rate of climb and increase airspeed.
B — Reduce climb speed and increase RPM.
C — Increase climb speed and increase RPM.

50.
3663. If an aircraft is loaded 90 pounds over maximum certificated gross weight and fuel (gasoline) is drained to bring the aircraft weight within limits, how much fuel should be drained?

A — 10 gallons.
B — 12 gallons.
C — 15 gallons.

51.
3675. (Refer to figures 33 and 34 on pages 172 and 173.) Which action can adjust the airplane's weight to maximum gross weight and the CG within limits for takeoff?

Front seat occupants . . . . 425 lb
Rear seat occupants . . . . 300 lb
Fuel, main tanks . . . . 44 gal

A — Drain 12 gallons of fuel.
B — Drain 9 gallons of fuel.
C — Transfer 12 gallons of fuel from the main tanks to the auxiliary tanks.

52.
3687. (Refer to figure 37 on page 160.) With a reported wind of south at 20 knots, which runway (10, 14, or 24) is appropriate for an airplane with a 13-knot maximum crosswind component?

A — Runway 10.
B — Runway 14.
C — Runway 24.

53.
3705. (Refer to figure 41 on page 156.) Determine the total distance required for takeoff to clear a 50-foot obstacle.

OAT . . . . Std
Pressure altitude . . . . 4,000 ft
Takeoff weight . . . . 2,800 lb
Headwind component . . . . Calm

A — 1,500 feet
B — 1,750 feet.
C — 2,000 feet.

54.
3710. Prior to starting each maneuver, pilots should

A — check altitude, airspeed, and heading indications.
B — visually scan the entire area for collision avoidance.
C — announce their intentions on the nearest CTAF.

55.
3715. During a night flight, you observe a steady red light and a flashing red light ahead and at the same altitude. What is the general direction of movement of the other aircraft?

A — The other aircraft is crossing to the left.
B — The other aircraft is crossing to the right.
C — The other aircraft is approaching head-on.

56.
3719. VFR approaches to land at night should be accomplished

A — at a higher airspeed.
B — with a steeper descent.
C — the same as during daytime.

57.
3765. (Refer to figure 48 on page 72.) Illustration A indicates that the aircraft is

A — below the glide slope.
B — on the glide slope.
C — above the glide slope.

58.
3789. Prior to entering an Airport Advisory Area, a pilot should

A — monitor ATIS for weather and traffic advisories.
B — contact approach control for vectors to the traffic pattern.
C — contact the local FSS for airport and traffic advisories.

59.
3813. What ATC facility should the pilot contact to receive a special VFR departure clearance in Class D airspace?

A — Automated Flight Service Station.
B — Air Traffic Control Tower.
C — Air Route Traffic Control Center.

60.
3844. Which statement best defines hypoxia?

A — A state of oxygen deficiency in the body.
B — An abnormal increase in the volume of air breathed.
C — A condition of gas bubble formation around the joints or muscles.

PRACTICE TEST LIST OF ANSWERS

Listed below are the answers to the practice test. To the immediate right of each answer is the page number on which the question, as well as correct and incorrect answer explanations, can be found.

Q. #	Answer	Page	Q. #	Answer	Page	Q. #	Answer	Page	Q. #	Answer	Page
1.	B	101	16.	C	53	31.	C	188	46.	C	250
2.	C	105	17.	C	54	32.	C	211	47.	C	249
3.	B	110	18.	B	40	33.	A	212	48.	B	263
4.	B	111	19.	A	45	34.	B	217	49.	A	50
5.	A	119	20.	A	42	35.	B	228	50.	C	166
6.	A	121	21.	C	41	36.	A	222	51.	B	175
7.	A	125	22.	C	40	37.	A	244	52.	B	161
8.	B	72	23.	C	154	38.	A	291	53.	B	156
9.	C	131	24.	C	288	39.	B	297	54.	B	75
10.	C	135	25.	C	187	40.	A	271	55.	A	74
11.	B	139	26.	C	47	41.	A	293	56.	C	289
12.	A	142	27.	C	191	42.	B	273	57.	B	72
13.	A	25	28.	C	196	43.	C	277	58.	C	77
14.	A	29	29.	C	192	44.	B	250	59.	B	132
15.	A	25	30.	A	189	45.	A	261	60.	A	179

APPENDIX B
INTERPOLATION

The following tutorial appeared in the FAA's *Pilot Handbook of Aeronautical Knowledge*.

Interpolation is required in questions found in the following two modules:

Chapter 5 - Airplane Performance and Weight and Balance

Module 5.2, Density Altitude Computations (pages 145, 153)

Module 5.4, Cruise Power Settings (pages 146, 158)

A. To interpolate means to compute intermediate values between a series of given values.

1. In many instances when performance is critical, an accurate determination of the performance values is the only acceptable means to enhance safe flight.

2. Guessing to determine these values should be avoided.

B. Interpolation is simple to perform if the method is understood. The following are examples of how to interpolate or accurately determine the intermediate values between a series of given values.

C. The numbers in column A range from 10 to 30, and the numbers in column B range from 50 to 100. Determine the intermediate numerical value in column B that would correspond with an intermediate value of 20 placed in column A.

A	B
10	50
20	X = Unknown
30	100

1. It can be visualized that 20 is halfway between 10 and 30; therefore, the corresponding value of the unknown number in column B would be halfway between 50 and 100, or 75.

D. Many interpolation problems are more difficult to visualize than the preceding example; therefore, a systematic method must be used to determine the required intermediate value. The following describes one method that can be used.

1. The numbers in Column A range from 10 to 30 with intermediate values of 15, 20, and 25. Determine the intermediate numerical value in column B that would correspond with 15 in column A.

A	B
10	50
15	
20	
25	
30	100

2. First, in column A, determine the relationship of 15 to the range between 10 and 30 as follows:

$$\frac{15 - 10}{30 - 10} = \frac{5}{20} \; or \; 1/4$$

a. It should be noted that 15 is 1/4 of the range between 10 and 30.

3. Now determine 1/4 of the range of column B between 50 and 100 as follows:

$$100 - 50 = 50$$
$$1/4 \text{ of } 50 = 12.5$$

    a. The answer 12.5 represents the number of units, but to arrive at the correct value, 12.5 must be added to the lower number in column B as follows:

$$50 + 12.5 = 62.5$$

4. The interpolation has been completed, and 62.5 is the actual value which is 1/4 of the range of column B.

E. Another method of interpolation is shown below:

1. Using the same numbers as in the previous example, a proportion problem based on the relationship of the number can be set up.

$$\text{Proportion: } \frac{5}{20} = \frac{X}{50}$$
$$20X = 250$$
$$X = 12.5$$

    a. The answer 12.5 must be added to 50 to arrive at the actual value of 62.5.

F. The following example illustrates the use of interpolation applied to a problem dealing with one aspect of airplane performance:

Temperature (°F)	Takeoff Distance (ft)
70	1,173
80	1,356

1. If a distance of 1,173 feet is required for takeoff when the temperature is 70°F and 1,356 feet is required at 80°F, what distance is required when the temperature is 75°F? The solution to the problem can be determined as follows:

$$\frac{5}{10} = \frac{X}{183}$$
$$10X = 915$$
$$X = 91.5$$

    a. The answer 91.5 must be added to 1,173 to arrive at the actual value of 1,264.5 ft.

FAA LISTING OF
SUBJECT MATTER KNOWLEDGE CODES

The next three pages reprint the FAA's subject matter knowledge codes. These are the codes that will appear on your Airman Computer Test Report. See the illustration on page 11. Your test report will list the subject matter code of each question answered incorrectly.

When you receive your Airman Computer Test Report, you can trace the subject matter knowledge codes listed on it to the next three pages to find out which topics you had difficulty with. You should discuss your test results with your CFI.

Additionally, you should cross-reference the subject knowledge codes on your Airman Computer Test Report to our listing of FAA private pilot test question numbers beginning on page 313. Determine which Gleim study modules you need to review.

Please check the Gleim web site for any FAA changes to these codes at:

www.gleim.com/Aviation/Updates/smkc-600.html

DEPARTMENT OF TRANSPORTATION
FEDERAL AVIATION ADMINISTRATION

SUBJECT MATTER KNOWLEDGE CODES

To determine the knowledge area in which a particular question was incorrectly answered, compare the subject matter code(s) on your Airman Computer Test Report to the subject matter outline that follows. The total number of test items missed may differ from the number of subject matter codes shown on your test report because you may have missed more than one question in a certain subject matter area.

Title 14, Code of Federal Regulations (14 CFR)
PART 1—Definitions and Abbreviations

A01   General Definitions
A02   Abbreviations and Symbols

14 CFR PART 39—Airworthiness Directives

A13   General
A14   Airworthiness Directives

14 CFR PART 43—Maintenance, Preventive Maintenance, Rebuilding, and Alteration

A15   General
A16   Appendices

14 CFR PART 61—Certification: Pilots, Flight Instructors, and Ground Instructors

A20   General
A21   Aircraft Ratings and Pilot Authorizations
A22   Student Pilots
A23   Private Pilots
A24   Commercial Pilots
A25   Airline Transport Pilots
A26   Flight Instructors
A27   Ground Instructors
A29   Recreational Pilot

14 CFR PART 71—Designation of Class A, Class B, Class C, Class D, and Class E Airspace Areas; Airways; Routes; and Reporting Points

A60   General - Class A Airspace
A61   Class B Airspace
A64   Class C Airspace
A65   Class D Airspace
A66   Class E Airspace

14 CFR PART 91—General Operating and Flight Rules

B07   General
B08   Flight Rules - General
B09   Visual Flight Rules
B10   Instrument Flight Rules
B11   Equipment, Instrument, and Certificate Requirements
B12   Special Flight Operations
B13   Maintenance, Preventive Maintenance, and Alterations
B14   Large and Turbine-powered Multiengine Airplanes
B15   Additional Equipment and Operating Requirements for Large and Transport Category Aircraft
B16   Appendix A - Category II Operations: Manual, Instruments, Equipment, and Maintenance
B17   Foreign Aircraft Operations and Operations of U.S.-Registered Civil Aircraft Outside of the U.S.

NTSB 830—Rules Pertaining to the Notification and Reporting of Aircraft Accidents or Incidents and Overdue Aircraft, and Preservation of Aircraft Wreckage, Mail, Cargo, and Records

G10   General
G11   Initial Notification of Aircraft Accidents, Incidents, and Overdue Aircraft
G12   Preservation of Aircraft Wreckage, Mail, Cargo, and Records
G13   Reporting of Aircraft Accidents, Incidents, and Overdue Aircraft

AC 61-23—Pilot's Handbook of Aeronautical Knowledge

H300   Forces Acting on the Airplane in Flight
H301   Turning Tendency (Torque Effect)
H302   Airplane Stability
H303   Loads and Load Factors
H304   Airplane Structure
H305   Flight Control Systems
H306   Electrical System
H307   Engine Operation
H308   Propeller
H309   Starting the Engine
H310   Exhaust Gas Temperature Gauge
H311   Aircraft Documents, Maintenance, and Inspections
H312   The Pitot-Static System and Associated Instruments
H313   Gyroscopic Flight Instruments
H314   Magnetic Compass
H315   Weight Control
H316   Balance, Stability, and Center of Gravity
H317   Airplane Performance
H318   Observations
H319   Service Outlets
H320   Weather Briefings
H321   Nature of the Atmosphere
H322   The Cause of Atmospheric Circulation
H323   Moisture and Temperature
H324   Air Masses and Fronts
H325   Aviation Weather Reports, Forecasts, and Weather Charts
H326   Types of Airports
H327   Sources for Airport Data
H328   Airport Markings and Signs
H329   Airport Lighting
H330   Wind Direction Indicators
H331   Radio Communications

H332   Air Traffic Services
H333   Wake Turbulence
H334   Collision Avoidance
H335   Controlled Airspace
H336   Uncontrolled Airspace
H337   Special Use Airspace
H338   Other Airspace Areas
H339   Aeronautical Charts
H340   Latitude and Longitude
H341   Effect of Wind
H342   Basic Calculations
H343   Pilotage
H344   Dead Reckoning
H345   Flight Planning
H346   Charting the Course
H347   Filing a VFR Flight Plan
H348   Radio Navigation
H349   Obtaining a Medical Certificate
H350   Health Factors Affecting Pilot Performance
H351   Environmental Factors Which Affect Pilot Performance

FAA-H-8083—Airplane Flying Handbook

H501   Choosing a Flight School
H502   Instructor/Student Relationship
H503   Role of the FAA
H504   Flight Standards District Offices (FSDO's)
H505   Study Habits
H506   Study Materials
H507   Collision Avoidance
H509   Pilot Assessment
H510   Preflight Preparation and Flight Planning
H511   Airplane Preflight Inspection
H512   Minimum Equipment Lists (MEL's) and Operations with Inoperative Equipment
H513   Cockpit Management
H514   Use of Checklists
H515   Ground Operations
H516   Taxiing
H517   Taxi Clearances at Airports with an Operating Control Tower
H518   Before Takeoff Check
H519   After-landing
H520   Postflight
H522   Terms and Definitions
H523   Prior to Takeoff
H524   Normal Takeoff
H525   Crosswind Takeoff
H526   Short-field Takeoff and Climb
H527   Soft-field Takeoff and Climb
H528   Rejected Takeoff
H529   Noise Abatement
H531   Integrated Flight Instruction
H532   Attitude Flying
H533   Straight-and-level Flight
H534   Turns
H535   Climbs
H536   Descents
H538   Slow Flight
H539   Stalls
H540   Spins
H541   Spin Procedures
H542   Aircraft Limitations
H543   Weight and Balance Requirements
H545   Maneuvering by Reference to Ground Objects
H546   Performance Maneuvers
H548   Airport Traffic Patterns and Operations
H549   Normal Approach and Landing
H550   Crosswind Approach and Landing

H551	Short-field Approach and Landing
H552	Soft-field Approach and Landing
H553	Power-off Accuracy Approaches
H554	Faulty Approaches and Landings
H555	Final Approaches
H556	Roundout (Flare)
H557	Touchdown
H559	Basic Instrument Training
H560	Basic Instrument Flight
H561	Use of Navigation Systems
H562	Use of Radar Services
H564	Night Vision
H565	Night Illusions
H566	Pilot Equipment
H567	Airplane Equipment and Lighting
H568	Airport and Navigation Lighting Aids
H569	Preparation and Preflight
H570	Starting, Taxiing, and Runup
H571	Takeoff and Climb
H572	Orientation and Navigation
H573	Approaches and Landing
H574	Night Emergencies
H576	VOR Navigation
H577	VOR/DME RNAV
H578	LORAN-C Navigation
H579	Global Positioning System (GPS)
H580	Radar Services
H582	Systems and Equipment Malfunctions
H583	Emergency Approaches and Landings (Actual)
H585	Airplane Systems
H586	Pressurized Airplanes
H587	Oxygen Systems
H588	Physiological Altitude Limits
H589	Regulatory Requirements
H591	Multiengine Performance Characteristics
H592	The Critical Engine
H593	Vmc for Certification
H594	Performance
H595	Factors in Takeoff Planning
H596	Accelerates/Stop Distance
H597	Propeller Feathering
H598	Use of Trim Tabs
H599	Preflight Preparation
H600	Checklist
H601	Taxiing
H602	Normal Takeoffs
H603	Crosswind Takeoffs
H604	Short-field or Obstacle Clearance Takeoff
H605	Stalls
H606	Emergency Descent
H607	Approaches and Landings
H608	Crosswind Landings
H609	Short-field Landing
H610	Go-around Procedure
H611	Engine Inoperative Emergencies
H612	Engine Inoperative Procedures
H613	Vmc Demonstrations
H614	Engine Failure Before Lift-off (Rejected Takeoff)
H615	Engine Failure After Lift-off
H616	Engine Failure En Route
H617	Engine Inoperative Approach and Landing
H618	Types of Decisions
H619	Effectiveness of ADM

AC 00-6—Aviation Weather

I20	The Earth's Atmosphere
I21	Temperature
I22	Atmospheric Pressure and Altimetry
I23	Wind
I24	Moisture, Cloud Formation, and Precipitation
I25	Stable and Unstable Air
I26	Clouds
I27	Air Masses and Fronts
I28	Turbulence
I29	Icing
I30	Thunderstorms
I31	Common IFR Producers
I32	High Altitude Weather
I33	Arctic Weather
I34	Tropical Weather
I35	Soaring Weather
I36	Glossary of Weather Terms

AC 00-45—Aviation Weather Services

I54	The Aviation Weather Service Program
I55	Aviation Routine Weather Report (METAR)
I56	Pilot and Radar Reports, Satellite Pictures, and Radiosonde Additional Data (RADATs)
I57	Aviation Weather Forecasts
I58	Surface Analysis Chart
I59	Weather Depiction Chart
I60	Radar Summary Chart
I61	Constant Pressure Analysis Chart
I62	Composite Moisture Stability Chart
I63	Winds and Temperatures Aloft Chart
I64	Significant Weather Prognostic Charts
I65	Convective Outlook Chart
I66	Volcanic Ash Advisory Center Products
I67	Turbulence Locations, Conversion and Density Altitude Tables, Contractions and Acronyms, Station Identifiers, WSR-88D Sites, and Internet Addresses

AIM—Aeronautical Information Manual

J01	Air Navigation Radio Aids
J02	Radar Services and Procedures
J03	Airport Lighting Aids
J04	Air Navigation and Obstruction Lighting
J05	Airport Marking Aids and Signs
J06	Airspace — General
J07	Class G Airspace
J08	Controlled Airspace
J09	Special Use Airspace
J10	Other Airspace Areas
J11	Service Available to Pilots
J12	Radio Communications Phraseology and Techniques
J13	Airport Operations
J14	ATC Clearance/Separations
J15	Preflight
J16	Departure Procedures
J17	En Route Procedures
J18	Arrival Procedures
J19	Pilot/Controller Roles and Responsibilities
J20	National Security and Interception Procedures
J21	Emergency Procedures — General
J22	Emergency Services Available to Pilots
J23	Distress and Urgency Procedures
J24	Two-Way Radio Communications Failure

J25   Meteorology
J26   Altimeter Setting Procedures
J27   Wake Turbulence
J28   Bird Hazards, and Flight Over National Refuges, Parks, and Forests
J29   Potential Flight Hazards
J30   Safety, Accident, and Hazard Reports
J31   Fitness for Flight
J32   Type of Charts Available
J33   Pilot Controller Glossary

Other Documents

J34   Airport/Facility Directory
J35   En Route Low Altitude Chart
J36   En Route High Altitude Chart
J37   Sectional Chart
J39   Terminal Area Chart
J40   Instrument Departure Procedure Chart
J41   Standard Terminal Arrival (STAR) Chart
J42   Instrument Approach Procedures
J43   Helicopter Route Chart

ADDITIONAL ADVISORY CIRCULARS

J??   AC 00-24, Thunderstorms
K??   AC 00-30, Atmospheric Turbulence Avoidance
K??   AC 00-34, Aircraft Ground Handling and Servicing
K0?   AC 00-54, Pilot Wind Shear Guide
K03   AC 00-55, Announcement of Availability: FAA Order 1130.21A
K06   AC 43-4, Corrosion Control for Aircraft
K11   AC 20-34, Prevention of Retractable Landing Gear Failures
K12   AC 20-32, Carbon Monoxide (CO) Contamination in Aircraft — Detection and Prevention
K13   AC 20-43, Aircraft Fuel Control
K20   AC 20-103, Aircraft Engine Crankshaft Failure
K23   AC 20-121, Airworthiness Approval of Airborne Loran C Navigation Systems for Use in the U.S. National Airspace System
K26   AC 20-138, Airworthiness Approval of Global Positioning System (GPS) Navigation Equipment for Use as a VFR and IFR Supplemental Navigation System
K40   AC 25, Inertial Navigation System (INS)
K45   AC 39, Airworthiness Directives
K46   AC 43-9, Maintenance Records
K47   AC 43.9, Instructions for Completion of FAA Form 337
K48   AC 43-11, Reciprocating Engine Overhaul Terminology and Standards
K49   AC 43.13-1, Acceptable Methods, Techniques, and Practices — Aircraft Inspection and Repair
K50   AC 43.13-2, Acceptable Methods, Techniques, and Practices — Aircraft Alterations
K80   AC 60, Pilot Spatial Disorientation
L05   AC 60, Aeronautical Decision Making
L10   AC 60, Stall/Spin Awareness Training
L15   AC 61-107, Operations of Aircraft at Altitudes Above 25,000 Feet MSL and/or MACH numbers (Mmo) Greater Than .75
L25   FAA 8082-11, Inspection Authorization Knowledge Test Guide
L34   AC 90-48, Pilots' Role in Collision Avoidance
L42   AC 90-87, Helicopter Dynamic Rollover
L44   AC 90-94, Guidelines for Using Global Positioning System Equipment for IFR En Route and Terminal Operations and for Nonprecision Instrument Approaches in the U.S. National Airspace System

L45   AC 90-95, Unanticipated Right Yaw in Helicopters
L50   AC 91-6, Water, Slush, and Snow on the Runway
L52   AC 91-13, Cold Weather Operation of Aircraft
L53   AC 91-14, Altimeter Setting Sources
L57   AC 91-43, Unreliable Airspeed Indications
L59   AC 91-46, Gyroscopic Instruments — Good Operating Practices
L61   AC 91-50, Importance of Transponder Operation and Altitude Reporting
L62   AC 91-51, Effect of Icing on Aircraft Control and Airplane Deice and Anti-Ice Systems
L70   AC 91-67, Minimum Equipment Requirements for General Aviation Operations Under FAR Part 91
L80   AC 103-4, Hazard Associated with Sublimation of Solid Carbon Dioxide (Dry Ice) Aboard Aircraft
L90   AC 105-2, Sport Parachute Jumping
M01   AC 120-12, Private Carriage Versus Common Carriage of Persons or Property
M02   AC 120-27, Aircraft Weight and Balance Control
M08   AC 120-58, Pilot Guide for Large Aircraft Ground Deicing
M13   AC 121-195-1, Operational Landing Distances for Wet Runways; Transport Category Airplanes
M35   AC 135-17, Pilot Guide — Small Aircraft Ground Deicing
M51   AC 20-117, Hazards Following Ground Deicing and Ground Operations in Conditions Conducive to Aircraft Icing
M52   AC 00-2, Advisory Circular Checklist

NOTE: AC 00-2, Advisory Circular Checklist, transmits the status of all FAA advisory circulars (AC's), as well as FAA internal publications and miscellaneous flight information such as Aeronautical Information Manual, Airport/Facility Directory, knowledge test guides, practical test standards, and other material directly related to a certificate or rating. To obtain a free copy of AC 00-2, send your request to:

U.S. Department of Transportation
Subsequent Distribution Office, SVC 121.23
Ardmore East Business Center
3341 Q 75th Ave.
Landover, MD 20785

CROSS-REFERENCES TO THE FAA PILOT KNOWLEDGE TEST QUESTION NUMBERS

Pages 313 through 321 contain the FAA private pilot question numbers from the private pilot knowledge test bank. The questions are numbered 3001 to 3915. To the right of each FAA question number* we have added the FAA's subject matter knowledge code. To the right of the subject knowledge code we have listed our answer and our chapter and question number. For example, the FAA's question 3001 is cross-referenced to the FAA's subject knowledge code A01, "FAR Part 1, General Definitions." The correct answer is B, and the question appears with answer explanations in our book under 4-1, which means it is reproduced in Chapter 4 as question 1. Non-airplane questions (omitted from this book) are indicated as NA.

The first line of each of our answer explanations in Chapters 1 through 11 contains

1. The correct answer
2. The FAA question number
3. A reference for the answer explanation, e.g., *FTH Chap 1*. If this reference is not practical, use the following chart to identify the subject matter knowledge code to determine which reference is appropriate for the question.

Thus, our question numbers are cross-referenced throughout this book to the FAA question numbers, and these 9 pages cross-reference the FAA question numbers back to this book.

FAA Q. No.	FAA Subject Code	Gleim Answer	Gleim Chap/ Q. No.	FAA Q. No.	FAA Subject Code	Gleim Answer	Gleim Chap/ Q. No.	FAA Q. No.	FAA Subject Code	Gleim Answer	Gleim Chap/ Q. No.
3001	A01	B	4-1	3021	A20	C	4-27	3045	A29	B	4-54
3002	A01	B	4-2	3022	A20	C	4-28	3046	A20	A	4-55
3003	A01	A	4-3	3023	A20	C	4-29	3047	A29	C	4-56
3004	A01	A	4-4	3024	A20	B	4-33	3048	A29	B	4-57
3005	A01	C	4-5	3025	A20	C	4-32	3049	A29	C	4-59
3006	A02	A	4-10	3026	A20	C	4-31	3050	A29	C	4-60
3007	A02	A	4-7	3027	A20	B	4-34	3051	A29	B	4-58
3008	A02	A	4-8	3028	A20	C	4-35	3052	A29	A	4-62
3009	A02	C	4-9	3029	A20	C	4-40	3053	A29	C	4-61
3010	A02	A	4-11	3030	A20	A	4-39	3054	A29	C	4-63
3011	A02	C	4-12	3031	A20	C	4-41	3055	A29	A	4-64
3012a	A02	A	4-13	3032	A20	C	4-44	3056	A29	B	4-65
3012b	A13	B	4-15	3033	A20	B	4-42	3057	A29	B	4-68
3012c	A13	C	4-16	3034	A20	A	4-43	3058	A29	C	4-69
3013a	A15	C	4-19	3035	A20	A	4-45	3059	A29	C	4-71
3013b	A15	B	4-17	3036	A21	B	4-46	3060	A29	C	4-70
3013c	A15	B	4-18	3037	A21	C	4-47	3061	A29	C	4-72
3014	A16	A	4-20	3038	A29	C	4-51	3062	A23	NA	
3015	A16	B	4-21	3039	A20	B	4-30	3063	A23	NA	
3016	A20	C	4-24	3040	A20	C	4-36	3064	A23	B	4-48
3017	A20	C	4-22	3041	A20	A	4-37	3065	A23	B	4-49
3018	A20	B	4-23	3042	A20	C	4-38	3066	A23	B	4-50
3019	A20	C	4-25	3043	A29	A	4-52	3067	A60	A	4-76
3020	A20	B	4-26	3044	A29	B	4-53	3068	A60	B	4-77

*In June 2001, the FAA test bank was released without the familiar four-digit FAA question numbers. We identified all of the new questions and added them to the end of our cross-reference chart using our own question numbering system. The first four digits of this code refer to the month and year the question first appeared. The remaining digits identify the question number used in that particular FAA test bank release.

FAA Q. No.	FAA Subject Code	Gleim Answer	Gleim Chap/ Q. No.	FAA Q. No.	FAA Subject Code	Gleim Answer	Gleim Chap/ Q. No.	FAA Q. No.	FAA Subject Code	Gleim Answer	Gleim Chap/ Q. No.
3069	A60	B	4-140	3111	B08	A	3-74	3153	B09	C	4-144
3070	B07	B	4-78	3112	B08	A	3-77	3154	B09	B	4-143
3071	B07	NA		3113	B08	B	3-76	3155	B09	C	4-147
3072	B07	B	4-115	3114	B08	C	3-75	3156	B09	C	4-146
3073	B07	C	4-113	3115	B08	B	3-78	3157	B09	B	4-148
3074	B07	B	4-79	3116	B08	B	3-73	3158	B09	B	4-149
3075	B07	B	4-80	3117	B08	C	3-49	3159	B11	C	4-150
3076	B07	B	4-81	3118	B08	B	3-50	3160	B11	B	4-151
3077	B07	A	4-83	3119	B08	A	3-52	3161	B11	B	4-153
3078	B07	A	4-84	3120	B08	B	3-29	3162	B11	C	4-155
3079	B07	C	4-82	3121	B08	B	3-27	3163	B11	C	4-157
3080	B07	B	4-87	3122	B08	NA		3164	B11	C	4-156
3081	B07	C	4-85	3123	B08	C	3-12	3165	B11	A	4-158
3082	B07	C	4-86	3124	B08	A	4-118	3166	B11	C	4-121
3083	B07	A	4-88	3125	B08	C	9-29	3167	B12	B	4-163
3084	B07	C	4-89	3126	B08	B	4-119	3168	B12	B	4-160
3085	B07	B	4-91	3127	B08	A	4-120	3169	B12	B	4-162
3086	B07	A	4-92	3128	B08	B	9-30	3170	B12	A	4-161
3087	B07	B	4-90	3129	B08	A	4-159	3171	B12	C	4-165
3088	B08	C	4-93	3130	B08	A	4-123	3172	B12	A	4-166
3089	B08	B	4-100	3131	B09	B	4-125	3173	B12	B	4-164
3090	B08	B	4-98	3132	B09	C	4-124	3174	B12	NA	
3091	B08	A	4-96	3133	B09	NA		3175	B12	NA	
3092	B08	A	4-94	3134	B09	B	4-73	3176	B12	NA	
3093	B08	B	4-99	3135	B09	B	4-74	3177	B12	NA	
3094	B08	C	4-97	3136	B09	C	4-139	3178	B12	B	4-167
3095	B08	C	4-95	3137	B09	A	4-131	3179	B12	B	4-168
3096	B08	B	4-101	3138	B09	B	4-132	3180a	B13	B	4-169
3097	B08	B	4-103	3139	B09	B	4-130	3180b	B13	C	4-184
3098	B08	A	4-105	3140	B09	B	4-134	3181a	B13	A	4-171
3099	B08	A	4-104	3141	B09	A	4-127	3181b	B13	A	4-172
3100	B08	B	4-102	3142	B09	B	4-133	3181c	B13	A	4-170
3101	B08	A	4-107	3143	B09	A	4-137	3182	B13	B	4-181
3102	B08	C	4-108	3144	B09	A	4-138	3183	B13	B	4-173
3103	B08	B	4-109	3145	B09	C	4-126	3184	B13	B	4-174
3104	B08	A	4-106	3146	B09	C	4-128	3185	B13	C	4-176
3105	B08	B	4-111	3147	B09	B	4-136	3186	B13	C	4-182
3106	B08	A	4-110	3148	B09	C	4-135	3187	B13	C	4-14
3107	B08	B	4-112	3149	B09	B	4-129	3188	B13	A	4-177
3108	B08	B	4-116	3150	B09	B	4-142	3189	B13	B	4-178
3109	B08	A	4-114	3151	B09	A	4-145	3190	B13	B	4-175
3110	B08	B	4-117	3152	B09	NA		3191	B13	C	4-179

FAA Q. No.	FAA Subject Code	Gleim Answer	Gleim Chap/ Q. No.	FAA Q. No.	FAA Subject Code	Gleim Answer	Gleim Chap/ Q. No.	FAA Q. No.	FAA Subject Code	Gleim Answer	Gleim Chap/ Q. No.
3192	B13	C	4-180	3234	H307	A	2-62	3276	H313	C	2-45
3193	B13	A	4-183	3235	H307	C	2-59	3277	H313	C	2-42
3194	G11	A	4-185	3236	H307	A	2-56	3278	H313	C	2-43
3195	G11	C	4-187	3237	H307	C	2-70	3279	H314	C	2-3
3196	G11	B	4-186	3238	H307	C	2-68	3280	H314	B	2-5
3197	G11	A	4-188	3239	H307	B	2-69	3281	H314	C	2-7
3198	G12	B	4-189	3240	H307	B	2-71	3282	H314	C	2-1
3199	G13	C	4-190	3241	H307	A	2-75	3283	H314	C	2-6
3200	G13	C	4-191	3242	H307	A	2-72	3284	H314	B	2-4
3201	H300	A	1-4	3243	H307	C	2-73	3285	H314	NA	
3202	H300	A	1-5	3244	H307	C	2-48	3286	H314	A	2-2
3203	H300	B	1-9	3245	H307	A	2-46	3287	H315	B	1-24
3204	H300	A	1-7	3246	H308	B	5-4	3288	H315	A	1-26
3205	H300	A	1-6	3247	H312	B	2-10	3289	H312	C	5-7
3206	H300	A	1-14	3248	H312	C	2-9	3290	H317	C	5-6
3207	H300	A	1-27	3249	H312	C	2-11	3291	H317	B	5-5
3208	H301	B	1-28	3250	H312	C	2-24	3292	H317	C	5-13
3209	H301	B	1-29	3251	H312	C	2-23	3293	H317	B	5-14
3210	H302	B	1-22	3252	H312	A	2-25	3294	H317	C	5-15
3211	H302	A	1-23	3253	H312	B	2-26	3295	H317	A	5-10
3212	H302	B	1-25	3254	H312	C	2-34	3296	H317	C	5-9
3213	H302	A	1-3	3255	H312	A	2-41	3297	H317	A	5-12
3214	H303	C	1-33	3256	H312	A	2-28	3298	H317	A	5-8
3215	H303	C	1-34	3257	H312	B	2-27	3299	H317	C	5-11
3216	H303	B	1-35	3258	H312	B	2-29	3300	H317	B	5-2
3217	H303	B	1-30	3259	H312	B	2-33	3301	H534	A	1-21
3218	H303	B	1-31	3260	H312	B	2-31	3302	H516	C	11-8
3219	H305	C	1-2	3261	H312	C	2-35	3303	H516	A	11-9
3220	H305	A	1-1	3262	H312	C	2-8	3304	H516	A	11-10
3221	H307	B	2-47	3263	H312	C	1-11	3305	H516	A	11-11
3222	H307	C	2-49	3264	H312	C	2-12	3306	H516	A	11-13
3223	H307	A	2-55	3265	H312	A	2-16	3307	H516	C	11-14
3224	H307	B	2-74	3266	H312	C	2-14	3308	H516	B	11-12
3225	H307	B	2-57	3267	H312	C	2-15	3309	H539	C	1-12
3226	H307	B	2-66	3268	H312	C	2-17	3310	H539	A	1-13
3227	H307	A	2-65	3269	H312	C	2-18	3311	H303	C	1-10
3228	H307	A	2-67	3270	H312	B	2-19	3312	H317	A	1-17
3229	H307	C	2-60	3271	H312	C	2-20	3313	H317	A	1-18
3230	H307	A	2-61	3272	H312	C	2-21	3314	H317	B	1-19
3231	H307	C	2-58	3273	H312	B	2-22	3315	H317	B	1-20
3232	H307	B	2-63	3274	H312	C	2-13	3316	H303	A	1-32
3233	H307	B	2-64	3275	H313	A	2-44	3317	H702	A	1-8

FAA Q. No.	FAA Subject Code	Gleim Answer	Gleim Chap/ Q. No.	FAA Q. No.	FAA Subject Code	Gleim Answer	Gleim Chap/ Q. No.	FAA Q. No.	FAA Subject Code	Gleim Answer	Gleim Chap/ Q. No.
3318	H703	NA		3360	O220	NA		3402	I24	C	7-20
3319	H703	NA		3361	O220	NA		3403	I25	B	7-51
3320	H703	NA		3362	O220	NA		3404	I25	A	7-52
3321	H703	NA		3363	O220	NA		3405	I25	A	7-44
3322	H703	NA		3364	O30	NA		3406	I25	A	7-45
3323	H703	NA		3365	O30	NA		3407	I25	C	7-46
3324	H703	NA		3366	O30	NA		3408	I25	A	7-53
3325	H703	NA		3367	O30	NA		3409	I25	C	7-43
3326	H705	NA		3368	P01	NA		3410	I25	B	7-42
3327	H705	NA		3369	P01	NA		3411	I25	NA	
3328	H703	NA		3370	P01	NA		3412	I25	A	7-50
3329	H748	NA		3371	P01	NA		3413	I25	A	7-47
3330	H748	NA		3372	P04	NA		3414	I25	C	7-48
3331	H748	NA		3373	P04	NA		3415	I26	B	7-38
3332	H749	NA		3374	P04	NA		3416	I26	B	7-37
3333	H745	NA		3375	P04	NA		3417	I26	C	7-21
3334	H745	NA		3376	P04	NA		3418	I26	B	7-22
3335	H747	NA		3377	P04	NA		3419	I26	B	7-40
3336	H727	NA		3378	P04	NA		3420	I26	C	7-41
3337	H727	NA		3379	P11	NA		3421	I27	C	7-6
3338	H709	NA		3380	P11	NA		3422	I27	A	7-8
3339	H702	NA		3381	I21	C	7-1	3423	I27	A	7-7
3340	N20	NA		3382	I21	A	7-2	3424	I27	C	7-49
3341	N21	NA		3383	I21	C	7-55	3425	I28	A	7-23
3342	N21	NA		3384	I21	A	7-54	3426	I28	C	7-24
3343	N22	NA		3385	I21	A	7-56	3427	I28	B	7-26
3344	N22	NA		3386	I21	A	5-1	3428	I28	C	7-25
3345	N27	NA		3387	I22	C	2-36	3429	I28	C	7-18
3346	N27	NA		3388	I22	B	2-32	3430	I29	C	7-19
3347	N27	NA		3389	I22	C	2-30	3431	I29	C	1-15
3348	N27	NA		3390	I22	C	2-37	3432	I29	A	1-16
3349	N27	NA		3391	I22	B	2-38	3433	I30	B	7-39
3350	N34	NA		3392	I22	A	2-40	3434	I30	B	7-14
3351	O155	NA		3393	I22	C	2-39	3435	I30	B	7-15
3352	O170	NA		3394	I22	B	5-3	3436	I30	A	7-11
3353	O170	NA		3395	I23	B	7-3	3437	I30	B	7-12
3354	O170	NA		3396	I23	NA		3438	I30	A	7-13
3355	O170	NA		3397	I24	C	7-28	3439	I30	A	7-16
3356	O220	NA		3398	I24	B	7-29	3440	I30	B	7-10
3357	O220	NA		3399	I24	A	7-32	3441	I30	B	7-9
3358	O220	NA		3400	I24	A	7-30	3442	I30	C	11-15
3359	O220	NA		3401	I24	B	7-31	3443	I31	A	7-35

FAA Q. No.	FAA Subject Code	Gleim Answer	Gleim Chap/ Q. No.	FAA Q. No.	FAA Subject Code	Gleim Answer	Gleim Chap/ Q. No.	FAA Q. No.	FAA Subject Code	Gleim Answer	Gleim Chap/ Q. No.
3444	I31	C	7-27	3486	I57	B	8-37	3528	H320	C	8-8
3445	I31	B	7-34	3487	I57	A	8-22	3529	H342	C	11-31
3446	I31	C	7-36	3488	I57	A	8-28	3530	H340	A	9-1
3447	I33	C	7-33	3489	I57	A	8-23	3531	H346	C	11-19
3448	I35	C	7-5	3490	I57	A	8-24	3532	H348	B	10-2
3449	I35	NA		3491	I57	C	8-27	3533	H348	C	10-10
3450	I35	C	7-4	3492	I57	B	8-26	3534	H346	B	11-32
3451	I35	NA		3493	I57	A	8-29	3535	H340	B	9-2
3452	I36	A	7-17	3494	I57	A	8-66	3536	H340	C	9-3
3453	I54	A	8-68	3495	I57	C	8-73	3537	H342	NA	
3454	I54	B	8-67	3496	I57	A	8-72	3538	H346	C	11-24
3455	I54	A	8-7	3497	I57	C	8-69	3539	H348	A	11-20
3456	I54	C	8-1	3498	I57	B	8-71	3540	H346	C	11-34
3457	I54	C	8-2	3499	I57	B	8-70	3541	H346	C	11-33
3458	I54	C	8-3	3500	I57	B	8-60	3542	H346	B	11-35
3459	I54	A	8-9	3501	I57	A	8-56	3543	H340	B	9-4
3460	I54	A	8-4	3502	I57	C	8-57	3544	H341	NA	
3461	I54	A	8-10	3503	I57	C	8-59	3545	H346	B	11-27
3462	I55	C	8-13	3504	I57	B	8-58	3546	H346	A	11-25
3463	I55	B	8-11	3505	I57	C	8-55	3547	H346	A	11-26
3464	I55	A	8-14	3506	I57	B	8-54	3548	H346	C	11-38
3465	I55	B	8-15	3507	I58	A	8-41	3549	H346	B	11-37
3466	I55	B	8-16	3508	I58	B	8-39	3550	H346	C	11-29
3467	I55	A	8-12	3509	I59	A	8-38	3551	H346	B	11-30
3468	I55	NA		3510	I59	A	8-43	3552	H346	B	10-3
3469	I55	NA		3511	I59	B	8-40	3553	H348	B	11-21
3470	I55	NA		3512	I59	C	8-42	3554	H342	B	11-36
3471	I55	NA		3513	I60	B	8-50	3555	H346	NA	
3472	I56	C	8-18	3514	I60	A	8-49	3556	H346	A	11-22
3473	I56	A	8-19	3515	I60	C	8-44	3557	H342	NA	
3474	I56	A	8-17	3516	I60	A	8-46	3558	H346	NA	
3475	I56	C	8-20	3517	I60	A	8-47	3559	H348	A	10-4
3476	I56	C	8-21	3518	I60	C	8-48	3560	H348	A	11-23
3477	I57	NA		3519	I60	B	8-45	3561	H348	C	10-11
3478	I57	C	8-25	3520	I64	B	8-64	3562	H346	A	11-39
3479	I57	C	8-33	3521	I64	A	8-62	3563	H346	A	11-40
3480	I57	A	8-30	3522	I64	B	8-61	3564	H346	NA	
3481	I57	B	8-34	3523	I64	A	8-65	3565	H346	A	11-28
3482	I57	B	8-35	3524	I64	C	8-63	3566	H348	A	10-5
3483	I57	B	8-36	3525	I62	NA		3567	H340	A	9-5
3484	I57	A	8-32	3526	H320	C	8-5	3568	H346	C	11-18
3485	I57	A	8-31	3527	H320	B	8-6	3569	H342	NA	

FAA Q. No.	FAA Subject Code	Gleim Answer	Gleim Chap/ Q. No.	FAA Q. No.	FAA Subject Code	Gleim Answer	Gleim Chap/ Q. No.	FAA Q. No.	FAA Subject Code	Gleim Answer	Gleim Chap/ Q. No.
3570	H348	C	10-7	3609	J11	A	9-48	3649	N27	NA	
3571	H340	C	11-41	3610	J11	A	9-40	3650	N34	NA	
3572	H340	B	11-42	3611	J11	B	9-39	3651	H307	A	2-50
3573	H340	C	11-43	3612	J11	B	9-41	3652	H307	A	2-51
3574	H340	B	11-44	3613	J12	A	3-66	3653	H308	A	2-52
3575	H340	C	11-45	3614	J12	A	3-67	3654	H308	B	2-54
3576	H340	A	11-46	3615	J12	C	3-68	3655	H308	B	2-53
3577	H348	C	10-8	3616	J25	C	8-51	3656	H309	A	2-76
3578	H348	B	10-9	3617	J25	A	8-52	3657	H309	B	2-77
3579	H348	A	10-6	3618	J28	A	9-11	3658	H311	A	11-5
3580	H348	C	10-12	3619	J34	B	9-18	3659	H311	B	11-7
3581	H348	C	10-13	3620a.	J37	C	9-16	3660	H311	B	11-6
3582	H348	C	10-14	3620b.	J37	A	4-66	3661	H316	A	5-41
3583	H348	B	10-15	3621a.	J37	C	9-8	3662	H316	C	5-42
3584	H348	C	10-16	3621b.	J37	B	4-67	3663	H316	C	5-43
3585	H348	A	10-17	3622	J37	A	9-7	3664	H316	B	5-44
3586	H348	C	10-18	3623	J37	C	9-6	3665	H316	B	5-50
3587	H348	B	10-19	3624	J37	B	9-25	3666	H316	A	5-52
3588	H348	C	10-20	3625	J37	C	9-26	3667	H316	B	5-51
3589	H348	C	10-22	3626	J37	B	9-19	3668	H316	C	5-53
3590	H348	A	10-23	3627	J37	B	9-14	3669	H316	A	5-45
3591	H348	B	10-21	3628	J37	B	9-24	3670	H316	B	5-46
3592	H348	B	10-24	3629	J37	A	9-17	3671	H316	C	5-47
3593	H348	A	10-25	3630	J37	A	9-43	3672	H316	B	5-48
3594	H348	B	10-26	3631	J37	C	9-36	3673	H316	B	5-49
3595	H348	C	10-27	3632	J37	C	9-35	3674	H316	A	5-56
3596	H348	B	10-28	3633	J37	A	9-15	3675	H316	B	5-54
3597	H348	C	10-29	3634	J37	B	9-32	3676	H316	A	5-57
3598a	J01	C	10-1	3635	J37	A	9-37	3677	H316	B	5-55
3598b	J01	C	10-30	3636	J37	C	9-38	3678	H317	C	5-24
3598c	J01	B	10-31	3637	J37	C	9-20	3679	H317	B	5-21
3598d	J01	C	10-32	3638	J37	A	9-21	3680	H317	B	5-22
3599	J08	C	9-28	3639	J37	B	9-22	3681	H317	B	5-20
3600	J08	B	9-27	3640	J37	C	9-23	3682	H317	C	5-23
3601	J09	A	9-13	3641	J37	B	9-49	3683	H317	B	5-26
3602	J09	B	9-9	3642	J37	B	9-31	3684	H317	C	5-27
3603	J10	A	9-34	3643	J37	C	9-33	3685	H317	C	5-29
3604	J11	A	9-42	3644	J37	NA		3686	H317	C	5-28
3605	J11	B	9-44	3645	J37	NA		3687	H317	B	5-30
3606	J11	C	9-47	3646	J37	NA		3688	H317	A	5-25
3607	J11	C	9-46	3647	N23	NA		3689	H317	B	5-34
3608	J11	C	9-45	3648	N27	NA		3690	H317	B	5-31

FAA Q. No.	FAA Subject Code	Gleim Answer	Gleim Chap/ Q. No.	FAA Q. No.	FAA Subject Code	Gleim Answer	Gleim Chap/ Q. No.	FAA Q. No.	FAA Subject Code	Gleim Answer	Gleim Chap/ Q. No.
3691	H317	C	5-33	3733	H720	NA		3775	J05	A	3-3
3692	H317	B	5-32	3734	H745	NA		3776	J05	C	3-4
3693	H317	B	5-35	3735	H747	NA		3777	J05	C	3-18
3694	H317	A	5-39	3736	H747	NA		3778	J05	C	3-5
3695	H317	B	5-40	3737	H747	NA		3779	J08	C	3-57
3696	H317	B	5-37	3738	H78	NA		3780	J08	C	3-55
3697	H317	C	5-36	3739	H738	NA		3781	J08	C	3-56
3698	H317	B	5-38	3740	H738	NA		3782	J08	C	3-58
3699	H317	NA		3741	H746	NA		3783	J09	B	4-122
3700	H317	NA		3742	H746	NA		3784	J09	NA	
3701	H317	NA		3743	H739	NA		3785	J09	C	9-10
3702	H317	NA		3744	H742	NA		3786	J09	B	3-45
3703	H317	NA		3745	H742	NA		3787	J10	C	3-53
3704	H317	NA		3746	H743	NA		3788	J10	C	3-51
3705	H317	B	5-16	3747	H743	NA		3789	J10	C	3-54
3706	H317	B	5-18	3748	H744	NA		3790	J11	NA	
3707	H317	A	5-17	3749	H743	NA		3791	J11	C	3-48
3708	H317	A	5-19	3750	I35	NA		3792	J11	B	3-69
3709	M52	B	9-50	3751	I35	NA		3793	J11	A	3-70
3710	H507	B	3-43	3752	I35	NA		3794	J11	C	3-71
3711	H582	A	11-17	3753	I35	NA		3795	J11	C	3-72
3712	H564	B	6-12	3754	I35	NA		3796	J11	A	3-62
3713	H564	A	6-13	3755	I35	NA		3797	J11	C	3-61
3714	H564	C	3-41	3756	I35	NA		3798	J11	C	3-60
3715	H567	A	3-37	3757	I35	NA		3799	J11	A	3-59
3716	H567	A	3-38	3758	I35	NA		3800	J11	C	3-64
3717	H567	C	3-39	3759	J01	A	3-83	3801	J11	A	3-65
3718	H568	B	3-10	3760	J03	B	3-28	3802	J11	A	4-75
3719	H573	C	11-16	3761	J03	A	3-22	3803	J11	B	3-63
3720	H76	NA		3762	J03	C	3-21	3804	J12	A	3-79
3721	H76	NA		3763	J03	B	3-20	3805	J13	B	3-19
3722	H76	NA		3764	J03	C	3-23	3806	J13	A	3-17
3723	H76	NA		3765	J03	B	3-26	3807	J13	A	3-13
3724	H76	NA		3766	J03	B	3-25	3808	J13	C	3-14
3725	H76	NA		3767	J03	B	3-24	3809	J13	A	3-15
3726	H76	NA		3768	J03	C	3-11	3810	J13	C	3-16
3727	H76	NA		3769	J03	B	3-6	3811	J13	A	3-46
3728	H76	NA		3770	J03	A	3-7	3812	J13	A	3-47
3729	H719	NA		3771	J03	B	3-8	3813	J14	B	4-141
3730	H719	NA		3772	J03	B	3-9	3814	J14	A	3-44
3731	H719	NA		3773	J05	B	3-1	3815	J15	A	11-1
3732	H720	NA		3774	J05	B	3-2	3816	J15	B	11-2

FAA Q. No.	FAA Subject Code	Gleim Answer	Gleim Chap/ Q. No.	FAA Q. No.	FAA Subject Code	Gleim Answer	Gleim Chap/ Q. No.	FAA Q. No.	FAA Subject Code	Gleim Answer	Gleim Chap/ Q. No.
3817	J15	C	11-3	3859	N21	NA		3901	O220	NA	
3818	J15	B	11-4	3860	N21	NA		3902	O220	NA	
3819	J22	B	3-80	3861	N21	NA		3903	O220	NA	
3820	J22	A	4-154	3862	N21	NA		3904	O220	NA	
3821	J22	C	4-152	3863	N21	NA		3905	O10	NA	
3822	J22	C	3-81	3864	N21	NA		3906	O220	NA	
3823	J25	A	8-53	3865	N21	NA		3907	O220	NA	
3824	J27	C	3-30	3866	N21	NA		3908	O30	NA	
3825	J27	C	3-33	3867	N21	NA		3909	O30	NA	
3826	J27	A	3-31	3868	N21	NA		3910	O263	NA	
3827	J27	C	3-32	3869	N30	NA		3911	P03	NA	
3828	J27	B	3-34	3870	N30	NA		3912	P11	NA	
3829	J27	A	3-36	3871	N30	NA		3913	P11	NA	
3830	J27	B	3-35	3872	N30	NA		3914	P11	NA	
3831	J28	B	9-12	3873	N30	NA		3915	P11	NA	
3832	J31	B	6-14	3874	N30	NA		3916	NA		
3833	J31	C	6-10	3875	N30	NA		3917	NA		
3834	J31	B	3-40	3876	N30	NA		3918	NA		
3835	J31	A	6-9	3877	N30	NA		3919	NA		
3836	J31	C	3-42	3878	N30	NA		3920	NA		
3837	J33	C	4-6	3879	N30	NA		3921	NA		
3838	J34	A	9-54	3880	N32	NA		3922	NA		
3839	J34	C	9-55	3881	N32	NA		3923	NA		
3840	J34	A	9-58	3882	N32	NA		3924	NA		
3841	J34	B	9-57	3883	N32	NA		3925	NA		
3842	J34	B	9-56	3884	N34	NA		3926	NA		
3843	J34	B	3-82	3885	O220	NA		3927	NA		
3844	J31	A	6-1	3886	O220	NA		3928	NA		
3845	J31	A	6-2	3887	O220	NA		3929	NA		
3846	J31	A	6-3	3888	O220	NA		3930	NA		
3847	J31	B	6-4	3889	O220	NA		3931	L05	A	6-16
3848	J31	A	6-15	3890	O220	NA		3932	L05	C	6-19
3849	J31	C	6-11	3891	O220	NA		3933	L05	C	6-20
3850	J31	B	6-7	3892	O220	NA		3934	L05	C	6-21
3851	J31	A	6-8	3893	O220	NA		3935	L05	B	6-22
3852	J31	B	6-5	3894	O220	NA		3936	L05	C	6-23
3853	J31	A	6-6	3895	O220	NA		3937	L05	C	6-24
3854	M52	A	9-52	3896	O220	NA		3938	L05	C	6-25
3855	M52	B	9-53	3897	O220	NA		3939	L05	A	6-17
3856	M52	C	9-51	3898	O220	NA		3940	L05	A	6-18
3857	N31	NA		3899	O220	NA		3941	NA		
3858	N31	NA		3900	O220	NA		3942	NA		

FAA Q. No.	FAA Subject Code	Gleim Answer	Gleim Chap/ Q. No.
3943	NA		
3944	NA		
3945	NA		
3946	NA		
3947	NA		
3948	NA		
3949	NA		
3950	NA		
3951	J13	C	3-84
3952	J13	A	3-85
3953	J13	A	3-86
3954	J13	A	3-87
3955	J13	B	3-88

INDEX OF LEGENDS AND FIGURES

AUTHOR'S RECOMMENDATIONS

The Experimental Aircraft Association, Inc. is a very successful and effective nonprofit organization that represents and serves those of us interested in flying, in general, and in sport aviation, in particular. I personally invite you to enjoy becoming a member. Visit their web site at http://www.eaa.org.

$40 for a 1-year membership (U.S. and Canada)
$56 for a 1-year membership (International)
$23 per year for individuals under 19 years old
Family membership available for $50 per year

> Membership includes the monthly magazine *Sport Aviation*.

Write to: EAA Aviation Center
              P.O. Box 3086
              Oshkosh, Wisconsin 54903-3086

Or call: (920) 426-4800
             (800) 564-6322

The annual EAA Oshkosh AirVenture is an unbelievable aviation spectacular with over 12,000 airplanes at one airport! Virtually everything aviation-oriented you can imagine! Plan to spend at least 1 day (not everything can be seen in a day) in Oshkosh (100 miles northwest of Milwaukee).

Convention dates: 2002 -- July 23 through July 29
                      2003 -- July 29 through August 4

The annual Sun 'n Fun EAA Fly-In is also highly recommended. It is held at the Lakeland, FL (KLAL) airport (between Orlando and Tampa). Visit the Sun 'n Fun web site at http://www.sun-n-fun.org.

Convention dates: 2002 -- April 7 through April 13
                      2003 -- April 6 through April 12

BE-A-PILOT: INTRODUCTORY FLIGHT

Be-A-Pilot is an industry-sponsored marketing program designed to inspire people to "Stop dreaming, start flying." Be-A-Pilot has sought flight schools to participate in the program and offers a $49 introductory flight certificate that can be redeemed at a participating flight school.

The goal of this program is to encourage people to experience their dreams of flying through an introductory flight and to begin taking flying lessons.

For more information, you can visit the Be-A-Pilot home page at http://www.beapilot.com or call 1-888-BE-A-PILOT.

AIRCRAFT OWNERS AND PILOTS ASSOCIATION

AOPA is the largest, most influential aviation association in the world, with more than 370,000 members--half of all pilots in the United States. AOPA's most important contribution to the world's most accessible, safest, least expensive, friendliest, easiest-to-use general aviation environment is their lobbying on our behalf at the federal, state, and local levels. AOPA also provides legal services, advice, and other assistance to the aviation community.

We recommend that you become an AOPA member, which costs only $39 annually. To join, call 1-800-USA-AOPA or visit the AOPA Web site www.aopa.org.

PILOT KNOWLEDGE TEST (WRITTEN EXAM) BOOKS AND SOFTWARE

Before pilots take their FAA knowledge tests, they want to understand the answer to every FAA test question. Gleim's *FAA Written Exam* books and *FAA Test Prep* software have set the standard in FAA knowledge test preparation. Gleim's easy-to-use format helps pilots learn and understand exactly what they need to know to pass. Each chapter includes a study outline, actual FAA questions, and answer explanations. Gleim's *FAA Test Prep* provides standard FAA tests under simulated exam conditions. Additional information can be found in our reference books.

Books

- *Private Pilot FAA Written Exam*
- *Instrument Pilot FAA Written Exam*
- *Commercial Pilot FAA Written Exam*
- *Flight/Ground Instructor FAA Written Exam*
- *Fundamentals of Instructing FAA Written Exam*
- *Airline Transport Pilot FAA Written Exam*
- *Flight Engineer FAA Written Exam*

Software

- *Private Pilot FAA Test Prep*
- *Instrument Pilot FAA Test Prep*
- *Commercial Pilot FAA Test Prep*
- *Flight/Ground Instructor FAA Test Prep*
  (includes *Fundamentals of Instructing*)
- *Airline Transport Pilot FAA Test Prep*
- *Flight Engineer FAA Test Prep*

REFERENCE AND FLIGHT MANEUVERS/PRACTICAL TEST PREP BOOKS

Pilot Handbook - A complete ground school text using an outline format with diagrams. This book augments and enhances Gleim's *FAA Written Exam* books in preparing pilots for the private, commercial, and flight instructor certificates and the instrument rating. A complete, organized, and detailed text makes it useful and saves time. It also contains a special section on flight reviews.

Aviation Weather and Weather Services - A complete rewrite of the FAA's *Aviation Weather* (AC 00-6A) and *Aviation Weather Services* (AC 00-45E) into a single, easy-to-understand book complete with maps, diagrams, charts, and pictures. Pilots can learn and understand the subject matter more easily and effectively with this book.

FAR/AIM - The purpose of this book is to consolidate the common parts of Title 14 of the Code of Federal Regulations (14 CFR) [formerly known as the *Federal Aviation Regulations* (FAR)] and the *Aeronautical Information Manual* (AIM) into one easy-to-use reference book. Gleim's **FAR/AIM** resets the standard with a better presentation, easier-to-read type, improved indexes, and full-color figures. Included are Parts 1,43, 61, 67, 71, 73, 91, 97, 103, 105, 119, Appendices I and J of 121, 135, 137, 141, and 142.

Gleim's *Flight Maneuvers* books are designed to simplify and facilitate flight training and will help pilots prepare for the FAA practical test. Each task, objective, concept, requirement, etc. in the FAA Practical Test Standards is explained, analyzed, illustrated, and interpreted so pilots will gain practical test proficiency as quickly as possible. The actual FAA Practical Tests Standards are included.

- *Private Pilot Flight Maneuvers and Practical Test Prep*
- *Instrument Pilot Flight Maneuvers and Practical Test Prep*
- *Commercial Pilot Flight Maneuvers and Practical Test Prep*
- *Flight Instructor Flight Maneuvers and Practical Test Prep*

PILOT KITS

Gleim's Pilot Kits provide everything a pilot needs to complete his/her training, except an airplane, local charts, and a flight instructor. Each kit contains the easiest, most effective, and least expensive pilot training materials available.

Private Pilot Kit *Instrument Pilot Kit* *Commercial Pilot Kit* *Instrument/Commercial Pilot Kit*

ONLINE REFRESHER COURSES

Flight Instructor Refresher Course is the first FAA-approved online CFI renewal program. Gleim's FIRC contains all of the lessons and tests required to renew your CFI certificate. Visit www.gleim.com/firc to try Lesson 1 FREE and begin your renewal today.

Private Pilot Refresher Course is a recurrent ground training course designed to increase pilot knowledge and safety. Gleim's PPRC is designed to meet the ground school requirement for the flight review. It also satisfies the "safety meeting" requirement for the FAA's Pilot Proficiency Award Program (Wings Program). Visit www.gleim.com/pprc to try Lesson 1 FREE.

Gleim Publications, Inc. **P.O. Box 12848** **Gainesville, FL 32604**	TOLL FREE:	(800) 87-GLEIM/(800) 874-5346	Customer service is available: 8:00 a.m. - 7:00 p.m., Mon. - Fri. 9:00 a.m. - 2:00 p.m., Saturday Please have your credit card ready or save time by ordering online!
	LOCAL:	(352) 375-0772	
	FAX:	(888) 375-6940 (toll free)	
	INTERNET:	http://www.gleim.com	
	E-MAIL:	sales@gleim.com	

Gleim's *PRIVATE PILOT KIT*

Includes everything you need to pass the FAA pilot knowledge (written) test and FAA practical test.
Our price is far lower than similarly equipped kits found elsewhere . . . . $119.95 _____

Gleim's *INSTRUMENT PILOT KIT*

Everything you need, just like our Private Pilot Kit. With CD-ROM . . . . $114.95 _____

Gleim's *COMMERCIAL PILOT KIT*

Everything you need to prepare for your commercial certificate. With CD-ROM . . . . $94.95 _____

SPECIAL COMBO: *INSTRUMENT/COMMERCIAL KIT* . . . . $189.95 _____

KNOWLEDGE TEST

	Books	Software*	Book/Software	Audios**	Book/Software*/ Audios**	
Private/Recreational Pilot	☐ @ $15.95	☐ @ $49.95	☐ @ $58.95	☐ @ $60	☐ @ $106.95	_____
Instrument Pilot	☐ @ $18.95	☐ @ $59.95	☐ @ $70.95	☐ @ $60	☐ @ $117.95	_____
Commercial Pilot	☐ @ $14.95	☐ @ $59.95	☐ @ $66.95	**Please select audio format.		_____
Fundamentals of Instructing	☐ @ $12.95	☐ } both for		☐ CDs ☐ Cassettes		
Flight/Ground Instructor	☐ @ $14.95	☐ } $59.95	☐ @ $66.95			_____
Airline Transport Pilot	☐ @ $26.95	☐ @ $59.95	☐ @ $77.95			_____
Flight Engineer	☐ @ $26.95	☐ @ $59.95	☐ @ $77.95			_____

*CD-ROM (Windows) includes all questions, figures, charts, and outlines for each of the pilot knowledge tests.

REFERENCE AND FLIGHT MANEUVERS/PRACTICAL TEST PREP BOOKS

FAR/AIM	$15.95	_____
Aviation Weather and Weather Services	22.95	_____
Pilot Handbook	13.95	_____
Private Pilot Flight Maneuvers and Practical Test Prep	16.95	_____
Instrument Pilot Flight Maneuvers and Practical Test Prep	18.95	_____
Commercial Pilot Flight Maneuvers and Practical Test Prep	14.95	_____
Flight Instructor Flight Maneuvers and Practical Test Prep	17.95	_____

OTHER BOOKS AND ACCESSORIES

Private Pilot Syllabus and Logbook	$ 9.95	_____
Instrument Pilot Syllabus	14.95	_____
Commercial Pilot Syllabus	14.95	_____
Flight Computer	9.95	_____
Navigational Plotter	5.95	_____
Flight Bag	29.95	_____

Shipping (nonrefundable): **First item = $5; each additional item = $1** $_____

Add applicable sales tax for shipments within the State of Florida.

Please FAX, e-mail, or write for additional charges for outside the 48 contiguous United States. **TOTAL** $_____

Printed 11/01. Prices subject to change without notice.

1. We process and ship orders daily, within one business day over 98.8% of the time. Call by noon for same-day service!

2. Please PHOTOCOPY this order form for others.

3. No CODs. Orders from individuals must be prepaid. Library and company orders may be purchased on account.

4. Gleim Publications, Inc. guarantees the immediate refund of all resalable texts and unopened software and audios if returned within 30 days. Applies only to items purchased direct from Gleim Publications, Inc. Our shipping charge is nonrefundable.

5. Components of specially priced package deals are nonreturnable.

NAME (please print) _____

ADDRESS _____ Apt. _____
(street address required for UPS)

_____

CITY _____ STATE _____ ZIP _____

_____ MC/VISA/DISC _____ Check/M.O.   Daytime
Telephone (_____)_____

Credit Card No. _____ - _____ - _____ - _____

Exp. ____/____   Signature _____
Mo./Yr.

E-mail Address _____

INSTRUCTOR CERTIFICATION FORM
PRIVATE PILOT KNOWLEDGE TEST

Name: _____

    I certify that I have reviewed the above individual's preparation for the FAA Private Pilot--Airplane knowledge test [covering the topics specified in FAR 61.105(b)(1) through (13)] using the *Private Pilot FAA Written Exam* book and/or software by Irvin N. Gleim and find him/her competent to pass the knowledge test.

_____   _____   _____   _____ _____

      Signed   Date   Name   CFI Number Expiration Date

* *

INSTRUCTOR CERTIFICATION FORM
RECREATIONAL PILOT KNOWLEDGE TEST

Name: _____

    I certify that I have reviewed the above individual's preparation for the FAA Recreational Pilot--Airplane knowledge test [covering the topics specified in FAR 61.97(b)(1) through (12)] using the *Recreational Pilot FAA Written Exam* book and/or software by Irvin N. Gleim and find him/her competent to pass the knowledge test.

_____   _____   _____   _____ _____

      Signed   Date   Name   CFI Number Expiration Date

328

Gleim Publications, Inc.
P.O. Box 12848
Gainesville, FL 32604

TOLL FREE: (800) 87-GLEIM
LOCAL: (352) 375-0772
FAX: (352) 375-6940
INTERNET: www.gleim.com
E-MAIL: sales@gleim.com

Customer service is available:
8:00 a.m. - 7:00 p.m., Mon. - Fri.
9:00 a.m. - 2:00 p.m., Saturday
Please have your credit card ready
or save time by ordering online.

Gleim Publications, Inc.
P.O. Box 12848
Gainesville, FL 32604

TOLL FREE: (800) 87-GLEIM
LOCAL: (352) 375-0772
FAX: (352) 375-6940
INTERNET: www.gleim.com
E-MAIL: sales@gleim.com

Customer service is available:
8:00 a.m. - 7:00 p.m., Mon. - Fri.
9:00 a.m. - 2:00 p.m., Saturday
Please have your credit card ready
or save time by ordering online.

Thank You FOR CHOOSING GLEIM

We dedicate ourselves to providing pilots with knowledge transfer systems, enabling them to pass the FAA pilot knowledge (written) tests and FAA practical (flight) tests. We solicit your feedback. Use the last page in this book to make notes as you use *Private Pilot and Recreational Pilot FAA Written Exam* and other Gleim products. Tear out the page and mail it to us when convenient. Alternatively, e-mail (irvin@gleim.com) or FAX (352-375-6940) your feedback to us.

GLEIM'S E-MAIL UPDATE SERVICE

update@gleim.com

Your message to Gleim must include (in the subject or body) the acronym for your book or software, followed by the edition-printing for books and version for software. The edition-printing is indicated on the book's spine and at the bottom right corner of the cover. The software version is indicated on the CD-ROM label.

	Written Exam		Flight Maneuvers
	Book	Software	Book
Private Pilot	PPWE	FAATP PP	PPFM
Instrument Pilot	IPWE	FAATP IP	IPFM
Commercial Pilot	CPWE	FAATP CP	CPFM
Flight/Ground Instructor	FIGI	FAATP FIGI	FIFM
Fundamentals of Instructing	FOI	FAATP FOI	
Airline Transport Pilot	ATP	FAATP ATP	
Flight Engineer	FEWE	FAATP FEWE	
		Reference Book	
Pilot Handbook		PH	
Aviation Weather and Weather Services		AWWS	
Private Pilot Syllabus and Logbook		PPSYL	
Instrument Pilot Syllabus		IPSYL	
Commercial Pilot Syllabus		CPSYL	
FAR/AIM		FARAIM	

E X A M P L E

For ***Private Pilot FAA Written Exam***, ninth edition-second printing:

> To: update@gleim.com
> From: your e-mail address
> Subject: PPWE 9-2

For ***FAA Test Prep*** software, Private Pilot, version 4.0:

> To: update@gleim.com
> From: your e-mail address
> Subject: FAATP PP 4-0

IT ONLY TAKES A MINUTE

f you do not have e-mail, have a friend send e-mail to us and print our response for you.

ABBREVIATIONS AND ACRONYMS IN
PRIVATE PILOT FAA WRITTEN EXAM

A/FD	*Airport/Facility Directory*	MH	magnetic heading
AC	Advisory Circular	MOA	Military Operations Area
AD	Airworthiness Directive	MSL	mean sea level
ADF	automatic direction finder	MTR	military training route
AFSS	Automated Flight Service Station	MVFR	marginal VFR
AGL	above ground level	NDB	nondirectional radio beacon
AIM	*Aeronautical Information Manual*	NFCT	nonfederal control tower
AIRMET	Airman's Meteorological Information	NM	nautical mile
AME	aviation medical examiner	NOTAM	notice to airmen
ANDS	accelerate north, decelerate south	NPRM	Notice of Proposed Rulemaking
AOE	airport of entry	NTSB	National Transportation Safety Board
ARTS	Automated Radar Terminal System	OAT	outside air temperature
ASEL	airplane single-engine land	OBS	omnibearing selector
ATA	actual time of arrival	PAPI	precision approach path indicator
ATC	Air Traffic Control	PCL	pilot-controlled lighting
ATIS	Automatic Terminal Information Service	PIC	pilot in command
CDI	course deviation indicator	PIREP	pilot weather report
CDT	central daylight time	RB	relative bearing
CFI	certificated flight instructor	SFC	surface
CG	center of gravity	SIGMET	Significant Meteorological Information
CH	compass heading	SM	statute mile
CT	control tower	STC	supplemental type certificate
CTAF	Common Traffic Advisory Frequency	SVFR	special VFR
DME	distance measuring equipment	TACAN	Tactical Air Navigation
DT	daylight time	TAF	terminal aerodrome forecast
DUAT	Direct User Access Terminal	TAS	true airspeed
DVFR	defense VFR	TC	true course
EFAS	En Route Flight Advisory Service	TH	true heading
ELT	emergency locator transmitter	TWEB	Transcribed Weather Broadcast
ETA	estimated time of arrival	UHF	ultra high frequency
ETD	estimated time of departure	UTC	Coordinated Universal Time
FA	area forecast	V_A	maneuvering speed
FAA	Federal Aviation Administration	VASI	visual approach slope indicator
FAR	Federal Aviation Regulation	V_{FE}	maximum flap extended speed
FBO	fixed-base operator	VFR	visual flight rules
FCC	Federal Communications Commission	VHF	very high frequency
FD	winds and temperatures aloft forecast	VHF/DF	VHF direction finder
FL	flight level	VIP	video integrated processor
FSDO	Flight Standards District Office	V_{LE}	maximum landing gear extended speed
FSS	Flight Service Station	V_{NE}	never-exceed speed
GPH	gallons per hour	V_{NO}	maximum structural cruising speed
Hg	mercury	VOR	VHF omnidirectional range
HP	horsepower	VORTAC	collocated VOR and TACAN
IAS	indicated airspeed	VOT	VOR test facility
ICAO	International Civil Aviation Organization	VR	visual route
IFR	instrument flight rules	V_{SO}	stalling speed or the minimum steady flight speed in the landing configuration
IR	instrument route		
ISA	International Standard Atmosphere	V_{S1}	stalling speed or the minimum steady flight speed obtained in a specific configuration
LLWAS	low-level wind-shear alert system		
mb	millibar	V_X	speed for best angle of climb
MB	magnetic bearing	V_Y	speed for best rate of climb
MC	magnetic course	WCA	wind correction angle
MEF	maximum elevation figure	Z	Zulu or UTC time
METAR	aviation routine weather report		

INDEX

Please forward your suggestions, corrections, and comments concerning typographical errors, etc., to **Irvin N. Gleim • c/o Gleim Publications, Inc. • P.O. Box 12848 • University Station • Gainesville, Florida • 32604**. Please include your name and address on the back of this page so we can properly thank you for your interest. Also, please refer to both the page number and the FAA question number for each item.

1. _____

2. _____

3. _____

4. _____

5. _____

6. _____

7. _____

8. _____

9. _____

We need your help identifying which questions the FAA is pretesting (but not grading - see page 6). After you take your exam, please e-mail, fax, or mail us a description of these questions so we can anticipate their future use by the FAA.

10. _____

11. _____

12. _____

13. _____

14. _____

15. _____

16. _____

17. _____

Remember for superior service: Mail, e-mail, or fax questions about our books or software.
Telephone questions about orders, prices, shipments, or payments.

Name: _____

Address: _____

City/State/Zip: _____

Telephone: Home: _____   Work: _____   Fax: _____

E-mail: _____

GLEIM BOOKMARK

Dr. Gleim's Recommendation: Cover the answers and explanations in your book with this bookmark to make sure you do NOT cheat yourself. The answers will not be alongside the questions when you take your exam. Use our test prep software, flight maneuvers/practical test prep books, audio lectures, and online programs to complete your training.

FAA TEST PREP SOFTWARE

CD-ROM version for Windows 95, Windows 98, and Windows NT. Outlines, figures, and questions are integrated in our new interface.

Private thru ATP available.

If you don't have it - GET IT!
FAA Test Prep software will enhance your effectiveness in passing your FAA Knowledge Test.

FLIGHT MANEUVERS / PRACTCAL TEST PREP BOOKS

These books are designed to replace or enhance the FAA Practical Test Standards reprints. Gleim integrates the FAA books, advisory circulars, FARs, Practical Test Standards, etc., into one easy-to-use text. In addition to being complete, each book is well organized and structured to focus on exactly what you need to know and do to pass your FAA practical test.

ONLINE LEARNING TOOLS

Gleim currently offers the following programs for aviation online learning:

Non-airplane Question and Answer Service

Go to: www.gleim.com/Aviation/nonairplane/
All non-airplane questions are listed by certificate & rating.

Flight Instructor Refresher Course (FIRC)

CFIs can renew their certificates at their convenience by using Gleim's online FIRC. Visit www.gleim.com/firc/ and try Lesson One for FREE.

Private Pilot Refresher Course (PPRC)

PPRC is a recurrent ground training course designed to increase your knowledge and abilities while preparing you for your flight review. Visit www.gleim.com/pprc/ and try Lesson One for FREE.

(800) 87-GLEIM • www.gleim.com